Municipal Management Series

Management of Local Public Works

The International City Management Association is the professional and educational organization for chief appointed management executives in local government. The purposes of ICMA are to strengthen the quality of local government through professional management and to develop and disseminate new approaches to management through training programs, information services, and publications.

Managers, carrying a wide range of titles, serve cities, towns, counties, and councils of governments in all parts of the United States and Canada. These managers serve at the direction of elected councils and governing boards. ICMA serves these managers and local governments through many programs that aim at improving the manager's professional competence and strengthening the quality of all local governments.

The International City Management Association was founded in 1914; adopted its City Management Code of Ethics in 1924; and established its Institute for Training in Municipal Administration in 1934. The Institute, in turn, provided the basis for the Municipal Management Series, generally termed the "ICMA Green Books." ICMA's interests and activities include public management education; standards of ethics for members; *The Municipal Year Book* and other data services; local government research; and newsletters, *Public Management* magazine, and other publications. ICMA's efforts for the improvement of local government management—as represented by this book—are offered for all local governments and educational institutions.

Contributors

John A. Bailey

Carey C. Burnett

Myron D. Calkins

Stephen Chapple

Sam M. Cristofano

William S. Foster

Robert H. Goodin

Stephen B. Gordon

Ronald W. Jensen

Tina Ann Lamoreaux

Martin J. Manning

Burton W. Marsh

James L. Martin

John Matzer, Jr.

Abraham Michaels

Ronald Miller

Larry G. Mugler

Wilfred M. ("Wiley") Post, Jr.

William A. Ramsey

Mires Rosenthal

Michael J. E. Sheflin

Frank S. So

Donald M. Somers

L. Scott Tucker

Municipal Management Series

Management of Local PublicWorks

Editors

Published in cooperation
with the American
Public Works Association

Sam M. Cristofano
Director, Department of
Public Works
Santa Clara, California

By the
International
City
Management
Association

William S. Foster
Retired editor
American City

Municipal Management Series

Library of Congress Cataloging in Publication Data

Main entry under title:
Management of local public works.

  (Municipal management series)
  Bibliography: p.
  Includes index.
  1. Municipal services—Management—Addresses,
essays, lectures. 2. Public works—Management—
Addresses, essays, lectures. I. Cristofano, Sam M.
II. Foster, William S. III. American Public Works
Association. IV. International City Management
Association. V. Series.
HD4431.M35   1986   363'.068   86–125
ISBN 0-87326-048-1

Printed in the United States of America.

92919089888786
54321

Foreword

When the International City Management Association published the first edition of this book, then titled *Municipal Public Works Administration*, in 1935, the coverage was limited to streets, sewerage, buildings, motor equipment, and construction, plus chapters on work measurement, budgeting, accounting, and records. Through six successive editions, culminating in this book, the coverage has expanded and changed as local public works has changed. Fifty years ago the municipal airport was a landing strip and a wind sock; today it is a small city with utilities, hotels, and shops. These and other highly visible services—such as freeways, computer-driven signal systems, floodplain control, and air quality control—are now provided in a context of management, information, communication, law, finance, and planning.

The public works director has moved from being the on-site supervisor to the environmental manager as he or she works with organizations and governing bodies, plans operating and capital programs, analyzes data and other forms of information, and tames and exploits technology.

Management of Local Public Works has been planned and developed cooperatively by the American Public Works Association and the International City Management Association to blend the experience and resources of two of the oldest professional organizations in local

government. It is a highly visible symbol of the ongoing efforts of APWA (founded in 1894) and ICMA (founded in 1914) to promote professional management of public works in cities and counties. APWA and ICMA have jointly produced this edition to reflect current practice in a volatile local government environment. It reflects the commitment of both associations and the sustained efforts of two editors, twenty-two individual chapter authors, and numerous advisers and reviewers.

As its title suggests, *Management of Local Public Works* does not dwell on technical details of public works operations; scores of books are available on the many specialties covered in this volume. Rather, the emphasis is on management, both in the front office and in the field. It is a book to prepare public works managers and those who aspire to management for the public works environment of the 1980s and 1990s.

Like other titles in the Municipal Management Series, *Management of Local Public Works* is a collective effort. We are grateful to the many people who contributed to the planning, writing, review, editing, and production of this book.

We are especially grateful to the editors of this book, Sam M. Cristofano—Director of Public Works, Santa Clara, California—and William S. Foster—retired editor, *American City* magazine. Their work was particularly vital to the book's planning, manuscript review, and substantive editing.

Next, we are grateful to the staffs of APWA and ICMA, who worked together at every stage of the book from the initial outline to the bound copies.

The APWA staff included Oliver S. Merriam, Director of Administrative Services; Rita Knorr, Director of Research; Rodney R. Fleming, Associate Executive Director for General Services; and Richard H. Sullivan, Associate Executive Director for Management and Research. In addition, the executive council of the Institute for Administrative Management of APWA provided valuable advice on the general content and scope of the book.

The ICMA staff included David S. Arnold, former Editor, Municipal Management Series; Barbara H. Moore, Editor, Municipal Management Series; Devorah Leibtag Mittelman, Editor; Mary Blair, Publications Assistant; Dawn Leland, Publications Production Director; Rebecca Geanaros, Graphic Designer; and Susan Gubisch, Production Assistant. Lending assistance to the ICMA staff were Venka V. Macintyre, who copy edited the manuscript, and Diana Regenthal, who prepared the index.

Other persons who helped at various stages in the planning and development of the book (with their affiliations at the time of publication) are Ronald A. Beckman, City Engineer, Oceanside, California; James E. Bihr, P.E., Executive Director, International Conference of Building Officials; Mari Cote, AIA, Director of Inspections, Savannah, Georgia; Clarence T. Daugherty, Director of Public Works, Collin County (McKinney), Texas; Robert H. Goodin, Director of Public Works, Rockville, Maryland; Paul K. Heilstedt, P.E., Deputy Executive Director, Building Officials and Code Administrators International; Robert E. Hendrix, County Administrative Officer, Humboldt County (Eureka), California; Ronald W. Jensen, Director of Public Works, Phoenix, Arizona; John M. Lang, Administrator, Bureau of Environmental Services, Portland, Oregon; Stephen T. Pudloski, Director of Public Works, Evanston, Illinois; William J. Tangye, P.E., Executive Director, Southern Building Code Congress International; and Max L. Whitman, Director of Public Works, Winnetka, Illinois.

Robert D. Bugher
Executive Director
American Public
    Works Association
Chicago, Illinois

William H. Hansell, Jr.
Executive Director
International City
    Management Association
Washington, D.C.

Contents

Introduction

At one time many Americans watched a popular television guessing game involving a set of well-known panelists who would try to determine which of three people was the real individual described by the master of ceremonies. "Will the real Congressman from Alaska [for example] please stand up?"

Today the master of ceremonies might ask, "Will the real administrator of the urban infrastructure please stand up?" Thereupon the director of public works would arise, not at all sure whether he liked this new title.

Infrastructure is a relatively new word referring to the support system that permits an organization to function more effectively. Although it originally referred just to the internal workings of NATO, it was so descriptive that others quickly adopted it. A secretary, for example, is an important part of an office infrastructure, as is the mail room, or the accounting personnel. In an urban complex, the director of public works is responsible for such infrastructure duties as maintaining the streets and clearing them of snow so that traffic can move safely; providing storm drains that prevent flooding; providing potable water; transporting liquid wastes to treatment facilities; collecting and disposing of solid wastes; designing and installing traffic-control facilities; and performing the multitude of other tasks that allow an urban complex to function. In addition, the urban infrastructure has to be able to respond quickly and effectively to catastrophic emergencies such as hurricanes, unexpected heavy snowfalls, earthquakes, and many other disasters so that the smooth delivery of services will be maintained.

Providing such services presents administrators with new challenges, complicated by an ever-widening chasm between how much money is required to maintain services at a desirable level and how much money is available. In response, administrators are learning to do more with less, to maintain productivity, and to reduce or eliminate certain programs and services. Some have ventured into the costly policies of deferred maintenance; but as long as neglect continues, the amount of repair work will increase and the persistent push of inflation will raise costs out of proportion to the "savings" gained by delay. Maintenance is always least costly when performed early.

Today's public works directors, as well as the directors of various functions such as airports, water supply and distribution, and liquid and solid waste collection and disposal, probably started as neophytes with civil engineering degrees who learned the elements of supervision and management by on-the-job exposure. But that is not enough!

The vastly expanded job of the director of public works goes beyond technical competence. It requires dynamics of leadership, communication, analytical skills, and foresight. In addition, the manager must have the stamina to work easily and comfortably with elected and appointed officials, union representatives, community leaders, homeowner associations, and individual citizens.

The text of *Management of Local Public Works* has drawn on the wisdom of some of the most successful administrators in the field and presented their advice and counsel in the various chapters. Like other titles in the ICMA Municipal

Management Series, *Management of Local Public Works* discusses some technical issues and operating or functional details, but its primary purpose is to address the key managerial issues of the future for the public works official, such as information, planning, communication, law, purchasing, finance, personnel, and interpersonal relations.

Four major changes are emerging in public works management. *Involvement* is the first. Since the mid-1960s, public works administrators have been forced to work with a variety of groups—local citizens and neighborhood groups, supervisors, planners, social workers, realtors, and developers—to attain genuine exchange of views and information and to recognize their adversarial differences.

Planning is the second change. In a broad sense, public works professionals are planners. Whereas the dimensions of traditional city planning used to be the master plan, the zoning ordinance, and subdivision regulations, today planning includes social, political, economic, intergovernmental, aesthetic, environmental, and managerial considerations. Planning is an integral part of preparing short- and long-term operating and capital budgets, developing floodplain regulations, consulting on air quality measures, and drafting or reviewing environmental impact statements.

Analysis is the third emerging change. Public works administrators have always analyzed, especially for project planning, cost estimating, and engineering design. Today, analysis has become much broader; it is an amalgam of techniques, processes, models, and, above all, systemic approaches. In simple terms, it says, "Let's look at the options before we decide."

This text contains many examples of analysis: value analysis and life-cycle costing as a part of the purchasing process; "total equipment management" for motor equipment, including preventive maintenance, work measurement, time standards, parts inventory control, and other steps for optimal balancing of costs and service; transportation planning for bikeways, public transit, and access for pedestrians, the elderly, and the handicapped; and tradeoffs on floodplain planning and regulation.

Technology is the fourth major emerging change. It gives public works managers frequent and dependable access to job status reports and other data, computer-generated maps where variables can be compared in visual form, computer monitoring and feedback for energy conservation in public buildings, and an extraordinary range of refuse-collection trucks able to increase productivity.

Technological advances also affect management of the infrastructure. Take for example a calcium-chloride admixture to asphalt mixes that, when placed on a street, melts snow and ice as they appear, a development that most would not have believed could ever occur; or elevated water reservoirs (supported by fluted cylinders) that provide space for offices, storage, fire stations, university classrooms, and in one case, a theatre in the round. Consider the adoption of sloped tubes in a settling tank to hasten the settling process, or the recent introduction of an egg-shaped sludge digester for sewage treatment plants. Consider, too, the growing use of a harsh, vibrated concrete for bridge floors that has demonstrated an ability to resist deterioration from salt applications.

Technology is not all good news, however. Public works managers must deal with air pollution and solid-waste disposal hazards that in the past were insignificant or unknown. They must worry, too, about increasingly strict sewage treatment standards and water quality controls that no one thought would ever be imposed.

Public works is a dedicated profession with origins in antiquity. Municipal engineers were one of the earliest professional groups in local government, tracing their formal organization in the United States to the first meeting in 1894 of the American Society for Municipal Improvements. This organization and others have combined to form the American Public Works Association with a membership of about 20,000.

Public works managers today are reaffirming those duties and responsibilities to serve the public that have made it possible for the United States to achieve a high standard of living—one that depends largely on the services provided by local governments. Like its predecessors, going back to the publication of *Municipal Public Works Administration* in 1935, *Management of Local Public Works* builds on the history and traditions that have enabled public works managers to provide the physical backbone of the cities and counties that constitute Urban America.

Part one: Central management

What is public works?

The answer to the question, "What is public works?" is simple when only the physical facilities are considered. Is it public? Does it work? If the answer is yes to both questions, it qualifies. Our concern, however, goes much further than the facilities themselves, as will be seen later.

Public works is	Public works is not
A straight way to service	A road to riches
A challenge to change	A fairway to fame
An invitation to innovation	A gangway to glory
An incentive to improvement	A recipe for recognition.
An avenue to advancement	
An anecdote to ennui.	

The context of public works

Public works provide the physical facilities that make communities and societies possible. As noted in Chapter 10 of this book, public works is the "application of scientific, economic, and management principles to the solution of physical, service, and system problems to implement community plans, meet community goals, and achieve optimum costs of construction, operation, and maintenance."

Many other definitions have been proposed for public works. Donald C. Stone defines what public works *are* and lists eighteen examples.[1] The predecessor to this book, *Urban Public Works Administration*, describes what public works *do*.[2] *Webster's Third* defines public works in terms of *why*.[3]

To this imposing array should be added the men and women who make public works possible. These are the people who maintain existing facilities to serve the public need and provide the imaginative planning, conceptual design, organizational leadership, and financial acumen that make up the management of public works.

Therefore, the definition of public works should contain a qualifying condition: "managed by experienced, intelligent, dedicated professionals." Thus, Donald C. Stone's definition (see endnote 1) might read:

Public works are the physical structures and facilities that are developed or acquired by public agencies to house governmental functions and provide water, power, waste disposal, transportation, and similar services, *and are managed by experienced, intelligent, dedicated professionals to facilitate and ensure continuously better service to the public.*

In the public works profession praise must come from within. The reward is the satisfaction for a "job well done." Expect no applause and very little rec-

This chapter was prepared by Carey C. Burnett, with minor portions added by the editors.

ognition. This fact should not discourage the aspiring public works official, since the rewards for dedicated public service far outweigh the lack of public acclaim. Personal job satisfaction and pride in accomplishment—a river bridged, a canal constructed, a drainage problem solved, a better water source developed, an unsanitary sewage condition eliminated—give deep and lasting satisfaction.

Public works, the civilizing force

Public works provide the physical base essential to the social and economic development of American civilization. Designed to protect and enhance the human environment, they represent investments in the future for the people who create them and for succeeding generations. The transportation networks; the facilities that control floods and provide drainage; the systems that supply water for domestic, agricultural, industrial, and power-generating needs; the public buildings required for health services, education, defense, housing, and recreation; the waste collection, treatment, and disposal systems as well as the facilities that harness the power of the atom and explore space—have all contributed significantly to the growth of the nation.

Public works have made it possible for the people of the United States to achieve the highest standard of living in the world. Yet clean water at the turn of the tap; fresh vegetables year

around; light and power at the touch of a switch; hard-surfaced roads that, during winter or summer, provide for the movement of people and goods; modern airports that make safe and convenient air travel possible; extensive educational facilities, hospitals, public libraries, theaters, stadiums, parks; and many other types of public works are often *taken for granted by contemporary society*. They did not, however, just appear when they were needed. They were created through the efforts of many people working together within the framework of the American system of government. Dedicated men and women dreamed, planned, and worked for a better life. And the nation's engineers, contractors, and public officials joined with them to make their dreams a reality.

Source: Ellis L. Armstrong, ed., *History of Public Works in the United States: 1776–1976* (Chicago: American Public Works Association, 1976), dust jacket copy. (Emphasis added.)

An honorable profession

Public works as a profession is undoubtedly one of the oldest professions in the world, predating the Pyramids. Outstanding, intelligent, dedicated public works officials have served humanity as long as people have congregated in cities instead of in caves.

The ancient cities of Athens, Rome, Pompeii, Babylon, and many others dating back to 600 B.C. and beyond, are known to have been served with such public works facilities as roads (see Figure 1–1), bridges, canals, aqueducts (Figure 1–2), water and sewer systems, and even, in some instances, indoor plumbing.[4] Early road systems go back as far as 2500 B.C. in China and Egypt.[5] One example of such an early system is the Old Silk Trade Route, which ran over 6,000 miles, connecting China with Rome and pre-Christian Europe.[6]

As one authority points out, Rome led the way for centuries:

The most enduring monuments of Rome are not the ruins of empire . . . [but rather] those overwhelming Roman roads . . . those Roman *viae*—each like a gigantic thread weaving together all the then-known world. . . . It is not possible to overrate the value of these great *viae* in the history of man's development. Rome became a mobile civilisation and the mistress of the world because of her systematic control of world-space through her roads. . . . These continuous, well-engineered public roads went to the Rhine and the Danube, . . . [to] the Black Sea, to the Euphrates, to

Africa, to Arabia and even along the outside edge of India. . . . These 53,000 miles of communications were taut strings of civilisation, great life-lines that went off to the edge of every horizon. . . . The Roman engineers [public works officials] did not evade nature, they conquered her; if they met a river it was bridged, if a marsh intervened the road became a causeway. . . . It took Rome centuries to build its thousands of miles of all-weather roads—roads that stretched from Hadrian's Wall in Scotland to the Persian Gulf, from Spain to Caucasus, from the sand-seas of Libya to the gloomy forests of . . . Germany.[7]

The fact that many of these ancient public works facilities—roads, aqueducts, canals—are still in use today attests to the skill, genius, and dedication to public service of the men who conceived, built, maintained, managed, and improved these valuable public necessities over the centuries. We who are engaged in the profession today can be justly proud of its long history of service to mankind. In a flyleaf inscription in an old textbook, *Handbook of Water Control*, David C. Beaman expresses this thought:

Although the tomb of Moses is unknown, the traveler of today slakes his thirst at the well of Jacob. The gorgeous palaces of the wisest and wealthiest of monarchs, with their cedar and gold and ivory, and even the great temple of Jerusalem, hallowed by the visible glory of the Deity Himself, are gone; but Solomon's reservoirs are as perfect as ever. Of the magnificent and costly architecture of the Holy City, not one stone is left upon another, but the pool of Bethsaida commands the pilgrim's reverence at the present day. The columns of Persepolis are moldering into dust, but its cistern and aqueduct remain to challenge our admiration. The golden house of Nero is a mass of ruins, but the Aqua Claudia still pours into the City of Rome its limpid stream. The Temple of the Sun at Tadmor in the wilderness has fallen, but its fountain sparkles in the rays of the morning as when thousands of worshippers thronged its lofty colonnades. And if any work of this generation shall rise over the deep ocean of time, we may well believe that it will be neither palace nor temple, but some vast aqueduct or reservoir; and that if any name shall hereafter flash brightest through the mist of antiquity, it will probably be that of the man who in his day sought the happiness of his fellow men, and linked his memory to some such work of national utility or benevolence.[8]

Lest we become giddy in such a rarefied atmosphere of professional admiration, an article in *Smithsonian* magazine by James R. Chiles may bring us back to earth.[9] The article recounts ancient wonders that did not survive (see Figure 1–3) and compares three modern-day structures—namely the World Trade Center in New York, the Gateway Arch in St. Louis, and the Grand Coulee Dam on the Columbia River in Washington State. On the basis of research and consultation with structural engineers, geologists, and mechanical engineers most intimately familiar with each, the author projects what the life span of each might be.

The first to go would be the World Trade Center because of flooding of the basement by the Hudson River and the ravages of rust and corrosion. No timetable is given for the final collapse but the basement is expected to be filled with seawater in 100 years and total destruction is predicted in less than 1,000 years.

The next to go would be the Gateway Arch, falling victim to high winds within several hundred years, when the top of the arch would go. But the two concrete pillars standing 300 feet high might last 5,000 years.

Like the surviving structure in Mr. Beaman's unforgettable prose poem, the most permanent one here is a "vast reservoir," the Grand Coulee Dam. The life span of this tremendous mass of concrete is projected to extend over 10,000 years, or until the next Ice Age, when glacial flooding would finally be its downfall.

It is significant, however, that this timetable is based on *zero maintenance*. It is predicated on the assumption that all three structures will be left *unattended*,

Figure 1–1   Ancient cities were served by extensive networks of roads.

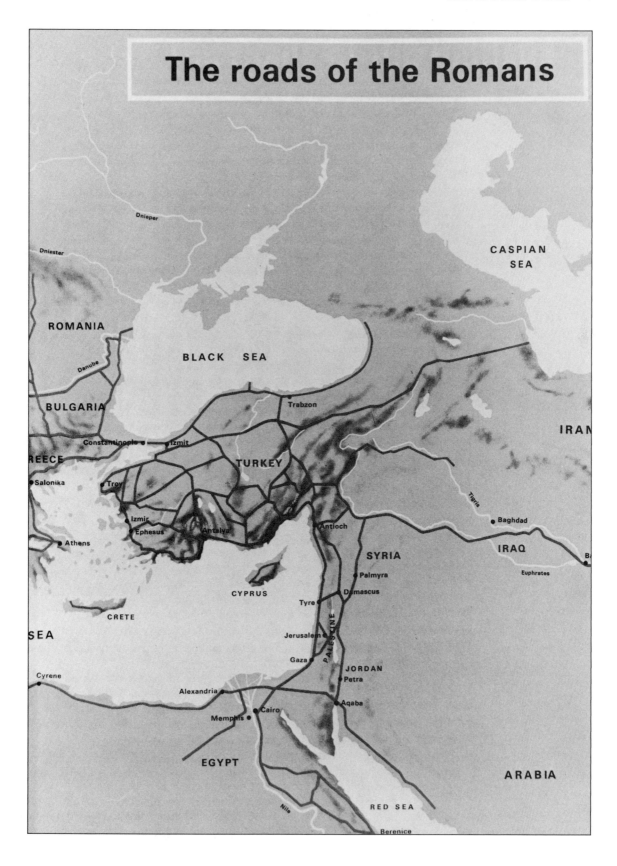

The roads of the Romans

Figure 1–2   Aqueduct at Segovia, Spain. Built under the Emperor Trajan (A.D. 53–A.D. 117); it is still working today.

as if the public works departments responsible for the maintenance of these facilities just walked off the job one day and never came back.

Mr. Chiles quotes the structural engineer who designed the World Trade Center, Les Robertson, as follows: " 'The idea of a 50- or 100-year life span for buildings is patently ridiculous. There's no structural reason not to go on and on and on. The effective life span is completely dependent on those who maintain them. Properly maintained, a building is ageless.' "[10]

The truth of this statement is evident to anyone who has visited the ancient cathedrals of Europe or the British Isles. These magnificent structures are undergoing constant repair and replacement, as they have throughout the ages. The life of the facility therefore depends on ongoing maintenance and repair, which generally is given only to those facilities that are regularly used by the public and that fill a vital public need. In other words they are "public" and they "work." These facilities have outlived other famous monuments because, once placed into service, they served such a vital public need that their maintenance and upkeep were not only assured but mandated by future generations.

King Croesus built the Temple of Artemis at Ephesus about 550 B.C. Invading Goths destroyed it in A.D. 262.

Built about 280 B.C., the lighthouse on Pharos stood at least until the 12th century; its fate is unknown.

The Colossus of Rhodes broke off at the knees in an earthquake about 225 B.C., 55 years after completion.

Phidias of Athens completed this 30-foot statue of Zeus about 430 B.C.; temple was destroyed in A.D. 426.

Tomb of Mausolus, begun in 353 B.C., probably was destroyed by quake between 11th and 15th centuries.

Nebuchadnezzar's Hanging (more likely rooftop or terraced) Gardens of Babylon may be apocryphal.

Figure 1–3   Six ancient wonders that did not survive.

A case in point is the Seven Wonders of the Ancient World as compared with the ancient roadways, aqueducts, canals, and drainage systems constructed prior to or during the same period. Of the Seven Wonders, only the great Pyramids of Gaza in Egypt are still standing, yet many of the ancient public works facilities are still in use.

Dedication to duty

One of the most famous of early public works officials was Sextus Julius Frontinus, a water works superintendent, if you will, who was appointed *curator aquarum*—Water Commissioner of the City of Rome—by Emperor Nerva in A.D. 97.

The writings preserved from two books by Frontinus provide virtually all the known facts about the first nine aqueducts and the ancient water supply system that delivered water to the city of Rome and the surrounding urban areas (see Figure 1–4).[11] The aqueducts were constructed over a 400-year period prior to A.D. 90, by which time the system was servicing a population of 1.2 million[12] and was providing about 85 million gallons of water per day.[13] (It is interesting to note that water usage in the city of Rome 1900 years ago averaged 80 to 100 gallons per person per day, which is almost the same amount used in the United States today.)

The writings of Frontinus were discovered by Clemens Herschel, chief engineer for the East Jersey Water Company and inventor and developer of the Venturi Tube, which is widely used in measuring the flow of liquids. Herschel discovered the Frontinus manuscripts at the Benedictine monastery at Monte Cassino, Italy, in 1897, and translated the writings into English.

In his writings Frontinus recorded the source of water; the condition, length, slope, cross sections, and capacity of each of the nine aqueducts; and the quantity

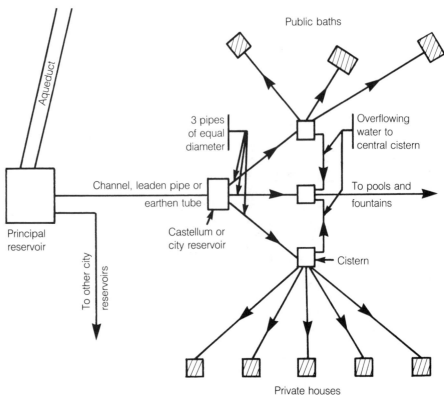

Figure 1–4   Water supply of a Roman city.

of water each delivered daily into the city. He also described the devices used to regulate the flow to each water customer—bronze "*calices*," which were short lengths of pipe approximately three-quarters of an inch in diameter (the size of the average house water service today).[14] Frontinus took on his work with diligence, zeal, and faithfulness, stating that "the first and most important thing to be done [is] . . . to learn thoroughly what it is I have undertaken."[15] This is the essence of the professional pride that provides the foundation for those who follow. The American Public Works Association has recognized many such pioneers in its periodical, *The APWA Reporter*. Here are five examples of persons who have made distinctive contributions to public works.[16]

Imhotep (ca. 3000 B.C.). Father of masonry construction. Builder of the first pyramid of stone for King Zoser at Sakara. First known public works engineer.

John Loudon McAdam (1756–1836). Originator of the basic road-building system known today as "macadam," which is said to have ushered in the Industrial Revolution.

Robert Mills (1781–1855). Designer of the Washington Monument, Mills was also responsible for many public works projects such as roads, bridges, canals, and river navigation improvements for his native state of South Carolina.

John Augustus Roebling (1806–1869). Designer and builder of the Brooklyn Bridge and inventor and first manufacturer of the wire cable used on all suspension bridges.

Ellis S. Chesbrough (1813–1886). City engineer of Chicago from 1855 to 1879. Responsible for the Sanitary and Ship Canal, which reversed the flow of the Chicago River to prevent sewage from flowing into Lake Michigan. Also famous for the tunnel built under Lake Michigan to obtain a pollution-free water supply for Chicago.

The roles of the public works manager

The public works manager of today must wear many hats, play many roles, and be able, as Kipling's "If" so aptly states, to "walk with Kings, nor lose the common touch."

No other position in city or county government depends so completely on a wide variety of experience as does that of the public works director. First, he or she must be in constant face-to-face contact with the various foremen, engineers, equipment operators, and construction contractors who are daily on the front lines of public works operations. The director must render almost daily operating decisions, usually through the supervisors, and must be able to make professional and political judgments involving streets, water, sewers, storm drainage, solid waste, vehicle maintenance, inspections, and codes. Nowhere can a phony or a pretender to the field be more quickly spotted.

The public works director must frequently be in personal contact with the city or county chief administrator and key department heads, chiefly those in finance, personnel, planning, and purchasing. He or she must meet regularly with the city or county council, the planning commission, and other officials.

A recent example taken from an actual county government situation illustrates the various roles that the public works manager must fill and the need for wide experience. The county in question is relatively large, roughly sixty miles by forty miles, and its population in 1980 was 215,000. The county seat is a city of 40,000 with council-manager government. The county encompasses fourteen separate incorporated towns, all with populations of 5,000 or less, their own elected councils, and few public works services.

A new state constitutional amendment had required a home rule form of government for the county, and, by popular referendum, the elected county supervisor system was replaced by a county council/administrator system. The newly appointed county administrator appointed the county's first public works director over considerable objection from certain county council members. The new director would not only be responsible for the Roads and Bridge Division, which the supervisors had controlled, but would also administer the Engineering, Solid Waste, Vehicle Maintenance, and Animal Control divisions that had previously operated independently.

When the new public works director took office, he was faced with the maintenance responsibility for 1,500 miles of county roads and 180 county bridges. He was also put in charge of solid waste collection and disposal for 200,000 people; maintenance for 375 motor vehicles; and animal control for an estimated 84,000 stray dogs.

The total departmental work force consisted of 126 permanent county personnel plus 81 temporary CETA[17] workers and 18 supervisors answering personally to the director.

County maintenance of roads and bridges was handled by five separate sections (former prison camps) located throughout the county. Specialized construction, such as paving and storm drainage, was done by five special work sections dispatched from the public works headquarters complex. Solid waste was collected from thirty-seven separate "green box" locations that were dispersed throughout the county in either 4-cubic-yard or 40-cubic-yard open-top containers.

Shortly after taking office the new public works director was faced with three emergencies:

1. The state revenues, on which the county depended for a large portion of its budget, were slashed drastically at midterm in the budget year.
2. The CETA program, which supplied the entire county labor force of some eighty-one workers, was discontinued.
3. Ninety of the 180 county-owned bridges were declared unsafe for school buses or fire trucks by the new state highway bridge inspection team, and 11 of these were cited for immediate closure.

The newly established department had to rework its entire budget in midstream and come up with major operational changes that would keep costs within the reduced revenue over the next several years while still maintaining as much public service as possible.

The department was called on to cope with the loss of eighty-one laborers without adding to the budget.

The department was also called on to take steps to reopen the eleven closed bridges to at least minimum passenger car traffic, and to make preliminary plans and estimates for a major bridge replacement program for the remaining seventy-nine unsafe bridges.

The roles that the public works director and staff in this example were required to assume, although concentrated to an unusual degree, nevertheless typify the roles most public works managers must play from time to time; namely, design and construction engineer, personnel officer, budget officer, purchasing agent, construction supervisor, solid waste manager, vehicle maintenance administrator, planning official, hydrologist, and environmentalist. The fact that this department was able to meet the challenges successfully is not unique to the profession.

Some of the management techniques employed in this county are described in the following section.

Management of the infrastructure

In many respects, the demands and duties placed on the public works director of today are comparable to those faced by the city or county manager of a decade or more ago.

In keeping abreast of the advancements in technology and their application to management of the infrastructure, public works managers and supervisors are improving a whole range of methods for resurfacing streets, replacing sewers, collecting refuse, disposing of waste, upgrading bridges, controlling traffic, expanding utility systems, maintaining vehicles, providing recreation, protecting the environment, and financing improvements. These managers and supervisors are applying new ideas and methods to personnel management, budgeting, financial reporting and control, and land use planning. To these traditional management responsibilities, managers and supervisors are adding new responsibilities that used to be considered peripheral to the "real" job of the public works manager: interpersonal communication, working with citizen groups, information systems, public/private cost comparisons, life-cycle costing, franchises and antitrust, motor equipment leasing, and environmental impact statements.

The demands placed on smaller cities or counties are and have always been somewhat less complex than those encountered in larger ones. However, the limited financial resources of the smaller units have frequently prevented them from employing outside consultants in the fields of engineering, sanitation, streets, buildings, and personnel, and therefore the public works director and staff have had to be able to meet these demands.

Many of the ideas and methods discussed in this book were used by the county described in the preceding section. This county had to resolve three emergencies. Working closely with the county administrator and key staff, the department was able to respond to the challenge by the following methods.

Drastic cutback in state revenues

The department was able to respond to the decrease in revenues by:

Reorganizing and consolidating the entire public works operation.

Reducing the manpower of the Roads Division from seventy-two to forty-six.

Consolidating five separate specialized work sections into one Support Services Section.

Reducing the number of road and bridge supervisors reporting directly to the director from eleven to two.

Reducing the number of county maintenance sections from five to four by redividing the county into larger work areas.

Reducing the number of county roadside, solid waste ("green box") collection stations from thirty-seven to fourteen by constructing residential solid waste compaction stations and cluster stations.

Reducing the cost of outside consulting services by performing design and construction of major projects "in-house."

Establishing a chain of command whereby work could be centrally planned and jointly executed.

Reducing the number of county vehicles being taken home at night from twenty-four to seventeen by limiting the practice to those subject to twenty-four-hour call.

Creating a motor pool operation for storing and performing preventive maintenance on all rolling equipment not in everyday use.

Establishing a night shift for vehicle maintenance to repair and maintain equipment while the work force is off duty, thus reducing down time.

Instigating a seal coat program to preserve existing pavement needing resurfacing until the budgetary "crunch" saw some relief. This program, giving five or more years' extra life to roadways at one-fourth the cost of full-scale tar and gravel resurfacing and one-seventh the cost of hot-mix asphalt resurfacing, made it possible to protect more than seventy miles of roads in one year.

Installing a computerized, card-controlled system for dispensing gasoline and diesel fuel, which eliminated possible theft and made it possible to keep accurate records of each vehicle and driver. Under this system service is cut off when a card has been lost or stolen, no gas attendant is required, and pumps are placed outside the fenced enclosure to allow law enforcement and other night operations to refuel.

Installing a portable filter system for recycling and reusing old crankcase oil by feeding it back into the vehicle from which it came.

Instigating a pilot program for using propane gas instead of gasoline for county vehicles.

Following these operational improvements, the overall budget was reduced by approximately $350,000 per year in operating costs, or roughly one-tenth of the department's annual budget.

In spite of personnel reductions, the department effectively handled the worst snow and ice storms the county had experienced for many years with a minimum of delay to the traveling public.

Discontinuance of CETA program

The department responded to this emergency by instigating a prison labor program to replace the loss of the CETA workers. Prison inmates from a nearby state correctional institution were given the opportunity to reduce their sentences (roughly one day off for three days' work) by volunteering to work for the county.

To accomplish this major move the department established a new position of "inmate services coordinator." Eighty to one hundred inmates per day were screened and transported to and from county work sites at no other cost to the county. By and large, the inmates replaced the labor force supplied by the CETA program and also provided a certain number of skilled workers such as carpenters, masons, concrete finishers, welders, and the like.

It is recognized that the use of prison labor is controversial, is opposed by labor unions, and is not permitted by law in some states. In this situation, however, the public works director realized that regular county employees were not being laid off. It seemed proper therefore to improvise with resources that were available and acceptable locally.

Declaration of unsafe county bridges

The department instigated a crash program for bridge replacement, funded initially by a transfer of $500,000 from the last of a road-paving bond issue. The department performed design and construction work "in-house" and replaced fifty narrow, unsafe timber bridges subject to frequent flood topping in less than two and one-half years at an average cost of $20,000 per bridge. The bridges built were full-size, reinforced concrete structures designed to meet state highway department standards (Figure 1–5).

Figure 1–5   One county replaced fifty unsafe bridges in less than two and one-half years.

Managing the public works infrastructure means overseeing personnel as well as physical resources. In the example above the critical element was the reorganization of the work force and the reassignment of key personnel. Transfers between divisions made it possible to set up a smooth working team to replace a formerly fragmented department. On the retirement of one division head, an entire chain of strategic moves could be introduced involving both promotions and reassignments.

Other examples

Many other examples can be cited of ways in which the infrastructure has been managed for the public good. In one instance a small town with limited resources was able to launch a major street-paving program by establishing a construction revolving fund to be replenished each year by front-foot property assessments. In that way twenty-two streets were paved by city forces over a three-year period for roughly one-fourth the amount of capital outlay that would have been needed.

In another instance the problem of how to provide the money to extend the water and sewer systems, when development on unserved streets was planned or had occurred, was solved by issuing small-denomination ten-year-maturity utility bonds. The proposed developers thus financed the extension by purchasing the bonds, in amounts as low as $500 each. The city was able to redeem the bonds with interest at maturity from the revenue derived from the water and sewer fees.

In another example, a city badly in need of a downtown parking garage was unable to buy the land and finance the construction with revenue bonds as a result of poor projections of parking revenues. This problem was solved by constructing shops on the ground floor and selling them to a private owner by competitive bidding and by reserving air rights above the shops for the multilevel parking garage, which was city owned and operated. The plan proved so successful that it was repeated twice, once by the city and once by private developers.

An alert public works director can discover many ways to save money and improve his or her department. Many of these can be picked up by reading the trade journals. Both the articles and the ads are informative. Manufacturers' representatives are a readily available source of ideas; although biased in favor of their own products, they can provide valuable information. Public works officials in other city, county, and utility operations are always one of the best sources. State highway department officials, particularly in maintenance, can be most helpful in narrowing down equipment selections and paving methods. Taking advantage of opportunities to observe construction in progress is one of the best ways to learn about the various fields in which the director must be knowledgeable.

Public versus private services

The question of whether to provide a particular service "in-house" or to contract out is ever recurring. Newly elected council members in particular are frequently interested in contracting out since it offers the apparent panacea of a budget reduction plus the attractive potential of garnering private enterprise approval. At certain times the "privatization" of a selected public service is not only feasible but also cost effective. Here are some examples in which public service by private contract has made sense as a temporary alternative:

1. A city annexation had not been included in the budget, and it was too costly to service the newly annexed area without a large tax increase, which could not win public approval through a referendum.
2. A wildcat strike seriously endangered the health of the general public by stopping solid waste collection service in midsummer.
3. A poorly managed, debt-ridden city was faced with a serious reduction in essential, life-supporting services.
4. A newly obligated service was beyond the existing financial capability of the city.

In these cases, the possibility of going "private" did offer temporary relief. The method could be either to contract outright for a particular service, or to approach the transition in stages.

Annexation

In the case of the newly annexed territory that had been promised city services, the equipment needed, namely police cars, was obtained by lease, which also covered all maintenance. The lease reduced the large capital outlay necessary, but the manpower was furnished by the city at an increase in city payroll cost. However, the solid waste collection was obtained through a private contract hauler on a two-year contract.

Strike

In the case of the wildcat strike, the transfer of a solid waste collection and disposal operation from public to private service proved to be cost effective. This was an illegal strike that endangered the health and well-being of the general public, and so a private hauler was employed. Arrangements of this type have ample precedent in cities and counties. A major advantage of such an arrangement is financial certainty; the contract is for a fixed rate for two or more years. Another advantage here was that the improved equipment provided cleaner, quicker service to the public. The equipment was installed by the contractor without the usual wrangling and delay associated with purchase requests for such equipment at budget time.

Subsequently, however, offsetting disadvantages were discovered. Among these was the difficulty the public works department encountered when the contractor began to lose money and to favor other, more profitable enterprises. When the contract had a year to run, the quality of collection began to decline and the department was plagued with more and more citizen complaints about missed service, sloppy pickup, and loose garbage spills. The contract was canceled by negotiation.

Thus the practice may carry a built-in liability when termination time comes. At such a time, unless a satisfactory contract with another service provider can be negotiated, the city or county is faced with the necessity of purchasing new or used equipment and employing new solid waste personnel. Collection routes are generally complicated and always require a considerable shakedown period before new drivers learn their routes. Thus the ease of getting out may be offset by the difficulty of getting back in.

Debt overload

For the debt-ridden city, the possibility of contracting out several of the vital, essential services that were in serious trouble became a viable alternative when accompanied by an offsetting reduction in payroll costs by employee layoffs. This move provided improved service and regained public approval, and it was instrumental in putting the governing body on the road to recovery. However, if the underlying cause of the trouble—that is, management—had not been corrected, the recovery, if any, would not have lasted.

Service obligations

In the fourth example, an annexation referendum carried a commitment for specified city services: solid waste collection, police protection, and ambulance service. The solid waste collection was contracted to a private hauler; the police protection was provided by a rental contract for patrol vehicles; and the ambulance service was obtained by a management contract with a company already providing a military establishment with the service. All were for a two-year period and gave the city a chance to catch up financially.

Contracting criteria

Contracts can cover most city services—fire protection, water and sewer, parks and recreation, and others. When the need is apparent and the obligation is real, performing the service by private contract may be a necessary and in fact a welcome opportunity. But the contract should be carefully written, with workable termination clauses. One method that has been used successfully under similar conditions is a "management contract." The city or county contracts for the labor and rolling equipment, and it supplies the land and permanent materials and equipment. Pipe material and supplies, water and sewer facilities, pumping stations, fire stations, ambulance stations, and landfill sites are examples of property owned by the city or county. Trucks, crawlers, backhoes, cranes, and ambulances are examples of equipment the contractor furnishes.

The contractor also employs the workers and retains management control. The employees of the contractor read the meters and make service connections, but the city or county owns the taps and handles billing and collections. Ambulance fees, when paid on the spot, are collected by the contractor and turned over to the city or county, and fees paid by mail are handled by the city or county. The contract termination clause should contain provisions for the city or county to purchase equipment owned by the contractor and provide for the contractor to train new personnel if the local government is to assume full service responsibility.

Private sector contract service may cost less than city or county government provision of the service for a number of reasons. The contractor may have an advantage in wage rates and may be able to employ part-time and seasonal workers to cover peak periods, spread equipment costs over a larger number of jobs, operate with less overtime, and incur less overhead.[18]

Contracting has advantages and disadvantages, as shown in Figure 1–6. It is obvious that costs should be compared between public and private provision of service, but other factors should also be considered, including legal restrictions, personnel rules, union contracts, availability of capable local contractors, quality of service, and cost-benefit ratios.

The future of public works management

The management of public works in the 1980s and 1990s will be moving in the same direction as local government management generally—that is, from techniques and procedures to planning, analysis, measurement, evaluation, human relations, automated systems, legal concerns, working with elected and appointed officials, and education. It is not an either/or setting. Traditional management as expressed through techniques and procedures is still basic, but the management job is much broader than it was in earlier decades. Subsequent chapters in this book cover these broader concerns, both in Part 1, "Central management," and in Part 2, "Public works operations." The balance of this chapter

Figure 1–6 Advantages and disadvantages in local government contracting.

Advantages

May cost less

May provide better performance

Limits the growth of government

Avoids large, initial capital costs

Permits greater flexibility in adjusting program size

Provides a yardstick for comparison

Produces better management.

Disadvantages

May cost more

May result in poor service to citizens

May increase the chance of corruption

A contractor may not complete operations

Displaces public employees and draws opposition from municipal unions

Creates problems in formulating adequate contracts

May be restricted by law

May entail problems in enforcing public policy

Fails to guarantee adequate competition for certain contracts.

briefly touches on the last two elements mentioned above, working relations and education, because of their fundamental importance to the entire book. It then concludes with a few guidelines on management behavior.

Working with elected and appointed officials

The varied roles of today's public works director include close working relations with both appointed and elected officials—city and county managers, special service directors, mayors, council members, and board members. The need for coordination between the public works department and these variously related agencies has expanded rapidly in recent years owing to expanding urban and suburban populations, the increasing interaction of various levels of government, centralization of formerly independent urban functions under the administrative responsibility of the public works department, and rising public expectations.

The director and top management must be able to relate effectively with the city or county administrator, the city or county elected governing body, and various elective or appointive boards and commissions, both public and private, that constitute the fabric of today's complex urban structure.

A friendly, easy relationship on a one-to-one basis with each individual involved is not always easy to achieve, but it is always to be sought. Such a relationship is critical to the success of the public works department's goals and objectives and often to the city's or county's goals as well.

Public works education

The educational demands for all public professions, occupations, and trades are high today for many reasons. Technology is often cited, but in public works some special reasons include the growth of special districts, the growth of environmental controls, the growth of data-oriented systems (and the computer hardware and software to undergird such systems), the availability of sophisticated motor vehicles and construction and maintenance equipment, emergency planning, and much greater responsibility for dealing with all kinds of people, groups, and organizations. Engineering, construction, and maintenance are still basic, but the *context* is much larger than it used to be.

The educational level of public works, as measured by the degrees held by public works directors, has been high for decades. The data over the past generation bear this out. The Municipal Manpower Commission noted in 1962 that public works directors were among the best educated people in local government. At that time, 61 percent of the public works directors in cities over 250,000 and 48 percent in cities under 250,000 had college degrees.[19] An APWA survey in 1969 showed that 67 percent of the public works directors had bachelor's or master's degrees. The ratios were still higher in 1980, when another APWA survey found that 81 percent of the public works directors in the United States had college degrees (62 percent held the bachelor's, 19 percent the master's).[20]

These data cover only the degrees held. Another survey conducted in 1980 looked at undergraduate catalogs of 50 of the 200 colleges and universities in the United States with civil engineering programs.[21] Five of those fifty programs offered a senior elective course on the administrative aspects of the work of the municipal engineer. Three other programs offered similar courses at the graduate level. It is a small ratio in the totality of civil engineering education, but it is a start.

This book addresses the major management concerns of public works, including the intangibles of communication:

You will probably spend more time dealing with government than with other engineers. . . . You will appear before committees and commissions seeking the right and permission to build, to design and to enlarge the national horizons. Then you will appear before them to explain why you did what you did, even though you had permission to do what you did.[22]

Civil or municipal engineering education in the traditional sense does not provide the management skills needed to deal with the interrelatedness of the many communities that make up urban society. The raison d'être for this book has been well put by a teacher at the University of New Brunswick:

Newly graduated municipal engineers soon discover that the technical expertise acquired at a university imparts only some of the skills needed to function within public organizations. If they are employed by the public sector or provide consulting service to it, they need to more fully comprehend their role as a policy adviser to elected officials and an implementer of their policies. Engineering students must be made aware of the political and bureaucratic processes operating within our society.[23]

Guidelines for behavior

Much is written these days about how to get along with people; how to negotiate, mediate, and facilitate; assert yourself; sell a proposal; reduce your stress level; and balance your professional and personal lives. *Management of Local Public Works* cannot deal with all of these and related topics. That would be another book, but this chapter can conclude with a few aphorisms that work well in management.

Trust   Trust is the foundation for working effectively. Trust includes respect for others, openness, and honesty. When trust is destroyed, working relations of all kinds are undermined or destroyed.

Sense of humor   Take your work seriously but never take yourself solemnly. A sense of humor helps in understanding others and accepting people and situations, especially those that cannot be changed.

Information   Information is meant to be shared. There are a few exceptions (personnel records, proprietary data, and the like), but most information keeps the organization moving. Strive to keep managers, supervisors, and elected officials informed and channel information through the chief administrator.

Evenhandedness   Show no favoritism. Treat everybody with respect.

Prior approval   Do not commit personnel and equipment to a project that has not been approved by the chief administrator, or, in his or her absence, by a formal vote of city council or county board. Nobody likes surprises.

Dignity and self-respect   The person who has self-respect is more likely to treat others with respect. Do not abuse the self-worth of others. Robert Henri, the American painter, once remarked that he liked to paint "people through whom dignity of life is manifest." That includes most of us.

1   Public works are "the physical structures and facilities that are developed or acquired by public agencies to house governmental functions and provide water, power, waste disposal, transportation, and similar services to facilitate the achievement of common social and economic objectives." Cited in William E. Korbitz, ed., *Urban Public Works Administration* (Washington, D.C.: International City Management Association, 1976), p. 3, from Donald C. Stone, "Professional Education in Public Works/Environmental Engineering and Administration" (Chicago: American Public Works Association, 1974), pp. 2–3.

2   "Public works provide the physical infrastructure (facilities and services) essential to urban society and to economic and social development. They constitute the main fabric of what may be called urban physical systems linked to national and regional sys-

tems. Public works make human settlement and nations possible." Cited in *Urban Public Works*, p. 4, from Stone, "Professional Education," p. 3.

3   *Webster's Third New International Dictionary*, 1981 ed., s.v. "public works." Public works are "works (as schools, highways, docks) constructed for public use or enjoyment especially when financed and owned by the government."

4   Charles Singer et al., *A History of Technology* (Oxford: Oxford University Press, 1958), vol. 2, pp. 665, 667, fig. 610.

5   *History of Technology*, vol. 1, p. 714; vol. 2, p. 494.

6   *The World Book Encyclopedia* (1984 ed.), vol. 16, p. 338.

7   Victor W. Von Hagen, *The Roads That Led to Rome* (London: Weidenfeld & Nicolson, 1967), pp. 8, 10, 13.

8   David C. Beaman, in Armco Drainage and Metal Products, Inc., *Handbook of Water Control, For the Solution of Problems Involving the Development and Utilization of Water* (Berkeley, California: Lederer, Street, and Zeus Co., Inc., 1946).

9   James R. Chiles, "Engineers versus the Eons, or How Long Will our Monuments Last?" *Smithsonian*, vol. 14 (March 1984), 56–57.

10 Les Robertson, in Chiles, "Engineers," *Smithsonian*, p. 67.

11 Sextus Julius Frontinus, *Water Supply, City of Rome*, trans. Clemens Herschel (Steedham, Mass.: New England Water Works Association, 1973).

12 Ibid., p. 5.

13 *World Book Encyclopedia*, vol. 1, p. 545.

14 Ibid., p. 14.

15 Frontinus, *Water Supply, City of Rome*, pp. 4–5.

16 *APWA Reporter*, magazine section, "People in Public Works," March 1983, April 1980, March 1978, February 1978, and February 1977.

17 CETA refers to the Comprehensive Employment and Training Act, a federally funded program established in 1973 and expired in 1982.

18 Donald Fisk, *Issues in Contracting for Public Services from the Private Sector*, Management Information Service Report, vol. 14, no. 5 (Washington, D.C.: International City Management Association, May 1982), pp. 3–5. This report concisely reviews positive and negative factors in local government contracting.

19 Ellis L. Armstrong, ed., *History of Public Works in the United States: 1776–1976* (Chicago: American Public Works Association, 1976), pp. 687–88.

20 American Public Works Association, *Public Works Management: Trends and Developments*, Special Report 47 (Chicago, 1981), pp. 80–81.

21 J. Hunter, ed., *Peterson's Annual Guide to Undergraduate Study: 1981 Edition* (Princeton, N.J.: Peterson's Guides, Inc., 1980).

22 W. F. Light, "Grim Lot for the Engineers," *Engineering*, vol. 14, no. 7 (July 1980), 2, cited in Michael C. Ircha, "Municipal Engineering: Shifting to a Maintenance Perspective," *Engineering Education* 72 (May 1982).

23 Michael C. Ircha, "Municipal Engineering: Shifting to a Maintenance Perspective," *Engineering Education*, 72 (May 1982), 815-17.

2 Public works organization

A growing trend in the twentieth century has been to group a local government's physical development activities and its delivery of operational services in a public works department. It seems inevitable that this should have happened in view of the ever-increasing number of physical services provided by local jurisdictions during the middle and latter parts of the nineteenth century.

Even before the Revolutionary War it was evident that the citizens beginning to cluster in urbanized areas needed certain basic services. In the early stages of the country's development, delivery of these services was often fragmented. Each service was usually individually provided as the need arose and similar services were not necessarily grouped together in any form of "public works department" as we know it today. As urbanization spread in our developing country, it became increasingly necessary to administer a variety of improvements and operational services in these urban areas. In the twentieth century many of these activities and services have come to be grouped under the general heading of "public works." In earlier times there was never a prescribed procedure for the formation of a public works department because of the many activities that were generally described as "public works." Even today the activities grouped under this general term may not all fall into the same category. In more recent times, however, the trend in small, medium, and fairly large jurisdictions has been to group most development activities along with the provision of physical services under public works (see Figure 2–1).

In the very large and complex jurisdictions, however, this grouping has become unwieldy. As a result, many such jurisdictions have further divided public works activities into several departments in order to be able to administer them effectively. Thus, although the discussion in this chapter focuses on the public works organization as a department of urban government, it should be remembered that very large jurisdictions no longer consolidate all these functions in a single department.

Organization of the public works department

Any group of activities must be effectively organized if those activities are to be efficiently performed. Nowhere in local government is the need for such organization more apparent than in public works. Unlike many other local services, the public works activities of any jurisdiction are usually so varied and widespread that effective organization is imperative. This "effectiveness" can be achieved through a variety of organizational structures, depending on the requirements of local agencies.

As indicated in a report published by the American Public Works Association in 1981, more than three-quarters of the city respondents to a survey of cities and counties in the United States and Canada indicated that their public works activities were centralized within a public works department. The extent to which local jurisdictions have public works departments is shown in Table 2–1.

The percentage of cities in the United States with public works departments (75 percent) is much higher than that of counties (53 percent). This is not

Table 2–1 Status of
public works departments
in U.S. and Canadian
cities and counties,
by region, 1981.

Classification	% with public wks. dept.[1]	Year established (%)[2]			Dis- solved (%)[3]	Never had (%)[4]	No response (%)
		Before 1960	1960– 1969	1970– 1979			
U.S. cities	75	53	24	23	5	8	12
Northeast	76	56	21	24	1	10	13
North Central	76	53	25	27	3	9	12
South	72	49	28	23	4	8	16
West	73	54	22	25	11	6	10
U.S. counties	53	27	23	50	1	30	16
Canadian cities	82	51	21	28	2	3	13
Atlantic	80	51	38	13	0	7	13
Quebec	70	71	14	14	10	0	20
Ontario	79	47	22	31	3	3	15
Prairies and British Columbia	92	55	14	32	0	3	5
Canadian counties	77	40	20	40	0	8	15

Source: American Public Works Association, *Public Works Management: Trends and Developments* (Chicago: American Public Works Association, 1981), p. 30.
1 1,214 respondents.
2 735 respondents.
3 1,217 respondents.
4 1,206 respondents.

surprising if public works are associated with a high degree of urbanization. Counties did not begin to provide urban services on a large scale until the 1960s.

It is interesting to note that a rather large number of places in both the United States and Canada do not have a public works department. Presumably, the functions of street maintenance, street lighting, solid waste service, traffic engineering, and the like are provided by other departments and agencies as well as by other local governments serving the same geographic area.[1]

The wide variety of activities assigned to public works departments in urban areas makes it difficult to compare one jurisdiction with another. Local requirements invariably dictate what emphasis is placed on various functions, how these functions are grouped together, and how many are allocated to the public works department. The functions most often allocated to public works departments are shown in Table 2–2.

Many additional functions performed by local government from time to time have been recognized as public works functions. These additional functions, which are quasi–public works in nature, are most often assigned to other departments of city or county government. These additional functions (see Table 2–3) indicate the substantial number and variety of activities that are related to public works but usually administered elsewhere.

It would be difficult, if not impossible, to find a public works department anywhere that would encompass all the activities listed in Tables 2–2 and 2–3. Despite the great variation, however, it is interesting to note the *basic* similarity in the way public works activities are grouped. In most jurisdictions the functions allocated to the public works department can generally be categorized as either "developmental" or "operational" functions, with an "administrative" grouping to furnish staff support for these two general divisions.

Structure of the public works department

The specific structure of most public works departments is depicted by an organization chart. These charts came into common use in the early part of the twentieth century as more activities were added to the public works department's

Table 2–2   Number of U.S. and Canadian cities and counties providing public works functions within the public works department, 1981.

Function	Total	U.S. cities	Canadian cities	U.S. counties	Canadian counties
Street maintenance	714	568	77	66	3
Street cleaning	697	560	79	56	2
Catch basin cleaning	683	546	76	58	3
Street/traffic sign maintenance	647	503	75	66	3
Catch basic maintenance	645	509	78	55	3
Street/traffic sign installation	643	503	73	64	3
Public works vehicle maintenance	601	473	72	53	3
Street striping (marking)	564	446	58	57	3
S.C. collector maintenance[1]	560	457	74	27	2
S.C. interceptor maintenance[1]	554	450	75	28	1
Snow removal	525	400	78	45	2
Stationary equipment maintenance	491	389	62	38	2
W.C.S. collector maintenance[2]	491	396	72	22	1
Street tree maintenance	466	370	49	45	2
Street design	460	341	60	56	3
W.C.S. interceptor maintenance[2]	447	362	65	20	0
Street/traffic sign manufacturing	446	353	40	50	3
Surveying	440	314	64	60	2
Bridge maintenance	424	305	53	63	3
Traffic engineering	417	318	47	50	2
Street construction	416	306	58	49	3
S.C. retention/collection maintenance[1]	415	340	52	22	1
Weed control	413	328	46	37	2
Solid waste collection	410	338	52	19	1
Police vehicle maintenance	398	341	25	32	0

Source: American Public Works Association, *Public Works Management: Trends and Developments* (Chicago, 1981), p. 20.

1 S.C. = Stormwater control.
2 W.C.S. = Wastewater collection system.

responsibilities. New physical activities initiated by city governments were usually allocated to the public works department because the activities did not seem to "fit" into any other structured department of the city government. Accordingly, organizational charts had to be revised frequently to incorporate changes. Such charts tended to depict an autocratic grouping of activities and to emphasize the rigidity with which many departments appeared to function. The organization chart obviously established a "chain of command" and reinforced the idea that a single individual formulated the plans and controlled the destiny of the department. In many areas, this type of organizational control was the accepted norm during the first half of the twentieth century. Although organization charts are still used to indicate lines of authority and responsibility, they are now less reflective of the actual processes by which public works departments operate.

An important point to note about organizational structure in general is that its effectiveness depends on two basic factors:

1. No matter what structure is adopted, an organization's ability to achieve results is directly related to the effectiveness of its key employees.
2. Any detailed organizational structure will not remain fixed for any

Table 2–3 Number of
U.S. and Canadian cities
and counties providing
public works functions
within "other" departments,
1981.

Function	Total	U.S. cities	Canadian cities	U.S. counties	Canadian counties
Park maintenance	424	340	39	42	3
Zoning	409	327	34	45	3
Code enforcement, housing	393	308	36	47	2
Code inspection, buildings	357	283	30	41	3
Planning (physical)	301	235	24	38	4
Animal control	290	228	30	32	0
Fire vehicle management	289	237	40	11	1
Meter reading	272	244	17	11	0
Building custodial services	265	190	23	51	1
Fire vehicle maintenance	250	210	30	9	1
Building maintenance	250	178	19	52	1
Animal pound	245	190	23	32	0
Dead animal control	241	187	26	26	2
Abandoned vehicles	233	212	8	13	0
Street trees maintenance	222	184	29	9	0
Pumping operation	208	189	9	10	0
Subdivision review	208	171	15	19	3
Water distribution maintenance	206	186	10	10	0
Map maintenance	205	163	14	25	3
Water distribution operation	204	185	10	9	0
Mapping	202	161	13	24	4
Water service installation	192	172	10	10	0
Inspection construction	188	154	15	18	1
Weed control	176	139	9	17	1

Source: American Public Works Association, *Public Works
Management: Trends and Developments* (Chicago, 1981),
p. 21.

extended period of time. As a community's needs and personnel change, the structure must be adjusted to retain its effectiveness.

Figure 2–1 shows a general organization chart for a hypothetical public works department. As can be readily observed, this particular chart includes most of the functions that might be allocated to any public works department. It indicates how a broad variety of activities might be grouped and how they would interact. Although this organization chart could be arranged in many other ways, depending on the needs of any specific community, many basic components would remain the same.[2]

The director and administrative staff

The management and controlling mechanism for the entire department consists of the director—whose responsibility is to interpret existing city policies and guide the development of departmental policies to effectively implement the directions of the city council—and administrative staff. In a large and complex departmental organization, the director may have a deputy to assist in coordinating the volume and variety of services provided by the department.

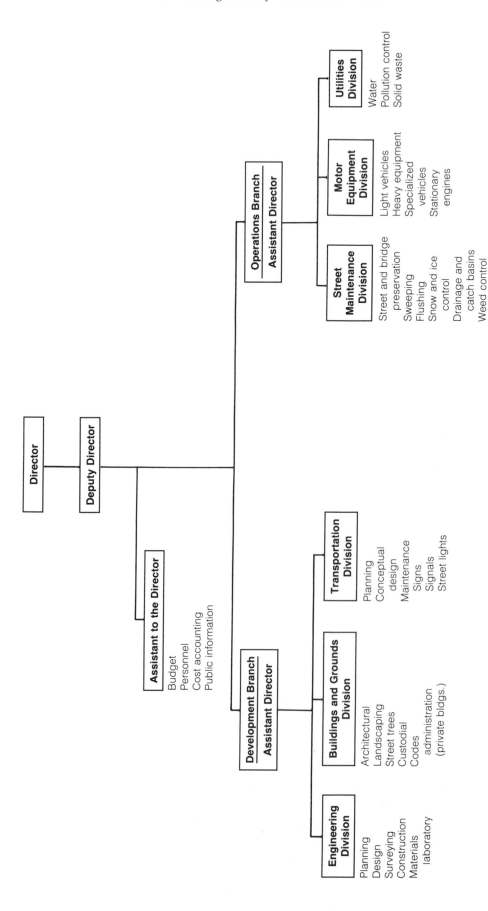

Figure 2–1   Basic public works organization. This hypothetical organization chart suggests the structure and functions that should be evaluated in setting up or restructuring a public works department. The deputy director and the two assistant directors probably will not be needed in smaller city and county departments, and these departments may also combine some of the divisions. These smaller departments, however, will still be providing most of the functions and services shown here.

The administrative staff normally provides support services for all divisions of the department. These services would consist of the assembly, adoption, and control of the departmental budget; all personnel transactions; and control of cost accounting. Other important activities might include processing departmental contracts and managing a public information office.

Administrative support staff may also oversee the centralization and control of complaint responses. By their very nature, public works activities generate many citizen requests for information and additional services. Many development and operational divisions have the basic information to respond to these requests but lack the inclination or ability to do so effectively. Nonetheless, citizens' requests should be answered promptly and with accurate information. Moreover, the answer should be presented tactfully. Although some technical employees lack the skills to provide complaint responses effectively, it is still possible to coordinate the appropriate information for a diplomatic and informative reply.

The administrative group may be responsible for developing and implementing data-processing programs for management information and departmental procedures. Such data facilitate managerial adjustments by providing the results of a huge variety of departmental activities.

The objectives of the administrative staff are to support the development and operations divisions so that their personnel can effectively concentrate on accomplishing their objectives.

Development branch

The development branch of a public works department is usually concerned with planning, designing, constructing, and, in some cases, maintaining the physical improvements within a city. It may be managed and coordinated by an assistant director whose function is to verify that all division activities are related to departmental goals. The primary divisions of this branch are engineering, buildings and grounds, and transportation.

Engineering division   The engineering division is responsible for planning, designing, and constructing public improvements. It is often advantageous to consolidate design and construction for other divisions of public works within the engineering division. In this manner planning can include all public improvements necessary for the development and operations branches of the department. The planning function, one of the most important activities of the engineering division, requires professional judgment in developing physical improvements in their proper sequence.

The design function has to do with the procedure by which general plans for physical development are translated into detailed plans and specifications for construction. This section is responsible for developing design alternatives before a final one is chosen. It also completes standard designs for certain elements of improvement projects to be used throughout the city.

Personnel in design need to have ready access to survey crews, who may be directly responsible to the construction section, so that plans can be developed from survey notes provided by field parties.

The construction section is normally responsible for translating design plans and specifications into the finished construction project. Its work starts with the execution of a construction contract. The section provides inspection during construction to verify that plans and specifications have been followed.

Construction personnel normally supervise field survey crews as well and thus are able to ensure that crews are available to establish field control points governing the precise location of the project under construction. The construction section also certifies that the project has been completed, sees that appropriate information is developed and processed for final payments, and assembles project data for permanent city records.

Buildings and grounds division   The buildings and grounds division normally has jurisdiction over the planning, construction, and overall maintenance of all public buildings and their grounds. In addition, it may have other functions, including responsibility for street trees, custodial operation of public buildings, and the administration of building codes where they apply to private building construction. Because of the variety of its functions, this division may be more complex in organization than other divisions of the public works department.

The planning, design, and construction of public buildings are generally considered to be architectural activities, and personnel skilled in this discipline usually perform these tasks.

The planting and maintenance of street trees, the custodial operation of public buildings, and the administration of building codes for private construction are substantially different activities and may require employees who are more skilled in various crafts and trades. Any of these activities may be of sufficient volume to require separate divisional status.

Transportation division   Transportation responsibilities normally include the conceptual planning for controlled intersections; the design, sequencing, and computerization of required signal equipment; and the development of specific locational plans for traffic signs throughout the city. Necessary street lighting for traffic and pedestrian separation can also be assigned to this division.

The detailed design and construction of specific improvements planned and conceptualized by the transportation division can be handled by the engineering division in the course of its normal activities. Continuous coordination between the two divisions can usually produce the construction of the required elements for transportation control as an integral part of the construction of street improvements. Obviously separate design and construction sections can be maintained by the transportation division, but such an arrangement is liable to result in the duplication of personnel assigned to design and oversee construction projects.

A separate maintenance section is usually warranted within the transportation division, however, for the specific maintenance required for traffic signals, street lights, traffic signs, and traffic striping. Many of these activities require preventive maintenance schedules and specialized equipment. The activities of the transportation division also have to be coordinated with those of the street maintenance division so that the street striping of traffic lanes and crosswalks and the adjustment of traffic signal activators can be closely coordinated with the resurfacing programs of the street maintenance division.

Operations branch

The operations branch of the public works department usually contains service-oriented activities for streets, motor equipment, and utilities. The activities of this branch may also be led by an assistant director to ensure responsiveness to departmental goals. Figure 2–1 shows a typical grouping of these functions.

Street maintenance division   Although it might be argued that street maintenance is logically a part of the engineering or transportation division, it is usually such a substantial and important activity of the department that it warrants divisional status. This is one of the divisions that employs the most people.

The obvious emphasis in street maintenance is the preservation of streets and bridges throughout the city. This embraces a variety of activities ranging from substantial resurfacing programs to shoulder mowing for weed control. Extremely important activities include periodic condition-reviews of bridge structures, patching of street surfaces, sweeping and flushing of improved streets, and controlling snow and ice accumulations on street surfaces. Street maintenance also includes drainage control, catch-basin maintenance, and the removal of weed growth on streets.

This division needs an extremely flexible plan of operation because of seasonal variations in the demand for its services. Street patching is usually needed most at the time of spring thaws. Clearing drainage channels and catch basins is also of prime importance in the spring. Summertime is the period for extensive resurfacing and sealing of street surfaces. Although street surfaces have to be swept and flushed throughout most of the year, they need special attention in the fall, when leaves collecting on streets can impede motorist and pedestrian traffic. Snow and ice control is the primary task of the street maintenance division in areas of extreme winter weather.

At one time or another, most of these activities take place in the face of an emergency. Springtime flooding and wintertime snow and ice are common examples of emergencies that can be anticipated annually. Operational plans should be developed so that effective responses to these emergencies can be delivered.

Motor equipment division   The motor equipment division is charged with drafting specifications and procuring and maintaining all mechanized equipment used by other public works divisions and other departments of the city. This internal service plays a major role in enabling other divisions and departments to deliver their services to the citizens.

Most of the activities of the motor equipment division have to do with the maintenance of automobiles, vans, and other relatively lightweight vehicles used by the city. Employees with average maintenance skills can be assigned to this part of the vehicle fleet, and the maintenance required can be fairly well standardized if established practices are followed in the procurement of automobiles and other lightweight vehicles.

Another extremely important part of public works activities is the maintenance of the heavy-equipment fleet. Heavy equipment normally includes refuse packers, dump trucks, graders, sweepers, flushers, and other types of specialized motor equipment. Because these kinds of vehicles are purchased infrequently, the fleet usually contains a variety of types. Accordingly, maintenance employees assigned to them usually require a greater degree of skill in analyzing problems and performing necessary maintenance. Some jurisdictions divide their heavy-equipment mechanics into geographical units that coincide with the locations where the heavy-equipment vehicles are headquartered.

This division's employees must be prepared to respond to emergency situations in much the same way that street maintenance employees do. They must also maintain all pieces of equipment in operating condition, particularly when emergency conditions are liable to occur. Although seldom recognized, employees of this division can perform just as important a part of the services required by citizens as those employees actually involved in service delivery.

Another responsibility that can be assigned to the motor equipment division is the care and maintenance of specialized types of automotive equipment such as vehicles assigned to the fire-fighting fleet. If such an assignment is made, employees often require specialized training to learn the proper techniques necessary for maintaining aerial ladders, pumps, and other unusual pieces of fire-fighting equipment.

The motor equipment division may also be asked to maintain all of the city's stationary motor equipment. Employees assigned to this task must have a great degree of mobility to complete maintenance schedules on all of this equipment within the city.

Utilities division   Many utility services provided by public works departments are organized as separate utility operations because of the financially self-supporting nature of such services. The common city utilities are water supply, liquid waste control, and solid waste collection and disposal.

These three utilities lend themselves to a utility structure of pricing, accounting, and revenues for several reasons. First, the costs of capital investment, debt service, and operating expenditures can be planned and accounted for with a high degree of accuracy. Second, citizen usage fluctuates widely. For residential users, water requirements vary with income, personal desires, size of family, and other factors directly related to usage. Third, if revenues exceed cost, the surplus can be used to reduce utility fees or to increase other local government services in locations where this is legally possible. Finally, there is strong public support for the idea that water supply and distribution, sewerage and liquid waste service, and refuse collection and disposal should be paid for by the direct users of these services.

The water utility is probably the oldest revenue-producing service provided in urban areas. The need for pure water delivered in useful quantities has been recognized since the earliest days of urban settlement. Since there was agreement on the need for ample quantities of pure water, it was natural that the sale of this precious commodity would become a recognized necessity. Obviously precisely measured costs were involved in the procurement and purification of water supplies and in the delivery of the purified water to required locations.

Although good reasons may exist for a completely self-sufficient and independent water utility, some of its services can still be performed by other parts of the public works department with appropriate charges to the utility. For example, the engineering required for water plant expansions, pumping stations, and water main extensions could be assigned to the engineering division. A system of internal charges can be established so that such engineering services can be properly accounted for and reimbursed to the engineering division from water utility revenues. Motor equipment maintenance and repair services can be performed in a similar manner by appropriate charging between the water utility and the motor equipment division.

The idea of having a separate utility for the collection and treatment of sewage and liquid wastes is of more recent vintage. With the establishment of federal requirements for sewage treatment before such waste material is discharged to receiving waters, however, a separate utility operation has become much more readily accepted. Necessary charges for building and operating sewage treatment plants to meet these requirements has now become a recognized part of required city services.

Similarly, some public works departments have organized a separate pollution control utility when it has been necessary to separate and account for all revenues from this operation. Such a pollution control utility may be a part of an existing water utility (keeping separate accounts), or it may be completely separated. What is important is that all revenues received for these purposes be separated from other city revenues so as to ensure that they are used solely for the necessary expenses of each utility.

In a similar manner, a solid waste collection and disposal utility may be a part of the public works department in certain jurisdictions. A separate utility for this purpose is much less common than one for water and pollution control. Many cities are still providing the cost for solid waste collection and disposal from general revenues. Accordingly, a service charge is not rendered and separate utility operations are not required. However, as the competition for general city revenues increases to cover new types of programs, waste disposal is a specific service for which a user fee can usually be more easily established than for other city services.

As requirements for solid waste disposal become more stringent, it is likely that more cities and counties will assume direct control over waste collection and disposal practices to safeguard the quality of the environment. As this occurs, user charges will become more widespread, and a separate utility operation can be expected.

Participative management

The formal lines of authority and responsibility emphasized a couple of decades ago have given way to new ideas about organizational structure. Although the structure for the public works department still needs to be defined, the formal organization chart has become more of a set of guidelines, a method of communicating the way the department is generally operated, than a visual representation of a hierarchy.

In practice, the widespread need in recent years to increase production with the same or lesser amount of revenue dollars has led to a more participative form of management than the rigid organization chart would indicate. Participative management means developing and implementing policies by pooling ideas from many sources—individual employees, their supervisors, their division heads, and others within the department. Participative management has evolved into more of a team approach in the setting of goals and objectives. In some cases, however, it is difficult to determine whether an effective team approach to goal setting and problem solving exists or can be created within any particular public works department.

Figure 2–2 represents an interesting exercise by which a department director and departmental division heads might determine whether their organization was actually functioning as a team in approaching common problems. An objective analysis of the answers will indicate whether the organization is functioning as a team operation.

Most public works directors and other local government managers now hold that the team concept in organization must be applied if maximum results are to be achieved. Some department heads, however, may not be convinced of the value of a team approach or understand what such an approach really encompasses. It does not mean simply that employees and their supervisors conduct "brainstorming" sessions without reaching specific conclusions. It does not mean that specific responsibilities for reaching decisions and acting upon them are abandoned. Nor does it mean that employees at all levels share their ideas and then pool their valid suggestions in adopting improved managerial procedures. It does mean the realistic consideration of ideas from all sources in the process of developing goals that are adopted and followed.

Lee Iacocca, the remarkably successful chairman of the Chrysler Corporation, has developed a philosophy of team leadership that has been described in the following manner:

Potent responsiveness requires responsibility. Listening, talking and even understanding is not enough. . . . Iacocca uses a quarterly goal-setting session with each of his subordinates. He institutes this process down the managerial line.

Those subordinates come to these sessions with their hopes, plans and priorities. The dialogue with their manager focuses on a 90-day projection of what's to be accomplished and how. This process makes the employees accountable to both themselves and their bosses. It also creates a dialogue between levels of management which encourages good working relationships.

Responsive, planful, action-oriented management needs a decisive manager. Iacocca says, "if I had to sum up in one word the qualities that make a good manager, I'd say that it all comes down to decisiveness." He knows that passivity equals no response, no leadership and no movement.

Decisiveness requires a certain amount of risk-taking. Committees are fine for

Figure 2–2 Do you really have a team?

To find areas for improvement toward the positive aspects of a functioning team, use the following scales to evaluate your work group. Score it three times, either by color coding the response or reproducing the form. First, how would *you* score *your* department? Second, how would *your employees* score the department? Finally, evaluate all your municipal departments as a cooperative unit. How does your municipality score as a team?

	1	2	3	4	5	
Communications
Guarded, cautious	___	___	___	___	___	Open, authentic
Department goals and objectives
Not understood by team	___	___	___	___	___	Clearly understood by team
Priorities
Not understood	___	___	___	___	___	Clearly understood
Not accepted	___	___	___	___	___	Accepted
Conflicts
We deny, avoid, or suppress conflicts	___	___	___	___	___	We accept conflicts and "work them through"
Member resources
Our abilities, knowledge, and experience are not used	___	___	___	___	___	Our abilities, knowledge, and experience are fully used
Control
Control is imposed on us	___	___	___	___	___	We control ourselves
Department environment
Restrictive, pressure conforming	___	___	___	___	___	Free, supportive, respect for individual differences
Roles of team members
Not understood	___	___	___	___	___	Clearly understood
Not agreed upon	___	___	___	___	___	Agreed upon
Decision making
Not understood	___	___	___	___	___	Clearly understood
Not agreed upon	___	___	___	___	___	Agreed upon
We are not involved	___	___	___	___	___	We are involved

generating and sharing ideas. Individuals make decisions. Iacocca acknowledges the mix of intuition and facts needed for decisions. He's critical of "bean counters" who want to wait for all the facts before making a decision. By the time all the facts are in, it's too late.

The good manager takes a modicum of data and uses it to examine possible options and scenarios. Iacocca wants to consider a choice between vanilla and chocolate before making a decision. If it's a big ticket decision, he'll also consider strawberry.

Although some of Iacocca's critics portray him as "shooting from the hip," he denies this. With his usual wry sense of humor he suggests that practice has given him the ability to hit a moving target.

Iacocca makes it clear that good management combines experience and education. He is not a born manager. He freely acknowledges those who taught him valuable lessons. He recognizes the paradoxes of good management. It means being both tough and generous.[3]

This description indicates how an effective leader uses the team approach. It allows for sufficient input, but it leaves no doubt about how the final decision will be reached. This approach gives each team member adequate opportunity to be heard, but it also recognizes that the final determination is the responsibility of the team leader.

Alternatives for public works organization

In many cities and counties the public works department does not include all public works activities, usually because such an organization would be excessively large and unwieldy or because some services—utilities are a common example—generally develop their own constituencies and revenue sources. Some examples of organizational alternatives are described in the following paragraphs.

Department of community development

An alternative to consolidating all public works activities into one department is to establish other departments for certain public works functions. A department of community development normally combines some of the activities of public works planning and engineering with a focus on the physical development of the community. A few community development departments also provide overall community planning, including land use planning, zoning and subdivision regulation, economic base studies, transportation planning, and other components of the comprehensive planning program.

The primary goal of a department of this type is to develop an effective capital improvements program that can be implemented over the next five or six years. Such a department may also be responsible for attracting new private development to the city as well as keeping the existing developments satisfied. Such efforts will lead to the establishment of short- and long-range capital improvements programs that will integrate public improvements desired by private developers with those desired by resident citizens. This approach recognizes that public and private interests must work together if the community as a whole is to benefit.

Department of utilities

As mentioned earlier, revenue-producing services provided by the city are often assigned to separate departments. This approach recognizes that revenues received for a specific purpose need to be accounted for separately and used only for expenses required to achieve that purpose. Normal public works activities that lend themselves to a utility status are water, pollution control or sewage treatment, and solid waste collection and disposal. A utilities department in a city could adequately manage all three of these.

In a department of utilities each separate service would undoubtedly be given divisional status. Each division would operate autonomously but under the general control of the department director. Some common administrative functions could be shared with appropriate charges being made to each utility division for its share of these functions. Annual audits of each utility should normally be provided in order to verify that user fees have been properly allocated and expended for the purposes intended.

In larger jurisdictions the various utilities can become so complex that a separate department may well be needed for each. Even in this event, however, common administrative requirements should be consolidated to eliminate duplication of effort. Suitable overhead charges accounted for and made to each utility department can divide the cost of these common services.

Department of transportation

In recent years the transportation needs of citizens in congested urban areas have become so complex that many of these areas have formed a separate department of transportation. Historically, the transportation or traffic operation in a public works department was concerned with establishing and maintaining traffic signals and signs and with striping traffic lanes on arterial streets.

As multiple forms of transportation have increasingly affected urban communities, the transportation function in many areas has expanded to include port maintenance and operations; airport construction, maintenance, and operation; and the provision of appropriate mass transit services for the community. As a result, the transportation services within some cities have come to be closely integrated. A separate department is in a position to coordinate more effectively all of the various forms of transportation a community may have access to. In this manner adequate highway and transit facilities can be planned to serve private and public port operations, airports, and bus and railroad facilities.

Even though a separate department may exist for the integrated planning of all transportation needs, it may still be appropriate to use the public works department to develop construction plans and specifications for many of its capital improvements and to provide maintenance for vehicles and restricted roadways. One of the basic reasons why staff services within various city departments are duplicated is that many believe each department should be completely self-supporting. Proper assignment of and attention to common services throughout the city can help eliminate much of this duplication and thereby reduce administrative and overhead costs. When the demand for greater production and lower costs intensifies, the potential for increased efficiency develops.

Other forms of organization

Although the preceding discussion of organizational structure is applicable to most jurisdictions, there are certainly other forms of organization to consider. In small, completely developed cities, the engineering division that has such a prominent role in most public works departments may be eliminated. Most public works activities in smaller jurisdictions tend to emphasize maintenance and the delivery of operational services. In this situation, the required maintenance for all types of public facilities can be consolidated in one division, which might handle not only the physical maintenance of streets, bridges, public buildings, and equipment, but also custodial maintenance.

The other division of this extremely modified version of a public works department would include most of the utility operations previously discussed. Such a division would be responsible for the delivery of adequate water, provision of sewage treatment, and the collection and disposal of solid waste. Most of these services could be provided through contracts with adjacent communities or with private contractors.

Relations with independent and quasi-independent bodies

In providing the entire range of public works services, the department concerned will have to work with various types of boards and commissions. Some will be professionally organized and staffed with highly qualified employees. Others will be less professionally competent and will require a great deal of assistance. Examples of these boards and commissions are utility boards, transit commissions, and private utilities.

Utility boards

Some utility boards are completely outside the framework of city and county government. The rationale for such boards is that their geographical service areas do not have to coincide with the boundaries of individual jurisdictions, or with the continuing need, previously emphasized, to segregate user fees. Such utility boards normally receive enough financial support to provide staff who are professionally qualified to deliver the services they are responsible for.

A primary concern of most public works departments in dealing with utility boards is adequate control over the placement and maintenance of the utilities' facilities. Utility location and coordination committees contribute vitally to acceptable results. The establishment of "one-call" systems has helped to minimize the disruption of various utilities within an urban area. The one-call system requires that representatives from the utility board, other private utility companies, the city or county government, and perhaps the state highway department carefully plan and coordinate their overlapping activities for such installations as sewer lines, telephone lines, water mains, and cable television lines. Thus, only one call is needed for specific facility locations, curb cuts, pavement cuts, street tree trimming, and other services that must be provided so that utility installations can proceed in accordance with location and design standards and with a minimum of disruption and expense.

Transit commissions

A separate transit commission is also common. Such commissions usually supply transit services to an area that is much broader than that encompassed by the city limits. Some transit routes traverse several adjoining cities in order to provide adequate service. It is imperative that the construction of any separate transit facilities for rail or bus service be coordinated with the local governments they serve. It is also imperative that local public works departments retain current information on established transit and bus routes. This will ensure the necessary coordination of all mass transit activities through liaison with the transportation division of the public works department.

Private utilities

The public works department interacts with many private companies, including electric and gas companies, telephone companies, cable television companies, and railroads. All of these utility companies need to place their facilities along or across city streets in a variety of locations. These private companies provide necessary services to urban areas, and a coordinated effort is required to see that their facilities are properly placed. A utility location and coordination council can be used for this purpose. In addition, it is appropriate to execute long-term agreements between the city and the companies involved indicating the fair responsibilities of each in the maintenance of these private facilities.

Councils of governments

In recent years councils of governments (COGs) have been established in most metropolitan areas. The COG makes it much easier for cities and counties within a metropolitan area to work together on plans and projects of common interest by coordinating individual efforts to produce work that all can use. Here are two examples.

1. Through extensive cooperation, standard public works construction specifications can be developed and adopted for the entire metropolitan area.
2. The COG provides a clearinghouse for the exchange of information on *all* public improvements planned for the entire area. This is particularly useful in planning improvements for drainage areas, arterial streets, and other facilities that cross jurisdictional boundaries.

Relations with county, state, and federal agencies

In most jurisdictions, relations with other units of government usually revolve around (1) the effective use of grant money that may be available for new improvements, and (2) the coordination of services that may be delivered to citizens as a joint responsibility of more than one government. Local public works organizations must be continuously aware of the possibilities of any state and federal grants that might be used. Thus, they will be in a position to ensure not only that the greatest number of public improvements are achieved for the local area, but also that matching local funds available for a variety of projects are budgeted in the most effective manner.

Various governmental agencies may also have requirements for providing public works services that overlap with those of other jurisdictions. In such cases, close coordination can minimize duplication. Agreements can be developed between the various agencies to designate which one will take on individual responsibilities.

Conclusion

The basic organizational structure of public works for most city governments, and for many county governments as well, encompasses an extraordinary array of functions and activities that impinge on the physical environment. Figure 2–1 suggests this array, but it does not show either the many kinds of professions, occupations, and skills that make public works possible or the dynamics of participative management that make all the pieces fit together.

Public works is usually thought of as engineering, but it also includes and is involved with urban planning, architecture, landscape architecture, financial management, employee relations, and a wide variety of occupations connected with the construction and maintenance of physical facilities.

The formal organization of a public works department does not indicate the way in which most departments actually function. Participative management practices have generally been initiated in jurisdictions that are operated most effectively. This concept allows a sharing of the departmental management process so that all personnel have a part in the formulation of most public works policies and the development of most public works programs. Through this kind of management procedure and the effective coordination of public works activities with those of various other boards, commissions, and governmental agencies, local governments can provide a comprehensive approach to the creation of public works improvements and the effective delivery of public works services.

1   See American Public Works Association, *Public Works Management: Trends and Developments*, Special Report 47 (Chicago, 1981), pp. 30–31. This report, based on a survey of 1,218 cities and counties in the United States and Canada, provides a good overview of organization, finance, personnel, personal and educational characteristics of public works managers, and management concepts and issues.

2   Figure 2–1 and the following discussion are based on municipal public works departments, but they apply equally well to many county governments and their public works departments, especially counties that have substantial urbanized areas.

3   Sandra Eveloff, "Iacocca's Story Tells You How To Be a Good Manager," *Kansas City Business Journal*, January 7, 1985, p. 22.

3 Information systems

The concepts of modern management that evolved during this century originate in various schools of thought. The thread that runs through all the discussion about management, starting with Taylor's Scientific Management Theory, is the need for information. It may be called feedback or communication; whatever it is called, information remains a key ingredient of management.

Henry Mintzberg, in his study of managerial work, identified the central roles that managers perform.[1] Information is squarely at the center of the Mintzberg model. The informational roles constitute one of the three basic types of roles that managers perform. Information is critical to the function of management as it is now known.

Data versus information

Often technological advancements bring about new management concepts that produce a flurry of activity and new procedures for maximizing the use of a technology. The evolution of information systems, assisted by computer technology, is an example. Consequently, the purpose of this chapter is to assist public works managers in understanding the basic difference between data and information and between management information systems and data processing.

Data are pieces of facts, independent in nature and unlimited in number. Data can be an end in themselves, as in accounting records, street maintenance records, or vehicle repair records. The data items that make up these records have meaning for a particular event.

Information is the result of arranging data into meaningful knowledge. For instance, a vehicle record is composed of various pieces of data (see Figure 3–1). By processing several records, we can transfer the data into cost relationships—that is, cost per mile for the operation of a specific vehicle over a specific amount of time (see Figure 3–2). The data are the same, but now some pieces have been presented in relation to other pieces and thereby have meaning beyond the single fact each represents. Together, the relevant pieces constitute information. Consequently, information is always made up of data—but not all data produce meaningful information. Information can also be defined as knowledge since it helps to reduce uncertainty and enhance understanding (Figure 3–3).

Information revolution

Without doubt, technological improvements in this century have changed the way managers approach their jobs. Telecommunications, satellite hookups, and computer-enhanced networks have all been involved in the information revolution. In his book *Megatrends*, John Naisbitt notes the impact of moving from an industrial-based to an information-based society:[2] Information and its availability are reshaping management's approach to problems in the same way that Taylor's principles of scientific management revolutionized management itself. The rapid change that has been set in motion by the information revolution is realigning organizations. Furthermore, local government managers are being

Figure 3–1 Motor vehicle record data.

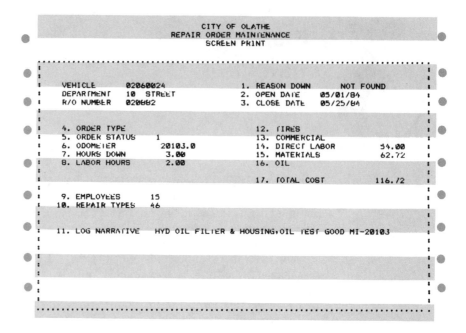

```
                        CITY OF OLATHE
                  REPAIR ORDER MAINTENANCE
                        SCREEN PRINT

   VEHICLE      02060024          1. REASON DOWN      NOT FOUND
   DEPARTMENT   10  STREET        2. OPEN DATE     05/01/84
   R/O NUMBER   020882            3. CLOSE DATE    05/25/84

   4. ORDER TYPE                 12. TIRES
   5. ORDER STATUS    1          13. COMMERCIAL
   6. ODOMETER        20103.0    14. DIRECT LABOR       54.00
   7. HOURS DOWN       3.00      15. MATERIALS          62.72
   8. LABOR HOURS      2.00      16. OIL

                                 17. TOTAL COST        116.72

   9. EMPLOYEES      15
  10. REPAIR TYPES   46

  11. LOG NARRATIVE    HYD OIL FILTER & HOUSING,OIL TEST GOOD MI-20103
```

asked to reduce the uncertainty of decisions and their impact on a community. The expectation levels of informed citizens and community groups are pushing governments to pursue efficiency, effectiveness, and economy with new zeal. All of this is happening because society now has a common resource—information.

Computer impact on information

The information revolution has been fueled by the computer, both by its hardware and by its software. The hardware is the machine part of the system, while the software represents the instructions that cause the machine to operate.

Hardware technology has improved in size, speed, cost, and storage capacity. The size of computers has been reduced from machines as large as a room to units the size of a television set. Early machines used vacuum tubes, which were replaced by transistors, and now these have been replaced by integrated circuit chips. The miniaturization of computer parts has also brought vastly increased speed and enlarged memory. The shorter the route, the faster an electric charge will reach its destination.

Reduced cost is another by-product of miniaturization. Mass production has helped to drive costs down. Certainly the reduced cost of computer data storage is as impressive as any of the advances. Entire reference libraries can now be stored off line but can be readily accessed by the computer's main processor.

As impressive as these advances are, hardware alone will not do the job. Many computer professionals cite the advances in software as the real catalyst that has triggered the computer explosion. Some argue that software developments have driven specific hardware developments. Now, for example, more than one station is able to use the computer and more than one program can be in operation at the same time. When the hardware and software developments are combined, it becomes obvious that impressive advances have been made in just two decades.

Data processing versus management information

Most managers have a systematic or organized way of developing information. In many instances, managers filter information they receive by informal means.

CITY OF OLATHE
MANAGEMENT INFORMATION SUMMARY
JULY 1965

DEPARTMENT 10 STREET

02050022 PICKUP

	YTD		TOTAL $	DOWN HRS	LIFETIME
FUEL $ 366	LABOR $ 338		YTD 843	YTD 21.25	USE (MI) 86,241.0
OIL $ 15	MATL $ 172		LTD 9,413	LTD 404.00	COST/MI FUEL .06
TIRE $	OUTSIDE $				COST/MI TOTL .11

02050027 BLAZER

	YTD		TOTAL $	DOWN HRS	LIFETIME
FUEL $ 484	LABOR $ 621		YTD 1,461	YTD 87.50	USE (MI) 88,552.0
OIL $ 15	MATL $ 321		LTD 16,177	LTD 907.50	COST/MI FUEL .06
TIRE $	OUTSIDE $ 18				COST/MI TOTL .18

02050421 PICKUP

	YTD		TOTAL $	DOWN HRS	LIFETIME
FUEL $ 174	LABOR $ 149		YTD 1,180	YTD 6.00	USE (MI) 26,421.0
OIL $ 34	MATL $ 19		LTD 4,355	LTD 33.50	COST/MI FUEL .10
TIRE $ 184	OUTSIDE $ 18				COST/MI TOTL .16

02060005 DUMP TRUCK

	YTD		TOTAL $	DOWN HRS	LIFETIME
FUEL $ 473	LABOR $ 2,314		YTD 6,303	YTD 247.75	USE (MI) 68,650.0
OIL $ 16	MATL $ 2,374		LTD 20,711	LTD 881.50	COST/MI FUEL .06
TIRE $	OUTSIDE $ 1,124				COST/MI TOTL .30

02060013 DUMP TRUCK

	YTD		TOTAL $	DOWN HRS	LIFETIME
FUEL $ 434	LABOR $ 1,255		YTD 3,294	YTD 144.50	USE (MI) 34,267.0
OIL $ 23	MATL $ 1,581		LTD 23,475	LTD 1,111.25	COST/MI FUEL .18
TIRE $	OUTSIDE $				COST/MI TOTL .70

02060014 DUMP TRUCK

	YTD		TOTAL $	DOWN HRS	LIFETIME
FUEL $ 440	LABOR $ 975		YTD 2,615	YTD 40.50	USE (MI) 28,687.0
OIL $ 17	MATL $ 282		LTD 25,809	LTD 1,237.50	COST/MI FUEL .14
TIRE $	OUTSIDE $ 900				COST/MI TOTL .90

02060016 DUMP TRUCK

	YTD		TOTAL $	DOWN HRS	LIFETIME
FUEL $ 660	LABOR $ 1,158		YTD 2,858	YTD 202.00	USE (MI) 84,217.0
OIL $ 30	MATL $ 369		LTD 32,997	LTD 1,544.00	COST/MI FUEL .11
TIRE $	OUTSIDE $ 639				COST/MI TOTL .39

Figure 3-2 Monthly motor vehicle cost data.

Figure 3–3   Hierarchy of data, information, and intelligence.

Data: recorded observations of real world phenomena

Information: level of knowledge needed to solve a problem or show patterns

Intelligence: essential factors selected from information and data

Knowledge: total concept of data, information, and intelligence with feedback loop

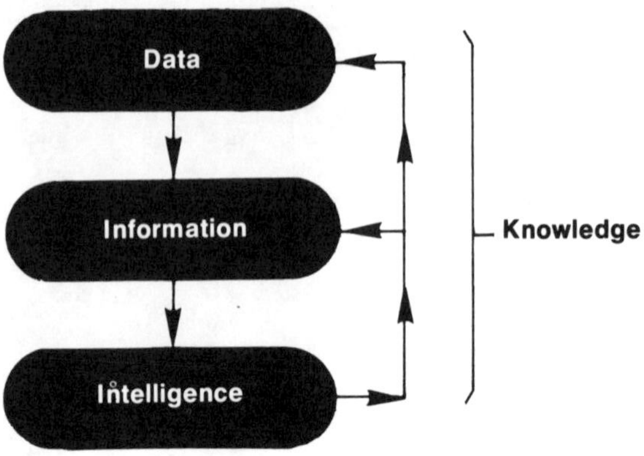

Informal information is made up of nonstructured, verbal, or observed bits and pieces of data and activity. Informal information is undoubtedly a necessary part of a manager's resources, but a formal, routine, and systematic means of obtaining information on the performance of the organization is just as important. The first management information systems were accounting systems that provided management with financial information. The advent of computer systems with data base capacity enlarged the focus of information systems to total organizational needs, not just finance.

Data processing (DP)

Data processing (DP) means performing operations through which facts and figures are collected, assigned meaning, communicated to others, and retained for later use. Data are facts and figures, and processing is the manipulation of those facts and figures. The following activities are the means by which data processing turns data into information: recording, classifying, sorting, calculating, summarizing, comparing, communicating, storing, and retrieving.

All data processing involves one or more of these activities and all are part of this basic data-processing cycle.

Input	**Processing**	**Output**
Record	Classify	Communicate
	Sort	
	Calculate	
	Summarize	
	Compare	

Management information system (MIS)

Data processing performs an internal operation function. The management information system (MIS) picks up where DP leaves off. That is, DP provides input for MIS, but other external data are also injected as input, and thus provide a wider scope of information for the manager. Typically, data processing and MIS are built up from the data base through control and planning, as shown in Figure 3–4. Note the changes in emphasis, depending on the level of management. One of the key points in the evolution of MIS is the movement from a financial system to a decision support system (Figure 3–5).

Figure 3–4   Interactions of data processing and MIS.

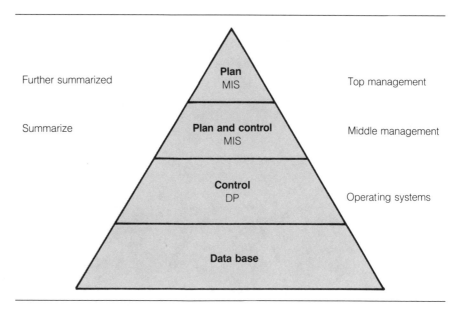

Further summarized	**Plan** MIS	Top management
Summarize	**Plan and control** MIS	Middle management
	Control DP	Operating systems
	Data base	

Decision support system (DSS)

Decision support systems, which are an outgrowth of data processing, recognize the fact that automated systems will not replace the manager. In effect, a DSS works to enhance the quality of management by reducing uncertainty. A DSS will accomplish one or more of the following:

1. Retrieve specific pieces of data
2. Analyze data elements in a data base
3. Interact with several data bases and analyze problems
4. Estimate the consequences of decisions
5. Propose decisions.

The system works for all levels—line, staff, and management—and is usually concerned with overall effectiveness. It focuses on the present as well as the future. In the final analysis, MIS provides the basic information, while DSS takes the information one step further by using it to make a decision.

MIS defined

MIS can be defined as a "network of computer-based data processing procedures developed in an organization and *integrated as necessary* with other manual, mechanical, and/or electronic procedures for the purpose of providing timely and effective information to support decision making. . . ."[3]

Most public works agencies have had to decide when to replace equipment. Figure 3–5 represents a step toward a DSS in vehicle replacement. If the vehicle that has been targeted for replacement cannot be replaced and operated at a lower cost, it stays in the fleet. The system has stopped the trade-out of vehicles just because they have reached a certain age.

According to the preceding definition, the development of an information system should be rather straightforward. However, the following factors must be taken into account in developing and producing the information:

1. *Timeliness*. Out-of-date information is of no use to the manager. Figure 3–6 is a weekly fuel report that automatically generates timely informa-

CITY OF OLATHE
VEHICLE REPLACEMENT ANALYSIS

VEHICLE TYPE A1 E SEDAN EMERGCY

EXPECTED LIFE (MI OR HR)
EXPECTED ANNUAL USE (MI OR HR)

		PROJECTED LIFE (YRS)		REPLACEMENT COST		PROJECTED CAPITAL COST/YR	
		VEHICLE	DEPARTMENT	PURCHASED			
YR MFGR	PURCH COST	OPER COST	MAINT COST	TOTAL COST	HOURS/MILES	TOTAL COST/MI(HR)	DOWN HOURS
77 CH CHEVROLET	02010012	13 COMMUNITY DEV		07/29/77			
LTD ->	4,232.45	1,576.52	2,084.59	3,661.11	4,188.0	.08	94.5
AVG/YR ->	533.71	198.80	262.87	461.68	5446.2	.08	11.9
77 CH CHEVROLET	02010013	22 UTILITIES		07/29/77			
LTD ->	4,232.35	1,744.78	2,139.20	3,883.98	31940.0	.12	127.2
AVG/YR ->	533.71	220.02	269.76	489.78	4034.0	.12	16.0
78 CH CHEVROLET	02010014	19 WATER PLANT		05/26/78			
LTD ->	4,519.20	1,932.47	2,337.84	4,270.31	42008.0	.10	178.5
AVG/YR ->	636.51	272.18	329.27	601.45	5916.6	.10	25.1
79 FD FORD	02010401	13 COMMUNITY DEV		06/18/79			
LTD ->	5,024.72	1,912.07	1,495.34	3,407.41	44570.0	.08	189.2
AVG/YR ->	831.91	316.57	247.57	564.14	7379.1	.08	31.3
79 FD FORD	02010402	13 COMMUNITY DEV		06/18/79			
LTD ->	5,024.72	2,365.46	4,448.52	6,813.98	39895.0	.17	351.2
AVG/YR ->	831.91	391.63	736.51	1,128.14	6605.1	.17	58.2
79 FD FORD	02010403	11 SERVICES		06/18/79			
LTD ->	5,024.72	1,423.36	1,555.98	2,980.34	53367.0	.06	116.5
AVG/YR ->	831.91	235.66	257.61	493.43	8835.6	.06	19.3
79 PL PLYMOUTH	02010304	14 HOUSING AUTH		06/08/79			
LTD ->	5,850.00	2,582.50	3,475.74	6,060.24	61058.0	.10	470.7
AVG/YR ->	963.76	425.45	572.61	948.39	10054.0	.10	77.6

Figure 3-5 Vehicle replacement analysis.

```
                              CITY OF OLATHE
                          WEEKLY FUEL USE REPORT
                           WEEK ENDING 7-31-85
```

FUEL TYPE	GALLONS	COST	TOTAL $	YTD TOTAL $	YTD TOTAL GALLONS
1 REGULAR	1576.0	1.026	1,616.98	43,643.19	45815.0
2 DIESEL	1766.0	.763	1,347.46	42,597.28	50327.0
3 UNLEADED	2087.0	1.056	2,203.87	61,949.68	62360.0
TOTAL	5429.0		5,168.31	148,190.15	158502.0

Figure 3–6 Weekly fuel use report.

tion. Comparing the information to that from a prior week or from the same period a year ago can be a significant indicator.

2. *Completeness*. All of the information must be included, particularly for a decision support system. Figure 3–7 is a street report showing sections of street needing an overlay as well as the history of the street. This type of report can be used by supervisors as well as by management. The total number of streets needing overlay, sealing, rejuvenation, or crack seal can also be used by city councils or county boards to determine levels of support (budget allocations) for maintenance.

3. *Conciseness*. In the computer environment of today, vast amounts of data can be dumped onto managers. The system must be able to summarize data. Figure 3–8 shows how the computer filters information for an exception routine. In this case all vehicles with a total monthly cost in excess of $500 will be reported. This routine allows a manager to zero in on a problem while operating within an information system that utilizes large volumes of data.

4. *Relevance*. Often information that was once critical has been modified to the point where it is no longer relevant. One of the goals of MIS is to produce information that will generate action or provide insight.

Computer use

Information systems depend on the computer. Consequently, computer system design will affect the information system. The basic computer system is composed of input, processor, storage, output, and data communication. The arrangement of the basic components or the manner in which they are managed will affect the information system.

Centralized versus decentralized data processing

In centralized data processing all assets are controlled and operated by a single department. All other data-processing users must go through the centralized department for computer support. In many cases centralized DP allows management to tightly control computer resources. Usually a committee will help referee who receives priority service.

Decentralized data processing means that each department has its own data-processing operation, funds its own requirements, and reports to higher management on the success or failure of its DP support. Obviously decentralization for a local government represents a move from concern for cost to concern for service. Decentralization encourages duplication since data files are structured by functional areas. Shared information is difficult to pass from one department to another.

CITY OF OLATHE
STREET MANAGEMENT REPORT

STREETS REQUIRING OVERLAY

STREET	LENGTH	DATE CHECKED	LAST REJUV	LAST CHIP	LAST OVRLY	LAST CRACK	TRAFFIC COUNT
119TH ST. - K.C. RD. TO RENNER RD.	.2	06/01/84					
AVALON - SUNVALE TERR. TO SUNVALE	.1	07/01/84					
BLACKBOB - SANTA FE TO 151ST ST.	2.0	06/01/84		81			
BURCH - SANTA FE TO LOULA	.2	06/01/84		82			
CATHY KCIR. - DIANE DR. TO WEST END	.1	06/01/84					
CEDAR - CLAIRBORNE TO MURLEN - 1	.5	06/01/84		82			
CEDAR - KANSAS TO K-7	.7	06/01/84		83			
CEDAR - KANSAS TO KEELER - 2	X	03/21/85		80			
CEDAR HILLS RD. - DENNIS TO SO. END - 2	X	06/01/84					
CHERRY - LOULA TO SOUTHGATE	.4	06/01/84		81			
CHESTER TERR. - LOULA TO ELM	.2	06/01/84					
CHESTNUT - LOULA TO SOUTHGATE	.4	06/01/84		82			
CHESTNUT - PRAIRIE TO NO. END	.4	06/01/84					
CHESTNUT - PRAIRIE TO WHITNEY - 2	X	06/01/84		83			
CHURCH - SHERIDAN TO LAKE DR.	.1	06/01/84		81			
DENNIS - K-7 TO LAKESHORE - 1	1.8	06/01/84					
DENNIS - ROBINSON TO LAKESHORE	1.8	06/01/84					
DIANE DR. - DENNIS TO NO. END - 1	.1	06/01/84		84			
DRURY LN. - RIDGEVIEW TO RIDGEWAY	.2	06/01/84			82		
EDGEMERE - SHERIDAN TO FROOST	.3	06/01/84			80		
EDGEMERE - WABASH TO SHERIDAN	.2	06/01/84		81			
FERRELL - DENNIS TO ALTA LN. - 2	.2	03/21/85			80		

Figure 3-7   Street management report.

CITY OF OLATHE
EXECUTIVE EXCEPTION REPORT
MTD TOTAL $ OVER   500
MONTH ENDING 7-25-85

VEHICLE	FUEL $	OIL $	LABOR $	OUTSIDE $	MATL $	TIRE $	MTD TOTAL $	YTD TOTAL $
DEPARTMENT 10 STREET								
02060016	81.05		405.00		488.93		974.98	3,833.39
02060018	329.35	14.95	182.25		82.66		609.21	3,420.32
02060025	68.74		128.25		497.59		694.58	1,432.88
02060094	19.84		985.50	30.00	199.45		1,234.79	1,234.79
02060099	150.31		216.00		247.48		613.79	3,858.89
02060029A	647.79						647.79	851.10
02060608	238.03	34.95	222.75	71.35	174.04		741.12	7,689.37
10000000	333.45	68.30	168.75	97.80	377.30		1,045.60	3,526.58
43011000	36.62		141.75		1,091.47		1,269.84	19,049.65
43231450			209.25	529.14	100.82		839.21	944.41
DEPARTMENT 11 SERVICES								
02010332	69.70		40.75	859.24			969.69	5,974.49
DEPARTMENT 12 SANITATION								
02060100	242.63	9.54	111.00		59.81	365.40	788.38	5,255.71
02060701	235.00	26.98	204.00		111.37		577.35	6,667.07
02060702	215.93	28.97	243.00		53.06		540.96	14,704.68
02060703	119.03	23.76	97.50		46.05	365.40	651.74	8,804.13
02060704	167.86	21.25	244.50		225.08	182.70	841.39	12,946.38
02060705	187.70	39.64	330.75	1,439.99	26.10		2,024.18	9,792.07
02070100	162.52	50.95	1,775.25	595.12	712.57		3,296.41	14,104.53
02070101	276.21	50.95	405.00	60.00	70.19		862.35	9,978.94
02070102	301.39		357.25		100.08		758.72	14,062.01

Figure 3–8 Monthly motor vehicle exception report.

The boundaries of MIS   A well-established MIS can do a great deal to help managers process information and make decisions. But of course there are limits to what an MIS can do.

Information boundaries   One way to view MIS boundaries is to consider them in terms of information. How much information does the system need in order to provide management with what it wants? For many kinds of tasks—planning and forecasting, for example—MIS must be able to reach for information far from the organization itself and at the same time collect information about the most minute in-house transactions. The boundaries here depend on the cost-benefit analysis. Is the benefit of having this information— or this capability—worth its cost?

Processing boundaries   MIS boundaries can be viewed in processing as well as informational terms. Just how complex a problem can MIS solve? MIS can easily process automatic, programmable decisions by using conventional decision rules and specific policies that are quantifiable. More sophisticated, however, is semiautomatic processing, which employs the user system interface to replace the completely automatic programming of decisions. The MIS still plays an active role in processing, but now there is a measure of human intervention in the decision-making process.

When still more sophistication is required, the role of MIS in decision making becomes negligible from the processing standpoint. Thus, MIS is also bound by its limitations in processing decisions.

Input–process–output boundaries
MIS boundaries can also be viewed in terms of inputs, processing, and outputs. In this framework, MIS starts where the captured data can be manipulated. In other words, the system begins where the processing starts. Information that leaves the process, that goes out into the environment, constitutes output. Information entering the process is input. The system includes all elements involved in converting inputs to outputs. All other elements are considered to be outside the boundaries of the system.

The MIS boundaries do not extend into the environment; they do not go beyond the organizational boundaries. Only the input data come from the environment, but the MIS itself consists only of the processing elements that translate input data—whether about the environment, about competition, or about internal affairs—into output information that is useful for operations and decision making.

Distributive data processing

Computer technology has assisted in resolving the problem of centralization versus decentralization. A compromise has been reached with the development of minicomputers and microcomputers, communication hookup advances, and software to allow computers to "talk" to one another. Distributive processing is the best of both worlds. A centralized data-processing department with a mainframe and overall management control for basic services deals with the cost concerns of top management. But, as in the decentralized configuration, each DP user is equipped with its own computer system, in most cases a minicomputer or microcomputer with some storage capability. The smaller system has stand-alone capability to process the unique requirements of a particular user. For organization-wide applications, the mainframe is used via the communication link. Selective data from each system can be sent back and forth as required. Consequently, the best of both systems can be utilized and the result is a cost-effective and service-driven data-processing system.

Microcomputers

Since the late 1970s, microcomputers have been increasingly used in local government. Recent technological advances have given micros the computing capability of earlier mainframes. As the capabilities of micros have increased and hardware cost has decreased, the use of micros has mushroomed. In many cases they are being used for stand-alone functions that might be too expensive to program on a mainframe. Examples of stand-alone functions include:

Fleet management	Project management
Traffic signal timing optimization	Inventory control
Sanitation routing	Capital improvement programs
Storm water drainage analysis	Spreadsheet analysis
Hardy cross-flow analysis	Word processing
Pavement management	Graphics.

The use of microcomputers in an organization has both advantages and disadvantages. For the data-processing operation, it frees up programming time, reduces storage requirements, and reduces the number of users on the mainframe (and thus speeds up response time). For the using department, the micro represents computing ability in the form of spreadsheet programs that are not available on mainframes. The micro also allows low-priority functions to be taken outside of the data-processing system. The end result for the user is that operational problems can be resolved at an earlier date.

The disadvantage of the microcomputer is the loss of control by top management. Some organizations have allowed the number of micros to expand without considering common functions, program interchange, or interface capability with the mainframe. By using proper procedures for determining DP needs and whether a micro is the best way to address those problems, managers can avoid the mistakes of early micro users.

Data bases

The data base makes an effective and large-scale MIS possible. Early data-processing systems revolved mainly around accounting transactions that were characterized by a large volume of redundant transactions with punched card input. However, managers were well aware of the power of the computer to do more than serve as an accounting machine. Other applications followed that allowed the speed and processing power of the computer to be exploited. The only problem was that each application required its own data file, which was unique to the problem addressed.

The data developed for one program could not be interchanged with other programs. The result was duplication—expensive duplication—of data. Because of the ensuing dissatisfaction, attention turned to developing standardized data elements—that is, data bases. The data base represents an integrated approach to shared data. Once it is inserted into the system, all application programs have access to the data. The advent of direct, on-line input hastened the use of data bases since the files could be updated easily. Data bases all provide for:

Mass storage of relevant data

Easy data access to the user

Real time (current) updates to the data base

Centralized management of the data base

A set of rules to standardize, commonly define, and organize data within the organization.

In addition to providing the advantages of shared data, new software for data base management takes the concept one step further. Data base management systems have the ability to sort, rearrange, and present the data for report purposes. A one-time report can be extracted from the data base using the data base management software. Under the former structured data file system, a special program would be required to generate the report, whereas the data base management system enables the user to develop the reports without the assistance of a programmer.

MIS at work

An information system can be built on a department level. Its purpose will be the same as that of an organization-wide MIS, to reduce uncertainty and provide a better foundation for decision making. One of the most beneficial products of a public works MIS is computer-assisted productivity and work analysis. Such systems provide for several needs, the most common being to:

Simplify and improve work planning and scheduling, including the integration of recurring and on-demand jobs

Measure and track work force productivity

Develop unit costs and measure the impact of resource allocation to various activities.

Work planning and scheduling can be assisted by a computer system in balancing crew work loads, identifying idle time by cause (equipment not available, training and meeting time, etc.), providing a list of backlogged work, calculating response time, and scheduling preventive maintenance for optimal utilization.

Work force performance can be assisted by comparing actual accomplishments against targets and checking work crew performance against performance by crews engaged in similar tasks. The following figures illustrate the various levels of a departmental information system and their uses for supervisors and managers. Figure 3–9 is a vehicle print used by shop personnel. The basic data about the vehicle are grouped together. By looking at the information the mechanic can review the maintenance history of the vehicle and update the maintenance log. Whereas the mechanic uses a vehicle printout for quick reference, the crew foreman can use the information to check productivity. Figure 3–10 is a street maintenance productivity report with indicators and targets that were jointly developed by supervisors and crew members. Each time a job is performed, a work ticket is completed. This device makes the supervisor, crew leader, and crew members aware of activity, productivity, and resource utilization (manpower, equipment, and materials).

In this day of computer graphics, a handy way to examine manpower utilization is depicted in Figure 3–11. This kind of graphic reporting is especially appreciated by the city or county manager, the mayor or county board chairperson, and members of the city council or county board.

Management reports can best be utilized if they focus on a critical activity and summarize the results as acceptable or unacceptable. Figure 3–12 is an example of a management report that fits these summarization criteria. The absence report provides a "bottom line" outcome. A financial system that has

[Text continues on page 54]

```
                                    CITY OF OLATHE
                                  FULL VEHICLE PRINT

VEHICLE          020060024
DEPARTMENT       10    STREET

DESCRIPTION      DUMP TRUCK
MODEL YEAR       80            BEGIN MONTH ODO OR HOUR METER      25833.0
PURCH DATE       09/04/80      CURRENT ODOMETER OR HOUR METER     25833.0
COST                6,390.84   LIFETIME MILES OR HOURS            31665.0
LICENSE #        J02/749       YEAR-TO-DATE MILES OR HOURS         2633.0
KEY #            C6

MFGR CODE        CH    CHEVROLET            FUEL TYPE          03    UNLEADED
TYPE CODE        A6    ONE TON TRUCK        YEAR-TO-DATE TOTAL GALLONS    996.0
                                           BEGIN MONTH FUEL METER      18226.0
VEH ID (VIN)     CCM63AV156219             CURRENT FUEL METER          18226.0
VENDOR           DENNIS CHEVROLET
MFGR MODEL #     CCM63 (1 TON--2 YARD)

MTD FUEL $                     YTD FUEL $       1,005.00   LTD FUEL $     8,011.73
MTD OIL $                      YTD OIL $           1/5.13  LTD OIL $         504.13
MTD TIRE $                     YTD TIRE $                  LTD TIRE $      1,101.45

MTD MATERIAL $          3.71   YTD MATERIAL $     142.11   LTD MATERIAL $   3,144.13
MTD LABOR $                    YTD LABOR $        371.25   LTD LABOR $      4,175.38
MTD OUTSIDE $          25.00   YTD OUTSIDE $       32.50   LTD OUTSIDE $    1,000.90

MTD TOTAL COST $       28.71   YTD TOTAL COST $ 1,725.94   LTD TOTAL COST $ 22,935.42

MTD TOTAL DOWN HRS             YTD TOTAL DOWN HRS  39.25   LTD TOTAL DOWN HRS   891.25

PARTS LIST

SEQ #    TYPE    R/O #    DESCRIPTION
000001   TIR              SIZE= 750-16LT H    QTY= 002
000002   TIR              SIZE= 750-16LT M    QTY= 004

MAINTENANCE LOG

LOG DATE    SEQ#    R/O #    NARRATIVE              DATE1        DATE2
11/17/80    01      6461     WARRENTY - ANTI-FREEZE LEAK    00/00/00    00/00/00
09/03/81    01      7368     WARRENTY 2-SPEED 8449 MI.      00/00/00    00/00/00
10/30/81    01      9300     SPEED METER (WARRENTY)
04/09/82    01      10203    VALVE JOB-LIFTERS
06/08/82    01               CLUTCH
```

Figure 3-9 Basic vehicle data for shop personnel.

```
                    CITY OF OLATHE
              UNITS OF PRODUCTION BY JOB TYPE
```

JOB TYPE	JOB DESCRIPTION	NO-OF JOBS	LABOR HOURS	LABOR COST

* UNITS OF PRODUCTION FOR ACTIVITY: SC — CONSTRUCTION

JOB TYPE	JOB DESCRIPTION	NO-OF JOBS	LABOR HOURS	LABOR COST
SC02	CHIP AND SEAL___LNMI	82	1872.0	22256.00
SC03	BLADE RURAL RD LNMI	55	292.0	3784.00
SC04	SPREAD ROCK_____LNMI	20	191.0	2312.00
SC05	CRACK SEAL	40	636.0	7896.00
SC06	DIRT HAULING___LOAD	10	200.0	2400.00
SC07	CURB REPAIR____LIFT	37	644.0	7440.00
SC08	SIDEWALK REP. LIFT	6	80.0	960.00
SC09	DUST CONTROL___LNMI	14	112.0	1432.00
SC10	SLUDGE HAULING_LOAD	3	16.0	200.00
SC12	OTHER CONSTRUCTION	66	1288.0	15332.00
** SUBTOTAL **		333	5331.0	64012.00

* UNITS OF PRODUCTION FOR ACTIVITY: SD — NON-PRODUCTIVE

JOB TYPE	JOB DESCRIPTION	NO-OF JOBS	LABOR HOURS	LABOR COST
SD02	MEETINGS	4	48.0	624.00
** SUBTOTAL **		4	48.0	624.00

* UNITS OF PRODUCTION FOR ACTIVITY: SF — DRAINAGE

JOB TYPE	JOB DESCRIPTION	NO-OF JOBS	LABOR HOURS	LABOR COST
SF02	UNDERGROUND DRAINAG	7	116.0	1336.00
SF03	OPEN DRAINAGE__FTCH	37	444.0	5252.00
SF04	OTHER DRAINAGE	1	16.0	160.00
** SUBTOTAL **		45	576.0	6748.00

* UNITS OF PRODUCTION FOR ACTIVITY: SL — CLEANING

JOB TYPE	JOB DESCRIPTION	NO-OF JOBS	LABOR HOURS	LABOR COST
SL01	ST. SWEEPING CBMI	121	956.0	12428.00
SL02	ST. FLUSHING LIMI	6	44.0	572.00
SL03	BRUSH REMOVAL__LOAD	4	48.0	480.00
SL05	CLEAN-UP LITTERLIMI	3	108.0	1080.00
SL06	MUD REMOVAL	4	26.0	260.00
** SUBTOTAL **		138	1182.0	14820.00

* UNITS OF PRODUCTION FOR ACTIVITY: SR — REPAIR

JOB TYPE	JOB DESCRIPTION	NO-OF JOBS	LABOR HOURS	LABOR COST
SR01	BASE REPAIR_____SQYD	173	6012.0	60432.00
SR02	POT HOLE REPAIR_#PH	12	240.0	2568.00
SR03	EQUIPMENT PREP	35	404.0	4944.00
SR04	SERVICE CENTER MAIN	4	144.0	1440.00
SR05	SPOT OVERLAY____SQYD	14	292.0	2944.00
SR06	OTHER REPAIR	14	272.0	2912.00
** SUBTOTAL **		252	7364.0	75240.00

* UNITS OF PRODUCTION FOR ACTIVITY: ST — TRAFFIC

JOB TYPE	JOB DESCRIPTION	NO-OF JOBS	LABOR HOURS	LABOR COST
ST01	SIGN MARKING___SIGNS	7	54.0	540.00
ST02	SIGN REP&INST SIGNS	77	596.0	5960.00
ST03	SIGNS/NEW DEV.SIGNS	7	32.0	320.00
ST04	PAVEMENT MARK LIMI	22	276.0	2856.00
ST05	CROSSWALK MARK LIFT	13	150.0	1500.00
ST06	STRAIGHTEN SIGNS	5	50.0	500.00
** SUBTOTAL **		131	1158.0	11676.00

Figure 3-10 Street maintenance productivity report.

EQUIPMENT COST	MATERIAL COST	TOTAL COST	UNITS-OF PRODUCTION	COST-PER UNIT
4324.00	12098.20	38678.20	79.00	489.59
3168.00	1294.22	8246.22	217.00	38.00
714.00	5090.31	8116.31	37.00	219.35
2298.00	2175.70	12369.70	2605.00	4.74
1084.00	0.00	3484.00	178.00	19.57
1714.00	2502.76	11656.76	1036.00	11.25
148.00	68.50	1176.50	100.00	11.76
216.00	16988.00	18636.00	0.00	0.00
184.00	0.00	384.00	0.00	0.00
4280.00	6926.95	26538.95	617.00	43.01
18130.00	47144.64	129286.64	4869.00	
0.00	0.00	624.00	0.00	0.00
0.00	0.00	624.00	0.00	
108.00	137.15	1581.15	0.00	0.00
2855.00	546.50	8653.50	3575.00	2.42
16.00	0.00	176.00	0.00	0.00
2979.00	683.65	10410.65	3575.00	
6692.00	0.00	19120.00	1354.00	14.12
88.00	0.00	660.00	28.00	23.57
48.00	0.00	528.00	7.00	75.42
108.00	0.00	1188.00	14.00	84.85
44.00	0.00	304.00	0.00	0.00
6980.00	0.00	21800.00	1403.00	
9222.00	49873.00	119527.00	10690.00	11.18
400.00	4670.00	7638.00	1667.00	4.58
68.00	0.00	5012.00	0.00	0.00
180.00	707.00	2327.00	400.00	5.81
392.00	1954.00	5290.00	434.00	12.18
684.00	1034.00	4630.00	140.00	33.07
10946.00	58238.00	144424.00	13331.00	
0.00	0.00	540.00	38.00	14.21
894.00	7380.82	14234.82	407.00	34.97
46.00	995.70	1361.70	18.00	75.65
384.00	2078.30	5318.30	215.00	24.73
158.00	997.50	2655.50	8340.00	0.31
60.00	68.40	628.40	9.00	69.82
1542.00	11520.72	24738.72	9027.00	

Figure 3-10   (continued).

Figure 3–11 Computer graphic showing employee utilization for street repair.

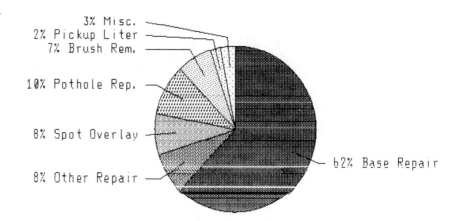

3% Misc.
2% Pickup Liter
7% Brush Rem.

10% Pothole Rep.

8% Spot Overlay

8% Other Repair

62% Base Repair

Figure 3–12 Department absence report covering 15 days.

```
                              CITY OF OLATHE
                       DEPARTMENTAL ABSENCE REPORT


DEPARTMENT  ALL      START DATE  04/01/85      END DATE  04/15/85  TOTAL DAYS   15


   EMPLOYEES     X     WORK DAYS   X  8   =    HOURS AVAILABLE
      59              11.0                       5,192.0


      TIME OFF ANALYSIS:

                                      PCT OF
                CODE      HOURS       AVAILABLE
                 PD       16.0         .31

                  S       93.5        1.80

                  V      104.0        2.00

                  W        8.0         .15

                TOTAL    221.5        4.27
```

Codes: PD = personal days; S = paid sick leave days;
V = paid vacation days; W = absent without pay.

Figure 3–13 Rolloff transaction summary.

```
                              CITY OF OLATHE
                       ROLLOFF TRANSACTION SUMMARY


   TRANSACTION                              COUNT        AMOUNT

001   DELIVER                                 17
002   EMPTY AND RETURN                       143       12,125.00
003   EMPTY AND NO RETURN                     11         850.00
004   MINUMUM MONTHLY CHARGE                   1          85.00
005   CONTAINER RENTAL CHARGE                 31         768.00
006   LEASE ON STATIONERY COMPACTOR           1         234.59

                                  TOTAL      204       14,062.59
```

```
                        CITY OF OLATHE
                   ROLLOFF BILLING REPORT
                        APRIL BILLING

CUSTOMER  0001   MANN FENCE           P.O. BOX 612, OLATHE, KS.  66061

CONT#   DATE       TRANSACTION                  TICKET   SERVICE ADDRESS        CHARGE

04019            CURRENTLY ASSIGNED
        04/17/85  002  EMPTY AND RETURN          03088   15415 SO. 169 HWY.      85.00
        04/30/85  005  CONTAINER RENTAL CHARGE   02781   15415 SO. 169 HWY.      30.00
                                                                    TOTAL       115.00


CUSTOMER  0002   PANIPLUS COMPANY     100 PANIPLUS ROADWAY, OLATHE, KS.  66061

CONT#   DATE       TRANSACTION                  TICKET   SERVICE ADDRESS        CHARGE

04201            CURRENTLY ASSIGNED
        04/02/85  002  EMPTY AND RETURN          03461   100 PANIPLUS ROADWAY    85.00
        04/09/85  002  EMPTY AND RETURN          03492   100 PANIPLUS ROADWAY    85.00
        04/15/85  002  EMPTY AND RETURN          03067   100 PANIPLUS ROADWAY    85.00
        04/18/85  002  EMPTY AND RETURN          03097   100 PANIPLUS ROADWAY    85.00
        04/24/85  002  EMPTY AND RETURN          03574   100 PANIPLUS ROADWAY    85.00
        04/29/85  002  EMPTY AND RETURN          02865   100 PANIPLUS ROADWAY    85.00
                                                                    TOTAL       510.00


CUSTOMER  0003   R.O. CORPORATION     525 EAST DENNIS, OLATHE, KS.  66061

CONT#   DATE       TRANSACTION                  TICKET   SERVICE ADDRESS        CHARGE

04020            CURRENTLY ASSIGNED
        04/02/85  002  EMPTY AND RETURN          03546   525 E. DENNIS           85.00
        04/04/85  002  EMPTY AND RETURN          03469   525 E. DENNIS           85.00
        04/08/85  002  EMPTY AND RETURN          03483   525 E. DENNIS           85.00
        04/11/85  002  EMPTY AND RETURN          03059   525 E. DENNIS           85.00
        04/16/85  002  EMPTY AND RETURN          03076   525 E. DENNIS           85.00
        04/19/85  002  EMPTY AND RETURN          03099   525 E. DENNIS           85.00
        04/22/85  002  EMPTY AND RETURN          03561   525 E. DENNIS           85.00
        04/26/85  002  EMPTY AND RETURN          02858   525 E. DENNIS           85.00
                                                                    TOTAL       680.00
```

Figure 3–14 Rolloff billing report.

built-in levels for management and finance is illustrated in Figures 3–13 and 3–14, respectively. The summary provides all the information needed for departmental management, while the same system provides the finance clerk with detailed transactions for each customer.

Finally, a department MIS must help affect decisions. Figure 3–15 is an example of a commercial sanitation route balancing report. Periodic review of this report provides the information needed to assist in balancing the work load.

Suggestions for developing a public works MIS

The information revolution has affected local government in two ways. First, it has changed the way local government operates. Detailed, exact data are now available to help set priorities and allocate resources. Detailed unit cost and productivity analyses are now within daily reach of public works managers. Consequently, the successful department manager is able to develop and extensively use an information system. Second, it has affected first-line supervision. The feedback on work accomplishments, backlog, and performance that is now readily available can be used to develop first-line supervisors. Consequently, a department MIS will help the manager with strategic planning and the foreman with work planning.

With these points in mind, consider carefully the following DOs and DON'Ts before embarking on an MIS odyssey:

DO: Talk to the data-processing manager before making decisions on budgeting, motor equipment, and other tasks that involve data.

DO: Learn about data processing to facilitate the exchange of facts and ideas with the data-processing manager.

DO: Consider the cost of computerization, which includes hardware, software, and employee time for data entry. Will the benefits be equal to or greater than the cost?

DO: Review operations thoroughly prior to computerization. An ill-defined problem will remain just that; computerization won't solve it.

DO: Evaluate the manual system now in place. In many instances, manually generated reports, especially nonrecurring reports, are more cost effective.

DO: Thoroughly understand the purposes, goals, and objectives of the operation. Establish performance indicators, activity benchmarks, and performance standards. *Then* think about the data and information needed to support MIS.

Figure 3–15 Commercial sanitation route balancing report.

CITY OF OLATHE
COMMERCIAL SANITATION
ROUTE BALANCING GRID

ROUTE 1 FRONT	MON	TUE	WED	THU	FRI	SAT	SUN	TOTAL
1YD	6	7	3	10	6	1		33
2YD	6	5	10	15	5			41
3YD	12	16	16	12	25	2		83
4YD	13	12	8	13	11	4		61
6YD	35	28	28	43	36	8		178
8YD	24	27	25	23	32	10		141
TOTAL UNITS	96	95	90	116	115	25		537
TOTAL YDS	508	497	471	570	607	151		2804

DON'T: Go out and buy a microcomputer before you know what you want it to accomplish.

DON'T: Buy a microcomputer without consulting with the data-processing manager about compatability and commonality.

DON'T: Ask the data-processing office for one-time reports that cost more to produce than the value received.

DON'T: Forget that MIS (computerized or manual) is a resource to *assist* the manager, reduce uncertainty, and improve decisions.

1 Henry Mintzberg, *The Nature of Managerial Work* (New York: Harper and Row, 1973).

2 John Naisbitt, *Megatrends: Ten New Directions Transforming Our Lives* (New York: Warner Books, 1982).

3 Donald H. Sanders and Stanley J. Birkin, *Computers and Management*, 3d ed. (New York: McGraw-Hill, 1980), pp. 69–72.

Public works finance

Governments exist to provide services that the private sector is unable or unwilling to provide. Richard Musgrave has identified three economic functions of government: stabilization, distribution, and allocation.[1] The stabilization function involves maintaining economic growth to control unemployment and inflation while improving society's standard of living. The distribution function involves redistributing wealth to provide a minimum standard of living to all citizens. These two functions are usually beyond the control of any particular state or local government but are managed at the national level of government. However, the third function, allocation, is a basic concern of local government.

The allocation function of government can be defined as the provision of socially desirable public goods. The private sector cannot be relied on to provide adequate levels of certain goods, such as police and fire protection, drainage control, and transportation services, because it is unable to charge enough to recover the costs of providing them and also make a profit.

The problem with public goods is twofold. First, it may be impossible to exclude persons from using the service even though they may not have paid for it. For example, access to public parks is impossible to control. Second, public goods may be used by many people concurrently. For example, automobiles and pedestrians both use public streets. These two characteristics of public goods are referred to as *exclusion failure* and *nonexhaustion*, respectively.[2] When both characteristics are present, the good is purely public and is usually financed with taxes. When one or the other characteristic is present it may be financed by a quasi price or user charge.

This chapter examines the financial environment in which local government carries out the allocation function. In particular, it looks at revenues and expenditures, budgeting, public works accounting, capital budgeting, and borrowing and debt management. Some statistics are presented, but merely by way of illustration. For more detailed information on local government finances the reader is referred to such standard sources as *The Municipal Year Book*, *Government Finance Services*, and the *Statistical Abstract of the United States*.[3]

Revenue

The public works administrator should be fully aware of the general sources of revenue that finance local government. State laws, city charters, and legal decisions create a wide assortment of local revenue sources. A general discussion of revenues can highlight only the main features of the significant types of revenue and indicate some possibilities that should be further explored. The two major divisions of local revenue are tax revenue and nontax revenue.

Tax revenue

Taxation generates an involuntary contribution from citizens that is used to fund municipal activities. Because of the involuntary nature of taxes, the policy considerations in imposing them are equity and efficiency. Equity is judged on two principles: ability to pay and benefits received.

The ability-to-pay principle states that taxes should be distributed among taxpayers in relation to their financial capacities. Those who can pay more should pay more. The benefits-received principle suggests that the tax burden should be distributed among taxpayers according to their benefits from public service. The two principles are often in conflict with each other. The choice of which prevails in a particular community depends partly on philosophic and partly on pragmatic reasons. Efficiency has to do with the administrative costs of collection, adequacy, and economic effects.

Property tax   Historically, the property tax has been the greatest source of *tax* revenue for local government. With the expansion of services demanded in cities and counties, the property tax is no longer able to provide enough revenue to remain the major source of funding. Property tax controls imposed through state laws by taxpayers have contributed to the declining proportion of property taxes in total municipal revenue. In the early 1960s property taxes constituted approximately one-half of local revenue.

As of the early 1980s, the picture was quite different. In 1982–83, property taxes accounted for only 17 percent of all city government revenues. For county governments in 1982–83, the ratio of property taxes to all revenues was higher (27 percent) but still a much smaller ratio than the 38 percent provided by intergovernmental revenues. Tables 4–1 and 4–2 provide an overview of all revenues for cities and counties in 1982–83.

An important reason for Proposition 13 and other taxpayer-imposed controls is the perception that the property tax is inherently inequitable. The tax is an "ad valorem" tax—that is, it is based on the current value of real property and does not necessarily reflect ability to pay.

Many states have adopted "circuit breakers" to reduce the total state-local tax liability for citizens who share a disproportionately high property tax burden. The circuit breaker provides property tax relief—often in the form of a tax credit or rebate—for property owners under a specified income limit. Many of the circuit breakers are restricted to the elderly, with eligibility beginning at sixty-two or sixty-five years of age.

The property tax is a function of the local tax rates and the assessed value of

Table 4–1   City government revenue, 1982–83, by source.

Revenue source	Amount (in millions)	%
Total revenue, all sources	$125,100	100.0
Intergovernmental revenue	32,200	25.7
Total revenue, own sources	92,900	74.3
General revenue own sources	65,163	52.1
Property taxes	20,964	16.7
Other taxes	19,154	15.5
Charges and miscellaneous	25,045	20.0
Utility revenue	22,270	17.8
Liquor store revenue	273	0.2
Insurance trust revenue	5,194	4.2

Source: U.S., Bureau of the Census, *City Government Finances in 1982–83* (Washington, D.C.: U.S. Government Printing Office, 1984), Series GF83, No. 4, p. v.

Table 4–2 County government revenue, 1982–83, by source.

Revenue source	Amount (in millions)	%
Total revenue, all sources	$73,037	100.0
Intergovernmental revenue	27,773	38.0
Total revenue, own sources	45,266	62.0
General revenue	42,805	58.6
Property taxes	19,609	26.7
Other taxes	5,608	7.7
Charges and miscellaneous	17,587	24.1
Utility revenue	727	1.0
Liquor store revenue	219	0.3
Employee-retirement revenue	1,515	2.1

Source: U.S., Bureau of the Census, *County Government Finances in 1982–83* (Washington, D.C.: U.S. Government Printing Office, 1984), Series GF83, No. 8, p. v.

a taxpayer's property. The same rate usually is applied to all property of the same class in a taxing jurisdiction. Therefore, the assessed value of a particular property is the basis for determining a taxpayer's share of the total tax burden. The most serious faults in property taxation arise from the difficulty of determining accurate assessed values of all property at the same time. The goal of assessors is to appraise the fair market value, or some percentage of it, of all property involved. As inflation and shifts in market demand occur, it becomes critical but extremely difficult to ensure that all property is valued fairly.

Property tax exemptions present another equity concern. States exempt certain types of property from the tax. Total exemptions are typically provided for religious, charitable, educational, and governmental institutions. Partial exemptions may be provided to other groups such as veterans, the elderly, and certain industrial properties.

Consumption taxes   Many local governments rely on general sales taxes or selective sales (excise) taxes to supplement general revenues. These taxes pertain to the consumption of commodities. Payment of the tax is typically collected by the seller of the commodity from the consumer, and is remitted periodically to the government. A general sales tax applies to all current retail transactions not otherwise specifically excluded. Food for home consumption and medicines are frequently excluded from the tax to improve its equity features.

Selective sales, or excise, taxes are often levied on specific transactions, including such items as motor fuels, alcoholic beverages, tobacco products, and admissions. These taxes are classified as sumptuary, benefit-based, and luxury taxes. Sumptuary excises attempt to discourage the use of specific products such as tobacco and alcohol. Benefit-based excises attempt to tax commodities from which benefits are received. Motor fuel taxes, for example, are paid primarily by highway users. Luxury excises apply the ability-to-pay principle by assuming that the purchase of luxury items reflects an extraordinary tax-paying ability.

Income tax   Some cities rely on the income tax as a source of revenue because of its equity and efficiency. Municipal income tax rates are typically very low in relation to state and federal income tax rates, but the equity and efficiency features of the tax make it an attractive option. The tax is usually collected by the state along with the state income tax and later distributed to the local government. The local tax uses many of the same adjustments, exemptions, and deductions to improve equity as does the state tax. Furthermore, the local tax is easily collected as a "piggyback" tax to state or federal income taxes and it grows automatically as incomes rise.

Nontax revenue

Municipal nontax revenue comprises intergovernmental revenue, fees, and charges. With the decline in the relative importance of the property tax as a revenue source, nontax revenues have grown significantly.

Intergovernmental revenue   Transfers from federal and state governments take the form of categorical grants, block grants, and revenue sharing. Each serves a different purpose.

Categorical grants are designed to contribute to paying the cost of specific local government activities that benefit an area larger than the local government boundaries. The costs of wastewater treatment and air pollution facilities are typically subsidized by a higher level of government because cleaner water and air benefit others residing downriver and downwind. Categorical grants operate on the correspondence principle, which relates the financing of an activity to the area receiving the benefits.

Block grants are distributed to local governments to finance broad functional programs deemed to be in the state or national interest. The local government has considerable discretion in how the funds will be specifically used within the broad program areas.

Revenue sharing is intended to address the issue of fiscal imbalance. The federal and state governments may recognize that the ability to raise revenue does not always coincide with fiscal need at the local level. Revenue may be distributed on the basis of a formula that considers the fiscal disparities of local governments. In addition, no or few restrictions are placed on how the shared revenue may be used by the recipient government.

Fees for licenses and permits   A fee is a payment made as a condition for a citizen privilege. Fees are imposed on business and nonbusiness activities to recover the costs of regulating those activities in the community interest.

Business license fees, for example, cover the cost of inspecting certain businesses such as restaurants to ensure that health standards are being met. Dog license fees, as another example, are imposed to ensure that the community is protected from rabies. Franchise fees may exist to recover the cost associated with regulating a monopoly business.

User charges   User charges are differentiated from fees because they are similar to private prices. Charges are applied for the direct sale of local government goods and services. To charge or not to charge is a policy question often debated by local legislative bodies. With the increasing stringency of local budgets, charges are becoming more widespread (operational details are discussed later in the chapter).

Two basic conditions must exist for charges to be effective: benefit separability and chargeability. The users or beneficiaries of the service must be identifiable and excludable from the service for nonpayment. And there must be a feasible method for calculating the appropriate charge and collecting it.

When the two basic conditions are met, charges may be imposed to improve equity and efficiency. Equity can be improved because the charge will apply to all users of the service, including nonresidents and tax-exempt properties. Charges distribute the financing burden to users who would not otherwise contribute to the cost of the activity. Charges can improve efficiency by better defining the demand for the provided service. Charges provide the government with important information about the type, quality, and quantity of services desired in the community.

The benefit separability and chargeability conditions may coexist in different degrees. Where they both clearly exist, the private sector usually meets the demand. Where neither exists, the service is a public good and should be supported by taxation. Where they exist to some degree, the service is a merit service and charges may be appropriate. These differences constitute their characteristics as shown in Figure 4–1.

Two main criticisms are leveled against user charges: first, that many priced services meet a need of all citizens in the community and therefore should be financed from general tax revenues; second, that low-income individuals may be excluded from government services that are priced. It is argued that the service should be provided to all citizens regardless of their ability to pay.

Perhaps more than any other city or county department, the public works department depends on user charges for revenue. With the property tax limitations and other financial constraints that have been imposed since the late 1970s, user charges are often the only significant revenue option left for local governments. The ones that are especially important for public works are bridge and tunnel tolls, airport landing and departure fees, water service charges, sanitary sewerage charges, stormwater sewerage charges, and refuse collection charges. In smaller cities, parking meter receipts may make up a substantial portion of

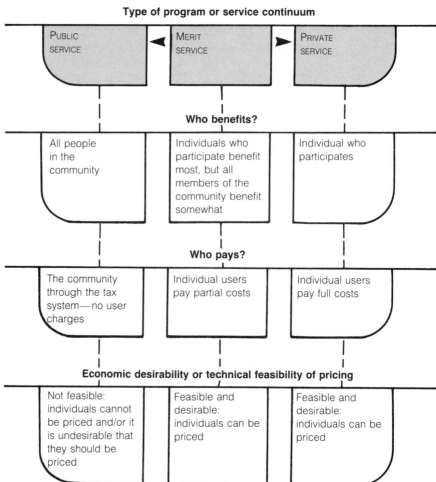

Figure 4–1   Difference between services exhibiting public, merit, and private characteristics.

Type of program or service continuum

PUBLIC SERVICE	MERIT SERVICE	PRIVATE SERVICE

Who benefits?

All people in the community	Individuals who participate benefit most, but all members of the community benefit somewhat	Individual who participates

Who pays?

The community through the tax system—no user charges	Individual users pay partial costs	Individual users pay full costs

Economic desirability or technical feasibility of pricing

Not feasible: individuals cannot be priced and/or it is undesirable that they should be priced	Feasible and desirable: individuals can be priced	Feasible and desirable: individuals can be priced

user charge revenues, especially if water and sewerage services are provided by the county government or a special district.

Pricing considerations

Pricing reflects the total cost of producing and delivering the service to the consumer. The cost of increasing the service output by a small amount is referred to as the marginal cost of production and distribution. Private firms generally charge a price equal to the marginal cost. Therefore, the price will be higher for consumers in areas where the transportation cost is higher. The consumer's willingness to pay the price depends on the satisfaction derived from the good or service. The relationship between marginal cost and consumer demand determines the price.

These pricing principles are relevant in the public sector as well. User charges should reflect the cost of providing the service and thus may vary by location within a jurisdiction. Solid waste collection charges, for example, may vary with the distance the refuse must be carried for disposal.

Three cost variables must be considered in pricing: output, distribution, and demand variation over time. The quantity of output of a service depends primarily on the density of development. High-density areas can generally be serviced at a lower cost in the long run (after the initial capital investment) than low-density areas. Distribution costs indicate the cost of service for different types of developments and densities, and their distance from the production site. The cost of services at different distances should be estimated. Once decisions regarding output capacity and locations to be served have been made, the demand over time, or "peak load" should be considered. If the same charge is applied at all times, users may at some point exceed the facilities' design capacity. The result may be user dissatisfaction owing to traffic jams, low water pressure, or brownouts, and overuse may reduce the life expectancy of the facility.

The design of the user charge must incorporate the three cost variables, but should also consider practical aspects of pricing. Administrative costs of billing, collecting, and maintaining data on demand should be reflected in the price. Citizen acceptance of user charges must also be considered. Because charges are voluntary for the user, they are not deductible for federal income tax purposes. This means that user charges are more costly to a citizen than local taxes. This aspect of charges is most significant for high-income residents and high-income communities where marginal income tax rates are higher.

Who gets what?   Budgeting is a public policy process. Almost every decision, activity, and program can be expressed in the financial language of the budget. The service-delivery implications of its dollar and cents are inescapable. . . . The budgetary process . . . is, essentially, the rationing of resources representing a multitude of sacrificed alternatives. . . . "Who gets what" is a statement of society's values, preferences, and priorities as expressed and carried out by local governments. The budget lies at the heart of politics; it is a political process conducted in a political arena.

Source: Lewis Friedman, "Budgeting," in J. Richard Aronson and Eli Schwartz, eds., *Management Policies in Local Government Finance*, 2d ed. (Washington, D.C.: International City Management Association, 1981), p. 91.

Budgeting

Budgeting is the process of allocating available resources among competing demands. Stated another way, the budget is a financial plan for a specific period of time. The sidebar "Who gets what?" stresses the political context of budgeting.

A key feature of local government budgeting is the requirement that expenditures not exceed revenues. As a result, one objective of budgeting is to ensure that administrators maintain acceptable levels of service delivery while keeping expenditures within legal limits.

The budgeting environment

The principal actors in the budgeting process are the "budget-spenders" and the "budget-cutters." Budget-spenders view their roles as performing a service; in their budget preparations they give higher priority to meeting professional standards and the demands of constituents than to observing revenue limits. Budget-cutters, usually chief executive officers and elected officials, see their role as holding the line on expenses. They consider the budget a way to meet revenue constraints.

The spenders-versus-cutters dichotomy generates certain universal trends. Aaron Wildavsky identified three administrator's goals in budgeting, which, in order of priority, are to (1) defend the base, (2) increase the base, and (3) expand the base.[4] To defend the base means to attempt to preserve the agency's share of total resources at the previous year's level. To increase the base is to receive a larger share of resources for existing activities at the expense of other agencies. To expand the base is to develop new programs.

Many techniques exist to achieve these goals. For example, constituent pressure may be brought to bear on elected officials. It is typical, however, for administrators to request more than they expect to receive. Such requests not only carry the hope of gaining additional funds, but also serve to meet the professional obligation of communicating the true needs of the department.

Elected officials have difficulty allocating resources in this type of environment. The result, therefore, is most often incrementalism—which is the tendency to look at the prior year's appropriations for police, fire, streets, debt service, and other ongoing commitments as a "given" and to focus only on the changes in an agency budget. Several budgeting methods have been adopted to overcome this tendency, but they have met with only limited success. Before these methods are examined, however, it is important to explain what budgets attempt to achieve.

The purposes of budgeting

Budgets exist for the purposes of legal control, management information, and planning. As a control tool, budgets prescribe, through a detailed description of proposed expenditures, how much and for what purposes funds may be spent. The purpose of this exercise is to prevent thievery and to ensure that legislative intent is carried out.

Budgets also provide management information to improve efficiency in agency operations. To this end, budgets focus on measurable performance activities. The important concern is the efficient use of resources in achieving desired program results. Finally the budget enables the agency to plan for service requirements. Budgets state the public policy agenda for the future. The period in which the budget is considered presents an ideal opportunity to consider the future implications of current decisions in a comprehensive, organized framework.

The budget cycle

Budgeting is a formal cycle of interconnected, institutionalized phases. Although specific activities may differ among governments, the basic phases are the same almost everywhere. The four principal stages are executive preparation, legislative consideration and adoption, execution, and audit.

Executive preparation involves identifying organization goals and estimating the revenues and expenditures necessary to accomplish the goals. Goals are typically set by the chief executive. Expected revenue and expenditures of service delivery are estimated by each agency. Agency estimates are aggregated by the budget office of the chief executive and reviewed to determine whether they are consistent with overall goals and constitute reasonable costs.

The chief executive (mayor or city manager) submits the budget to the legislative body for consideration and adoption. The budget submitted by the chief executive is his or her budget, not an aggregation of individual departmental requests. It represents a balancing of competing demands that always initially total more than projected revenues. The priorities are settled by the chief executive at this point so that a unified financial plan can be presented to the city council or county board.

Public hearings are held to enable citizens to participate in the process, and agencies are required to defend their requests at these investigative hearings. This stage culminates in the formal adoption of the budget, which legally appropriates money to specific purposes for the budget year. The annual appropriation may be modified from time to time by the passage of supplemental appropriations.

The third stage of the budget process is execution. Appropriations are spent and services are delivered within the approved appropriations level. Spending is constantly monitored to assure that expenditures do not exceed appropriations and that planned services are delivered.

The audit is the final stage of the cycle. The audit is primarily concerned with legal compliance. Expenditures are reviewed to ensure that money was spent legally for approved purposes. Sometimes audits are used as management tools to determine whether money was spent in an efficient manner to minimize waste. They may also examine whether desired programmatic results were achieved.

Types of budgets

The public works director may be required to present two separate budgets. The annual operating budget provides the financial plan for day-to-day, recurring costs of the agency for one year. The capital improvements budget is projected over a longer period of time (usually five years) for nonrecurring capital projects. This section considers types of annual operating budgets. Capital improvements budgets are addressed separately.

Budgets can be presented in several formats (Figure 4–2). Each attempts to reflect a different policy perspective on decision making. They have different orientations for management and different criteria for policymakers. The line-item budget is the oldest and most common type of budget format. It allocates specific dollar amounts to each item, or object, of expenditure. Expenditure items are systematically organized into categories or accounts. Line-item budgets are aimed at achieving economy through strict control.

Performance budgets have a management orientation. Revenues and expenditures are related to work loads and unit costs to achieve efficiency. The emphasis in the performance budgeting format is on how well an agency is utilizing its resources. The measures used include cost per citizen and cost per unit of output.

The program budget is oriented toward planning. Expenditures are presented in the form of programs and activities rather than departmental line items. Program budgeting defines the goals of an agency and classifies organization activities contributing to each goal. Data are presented by product output rather than a formal organization line in order to focus on goals and alternative programs for achieving them.

The planning-programming-budgeting system (PPBS) is similar to program budgeting in that it involves multiyear projections. PPBS is an attempt to carry

Figure 4–2   An analysis of budget formats.

Format	Characteristics	The question	Orientation	Criterion
LIB	Expenditures and revenues are related to commodities	What is to be bought?	Control	Economy
PerB	Expenditures and revenues related to work loads Elaborate array of organizational costs centers Unit costs display	What is to be done?	Management	Efficiency
ProB	Expenditures, revenues related to public goals Transorganizational cost centers	What is to be achieved?	Planning	Effectiveness
PPBS	Expenditures and revenues related to public goals and benefits Transorganizational cost centers Analysis of alternatives Multiyear projections	What is to be achieved?	Planning	Effectiveness
ZBB	Expenditures and revenues related to work loads Elaborate array of nonorganizational cost centers Alternative service and financing proposals Ranking procedures	What is to be done?	Management	Efficiency

out comprehensive policymaking. Although thinking about priorities, goals, and objectives for several years into the future is an admirable goal, PPBS has simply proved too difficult to do in the budgeting environment.

The zero-based budget (ZBB) format focuses on alternative levels of service delivery. It has a strong management orientation and attempts to achieve efficiency. In its pure form, ZBB attacks incrementalism by requiring agencies to defend their "entire" budget each year and, if warranted, set new priorities for the upcoming budget year. In practice, however, ZBB usually requires agencies to prepare three alternative service-level budgets for each program and present them as decision packages for the legislative body. The alternative levels may demonstrate, for example, the costs and consequences of (1) eliminating a program, (2) funding it at a reduced level, (3) funding it at the current level, and (4) funding it at an increased level.

The traditional line-item budget, however, remains the most common budget format, primarily because it is easy to use. But many local governments are recasting line-item data in order to present the financial plan as a management tool for meeting program objectives efficiently and effectively.

A few local governments are using the annual operating budget as a one-year installment in a three- or five-year projection of the operating budget. This provides an excellent linkage with the capital budget, which usually has a five-year base. No matter how it is designated—three-year operating budget, planning budget, or projected budget—this approach helps government anticipate revenue sources that are on their way up or down, plan for future operating and maintenance expenditures that will be needed when capital improvements are completed, and explore financial alternatives for the effects of inflation and changes in interest rates.

This approach to the annual operating budget provides department heads and other managers with an excellent opportunity to forecast future departmental activities. In Santa Clara, California, for example, public works managers are required to maintain five-year operating budgets.

Accounting

When several major cities experienced fiscal crises in the mid- and late-1970s, regulators, credit-rating firms, and bondholders began clamoring for a clear set of accounting standards. However, most local governments still maintain accounting systems in a way that is almost incomprehensible to all but a few experts.

Accounting standards for local governments were first developed in 1934 by the Municipal Finance Officers Association (now the Government Finance Officers Association) through its National Committee on Municipal Accounting. The committee issued its generally accepted accounting principles (GAAP) in 1968. Revised standards and interpretive documents were also issued by the committee during the late 1970s before the committee was replaced by the Governmental Accounting Standards Board (GASB), the organization that is now primarily responsible for establishing accounting standards for state and local governments. The standards established by GASB provide for uniform accounting and financial reporting for citizens, the bond market, state and federal granting agencies, and public accounting companies.

The most frequent exception to GAAP is "cash basis" accounting. Although cash basis accounting is inherently simple—it presents only receipts and disbursements—it is inadequate for management information and control. Full disclosure of financial results is essential to uncover abuse. Full financial information also provides management with the means to evaluate performance and to plan for future operations.

GAAP-based accounting focuses on changes in spendable financial resources from one period to another. The results of transactions for various programs are presented in "funds." The fund basis of accounting recognizes that most governmental assets are not "fungible" (interchangeable) and that government activities must be accounted for through a series of distinct accounting and reporting entities (funds) to control resources and ensure compliance with legal and budgetary requirements. Separate funds are established for specific types of activities on the basis of the following categories.

Governmental funds

The resources in governmental funds are intended to be expended within a specific period of time, usually the budget year. They consist of several types:

1. The general fund is used for ongoing government services that are not accounted for by any other fund type. Revenues in this fund are not designated for any specific purpose.
2. Special revenue funds account for the expenditure of revenues that have been legally dedicated to specific programs or projects.
3. Capital project funds account for revenues and expenditures set aside for purchasing or building major capital assets. Bond proceeds, grants, and loans are typical revenue sources for these funds.
4. Special assessment funds are used for public property improvements for which the beneficiaries are assessed special taxes. Sidewalks, water lines, and sewer lines are often financed, in part, with special assessments.
5. Debt service funds account for revenue set aside to make interest and principal payments on long-term debt.

Proprietary funds

Accounting for proprietary funds resembles business accounting. The resources of these funds are not meant to be exhausted within a specific time period, and the intent of the program is to recover the full cost of operations. There are two types of proprietary funds.

1. Enterprise funds account for programs that usually sustain themselves through user charges for services rendered.
2. Internal service funds account for services performed by one local

government organization for another, such as a central printing facility, maintenance garage, or computer center.

Agency and trust funds

Agency and trust funds record transactions of a fiduciary nature—resources that the local government is managing on behalf of someone else, such as pension funds.[5]

Reporting and auditing

Each local government fund is a self-balancing set of accounts in which assets equal liabilities plus reserves plus fund balance. This equation ensures that all transactions have been recorded properly. For every change in assets there must be a corresponding change in the other side of the equation. This concept is referred to as double-entry accounting.

Accounting provides management with periodic reports—daily, weekly, and monthly—with which to monitor the budget and to evaluate performance. Monthly reports are the most common. If such reports reach public works directors and other managers within five working days after the month closes, these managers have an excellent tool for management evaluation and control. If the reports are extremely late (four to six weeks after the close of the month), they are of little value except to generate panic when unexpected "overs and unders" are discovered.

Accounting also provides an "audit trail" that enables the independent auditors to perform their postaudit—the fourth phase of the budgeting cycle. The annual report shows the auditors' findings and is the most important document to investors and others who have an interest in the financial condition of the government.

Capital budgeting

Capital budgeting plays an important role in financial planning for most local governments. It complements the annual operating budget by evaluating needs and resources for certain projects several years into the future. Unlike PPBS, discussed earlier in this chapter, capital budgeting does not attempt to evaluate all programs and activities, but only capital projects. It is important at this point to define the major terms associated with capital budgeting.

1. *Capital outlay* or *capital expenditure* refers to any expenditure made to purchase a physical asset that is expected to provide services over a period of time, usually more than one year.
2. *Capital project* or *capital improvement* is an expenditure for the construction, purchase, or major rehabilitation of physical structures.
3. *Capital improvements programming* (CIP) is the selection and multiyear scheduling of public physical improvements.
4. *Capital budgeting* is the annual process of deciding which public improvements listed in the CIP are to be funded and analyzing the various methods of financing such projects, along with their impact, on the annual operating budget.[6]

Not all capital expenditures appear in the capital improvements program and capital budget. Typewriters, for example, have a useful life of one year or more but are not considered a capital improvement. To eliminate such items from the CIP process, most local governments further define a capital project with a minimum amount, say $50,000.

Benefits of capital programming

The CIP process is typically a planning function coordinated by the planning agency or the chief executive's office. Capital projects are often financed by long-term borrowing and will have a long-term economic and fiscal impact on the community. Capital project requests, therefore, require careful and deliberate analysis.

The benefits of capital improvements programming have been identified by the Government Finance Research Center as follows:

1. A capital improvement program allows for the orderly repair and replacement of capital facilities and equipment.
2. A CIP enables governments to develop useful information on the condition of their capital plant, to use these data to identify capital and maintenance needs, and to maintain current inventories of capital assets.
3. Multiyear capital plans serve as the critical link between a government's goals, objectives, and output, and its anticipated revenues or resources.
4. A CIP assists government officials to work out priorities between current and future development, identify needs and wants, and decide whether to rebuild or replace existing capital infrastructure.
5. A CIP is a valuable financial planning tool. The process calls for forecasting own-source revenues, borrowing power, and intergovernmental assistance to estimate the level of capital spending that the government can safely afford over the next several years.
6. The financial programming built into the CIP can help to smooth out the tax rate, maintain a balance between debt service and current expenditures, and determine debt capacity and debt service levels.
7. The process identifies capital projects several years ahead of actual need. This helps set aside adequate time for planning and design, and may enable governments to buy land, if necessary, on favorable terms.
8. The process is a useful way to gain intergovernmental assistance to address capital projects.[7]

Financing concerns

The capital programming and budgeting process will vary in complexity according to the size of the government. The review and analysis procedures of a large city may not be appropriate for smaller communities. The policy issue of how capital projects will be financed, however, is a basic question all local governments must address. There are three alternatives: pay-as-you-go, pay-as-you-use, and a mix of the two.

A pay-as-you-go approach emphasizes no borrowing. Only those projects that can be financed with current-year revenues, or revenues that have been saved or "reserved" are to be undertaken. The pay-as-you-use approach employs debt financing for capital projects and annually raises the revenue required to service the debt. The borrowing term, of course, should not exceed the useful life expectancy of the facility financed. The third approach represents a mixture of the first two, with a down payment from current revenues and the remainder to be debt financed.

In some instances several communities may cooperatively finance a capital project. A resource recovery facility, for example, may serve many communities and be beyond the financing capability of the individual community.

Local government borrowing

When a local government adopts the pay-as-you-use or partial pay-as-you-use approach to financing capital projects, debt will be incurred. This section reviews some of the basic factors involved in debt management. The discussion falls into two parts: types of debt and policy considerations regarding debt.

Types of debt

Debt obligations may be classified according to length of term, the security pledged for repayment, the methods of retirement, and purpose.

Length of term Debt may be issued as either short-term or long-term obligations of the local government. Short-term or temporary debt will usually be repaid during the current fiscal year and always within one year from issuance. Temporary debt is issued in anticipation of a current revenue such as taxes, grants, or long-term bond proceeds. The debt is to be repaid when the taxes or grants are received, or when the long-term bond is sold.

Long-term debt is an obligation with a maturity of more than one year from the date of issue. Typically, long-term debt is made up of bonds but may also include leases and installment contracts that extend beyond one year.

Security pledged General obligation and limited-liability bonds are the two basic categories of debt under this classification. General obligation debt is guaranteed by the full faith and credit of the issuing jurisdiction for repayment. The jurisdiction pledges to raise taxes to whatever level necessary to meet scheduled payments.

Limited-liability bonds are not guaranteed. They are sold on the basis that revenues received from the project financed will redeem the debt. User charges for wastewater treatment, for example, would pay the debt service after regular operating and maintenance costs are met.

Limited-liability debt includes six categories.

1. Revenue bonds: revenue from the project financed (toll bridge, water plant, etc.) redeems the debt.
2. Lease-rental bonds: facilities (office buildings, computer equipment, etc.) financed from the debt proceeds are leased to a government at a rent sufficient to cover debt service and operating cost.
3. Lease-purchase bonds: public works (school, hospital, etc.) constructed by a private firm from debt proceeds are leased to a government (the government receives title to the property when the debt is retired).
4. Industrial development and pollution control bonds: private facilities— ultimately owned by their user—are constructed by the municipal debt proceeds with rental payments by the users servicing the debt.
5. Special revenue bonds: projects financed by bonds are serviced from special revenues (parking garages financed by a special property tax on downtown property or sidewalks financed by a special assessment on property owners in the affected area).
6. Tax increment bonds: bonds financing area redevelopment are serviced from the additional taxes generated in the redeveloped region.[8]

Limited-liability debt is usually perceived as a greater credit risk to investors than general obligation debt. The creditworthiness of such projects can be enhanced by purchasing bond insurance. Because bond insurance protects the investor, the reduced interest resulting from an enhanced rating may offset the cost of insurance.

Method of retirement The basic categories of retirement methods are term bonds and serial bonds. Term bonds mature on one date. Interest and payments may be made periodically, but the principal amount is paid at one maturity date. Serial bonds, on the other hand, schedule partial principal repayments along with interest periodically throughout the life of the bond.

Another retirement distinction is that either term or serial bonds may be callable or noncallable. A call provision permits the issuer to redeem all or part of the bonds before the maturity date, should resources become available. When this provision is exercised, a premium is usually paid to compensate the investor for early redemption.

Purpose The purpose of the bond issue does not pertain to the project being financed but rather distinguishes between funding and refunding. Funding bonds are issued to retire outstanding floating debt (e.g., short-term notes or bank loans) and to eliminate deficits. Refunding bonds are issued to retire bonds already outstanding. Refunding bonds enable issuers to exercise the call provision of existing bonds and thus to take advantage of lower prevailing interest rates.

Debt policy

Long-term debt obligations provide resources that will be used in the present but will be repaid in the future. They create a rigid contract that commits future budgets and must therefore be used judiciously. Abuse of current debt authority can have significant implications for future residents of the local government. John Mikesell stated the issue this way:

> Improper use can disrupt lives of those paying taxes and expecting services in the future as debt service costs can impair the ability of the borrower to operate normally. The fundamental rule of debt construction is: do not issue debt for a maturity longer than the useful life of the project it is financing.[9]

The amount of general obligation debt outstanding at any given time is usually controlled by state law or state constitutional provisions. These limits are almost universally related to a percentage of assessed valuation, the property tax base. Nonguaranteed, limited-liability debt issues are evaluated separately because they are intended to be self-supporting or to be financed with special revenues.

Special districts and authorities have sometimes been created to evade the low general obligation debt limits of many city and county governments. Because each district or authority may have its own debt limit, these limits are viewed as a legal requirement but do not necessarily satisfy the considerations of a rational debt policy. A more meaningful consideration is total overlapping debt per capita, a measure that shows the aggregate debt of all local government jurisdictions applicable to the population in a defined area.

Another consideration in developing a debt policy may be to limit the cost of debt service to some percentage of the operating budget.

The use of debt is not inherently bad. It may be more inequitable to employ a pay-as-you-go approach that requires current residents to pay for facilities that future citizens will use. The important point is that debt must be carefully used only for those projects that will yield future benefits and not overburden future taxpayers.

1 Richard Abel Musgrave, *The Theory of Public Finance; A Study in Public Economy* (New York: McGraw-Hill, 1959).

2 Francis M. Bator, "The Anatomy of Market Failure," *Quarterly Journal of Economics* 72 (August 1958), 351–79.

3 *The Municipal Year Book* (Washington, D.C.: International City Management Association, annually); *Government Finance Services* (Washington, D.C.: U.S. Department of Commerce, Bureau of the Census, annually); *Statistical Abstract of the United States* (Washington, D.C.: Government Printing Office, annually).

4 Aaron Wildavsky, *The Politics of the Budgetary Process*, 4th ed. (Boston: Little, Brown, 1983).

5 Adapted from Price Waterhouse, *Understanding Local Government Financial Statements: A Citizen's Guide* (New York, 1984).

6 Lennox L. Moak and Albert M. Hillhouse, *Concepts and Practices in Local Government Finance* (Chicago: Municipal Finance Officers Association, 1975).

7 Government Finance Officers Association, *Building Prosperity: Financing Public Infrastructure for Economic Development* (Washington, D.C.: Government Finance Research Center, 1983).

8 John L. Mikesell, *Fiscal Administration: Analysis and Applications for the Public Sector* (Homewood, Ill.: Dorsey Press, 1982).

9 Ibid.

5 Public works planning

The words "planning" and "plans" are generic to life, business, and government. To most of us they convey the idea of getting ready for the future or getting from here to there. This seems simple enough. However, within the context of municipal government, and to the various professionals such as public works practitioners who work in it, these words can have a variety of meanings, depending on the situation. One popular dictionary defines "plan" in part as "any detailed scheme," then goes merrily along to define it also as "a proposed or tentative project or goal." The alert reader will note the sand is already beginning to shift!

In an effort to explain planning and plans, this chapter will describe what planners mean by the planning process, various levels and types of planning,

Planning and plans

Planning as a process

At the most abstract levels of planning and management, the planning process is divided into five major steps:

1. Basic goals. For urban planning this may mean: Do we want to grow? Do we want to arrest decline? Do we want to be a center for high-tech industry? What is the balance between highways and mass transit investments?
2. Study and analysis. Planners study land use, population trends, the economic base of the community, physiographic features relating to topography and water, and so on.
3. Plan or policy preparation. This means preparing a plan or a policy for the community as a whole or a segment of it. It is a basic statement of how the community will develop, in what direction, and perhaps at what pace.
4. Implementation and effectuation. This means carrying out the plans. For the planner it means using tools such as zoning ordinances, land subdivision regulations, capital improvements programs, and general guides for private development and public investments.
5. Monitoring and feedback. This is a step to determine how well the plans and policies are being carried out, whether the goals were realistic, whether the study and analysis foresaw new occurrences, and so on. If we pay attention to feedback, we will redesign the plans, and even the planning system.

The above description refers to an abstract process. From a practical standpoint, traditional city planning (and some public works planning as well) basically consists of three steps: (1) examining inventories and trends in land use, population, employment, and traffic; (2) forecasting the "demand" (in some ways this is a "free market" approach); and (3) planning facilities and services of sufficient capacity *to accommodate* future demand. This process is similar to market forecasting by business firms that see a growing need and plan to satisfy that need through the manufacture and distribution of products.

Unfortunately, this traditional method of planning is not particularly adequate. One reason is that it doesn't take sufficient account of the interactions between the systems of the city. For example, an urban expressway can be filled beyond capacity on the first day it is opened. Or, land values can increase astronomically when a new link to an interstate highway is completed and attracts new growth to one side of the city. This points out a basic problem: no matter how sophisticated the forecasting methods, it is difficult to forecast trends independently.

Another problem with this approach is that it does not take sufficient account of the public responsibility for guiding and shaping the future of the city. Some public works managers may be uncomfortable with this notion, yet it is at the core of planning. Even some high-growth cities of the Sun Belt, which initially welcomed a boomtown atmosphere, are now reassessing the role of public planning because of declining air quality, crowded streets and highways, and an inability to keep up with public service demands.

Multistep planning

Planning agencies are now shifting away from both abstract and traditional planning to a multistep process that seems to work better. The first step of this process consists of taking inventories and analyzing trends just as the other methods have always done. In the second step, however, the forecasts are made with a different frame of mind. Instead of assuming that the forecast is a given, the planning agency considers it to be a "what if" statement. Then, a community can think about the pluses and minuses of a particular forecast.

The third step is to identify the goals and objectives. Many communities have undertaken community-wide or business-led goal studies. These are useful projects if the objective is to get people to think about the city. This approach is a bottom-up approach, with widespread participation, in contrast to a top-down approach in which top officials set the goals. However, the planning agency doesn't dwell on the goals and objectives in terms of apple pie and motherhood statements. Instead, the most sophisticated agencies try to raise issues where there are choices. For example, what are housing choices in the city? Are all income groups adequately served by the private market? Everyone wants a clean river in town, but how do you define "clean" and how much will it cost to clean up the river? How do we compare minimum standards for air pollution, noise, and water quality with economic development opportunities? Do we want to establish maximum population density ceilings in a particular area?

The fourth step is to formulate alternative policies and plans to be tested and compared. Unfortunately, only the most sophisticated transportation planning agencies have the methodological capacity to be very precise about testing alternatives. The fifth step is to compare and evaluate alternative plans on the basis of such criteria as financial capacity, the extent to which goals of a community are met, public acceptability, the legal and social constraints in implementing the plan, and the degree to which limited resources or facilities would become overloaded.

The sixth step is to select the most acceptable plan and loop back through the forecasts and assumptions to see the degree of fit with the known data and the amount of compromise it took to bring the plan to this point. A seventh step is to prepare detailed plans for elements of the comprehensive plan, community facilities, and programs.

The eighth step is to implement plans and policies through both public and private means. Implementation usually involves regulation, some incentives, and some cooperation.

The final step is not a step at all but a continuous process—that is, a continuous evaluation of the process as a whole in order to discover blind alleys, redo plans that can't seem to be implemented, change regulations that are creating problems, and so on.

Throughout this process the planning agency conducts its own in-house work, hires consultants, consults with other city or county departments, establishes task forces and advisory committees, consults with other governmental levels, and has a seemingly endless round of meetings with officials, technicians, and the public. This is frustrating, yet seems to be the only way we know how to run local democratic planning processes.

Plans

The discussion above emphasizes the process of planning, but planning must produce products. These products vary depending on the type and level of plan that is being prepared, as shown in Figure 5–1. This section of the chapter describes the major types and levels of plans that make up "planning." The next section describes the dimensions of planning—legal, political, and other. Both the types and the dimensions interact in the planning process at the base of the discussion in these two sections.

At the most abstract, wide-scale, and comprehensive level is the comprehensive plan. At one time, it was called the master plan and has also been known as the general plan. More recently, products of this kind have been called strategic plans. The comprehensive plan is a document (in multiple volumes for very large jurisdictions) that is the result of relatively long and intensive study and analysis. The geographic scope is the entire city and its regional environment. The time scale is long-range or indefinite. It is comprehensive in that it tries to relate long-range objectives and the interrelationships between population growth, economic development, the use of land, transportation, and community facilities. A land use element, usually produced on a generalized map, indicates the area and location of major types of land uses: residential (by various types of dwelling units and density), business offices, retail trade, wholesale trade, industry and manufacturing, public open spaces, and public facilities.

The comprehensive plan will discuss the principal issues and problems of growth or decline facing the city. It will also point out the main trends that seem

Figure 5–1   Types and levels of plans.

I. **Comprehensive plans**
   Comprehensive plan containing basic policies for land use—residential, commercial, industrial, public—and general policies for public systems.

II. **Systems plans**
   Land use
   Sewers
   Water
   Storm drainage
   Transportation: streets and mass transit
   Solid waste
   Parks and recreation
   Libraries
   Government administration
   Police
   Fire
   Health
   Public works buildings and facilities
   Cultural
   Institutional

III. **Area plans**
   Central business district
   Industrial districts
   Civic and cultural centers
   Community district
   Waterfront
   Neighborhood

IV. **Subsystem components plans**
   Engineering detail plans for construction of trunk sewer line, major water main, or a street extension

V. **Site plans**
   Library, fire station, neighborhood park

inevitable and that need the attention of public or public-private programs. Plans usually contain a mixture of ideas that are being floated, proposals that don't yet have the means of implementation identified, and actual commitments of city governments. For at least a decade or more the tendency has been not to show plan proposals in map form, because of the difficulty of identifying precise sites or dimensions, but rather to present a series of policy statements. Although these policy statements are relatively abstract at times, if carefully drafted they can provide good guidelines or decision rules for the future. That is, if the policy guidelines are precise, they will help a city council or planning commission determine whether a particular proposal at a particular place achieves a plan's objectives, is in harmony with the policies, or is in conflict with them. A good comprehensive plan will point out the interrelationships between systems or parts of the city, and the relationship between economic and social development and public facilities. For example, the plan for an area designated for industrial park development would also point out the infrastructure needed to support it.

Depending on the size of the city, a comprehensive plan may also contain chapters on public utility and facility systems if general policies have been established. However, the degree of detail is nowhere near that shown in the next level of planning, systems plans.

The second level in Figure 5–1 shows systems plans. These are more detailed than the comprehensive or general plans, yet they do not necessarily approach engineering specifications. For the purposes of this discussion, a systems plan is defined as the plans, policies, and program for a specific network of citywide facilities—in other words, the entire sewer system, the entire fire protection plan, or the plans for parks and recreation.

Public works managers are probably most familiar with systems plans for sewers, water supply, storm drainage, transportation, and solid waste disposal. Perhaps they are most "comfortable" with this level because the plans deal with particular facilities in particular places. From the standpoint of comprehensive planning policy, however, these plans are frequently inadequate in two respects.

First, if these systems plans are based on population projections and land use trends (as they frequently are) and not on adopted planning policy, the assumptions are questionable. In effect, the systems plan has made the general policy decision, when no policy position has been made at all. A closely related problem is the tendency in some of these plans for demand responsiveness or for a perceived need to guide the direction of growth instead of the system itself. As a practical matter, public works departments or their consultants must forge ahead with systems plans, even if comprehensive plans are outdated or don't address issues related to new development. Yet, it would be best for the community if these issues were identified and discussed very early in a project. Perhaps such an examination would compel the community to update its comprehensive plans. In well-managed communities, comprehensive plans and systems plans move along together according to a specific schedule.

A second problem is that some systems plans fail to pay enough attention to their public finance component. That is, most plans make a first estimate of the costs of various components of the system, but at times these are "ballpark" estimates, to say the least. Sometimes they leave out critical factors such as land cost. Many systems plans also fail to create a loop in the work program whereby the entire system and estimated costs can be politically tested by the local governing body. What is needed is a second phase in which the political leadership determines the general funding that is available (or more importantly, that will be permitted) and the system planners identify the most essential or desirable elements of the system to be implemented on a priority basis.

The third level of plans consists of area plans. These contain greater details for some geographic parts of the city. The most common type is a plan for the central business district. Others include industrial districts, civic and cultural centers, the community or district making up several neighborhoods, the water-front if there is one, and the neighborhood.

In area plans, details may go down to the block level. The area plan identifies the particular issues and problems facing a particular geographic area and develops plans and proposals for the future. These plans must be comprehensive in the sense that they have to interrelate land use policies with the various utility and facility services that must serve the area. The basic purpose of area plans is to provide a public statement of plans and policies that will guide local decision makers when they review private development proposals and provide input into departmental planning for particular facilities needed to carry out the plans successfully.

The style of planning may vary from area to area. For example, a plan for a central business district may emphasize urban design components and involve the private sector to a great extent, whereas, neighborhood-level planning involves citizen groups and neighborhood organizations and can take a long time to prepare and complete. In both cases suspicion and acrimony frequently arise when groups become skeptical about how much influence they will really have over government planning decisions.

The fourth type of plan is the detailed engineering plan for components of subsystems, such as trunk sewer lines, major water mains, and street extensions. These plans are based on system-wide plans and are typically prepared under the direction of the public works department. The component would have been scheduled in the capital improvements program with sources of funds identified. The construction of such a system component requires extensive cooperation with all municipal departments involved in systems that are built within street rights-of-way.

One of the main reasons for considering this type of plan separately from the category of site plans (the last level in Figure 5–1) is that linear systems provide the basic network for planned development. If the systems (the first three levels in Figure 5–1) are not in, development may not occur. After they are constructed, development may in effect be accelerated because of the availability of utilities. In other words, these linear systems should be considered the growth shapers of urban development.

Finally, at the fifth level is the site plan for a facility such as a library, fire station, or neighborhood park that requires land purchase, architectural and engineering drawings, scheduling in the capital improvements program, possible public hearings for site selection, meetings with neighborhood or community groups to discuss services that will be provided at the site, and coordination with neighborhood development plans.

The dimensions of planning

The word "dimensions" is used in this discussion in the sense of the dimensions of a problem, or the dimensions of a character in a novel or play. It can also be thought of as a "parameter" of planning—that is, a variable that affects planning and must be an inherent part of any planning problem or project.

The *legal* dimension is generally straightforward and usually easy to deal with. Land use controls, such as zoning and land subdivision regulations, must be drafted and administered in accordance with state enabling statutes and relevant court decisions. When plans are prepared and techniques devised to implement them, the planner must always ask, "Is it legal?" State laws can also affect comprehensive planning. For example, a number of states, such as Florida, Oregon, and California, mandate that communities prepare comprehensive plans that contain specific plan elements. State law can also mandate consistency between plans and land use decisions.

That a planner needs to know and appreciate the law has been succinctly

---

The dimensions of planning These dimensions have traffic lights and warning signals that need to be observed. These dimensions are described in the text, but this checklist may also be useful.

Legal Is it lawful? Can it be done?

Political Is it acceptable?

Social Who wins? Who loses?

Economic What are the costs? What are the benefits?

Fiscal Where is the money?

Intergovernmental What agencies are directly responsible?

Aesthetic What are community preferences and values?

Environmental What is the impact?

Management Who's in charge?

---

stated by U.S. Supreme Court Justice William J. Brennan, Jr.: "If a policeman must know the Constitution, then why not a planner?"[1]

The *political* dimensions of planning can be extremely frustrating for the planner and the public works practitioner. Yet, this is the world in which they operate on a daily basis. Professionals in local government are trained to give objective evaluations and recommendations. When these recommendations are ignored for political reasons, professionals are frustrated. Frustration may be appropriate when political decisions are arbitrary and are aimed at benefiting special interests. However, recent years have also seen a new kind of urban politics emerge where political officials conduct strong political campaigns on urban development issues. One group is in office and favors growth and economic development. An "out" political group favors slowing down growth and increasing the city's concern with environmental quality. Both city councils and mayors have been known to change urban development policies after elections. This type of political dimension is entirely legitimate in a democratic government, and planners and public works directors must cope. These situations require the highest level of professionalism.

The *social* dimensions of planning can be seen in a variety of circumstances. City renewal efforts often displace low-income groups. This was a severe problem in the days of urban renewal and the building of urban links to the interstate highway system. With the slowing down of development in some cities, the problems have become more subtle, yet remain important. For example, some inner city neigborhoods are being rehabilitated and the word "gentrification" has been applied to high-income groups' driving up land and housing prices, which in turn forces low-income groups to move elsewhere. Neighborhood planning in central cities is to some extent social planning in that it provides social service facilities for dependent population groups. Social factors also influence suburban developments in terms of accommodating low- and moderate-income housing.

The *economic* dimension has always been a strong factor in planning. The earliest central business district renewal schemes had an economic objective. Cities in the Sun Belt and on the West Coast are experiencing significant amounts of high-tech industrial development. The older cities of the North have frequently reorganized or reoriented their planning programs so that economic development is the major focus of central city planning. Some cities now have both planning departments and economic development departments.

Economic development planning has become important not only because of the traditional reasons—that is, to maintain and increase the tax base—but also because it helps to create new job opportunites. The financial mechanisms to promote economic development are also undergoing significant change as a greater number of experiments are being conducted in public-private partnerships. Developers and cities are sharing more and more of the cost of development and cities are also using techniques such as tax increment financing or tax abatements to promote business and industrial development.

The *fiscal* element of planning is one that permeates planning for public systems and facilities. As the discussion below on capital improvements programming points out, the federal-state-local finance system has been undergoing significant changes during the 1980s. In general, there will be far fewer federal grants-in-aid for public facilities and planning programs. In addition, several states, such as Massachusetts and California, have had tax limitation referenda. Cities will have tough times ahead as they try to figure out how to finance new facilities and to maintain existing ones.

The *intergovernmental* dimension has been significant since World War II. Public works and planning departments must deal with federal agencies—to the extent that they are still involved in regulatory or grants-in-aid programs—with state agencies that build or regulate, and with metropolitan organizations such as water or sanitary districts, county highway departments, forest preserve and park districts, and so on. Cities are no longer built just by the cities themselves. There are planners, builders, and regulators at every level of government and this requires extensive coordination among governmental units and agencies.

The *aesthetic* dimension has been part of planning since the beginning. More recently, there has been a movement to prepare urban design plans, especially for central business districts and cultural centers. In addition, historic preservation planning is on the rise all over the nation. Even with new development, the appearance of commercial and industrial facilities is gaining attention. Zoning ordinances and land subdivision regulations contain more and more provisions relating to appearance, landscaping, and architectural and site plans. Sign regulation has always had a strong aesthetic element underlying the ordinances.

The *environmental* dimension of planning has been significant since the early 1970s. Major development decisions, whether public or private, frequently must pass the review of state environmental protection agencies. In some states, such as California, major public works projects must now contain an environmental analysis as part of basic planning and decision making. In suburban jurisdictions, regulations relating to soil conservation, hydrology, and the preservation of streams and stands of trees are becoming more common. In some Sun Belt and resort communities environmental factors are among the most important to be considered in planning and regulation.

Planners and public works officials in a number of states (such as Florida, Vermont, Hawaii, California, and Maine) must also deal with a state-level planning and land use control system that must be interrelated with local planning and land use control. The concepts of "regional impact" and "areas of state concern" refer to development decisions that must be examined by state planning agencies as well as local agencies. Local jurisdictions that have coastal lands, wetlands, large forests, and other environmentally fragile areas are often affected.

Finally, there is the *management* dimension of planning. Plans and programs can be designed, but they require managers to implement them. Since local government is generally fragmented into traditional departments, mechanisms must be created to provide a management perspective that is understood by all department heads. Mayor's or manager's cabinets are a common way of providing management input. Interdepartmental committees are another method. In some cities with city managers a system of deputy managers overseeing several departments has been created to provide management coordination. Good management has always been important, but in an era of fiscal constraints it is more critical than ever.

Zoning

Zoning, given its widespread use and the time that planning departments spend on it, is the workhorse of planning. Zoning is related to the general plan in that it carries out the land use plan portion. It is the strongest legal tool used in planning. Whereas a land use plan is general and long-range, the zoning ordinance is extremely precise: Every parcel of property is placed in some zone and specific regulations apply. The zoning function does more than carry out the general plan, because it is a regulatory instrument that may be used to regulate private property in accordance with commonly held community values, generally accepted notions of what is good development, and even such community prejudices as those that reject high-density, low-rent housing.

Zoning is defined as the division of a city or county into geographic districts contained on a zoning map, and the regulation within these districts of:

1. The uses of land and buildings that may or may not be permitted
2. The height, width, and length of the buildings and structures
3. The area of a parcel of property that may be occupied by structures, minimum dimensions between buildings and between buildings and property lines, and the size of required open spaces
4. The density of population by limiting the kinds and numbers of dwelling units permitted
5. A variety of development standards such as off-street parking and loading.

Legal aspects of zoning

Zoning is a police power that enables local governments to enact legislation protecting the health, safety, and general welfare of citizens. State enabling statutes that prescribe the extent of powers, together with state court decisions on zoning, control what a city may do in developing and administering a zoning ordinance. Many legal safeguards are built into the regulatory system because any regulation prohibiting an individual from using his or her private property as he or she sees fit must be exercised with care. Of particular importance for zoning is the concept of "due process," which requires that zoning bear a reasonable and substantial relation to protecting health, safety, and general welfare. If zoning regulations reach beyond these objectives, the effect in the opinion of many courts, is the taking of property without just compensation.

Although laws and court decisions vary from state to state, zoning has existed long enough for four broad principles to have emerged. First, local governing bodies may not treat any individual property owners in an arbitrary and discriminatory fashion. Second, although regulations may differ among zoning districts, within a particular district the regulations must be uniform for each class and kind of building. Third, there must be a reasonable basis for classifying areas in particular ways. Fourth, regulations must be reasonable as applied to a particular property.

Form and content of the zoning ordinance

Work and study are essential to preparing a new zoning ordinance. Although some of the information may have been collected if the city has recently completed a general plan, such a plan tends to emphasize broad policies and guidelines and may not provide nearly enough information on existing and proposed buildings and other facilities and resources. Thus, population and economic projections must be made in order to determine development trends. For example, how much, if any, new industry is anticipated? Will the central business district expand in land area or will it remain as it is today? What long-term changes are taking place in the housing market? So complex is the process of preparing an ordinance that it usually takes several years to prepare one for even a medium-sized city.

In the broadest terms, a zoning ordinance comprises two major elements: the zoning map and the zoning ordinance text. The zoning map must be sufficiently detailed and accurate to answer any question about the district classification for a particular land parcel, even a single building lot. The text of the zoning ordinance contains all the particular aspects of regulation, including descriptions of the zoning districts and of how the map may be changed. Most of the text is usually devoted to district regulations, with a separate chapter or section assigned to each district. A small city may have as few as three zoning districts: residential, commercial, and industrial; a large city may have dozens. Residential district zoning may differentiate between single-family and multifamily dwellings, and it may be subdivided further according to densities within various single-family or multifamily districts. Business districts may be categorized as neighborhood, community, or central. In addition, the more complex zoning ordinance will also contain a variety of special-purpose districts such as agricultural, educational, public use, and institutional.

The district regulations contain a list of permitted uses, a list of accessory uses, and a list of special or conditional uses. The typical ordinance prescibes precise standards for uses in terms of lot areas; setbacks; front, side, and rear yards; open space; lot coverage; and building height. Apartment regulations may prescribe the minimum lot area per dwelling unit, a factor that may vary depending on the number of bedrooms contained in a unit. In commercial districts, the ordinance specifies the types of businesses—retail or wholesale; or offices, bakeries, or shoe stores. Industrial district regulations may be far more complex. Thus, in different industrial districts, the use—such as watch manufacturing, automobile assembly, or machine shop—is not specified; instead, the specific amounts and degrees of noise, smoke, odor, heat, vibration, dust, and glare that are permitted are specified by numerical values.

District regulations may specify the number of parking spaces required and, for business and industrial uses, the number of truck-loading berths required.

Other sections of the text usually deal with definitions, procedures for obtaining zoning or occupancy permits, procedures for amending the ordinance, general provisions that apply to all districts, and special procedures and standards for planned unit developments. Several of these types require additional discussion.

Amending the ordinance   No matter how well the ordinance is written, changing conditions will require that it be amended from time to time. The less common type of amendment is the text amendment. The more common type is the map amendment, whereby the zoning designation for a particular parcel is changed. The map change generates the greatest amount of administrative work, public controversy, and court litigation.

Most map changes come about because of property owner initiative and petition stimulated by forces in the real estate market. The early literature of planning and zoning tended to overemphasize the ability of planners to predict with accuracy how land would be used in the future. What was frequently overlooked was that most land development decisions are made by private owners who have their own conception of what is profitable or desirable. Thus, zoning maps reflect economic realities at the time they are adopted, and it is difficult to use zoning as an effective barrier to economic forces. For example, almost all planners agree that business uses should not be strung out along major arterial streets. A glance at any city, however, will show that this strip development is rarely prevented.

These market factors should not be seen as a cause for despair; rather, they illustrate the need for effective, impartial, and professional administration of zoning amendments. A good zoning ordinance would require that a staff study be undertaken of any area larger than a single parcel or a block when rezoning requests are made. Such a study would determine whether a particular request was a forerunner of strong economic forces, whether it was a request to gain special advantage, or whether such public facilities as streets and utilities could in fact absorb more intensive development.

Variances The variance, in some states called the variation, is a safety valve. It recognizes that the drafters of a zoning ordinance cannot be aware of precisely how regulations may apply to *every* parcel, and in particular how regulations can create an unnecessary hardship that serves no broad public purpose. For example, a particular property may have a small stream or an easement running through it that would make it necessary to locate a structure close to a property line. A variance would allow the structure to be placed closer to the lot line than the ordinance allowed if appropriate evidence of hardship were shown at a public hearing.

Unfortunately, the variance power is often misused through ignorance or abused with full knowledge—or a combination of both. An example of a misuse would be allowing a use that could not be permitted legally unless a map amendment were made, or allowing an apartment developer to add dwelling units above the number permitted by the district regulations because of an alleged economic hardship.

Nonconformity There are two types of nonconformity: nonconforming structures, which do not meet yard, height, or bulk requirements specified in the zoning ordinance; and nonconforming uses, which employ a structure for an activity not permitted within the zoning district (for example, a structure in a residential area might be used as a store). Clearly, the latter is the more important and the one that creates most problems. The nonconforming use provision of a zoning ordinance specifies that uses that were legal on the effective date of the zoning ordinance but that thereafter do not conform to the use regulation of their district may legally continue.

The most common examples are the corner grocery store or isolated apartment structure in a single-family district. Most ordinances, however, provide that if the use is discontinued because of fire, or for some other reason, it may not be resumed. Nonconforming uses usually may not be expanded unless an administrative hearing is held and permission granted to do so.

Administration Administrative practices vary, but some typical patterns emerge. In small communities, the zoning officer is usually the building inspector. In larger communities, enforcement may be carried out by the zoning division of the public works or planning department. In both cases, personnel process building and zoning permit applications, check plans for conformance, handle inquiries, and prepare applications for map amendments, variance requests, special uses, and planned unit developments. In practice, the small community's building inspector usually has neither the time nor the professional skills to prepare extensive studies on applications. In a large city, however, the planning department staff spends a considerable amount of time making such studies.

Another typical component of zoning administration is a lay commission or board appointed by the city's chief executive with the concurrence of the city council. In a small community, a single body may function both as a planning commission and a zoning board of appeals, whereas a large community usually has separate bodies. The primary function of the planning commission in zoning administration is to conduct public hearings on rezoning requests and make recommendations to the governing body. The final decision, which requires the passage of an ordinance, is a legislative rather than an administrative action.

The zoning board of appeals handles appeals from decisions made by the zoning enforcement officer. At times the appeal may involve an alleged mistake on the part of the official, but more typically, appeals are for variances requested after a building or zoning permit has been denied.

Emerging techniques   Originally zoning was very limited in its regulatory scope. The earliest ordinances classified land into broad districts, regulated lot and building dimensions, required parking and off-street loading, and dealt with the size of signs. A wide variety of techniques have been built into zoning ordinances over the years to control many additional details of site and building development. The discussion below highlights some of these techniques.

Planned unit development (PUD) is a technique that allows the grouping of uses on smaller lots so that open space can be preserved. It was first applied to suburban residential developments that had a mixture of single-family and multifamily development, with perhaps some neighborhood-level commercial use. It has since come to be used in central city locations as well as in mixed-use developments in combinations of apartments, offices, hotels, vertical shopping centers, connections to mass transit facilities, and parking.

PUD has also evolved to the point where developments are reviewed under the provision relating to "site plan review," which can cover almost every element of site design. Examples of elements in site plan review are the size, color, and placement of signs; landscaping specifications for the perimeter of a site and within parking areas; pedestrian access; general architectural appearance relating to building mass, color, and texture; storm water drainage and retention; ingress and egress from the site; and many other site details.

The text of the zoning ordinance is no longer the sole means of authorizing large-scale land development. Such development is increasingly negotiated by the developer and the local government through intensive scrutiny of the PUD proposal, its site plan, and the facilities that must be provided.

Cities and counties, for example, frequently expect the developer to pay for *off-site* improvements such as access roads that must be built to accommodate the development. The two parties may therefore negotiate a swap: permission to increase the density within the site in exchange for the developer's promise to pay for additional off-site improvements.

Such negotiations often are extralegal. The zoning ordinance may not require the developer to provide off-site improvements, but he or she does so in exchange for higher density or other *on-site* provisions. Sometimes it is strictly a bargaining situation that depends on how much the city or county wants the development in comparison with the developer's opportunities to develop there or elsewhere.

A number of suburban communities are experimenting with new types of zoning controls, generally called "performance zoning," which allow more flexibility in site plan arrangements so that environmental features can be preserved. Houses may be clustered in one corner of a site to protect a significant stand of trees. Or, types of dwelling units may be mixed in a variety of ways as long as the underlying density remains the same. Requirements for streets and landscaping may vary considerably, depending on landscape features. Rather than being separated by type of use, districts may be combined in innovative ways.

Another technique is the transfer of development rights (TDR). Our traditional concepts of real estate are that the property owner owns a "bundle of rights" for a piece of property that extends down into the earth and up into the sky. A common example of TDR involves the development rights on a farm within a zoning district that permits higher densities. The farm owner could sell those development rights to an adjacent landowner, who could then build to a higher density in exchange for agreeing to let the farm be kept as a farm. Although the density on the developed site would increase, the farmland would not be developed, and the overall density of the zoning district would stay the same.

Another common example might involve a city's central business district where the underlying zoning in a particular block may permit twenty-story buildings. On a particular site there may be a ten-story building of great architectural quality. The owner of this building would sell the remaining "ten stories of development rights" to an adjacent owner, thereby making it economically feasible to preserve the historic building.

Zoning can also be used for social purposes. For example, in order to provide more low- and moderate-income housing in the suburbs, the zoning ordinance may require a developer to set aside a certain proportion of the land or dwelling units for lower cost housing. In a number of large cities studies are under way to determine the feasibility of requiring developers of office buildings to pay money into funds that would later be used by the community to construct low- and moderate-income housing.

Land subdivision regulations

Land subdivision regulations control the conversion of vacant unimproved land into building sites. The administration of land subdivision regulations deals largely with single-family residential subdivisions and planned unit developments that contain a mixture of residential and business uses.

The public works manager is intensely involved in subdivision development because the subdivision ordinance regulates the location and design of public improvements.

As is the case in zoning and other police powers, a municipality's right to adopt subdivision regulations is based on state enabling legislation. The antecedents of modern subdivision regulation date from precolonial times when European monarchs devised rules and regulations governing the layout of new towns in Europe. In the twentieth century the concept has gone through four principal phases:

1. The period before 1930, when the essential concern of local government was to ensure that subdivisions were accurately surveyed to protect the prospective purchaser and that new streets were coordinated with the city's existing street system
2. The 1930s and early 1940s, when the concept of subdivision regulation was expanded from an engineering and real property legal device to a tool for carrying out city plans
3. The period after World War II, when cities began to require the installation of physical improvements as a prerequisite to subdivision plat approval
4. The period since the mid 1970s, when concepts of growth management—especially the timing of development—and the question of who pays for local infrastructure came to the fore.

The substance of regulations

Although organization and administrative procedures vary, the substance of subdivision regulations is similar among local governments across the country. Such regulations have been strongly influenced by the model ordinances prepared by professional associations, state municipal leagues, and other bodies and built around plat specifications; standards for blocks, lots, and streets; and required improvements.

Plat specifications Subdivision regulations require that certain information be provided on the plat, or map, that eventually will be recorded in a county's records of deeds. Information that is usually required in the final plat includes:

1. Street, lot, and setback lines and other graphic presentations
2. Precise dimensions, angles, and bearing and other engineering data that make it possible to transfer lines to the ground
3. Monuments
4. Lot numbers, street widths, and names
5. Details on adjoining streets and properties
6. A variety of other technical data such as graphic scale and true north point.

Such data provide basic property records for land transfers and precise dimensions for public rights-of-way. A preliminary plat contains similar information, but lacks precise engineering details. It also relates the plan of the subdivision to existing conditions, particularly topography. In most jurisdictions, the crucial decisions and adjustments are made at this earlier stage. If the final plat follows the outlines of the preliminary one, approval is usually a mere formality.

Standards for blocks, lots, and streets A section of subdivision regulations entitled "design standards" will state the minimum dimensional requirements for blocks, lots, and streets. Some ordinances will state only that minimum dimensional requirements for lots shall be the same as required in the zoning district in which the subdivision is located. Other regulations may prescribe minimum area, width, depth, and width-to-depth ratios for lots. Minimum lot size requirements may also be based on the availability of public sewer and water facilities. In regulating the size of blocks, communities must specify that streets are to appear at certain intervals, usually at least every 1,000 to 1,200 feet. Modern subdivisions designed with curvilinear streets must provide pedestrian rights-of-way through blocks for access to schools should the street design fail to provide a direct route.

Streets standards generally are specified in terms of minimum right-of-way, depending on the street's function: arterial, local, or collector. Arterial streets provide for the through movement of traffic; local streets provide access to abutting residential property; and collector streets feed traffic from local to arterial streets. To preserve adequate driver sight distances on streets, specifications for vertical and horizontal design are required, as are design standards for street intersections.

Subdivision regulations govern the design and placement of easements for utilities should the utility leave the street right-of-way. Regulations also specify the community's street naming and house numbering systems.

Required improvements In addition to preventing land speculation, required improvements ensure that a new residential area is complete at the time of occupancy by residents and that all the physical facilities essential to a healthful, safe, and convenient physical environment are in place.

The most common requirements relate to street improvements. These vary depending on the function of the street within the subdivision—usually either collector or local—and the residential density. Ordinances deal with pavement widths, subgrade and paving materials and thicknesses, general physical characteristics relating to load-bearing capacity, and variations based on soil characteristics. The degree of detail in construction standards and engineering design will vary, but the common practice is to include only general requirements in the subdivision regulations and to put material specifications in the local public works standards. This practice allows for flexibility as technical standards change.

Closely related to street requirements are those for curbs, gutters, and drainage facilities. Requirements frequently specify whether culverts and ditches are permitted or whether complete storm drainage systems must be built. Regulations may require the construction of sidewalks on one or both sides of a street, and usually specify whether curb lawns are required. Considerable variation exists in the requirements for the provision of street lighting, street-name signs, and street trees.

Subdivision regulations deal with soil erosion during and after the construction of a development. Each year millions of tons of soil are lost owing to poor control of storm water runoff in construction areas. A developer is generally required to provide a plan that contains, as a minimum, topographic information about the area, a soils study, and a survey that identifies critical areas in the subdivision that would require soil and water conservation work and/or special drainage facilities (spillways, sediment basins, drain tile systems). Further, the developer is required to minimize excavation and to expose only the smallest practical area of land for the shortest possible time, so as to reduce erosion.

Recent issues in improvements Two trends relating to improvement standards began to emerge in the 1980s: (1) increasing reassessment of physical improvement standards, and (2) reconsideration of who pays for the improvements.

In the late nineteenth and early twentieth centuries, cities were laid out in block and street patterns that often did not differentiate between the streets to be used for local access to residential properties and those to become major streets. Thus the tendency was to require relatively wide rights-of-way to ensure that enough space would be available to develop wide streets if later traffic volumes justified street widenings. After World War II developers began to change the design of residential neighborhoods in order to discourage through traffic, first by constructing curvilinear streets and second by classifying streets as residential (i.e., designed for local access, not through traffic) or as collector and arterial, with the appropriate right-of-way and pavement widths. More recently, these standards have been reexamined with an eye toward reducing the costs of municipal maintenance and of the improvements so as to reduce the cost of housing.

In consequence, a number of communities have determined that if certain streets serve only a limited number of residential units, then right-of-way and pavement widths can be narrowed. Measurements of average daily traffic show that low-volume streets can indeed be narrower. In addition, increasing concern with storm runoff has created a desire to reduce the land area covered by impervious surfaces. Thus, residential subdivisions in planned unit developments or in hilly areas may have narrower streets than in the past.

Another impetus to reexamine development standards came about in the late 1970s and early 1980s when high inflation and high interest costs drove up the cost of housing. A number of communities are experimenting with planned unit developments on smaller lots and zero-lot line developments and are cautiously reconsidering improvement standards. This trend will undoubtedly continue, but it should be emphasized that public works managers should approach proposals for lower standards with great caution.

The second trend pertains to who pays for improvements. The earliest days of subdivision regulation required developers to construct physical improvements such as streets, sewer lines, and water mains. In the 1960s it was considered innovative to require that park and school land be reserved or dedicated. Somewhat later, when school and park officials discovered they did not need a site in every neighborhood, the concept of fees in lieu of dedication evolved, wherein the developer was required to pay a fee into a common fund that would cover park and school services in a wider area. Throughout this period, major facilities, such as trunk sewer lines and treatment plants, were paid for by the community as a whole through general obligation or revenue bonds.

Urban growth in the late 1970s and 1980s, coupled with declining municipal revenues, forced many communities to reconsider who pays for what. Thus, developers are now required to pay for many more improvements that may serve other areas as well as their own. A number of communities require developers to construct oversized or off-site sewer and water lines because the community cannot afford to build them through traditional financial means. Thus, the cost of off-site infrastructure has shifted to the developer's budget. Some communities have entered into "recapture agreements," wherein developers recover portions of the cost from other developers as they tap into the sewer or water lines.

Developers of commercial and industrial properties are frequently required to construct acceleration and deceleration lanes on adjacent roads. A number of communities are even measuring the traffic impact of large-scale development and are requiring special fees to support system-wide road and street improvements. Communities are also experimenting with impact fees or facilities benefit assessments that require contributions toward system-wide construction and maintenance.

The courts, too, have been involved in that some developers have brought lawsuits against cities and counties over issues such as the reasonableness of improvement standards, the rational connection between requiring fees and the actual impact of the development, and the definition of a tax or fee. Since state courts differ widely in their rulings, the public works practitioner, the planner, and the city attorney must carefully study the new types of improvement fee.

Growth management

Traditional comprehensive planning was based on the assumption that studying trends, making projections, analyzing alternatives, and adopting plans constituted a sound approach to making decisions about new development. The most important tools in implementing comprehensive plans were the zoning ordinance, subdivision regulations, and the capital improvements program. Experience in using these concepts and tools led many planners to conclude that growth—especially in high-growth communities—could not be planned and controlled very well with just these tools. A set of interrelated problems began to emerge concerning the *rate* of growth, the *location* of growth, the community's *infrastructure capacity*, the effects of new development on the *environment*, and the increasing desire of *citizen and environmental groups* to have a say in how their communities are developed.

A number of communities in widely scattered locations throughout the nation began to develop sets of policies, ordinances, and concepts that came to be known as "growth management." These programs had a number of characteristics in common.

1. A concern with dealing with the rate of growth. Unquestionably, many communities felt they were growing "too fast" and were losing some of their "character." Some communities experimented with population growth limits or limits on the number of dwelling units constructed in a year (these were not always upheld by the courts).
2. Coupling the rate of growth with a plan for providing and financing infrastructure. Local officials felt that the rate of growth had to be controlled in some way if they were to intelligently program expenditures for infrastructure. Often these plans were carried out through the adoption of ordinances regulating utility extension policies, and who paid for extensions—community, developer, or some combination of the two.
3. A concern with the location of development, especially in relation to infrastructure improvements. A number of communities adopted ordinances establishing urban limit lines, utility extension policies, or utility districts. All were concerned with trying to channel growth into

areas where infrastructure improvements were in place or were programmed for the near future.

4. A belief that unlimited growth should not be an end in itself. Americans, especially those who own real estate, love a boomtown because of the profits. But those who move to such communities seeking a pleasant environment find that growth can damage the environment they sought. Unfortunately, some of these attitudes also created equity problems in trying to keep out newcomers.

5. Increasing attention to issues of environmental planning and quality through the adoption of ordinances relating to coastal zone management, agricultural land protection, stream and woodland protection, and performance-oriented land development ordinances.

Although growth management systems have not always achieved their objectives, for the most part they have helped develop a closer fit between long-term plans and day-to-day land development regulation and management. Planning practice has been improved through the coupling of land development management with infrastructure capacity, the systemic approach to environmental assessment, and the analysis of costs and revenues associated with community growth.

Capital improvements programming

The 1909 Burnham plan of Chicago is the benchmark for the beginning of modern city planning. This plan is usually mentioned together with the City Beautiful Movement. What is generally not said is that the plan contained a discussion of how bond issues would be required to finance the plan's public works proposals. Chicago built $300 million (about $3 billion in 1985 dollars) of public improvements to implement the plan in the first fifteen years. In retrospect, it was an astonishing achievement.

Although the Chicago experience taught the significant lesson that public works expenditures contribute a great deal toward implementing comprehensive plans, it was not until the late 1920s that the concept of capital improvements programming began to emerge as a *continuing* element of municipal planning and fiscal management. Planning and public works officials began to realize that planning capital improvements was decisively different from annual budgeting. In essence, as capital improvements were increasingly financed by public borrowing, it became necessary to undertake financial analyses of the community's ability to pay in the future; the ways in which debt was to be amortized; and the inevitable choices that had to be made when the number of proposed improvements exceeded the financial capacity of a community.

Experiences during the Great Depression, when numerous cities became bankrupt, and during World War II, when many cities postponed public improvements, gave communities a new incentive to plan public facilities with care. Basic concepts of capital improvements programming have come down to the present generally intact. Thus, the capital improvements program has become a thoroughly tested and useful planning tool.

Definitions

Capital improvements programming is the multiyear (five or six years) scheduling of public physical improvements, which is based on studies of fiscal resources, and the choice of specific improvements to be built. The capital improvements *budget* refers to those facilities that are programmed for the next fiscal year. A capital improvements *program* (CIP) refers to the improvements that are scheduled in the succeeding four- or five-year period. An important distinction between the capital improvements budget and the capital improvements program is that the former may become a part of the legally adopted annual operating budget, whereas the longer-term program does not necessarily commit a government to a particular expenditure in a particular year.

The definition of a *capital improvement* may be different in different cities. The common definition includes new or expanded physical facilities that are relatively large, expensive, and permanent, such as streets, expressways, public libraries, water and sewer lines, and park and recreation facilities. In small communities the purchase of a fire engine may also be a capital expenditure. The important fiscal planning principle underlying this definition is that capital improvements should include *only* those expenditures for facilities with relatively long-term usefulness and permanence. Capital improvements *should not* include expenditures for equipment or services that prudent management defines as operating budget items and that ought to be financed out of current revenues.

The benefits of a CIP

The CIP process has many benefits for local governments. It ensures that plans for community facilities are carried out; allows improvement proposals to be tested against a set of policies; schedules public improvements that require more than one year to construct; provides an opportunity, assuming funds are available, to purchase land before costs go up; provides an opportunity for long-range financial planning and management; helps stabilize tax rates through debt management; avoids such mismanagement as paving a street one year and tearing it up the next to build a sewer; offers an opportunity for citizens and public interest groups to participate in decision making; and contributes to better overall management of city or county affairs.

How capital improvements are financed

Because most capital investments involve the outlay of substantial funds, local governments can seldom pay for these facilities through annual appropriations. Therefore, numerous techniques have evolved to enable local government to pay for capital improvements over a longer period of time than a single year. Most but not all of the techniques involve financial instruments, such as bonds, in which a government borrows money from investors (both institutional and individual) who then receive the principal and interest over a number of years.

State laws governing local government finance and the literature of public finance classify techniques that are used to finance capital improvements. These techniques are discussed below.

Current revenue (pay-as-you-go)   Pay-as-you-go is the financing of improvements from current revenues such as general taxation, fees, service charges, special funds, or special assessments.

Reserve funds   Reserve funds are accumulated in advance for capital construction or purchase. The accumulation may result from surplus or earmarked operational revenues, funds in depreciation reserves, or the sale of capital assets.

General obligation bonds   Some projects may be financed by general obligation bonds. Through this method, the full taxing power of the jurisdiction is pledged to pay interest and principal to retire the debt. General obligation bonds can be sold to finance permanent types of improvements such as schools, municipal buildings, parks, and recreation facilities. Voter approval may be required.

Revenue bonds Revenue bonds are frequently sold for projects that produce revenues, such as water and sewer systems. A type of revenue bond developed during the late 1970s to promote economic development was the industrial revenue bond. Because such bonds are exempt from federal taxation, some have questioned the appropriateness of the method. At some point Congress may severely restrict their use.

Lease-purchase Local governments using the lease-purchase method prepare specifications for a needed public works project that is constructed by a private company or authority. The facility is then leased to the jurisdiction. At the end of the lease period the title to the facility can be conveyed to the local government. The payments over the years will have paid the total original cost plus interest.

Authorities and special districts Special authorities or districts may be created to provide a single service such as schools, water, sewage treatment, toll roads, or parks. Sometimes these authorities are formed to avoid restrictive local government debt limits and also to finance facilities serving more than one jurisdiction. They may be financed through revenue bonds retired by user charges, although some authorities have the power to tax.

Special assessments Public works that benefit particular properties may be financed more equitably by special assessment: That is, they are financed by those who directly benefit. Local improvements often financed by this method include street paving, curbs, street lights, sanitary sewers, and water mains.

State and federal grants There has been a general decline in state and federal grants-in-aid to finance local programs. Much of this money has been used to finance capital improvements.

Tax increment financing Tax increment financing may be used to provide front-end funds in an area where large-scale redevelopment is feasible. A district around the proposed development is designated with a tax base equivalent to the value of all the real property within the area. The tax revenues paid to taxing units are computed on the tax base initially established during the redevelopment period, which is usually the expected life of the project. The area is then redeveloped with funds from the sale of tax increment bonds. These bonds are sold by the municipality or a specially created taxing district for acquisition, relocation, demolition, administration, and site improvements. Because of the higher value of the newly developed property in the district, more tax revenue is collected and the tax increment above the initially established level goes into a fund to retire the bonds. After the development is completed and the bonds are retired, the tax revenues from the enhanced tax base usually become part of the general revenues of the local government.

Public/private As government budgets have tightened, a number of techniques have been developed to pay for capital facilities—especially facilities that serve a specific development project. These techniques include privatization, whereby a facility is built and maintained by a private company; cost sharing, wherein a developer pays for some facilities and the public pays for others; upfront payment by developers; the creation of quasi-public corporations that build facilities; tax abatement for a specified period of time for new businesses; contracting with private companies to run public facilities; and state capital fund revolving loan programs.

Recently there has been considerable interest in variations of traditional debt instruments. Examples are commercial paper, zero coupon bonds, and others that go beyond the scope of this chapter. As a result, today's public works practitioner must know more about public finance than ever before.

Fiscal policies

Careful long-range fiscal analysis and the adoption of specific fiscal policies must be the foundation of a local CIP. Such analysis includes the preparation of tables showing the amortization of all outstanding debt. Since local government can issue bonds that mature over long periods of time, this analysis will have to look ahead for more than a decade. In practice, the analysis and forecasting covering the first five years are more intensive and focus on the local economic situation and the extent to which it may affect long-term local government revenues. For growing communities the analysis may show the degree to which various categories of revenue—property taxes, fees and licenses, state aid, income taxes, and other sources—are expected to grow in the future. For stable or declining communities (for example, mature central cities), such an analysis may show that because the economic base of the city is declining (for example, manufacturing and retailing establishments are moving to the suburbs), the local tax base may also be declining.

Anticipated revenues and expenditures for capital improvements, personnel services, pension plans, and other costs are projected to determine whether projected revenues and expenditures are in balance. The analysis then leads to the development of fiscal policies that should address the major problems identified in the financial analysis and provide specific guidance to the budget and planning departments as well as the operating departments that propose capital improvements. Policies might address such issues as the maximum amount of debt the local government is willing to take on; the types of revenue devices that will or will not be used; the annual amount of debt service that the operating budget can absorb; the specific types of projects or facilities that must be made self-sufficient through user fees or other charges; and the degree to which local government will seek state or federal grants-in-aid.

In recent years communities have begun to adopt fiscal policies that are related to strategic community objectives. Mature central cities, for example, are adopting policies that relate expenditures to economic development. These cities may adopt policies to finance improvements that are most likely to maintain or attract an industrial or commercial base, create new jobs for local residents, or generate private investment in neighborhood revitalization.

Many rapidly developing communities are adopting fiscal policies that promote environmental objectives, for example, by purchasing critical environmental areas or parklands, or by creating greenbelts that will help shape urban growth. These communities are also paying more attention to the secondary impacts of capital investments with the result that capital facilities, such as major sewer trunks and major expressways, are being located and programmed in areas where the community wants growth to occur and are being denied or delayed in areas the community does not want to see developed.

The CIP administrative process

The capital improvements process is often administered through separate budget channels of local government, the reason being that the planning agency may be the key coordinator for capital expenditures, while a budget office or city manager's office may be the coordinator for all operating expenditures. Obviously, the process varies from city to city, but the description below should be considered relatively typical.

The first step in a CIP process consists of analyzing the fiscal resources of the community—the revenue and expenditure projections discussed above. This is typically conducted by the finance office. The manager or mayor will meet with key aides and council members to discuss the implications of the analysis for setting fiscal policies.

Next, a directive is issued by the chief executive officer to all department heads requiring them to submit proposed capital improvements projects to the agency administering the CIP. The directive will include the fiscal policies discussed above as well as forms, deadline dates, and dates of key meetings.

Departments will be asked to rank their proposals so that all of them can be evaluated within the framework of five to six years. It is a long and hard process every year to evaluate the new proposals vis-à-vis those already in the CIP. During the process the key agencies are likely to be the planning department, from the community development point of view; the public works department, from the construction, maintenance, feasibility, and cost point of view; and the budget office or finance department, from the revenue/expenditure point of view.

After all project proposals have been submitted to the CIP agency, numerous meetings are held at which time the planning director, public works director, finance officer, local government manager, mayor, and department heads discuss, critique, and hammer out project proposals. The objective at this juncture is to pull together a CIP that is sensitive to official policies, contains projects related to city development objectives, and produces a product that the manager or mayor can submit to the city's governing body.

The CIP is presented to the jurisdiction's governing body by the chief executive officer together with any special budget messages. Depending on local practice, the CIP and the operating budget may be discussed separately or together. Normally, the governing body holds numerous meetings and public hearings.

After the governing body determines its own priorities and choices, the CIP is adopted. "Adopted" should be understood to mean that the first year of the program—the year of the capital budget—is considerably different from the remaining years. The choices for the first year are firm, whereas in subsequent years the CIP is concerned basically with policy direction rather than with a specific and firm choice about projects. Even though the CIP may be adopted with the annual operating budget, it will still be necessary for the governing body to pass ordinances appropriating specific funds during the budget year for specific projects. Ordinances are also required to authorize the issuance of bonds or other financial instruments.

The problem of choice: priorities

The CIP process has been at work for decades in the planning, public works, and management fields. Nevertheless, the setting of priorities continues to be vexing. Choosing projects is the most crucial step in the CIP process, yet it continues to be troublesome. For example, how does a city decide what is more important—extending a waterline, building a new library, purchasing more parkland, or repaving a street? In a more "quaint" era planners thought that they could simply evaluate each project according to whether it was covered by the comprehensive plan and the facility plans; the project was either in the plan or not. However, plans never specifically identified all the potential projects that could come up through the line departments of city government. Moreover, now that comprehensive plans have become more policy oriented, they rarely identify all specific projects. And some communities have plans that are completely out of date or are still under preparation.

One traditional system of assigning priorities divides proposed projects into four categories: essential, desirable, acceptable, and deferrable. These categories are usually further defined in terms of whether a project contributes to public

CRITERION	3	2	1	0	P	S	W	T
Public health and safety	Project needed to alleviate existing health or safety hazard.	Project needed to alleviate potential health or safety hazard.	Project would promote or maintain health or safety.	No health or safety impact associated with project.	A		3	
External requirements	Project is required by law, regulations, or court mandate.	Project required by agreement with other jurisdiction.	Project will be conducted in conjunction with another jurisdiction.	Project is City only and not externally required.	A		3	
Protection of capital stock	Project is critical to save structural integrity of existing City facility or repair significant structural deterioration.	Project will repair systems important to facility operation.	Project will improve facility appearance or deter future expenditure.	No existing facility involved.	A		3	
Economic development	Project will encourage capital investment, improve the City's tax base, improve job opportunities, attract consumers to the City, or produce public or private revenues.			Project will have no significant economic development impact.	A		3	
Operating budget impact	Project will result in decreased costs in the operating budget.	Project will have minimal or no operating and maintenance costs.	Project will have some additional operating costs and/or personnel additions will be necessary.	Project will require significant additions in personnel or other operating costs.	A		3	
Life expectancy of project	Meets the needs of community for next 20 years or more.	Meets needs of community for next 15 to 19 years.	Meets needs of community for next 10 to 14 years.	Meets needs of community for less than 10 years.	A		3	
Percentage of population served by project	50% or more	25% to 49%	10% to 24%	Less than 10%	B		2	
Relation to adopted plans	Project is included in formal plan which has Mayor/Council approval.	Project is included in written plan adopted by City board/commission.	Project is included in written plans of City staff.	Project is not included in any written plans.	B		2	
Intensity of use	Project will be used year-round.	Project will receive seasonal and as-needed use.	Project will receive only seasonal use.		B		2	
Intensity of use	Project will be used year-round.	Project will receive seasonal and as-needed use.	Project will receive only seasonal use.		B		2	
Scheduling	Project to be started within next year.	Project to be started within 2 to 3 years.	Project to be started within 4 to 5 years.	Project is uncertain.	B		2	

Figure 5–2   System for establishing priorities among proposed capital projects, city of New Orleans. Codes: P = priority; S = score; W = weight; T = total.

safety, prevents hazards, satisfies a critical need, or would be of benefit but is not essential. Another system ranks projects on the basis of criteria such as protection of life, public health maintenance, conservation of natural resources, and replacement of obsolete facilities.

Some communities have constructed scoring or point systems whereby a project is evaluated in terms of particular criteria (for example, contributing to public safety); the score may be registered on a scale of 1 to 10, for example. According to the internal logic of such systems, projects that have a high score are more desirable.

A priority rating system developed for the city of New Orleans is shown in Figure 5–2. In addition to the traditional criterion of public health and safety, this system makes the analyst think about other criteria, such as impact on the operating budget, economic development objective, energy consumption, and public support. The criteria are weighted within a single criterion and among them to obtain a score.

These and other rating systems have limitations and should be used with caution. Such systems do not show what is absolutely essential. Nor do they replace professional judgment. Perhaps the most serious objection is that rating system scores are not the same as political judgments. If elected officials decide

CRITERION	3	2	1	0	P	S	W	T
Benefit/cost	Return on investment for the project can be computed and is positive.		Return on investment cannot be readily computed.	Return on investment can be computed and the result is negative.	B	2		
Potential for duplication		No similar projects are provided by public or private agencies outside of City government.		Project may duplicate other available public or private facilities.	B	2		
Availability of financing	Project revenues will be sufficient to support project expense.	Non-city revenues have been identified and applied for.	Potential for non-city revenues exists.	No financing arrangements currently exist.	C	1		
Special need		The project meets a community obligation to serve a special need of a segment of the City's population, such as low/moderate income, aged, minorities, handicapped, etc.		The project does not meet particular needs of a special population.	C	1		
Energy consumption	Project will reduce amount of energy consumed.	Project will require no increase in energy consumption.	Project will require minimum increase in energy consumption.	Project will require substantial increases in energy consumption.	C	1		
Timeliness/ external	Undertaking the project will allow the City to take advantage of a favorable current situation, such as the purchase of land or materials at favorable prices.			External influences do not affect the timeliness of this project.	C	1		
Public support	Public has clearly demonstrated a significant desire to have the City undertake the project by way of neighborhood surveys, petitions, or other clear indicators.		City staff reports that the project is desired by the community to be served.	Public has not expressed a specific preference for this project.	C	1		
				TOTAL SCORE				

Figure 5–2 (continued).

that a project must be put in the CIP or moved to top priority, then they are applying their own rating system, which overrides any other.

Despite all of these warnings and objections, are rating systems useful? Of course they are. First, they provide a uniform structure for evaluating capital projects. Everybody must play by the same rules until the proposals go to the governing body for decision. Second, they force all department heads, and many others as well, to think about projects systematically and analytically. Finally, they provide the same base for reevaluating projects in the CIP every year until the projects are either built or dropped.

The CIP process and intergovernmental relations

The pattern of intergovernmental relations in metropolitan areas has profound effects on the local CIP process. Most metropolitan areas contain small fragmented municipal governments and a number of separate special districts that build important facilities, especially sewage treatment plants and their related major sewer trunk lines, and major expressways and highways. As is becoming increasingly understood, these key facilities can trigger, accelerate, or retard the speed and pattern of urban growth—in other words, they are the growth shapers. The decisions of the units that plan and construct these facilities have a great effect on local government, and it is the local government that must then provide the local capital facilities and public services to serve the growth thus generated. Local government does not always have complete control over its destiny.

A number of steps have been taken to coordinate such planning and development at the metropolitan level. Many metropolitan planning agencies are adopting metropolitan development policies and trying (often struggling) to influence these key investment decisions. A handful of metropolitan agencies have areawide capital improvements inventories. These programs attempt at least to identify the capital investments being made by various governmental levels and then inform major decision-making units of government.

A local government itself can survey capital investment plans of overlapping governments and special districts that will be built within the jurisdiction. This can at least inform local officials, who may then want to take political action; it also provides an opportunity to coordinate projects that will be built by different units in the same part of the community. Some communities have organized intergovernmental bonding committees that attempt to keep each other informed as to bonds that will be issued by the governments involved. This is a particularly important step, because when a community's bonds are rated by investment services the amount of overlapping debt on taxpayers affects the safety of the security.

Interactions of planning and public works

Because the tasks of the public works and the planning departments in any local government are related, close cooperation between the departments is essential. The degree of cooperation will depend on tradition, the specific functions assigned to each department, the degree of mutual understanding, and other factors.

Planning and public works departments can work together in a variety of ways. These fall into two categories: administrative devices and specific elements of the planning program.

Administrative devices

Information The simplest way to cooperate is to provide each other with information. Information from the planning department may include population projections, economic studies, the zoning designation for specific pieces of property, statistics on building activity, the content of general or neighborhood plans, and the like. Information from public works to planning might include costs of providing specific services on a per capita basis, widths of specific streets, sizes of water or sewer lines in particular areas, estimated capacities of existing and planned facilities, and capital and operating costs of public facilities.

Advice The difference between providing information and advice is often ignored. For example, either department may be involved in a project and may have secured specific kinds of information from the other. As the project nears completion and presentations are made to the legislative body, a council member may ask, "What does public works [or planning] think?" Although information has been requested and supplied, if no specific opinion was ever explicitly solicited or given, the answer will be less than satisfactory.

Technical advisory committees The planning and public works departments can exchange information and views through technical advisory committees. There are many cases in which one department has served on committees established by the other department or by other governmental agencies. The advisory committee is useful when many agencies or governmental units are interested in a particular project. It is less useful on a continuing basis or when only the two departments are involved.

Subcontracting Particularly strong interdepartmental relations can be fostered when departments subcontract work to each other. Such cooperation might occur when projects are large enough to warrant staff work of a scope and depth beyond that required merely for an exchange of information, or when one department possesses technical capabilities not available to the other staff (e.g., computer programs, models, a trained systems analyst). This type of interdepartmental work assignment gives each department an opportunity to inject its own point of view and to learn more about the views of the other.

Task forces Such projects as a major refuse disposal study or a continuing program for transportation planning may provide opportunities for cooperative projects in which each department provides staff to a task force that may be established on either an ad hoc or a continuing basis. For example, in planning its major streets and expressways within the city limits, one western city is aided by a task force made up of staff members from the public works, planning, and traffic departments. Staff are assigned to the task force on a more or less permanent basis—in effect, as chief liaison officers between the respective departments—but they maintain organizational ties with their own departments.

Building in-house staff capabilities   Most planning and public works departments could benefit from having professionals from the other fields within the department. A planner who is also an economist or a sociologist could be on permanent loan to the public works department, or an environmental specialist from public works could be on loan to the planning department. Each department could also seek to establish a permanent position and fill it as a part of the regular organization.

Informal methods   The public works director and the planning director usually see each other at city council meetings, meetings of the mayor's cabinet, or sessions with the city manager. If this is the extent of the relation, however, it will not be meaningful. Effective, cordial, and lasting relations are built from informal contacts, such as having lunch together, picking up the telephone for a direct personal opinion on some matter, or chatting in the corridors of the municipal building. These occasions offer ample opportunity to exchange information and views about what each department is doing or what is coming up in the near future and to discuss mutual problems.

Specific elements of the planning program

General plan   The degree of cooperation between public works and planning in the preparation of the general plan will vary with the level of detail, specificity of the plan, and the size of the community. If the general plan is a broad policy statement, the public works department will have little opportunity for technical work. If, however, the general plan is detailed and has many separate elements, the opportunity to provide technical input increases substantially. For example, public works would make a large contribution in preparing plans for major streets, sanitary sewerage and storm drainage, the selection of refuse disposal sites, and other facilities or services under the operating jurisdiction of the public works department. The greatest degree of technical coordination may occur in medium-sized communities.

The small public works department may have little technical expertise or input to lend, whereas the large and specialized planning staff may have engineering skills of its own.

Whatever type of plan is being prepared or whatever the size of the community, the planning department must obtain technical advice from the public works department on a regular basis. The public works director, together with other department heads, may serve on a technical advisory committee for general plan preparation. The role of such a committee differs substantially from that of the citizen planning commission and is no less important. Not only can it give technical advice, but it can also serve as a vehicle for the formal exchange of information and opinions, as well as an informal coordinating mechanism within the local government. A general plan in which public works personnel have participated will be technically sound and will have the support of the department when the plan is discussed with the city's chief administrative officer, the city council, the planning commission, and the public at large.

Zoning The public works manager must participate in determining the provisions of the zoning ordinance as they relate to sewer and water connections, the handling of surface drainage, possible street openings, and driveway cuts. The public works department can play a role in the preparation of the zoning map by providing basic data on street and utility capacities in various sections of the city. Such data will help the planning department make sound recommendations as to population density and intensity of development. This advisory role would also extend to the actual administration of the ordinance when map amendments are being considered. The two departments should determine what kinds of data are needed, when amendments are important enough to be discussed at interdepartmental staff meetings, and whether public works should either prepare written opinions or testify at public hearings.

Subdivision regulations Because subdivision regulations specify the type and character of public improvements to be built in new developments, close cooperation between the planning and public works departments is essential over the entire range of activities from ordinance preparation through administration. Sections of subdivision regulations containing technical specifications for required improvements might be prepared entirely by the public works department. Because most subdivision regulations involve opening new streets and installing utilities, the public works department will be heavily involved in administering and processing new developments. In many jurisdictions the public works director must sign the subdivision plat, a requirement not to be taken lightly.

The subdivision review often involves zoning and other planning considerations. Primary administrative responsibility lies in the planning department. However, many cities have a subdivision review committee of which the public works director is a member. This committee may include other department heads and at times may involve several planning commissioners. Such a committee determines whether a proposed subdivision conforms to city regulations, has a well-designed layout, and provides street and utility capacities that serve the subdivision; it also determines how the subdivision fits into connecting street and utility systems. As the typical subdivision approaches the construction stage, the planning department's role in inspection and supervision declines substantially and the role of the public works department increases to the point where it becomes involved in checking detailed engineering drawings and making field inspections.

Community and economic development This process is one of the most complex undertakings of local government, and the planning and execution of a project will involve the public works department heavily. Although such questions as the delineation of project boundaries and new uses may be the prime responsibility of the planning department, issues concerning streets and utilities demand the close attention of public works, particularly when the facilities are an integral part of the plan. New streets may thus be constructed and new utility lines installed. At other times, streets may be vacated completely and utility lines rerouted, or streets may be vacated but the actual easement for utilities retained. The public works department will obviously be heavily involved in planning and executing projects concerned with streets and utilities, but its involvement must begin at the earliest possible stage of development so that it may contribute to determining the engineering and financial feasibility of replanning an area. Changing street and utility patterns in built-up portions of older cities can become extraordinarily complex and expensive, and potential problems must be identified as early as possible in the planning process.

Capital improvements programming   During the annual preparation of the capital improvements program and capital budget, the planning and public works departments will come into close contact for periods of several months. Cooperation is essential if only because the typical public works department is responsible for spending the largest portion of the capital program. Although certain procedures will be established by local ordinance and through directives of the city council, the two departments must agree on specific dates for capital project submittals; the kinds of reporting forms to be used; the technical information to be presented on projection descriptions, financing, and the like; and the way in which priorities should be determined. In addition, many cities establish a CIP committee made up of various department heads as a technical and bureaucratic forum in which the final program is hammered out before being presented to the chief executive officer and the council.

Summary

This chapter has presented an overview of basic planning concepts, the role of the general system and area plans, zoning, land subdivision regulations, capital improvements programming, and the interaction of the planning and public works functions. The applicability of the methods and procedures discussed will depend on the size of the jurisdiction, its economic condition and prospects for growth (or, for that matter, decline), and its political and administrative traditions. Many of these factors will be outside the control of the local government manager, although that manager will be expected to rise to the challenge that they present, both in the public works department and in the local government as a whole. In the later 1980s, the allocation of goods and services, as they affect planning and public works functions, will probably be carried out in a climate of limited resources.

1   *San Diego Gas and Electric* v. *City of San Diego*,
    450 U.S. 621.

6 Managing people

Public personnel management is in a state of evolution owing to the shift in traditional employment relations. Work force demographics, attitudes, and expectations are changing. Employees are questioning authority, seeking meaningful work, participating in decisions affecting them, and looking for personal recognition. They place more value on leisure and personal affairs. Public organizations are striving to match the need for human resources with the new needs of the work force. Merit pay, civil service reform, employee motivation, productivity bargaining, comparable worth, participatory management, and the impact of technology are just a few of the issues confronting public managers. In response to these and other issues, existing personnel activities are changing as new techniques are being developed.

Public works managers and supervisors and other local government officials need to be informed about changing personnel issues and techniques. Productivity improvement, increased job satisfaction, improved labor-management relations, and more effective service delivery all depend on how well public works and other managers utilize their human resources. Both traditional and new personnel management techniques can help public works managers guide their personnel more effectively.

Organization of the personnel function

The basic framework for organizing the local government personnel function is usually set forth in state statutes or local charters and ordinances. Personnel organizational structures include the independent civil service commission, the executive personnel system, or some combination of both. Civil service commissions may have only advisory powers or they may be responsible for the direct administration of the personnel function. Common functions of civil service commissions include establishing qualification standards, approving classification standards, overseeing salary schedules, developing internal standards for promoting personnel, serving as an adjudicator for appeals, and approving personnel rules.

Civil service reform efforts are directed at improving personnel systems in accordance with common merit principles. Basic elements of civil service reform include the creation of centralized management personnel systems separated from quasi-judicial activities; decentralization of such personnel activities as recruitment, examinations, and position classification; development of objective job-related performance evaluation and merit pay systems; establishment of career executive programs; and creation of broad job classes.

The size and scope of the local government personnel program depend upon the form of government, the number and diversity of functions performed, and the number of employees. Some local governments have personnel departments headed by full-time personnel professionals whereas others assign personnel management to officials who have other responsibilities. Large personnel agencies employ a number of specialists in such areas as classification, testing, pay, training, and labor relations. In some instances the labor relations function is separated from the personnel function.

The effectiveness of the personnel system depends upon its legal basis, staffing, and financial resources as well as the political environment. Personnel resources available to public works managers therefore vary among local governments. For this reason, public works managers should become familiar with their personnel system and its capabilities. This involves reading those sections of the law establishing the personnel system and the written policies, rules, and regulations that have been prepared for administration of the system. Such information along with discussions with those responsible for personnel will acquaint public works managers with the types of personnel services available to them and the constraints under which they must operate.

Position classification and job analysis

Position classification is the foundation of personnel systems. It serves as the basis for pay, selection, promotion, performance evaluation, and training. Position classification is a system of grouping similar positions under common job titles on the basis of the kind of work, the level of difficulty and responsibility, and the qualifications required. A position comprises a group of duties and responsibilities assigned to one employee, whereas a class is a group of positions that are similar in duties and responsibilities, require approximately the same qualifications in education and experience, can be filled through similar testing procedures, and can be assigned the same job title and salary. A class specification is the description of the duties, responsibilities, and qualifications of positions in the class. The classification plan includes all the classes and class titles that have been established, the specification of each class, and the procedures for maintaining the plan. Public works managers should become acquainted with the position classification plan and the job descriptions for positions in their areas of responsibility.

The basis of a position classification plan is job analysis, which consists of gathering and evaluating facts about jobs, including the tasks involved; methods or tools used; services produced; qualifications needed to perform the job; and the level of performance required of the worker. Job analysis is a means of identifying the skills, behavior, knowledge, and abilities employees need to perform a job successfully. Direct observation, interviews, and questionnaires are employed in job analysis. Job analysis is time-consuming and expensive and requires skilled and experienced analysts.

Information gathered in a job analysis will aid the public works manager in gaining a clear understanding of what makes up a job, what an employee is responsible for, and what an employee needs to do in order to perform the job well. The public works manager should fully cooperate in the job analysis process by reviewing the information gathered to confirm its completeness and accuracy in relation to the requirements of the job. Managers have a responsibility to explain the purpose and importance of job analysis to their supervisors and employees and to support the effort.

There are four basic approaches to position classification.

The whole job-ranking system uses a panel to rank job descriptions obtained for each job on the basis of difficulty. This system is nonquantitative and does not use predefined factors and point scales for job comparisons. Attention is focused only on the most significant factors.

The grade description system establishes a number of pay groups and levels (such as craft, clerical, and professional) that are based on differences in skill, responsibility, and job similarities. A written standard is established for each class, and jobs are compared to the class standard.

The factor point system utilizes predetermined factors such as skill, knowledge, amount of problem solving, accountability, and work conditions. Numerical points are used to indicate how strongly each factor is represented in the job. Factor values are often determined by evaluation committees. The points for all factors are added to arrive at a total for a job.

The factor comparison system combines the whole job-ranking and factor point system. A committee ranks jobs by comparing them to key jobs, one factor at a time.

Public works managers have an important role to play in position classification. They and their employees will be involved in the mechanics of classification by completing questionnaires, participating in work audits, and serving on committees to review factors and allocate points. Strong management support is required to make the classification effort successful. Public works managers should impress upon their employees the importance of cooperating in classification studies. They should constantly review the integrity of the classification system by checking to see if their employees believe the system is equitable. Job descriptions should be periodically reviewed to determine if they accurately define the physical and environmental characteristics of work. Classification plans also need to be reviewed periodically to ensure that they reflect the changing nature of work, the need for new skills and qualifications, changes in organizational structure, and changes in the scope and level of services provided.

Total compensation

With the increasing weight and cost assigned to deferred compensation, health insurance, retirement plans, and vacations, among other benefits, it is no longer possible to depict employee earnings accurately by looking only at wages and salaries. For this reason the term "total compensation" often is used to signal that pay and benefits make up one package. Equitable and competitive pay/benefit plans are essential in assuring a high level of employee performance and in attracting and retaining good workers.

Pay plans

A pay plan is a listing of all the position classes together with the pay rates or ranges assigned to each class. The orderly grouping of positions resulting from the position classification plan enables management to develop a systematic and equitable salary structure. A local government pay plan generally includes a series of different pay ranges of three to seven steps including minimum and maximum steps. The range structure should be realistic, with an adequate spread between minimum and maximum to differentiate between performance levels.

Formal policies and procedures should exist to guide managers in implementing the pay plan. These policies will cover such matters as placement of newly appointed or promoted employees on the salary schedule and periodic salary adjustments. Other matters covered include appointment within the salary range, recognition for outstanding service, education-incentive pay, overtime, longevity, pay for part-time, seasonal, and temporary employees, and pay-rate adjustments for transfers, promotions, demotions, severance, and cost-of-living changes. Public works managers should carefully review the pay plan and policies pertaining to its administration. They should also participate in recommending agencies that should be included in pay surveys and in identifying and documenting pay problems associated with employee recruitment and turnover.

The purpose of merit pay is to link pay adjustments to superior individual performance. Performance appraisals provide the basis for merit increases. Merit pay is aimed at motivating employees, recognizing and rewarding quality performance, and helping to retain employees.

Appraisal systems used for merit pay purposes should include performance levels or standards that will characterize the quality, quantity, and timeliness of an employee's performance. Weights are assigned to each standard or objective to determine the amount of merit pay to be given. Important components of a merit pay system include:

Objective appraisal system based on behavior

Comprehensive measures of performance that directly relate to the duties and responsibilities of the position

Employee involvement in setting performance standards

Substantial percentage increase or lump sum bonus for outstanding performance

Two-way communication between supervisor and employee.

Linking pay to performance is difficult and emotional both for supervisors and for employees. A merit pay system is not suited to every organization. There must be strong commitment, proper system design, and adequate communication and training. Merit pay systems often fail because of the lack of measurable performance criteria, supervisory resistance, lack of adequate financial and top management support, and inadequate rewards.

A major pay issue today is comparable worth, or equal pay for work that has comparable value. Comparable worth is based on the idea that men and women whose jobs make equivalent demands on them and call for comparable skills or are considered of comparable worth to the employer should receive equal pay. The concept of comparability is being studied in several states and cities to see if existing job classification systems involve sex discrimination. Job or evaluation studies examine established job classes and evaluate the skills and education required and the related salary ranges as they affect men and women. Some of the new evaluation studies use complex scoring systems based on mathematical formulas that assign worth points to components found in most jobs such as knowledge and skills, mental demands, accountability, and working conditions. Critics say comparable worth is an arbitrary and subjective standard. Proponents contend that the object of the studies is to provide a means of overcoming generations of discrimination in the way salaries are set.

Benefits

Employee benefits are part of total compensation and are growing twice as fast as salaries and wages. In the public sector they constitute 30 to 35 percent of basic pay. Employee benefits are growing in number and complexity owing to collective bargaining and the desire of employees to increase personal security. Benefit packages are changing to meet different needs, which may vary with age, financial and family position, attitudes, and life style.[1] Trends in the 1980s have shown that there is considerable interest in alternative work schedules, more holidays, longer vacations, personal counseling, early retirement, payment of unused sick leave, and deferred compensation.

Deferred compensation is a valuable benefit because of the deferred income tax liability. Many local governments make it possible for employees to participate in deferred compensation plans such as those offered by the ICMA Retirement Corporation and the U.S. Conference of Mayors. These plans provide a way of sheltering income and planning for retirement. Although tax-deferred accounts can be a problem, because of possible IRS restrictions, they are a benefit option that should be explored.

Health insurance programs are being expanded to include treatment of mental illness, maternity benefits for unwed mothers, paternity leaves, and dental and vision plans.

Flexible benefit plans are another innovation that offers choices of benefits. Several types of plans are available. Under a cafeteria plan, all employees have minimum levels in each of several benefit areas in addition to a choice beyond the minimum coverage. A buffet plan provides the employees with the option of retaining the same benefits they previously had or choosing lower benefits and obtaining credits that may be used to purchase other benefits. An alternative diner's plan creates sets of benefit packages that are offered to target groups of employees such as single employees and single parents.

Flexible benefit plans help to shift some of the benefit cost to the employee and serve as a method of introducing new benefits. Such plans also aid in improving employee relations and attracting and retaining personnel. Flexible benefit plans are likely to be complex and costly. They involve considerable administration and record keeping and generally require computers. Specialized counseling and education are necessary to explain the complex options and eligibility requirements. Unions are usually cool to such plans because they fear some employees will eliminate benefits that they need.

Public works managers should keep up with new developments in fringe benefits and should closely monitor employee complaints and concerns relating to benefit administration. Current employee handbooks and annual benefit statements that show the type and value of the benefits earned by each employee are valuable employee relations tools.

Recruitment and selection

Employee selection decisions are among the most important and difficult facing public works managers. Hiring an employee generally comes after a two-part sequence of recruitment and testing that may range from a few days to several months.

Recruitment

Recruitment involves seeking out potential employees for a specific position. The public works manager should participate in the process by providing information on the position to be filled, checking the recruitment announcement to make sure that it clearly defines the requirements and qualifications of the job, and suggesting sources of qualified candidates. Public works managers can also identify professional association placement services and recommend magazines, journals, and newsletters for recruitment ads. Internal posting of job announcements is critical for employee morale and may be a legal requirement.

Executive search firms are often used to recruit top public works management and technical personnel. Such firms usually have broad contacts and can approach qualified individuals who may not be actively seeking a position. Substantial time and effort can be saved by having search firms screen applications and check references. The firms work closely with their clients and develop detailed profiles of the positions being recruited. Executive search firms are not without critics, who allege that some firms promote favored candidates, do not fully identify the needs of their clients, and sell other consulting services to individuals they have placed.

Testing

Testing is the second part of the selection process. Although testing is a specialized field, public works managers need to understand the process because they will be involved. Selection devices include application forms, résumés, oral and written tests, interviews, evaluations of education and experience, performance tests, reference checks, physical and psychiatric examinations, and assessment centers. The identification and preparation of appropriate testing devices requires considerable skill. Public works managers should work closely with test specialists in the selection and preparation of the desired tests by verifying information on the scope and qualifications of the job, suggesting questions, and evaluating exercises and criteria for performance tests. Frequently public works managers will be asked to serve on test panels.

Definitions

Reliability—degree to which the selection device produces consistent and trustworthy results.

Validity—degree to which the selection device measures what it is intended to measure.

Job relatedness—degree to which the selection device measures skills and behavior directly related to the requirements of the job and job performance.

Objectivity—degree to which the selection device produces results that are observable and measurable.

Those responsible for testing have an obligation to strive for reliability, validity, objectivity, and job relatedness. Adherence to the federal Uniform Guidelines on Employee Selection is a major objective. Usually a combination of devices is used since such traits as loyalty, industriousness, integrity, stability, and dependability cannot be determined by written and oral tests.[2] Selection interviews can be validated and made more reliable by structuring them through the use of lists and guidelines. Information should be obtained on specific performance-related experiences, and multiple interviewers should be used. Every effort should be made to ask job-related questions.

One selection device that receives high scores for job relatedness is the assessment center, which uses a number of methods to identify and measure the behavioral components and skills of a job that are crucial to successful job performance. Assessment centers incorporate group and individual exercises, including written tests, interviews, role playing, leaderless group discussion, problem analysis, and in-basket, speech, and nonverbal exercises. All of the exercises are designed to simulate the job environment.

The steps involved in setting up an assessment center consist of job analysis, selection and training of assessors, design of exercises, observation, feedback, evaluation, and validation. Assessment center success depends especially on the use of trained assessors and adequate feedback. Judgments of the performance of participants are based on information pooled from the assessors and an overall evaluation of each participant's behavior.

Assessment centers are not problem-free. They are costly to develop and administer. Inadequate assessor training and poorly designed exercises can bring about the failure of a center. Some participants find the center experience stressful because of the competitive exercises and thus refuse to participate.

Even with these limitations, assessment centers are a sound diagnostic tool for identifying training and development needs. Information obtained through the centers is used to develop training courses directed at meeting needs that have been identified. Centers are used for promotion, the design of upward mobility programs, and the development of performance appraisal systems. Because of their cost, assessment centers are generally used for upper- and middle-management positions.

Assessment center exercises

1. *Assigned role group discussion*
In this leaderless group discussion, participants acting as department heads of a hypothetical city must allocate revenue sharing money in the time allotted or make other judgments on the varying proposals offered. Each participant is assigned a role (point of view) to sell to other team members and is provided with a choice of projects to back and the opportunity to bargain and trade off projects for support.

2. *Nonassigned role group discussion* This exercise is a cooperative, leaderless group discussion in which four short case studies dealing with problems facing the city are presented to the group of participants. The participants act as consultants who must make group recommendations on each of the problems. Assessors observe each participant's role in the group and the handling of the content of the discussion.

3. *In-basket exercise* Problems that challenge middle and upper level executives in local government are simulated in the in-basket exercise. These include relationships with department superiors, subordinates, peers, representatives from special interest groups, executive and legislative branches, the public, the news media. Coming back from vacation, the participant must deal with memos, letters, policies, bills, etc., found in his/her

in-basket. After the in-basket has been completed, the participant fills out an extensive form concerning his/her handling of the various items.

4. *Speech exercise* Each participant is given a written narrative description of a policy, event, situation, etc., and specific situational problems related to the narrative which require a response. The participant is required to make a formal oral presentation, based upon the background narrative description (before the city council, at a news conference, before an employee group, etc.).

5. *Analysis problem* The analysis problem is an individual exercise. The participant is given a considerable amount of data regarding a particular problem of your choice, which he/she must analyze and about which he/she must make a number of management recommendations. The exercise is designed to elicit behaviors related to various dimensions of managerial effectiveness. The primary area of behavior evaluated in this exercise is the ability to sift through data and find pertinent information to reach a logical and practical conclusion.

Source: Debbie Cutchin and David Alonso, *Solving Personnel Problems through the Assessment Center*, Management Information Service Report, vol. 13, no. 2 (Washington, D.C.: International City Management Association, February 1981), p. 8.

Performance appraisal

Once an employee is hired he or she will need continual evaluation and feedback about performance. Few personnel topics receive more attention than performance appraisal systems, which are usually the basis for decisions concerning pay, promotions, discipline, transfers, training, and employee development. Appraisals can help improve motivation and productivity and assist in career development.

There are a number of performance appraisal systems. The narrative or essay appraisal system consists of written statements prepared by supervisors, employees, peers, or some combination of these. The statements vary in length and content and identify strengths, weaknesses, and potential for development. However, such systems lack the quantified information required for personnel decisions, tend to be unstructured, and depend on the appraiser's writing ability. Essay appraisals do offer an opportunity for a two-way exchange between supervisor and employee and are used in jobs requiring abstract knowledge and skills. They are most effective if related to performance standards.

Graphic rating scales or report card ratings are widely used. They consist of a set of statements or factors that call attention to certain personality or character traits such as quality of work, attitude toward job and others, initiative, cooperativeness, loyalty, dependability, appearance, and judgment. Adjectival or numeric scales are used to rate the employee according to such categories as unsatisfactory, below average, average, above average, and superior. Provision is usually made for written comments by the rater. These systems are easy to develop and use for a broad range of jobs and are more consistent than essay appraisals. Several pitfalls are associated with the graphic rating scale, however. One major weakness is that they are based on ambiguous terms. Supervisors tend to be lenient and allow judgments on one element to influence all others. Graphic rating systems are highly subjective and have little to offer in the way of feedback and training. Most supervisors resist commenting and tend to give "satisfactory" ratings. In some cases raters are instructed to force ratings into a normal or bell-shaped curve in order to reduce bias.

In a forced choice system the rater completes a form, choosing from a set of statements the one that best describes an employee. The statements of behavior represent poor to outstanding performance, but the terms in each set are matched so that they appear equally favorable or unfavorable to the rater. The rater does not know what the scoring weights are for each statement. Trained specialists construct the appraisal instrument. A third party interprets the results of scores and explains them to the rater, who in turn explains the results to the employee. It is difficult to provide constructive feedback, counseling, and advice on career development under this system because the ratings are interpreted by someone else. Forced choice rating systems are expensive to use and different sets of items must be developed for each occupation. Such a system is usually limited to middle- and lower-management positions.

Behaviorally anchored rating scales employ statements that are developed by job knowledge experts to describe incidents typical of successful job performance. Job analysis and statistical analysis are used to identify those kinds of behavior that distinguish effective from ineffective performance. Employees are rated on a numeric or adjectival scale to measure the frequency with which they engage in each kind of behavior. Examples of statements for a supervisor include "explains why the change is necessary," "discusses how the change will affect the employee," and "listens to the employee's concerns." Each supervisor would be rated on a scale such as:

almost never   1   2   3   4   5   almost always.

Behaviorally anchored systems are costly and time-consuming to develop. Not all performance dimensions can be reduced to specific kinds of behavior, especially when the position involves the exercise of judgment and discretion.

In a critical incident-based system, the supervisor and employee identify incidents critical to successful job performance. Raters match actual incidents against a predetermined critical incident scale to which numeric values can be assigned. The process is time-consuming and costly if technicians are used to identify critical incidents; furthermore, job analysis is essential to the development of the system. A less formalized approach has supervisors keeping records of actual incidents of positive and negative behavior. This information is used in discussing performance with employees but has limited application with respect to future performance.

Another approach is to appraise performance by means of comparative rankings. Individuals in a given category are compared with others doing the same

How to make criticism sessions productive   Criticizing a subordinate can be a real test for even the most seasoned manager. Too often what is supposed to be a constructive session turns into a futile confrontation, with mutual gripes and hard feelings, but no solution of the problem.

Five simple suggestions can help the manager make criticism sessions more productive and problem-solving.

Step 1. Get to the point. Don't evade the issue. Skip the small talk and go straight to the target: "Bob, I want to talk to you about your late reports"; or "Barbara, I called you in to discuss your personality conflict with the director of sales."

This advice appears cold and heartless. You probably feel that a warm and friendly opening, such as, "Bob, how are the kids?" or "Barbara, how's that training for the marathon coming along?" will relax your subordinate and ease the path to solving the problem.

But it rarely works out that way. Stalling and beating around the bush usually only increase the anxieties on both sides.

Step 2. Describe the situation. Use a descriptive opening that is specific, not general. Avoid evaluative openings at all costs.

Evaluative: "Bob, I can no longer deal with your late, sloppy reports." Descriptive: "Bob, you've been late on three reports in the last two weeks. That caused us two shipping delays and cost us $5,000."

Evaluative: "Barbara, you're nasty and abrasive." Descriptive: "Barbara, the sales director has just informed me that you refuse to communicate with him."

Evaluative openings are damaging because they prejudge your subordinate's point of view. This can only pave the way to a confrontation. By being descriptive you set the tone for a factual recounting of the situation *without* prejudging. The subordinate will feel much less threatened, and more willing to cooperate.

Step 3. Use active listening techniques. Encourage the subordinate to tell his side of the story. It will reduce defensiveness, clarify the situation and provide both parties with an opportunity to think the problem through.

It helps to ask open-ended questions that invite discussion, and cannot be answered with a simple "yes" or "no." Begin questions with *what* or *how*, or sometimes *tell me* or *describe*.

Bad: "Do you like our new computer system?" Good: "How do you feel about our new computer system?"

---

job. Under paired comparison, each employee is compared with every other employee. Every possible combination of everyone being rated is presented to the rater. An employee's relative position in the final ranking is determined by the number of times one individual is preferred over another. Weaknesses of this approach include the large number of ratings that must be made, possible bias toward specific employees, and difficulties in distinguishing degrees of difference between employees rated.

Alternation ranking consists of deciding who is most valuable and who is least valuable until a rank order list is established. Ranking systems are simple to use but can be easily manipulated, and they score low in reliability and validity. Little insight is provided about the intervals between ranked individuals. Ranking techniques are useful for making decisions about employees where multiple judgments are used.

Management by objectives (MBO) rating systems focus on the number and difficulty of objectives reached. Skill in formulating accurate and realistic objectives is necessary. Consideration must be given to the fact that many objectives

Nodding the head, restating the subordinate's statement in your own words, encouraging more information through silence are other examples of active listening techniques. They invite your subordinate to open up, and reassure him you are interested in and sensitive to his viewpoint.

Step 4. Agree on the source of the problem and its solution. It's essential that the subordinate agree that there is in fact a problem. If he doesn't, there's little likelihood the problem will be solved.

Once you and the subordinate have identified and agreed on the problem, work together to identify the source, and let the subordinate get involved in coming up with a potential solution.

For example, if the problem stems from lack of knowledge, a training program might be the answer. A lack of motivation might be resolved by exploring ways to make the subordinate's job more meaningful or stimulating. If there's a personality conflict between subordinates, you might want to transfer one of them, or get them to work out their difficulties between themselves. You may discover that the subordinate you're criticizing isn't the cause of the problem at all; in that case, you may want to look elsewhere in the chain of command.

No one likes to be ordered around. But by allowing the subordinate to participate in your decisions about resolving a problem, you can be better assured of his active cooperation.

Step 5. Summarize the meeting. Have the subordinate synopsize the discussion and the agreed-upon solution. Both subordinate and manager should leave the session with the same understanding of what was decided. Establish a follow-up date which allows the subordinate reasonable time to correct the situation.

In closing the session, you should reassure the subordinate that you're always available to discuss his progress.

The ultimate measure of your success will be whether the problem that worries you is solved. That's not always possible. But constructive criticism is a skill that can and must be mastered by the manager who is dedicated to improving employee performance, productivity and morale.

may not be within easy reach of the employee being rated. Technically, MBO-type systems are not considered appraisal systems because they are not evaluative.[3] The system documents performance expectations rather than outcomes. Such systems are useful for coaching purposes and as a motivational tool. MBO systems are most applicable for managerial and staff positions.

Each appraisal technique has its own strengths and weaknesses. Selection of a technique should be related to the desired objective and the unique characteristics of the organization. Some techniques are appropriate for making pay decisions whereas others are better suited for career counseling, organization development, and motivation. Effective performance appraisal systems have some of the following characteristics:

1. The system is based on job analysis.
2. The purpose of the system is clearly defined.
3. The system is based on job-related behavior and clearly defined performance standards.

4. Appraisals are conducted on an ongoing basis.
5. Appraisers receive extensive training in the use of appraisal techniques and in counseling employees.
6. Provision is made for appraisal discussion and positive feedback. Performance strengths and weaknesses are clearly spelled out along with a clear plan of action of what is needed to correct faults and improve performance.
7. There is a clear link between good performance and a reward system.

Appraisal systems frequently produce disappointing and unsatisfactory results. Public works managers therefore not only need to know about the different types of appraisal systems but also the pitfalls associated with them. Obstacles to effective systems include the lack of a clear idea of what the system is supposed to do and failure to plan for ways to meet supervisory resistance. Many systems merely measure what employees are doing instead of results. Job requirements may not be defined in terms of desirable performance. In some cases supervisors are not adequately trained and do not properly communicate with their employees. Employee performance may not be documented in clear behavioral and job relevant terms.

Improved employee motivation and productivity depend on appraisal systems that provide for continuous supervisor-subordinate interaction involving counseling and coaching. Attention should not only be directed at past performance but also toward future career development opportunities. Public works managers must develop and establish performance standards as a basis for measuring progress toward results. They need to closely monitor the appraisal process to determine its workability. The absence of an appraisal system does not mean evaluation will not take place. Supervisors inevitably form judgments about their employees. For this reason it is important that supervisors be trained to counsel their employees properly.

Coaching and counseling

Poor employee performance is often related to personal problems, and working with these employees to correct the situation is one of the toughest jobs a supervisor can face.[4] Personal problems can lead to low morale, reduced productivity, poor performance, turnover, increased costs, staff conflict, absenteeism, accidents, increased medical and insurance costs, work disruptions, and disciplinary problems.

Supervisors need to be trained in the four steps they should take in dealing with declining job performance: identification, documentation, confrontation, and follow-up.[5]

First, supervisors must recognize that a performance problem exists. Symptoms include absenteeism, tardiness, employee conflicts, not working up to established standards, disobeying rules, and poor performance. After recognizing that a problem exists, the supervisor should keep accurate and specific records of the employee's poor performance. The most difficult aspect of dealing with a troubled employee is discussing the evidence of deteriorating performance. Such discussions should take place as soon as possible after the poor performance. Supervisors need to cite specific examples and offer suggestions for improvement. In some cases disciplinary action may be needed.

Employees with alcohol, drug, financial, legal, marital, health, and psychological problems should be referred to appropriate counselors. Many local government agencies have employee assistance programs that offer early intervention and treatment to employees with personal problems. Employee assistance programs ensure confidentiality and provide supervisory training, professional administration, and follow-up. Supervisor follow-up is critical in helping the

The boss/subordinate meeting

Some questions: before, during, and after the meeting.

Are you meeting with the right people to solve the situation?

To what extent will you involve the employee in diagnosing the situation? How about involvement in the entire problem solving process?

To what extent have you prejudged the situation and how rigid is your position regarding the problem, cause, and solution?

What is the trust level between you and the employee? How might this influence your behavior and that of the employee?

How well did you listen? How many times did you interrupt, change the topic abruptly, not answer a question, withdraw (physically or mentally), or give advice?

Did you get defensive?

Have you followed a problem-solving model? Are you thinking of solutions without first diagnosing the entire situation?

Does the situation point to a need for you to confront your boss?

How willing are you to take that step?

Did you treat the employee as a child rather than as an adult? Why?

Did you deliberately raise false expectations in the subordinate?

How often were you deliberately evasive or ambiguous? Why?

Did you avoid a necessary confrontation or did you confront the issues and work toward their resolution?

Did you have a hidden agenda? If so, how difficult was it to keep the agenda hidden? How necessary was it to keep the agenda hidden? Have you weighed the consequences of not divulging the agenda versus the consequences of stating the hidden agenda?

At the end of the meeting, did you arrive at a mutually agreeable, mutually understood "contract" regarding the next steps?

Did you tell the employee your reaction to, or feelings about, the situation?

If you were the employee, how satisfied would you be with the meeting? Why?

Did you get the employee's reaction to the meeting? Did you tell the employee your reaction to the meeting?

Source: Peter Muniz and Robert Chasnoff, "Counseling the Marginal Performer," *Supervisory Management* (May 1982): 8. Reprinted by permission of Peter Muniz & Company, © 1980. All rights reserved.

employee to readjust to the workplace and to determine if disciplinary action is necessary because the counseling or treatment has not been successful. In dealing with troubled employees, the supervisor should not diagnose the cause of the problem, provide treatment, or try to be a professional counselor.

Some do's and don'ts for supervisors to follow in confronting employees with personal problems are:

1. *Do* let the employee know that the company is concerned with *work performance* only.
2. *Do* be aware that personal problems generally get worse, not better, without professional help.
3. *Do* emphasize confidentiality.

Tips on criticizing effectively

Avoid the "sandwich technique"—two slices of praise surrounding one of criticism. Usually it's a device for burying a serious problem between some trite words of praise. It can create confusion and mistrust.

Be serious. Criticizing someone is serious business. If you want a serious response from the employee, make sure he or she knows you're serious about the problem.

Be careful about timing. Don't save up a significant issue until long after the incident occurs. The employee may worry that you've got other things saved up or that you're keeping a dossier of problems. Also, experts recommend that you criticize early in the day and early in the week (never on Fridays). That way, you give the employee a chance to get back on the job and perform better right away rather than stewing at home over night or all weekend.

Be specific. All feedback should be specific, especially when you're expecting a significant change. Talk about actions rather than behavior. Tell the employee *exactly* what you were dissatisfied with and why. Don't generalize.

Identify action steps jointly. Give the employee a chance to respond to your criticism and come up with specific steps together. Encourage the employee to suggest ways of improving performance or avoiding future problems. Agree on action steps and set a time frame.

Touch bases again soon. An employee who has received some heavy criticism probably will hurt and worry. Make an extra effort to interact with that employee during the next few days—just to let him or her know you have confidence and still care.

Source: "Criticism—A Boon or A Bomb," *Personnel Advisory Bulletin*, number 822 (Waterford, Conn. 06386: Bureau of Business Practice, November 25, 1980).

4. *Do* explain that going for help does not exclude the employee from standard disciplinary procedures, and that it does not open a door to special privileges.
5. *Do* explain in very specific terms what the employee needs to do in order to perform up to . . . expectations.
6. *Don't* diagnose; you're not an expert.
7. *Don't* discuss personal problems unless they occur on the job.
8. *Don't* moralize—restrict the confrontation to job performance.
9. *Don't* be swayed or misled by emotional pleas, sympathy tactics or "hard-luck" stories.
10. *Don't* cover up for a friend. . . .[6]

Public works managers can also improve employee motivation and productivity through coaching, an ongoing process by which the supervisor and the employee collaborate to achieve increased job knowledge, a higher level of job satisfaction, improved job skills, a more positive working relationship, and opportunities for personal development.[7] Coaching enables the supervisor to guide and shape the job behavior of subordinates. In coaching, emphasis is placed on the job rather than the individual. It is an ongoing participative process that focuses on an employee's strengths and identifies ways in which the employee can improve his or her knowledge and skills. Particular attention is given to analyzing the employee's needs and values, exchanging ideas, and providing feedback on how performance can be improved.

Public works managers can contribute to improved employee performance by arranging for their supervisors to be trained in coaching and in working with employees with problems. Supervisors should be encouraged to let management know about the problems they encounter and the need for employee assistance programs and new types of training programs.

Poor performance is not only related to personal problems. A failure to establish and communicate job standards, careless selection, poor communications, lack of positive feedback, the failure to define job duties and responsibilities, the discouragement of new ideas, and unnecessary and embarrassing criticism—all have a detrimental effect on performance. Public works managers and supervisors should work to identify and eliminate these causes.

How to give supervisors recognition

Listen and respect

Solicit information, suggestions, opinions.

Keep supervisors informed on the status of their suggestions.

Minimize distractions and maintain attentive eye contact and body posture.

Convey interest in supervisor as an individual.

Positive reinforcement

Verbally acknowledge significant accomplishments.

Describe specific behavior in an honest and timely fashion.

Include positive accomplishment in supervisor's personnel folder.

Don't wait for perfection!

Rewards

Select meaningful rewards for each supervisor.

Recommend promotions, merit increases, offer bonuses, incentives, special privileges, profit sharing.

Enhance job—vary duties, enlarge scope, allow for special projects of interest, increase accountability.

Involve supervisor in problem solving and decision making concerning his/her department.

Source: Cheryl K. Needell and George W. Alwon, "Recognition and Reward: Keys to Motivating Supervisors," *Management Review* (November/December 1982), p. 55. Reprinted by permission of the publisher. © 1982 AMA Membership Publications Division, American Management Associations. New York. All rights reserved.

Information on the quality of work life and associated problems such as turnover can be obtained through exit interviews. Proponents of exit interviews believe that they help reduce turnover and address work environment problems. Opponents contend such interviews are seldom used and of limited value. A study of exit interviews in eighteen major organizations found that about two out of three organizations conduct exit interviews; exit interviews are conducted by the personnel staff; only half of the organizations used the information collected; and most organizations made no effort to compute turnover or exit interview costs.[8] Results of the study indicated that exit interviews are not effective unless the information gathered is used to correct problems and to compare exit interview and turnover costs.

Motivation

Employee motivation is a prime concern of all managers because it strongly affects performance. Thus, in the face of today's changing work force, new ways must be found to integrate organizational and employee goals. Changing work values, a diminishing work ethic, more guaranteed wages and benefits, decreased employee loyalty, adverse public opinion, and diluted management authority have been cited as some of the causes of declining motivation. Employee attitude surveys attribute worker dissatisfaction to changing worker attitudes, the job environment, demeaning and inept supervisors, authoritarian management, favoritism, poor communication, inadequate organizational policies, the nature of work itself, and peer and client relationships. Employee dissatisfaction is reflected in increased turnover, waste, absenteeism, accidents, sick leave, griev-

A psychologist looks at motivation "Motivation is something that comes from within," says clinical psychologist Dr. Peter Whitmer. "It's up to the manager and the company to set the stage to allow employee's internal motivation to appear."

To do so, "you need to tailor rewards and recognition to individual motivation. Any kind of reinforcement should be geared to each individual's motivation. Any kind of reinforcement should be geared to each individual's scheme of needs or psychological support," Whitmer explains. "Finding out what makes an individual tick is very complex, and individuals are not always reinforced by the same things all the time."

Whitmer, a consultant with Smith and Donahue, Inc. in Wellesley, Massachusetts, identifies three basic concepts of motivation: power, affiliation and achievement.

For those motivated by achievement, Whitmer says, you give them bigger and better jobs and a chance to show they can do these jobs. "Sometimes, achievement oriented employees will take bigger and better jobs even with a pay cut," says Whitmer.

For those motivated by affiliation, recognition means acceptance by a peer group. And for those motivated by power, recognition is the ability to command more troops (authoritative-types) or to work through more people (cooperative types).

What does this mean for personnel practices? "You have to compensate or recognize the individual differences which make people tick. For some,

financial reward is what I call their 'hot' button, for others it's something different," says Whitmer. "You have to tailor the recognition to the individual," says Whitmer. "If you don't, you risk giving the wrong kind of award."

According to Whitmer, this approach is particularly important for management- and vice-presidential level employees. For more general programs aimed at larger groups of employees, Whitmer suggests offering, at the minimum, a "smorgasbord approach" to recognition awards because it allows individuals to choose the award that makes them tick.

Whitmer also points out that recognition programs should not remain static. "When we give a bonus or a trip to Hawaii, we call it an incentive," says Whitmer. "What it really is, is a reward for a particular behavior and an attempt to encourage similar behavior in the future."

"But once an award is given, it loses its potency to motivate, because it becomes expected." The result, says Whitmer, is that we continually have to create different ways to recognize and reward employees. And in recognition and reward, Whitmer suggests that we shouldn't overlook job enrichment and job development, along with performance appraisal, as part of our recognition program.

Source: Margaret Magnus, "Employee Recognition: A Key to Motivation," *Personnel Journal*, copyright February 1981, p. 106. Reprinted with the permission of *Personnel Journal*, Costa Mesa, Calif. All rights reserved.

ances, and disciplinary actions, which reduce productivity and increase costs and health and personal problems.

Many supervisors understand very little about what motivates their employees. Surveys continually show a lack of agreement between supervisors and subordinates on motivators. Substantial evidence exists that employees are motivated by various factors such as money, affiliation, a desire to achieve, a feeling of responsibility, recognition, power, and interesting work. Motivation is influenced by personality, physical and emotional states, organizational structure, policies and rules, the nature of the job, and interpersonal relations. Motivational strategies should be tailored to each employee's wants, concerns, interests, needs, and purposes and cannot remain static.

No single motivator works for all employees all the time. Motivators must be capable of satisfying the most intense employee needs. Individual differences mandate that a wide selection of motivators be devised and offered. Achievement-oriented employees are motivated by job enlargement and enrichment. For many employees improved compensation and benefits are key motivators. Power-oriented employees seek opportunities to direct work through others. Many employees respond to recognition.

Numerous techniques are available for motivating employees. These include job redesign, a full range of monetary and nonmonetary incentives, quality circles, quality of work life programs, labor-management committees, employee assistance programs, and employee attitude surveys. In selecting and using motivational techniques, public works managers need to learn how contemporary workers think and what motivates them. Human relations skills need to be sharpened. Public works managers and supervisors can take a number of important steps in this direction:

1. Carefully define an employee's job and expected results.
2. Mutually establish understandable and acceptable job standards.
3. Involve employees in decision making.
4. Work with employees in setting work and career goals by encouraging career development, pointing out opportunities for achievement, and providing assignments that advance career development.
5. Redesign and enlarge jobs to make them more interesting and to encourage better use of skills, knowledge, and experience.
6. Freely delegate the tasks that can be done effectively by someone else.
7. Engage in open communications with employees and give them continual positive feedback. Interact with employees on a regular basis.
8. Provide a satisfactory physical work environment.
9. Ensure that employees have adequate resources and equipment.
10. Give recognition, praise, and credit.
11. Provide training, technical assistance, direction, and guidance.
12. Remove organizational and supervisory roadblocks.
13. Match jobs with personal motives. Treat employees as individuals.
14. Offer a broad range of incentives.

Incentives

Incentive programs are techniques for rewarding employees on the basis of performance equal to or above preestablished levels. Local governments have used a diverse number of monetary and nonmonetary incentive programs to increase motivation, production, safety, and efficiency.

Monetary incentives include merit increases, performance bonuses, safety awards, shared savings, attendance awards, competition and contest awards, suggestion awards, and education incentives. Such incentives, when based on objective, outcome-oriented performance criteria, have significant positive effects.[9]

Nonmonetary incentives consist of job redesign and enlargement, team management, job rotation, job sharing, task systems, autonomous work units, alternative work schedules, service awards, career development programs, work standards, and performance targets.

Obstacles to meaningful incentive programs include legal prohibitions, restrictive labor agreements, labor opposition, and administrative, fiscal, and political constraints. Incentive programs are likely to fail because:

1. They do not meet the personal needs of employees.
2. They are improperly designed and poorly administered.
3. They include standards that are difficult to achieve and are increased too frequently.
4. They do not provide meaningful rewards in a timely manner.
5. They do not provide benefits for supervisors.
6. They threaten the hierarchy within work groups.

Criteria for successful incentive programs include:

1. Objective and attainable measures of work performance
2. Employee and union involvement in the design and implementation of the program
3. Frequent and diverse rewards
4. Administrative simplicity, including brief and understandable rules
5. Supervisory involvement in developing the program
6. Consideration of employee fears
7. Supervisory coverage in the program
8. An adequate budget
9. Promotion of the program
10. Appropriate monitoring and appeal provisions
11. Frequent redesign of the incentives to maintain interest.

Public works managers can improve their operations and the level of job satisfaction and performance by recognizing the importance of motivation. Productivity improvement depends on managerial and supervisory understanding of the factors that influence employee productivity, including individual employee abilities and needs and formal and informal organizational conditions. Formal organizational factors affecting productivity consist of the organizational structure, working conditions, management climate, communications, personnel practices and policies, and leadership style. Informal organizational factors include group dynamics and cohesiveness, and peer standards.

Training

Public works productivity and effectiveness are directly related to the training provided for public works employees. Many advantages accrue from training, including improved morale, motivation, productivity, level of supervision, citizen relations, and quality of services.

An effective training program depends on a needs analysis, provision of a full range of training programs, and training evaluation. Public works managers should carefully define training needs in their departments through discussions with supervisors, employee training surveys, diagnostic tests, exit interviews, assessment centers, analysis of grievances, performance evaluations, disciplinary actions, and turnover. Public works supervisors play a prominent role in defining training needs and making recommendations for training courses.

After the training needs analysis is conducted, training objectives should be defined and training policy established. Training objectives relate to the degree of change desired in behavior, attitude, skill, and knowledge. Written training policies cover such matters as who is to receive training, the types of training to be offered, the length of training, and whether the training will be conducted on or off the job. Other policy matters include leaves of absence for training, the extent to which tuition reimbursement and educational incentive programs will be used, the extent of optional and compulsory training, and the relations between training, promotion, and pay increases.

Public works managers and supervisors should help develop and take part in lectures, conferences, case studies, demonstrations, role playing, field trips, and simulated problem-solving sessions. Public works managers should identify training resources and encourage development of train-the-trainer programs. The American Public Works Association, other public works professional associations, and the International City Management Association are excellent sources of information on training programs and materials.

Training benefits such as changes in work behavior, success in promotional examinations, introduction of new ideas, cost savings, and employee satisfaction should be documented and evaluated. Training evaluation should (1) examine the methods used to select trainees and measure trainee reaction to the training materials; (2) assess learning of information or skills; (3) evaluate attitudinal or behavioral changes; (4) examine the effectiveness of training techniques; and (5) determine the relevance of the training to the work situation. Evaluative tools include attitudinal surveys, on-the-job observations, standardized tests, long-term studies of trainee behavior, interviews with supervisors and employees, and performance reports.

Top public works management must take an active role to ensure that training courses are used, that they are taken seriously, and that training results are tracked and reported.

Labor relations

Public works employees are highly unionized, and this produces a dramatic effect on the traditional patterns of employee relations. Employees and their union representatives demand a direct voice in negotiating and setting pay, hours of work, benefits, working conditions, and other personnel policies. Public managers and supervisors, therefore, must be active in all the major stages of labor relations, from contract negotiations to contract administration.

The first step for public works managers is to check that their personnel houses are in order. This involves a close review of classification and pay plans, fringe benefits, performance evaluation systems, grievance procedures, and training.

The next step is to participate in the determination of bargaining units. Their importance is reflected in organization, composition of work units, and labor contract negotiations. Public works managers are in the best position to recommend the structure of bargaining units in relation to work programs and tasks and to identify the positions that should be excluded from bargaining, such as management, supervisory, confidential, and part-time jobs.

Of the many management elements of labor relations, three are separated here for emphasis: grievance procedures, discipline, and management training.

Orderly procedures for settling grievances expeditiously and equitably are the backbone of effective labor-management relations. Such procedures need to be continuously publicized, well understood, and conscientiously and consistently followed.

Orderly disciplinary procedures are equally important for settling problems expeditiously and equitably. Progressive disciplinary steps—which include oral reprimands, written reprimands, suspensions, demotions, and discharges—should be well understood and followed.

Labor relations training helps managers and supervisors work with union representatives and other employees efficiently so that the rights and prerogatives of both employees and management are recognized and observed. Such training should cover the history and definition of labor relations, legal status, represen-tation procedures, negotiation techniques, contract preparation, contract administration, and methods of handling impasses and strikes.

Contract negotiations

Service on the negotiating team is a major responsibility of public works managers and supervisors. The public works representative is expected to answer questions, provide expert advice to the chief negotiator of the impact of union proposals, management proposals, and contract language. Several steps should be taken by management prior to negotiations.

The language of the contract should be thoroughy reviewed to identify ambi-guities, bargaining issues, and provisions that should be added, changed, or deleted.

Grievances should be analyzed to identify subjects of negotiation. The poten-tial effect of union proposals on public works procedures, policies, work rules, and practices should be assessed. Particular attention should be directed to restrictive contract provisions that limit productivity and management's ability to control change. Examples of such contract clauses include those that mandate crew size, impose limits on outside contracting, limit work done by supervisors, provide pay for time not worked, and require union notification, consultation, and posting.

Past practices should be reviewed, especially unwritten rules, customs, and traditions that have the force of contractual language and severely limit man-agement flexibility. Every effort should be made to exclude prevailing rights or maintenance-of-benefits clauses from the contract. Such clauses continue for the duration of the contract all practices and conditions not specified in the contract.

Finally, an effort should be made to include contract language that promotes productivity.

When agreement is reached, the final contract language should be reviewed by managers and supervisors to ensure that it is understood and does not have a negative impact on public works operations.

Contract administration

After the contract has been signed, copies should be distributed to all public works supervisors. In the orientation sessions that follow, the management team sets forth its expectations regarding implementation and enforcement. Each provision of the contract should be interpreted in terms of how it affects super-visors and their work. Contract review sessions offer an opportunity to explain in simple language the intent behind contract clauses, to use examples to explain sections of the contract, and to review procedures that need to be instituted or changed.

A major aspect of contract administration is handling grievances. Most con-tracts provide for grievance procedures relating to the interpretation and application of the specific terms of the contract. Public works supervisors must adhere to the steps defined in the grievance procedure and the time limits required. They should also maintain records of all oral and written grievances and periodically tabulate the grievances by type. The skillful handling of complaints by public works supervisors in the early stages is essential because a backlog of unconsi-dered and unresolved grievances creates major labor relations problems.

Public works supervisors should receive training in grievance handling, coach-ing, counseling, techniques of supervision, and relations with union representatives. Many grievances are the result of supervisor antagonism, ridicule, open criticism, the lack of consistent and equitable enforcement of rules, the failure to comply with contract terms, and poor communication. Supervisors must be warned that informal agreements and modifications and exceptions to personnel rules and contract clauses will violate the contract.

Some contracts include binding arbitration as the final step for the grievance procedure. Considerable care is exercised in selecting the outside arbitrator, preparing for the arbitration hearing, participating in the hearing, and implementing the arbitrator's decision. Public works managers and supervisors can expect to appear as witnesses and to assist in the preparation for the hearings. Implementation of the arbitration decision is a major responsibility of the public works supervisor, who must be prepared to explain and smoothly implement it. Grievance arbitration can be time-consuming and costly.

Impasses and strikes

Not all negotiations produce agreement and public works managers need to know about the alternatives available for resolving disputes: mediation, fact finding, and arbitration. Understanding the methods, advantages, and disadvantages of each is important because public works supervisors will be expected to keep rank-and-file employees informed of progress in resolving disputes.

Although impasse resolution techniques exist, public employees nevertheless strike and engage in other forms of work interruptions, including work slowdowns, sick calls, and "working by the book." A well-prepared strike contingency plan can minimize the impact of work actions on the maintenance of public services during a strike. Components of a strike plan include listing the supervisors and employees who will remain on the job; identifying essential services that will be needed; drafting contingency plans for security, mutual aid, shared equipment, supplies, jobs requiring special licenses, communications, and strike records; and reviewing personnel policies that will be applied to both nonstriking and striking employees. Training sessions should be conducted to prepare management employees for strike duties.

After the strike, public works managers and supervisors need to reestablish sound working relations with employees. Supervisors will have to deal properly with the hard feelings and possible verbal and physical abuse from striking employees. Tact and sound judgment will be needed to restore conditions to normal. Supervisors should receive training in how to handle employee relations following the strike.

Public works managers must become acquainted with all phases of collective bargaining and help develop overall labor relations policies and programs directed at building constructive labor-management relations. Public works managers should keep informed about changes in the collective bargaining environment and of new developments in labor-management relations, such as concession bargaining, productivity bargaining, and labor-management committees.

Conclusion

Personnel management is a major responsibility of public works managers. A knowledge of personnel techniques and issues will greatly assist both managers and supervisors in managing their operations more effectively. Local government personnel management is undergoing radical changes, and conventional personnel policies and practices are no longer adequate to meet social, economic, legal, and technological forces reshaping the management of human resources.

Public works managers can better respond to the changing needs of their work forces by:

1. Being informed about their personnel system, particularly the personnel policies, rules, and regulations

2. Keeping up to date on the changing character of their work force, particularly new attitudes and expectations
3. Learning about the factors that influence employee motivation and the use of different motivational strategies
4. Keeping informed about new personnel issues
5. Developing close working relations with personnel professionals
6. Identifying personnel problem areas and recommending solutions
7. Supporting training for all employees
8. Fostering new approaches to labor-management cooperation
9. Orienting public works supervisors and middle management to the changing environment of personnel management
10. Experimenting with new and innovative approaches to personnel management
11. Assessing on a regular basis the effectiveness of the personnel system
12. Recognizing the human resource problems associated with the introduction of technology
13. Learning to use the personnel system more effectively in order to improve productivity and employee motivation
14. Supporting the efforts of personnel professionals to apply creative solutions to personnel problems.

1   Kenneth A. Kovach, "New Directions in Fringe Benefits," *S.A.M. Advanced Management Journal* (Summer 1983):63.

2   Hall A. Acuff, "Employee Selection Simplified," *Management World* 11 (November 1982):28.

3   J. Peter Graves, "Let's Put Appraisal Back in Performance Appraisal: Part I," *Personnel Journal* 61 (November 1982):846.

4   Ron Zemke, "Should Supervisor Be Counselors?" *Training/HRD* 20 (March 1983):44.

5   John H. Meyer and Teresa C. Meyer, "The Supervisor as Counselor—How to Help the Distressed Employee," *Management Review* 71 (April 1982):44.

6   Zemke, "Should Supervisors Be Counselors?" p. 48.

7   G. Eric Allenbaugh, "Coaching—A Management Tool for a More Effective Work Performance," *Management Review* 72 (May 1983):23.

8   Pamela Garretson and Kenneth S. Teel, "The Exit Interview: Effective Tool or Meaningless Gesture?" *Personnel* 59 (July–August 1982):76.

9   John M. Greiner, "Motivating Improved Productivity: Three Promising Approaches," *Public Management* 61 (October 1979):5.

7 Communication management

As public works managers and supervisors well know, local public works have expanded from streets, roads, water, sewers, and public buildings to the entire built-up environment. So it is with communication management. Communication used to be just a way to get messages from one place to another. Today it is perceived as an integral part of management—explaining assignments to employees, listening to citizen complaints, persuading the city council or county board, providing information for news reporters, writing letters and reports, working with neighborhood groups, and resolving citizen complaints.

This chapter explores communication methods that are especially useful for managers and supervisors in public works who must deal with an unusually wide range of elected officials, employees, and other people. From organizational communication to reporting to the public, suggestions are offered that will help build communication into management.

Communication linkages

The need for precision in communication has increased with the growing reliance on legal staff by contractors and public agencies endeavoring to ensure that the expectations of contracted work are met by both parties. The increased professionalism among public works managers and improved general management training of key personnel have also contributed to this change, the result of which is greater emphasis on communication management. The various elements within the scope of communication management now range from cable television and the adversarial press to union negotiations, the preparation of materials for city and county managers and elected councils, and the preparation of letters, memos, and testimony—all for more sophisticated audiences. The traditional need for prompt response is still there, but those responses, both written and oral, are much more diverse and technical than they used to be.

Communication between public officials and the citizenry is a crucial link in the democratic process. Successful appointed and elected officials understand the importance of becoming effective communicators. Information received from the public is always significant, as is the willingness of officials not only to listen to such information but to seek additional information from all parts of the community.

Ideas, comments, criticisms, and suggestions flow easily from some groups such as service clubs and neighborhood associations, but other groups—particularly the poor, the undereducated, the young, and the aged—are typically hard to reach, possess little leadership, and often cannot express their needs and desires clearly.[1]

Cable television is a significant new development in communication technology that makes it possible not only to broadcast public meetings at length, such as city council meetings, but also to use interactive (two-way) methods of interviewing viewers, taking polls and surveys, or simply gathering information. Further, cable television can provide for training, conferences, and at-home work. Digital (nonvideo) information such as meter reading, traffic control, fire early-warning systems, burglar alarm systems, and computer data interface are all part of the potential for cable TV.[2]

Organizational communication

To manage is to communicate. Although this has always been true, today more people are involved, more messages are sent, more information flows in and out, more people depend on information, and, hence, there is much greater need to manage communication. Even a generation ago a governing body, through its chief administrator, department heads, and experts, could write its ordinances, regulations, and directives with only perfunctory public input.

Today, however, everyone not only wants to be involved but becomes involved. Frequently council and board agendas include a "citizen's forum" with specific time set aside at each meeting for communication between any resident of the jurisdiction or his representative and the governing body.[3]

Perhaps the technical experts have been offended by the ordinary citizens who have expressed their opinions about some complicated issue ("Everyone is an expert on traffic engineering," said Henry Barnes, the imaginative traffic engineer of Baltimore, a generation ago). Yet, sensitive technical administrators will use these forums, even if they are gripe sessions, to sift out the elements of truth and seek the technical expression of those truths. Few people take the time to complain at a public meeting about something that is not significant to them.

The mayor and council must often deal with citizens on both sides of a technical issue (the "No turn on red" signs relieve the traffic bottleneck but also increase pedestrian hazards). For the most part, however, a composite of the elements of truth from citizens' concerns can form the basis for an intelligent investigation (and perhaps even a solution that can satisfy all). Willingness of the mayor and council to hear constituencies is an obvious plus both for the elected officials (they are sensitive to the needs of the citizens) and for the managers (they obtain information about opportunities to provide improved services).

Communication within the agency between its elected or appointed representatives continues to be a high priority for public works managers. Clear directives to subordinates take on added significance as the cost of the labor, materials, and equipment used to carry out those directives increases. Whatever the management style in an agency or the underlying theory of management, department and division heads need to interpret the directives of their superiors for all their subordinates within the department. They are information managers.

Top management must be apprised of the actions of subordinates if it is to understand department and division progress. The delegation of authority coveted by so many, yet genuinely achieved by so few, relies on adequate feedback. The new matrix management approach places an additional strain on both top management and department and division heads because of the crossed lines of authority. In matrix management the traditional hierarchy is subordinate to task-oriented groups that may cut across departments, divisions, or other sections of an organization. The objective of assembling a group (a "task force") is to accomplish some element of work. The efficiency of such a task force depends on the quality and quantity of internal communication. When everyone is informed, everyone benefits. Both superiors and subordinates on a task force must be committed to making the task force succeed.

Department and division heads should take the opportunity to communicate with the city or county manager (or the elected council if the public agency has no manager) beyond providing mere feedback. They should report all actions in a way that sets forth the reasons for a specific action. Consider, for example, the difference between straight feedback, "We patched the hole at 100 Elm Street as requested," and the explanation, "We were delayed over two weeks in patching the hole in front of 100 Elm Street because of the abandoned vehicle with no wheels which was finally moved by the owner." Such an explanation can blunt criticism for not meeting some specific need earlier.

Classical line and staff conflicts can be reduced or eliminated through communication. Line functions (doing the work of the city) and staff functions (supporting the line personnel) in public agencies break down when staff members attempt to follow procedural guidelines at the expense of substantive action toward accomplishing agency goals. The chief administrative officers who clearly instruct their "staff" personnel to support the "line" personnel will successfully accomplish their agency's mission. The concept of experts being "on tap" and not "on top" has relevance here. Ultimately, the specialists must answer to the line personnel. Setting broad guidelines that instruct departments and divisions to show city interests first and department and division interests second will also enhance organizational responsibilities. Training top department staff to recognize city interests first must be backed up by a policy of top management support for key department functions.

Peer relations require tactful communication, and although interdepartmental problems can never be eliminated, mutual support between departments can be fostered.

Interpersonal communication

Support for caring interpersonal relations facilitates successful organizational communication. Modern organizations can assume that technical matters are met by employees who are trained to supplement and keep current on their entry skills and education. Obviously if the technical requirements are not met, then the functions of the organization quickly break down. Such an assumption cannot be made, however, for interpersonal skills, which are more subtle and not as well understood.

Relations between department heads, division heads, superintendents, supervisors, foremen, crew chiefs, and employees that are based on mutual caring will help achieve agency goals. A department is the people who work for it. If people are respected at whatever level of service they perform and despite whatever limitations they possess, agency goals will be successfully met and the right atmosphere created for improving education and training.

Employees in an organization have two principal loyalties: the first stems from their technical, job-related responsibility as defined by a job classification for their specific level in the organization; and the second is a personal loyalty between the two individuals who occupy those classifications in a superior/subordinate relation.

Developing good interpersonal relations involves both formal and informal communication within the organization. Formal communication provides the information links between management and workers on roles and expectations, new assignments, legal and organizational changes, and clarifications of management policies. Informal communication, the "open door" policy, provides personal assurance and back-up for subordinates who are taking on new assignments, praise and recognition for good work, private criticism and help where performance is shaky, and a psychological climate of trust. Many methods can be learned for improving interpersonal communication. How to say "no," illustrated in the sidebar, is an example.

Standard work procedures should be reviewed to recognize both the gifts and limitations of individuals occupying diverse jobs. If an organization is to run efficiently, standard procedures should be few and not too detailed for supervisors who must apply the procedures on the job. It is essential for supervisors to work with the work crews they have rather than the work crews they wished they had.

The principle of reinforcing positive results is a psychologically sound communication tool that can help employees function more effectively. If correct behavior is praised publicly, and incorrect behavior is criticized privately, then the rewards of personal recognition go with the correctly performed task and the pressure is to perform well for recognition. Indiscriminate criticism and erratic discipline are self-defeating. Obviously wrong behavior has to be corrected, but the way to do this is to key management's attention and pleasure to the correct performance.

How to say yes and no Let your "yes" be "yes" and your "no" be "no, but. . . ." Encouraging staff suggestions for constructive change is an ongoing proposition. Follow the rule that any suggestion from an employee that is acceptable to management should be implemented as soon as possible, given with the credit for the employee, and circulated as widely as possible to all those who would be affected by the change. However, if the answer must be "no" to some suggestion, always add the reason why. Employees will accept a "no" if they are given a logical, reasonable, and caring explanation of why something they have suggested (their "creation") could not be carried out. Most people want to support the organization they work for and would like to have a part in improving its effective operation. A "no" without any explanation will only turn off a source of future suggestions

Source: Unpublished notes from workshop conducted by the American Public Works Association.

Two ways to say no.

Like the sergeants in the military, the first-line supervisors are the ones responsible for the working employees and thus need top management's support in their efforts to get the job done well. It is usually at this level that the talents and shortcomings of individual employees are apparent. First-line supervisors who are permitted to respond to those talents (and have management's backing for such individual actions) make the most effective use of their personnel.

Training opportunities must be constantly available for employees and supervisors. All training must be voluntary if it is to be effective. If new state requirements, for example, indicate that all water plant operators must be certified, then the present water plant operators need to be offered appropriate training. In providing the opportunity for training, management shows that it wants to open the pathway for certification, yet leave the decision up to the employee. In this way management can adapt to individual circumstances and communicate a caring attitude. It is obvious that water plant operators need to be certified to stay on the job, but if those employees have the respect of the supervisor, they can retain their dignity by making their own decisions about additional formal training.

Meetings as communication

Small group communication is a special kind of internal communication. Communication with groups is successful first where the group leader plans ahead, perhaps through an agenda, so that individuals can come to the meeting well prepared, and second where the leader follows up on the meeting with an action plan. With consensus and follow-through on specific actions, the group will accomplish its goals. Whenever eight people meet for one hour, that is eight man-hours or one day of activity for which the committee chairperson is responsible. Time spent on thinking through the subject matter of the meeting and anticipating questions can save time and money at a ratio of eight to one.

Small groups need to know the purpose of the meeting. Therefore, it helps to circulate in advance a simple outline of topics to be covered. Back-up in the form of reports and other documents should be kept to a minimum (many people won't read them). When the meeting starts, the chairperson or moderator should state briefly what the group hopes to get done and what the persons who are there can contribute. These points may seem obvious, but many meetings fail because of a lack of clear purpose and expectations.

Whenever conclusions are reached or actions are determined, they should be summed up by the chairperson at the end of the meeting with some statement of "Here's what I expect to happen after you leave today. . . . " It is often helpful to follow up the meeting with a written summary and to send it to each participant. Such a summary can be the basis of a follow-up meeting to review progress and to see if changes need to be made.

Space, attractiveness, quiet, and other amenities in the physical surroundings help the group work efficiently. There should be no distractions, whether they be the noise generated by equipment running in a nearby shop, inadequate ventilation, poor acoustics, or uncomfortable furniture.

Working with elected officials

Working with elected officials involves another special kind of internal communication.[4] Frequently chief administrative officers (CAOs) will permit and even encourage direct contact between elected officials and department and division heads. To be successful, the CAO must insist that major contacts generated by elected officials with individuals in an organization be reported to the department head and the CAO. First contacts with newly elected officials are most significant. These officials need to know where to go for information and how to deal with department heads and others in a tactful and constructive way. One approach to this kind of political and professional partnership is shown in the sidebar, "Dear Alderman Jones. . . ."

It is the job of the city manager, the county manager, the public works director, and other managers to keep the communication channels open to the city council, the county board, the planning commission, the zoning board, and other boards and commissions.

Council and board members, like city and county managers and department heads, hate surprises. They need, and expect, to be kept up to date on meetings, agendas, problems, complaints, and decisions. A weekly or biweekly newsletter or informal report to the council always is appreciated. Agenda back-up reports and other materials are obligatory. Council and board members like to know about the people involved, especially citizens representing other governments, local businesses, and community and neighborhood groups who are pressing for answers to be given and actions to be taken. During this process (which is continuous in local government), managers have a special obligation to keep all officials informed on equal terms.

Dear Alderman Jones . . . Welcome to the city council! I am pleased to respond to your question directed to the city manager and the various department heads asking how Aldermen and the staff can work together most effectively to improve the quality of life in our city. I appreciate the opportunity to give you my candid views.

Department heads respect the council's role as the elected body through whom our citizens speak to us. We are accountable to you; you are not accountable to us. Our job is to satisfy your requirements. You represent the people of our city. We do not.

By now, you have received copies of the city code, zoning ordinance, 10-year plan, current budget and recent audit from the City Manager. I have forwarded to you our refuse collection regulations, our flyer, "Ten Steps to Obtain a Building Permit," our zoning-board rules, and several other pamphlets which are routinely given to our residents to help them understand the services that you, as Aldermen, have instructed the Department of Public Works to provide. As you examine these, if you find anything that is not clear, please let me know. Sometimes we get a little close to the activities, and a fresh review by a newly elected alderman can help to clarify confusing points for our residents.

My intention is to work with you and the other council members as a team, and certainly *not* in competition. I hope that you will feel free to call on me for addi-

tional information at any time. When you do, you will receive accurate, brief and complete reports.

Whenever you, or any other alderman asks me a question I will generally prepare a written reply and distribute it to all council members and the city manager so all will be equally informed. Your questions (and my answers to them) will probably be of interest to other council members.

On Council items requiring action, and involving the Public Works Department you can expect reports thoroughly analyzing the subject with a list of alternate conclusions and a recommendation. My role is to help provide you with decision-making tools. I will give whole-hearted support to your decision, even if it is exactly opposite to my recommendation. My obligation is to provide you with the alternates, and your obligation is to select the one that you feel serves the city best.

Some action items will be tough. May I encourage you not to commit yourself to a citizen or group of citizens before the Council as a whole meets to discuss the matter. If a resident asks for an answer, we urge you to reply that you will investigate and report back. Theoretically, council members make decisions as a Council, and not as individuals. You should not have to answer as an individual.

Our state has an "open meetings" statute. Let me urge you *not* to use telephone votes or informal meetings which can only undercut effective gov-

---

In cities and counties with the council-manager plan, the manager serves at the pleasure of the city council or county board. Therefore, the council expects the manager to provide information for all members of the council. Department heads who do not observe this courtesy embarrass the manager and jeopardize their neutral status. A good rule for department heads is to report all substantive contacts with elected officials to the manager and to send copies of any documents that might have been prepared for individual council members to the manager.

Informal contacts with the mayor and leading council members can help to keep everyone informed and avoid surprises. Such informal contacts with the elected officials will keep staff members aware of any potential changes in policy and will avoid embarrassing either elected officials or staff.

ernment. Such informal actions might expedite some decisions, but usually will complicate our actions later.

I hope that you will not consider your role on the Council as an extension of your professional specialty. Occasionally, your professional training will assist the council, but I sincerely hope that you will not second-guess the staff research.

Your job will be much easier and more effective if you expect the detailed staff work to be performed by the staff. We anticipate that you will ask appropriate questions and insist that the staff work be done with thoroughness and credibility, so that you can rely on it for policy determination.

If you get complaints or requests for service, please direct them to the City Manager or to the appropriate department head. You will find that handling complaints yourself is time consuming and implies a bias in favor of an individual. Be assured that we will respond promptly to each inquiry.

You may hear from a resident that he has complained of a problem to "city hall" but has received no results. If this is true, it could mean that the person is simply not entitled to the service. In any case, we can help you with these, and explain the merits and liabilities as we see them before you take a position with the resident.

If you receive any complaints about discourtesy or inaccuracy on the part of a public works staff member, please

report them immediately to me directly. If they involve other departments, report them to the city manager or the appropriate department head. You should demand that your staff be capable, conscientious, and dedicated. We recognize our responsibility not only to do well, but to give the appearance of doing well.

One last point, Alderman Jones. I don't want you to interpret anything in this letter to infer that Public Works is "more important" than the Police, the Fire or any other department. The question of values is for you and the Council to decide. Some of your toughest decisions will involve a choice between, for example, improving some social service, and buying a new piece of public works equipment. The best that I can do is to describe how the equipment will be used, what advantages it will bring, and how it will improve the quality of life in our community. But you have to make the crucial decision of where the dollars should go.

Again, I appreciate your question on effectiveness. I will do my best to provide succinct and accurate information to the Council, giving realistic alternatives and a recommendation. You can also be sure that when you have reached a decision, we will provide prompt, thorough and cheerful follow-up, even though the decision will not necessarily be the one we had hoped for.

Source: Robert H. Goodin, "Dear Alderman Jones," *American City & County*, December 1979, p. 53. Reprinted with permission.

If a division head in public works is the staff liaison to an appointed board or commission, the same general rules apply for circulating copies of agendas, supporting information, and minutes of the commission meetings to the department head as well as the CAO, who in turn reports to elected officials. Board and commission members who hear public testimony need to follow specific ordinances in reporting the results of those public hearings. Division heads will have the added burden of meeting the ordinance requirements and helping commission members to do so, as well as merely providing information. In potentially difficult cases a willing city attorney will be helpful in assuring that not only are ordinance requirements met but that the choice of words meets the most current "case law" requirements for the agency.

As a rule, department and division heads should "take the heat" from public responses on difficult or sensitive matters, and, on more positive matters, give the exposure to the boards and commissions. The department head who staffs a board or commission can easily meet informally with the board chairperson to establish the working rules to be followed. Anything unusual should be checked with the CAO or agency attorney if necessary, but generally the informal desires of the chairperson should prevail.

Because of established procedures as well as ordinances and statutes, there is considerable *formal* communication between administrative staff and elected officials, but good informal contacts should also be established. Frequently, responding to the inquiries of individual council members helps maintain informal relations and keeps the CAO abreast of mayoral and council interests.

Informal "study sessions" are also helpful. These can precede or follow formal meetings, and the press and public can be permitted to attend.

Several cities use the format of an informal meeting between city staff and elected officials on some particular topic and invite the public to attend, but discourage conversing with the elected or administrative officials during the course of the meeting. This keeps the session from becoming a public hearing or a sounding board for interested citizens but maintains the open-meeting atmosphere. The press and citizens alike have access to the discussions. Obviously, no votes should be taken during these meetings, but summary reports, including information requested at the meetings, can be made available to the public.

Listening to citizens

As far as public works managers are concerned, citizen participation should be nonadversarial. Although the department head and employees must follow the policies and procedures established by the mayor and council, it is essential that relations with citizens be kept at a supportive, or at least a "neutral," level. Generally the city staff is doing what the mayor and council wish to have done. If there is a conflict with a citizen's desire, then he or she needs to know that it is a conflict with the entire city policy, not a random action directed at the citizen or some "bureaucratic" determination that may have another outcome for another person.

Phone calls or letters by irate citizens should be answered carefully. Even the most abusive phone call is really not directed at the individual who happened to answer but, for whatever reason, to the "city" that instigated the point at issue. An understanding employee can always neutralize an unreasonable phone call by listening and responding only to the substance of the conversation.

Consider every irate phone call as coming from a relative of the mayor! Is what you say to that relative something that could be recited verbatim to the mayor or city manager? Some employees do not believe that they have to take a phone call from an irate citizen, but all rights have equal responsibilities, and effective communication with an irate citizen is one of them.

Some of the most effective communication at the city hall or county courthouse is initiated by employees with the skill to respond to irate citizens. The only difference between an irate citizen and a mere request for service is the way in which the request is given. The most unreasonable complaint is merely a request for service in disguise. An effective employee can look behind the disguise, brush off the unreasonable and intemperate language, and respond to the request.

One technique a manager can use to influence staff attitudes toward complainants is to discourage the staff from referring to such resident concerns as "complaints" and from using such words as "complaint form," "complaint report," or "complaint summary." They should encourage instead the use of the term "service requests." Looking at all calls from residents as requests for service,

---

The user friendly telephone The telephone is a popular way to handle questions and complaints. It is quick, easy, and inexpensive. Think about how you may sound on the phone. You may think your phone voice is businesslike and efficient, but the person on the other end of the line may think it is brusque or cold. To make the best use of the telephone, the following guidelines should be observed.

Answer the phone promptly.

Identify yourself and your department.

Speak clearly, naturally, and distinctly.

Keep a pencil and paper next to the phone to note important information and messages.

If the caller is upset, remain calm, listen carefully, and do not argue. Get the facts.

If a call must be transferred, relay all pertinent information to the person to whom the call is transferred, so that the caller does not have to repeat the question or complaint from the beginning.

Do not keep the caller waiting while you are looking up information. If necessary, tell the person that you need time to look up the information and that you will call back as soon as possible.

Be careful with the "hold" button! If you put someone on hold, make it short—twenty to thirty seconds at the most.

Deliver all phone messages promptly to prevent delays in returning calls or embarrassment to the person for whom the call was intended.

End the telephone call as courteously as it began; a good final impression is important.

Source: David S. Arnold and Howard N. Smith, Jr., "Working with the Public," in *Effective Supervisory Practices*, 2d ed. (Washington, D.C.: International City Management Association, 1984), p. 207.

---

however vociferously they may be phrased, will help the staff to understand their service role.

If a city ordinance or city policy does not permit a positive response, then the citizen must be told that the request is not a service that the city provides. If the citizen then asks for the name of the employee's superior, it should be given out unhesitatingly. As soon as the citizen hangs up the telephone, the employee should tell his or her superior to expect a call.

With irate or intemperate letters, the administrative official should never write an offensive reply, and should always expect an intemperate reply to be taken out of context and shown as an example of the writer's personality. In writing a reply to any request for service, the letter should begin with a "Thank you" for the letter received. This sets the tone for the letter and in no way can be misinterpreted.

A reply that expresses understanding of the concerns of the irate citizen also helps to neutralize the problem. It should restate the key problem but not refer to the hostile words or negative tone of the citizen's letter. After restating the problem, the response should include an explanation of your understanding of the incident, especially if it was at variance with the description given. If the incident described was contrary to departmental policies, then clearly state that it was and express regret that it happened. Finally, list appropriate alternatives, if possible, as to what might be done next.

The easiest letters to answer are those in which the resident points outs that a city or county employee did, in fact, do something wrong. That gives the respondent a chance to acknowledge the citizen's observation, thank him or her for reporting it, and correct something that shouldn't happen a second time anyway.

It is important to send a copy of the letter and the reply to the city manager. If the letter includes a reference to either the mayor or a council member, then include copies of both letters for the mayor and all council members. Sometimes a statement in the letter of reply saying something to the effect that "because this matter may be of interest to the mayor and council, I am including your letter and my reply for their information" may head off any irate calls to them.

Policy changes are frequently made after citizens have reported an unfortunate development caused by the current policy. If the mayor and council make a change, then take a second opportunity to reply to the citizen saying that the mayor and council favorably considered his or her request for service and that beginning on a certain date a new policy will be followed. Then thank the resident for expressing concern so that there is no hint of displeasure.

Residents may bring up matters over the phone that they would never write down, such as allegations of graft, racial bias, religious bias, or some other emotional matter. Upon completion of such a call, it is prudent to write up notes or a memorandum on the call, including the allegations, and to send the information to the immediate supervisor. There may be some element of truth to what was said, and notification gives the supervisor a chance to follow up.

All employees must understand how such contacts with residents should be made. A formal policy may direct that only supervisors are to answer inquiries. Then employees need only tell the resident that they would like to have their supervisor respond to the inquiry. At least it would permit a smaller number of persons to give "official" response. Sometimes the employees do not have all the information about a certain matter, and their answers may add to the problem rather than solve it.

First-line supervisors should be trained to answer inquiries. For example, merely explaining to a resident what went wrong (broken equipment, bad weather, etc.) is usually not a satisfactory reply. Instead such replies should indicate how the situation will be corrected next time; it is best to avoid dealing specifically with the past event.

A supervisor should also keep the perspective of his or her department in mind. To the refuse collection crew with a flawless record, the accusation of a missed collection is an insult. To the supervisor it may simply be another problem to be dealt with by making a special collection (if warranted).

A city with 10,000 residences and semiweekly refuse collection will make over 1,000,000 collections each year. With that number of collections, there is bound to be some conflict between the expectations of residents for year-round, flawless service and departmental requirements to keep staff and equipment on the road every working day of the year.

Sometimes a complaint can be answered with a question: "How would you suggest we change our service?" This moves the situation from the negative to the positive. It is absolutely necessary, however, to follow up, tell what happened, and explain if the idea could not be followed.

In the case of refuse complaints, when a violation of collection rules or regulations clearly exists, it is effective to simply allow the citizen to vent displeasure and then take the material away. This is a way for everybody to save face.

In replying to a citizen's concern, don't blame another city (or county) department for deficient service. To the resident, a city employee is just that—a city employee—not the public works or police employee. If the answer should be given by another department, then it is appropriate to refer the individual to the other department. This referral, however, should be done with a positive attitude: "The reply to your question should really come from our chief of police, Chief Jones. I'm going to switch your call to him. If we get disconnected, or if

Chief Jones cannot satisfy your request, call me back. I am Bob Smith on extension 111."

The effect of that statement is that you are not abandoning the caller to the telephone system, that you are saying the "buck" stops at your desk (at least in part), and that the citizen has a real person at city hall to contact for additional help. Similarly, if the referral must be made to an agency outside of city jurisdiction (often the school district, the county government, or the local courts), give the appropriate phone number to call and again invite the resident to call back if he or she is not satisfied with the answer.

Sometimes an accusation will be so outrageous that it has to be untrue ("Your refuse collector turned his barrel upside down in my garden and deliberately dumped all of his garbage on my flowers"). One reply to that kind of question is to say: "The action you have described of our employee on your property should not have happened." That way you do not have to decide whether the resident was telling the truth but can merely agree that any such outrageous act (whether it happened or not) is not a part of your policies.

It is frequently better to have lower level supervisory staff settle problems. If the supervisors have been delegated responsibility to make adjustments, then a considerable number of calls can be diverted to their offices. Guidelines should be clear for following up on complaints. For example, a rule might be that no refuse collections could be made at some specific location. If your supervisor knows that you will back him or her up on a judgment call, then he or she will be free to use personal judgment, make the decision, and report it to you. You can then give a "post audit" to the action that might help the supervisor make a judgment next time. The goal of complaint handling should be to have the situation resolved at the lowest level of the supervisory system. There is then ample time to amend the system and thus to prevent recurrences.

Listening to neighborhoods

In working with citizen groups and associations, the public works department must be meticulous in providing correct information and current policies of the city toward whatever technical matter may be discussed. When meeting with groups, a division or department head has the advantage of being a "guest" in someone's home or someone's neighborhood. This tends to lower the emotional intensity (compared, for example, to meeting in the city hall). In a group, one or more persons usually will understand that your role is to state the city or county policy, to give reasons for proposed mayor and council actions, and to be a conduit for comments and suggestions to be taken to the policymaking board. Sometimes it is possible to offer alternate courses of action to give added dimension to the discussion. A simple statement of the increased cost or potential benefit related to the interest of the group (financial, service, etc.) can broaden the neighborhood's interest.

After the meeting, be sure to write and thank the chairperson of the neighborhood group for having provided the opportunity to speak to them and answer questions. If you send a report of the meeting to the city manager, mayor, and council, also send a copy to the neighborhood group (appropriately informing all parties of your actions) so that there will be no appearance of biased reporting. If a neighborhood group receives your memorandum and writes back taking issue with it, that gives you a chance to further present to the mayor and council the views of the neighborhood and to offer a specific critique of whatever was suggested by the neighborhood group.

Neighborhood meetings provide a good opportunity to get to know people who are capable and useful. Those who are interested enough to turn out at night on their own time are the people who can be allies as well as adversaries.

They are not always the officers of various associations, but they are visible at meetings through their interest and participation. A few may be opponents forever, but many will listen, ask intelligent questions, and, if convinced that the city or county proposal has merit, join forces with the local government. When you meet people like that, it is appropriate to keep in touch for advice, clarification, and review. It is even possible, with discretion, to solicit their views on tactics and procedures that are suitable for the neighborhood.

One technique in working with a neighborhood group is not to have "all the answers" but to carefully record the questions that are being asked and then write a well thought-out response later. Take the names and addresses of everyone attending the meeting who would like to have a reply to the questions and then mail the answers to them. Almost any effort to inform groups of residents or to provide channels of information or merely to be an understanding staff member at city hall will be welcomed. The hosts or sponsors of such meetings should be thanked for giving you a chance to be heard.

Providing information for neighborhood organizations is also effective. Unless there is some obvious conflict between mayor and council policies and a specific neighborhood subject, the employee who devotes time to that neighborhood group will find the invested time fruitful. An hour spent with one hundred neighbors at a meeting is the equivalent to two and one-half working weeks. The payoff for the time invested is often support from those who are active in the neighborhood group. They are probably the leaders in the community and the ones who would support or oppose mayor and council policy. Some cities help neighborhood organizations build structured neighborhood associations, and even provide handbooks and guidelines on how this might be done.

Working with the media

Public works managers may often think that newspaper, radio, and television reporters thrive on goading "city hall," always seeking the sensational, ever in pursuit of an exposé. It is not that bad, but the media do have values and work methods that include adversarial relations. To be effective, a journalist must be disinterested, an outside observer. If a journalist is co-opted (an accusation often made of the Washington press corps), his or her objectivity is destroyed.

Therefore, when dealing with reporters, recognize at the beginning that you are not a professional performer or a journalist and that in any confrontation you are not going to be "one up" on the professional journalist. The journalist represents a corporation that has certain policies that may include not trying to resolve issues but concentrating on inconsistencies, negatives, and problems.

Therefore, if a real problem is uncovered, admit it and describe what you are going to do about it. If there are questions that cannot be answered, it is certainly appropriate to respond that you do not have a comment. Although you do not want to appear completely uninformed, it is much better to state that you do not know than to guess incorrectly. Tell the journalist that you don't know the answer but that you'll get back to him or her within a certain period of time. That gives you time to find and assemble the information.

On a badly written newspaper story, it is generally not advisable to enter into a letter-writing match with the journalist. The newspaper always has the last word. Although it is helpful to correct the facts, a "correction" of the interpretation of an incident probably leads nowhere.

The positive part of dealing with the media can include seeking out the journalist who covers "city hall," talking to him or her about newsworthy stories such as forthcoming construction projects, and offering suggestions on possible feature stories and photo opportunities such as a large sewer installation, nighttime work, and new kinds of equipment. Your effort to inform the journalist of possible news stories will increase your credibility.

Guidelines for working with the media Those responsible for public relations can promote improved news media relations by adhering to the following guidelines:

See that information given to reporters is accurate and complete.

Practice a genuine open-door policy for reporters. Be available for interviews that will help them meet their deadlines.

Encourage reporters to talk to elected officials, department heads, and other employees. Never attempt to block their access to any city or county official or employee.

Learn to live with the skepticism that is built into reporters' professional backgrounds—a skepticism that has come from trying to learn the facts and from having learned that they are not always what somebody would like one to believe. Always handle newsbreaks among competing media as impartially and objectively as possible.

Take time to orient reporters to city hall or county courthouse operations.

When an article or series of reports is especially good, phone reporters and

tell them. Send a commendatory letter to the editor or publisher of the paper.

Ignore minor errors of fact and interpretation in news stories, but talk to reporters about major errors.

Use letters to the editors sparingly. Generally, they should be limited to public explanation and correction of complex technical issues.

Encourage the county board, city council, or their committees to hold closed meetings only when the nature of business really requires it.

Work with the news editors to set up ground rules for restrictive news coverage, and especially for such coverage of those matters that must be considered in closed sessions of the board, council, or committees.

Source: James M. Banovetz, "Communicating with the Public," in James M. Banovetz, ed., *Small Cities and Counties: A Guide to Managing Services* (Washington, D.C.: International City Management Association, 1984), p. 288.

How do you deal with a negative newspaper? The first step is to recognize that it is a two-way relationship. Local government news is of great interest to many people. The second step is to prepare news releases that are clearly written, short, and factual. Such releases should be sent to radio and television stations and to newspapers in neighboring cities and counties. The local newspaper seldom has a monopoly on local news coverage. The third step is to strengthen and diversify local government reporting. Cities and counties have their own channels for disseminating news.

Reporting to the public

Common forms of reporting city and county activities are newsletters, mailings with water bills, calendars, annual reports, budget reports, cable TV reports, mayor and council agendas, and neighborhood group meeting records. A simple newsletter mailed regularly to all residents can provide information and a point of view that may not be covered by the local news media. If the material is accurate, it will be relied upon by the public. Running timely articles about seasonal changes in operations (playground schedules, refuse collection routes) will build credibility. Responding to citizens' questions in the newsletter will show an interest in specific concerns and problems.

Brief notices of particular importance to the city or county can be included with water bills. If the bill is a postcard, it might be possible to use the "postage meter space" for a simple announcement such as "Motor vehicle fees are due," or "Summer swim passes are available." Many cities distribute trash bags around the winter holidays along with a calendar of specific events such as special refuse collection schedules and special newspaper collections.

An annual report can highlight important events within the department as well as give a complete record of accomplishments. Many annual reports are organized by specific divisions within a department to recognize key individuals within the department, key responsibilities of interest to residents, specific accomplishments for the current year, and proposed work for the coming year. Numerous photos of action by construction and maintenance crews will make the publication more direct and immediate.

A budget document can frequently be used not only to list relative expenses in divisions and departments but to state the city's broad policies: For example, "Clear all major and secondary streets of snow within six hours."

Conclusion

This chapter has emphasized the intangibles of communication, including organizational and interpersonal communication as well as the art of dealing with citizens, elected officials, and others. Much of communication management involves public relations in terms of service, trustworthy information, good appearance, friendly attitudes, courteous demeanor, and a genuine desire to serve the public. It cannot be faked. The employee who likes his or her job and is proud of the city or county government will convey that attitude to everybody he or she works with. The public works manager who is tactful, but not manipulative; interested in others, without invading their privacy; proud of the work of the department, but willing to admit mistakes, is the manager who builds credibility and trust, the base for effective management.

1 James M. Banovetz, ed., *Small Cities and Counties: A Guide to Managing Services* (Washington, D.C.: International City Management Association, 1984), pp. 278–79.

2 Banovetz, *Small Cities*, pp. 292–94.

3 David S. Arnold, Christine S. Becker, and Elizabeth K. Kellar, eds., *Effective Communication:* *Getting the Message Across* (Washington, D.C.: International City Management Association, 1983), p. 3.

4 Useful information on communicating with elected officials can be found in Arnold, Becker, and Kellar, pp. 46–68.

Legal aspects of public works

Local government officials, including public works directors and managers, are empowered, compelled, buffeted, limited, and governed by law. Second only to nuclear power production, local government may be the most regulated industry in the United States. The legal system under which local government officials operate is in every way as complex, and sometimes convoluted, as the physical infrastructure of a large city. Levels of need and responsibility, gradations in quality, maintenance of the integrity of the system, simple or devastating system failures, and the obligation to provide essential services are all standards that are as familiar to a local government attorney as they are to the public works director or the airport manager.

What one discovers on reflection is that many of the skills that make a good manager in public works or any other city department are the same skills needed to oversee the legal needs of the organization. Notably, these skills include an overall understanding of the organization and its goals, an awareness of the legal framework under which it operates, and the recognition of the need for expertise to address particular problems when they arise.

Overview

This overview discusses some of the fundamental legal concerns that managers must have in operating their departments or divisions. In addition, it provides a short discussion of the application of these principles to various aspects of public works management. The remainder of the chapter examines the very important role of each manager in fulfilling the legal obligations of the city by careful contemplation, use of risk management and reduction techniques, and adherence to management and policy goals. Several topics of substantial and ongoing interest to public works management, such as antitrust and contracting out, are also covered.

In this chapter the term *city* is used generically to mean any unit of general-purpose local government, including cities, counties, townships, and the like. The legal principles applicable to general-purpose local governments are quite similar in most states. Special-purpose districts and authorities often operate under more restrictive state legislation. Where applicable, these differences are noted.

Fundamental obligations—the legal context

This section focuses on five different duties that appear to crosscut all other activities of local government managers. There are, of course, many more crosscutting responsibilities, but attention to the following will enhance the likelihood of compliance with applicable legal principles.

Awareness of developments and issues It is standard advice that managers must be aware of new developments that might affect their areas. In the legal context, however, this advice is even more compelling. Most court decisions are effective the day they are decided; some are retroactive at least to the time period covered by the statute of limitations found in the law under which the case was decided. Consequently, if the state supreme court decides that local governments in the state are no longer entitled to sovereign immunity for their acts, or that a state statute limiting the amount of damages for negligent acts by local governments is unconstitutional, cities and counties may, from that day forward, be liable in money damages for those acts.

If the United States Supreme Court decides that the federal Fair Labor Standards Act provisions on hours, wages, and overtime can be applied to local government employees, as it did in February 1985,[1] the city or county's liability for wages and scheduling begins as of that date. It is even possible that that decision may be applied retroactively.

Similarly, actions by the Congress and the state legislature can have immediate effects that can significantly alter a departmental budget, plan, or mode of operations. A congressional decision to eliminate General Revenue Sharing, for example, after the anticipated amounts have been factored into a departmental budget, will certainly have a deleterious effect on departmental operations. This is even more true where the federal, state, and local governments have overlapping fiscal years and the current budget of one entity is subject to the planning budget of another entity on a different cycle.

Actions by federal and state regulatory agencies can also have immediate and unanticipated effects on operations and budgeting. Major environmental efforts at all levels of government dealing with potable water, sewage and solid waste disposal, and the transportation of hazardous waste fall on local public works departments.

State and national organizations representing local governments and professionals are some of the best sources of the information needed to maintain sufficient levels of awareness: The State and Local Legal Center deals with Supreme Court decisions; for legal issues on a local level, consult with the National League of Cities, the U.S. Conference of Mayors, and the National Association of Counties. As indicated below, however, ongoing attentiveness to the daily flow of information received from citizens, newspapers, magazines, and other media, along with an effort to correlate that information with the daily workings and problems of the department, will go a long way toward anticipation of problems.

The city or county attorney is an indispensable ally in maintaining this awareness. The Supreme Court has recently ruled that most public officials can be immune from legal damages for violations of rights where they can show that even through due diligence they could not have known of the illegality of their actions. Consultation with the city or county attorney is a good benchmark of due diligence. (Further discussion appears in the section on civil rights.)

Nondiscrimination—fairness and openness in dealing   Governmental service is a public trust. Throughout the discussions that follow, particularly on civil rights and conflict of interest, a recurring theme is the fair treatment of citizens, neighborhoods, and employees in all activities from the provision of services to the allocation of resources. The United States Constitution and all state constitutions provide explicit and enforceable protections that essentially say that a government of the people must be fair to all of the people. Broad "government in the sunshine" (open meeting) and freedom of information (open records) laws coexist with competitive bidding and other laws in many states. They are designed to ensure responsiveness to the citizenry and to guarantee that the conduct of the public's business is undertaken in the best public interest. Penalties for violations of these constitutional and statutory provisions can be substantial, ranging from criminal actions to the awarding of personal damages against intractable officials.

The principles are fairly simple. Favoritism is not allowed; personal dealing for profit or advantage will be punished; and discrimination on the basis of race, age, creed, sex, or religion will not be tolerated. Local governments and their officials have been found liable for the misallocation of resources between pre-dominantly white and predominantly black neighborhoods in the construction of sewers, or the curbing of streets, or the building of schools.[2] Local government officials with personal interests in contracts have found themselves in jail and often subject to enormous civil damages. Local government officials who have treated employees unfairly on the basis of age or sex or race have found them-selves and their employer liable for damages, for back pay, and for other remedial relief.

In the text that follows, notions of due process, equal protection, and simple fairness under the law are discussed. This overview only means to stress that a manager's notion of fairness and fidelity to duty may be the best instinctual guides to fulfillment of the public good.

Use of the city or county attorney   Just as a public works director keeps pace with developments in his or her field, the local government attorney is the linchpin to new developments and appropriate dealings where the manager's efforts intersect with legal questions. The basic rule should be: When in doubt, ask! For example, an important distinction in the law is drawn between the "discretionary" and "ministerial" functions of local government officials. A divi-sion manager's decision to issue a permit once all the prerequisites for the permit are met is ministerial; courts are not hesitant to order an official to perform a ministerial act. The decision over whether the prerequisites have been met, such as whether water lines have been laid according to requirements as to grade, is basically discretionary; courts are hesitant to second-guess the expertise of profes-sionals over discretionary decisions.

This distinction, however, is fraught with difficulties. The city or county sur-veyor, for example, can demonstrate an expertise in assessing the impact of inclines and declines. Can the surveyor show the same expertise in the man-agement of people in a decision to fire or discipline an employee? In the latter case, the expertise of the personnel manager is essential, as is the expertise of local counsel, in assuring that the steps to be taken in the firing or disciplining are properly sorted out between the surveyor and the personnel manager. Almost invariably, attorneys would rather put the hour or so of time into the assessment process than to have to spend a year or so in litigation over the appropriateness of the decision.

Intergovernmental relations   Local governments operate in an enormous web of overlapping, duplicative, contradictory, and conflicting governmental rules and standards. The Advisory Commission on Intergovernmental Relations has described the system as being more like a marble cake than a layer cake.

Responsibilities for programs and service delivery often mesh federal funding with state authority and supervision and local implementation. Each level has its own rules regarding personnel, finance, accounting, budgeting, record keep-ing, and the like. Even with the best advice, adherence to these rules may be impossible. The rules are flexible, constantly changing and always subject to a new interpretation by federal or state courts or by any one of the levels of government involved in the process.

This complexity takes on additional importance in times of budget reductions and fiscal restraint, as the substantive rules often remain on the law books while the funding to conform to the rules withers away in the face of diminished resources. For example, the federal rules regarding the effluent from sewage treatment plants are not eased when a decision is made by the Congress to reduce or eliminate federal funding for wastewater treatment plants. In addition, the rules that allow citizens to sue local governments for violation of the effluent rules remain in effect. Thus, as the commitment of the intergovernmental financing system to clean water wanes, the law remains that can force conformance to standards that assumed a certain level of financing.

One can hardly underestimate the importance of the legal consequences of intergovernmental cooperation. Grant and contract agreements that were workable with full funding become difficult when the funding scheme fails. Intergovernmental cooperation may even serve as the basis of a lawsuit for conspiracy or monopolization.[3] The local manager should be constantly vigilant in recognizing the legal relationships mandated by the intergovernmental system.

Anticipation, prevention, and reduction of risks   In the past decade a great deal of attention has been paid to the role of risk management and reduction in local government. The International City Management Association has been publishing survey data and research reports since the early 1970s. A further step was taken in 1978 with the organization of the Public Risk and Insurance Management Association (PRIMA) to bring together the professional risk management activities of local governments. This emphasis on risk management and reduction is particularly valuable in the legal forum. Most legislation, regulations, and court decisions, while not predictable as to final results, at least are predictable as to potential results. Just as an attentive waterworks manager can anticipate potential systems problems, an attentive city or county attorney is familiar with the themes underlying pending cases or legislation.

Staff training and the improvement of systems for purchasing, contracting, construction, and ongoing maintenance can all serve to minimize legal vulnerability. Again, the local government attorney should be an essential actor in the design and implementation of departmental risk management programs. These efforts and analyses will lend predictability to budgeting and insurance costs and will, in fact, substantially reduce the possibility that departmental errors or oversights will lead to lengthy and costly litigation.

Application to staff functions of the department

This section, and the one following, set forth the application of the obligations outlined above to various areas of activity commonly undertaken by public works departments. "Staff functions" are generally defined as the array of activities—such as personnel management, planning, and budgeting—that must take place for the department to deliver "line" services, such as water and sewer services, street paving, and sanitation.

Personnel management and labor relations   The legal problems and complexities surrounding this area appear to be almost intractable. Recent legislation at both the state and federal levels, along with the spate of civil rights suits involving public employees, have exacerbated the general turmoil found in personnel management.

The courts, of late, have been quite generous in sustaining congressional actions that impose duties on local governments in their relations with employees. In February 1985, the Supreme Court overruled *National League of Cities* v. *Usery*, a 1976 decision that had attempted to set limits on the ability of the federal government to intrude on the employment activities of local governments when those governments were acting in traditional governmental areas.

At this writing, it is unclear what impact the new case, *Garcia* v. *San Antonio Metropolitan Transit Authority*, will have on governmental labor relations, but it is certain that the Congress and the federal regulatory agencies will feel that they have a much freer hand in defining those relationships. It is entirely possible that legislation concerning public-sector pension plans and public employee labor relations activities will be introduced and possibly passed in the wake of *Garcia*. Similarly, the Supreme Court has upheld the application of the Age Discrimination in Employment Act, which generally disallows mandatory retirement prior to age seventy for most government employees; this rule now applies to uniformed safety officers such as police officers and fire fighters.[4] These decisions preempt both state and local law. Consequently, reliance on state statutes or constitutional provisions will fail against a federal challenge.

The Supreme Court and the lower federal courts have been somewhat more sympathetic to the needs of local government managers in the control and discipline of the workplace. At least two recent cases have held that public employees' First Amendment rights to speak freely were not violated when they were disciplined for abusive or disruptive on-the-job activities. Although the employees' complaints had some features that might warrant protection, the effect on the efficiency and smooth operation of the workplace was sufficient to justify the imposition of the discipline.[5]

Finally, of course, the obligation to be fair and nondiscriminatory arises on a daily basis in public employment. State and federal courts have been vigilant in enforcing statutes designed to assure that factors such as age, sex, race, national origin, religion, and handicap are not considered in equations dealing with the hiring, promotion, retention, or compensation of employees. The advice of local counsel in these areas is critical. Very difficult questions arise over equal pay for equal work, pregnancy-related discrimination, affirmative action goals, compliance with a quagmire of federal, state, and local laws, and a relatively new area, comparable worth. The premise underlying comparable worth is that the salary discrepancies often found between jobs traditionally held by women and those traditionally held by men (for example, nurse or secretary versus sanitation worker or carpenter) are the result of long-standing societal biases that undervalue the jobs performed by women. Very extensive litigation is proceeding on this theory.

Planning, design, and finance The doctrines here range from disparate treatment of neighborhoods (see endnote 2) to the imposition of liability for failure to comply with local building and construction codes (see the section on torts later in this chapter). Planning and finance (or budgeting) are some of the best areas for early recognition, intervention, and reduction of legal risks facing the city or county.

Clearly, the design of traffic systems that minimize the potential for death or injury to travelers will also minimize the exposure of the local government to tort suits. Effective budget oversight will ensure the fairness of the allocation of resources, and will also assist in the recognition of the need for equipment, facilities, or street maintenance or replacement. Public managers should take full advantage of these staff functions so as to provide a vital link between policy and implementation.

Purchasing and contracting out The principles outlined above, particularly regarding fairness and openness in dealing, and the general principle of protection of the public treasury, have generated a significant body of law and regulation over local government procurement. The requirement for competitive bidding is almost universal among governments and usually includes very detailed steps that require strict compliance with the law to ensure the validity of contracts.

Recent budget reductions at the federal level, combined with reduced tax revenues available to state and local governments under various tax limitation measures, have forced many local governments to look to the contracting out or "privatization" of some services. This is particularly true for activities where significant initial capital investments are required—for example, the development of solid waste disposal plants. These programs are all fraught with legal

Antitrust issues affecting local governments The antitrust laws of the United States prohibit unreasonable restraints of trade or the monopolization of activities. Most states have similar laws. Until 1978 it was generally assumed that these laws did not apply to local governments. In *City of Lafayette* v. *Louisiana Power and Light Co.*, 435 U.S. 389 (1978), the U.S. Supreme Court held for the first time that local government activities could be reviewed under the Sherman Act. A 1982 decision, however, *Community Communications Co.* v. *City of Boulder, Colorado*, 455 U.S. 40, generated a flood of litigation that has engulfed local governments over the past three years.

The city of Boulder attempted to regulate its cable television franchisee by imposing a ninety-day moratorium on construction and expansion of the cable system while the city sought additional bidders to provide cable services to city residents. Boulder attempted to do this under the power granted in its home rule charter. The Supreme Court found that an antitrust exemption is only available where the *state*, through the state legislature, had expressed its intent that the local government should act in a manner that had anticompetitive results.

At least 250 antitrust lawsuits have been filed against local governments since 1982. Many of them relate to activities commonly carried out by public works departments such as solid waste disposal and the allocation of trash pickup routes. A major case has focused on the determination by a city that required that all solid waste collected in the city be delivered to the publicly financed solid waste plant. The object of that ordinance was to assure that it would have sufficient feedstock to produce the energy and steam needed to amortize the revenue bonds issued to finance the facility. *Hybud Equipment Corp.* v. *City of Akron, Ohio*, 742 F.2d 949 (6th Cir. 1984).

The federal courts have been quite sympathetic to the needs of local governments to carry on the public's business relatively unfettered by threats of antitrust litigation. The Congress, in late 1984, adopted the Local Government Antitrust Act, P.L. 98-544 (15 U.S.C. §35), which eliminates all money damages against local governments and their officials when they are acting in their "official capacity." In addition, local governments, operating under sufficient state authorization, are able to extend the same money damage immunity to private parties where the city or county "directs" the anticompetitive action.

---

difficulties: the use of bonding authority under federal tax law and state law; the use of state contracting law and federal substantive (e.g., solid waste or hazardous waste) law; or the application of federal antitrust or civil rights laws (see later discussion). Advice of counsel in these areas is critical, particularly since these programs represent new and innovative techniques for the provision of public services subject to a constantly changing matrix of laws.

As one example, the Supreme Court has held that local governments can be found responsible for price discrimination under federal law where they use their governmental power to the disadvantage of local retailers.[6] In this case, a county hospital was purchasing drugs at discounts based on the fact that it was buying in large quantities and that it was a governmental entity. The county then resold the drugs at the hospital pharmacy in direct competition with retail druggists in the city. It is still unclear where this line of reasoning will go, but any city or county department, such as a public works agency, that makes substantial purchases needs to be aware of these developments in the law. Similar problems arise in franchising, where the local government confers a special status on a private party to undertake public or quasi-public activities.

Still, local government managers should be acutely aware that the federal act does not relieve them from suit under the antitrust laws. Injunctive relief is still available, and, more often than not, the antitrust suit is also brought as a civil rights suit and money damages are available in civil rights suits.

Actions not taken in "an official capacity" may still subject the city or county and relevant officials to the full panoply of antitrust damages. Undoubtedly, the term "official capacity" will be interpreted to include both the appropriateness of an action under state law and local ordinances, the fairness and openness in dealing, and the potential for conflicts of interest. Of course, other federal and state laws concerning bribery, extortion, and other criminal acts remain in full force and effect.

The potential for protection of private parties under the 1984 law will cause existing franchisees and contractors, and new bidders for projects, to seek adequate "direction" when they participate in local government efforts. This provision of the act will loom large in all local government negotiations where attempts are made to allow private parties to assume functions that once were governmentally operated (e.g., solid

waste disposal and hazardous waste monitoring and control).

The watchword for local government managers in antitrust is to look for state law authorization to undertake activities that may have substantial anticompetitive effects on private parties. A decision, for example, to allow one builder to hook into the city or county sewer system while denying the same right to another builder has inherently anticompetitive economic results. The public policy justification for such a decision should be very clear and well documented under both state law and local ordinances.

In March of 1985 the Supreme Court decided two very important cases regarding the application of the antitrust laws to local governments. *Town of Hallie* v. *City of Eau Claire, Wisconsin*, 105 S.Ct. 1713 and *Southern Motor Carriers Rate Conference* v. *United States*, 105 S.Ct. 1721. These cases substantially simplify the ability of local government officials to show that their actions were taken pursuant to state law and thus should be immune from antitrust scrutiny. Still, managers should be aware that this area of the law is still quite unsettled, and they should proceed with the cautions outlined above.

Applications to line functions

Just as the manager must attend to the dictates of the law in overseeing the process of service delivery, equal attention must be paid to the effect or impact of the services actually delivered. From basic services, such as the construction and maintenance of streets and roads, to the enormously complicated tasks of operating a municipal utility, all the activities of the local government will be subject to scrutiny in the press, in the political arena, and in the courts. The principles remain the same, however, and the sections below will provide managers with additional information on which to base their decisions within several aspects of the law.

Civil rights obligations under Section 1983

The massive proliferation of lawsuits against local governments and officials under the Federal Civil Rights Act of 1871 (42 U.S.C. Section 1983) makes awareness of this area essential for local government officials. Knowledge of

A primer on remedies and liability   This chapter uses several terms that have fairly explicit legal meanings. Those concerning liabilities and remedies are particularly important as they give an indication of the risks, personal and municipal, that certain actions may engender. This primer is essentially a definitions section designed to clarify these various terms.

Equitable or injunctive relief. This is generally prospective relief, that is, the court uses its equity powers to compel or prevent the defendant from taking an action. For example, a court might issue an order stopping a public works department from removing signs under a new city sign ordinance if it appears that the sign ordinance might be invalid. Similarly, a court might order a city or county to reallocate its resources to benefit parts of the town that have received inadequate services in the past. The equity powers of courts act on the person. Rather than saying that a wrong committed by the person can be remedied by forcing him or her to pay money damages, the court finds that the wrong that is being commmitted is so substantial that the court should use its powers to end the activity immediately. More often than not, the punishment for violation of an injunction is to go to jail. The traditional legal argument is that the person committing the wrong "holds the keys to his own release"; once the person agrees to comply with the injunction, the court will release him or her from jail. Recent examples include reporters who refuse to disclose their sources on controversial articles. The judge orders them to jail until such time as they are willing to comply with the mandate to disclose their sources.

Monetary or legal damages. Legal (money) damages are awarded for several purposes including the punishment of wrongdoers, the compensation of victims, and the creation of a deterrent to negligent or willful behavior that might injure people. It is important to look at the responsibility for payment of damages, the nature of the damages (punitive or compensatory), and the means for ensuring payment.

1. *Individual or personal damage liability.* There is a host of areas where public officials can be held personally liable for their actions. Personal liability will allow the prevailing plaintiff the right to collect money damages from the personal assets of the official, including his or her bank accounts, capital assets, wages, and savings. Many of the areas where personal liability might attach include antitrust, civil rights, and, in some instances, torts. It is often the case that some showing of personal animus or indifference to problems would have to be made before personal damages can be awarded to the plaintiff against a supervisor or someone other than the tortfeasor.

2. *Municipal liability for the official acts of officers and employees.* Local governmental entities can be held liable for the acts of their employees and officers. In the civil rights area, this liability is absolute, even where the employees and officers cannot themselves be held responsible for money damages. Local government entities are very often the objects of lawsuits simply because they are perceived as having "deep pockets." Consequently, a plaintiff in a one-car accident who has sustained substantial injuries will be tempted to sue the local government that constructed and maintained the road, alleging negligence in those activities in the hope of finding some party to pay the costs of repairing injuries and damages.

3. *Actual damages versus punitive or exemplary damages.* Actual damages are meant to compensate the plaintiff for his or her losses. Generally they include out-of-pocket expenses along with anticipated losses such as lost wages. Thus in an automobile accident, where a city employee operating a vehicle on official business negligently injures someone, the plaintiff can sue for actual damages covering medical expenses, wages from time lost from work, other losses to his or her family, and property losses. An employee who is wrongfully discharged may sue for back wages, reinstatement, reestablishment of seniority, and other actual monetary losses he or she can demonstrate resulted from the discharge. Punitive damages are designed to deter behavior that is unacceptable. They are often defined by statute. The federal antitrust laws, for example, mandate a trebling of actual damages by the court. Thus if a jury finds that a local government's unlawful action did $9.5 million in damages to a plaintiff, a court applying the Sherman Act must multiply that amount by three, to $28.5 million, as happened in the Lake County, Illinois, case. Under current civil rights laws, local governments themselves cannot be held liable for punitive damages, but the standard for imposing punitive damages on individual employees and officers is quite lax.

Attorney's fees. Many statutes, federal and state, now allow for the award of attorney's fees to prevailing plaintiffs. This represents a change from the so-called "American Rule," which traditionally has required each side in court proceedings to pay its own attorney's fees. This cost can be enormous, even where small actual damages are awarded. In a recent antitrust case, a utility was made to pay over $150,000 in attorney's fees based on a finding of actual damages of less than $10,000.

Defenses to damages—immunities. It is often the case that some affirmative defense is available to local governments and their employees and officials seeking to avoid damage claims. Some officials are entitled to absolute immunity from damages. Under federal law officials are entitled to an immunity from damages where they acted reasonably and could not have known, through due diligence, that they were acting in such a way as to violate someone's rights. Several states continue the doctrine of sovereign immunity under which local governments and their officials cannot be held liable for money damages. However, those state statutes are no defense against a federal antitrust or civil rights claim for damages.

Reduction of individual or municipal risk insurance. In most states it is possible to purchase errors and omissions insurance to assist in payment in the event that liability is found in a lawsuit. However, given the torrent of litigation against cities and counties, this insurance has become quite expensive and is not available for some activities. There is also a question of whether insurance can be purchased that would pay punitive damages as it may be against public policy in some states to allow local governments and their officials to be free from the deterrent effect that the threat of punitive damages imposes on their actions. Of course, the use of risk management, reduction, and training techniques may well be the greatest assets available to public managers in their efforts to minimize their exposure, that of their employees, and of their local government to potential damage claims.

Section 1983 and interpretive court rulings regulating local official actions and decisions is essential to avoid or minimize liability under the statute.

Section 1983 states that "every person who, under color of any statute, ordinance, regulation, custom or usage of any state or territory" deprives anyone of "rights, privileges, and immunities secured by the Constitution and laws" shall be liable to the injured party.

Elements of a civil rights violation under Section 1983

The enforcement of rights "secured by the Constitution and laws of the United States" encompasses violations under the due process, equal protection, and privileges and immunities clauses that are guaranteed under the Fourteenth Amendment of the U.S. Constitution.

The guarantee of due process protects a broad spectrum of activities, which includes the essential safeguards for the protection of individual rights such as notice, hearing, and an opportunity to defend one's rights.

The equal protection clause assures uniform treatment of individuals in similar circumstances. Equal protection challenges have involved claims of unequal treatment in employment classifications, wage standards, and the provision of public services, for example.

A Section 1983 action may be brought against a local government for deprivation of a federal statutory right as well as a violation of a constitutional right. The Supreme Court has concluded that "laws" under Section 1983 encompass federal statutes such as Social Security and environmental acts in addition to civil rights statutes.

Municipal officer liability

Since 1978, Section 1983 has been broadly interpreted by the U.S. Supreme Court against local officials and municipalities. This attention has in recent years turned to deep concern about the increased costs of litigation and the potential liability of public officials.

Public officials can be found personally liable under this section. Such liability may result in the award of nominal, compensatory, or punitive monetary damages against a municipal officer. City officials are subject to liability for official acts performed under color of state or local law that violate the established constitutional or statutory rights of an individual. Although the statute covers a broad spectrum of protected rights, the federal doctrine of official immunity ultimately determines personal liability under Section 1983.

Official immunity

All municipal officers and employees are afforded some protection against personal liability for damages under Section 1983, although this protection is not embodied in the specific statutory language. The extent to which an officer is protected by official immunity is based on the scope and type of duties performed.

There are two types of official immunity, absolute immunity and qualified immunity. State and local legislators and judges are entitled to absolute immunity from damages in Section 1983 actions. Most other state and local officials have only a qualified immunity from damages in Section 1983 actions in their exercise of administrative, ministerial, or executive powers.

The scope of the qualified immunity defense was clarified in the 1982 United States Supreme Court decision *Harlow* v. *Fitzgerald*.[7] In *Harlow*, the Court specifically held that "government officials performing discretionary functions generally are shielded from liability for civil damages insofar as their conduct does not violate clearly established statutory or constitutional rights of which a reasonable person should have known."

Applying this test, a public official is required to be familiar with clearly established law governing his or her conduct. Thus, a public official will not be afforded the benefit of qualified immunity if he or she knows or reasonably should have known that such conduct could violate an individual's civil rights. Accordingly, the qualified standard is troublesome in that it has not yet evolved into a comprehensive test that allows an individual to identify clear constitutional or statutory rights that must be protected as he or she performs official acts on behalf of the government.

It is important to note that a public official is more likely to be protected by qualified immunity where he or she has consulted the city attorney when in doubt as to the propriety of his or her proposed actions. Moreover, if such advice is coupled with other evidence that the official followed applicable departmental procedures and regulations, immunity should attach.

Entity liability of local governments

State and municipal officials are not the only "persons" subject to suit within the meaning of the statute. The Supreme Court has determined that municipalities are included in the definition of persons to which Section 1983 is applicable. Local government entities have no protection under the absolute or the qualified immunity defenses. As a result, municipal liability is absolute when a federally guaranteed right is violated. Even if a municipal official can establish personal or official immunity, that immunity will not shield the local government from liability for Section 1983 violations. In the wake of recent Supreme Court decisions, local governments are in effect strictly liable for acts or policies that violate an individual's civil rights.

Color of law—official policy

A city may be sued under Section 1983 when the conduct of its officials that gives rise to the claim is performed "under color of any statute, ordinance, regulation, custom or usage of any state or territory." This language has been interpreted to include all acts that reflect an official custom or policy of the municipality. Municipal customs or policies include express statements, such as an ordinance or resolution, as well as any unwritten policies or practices that through continued usage take on the force of law.

Although it is often difficult to determine what constitutes municipal custom or policy, it is relatively clear that a single act of official misconduct will usually not be sufficient to establish municipal liability. In egregious circumstances, however, this rule has not been followed.[8]

Similarly, *mere* negligence by employees is not sufficient to create municipal liability under Section 1983. Rather, an affirmative link must be shown between the official misconduct and an express or implied municipal authorization of such action. Deliberate indifference by the municipality, once it is put on notice of acts or probable acts causing deprivations of an individual's civil rights, may well create municipal liability. Such a challenge might allege that the municipality is responsible for the local official's disregard of known facts or gross negligence pertaining to a Section 1983 violation.

Liability for the conduct of subordinates

A municipality cannot be held liable under Section 1983 solely on a *respondeat-superior* theory. In other words, liability cannot simply be premised on an employer-employee relationship. There must be evidence that the municipal employee's impermissible conduct was based on a municipal policy or custom or on indifference.

The courts have held that local governments and their officials may be liable for the acts or omissions of their employees. Although an official cannot be held liable for the acts of subordinates based on a *respondeat-superior* theory, direct participation by an official in an alleged civil rights violation will result in liability. Moreover, the cases suggest liability for any showing of the official's personal responsibility for his subordinate's acts. Other instances of municipal supervisor liability include any direct or indirect approval, participation, sanction, promotion, or knowledge of a subordinate's misconduct resulting in a civil rights violation.

Liability for damages under Section 1983

Municipalities are often the subject of Section 1983 civil rights suits since they are perceived to have deep pockets. Section 1983 damage awards against local governments and their officials can be quite substantial, but the U.S. Supreme Court has established limits on the amount of municipal liability. A city may be subject to liability for nominal and compensatory damages only; punitive or exemplary damages cannot be awarded against a municipality under the statute.

Attorney's fees

Although local governments cannot be held liable for punitive damages, Section 1983 litigation can be even more costly by an award of attorney's fees under the Civil Rights Attorney's Fees Awards Act of 1976 (42 U.S.C. Section 1988). The statute provides that the court in its discretion may award reasonable attorney's fees from a local government, or its officials personally, to a prevailing plaintiff. Application of the statute by the courts operates substantially in favor of Section 1983 plaintiffs. Plaintiffs can collect attorney's fees under Section 1988 even where the damage award is nominal, and where simple injunctive relief is acquired. Moreover, a plaintiff may be deemed a "prevailing party" and awarded fees by means of a favorable settlement or success on the significant issues of the litigation.

Decisions on the awarding of attorney's fees for defendants have not been so generous. To the contrary, the Supreme Court has held that a defendant can obtain attorney's fees only when the plaintiff's claim is meritless or frivolous.

Local government tort liability

Understanding tort liability is particularly important given the nature of public works activities and the role of public works in overall local government operations. In recent years there have been an increasing number of court decisions requiring local governments to pay large damage awards because some fault or failure was ascribed to the city. This section focuses primarily on the tort liability of public works officers and employees as well as the municipality's liability for wrongful acts or omissions.

Introduction to tort principles

Liability for the actual construction, maintenance, and repair of public works projects arises from a failure of duty. The injured party must prove negligence as a prerequisite to individual or municipal liability. Generally, municipal officers acting within the scope of their authority and without negligence are not personally liable for damage resulting from their acts. However, employees and officials are responsible for negligent or improper acts committed during the performance of their duties.

Proof of a negligence claim requires a showing that the officer or employee had a duty to the public and to the particular injured party and that the failure to perform that duty with requisite care and skill was the cause of the plaintiff's injury.

Public officers and employees have duties that are defined by federal, state, and local statutes. Each of these statutes regulates, to some degree, the facilities and services provided by the public works department, thereby creating an affirmative statutory duty to operate within established legal parameters. Tort liability is an area governed almost completely by state law. The extent to which specific legal tort doctrines apply to specific acts varies from state to state so the discussion below is necessarily general.

Once legal duties have been established or created, either by internal departmental custom and policy or by statutory standards, public works personnel have to conform to the duty to act with reasonable care and skill.

A breach of these duties may occur in two ways:

1. The improper performance of an affirmative act
2. A failure to act (e.g., if the city undertakes a reduction in services based on fiscal cutbacks, the subsequent failure to provide services may result in a tortious injury).

The element of causation exists when the municipality takes affirmative action that encourages reliance by the public, or an individual, thereby creating a duty relationship that may give rise to tort liability.

By way of example: The city decides to design and construct sidewalks for a residential street. Once the city decides to make sidewalks available to the public, it must exercise reasonable care to design, construct, maintain, and repair them safely for public use. When snow and ice accumulate on the sidewalk, the creation of this dangerous condition may give rise to a duty on the part of the city to use reasonable care to remove the dangerous condition. If the city fails to remove the snow and an individual slips and falls, the city's failure to act may be said to have caused or contributed to the individual's injury, thereby creating a negligence claim against the city. The city may have a defense to the claim, for example, that the snowfall created an emergency condition to which it could not immediately respond. However, once the snow is removed and the city is put on notice of a large crack in the pavement resulting from the snowfall, responsibility may well arise for any resulting injury.

The amount of damages that a plaintiff may recover can have a significant impact on a city or county already financially burdened by the increased costs of essential services. Therefore, the importance of close cooperation between the city attorney and the public works director is reemphasized in the handling of damage claims against the city. The city attorney can provide advice as to the nature and extent of the city's liability and may suggest precautions to avoid such actions in the future.

Municipal liability

The great variation in state tort law makes it difficult to detail the circumstances under which, and the extent to which, municipalities may be held liable for the acts of their employees.

The discussion of the scope and extent of local government liability hinges on a determination of the circumstances under which a governmental entity is immune from tort liability. All state and federal jurisdictions grant some form of sovereign immunity under specific circumstances. There are some states,

Legal complexities In the course of their work, public works managers and supervisors may face complex and difficult situations with legal (and often ethical) implications. Here are some hypothetical scenarios accompanied by questions to provide food for thought.

A former supervisor of operations has been promoted to the position of fleet manager for all of the local government's public works vehicles. For years this supervisor has exchanged gifts at Christmas and other occasions with a high school friend who now owns a local truck and heavy-equipment dealership. The gifts are of nominal value, although as each friend has become more successful over the years, the value of the gifts has increased accordingly. This year's gifts fit well into this pattern. In addition, the friends and their families socialize on a regular basis. The city, with the fleet manager in charge, puts out a request for bids to purchase several heavy vehicles including trucks and earthmovers. The fleet manager, in reviewing the bids, finds that the dealership owned by her friend has submitted a bid which, while it is very competitive, fails to meet an essential technical aspect of the request. By virtue of their personal friendship, the manager knows that the dealership can almost certainly meet the technical requirement. Should the manager call her friend? Should the manager issue clarifying letters to all

bidders, even those that have fully complied with bid specifications, to assure that each and every seller understood the technical requirements? Should the manager remove herself from further consideration on the contract despite the fact that the position of fleet manager exists because the city needs the expertise offered by the manager in its decision to make a substantial equipment purchase? Should the manager seek the advice of the city attorney in this situation?

The local government's public works capital budget has been subjected to severe scrutiny by the mayor and city council. The public works director has requested an ordinance from the mayor and council that would require substantially greater concessions from developers in financing the street, sewerage, and lighting facilities that will be needed for the developer to complete its project. Word gets back to the director that one crucial vote on the council for the proposal has a sense that the channeling of work by the developers to local subcontractors would be very helpful to the political fortunes of the existing administration which, after all, employs the director. Should the director seek to have the developers comply with a condition like this to assure that the needed public works facilities are installed? Would such an action by the director induce a sufficient fear of economic loss in the developers that it could be called

however, where municipal liability is the rule and immunity the exception. In other states, however, immunity is the rule and liability is the exception. Ultimately this means that state laws may impose liability on the basis of the power under which the city has acted (i.e., whether the act is a governmental or a proprietary function of the city).

Although the governmental-proprietary distinction is quite difficult to determine, liability and immunity for local government tort actions are often based on this distinction. It is important to remember that immunity and liability may appear to be hopelessly interwined, but are two separate and distinct issues.

The standard for liability for negligence by a city employee is the same as that defining individual liability: There must be a showing of a duty owed to the injured person that was breached by the city and thereby allegedly caused the injury.

Unlike the civil rights area, tort liability frequently results under the doctrine "extortion"? Is it the responsibility of the director to ascertain the motives for the request from the "crucial vote"? Was the director correct in the first place in seeking this authorization from the mayor and council? If the director was correct, how can he seek to remove the apparent taint that has now intruded itself into this process so as to serve the needs of both the developers on one hand and the mayor and city council on the other to get on with the public works projects that need to be completed? Should the director seek the advice of the city attorney in this situation?

The public works director has a division in the planning department that is largely financed out of federal water pollution control grants. The county is on notice that federal money under this grant program may end in the near future. One employee of the division, who has an exemplary record, is a minority female. She has complained to her immediate supervisor that her co-workers have been making disparaging remarks to her having to do with both her sex and her minority status. The supervisor has passed these complaints on to the division director seeking guidance. The division director has failed to act. The employee, along with several other employees in the division, is given notice of termination based on the loss of federal funding for their efforts. What could any one of the supervisory personnel have done to avoid the lawsuit that is certain to come, and should come, from this situation? Is there an inadequacy in the supervisory or personnel system that has allowed this complaint to progress so far? What advice could the city attorney have provided to the managers facing this complicated scenario? Who is liable here: the immediate supervisor, fellow employees, the division director, the department director, the county council, and/or the county?

An employee complains that the county's public works sanitation trucks are operating in an unsafe condition because the tires on the trucks, rated to go 50,000 miles, are being used for 75,000 miles. The supervisor explains that budget cuts necessitated by reduced revenues have forced the department to extend the life of material such as tires. A county sanitation truck fails to stop in an emergency situation because the pavement is wet. The lawyers for the injured employee, and the injured occupants of the car hit by the truck, bring in expert testimony that if the truck had had adequate treads, it would have been able to stop in time to avoid the accident. What next? More important, what could have been done to reduce the risks that this situation presents. Who is liable here: the employee who was driving the truck, supervisory personnel, and/or the county?

of *respondeat superior*: The municipality is accountable to an individual who suffers a direct injury caused by the negligence of a municipal employee acting within the scope of his or her employment.

Municipal officer and employee liability

The liability of an employee is a separate issue from municipal liability. Generally, municipal officers are immune from personal liability when acting in good faith, without negligence, and within the scope of their authority. Under many state and local statutes, however, municipal officers and employees can be held personally liable for damage or injury resulting from public work performed if such injury resulted from the negligent or improper performance of the work.

This admixture of "official" liability and liability in one's "personal capacity," when played against the potential liability of governmental entities themselves, creates vexing problems in litigation and in the defense of lawsuits. As all of these areas are in a substantial state of flux, public officials should always consult with the jurisdiction's lawyers whenever potential litigation appears.[9]

Conflict of interest

Local government officials and employees are required to act with the utmost good faith, fidelity, and respect as fiduciaries of the municipality and the public trust. This duty mandates that public officials must maintain a high degree of propriety in the performance of their obligations. They must be mindful of the appearances of, or actual, conflicts that might arise from their actions. A conflict of interest may occur in a variety of forms relevant to holding public office, including outside employment interests, private financial interests, personal relations, acceptance of gifts, and abuse of office or position.

Many of these conflict-of-interest areas are governed by state or local statutes or charters. The most familiar application of the conflict-of-interest prohibition is clearly exhibited in the area of municipal contracts. Generally, state law prohibits public officials from contracting with an agency they represent, or from having a private interest, direct or indirect, in city contracts. As such, municipal officers are held to a strict standard of accountability when dealing on the city's or county's behalf.

The interest of an employee or officer in a public contract may be a pecuniary one, which benefits the officer either directly or indirectly. Here is an example of a direct conflict. A public works officer contracts with a private company to purchase materials and equipment for the repair of city street surfaces. If the official receives a commission as a result of the awarding of the contract, the contract can be held void as against public policy.

Similarly, an indirect conflict would arise if the contracting official is related to an officer or director of the private company or is financially interested in the company as a stockholder. In addition to the invalidation of the contract, further adverse consequences to the official may result. A violation of the conflict-of-interest requirements may include removal from office, liability for all profits received, and possibly criminal prosecution and fines. This prohibition of an officer's personal and financial interest extends through all stages of contract formation and performance.

In addition to avoiding private interest in public contracts, public officials must avoid situations that appear inconsistent with the proper performance of their duties. Awareness of potential conflicts is essential; even the most innocent or harmless situations may be tainted with the appearance of self-interest or self-dealing. These general principles apply in the following four areas:

1. *The receipt of gifts, commissions, or bonuses.* The receipt of anything of value that may directly or indirectly influence a public official in his or her actions is clearly illegal and is easily traceable.
2. *Interest in the contracting corporation.* The ownership of stock or the holding of office in a corporation with which an officer contracts on behalf of the public, either directly or indirectly, is prohibited. The general rule includes not only ownership or holding of office by the public official but includes the spouse or other immediate family member of the public official.
3. *Personal relationships.* Public officials must avoid situations in which their actions may be affected by personal relationships. Familial and personal ties that interfere with an official's obligation to pursue the public good or that create an appearance of special interest are forbidden.
4. *Political contributions or considerations.* An officer must refrain from making or receiving contributions or considerations that benefit his or her

political interests or the interests of someone with managerial or political authority over the official. This area is closely regulated by federal and state statutes.

Conclusion

Awareness of issues, adherence to duties and established policies, the willingness to seek legal assistance when in doubt, and a continuing commitment to the pursuit of the public welfare should be the guides to management. Changing political winds, traumatic budget changes, and other seemingly great problems can, in most cases, be minimized and handled through conscientious application of these basic principles.

1 *Garcia* v. *San Antonio Metropolitan Transit Authority*, 105 S.Ct. 1005 (U.S. Supreme Court, February 19, 1985). On November 7, 1985, Congress passed the Fair Labor Standards Amendments of 1985, P.L.99-150, signed by President Reagan on November 13, 1985. The act represents a compromise between state and local representatives, labor groups, and Congress. Among other things, the act amends the FLSA to allow state and local employers to grant compensatory time in lieu of paid overtime at a rate of time-and-a-half as of April 15, 1986. It also allows public safety and "seasonal" workers (intended to apply to many public works employees) to accumulate up to 480 hours of compensatory time before they must be paid cash overtime. "Regular" employees may bank up to 240 hours.

2 See *Johnson* v. *City of Arcadia, Florida*, 450 F.Supp. 1363 (N.D. Fla. 1978).

3 In *Unity Ventures* v. *County of Lake*, a U.S. District Court found Lake County, Illinois, a village, and three public officials liable for denying access to a developer who wanted to connect with the county's sewer interceptor system. This antitrust case was based on the claim that a "sphere of influence" agreement signed between the village and the county was an "agreement in restraint of trade" in violation of the Sherman Act. There was no claim in this case of improper dealing for personal gain. The county and the village had an agreement stating that their preference for the extension of sewer services would be to developments in incorporated areas. A jury award of $9.5 million under the Civil Rights Act and the Sherman Antitrust Act was trebled by the judge under the provisions of the Antitrust Act to $28.5 million. The village's annual tax levy that might be available to pay damages was, in 1983, $87,029. This case is still under appeal.

4 *EEOC* v. *Wyoming*, 460 U.S. 226 (1982); and see, *EEOC* v. *Mayor and City Council of Baltimore*, 731 F.2d 209 (4th Cir. 1984); *reversed*, June 17, 1985, 105 S.Ct. 2712.

5 *Connick* v. *Meyers*, 461 U.S. 168 (1983); and see *Pickering* v. *Board of Education*, 391 U.S. 563 (1968), *Perry* v. *Sindermann*, 408 U.S. 593 (1972), and *Branti* v. *Finkel*, 445 U.S. 507 (1980).

6 *Jefferson County Pharmaceutical Assn.* v. *Abbott Laboratories*, 460 U.S. 150 (1983).

7 *Harlow* v. *Fitzgerald*, 457 U.S. 800 (1982); in the summer of 1985 the Supreme Court returned to the "qualified immunity" questions raised in *Harlow* and handed down a case which should provide substantial guidance to local government lawyers in advising public officials. *Mitchell* v. *Forsyth*, 105 S.Ct. 2806 (June 19, 1985).

8 Cf. *City of Oklahoma City* v. *Tuttle*, 105 S.Ct. 2427 (U.S. Supreme Court, June 3, 1985).

9 There will, of course, be times when the interests of the city or county and the interests of the individual employee are in conflict; often, in those cases, the individual employee is well advised to seek his or her own counsel. The city attorney generally has an ethical obligation fairly to advise individual employees of these circumstances. Still, the area is quite confused and caution is warranted. Compare, e.g., *Brandon* v. *Holt*, 105 S.Ct. 873 (U.S. Supreme Court, January 21, 1985), in which a suit against an official "in his official capacity" imposes liability on the jurisdiction he represents even where the jurisdiction itself was not a named party; with *Kentucky* v. *Graham*, 105 S.Ct. 3099 (U.S. Supreme Court, June 28, 1985), in which a state cannot be made to pay the attorney's fees of a public employee sued "in his individual capacity." See, also, *Oklahoma City* v. *Tuttle*, cited in note 8, above.

Purchasing

Of the many activities of local government, purchasing is unique in at least one respect: It offers all departments and offices an opportunity to save money without cutting back or eliminating services, discharging employees, or otherwise disturbing the operations of the local government. The opportunities for savings through sound purchasing are enormous because purchases represent up to 40 percent of the annual budgets of many jurisdictions.[1] As one scholar noted more than forty years ago, purchasing—if it is centralized and properly administered— can be the "sentry at the tax exit gate."[2]

This chapter covers the fundamentals of centralized purchasing, with specific emphasis on support for a public works program. It is based on the premise that:

purchasing is an operation of government that ought to be run in a business-like way, ought to produce good results, and ought to serve the best interests of everyone concerned: the departments, their employees, the vendors and the taxpaying public. [It presumes that] it is assuredly good administration . . . and . . . ought to be considered good practical politics . . . to run an efficient, economical purchasing operation.[3]

Management, purchasing, and public works

Central management, finance, purchasing, and public works all have a stake in effective purchasing. Central management is concerned not only with potential dollar savings but also with the thorny questions of buying locally, balancing competing demands of quality and cost, and the ever-present threat of conflict of interest. The finance department has its concerns with accounting practices, scheduling purchases vis-à-vis cash flow, and a variety of financial controls. The purchasing department has its job to do, as described throughout this chapter, but one of its constant concerns is maintaining good working relations with all of the other agencies in the city or county government. The public works department is concerned with the long-term reliability and value of many products and services that are difficult to specify, costly and time-consuming to get bids or proposals on, and expensive to pay for.

The term *purchasing* is used throughout this chapter to describe the process of supplying needed goods and services to using agencies. It encompasses efforts that may be known variously as purchasing, materials management, or procurement programs.

The centralized purchasing department must satisfy the requirements of using agencies in a timely and economical way, while complying with legal and regulatory requirements, *and* promoting maximum value for the public dollar. Such a job cannot be performed properly without the unwavering support of the chief administrator, the public works director, other administrators, and their employees. Management commitment must reflect the supreme importance of integrity in public purchasing, even when standing behind that commitment may mean passing up a short-term opportunity to save money or enhance the quality of a

Figure 9–1 The cons
and pros of centralized
purchasing.

Con	Pro
It casts doubt on ability of department heads.	It helps department heads by providing better goods and services.
How can one person or agency know so much?	It sets up a clearinghouse for information on product and service innovations and problems.
Each department knows its needs better than purchasing. Everything is o.k. now, so why change?	Maybe so, but purchasing's job is to buy . . . not determine need. Centralized purchasing will save money and help all using departments by reducing unit prices for items purchased, paperwork, overhead costs, and duplicated effort.

service. Public works and other operating agencies should work with, and through, purchasing officials, rather than around them, to ensure that the purchasing system works to the maximum benefit of all, including the taxpayers. The case for centralized purchasing—concentrating the authority and responsibility for purchasing in a single administrative unit—is summarized in Figure 9–1.

Purchasing is, above all, a service agency with service, staff, and line responsibilities. It must work with administrative agencies in a spirit of cooperation and support to ensure that needed goods and services are provided on time, and at the lowest total cost. Purchasing, in order to be completely effective, must be neither a clerical "stooge" nor a self-appointed dictator.

The potential for conflict between central purchasing and public works should be acknowledged. Both have professional standards, which may come into conflict, and professional pride in their work. Cost need not mean haggling over nickels and dimes. Nor should quality be in opposition to economy. In the imperfect world of local government, however, conflicts can arise. If this unhappy event should occur, the best way to resolve it is for the two agencies to work it out themselves. If that cannot be done, then central management must step in and settle the issue, but that is almost always the solution of last resort. The most likely causes of conflict are schedules, priorities, manpower, technical opinion/performance tradeoffs, administrative procedures, and cost.

Purchasing must assume the responsibilities listed in Figure 9–2. These and other purchasing responsibilities are discussed in this chapter under the headings of "Planning and scheduling purchases," "Establishing contracts," and "Administering contracts."[4]

Planning and scheduling purchases

Although planning and scheduling are related and tend to overlap, planning is primarily concerned with how best to acquire goods and services, and when best to acquire such items. Five specific opportunities for improving local government purchasing through planning and scheduling are discussed here: consolidating requirements, managing inventory, market research, value analysis, and scheduling acquisitions.

Purchasing and the using agencies, in coordination with the finance department and top management, can work together to ensure that needs are met at the lowest total cost. In today's complex marketplace, this means agreeing on acceptable quality levels, deciding how and when to buy, determining whether to carry an item in inventory, and evaluating financing options in contract award decisions.

Figure 9–2 Service, staff, and line responsibilities of the procurement function.

Service responsibilities
To provide adequate and timely support in a tactful and courteous manner.

To be receptive to advice from personnel in other departments, and to be guided by such advice when it benefits the organization.

To maintain good relations with all personnel in other departments.

To ensure that various departments are kept informed of each other's needs, problems, and methods of operation.

To keep in mind that procurement is essentially a service function.

Staff responsibilities
To keep management and other users advised on:

General market conditions with particular reference to the principal commodities or services used.

New products or services that may be substituted for ones currently used.

Changes and trends in prices.

Improvements in available products or services.

Line responsibilities
To evaluate feasibility and (as appropriate) implement:

Value analysis of specification requirements.

Life cycle costing.

Value purchasing.

Consolidation of requirements.

Standardization.

Make-or-buy analysis.

Lease-or-buy analysis.

Cooperative and/or consolidated procurement.

Consolidating requirements for products and services

The generally lower prices brought about by buying in quantity are one of the obvious assets of centralization. Even so, public works and other using agencies often do not consolidate their requirements for the items that they, as individual departments, use repetitively—much less pool their requirements for the common-use items that they and other departments use. The reasons for not consolidating requirements vary, but the harmful results always include lost opportunities to save money through lower prices and reduced administrative time and cost. Using agencies must communicate with purchasing, and with one another, to consolidate requirements for repetitive and common-use items. Either they, or purchasing, must accumulate, maintain, and periodically analyze such historical data as quantities purchased, ordering frequencies, unit prices per transaction, and vendor performance, to help decide how and when items should be purchased. The purchasing agency might suggest, for example, scheduling one or more definite quantity purchases, with preestablished delivery dates and points, during the year and establishing a term contract (discussed below) based on projected usage.

Most public officials are familiar with one-time, definite quantity purchasing because it is the approach almost always used to acquire commodities, supplies, and equipment. This familiar, straightforward process involves requisitions, bids and contracts, delivery, inspection and possibly testing, and payments to vendors.

A jurisdiction's annual requirement for a repetitive or common-use item may be of such a small dollar value and so intermittent that it does not justify the effort and expense of obtaining competitive quotes or bids. Even so, purchasing should consider making a one-time definite quantity purchase, at the very least. Applicable laws, regulations, and procedures will govern whether competitive small-purchase procedures should be used to obtain informal quotes, or whether formal, competitive bids should be obtained, but some competition should be obtained, even if the requirement is only for a couple of hammers.

When an item is to be purchased at a specific time every year, or at periodic intervals throughout the year, scheduled buying should be used if term contracting cannot be used. In essence, scheduled buying involves one or more purchases of definite quantity and volume that have been scheduled in advance. Perishables and similar items with a short shelf life lend themselves to scheduled buying, as do items that are required in volume but have inconsistent usage. Schedules for such buys should be established in accordance with using agency consumption patterns, warehousing capacities, and seasonal factors.

To the extent possible, however, purchasing should encourage using agencies to put repetitive-use and common-use items on term contracts. Term contracting, according to one definition, is "a technique in which a source or sources of supply are established for a specified period of time, usually characterized by an estimated or definite minimum quantity, with the possibility of additional requirements beyond the minimum, all at a predetermined unit price."[5] Within this definition are a number of conventional arrangements, including, in order of desirability, definite quantities for a definite period, approximate quantities for a definite period, indefinite quantities for a definite period, and indefinite quantities for an indefinite period.

Term contracting has advantages for both the vendor and the local government. For the vendor, a term contract represents volume business spread over a period of time. Term contracting spares all vendors the administrative time and expense of repeatedly preparing bids. For the contractor, it reduces sales expense and permits redirection of sales efforts.

Many of these advantages also can be realized by the local government. Through term contracting, the jurisdiction can eliminate the administrative time and expense of repeatedly preparing and issuing invitations for bids for the same items, and of receiving, processing, and evaluating the offers that are received. Term contracting makes it possible for fewer personnel to handle larger volumes of purchases and for local governments to reduce, and sometimes almost eliminate, the problems and costs of maintaining inventories.

Purchasing must work with public works and other departments to help them identify the most cost-effective and reliable methods of purchase, even for low dollar value items. At the very least, everyone involved in the purchasing process must do his or her best to ensure that emergency purchases are minimized because, as an Alaskan statute indicates, "true emergencies are rarely known to exist." Emergency purchases are costly and often are caused by poor planning.

The extent to which a jurisdiction can, or cannot, consolidate its requirements for repetitive-use and common-use items will depend largely on top management's commitment and the jurisdiction's ability to maintain and analyze such historical information as which agencies bought how much of which items, when, and at what prices. It will also depend on other factors such as the type of good or service being purchased, inventory management policy, purchase timing policy, market conditions, trade and seller distribution practices, the degree of competition, pricing and quantities, and the required lead time for the item.[6]

Managing inventory

Inventory management is a subject in its own right, so only a brief overview can be provided here.[7]

The goal of effective inventory management is to ensure the immediate availability of certain items and, at the same time, to minimize both the jurisdiction's investment in inventory and the administrative and overhead costs associated with acquiring, storing, and issuing those items.

Traditionally, many local governments have maintained inventories for a variety of items, but the trend now is away from maintaining warehouses and stores toward relying on "stockless" term contracts.

On the plus side, an inventory provides a buffer that can absorb unexpected changes in demand or interruption in services; permits quantity purchasing, with lower prices; makes forward buying, and even speculation, possible in times of rising prices; and provides flexibility in usage and units of issue. On the other hand, inventories present problems that include (1) more assets on hand than can be used, because of abrupt changes in user programs, errors in reporting data, technological changes, inaccurate usage factors, erroneous usage projections, and misinterpreted policies; and (2) losses resulting from abuse in handling, improper protection from the elements, the deterioration of items with short shelf lives, and pilferage.

If a local government decides to enter into inventory management and control, for one or more items, its objectives should include balancing inventory investment with user demands and ensuring that an adequate supply of essential items is on hand; physical quantities and dollar values of property on hand are those shown on inventory records; property is protected from loss or damage; a warning system flags understocked or overstocked positions; surplus, excess, and obsolete material is purged; and a data base is established to help determine requirements.

Conducting market research

In larger jurisdictions, keeping abreast of the latest economic and product/service information usually is a joint responsibility of purchasing, the using agencies, and the jurisdiction's economic analysts, if there are any. In smaller jurisdictions where purchasing staffs are small, however, gathering such information will usually be the responsibility of the using agency and the finance department. Regardless of who takes the lead, someone should be responsible for tracking market conditions for items bought on long-term contracts; noting changes in the requirements of using agencies for specific items; noting new and improved products and services; noting seasonal requirements or fluctuating markets; and, monitoring transportation costs and recommending cost-effective options.

Information on the market conditions for products and services can be obtained from a variety of sources, including magazines such as *Business Week*, newspapers such as *The Wall Street Journal*, services such as BidNet, and any number of product/service exhibitions.

Using value analysis

Value analysis (VA) refers to a body of related efforts directed at

analyzing the function of systems, products, specifications, standards, practices, and procedures for the purpose of satisfying the required function at the lowest total cost . . . consistent with requirements for performance, reliability, quality, and maintainability.[8]

According to the National Institute of Governmental Purchasing (NIGP), value analysis is a

management (not just purchasing) technique that involves the "right" group of people for a particular task and a "structured plan of approach in an effort to eliminate needless costs that are not essential to doing the job that needs to be done."[9]

In its simplest form, VA looks at an item (system, service, etc.) and asks four questions:

1. What is the function that must be performed?
2. How are we performing it right now, and at what cost?

3. What are the alternative means of accomplishing the required function, and how much would each of these alternatives cost?

4. Considering the cost of the current approach and the projected cost of each of the alternatives, which approach should we choose in order to perform the required function at the lowest total cost?[10]

The areas in which VA can be applied are wide and varied. They include but are by no means limited to (1) requirements analysis; (2) life-cycle cost bid evaluation; (3) value purchasing bid evaluation; (4) value incentive contracting; (5) "make or buy" decisions for services; and (6) lease versus purchase decisions. Each of these applications is discussed briefly below.

Requirements analysis   The most basic application of value analysis is in setting new and revised specifications and performance standards for products or services. VA might involve, for example, raising the minimum fuel efficiency requirement for passenger cars from seventeen miles per gallon to twenty-four miles per gallon, or it might involve specifying diesel (as opposed to gasoline) engines for trucks and heavy equipment. In both cases, the objective is to select cost-effective products. Requirements analysis can be used by itself or in conjunction with one or more of the next three applications of value analysis discussed below.

Life-cycle cost bid evaluation   This application of VA measures the total cost of "ownership," usually known as the life cycle, for a product or service that has been offered in response to an invitation for bids that prescribes how total costs will be calculated. Total costs are compared for all of the competing bids for the life cycle of the product or service. For example, a government might state in an invitation for bids that it is going to evaluate bids for a portable air compressor on the basis of the following formula:

$$EBP = P + FC, \text{ where:}$$

EBP = Evaluated bid price (the price that is to be compared for purposes of contract award)

P = Purchase price (the price that ordinarily would be considered for contract award)

FC = Projected fuel costs (for the compressor over the expected life of the vehicle).

The government, of course, would have to indicate the unit of measure for fuel consumption (gallons per hour), and it would have to state:

1. That bidders would be required to submit, with their bids, a fuel consumption rate for the current make and model they were offering to sell to the jurisdiction.

2. That the fuel consumption rate would be based on a single, specified procedure (the Compressed Air and Gas Institute Recommended Fuel Consumption Test Procedure for Portable Air Compressors).

3. That fuel costs would be projected on the basis of a specified formula, such as:

$$FC = CR \times OH \times LY \times PG, \text{ where:}$$

FC = Projected fuel costs

CR = Consumption rate (in the specified unit of measure, in accordance with the specified test procedure)

OH = Projected annual operating hours

LY = Projected lifetime in years

PG = Price of gasoline to the jurisdiction.

4. That evaluated bid prices, instead of just purchase prices, would be the basis for contract award.
5. That any bidder who failed to provide the required fuel consumption rate data would not be considered for contract award.
6. That the jurisdiction reserved the right to conduct its own tests to verify the test data submitted by the bidder, with the understanding that the costs of tests that did not substantiate the bidder's submittal would be borne by that bidder.

If the jurisdiction stated in the bid invitation that it intended to award the contract for an air compressor this way, it would have to do so. By the same token, if the jurisdiction said nothing about considering fuel costs in the award of the contract, it could not decide to do so, legally or ethically, once the bids were submitted.

Although it would be desirable to consider maintenance costs in determining the successful bidder on this type of equipment, doing so is difficult, if not impracticable, for at least two reasons. First, equipment and vehicle manufacturers are frequently coming out with new models, and neither they nor the purchaser have maintenance costs on such models. Second, cities and counties often prefer to do their own maintenance, and manufacturers and dealers will not commit themselves to a cost ceiling for maintenance work they do not control.

Bid evaluation formulas have been developed and used by local governments for a number of items, particularly motor equipment. So, before a government runs out and reinvents the wheel, its officials should contact the National Institute of Governmental Purchasing, which maintains an information clearinghouse for public purchasing agencies that belong to NIGP.

Most life-cycle cost bid evaluation formulas fall far short of establishing a true cost of ownership, but they do provide a wider basis for comparing competing products or services than would simply looking at purchase prices. Jurisdictions that use this approach, however, must state their intent and approach and then proceed exactly as stated.

Value purchasing bid evaluation   Similar in approach to life-cycle cost bid evaluation, value purchasing bid evaluation rewards a bidder for offering a product that has "more on the average" of a desired characteristic but is priced competitively. Life-cycle cost bid evaluation considers one or more additional costs of owning an item, but value purchasing bid evaluation considers one or more additional values that a jurisdiction would get if it purchased a particular bidder's product. Actually, as is shown below, a bid evaluation formula can reflect a jurisdiction's desire to consider both the costs and the value of owning a particular item.[11]

To illustrate how a "value" can be determined objectively, assume that a jurisdiction wanted its portable air compressor to be quiet as well as energy efficient. It then would modify the formula described earlier to read:

EBP = $P + FC - VNR$, where:

EBP = Evaluated bid price

P = Purchase price

FC = Projected fuel costs

VNR = Value of noise reduction.

In addition to what was stated earlier, the jurisdiction would have to indicate in the invitation for bids how noise output would be measured (in decibels, A scale), and it would have to state:

1. That bidders would be required to submit, with their bids, a noise output level for the current make and model they were offering to sell to the jurisdiction.
2. That this noise level output would be based on a single specified procedure (the U.S. Environmental Protection Agency Air Compressor Noise Test Procedure).
3. That the value of noise reduction would be calculated in accordance with a stated formula, such as:

VNR $= Y (P_{AV}) (N_n - N)$, where:

VNR $=$ Value of noise reduction

Y $=$ The percentage of the P_{AV} (see below) by which the jurisdiction would reward the bidder (for bid evaluation purposes only) for each decibel that his/her unit is quieter than the loudest unit offered responsively

P_{AV} $=$ The average of actual bid prices of the responsive bidder

N_n $=$ The noise level output of the noisiest unit offered responsively

N $=$ The noise level output of the unit for which the VNR is being calculated.

4. That *EBP* would be the basis for contract award.
5. That any bidder who failed to provide the required noise level output data would not be considered for contract award.
6. That the jurisdiction reserved the right to conduct its own tests to verify the test data submitted by the bidder, with the understanding that the costs of tests that did not substantiate the bidder's submittal would be borne by the bidder.

Once a jurisdiction has stated in the bid invitation its intention to consider the value of noise reduction in determining the lowest bidder and has explained how it will do so, it must do so.

An actual bid evaluation taken from a purchase of portable air compressors by Salt Lake City is shown in Figure 9–3. Salt Lake City considered both the projected cost of fuel and the value of noise reduction, along with price, in its bid evaluation formula.

Noise is the only characteristic for which governments have assigned a value in bid evaluation, but this will not remain the case for long. One major manufacturer of reflective sheeting is exploring the feasibility of encouraging local governments and state agencies to reward bidders for (1) offering sheeting that exceeds their minimum requirements for reflectivity, and (2) offering additional warranty periods beyond that required. A southern California city is also encouraging the state of California to consider the "value of cleaner air" in its purchases of automobiles, trucks, and heavy equipment.

Value incentive contracting This infrequently used form of value analysis is applied after a contract has been awarded but is based in, and guided by, a value incentive clause (VIC) that is included in the solicitation document. The VIC encourages the contractor (who has "won" the contract award on the basis of the requirements and conditions stated in the solicitation document) to pro-

"Raw" bids

Bidder	Manufacturer	Noise level (dbA)	Fuel consumption (gal./hr.)	Price
A	Atlas-Copco	76.0	2.214500	$10,598
B	Ingersoll-Rand	76.0	2.381375	10,627
C	LeRoi-Dresser	74.5	2.898800	10,189
D	Sullair	76.0	2.690300	10,905

"Revised" bids

Bidder	Price	(−) Value of noise reduction	(+) Cost of energy	Evaluated bid price
A	$10,598	$ 0.00	$34,546.20	$45,144.20
B	10,627	0.00	37,149.48	47,776.48
C	10,189	317.40	45,221.28	55,092.88
D	10,905	0.00	41,968.68	52,873.68

pose to the purchasing agency (in the form and manner established in the VIC) a better, less costly alternative to performing the required function "without impairing needed performance or quality of the product or service." Such a proposal, generally known as a value change proposal (VCP), may either be rejected or accepted and implemented by the purchasing agency, in the manner established in the VIC. If it is accepted and implemented, the government and the contractor "share" the savings (again, in the amount and manner established in the VIC), but the purchasing agency is under no obligation to accept a VCP.

Use of value incentive contracting has been confined primarily to the federal government, but in at least one instance a state government also implemented this form of value analysis. It is, however, unlikely that value incentive contracting will become a trend at any level because *most* of the products used by federal, as well as state and local, agencies are "off the shelf," standard items rather than items specially manufactured to fit particular needs. Nevertheless, there may be some special applications (such as the construction of a new facility) where value incentive contracting may be used to save money and possibly energy.

The Office of Federal Supply and Services, U.S. General Services Administration, has used value incentive contracting to save energy and money. In two instances, that large purchasing agency accepted value change proposals after manufacturers of air conditioners for computer rooms modified their products to achieve energy savings.[12]

Make or buy decisions for services Local governments are relying increasingly on private contractors to provide public services, many of which were previously provided in-house.[13] It is essential that local government officials make their decisions to provide services—either in-house or by outside contract—through a process that is both practicable and as impartial, rational, and formal as possible. The National Institute of Governmental Purchasing suggests a five step process:

1. Define the service in terms of the jurisdiction's broad goals, its specific requirements, and how the performance of those requirements will be evaluated.
2. Establish a case for providing the service in-house and by contract, considering the advantages and the disadvantages in both cases.
3. If in-house delivery is a feasible option, develop an in-house bid or

proposal on behalf of the department that is providing, or would provide, the service.

4. If contract delivery is a feasible option, develop a solicitation document and obtain offers (i.e., bids or proposals).

5. Evaluate both the in-house offer and the offer of the best qualified private contractor, in order to select the best provider.[14]

The city of Phoenix, Arizona, comes very close to conforming to this ideal approach.[15]

Some of the factors, aside from direct costs, that should be considered in make-or-buy decisions for services are legal constraints against in-house delivery or contracting out; possible resistance by certain interest groups; the ability of the jurisdiction, and of private firms, to provide the service, and their interest in doing so; the extent to which the in-house service (current or planned) can be defined and costed; and the capacity of the jurisdiction's staff to administer an outside contract.[16]

Lease versus purchase decisions   Recent years have witnessed a dramatic increase in lease/purchasing by local governments because of increasing difficulties in financing growth. This option allows many jurisdictions to obtain capital equipment despite tight budgets. The factors that the public works director, the finance director, and the purchasing agent should consider in determining whether to lease, lease/purchase, or buy a piece of equipment outright include those shown in Figure 9–4.

Scheduling

Purchasing should work with the using departments to establish an annual buy schedule for items the departments know they will need during the coming year. The schedule should include the date the using department will need the item; the date the contract will be awarded; the date that bids or proposals will be closed; the deadline date for requisitions; and a description of the item (or items).

Establishing contracts

The next step in the procurement process involves establishing contracts for goods and services by developing the bidders list, obtaining bids or proposals, evaluating the bids or proposals, and making the award.

Figure 9–4
Considerations
in lease, lease/purchase,
or buy decision.

In favor of lease or lease/purchase	Against lease or lease/purchase
Debt limit has been approached or reached	Local laws prohibit lease or lease/purchase
Chance for passage of bond issue is unlikely	Political opposition to either or both approaches
Useful life of item or changing technology makes bond issuance inappropriate	Equity considerations dictate the outright ownership of the asset
Cost of items is not large enough to justify bond issuance	Jurisdiction lacks the expertise to structure a lease or lease/purchase agreement
Duration of use does not warrant outright purchase	The "nonsubstitution" clause limits the jurisdiction's flexibility

Bidders list

Local governments must have an acceptable and broad list of vendors from whom to solicit bids or proposals; such a list is essential to fostering a competitive environment. There are, however, two schools of thought on just who should be included on the bidders list. One school says that *any* supplier should be included, and the other, that bidders should be prequalified (or screened) before they are put on the list. From a practical standpoint, some form of prequalification probably is necessary to keep bids or proposals to a manageable number, *but*, jurisdictions that prequalify must remember that they cannot preclude vendors who are not on their bidders lists from bidding.

Whether bidders lists are prequalified or not, they should be set up in accordance with a commodity coding system that organizes products and services by class and item. The commodity coding system will facilitate automation of the purchasing function, facilitate ordering, and provide data for statistical analyses. Two organizations have developed commodity coding systems for use by local jurisdictions and state agencies in organizing bidders lists and commodity files for automated procurement. One of the organizations is NIGP, which also has developed a software package that local governments can use with desktop computers to maintain bidders lists, select vendors for mailings, and keep track of performance changes.[17] The other is BidNet, an affiliate of the Dun & Bradstreet Corporation. BidNet's primary business is to notify vendors of upcoming purchases of their products or services by state and local governments.

Obtaining bids or proposals

Three basic methods are used in the competitive acquisition of supplies and services. Although the terminology will vary from state to state and jurisdiction to jurisdiction, these methods include competitive sealed bidding, competitive sealed proposals, and informal competitive bidding.

These three methods of "source selection" are discussed in this section. Requisitions and specification development are also discussed briefly.

What are bids and proposals?
"Bids" and "proposals" are terms that often are used interchangeably to describe offers by a vendor to provide a product or service. There is, however, a difference in the meaning of the two terms.

A bid is an offer that is made, and accepted, essentially on the basis of comparative price. The bidder agrees by its bid to perform without condition or reservation in accordance with the purchase specification, delivery or performance schedule, and all other terms and conditions of the invitation for bids.

A proposal is an offer made by a vendor in response to a request for proposal (RFP). The bidder submits price and other information requested by the jurisdiction, with the understanding that the contract will be awarded through the comparative evaluation procedure stated in the RFP. Proposal evaluation procedures allow jurisdictions to "rank" offers based on differing price, quality, and contractual factors. Quality factors generally include technical and performance capability, and the content of the technical proposal.

Competitive sealed bidding   Competitive sealed bidding is the method most often used by local governments for acquiring goods, services, and construction. It provides for award of the contract to the lowest responsive and responsible bidder whose bid price is lowest, thereby making the bid evaluation process more objective than it is when competitive sealed proposals (see below) are evaluated.

Competitive sealed bidding, which *does not* include negotiations with bidders after bids are opened, is normally used when:

Clear and adequate specifications are available.

Two or more responsible bidders are willing to do business with the government in accordance with the government's requirements and criteria.

The dollar value of the purchase is large enough to justify to both buyer and seller the expense associated with competitive sealed bidding.

Sufficient time is available for the solicitation, preparation, and evaluation of sealed bids.

Even though competitive sealed bidding is the easiest method to audit, there are certain circumstances under which this method may not be practical. Provided that they have the legal authority to do so, jurisdictions may find that multistep competitive sealed bidding, or requesting competitive sealed proposals, is more appropriate.[18]

Contracting for professional services From 1975 to 1984, the American Bar Association, with input from the National Institute of Governmental Purchasing (NIGP), the National Association of State Purchasing Officials (NASPO), and other groups, developed its *Model Procurement Code for State and Local Governments.* Although both NIGP and NASPO endorsed the concept of the ABA Code "with discretion in adoption responsive to the particular requirements of the jurisdiction," they took exception to two key points in the model statute.

These were the recommendation in Section 2-302 of Article 2, "Procurement Organization," that the authority to contract for "certain" professional services (e.g., accountants, clergy, physicians, lawyers, dentists) be lodged outside the central procurement agency, and the recommendation in Article 5, "Procurement of Construction,

Architect-Engineer and Land Surveying Services," that such surveying services be procured through a special, less price-competitive method commonly known as the "Brooks Bill" Approach.

The two professional purchasing organizations argued that the standard procurement methods set forth in Article 3, "Source Selection and Contract Formation," were fully adequate and most appropriate for procuring any and all services. NIGP and NASPO do not maintain that all services should be competitively bid, with awards always being made to the responsive and responsible bidder offering the lowest price to the government. Rather, their argument is that price always should be considered *up front*, in conjunction with other stated evaluation factors, in the award of *all* service contracts, including architect-engineers and other consultants.

Multistep competitive sealed bidding Multistep (generally, two-step) sealed bidding is a variant of the competitive sealed bidding method. It may be used when a jurisdiction wishes to award a contract on the basis of price, but available specifications are inadequate or too general to permit full and free competition without technical evaluation and discussion. It is a multiphased process that combines elements of both the request for proposals method (in the first phases) and "regular" competitive sealed bidding (in the final phase).

The first phase consists of one or more requests for information, or unpriced technical offers. The second phase resembles competitive sealed bidding. Bidders who submitted technically acceptable offers in the first phase are invited to submit sealed bids based on their technical offers. The contract is awarded to the lowest responsive and responsible bidder. Multistep bidding, if used properly and within appropriate circumstances, can introduce price competition into purchases of complex items.[19]

Competitive sealed proposals   If a jurisdiction has to purchase relatively new technology or a nonstandard item, it may choose to request competitive sealed proposals *if* its laws permit it to do so. Some reasons for going this route are:

The contract needs to be other than a fixed-price type.

Oral or written discussions may need to be conducted with offerors concerning the technical and price aspects of their proposals.

Offerors may need the opportunity to revise their proposals, including price.

The award may need to be based on a "comparative evaluation" that takes differing price, quality, and contractual factors into account.

Jurisdictions should be sure that they have the ability to use this approach fairly and effectively before they actually request sealed proposals. This method provides more flexibility than competitive sealed bidding, but it also allows more room for error.[20]

Informal competitive bidding (small purchases)   When a need arises for an item that has a dollar value less than that of the statutory minimum for sealed bidding, governments should still seek as much competition as possible. Although telephone bids are a good approach, written informal bids (usually in the form of a letter) are even better because they help resolve disputes with vendors and provide suitable documentation for audits. Governments that obtain informal bids should be sure to document the following information every time: the name of the firm quoting the price, the name of the individual quoting the price, the "make" and model offered, the unit price, the payment terms, and the promised delivery date.[21]

Requisitions and specifications   Good requisitions and specifications are fundamental to good public purchasing. Requisitions are the means by which the using agency communicates its needs to purchasing. Specifications are the means by which governments "tell" bidders what is required, and the means by which governments determine whether they have received what was asked for.

Requisitions are used to inform the purchasing agency of a using agency's needs, to identify the products or services required, and, in some cases, to give the purchasing agency the written certification that funds are available to pay for the item. All requisitions should show the information listed in Figure 9–5.

Figure 9–5 Basic items to be included in purchase requisitions.

1. Requisition number
2. Date
3. Department and name of contact person
4. Product or class identification number (if the local government uses a standard classification or codification system)
5. Item description and recommended specification
6. Statement of what the item will be used in, or functional purpose of item
7. Quantity
8. Possible vendors (advisory only)
9. Estimated cost
10. Account number to be charged
11. Delivery point and any special instruction (e.g., set in place and installation required, special rigging required, tailgate delivery, etc.)
12. Desired date of delivery
13. Certification of need and fund availability
14. Signature of authorized official (usually the department head)

The purchasing agency has a much better chance to be a service agency—to be of real help to public works and other departments—if departmental requisitions are accurate, complete, and on time. Departments can help their own cause by showing as clearly as possible what the requisitioned item is expected to do and by asking for a product or service that is readily available from commercial sources. It is helpful to show the product brands and models that are acceptable, always with the understanding that these are standards, not mandates. The purchasing agency can be of even more service if it prepares concise instructions on filling out requisitions; a checklist is the preferred format. If this information is not provided, then public works and other departments should work with purchasing to develop the information.

Intergovernmental cooperative purchasing Smaller cities should consider the benefits of intergovernmental cooperative purchasing (IGCP). IGCP enables cities, counties, and other jurisdictions with limited staff and financial resources to secure many of the advantages of centralized purchasing, including, most important, lower prices for goods and services and reduced administrative costs. Essen-

tially, IGCP refers to a variety of arrangements under which two or more governmental entities purchase a good or service from a supplier as a result of a single invitation for bids, or a single request for proposals. For additional information on how to set up or get involved with an ongoing IGCP program, contact the National Institute of Governmental Purchasing.

Specifications always are helpful, especially if professionally developed and tested. An efficient specification for a product or service will identify minimum requirements, allow competitive bidding, indicate the reproducible method for checking compliance with each specification requirement, and provide for an equitable contract award at the lowest possible cost.[22] Effective specifications depend not only on quality of content but also on consistent procedures, uniform formats, and inspection and testing (if necessary) of delivered items.

The format for specifications, if standardized and used consistently, will show bidders where to look for certain subjects and provide a checklist for using agencies to follow when developing final specifications. The specification format recommended by NIGP is as follows:

1. Scope and classification
2. Applicable publications
3. Requirements
4. Sampling, inspection, and test procedures
5. Preparation for delivery
6. Notes.

Performance specifications, which state what a product should do, should be used wherever possible instead of "brand-name-or-equal" specifications. For certain commercial products, however, public works and purchasing may not be able to justify the time and resources needed to develop a full-fledged specification. They may decide, perhaps because of the low dollar value represented, to use a brand-name-or-equal specification. The use of such specifications should be limited as much as possible because they tend to lessen objectivity in evaluating bids and making awards, provide unequal access and opportunity among bidders, and discourage competition.

Evaluating offers and awarding contracts

The topic of evaluation and award could be discussed at great length, but, for purposes of brevity, only two key points will be made.

First, contracts made in response to invitations for bids *should* be awarded to the responsible bidder whose bid is lowest in price and responsive to the invitation for bid. Second, contracts made in response to a request for proposal (with or without subsequent discussions) should be made to the responsible bidder whose offer is most responsive to the request for proposal if price and other factors are consistent with the request for proposal. The reader is referred to the NIGP text on *General Public Purchasing* for an in-depth discussion of this topic.[23]

Administering contracts

The final step in the purchasing process is often paid little heed by public jurisdictions despite its obvious importance. This step involves the following activities under the broad responsibility of ensuring that both parties to contracts live up to their obligations with respect to delivery and performance, inspection and testing, and payment.

Delivery and performance

Contract terms must clearly show when items are to be delivered and services are to be performed. Among the terms that must be addressed are the point, date, and time; different delivery places and receiving times, if appropriate (e.g., if more than one item is covered by the contract); and liquidated damages, if any, for nondelivery or late delivery.

If delivery problems develop, a jurisdiction's options include contacting the vendor's representative for assistance, initiating collect phone calls or telegrams, or (if things look hopeless) canceling the contract and applying the liquidated damages clause (if one was included in the contract). Several factors must be considered when deciding which action to take, including the needs and requirements of the user, contract terms, availability of the item(s) from other sources, and the time it would take to order the item(s) from another source.

Whatever action is taken should be fully documented. In some circumstances a local government may wish to accept partial deliveries or substitutions, but the conditions under which they will be accepted should be covered in the contract. Each decision regarding such acceptance should be made case by case on the basis of established policy.[24]

Inspection and testing

The importance of inspecting and (if necessary) testing products and of monitoring services seems obvious. Nevertheless, most jurisdictions have a haphazard approach to ensuring that they get what they have paid for. Governments therefore should establish policy and procedures for checking goods at the time of receipt to assure compliance with specifications and requirements for quantities and packaging, and to detect any damage or defects.

Depending on the item, it may also be necessary to perform in-house tests or to have an outside laboratory perform tests on behalf of the jurisdiction. Gasoline is an example of an item that should be tested upon receipt to ensure that it contains the correct blend of components.

The following points should be followed in inspection and testing:

1. Contract terms and conditions should clearly indicate how and under what circumstances inspections will be made and what tests will be performed.
2. Specifications should clearly indicate the name of the test procedure that is to be used, if testing is or may be performed.
3. Inspection and testing will cost money, but it is important, especially if failure to detect defects can result in equipment failure, injury, or death.
4. Inspection and testing must be thoroughly documented.[25]

Payment

There are several methods for paying invoices for goods and services. Certain conditions offer advantages to both the jurisdiction and the seller, depending on which method is used. Briefly, the methods include:

Full payment, which is self-explanatory

Advance payment, which might facilitate the agreement or contractual operations

Partial payment, which would be related to the completion portion of a project or service, or to several separate deliveries under a single contract

Progress payments, which could be made to assure acceptable progress and performance under a contract

Assignment of payment, which provides for payment to someone other than the vendor.[26]

The key point for public works officials to remember is that payments should be made on time. Failure to pay bills on time often causes vendors to lose interest in bidding on the jurisdiction's contracts and gives vendors who have contracts no incentive to perform above the minimum, required level.

Conclusion

This chapter has briefly described a complex and important service function for public works. Purchasing, when properly administered, is a valuable partner. Purchasing can help public works provide the very best service possible—in spite of complex and onerous laws, regulations, and procedures governing the purchasing activity in local government—*if* purchasing and public works put aside their self-interests and sit down together to resolve their common problems.

1   Harry Robert Page, *Public Purchasing and Materials Management* (Lexington, Mass.: Lexington Books, 1980), p. xiii.
2   Russell A. Forbes, *Centralized Purchasing: A Sentry at the Tax Exit Gate*, rev. ed. (New York: National Association of Purchasing Agents, 1941).
3   National Association of Counties, "The Case for Cooperative or Centralized Purchasing," *Information and Education Service Report*, no. 17 (1962), p. 1.
4   For further information, see National Institute of Governmental Purchasing, Inc., *Public Procurement Management* (Falls Church, Va., 1985).
5   National Association of State Purchasing Officials, prepared by NASPO and Peat, Marwick, Mitchell and Co., *State and Local Government Purchasing*

(Lexington, Ky., 1975), p. D.15–16.
6   National Institute of Governmental Purchasing, Inc., *General Public Purchasing* (Falls Church, Va., 1977), p. 79.
7   This discussion is based on Page, *Public Purchasing and Materials Management*, pp. 175, 177–78.
8   National Institute of Governmental Purchasing, Inc., *Public Purchasing and Materials Management* (Falls Church, Va., 1983), pp. 106–7.
9   Ibid., p. 107.
10 Ibid.
11 This example is based on a bid evaluation procedure developed by the National Institute of Governmental Purchasing, Inc., during the "Buy Quiet" Program. Buy Quiet was a joint effort of the NIGP and the National League of Cities, directed at help-

ing cities buy quieter, better equipment through the competitive bidding process.

12 National Institute of Governmental Purchasing, Inc., *Public Purchasing and Materials Management*, p. 111. A sample value incentive clause is available from NIGP.

13 Martha A. Shulman, *Alternative Approaches for Delivering Public Services*, Urban Data Service Reports, vol. 14, no. 10 (Washington, D.C.: International City Management Association, October 1982).

14 National Institute of Governmental Purchasing, Inc., *Public Purchasing and Materials Management*, pp. 187–97.

15 Mark Hughes, "Contracting Services in Phoenix," in *Public Management*, vol. 64, October 1982, pp. 2–4.

16 National Institute of Governmental Purchasing, Inc., *Public Purchasing and Materials Management*, p. 192.

17 For additional information on the class-item code and the software package for purchasing, contact the National Institute of Governmental Purchasing, Inc., 115 Hillwood Avenue, Falls Church, Virginia, 22046.

18 National Institute of Governmental Purchasing, Inc. *Public Purchasing and Materials Management*, pp. 119–20.

19 Ibid., pp. 120–21.

20 Ibid., pp. 121–26.

21 National Institute of Governmental Purchasing, Inc., *General Public Purchasing*, p. 126.

22 Ibid., p. 47.

23 Ibid., pp. 127–39.

24 Ibid., pp. 142–46.

25 Ibid., pp. 146–49.

26 Ibid., pp. 150–51.

Part two:
Public works
operations

Engineering and contract management

With this chapter the book turns to the technical and operational aspects of managing public works. It is appropriate to begin this part of the book with a discussion of engineering and contract management because engineering underlies almost all public works activities and because good contract management helps to ensure the successful use of public improvements once they are built. Engineering, technical, and economic decisions affect long-term operation and maintenance costs and the nature and timing of major rehabilitation and replacement. Although public works engineering still focuses on traditional tasks and services such as design, surveying, maintenance, and operations, the complexity of government today calls for integrity, skill, ingenuity, community awareness, and administrative ability in this profession. Furthermore, for public works, engineering generally includes architecture.

The purpose of this chapter is to examine five areas of local public works engineering and contract management:

The planning and design process

Construction management (including inspection)

Surveys, maps, and records

Engineering management and private activity

Retention and use of consultants.

All five areas are affected by financial, legal, ethical, planning, environmental, sociological, and political factors. Without professional integrity, good management, and attention to proper procedures, any of these factors could embroil the public works department in controversy.

Public works engineering represents more than just a linkage of economics and science. A broader definition would be: the application of scientific, economic, and management principles to the solution of physical, service, and system problems to implement community plans, meet community goals, and achieve optimum costs of construction, operation, and maintenance.

Engineering and contract management for local public agencies must deal with and coordinate a wide variety of facilities and activities that are often directly related or mutually dependent. Emphasis must be placed on both economy and competence when choosing between in-house forces or outside firms.

Local public works engineering is concerned with streets, bridges, alleys, sewers, drainage, water supply and distribution, wastewater treatment, public buildings, parks, lighting, traffic engineering, parking, and solid waste management. In addition, it may be directly involved in or play an advisory or oversight role for other activities such as gas and electric utilities, public transportation, airports, and communications. Coordination of engineering and contracts (both internally and externally) maximizes savings and convenience, minimizes conflict and disruption, and is expected by elected officials and the public. State laws establish most of the basic powers and duties that govern public works engineering and contract administration for the different types of agencies.

The top public works managers are seldom free from considerations of engineering and contract management even though only a small portion of their work time is devoted to purely technical subjects. Generally speaking, they must have a working technical knowledge of all facets of the agency's public works activities, and they must be expert in at least a few of them. The department may be engaged in report preparation, investigations, survey and geotechnical work, capital improvement program and project planning (both long and short range), engineering design, construction contract administration, inspection and quality control, the development of standards and procedures, map and records management, advising other governmental units and the public, expert witness appearances, benefit assessments, right-of-way determination and acquisition, administration of land subdivisions, emergency operations, and other related work. There are important interrelations between many of these tasks, even though the work may be done by agency personnel, contractors, or consultants. Citizens, businesses, and legislators will be daily participants and commentators as the department discharges its responsibilities.

Engineering for operation and maintenance is more than just design and construction. Managers of line divisions such as street maintenance and water must have some engineering ability; for further information and assistance they may rely on others within the agency or on consultants. As a manager and advisor, each agency engineering administrator must strive for consistency, uniformity, and harmony of engineering policy and technical procedures throughout the various operating and staff units of the organization. Public works engineers must provide advice on such matters as the safety of older buildings, sewage flow problems, and optimum performance of energy systems. During emergency operations they may be called upon for comments and advice by elected officials, the chief administrator, fire and police departments, and others, and they usually have to respond quickly, without the degree of thought and investigation that would ordinarily be desirable.

The design and construction linkage shows the total interdependence between design and construction management (especially inspection), because an inadequacy in one hampers or causes failure in the other. Local public works managers must ensure that cooperation, coordination, and communication exist between design and construction personnel and processes.

The use of staff versus outside services is a perennial question for public works managers since one of their vital functions is to formulate recommendations to the legislative body on in-house work and outside services. An agency may use contractors or its own forces (subject to applicable law) to do its construction, and there are advantages and disadvantages to each.

With agency forces, plans and specifications may be simplified, construction can be more easily controlled, and inspection can usually be done by the crew supervisor. However, the agency must buy or lease expensive construction equipment, handle personnel problems, and be concerned about matching staffing and activity levels.

With contract construction, special knowledge, techniques, and equipment are more readily available; the agency takes fewer risks; and sealed competitive bids generally produce a firm and realistic price. On the other hand, plans and specifications must be more explicit (and may be quite complicated, even on small jobs); bidding and awards take time and create added expense, and the work must be carefully inspected.

Decisions whether to use consultants or staff for planning and design involve similar considerations. The staff will be more familiar with local conditions and project goals, but consultants offer special expertise and wider experience; consultants fit better into workload fluctuations, but staff are still needed to work with and monitor the consultants. In any case, clear and consistent policies should be established regarding the retention of both contractors and consultants.

Education and training of staff is a continuous process. Agency engineers and other technical personnel must be fully informed about topics connected with their duties and responsibilities.

Engineers usually acquire formal training from an accredited college or university where, besides learning about technical subjects, they receive some instruction in the humanities, communications, planning, economics, and environmental science. More emphasis is now placed on graduate study in engineering or public administration for persons desiring to advance to top management jobs. Most agencies require professional registration above the lowest levels of technical management (and for the heads of operating divisions in larger organizations).

Technicians (surveyors, inspectors, delineators, aides, etc.) normally have some formal training from a trade school or two-year college, and they have specialized in calculation, drafting, and the use of survey instruments. Experienced technicians can perform simple or routine design and plan checking under the supervision of an engineer. Both engineers and technicians must be familiar with public works computer applications. The public works director must support and encourage management and promote the technical advancement of subordinates through supplemental education, training, and professional registration.

The planning and design process

Local government planning and engineering depend heavily on each other. Public works provides support and information, especially with respect to public infrastructure requirements, during the preparation of general and specific community plans. It also provides advice on the relative feasibility of development in different areas under consideration. Once adopted, those plans form the basis for systems, such as roads, water, and sewers, and will be used to develop long-range implementation and financing programs and to select shorter range capital improvements. The planning and design process should be viewed as a continuous flow, even though time frames may be long and a number of projects stem from the same planning base. Because of the nature of some systems and fund sources, annual work programs may contain either an array of projects (streets, for example) or simply free-standing or one-time projects (such as fire stations and convention complexes). Whatever the case, the purpose of capital improvement projects is to implement adopted plans and achieve specific community goals, such as economic development, urban renewal, and health and safety.

Management of capital improvement programs

The capital improvement program is very important to elected officials because it represents a large allocation of overall resources, and highly visible projects can be pointed to during election campaigns. Timely and successful completion is politically positive, whereas delays and problems are embarrassing to legislators. Therefore, effective capital improvement delivery can greatly influence the reputation of public works.

Public works is often asked to carry out most of the approved capital improvement program. In particular, public works proposals should consider need and the opportunities for special savings or coordination; rehabilitation and reconstruction are often given preference in order to preserve existing investments. A realistic program, when it is being formulated, requires engineering expertise in a number of areas: costing, scheduling, coordination, project scope refinement, and right-of-way needs. Top officials must be interested and directly involved, to ensure that the planning and design process is carefully controlled through the identification of key steps, assignment of competent staff or consultants, and establishment and monitoring of schedules. A project manager should be identified at the very beginning of the process so that problems can be attended to as soon as they crop up, and liaison can be established with the many others whose support and actions are critical to project implementation, such as financial and legal people, regulatory authorities, right-of-way agents, utility representatives, and citizen groups.

Almost every project has some activities that cannot be directly controlled by the engineer, such as securing data on existing underground installations and timely adjustment of, or additions to, facilities owned by others prior to project construction. Cash flow and debt financing time frames must be managed, as must regulatory and other clearances. Furthermore, every project and system plan must be fully considered and developed in its physical, environmental, and community setting. Inadequate research or investigation or attempts to bypass or minimize procedural steps usually cause serious delay and amount to a wasted effort. Environmental and citizen participation requirements demand special management attention. Lead times, scheduling, and proper sequences are so important that the critical path method (CPM) or program evaluation and review technique (PERT) may have to be used.

Project planning

The purpose of project planning is to acquire adequate information to support sound project decisions for the short and long terms. Project planning can include an entire system, phased implementation, or a single site, and it may combine several types of facilities that would ordinarily be handled separately. Project planning sometimes identifies alternatives for a final selection to be made at a later stage.

Many questions must be answered in the project planning process. Who are the users? Will they be using the facility as individuals or as groups? Who will operate and maintain the facility? Will it serve the public directly or be a support facility? How much service or capacity must be provided, and for how far into the future? Should future expansion capabilities be built in, and can they be based on accurate predictions or just a contingency allowance? What laws, regulations, and standards affect its design, and what are the relevant public safety and environmental considerations? Is the budget fixed or flexible, and how does this relate to the scope of the desired project? What are the implications of any unusual site conditions that are present or suspected? Some of these are technical questions and some pertain to policy, but the answers will largely determine the usefulness and present and future costs of the finished product.

Considering future needs   For some capital projects, capacity is relatively easy to add later at a reasonable cost (as in the case of wastewater treatment digesters), but in others difficult economic and policy issues have to be settled first. Suppose, for example, that a new trunk sewer is being designed, and that once the line is sized and built its capacity will be fixed, so that a whole new line would be needed to add future capacity. Public policy dictates that fees from new development in the service area must be the only funding source, so a difficult issue will be to reconcile the twenty-year land use (and therefore fee) horizon with the fifty-year minimum useful life of the new trunk line. Decisions on policy questions such as this influence the acquisition and use of project technical data.

Background information   Usually the first step in project or system planning is to assemble existing data from records, studies, and investigations. Although more facts than are available might be useful, some information is not cost-effective to obtain. For example, information about the precise locations of underground lines could be valuable, but it is more practical to rely on owner's records supplemented by actual field checks of critical points. Another essential planning and design element, criteria for sizing overall systems and individual projects, can be taken from applicable standards used by others or can be based on local experience.

Specific design criteria should be selected and adopted for all common types of facilities (streets, sewers, water, lighting, etc.). Beyond technical and site data, information on user needs must be secured and a "team" approach employed to ensure cooperation between the planner/designer and facility user/operator so as to avoid later problems. Users should provide statements of project needs and objectives, should participate in decision making that could affect meeting their goals (including consultant selection), and, if appropriate, should sign off at landmark points in the process. Background information for planning and design includes participation by citizens and community organizations and conditions resulting from approval of permits and other clearances.

Clearance and participative steps   Good project management means getting issues and problems out in the open early so that they can be resolved within the schedule and so that no surprises will be in store at public hearings. Whenever possible, land use and environmental clearances and required permits should be obtained during the planning phase, as should special aesthetic or historical approvals.

Most clearance and regulatory entities will be helpful if approached during the project's formative stages. They can provide information on application requirements, schedules, hearings, and the like. Data on size, appearance, function, location, and impacts usually have to be submitted before clearances can be processed and permits obtained. If these tasks are approached on a positive note, approval time and problems can be minimized. Further, many federal and state regulations and local policies mandate citizen participation and comment, which are best approached with an open attitude. Valuable ideas often surface at informational meetings, and it is much easier to deal with concerns and explanations while the project is in the formative stage rather than later when the design is nearly finished.

Principal affected parties such as the development industry, other units of government, and organized citizen or business groups should be involved as soon as possible and kept up to date as the project progresses. Such groups can be most influential, and their support at hearings or in reports usually brings credit to the public works department. Because project planning may not always uncover all the important information available from citizens, further contacts during design can have beneficial effects on construction. In one case, for example, direct contact with affected property owners during the design phase appeared to be the sole reason that no complaints were filed when contractor delays and rock blasting became unavoidable. Well-handled community involvement adds a human touch to technical factors in managing a successful project.

Project design

The purpose of design is to produce enough defined information to allow agency or contract forces to do the construction work with the confidence that the intended objectives will be achieved within the anticipated cost. Project planning information is used in design, but it must be supplemented with data from field surveys (control and physical data) and soils investigations, as well as facts concerning detailed codes and regulations, mandated or adopted standards, and utility conditions. The designer must pay particular attention to developing adequate data on special site conditions and unique project features.

Drawings and specifications are the two main outputs of the design process (estimates are prepared too, but as a measure of the harmony of design and budget). Standard drawings and specifications are used for common items of construction but special drawings and specifications must usually be prepared for each particular project.

Drawings The drawings must be clear and concise, and after the project has been completed they should be revised to reflect "as built" conditions. Standard drawings for such items as curbs and gutters, manholes, and fire hydrants offer considerable savings in project plan preparation and ensure compatibility and uniform quality throughout the system (standard drawings of other agencies can sometimes be adapted at minimal cost).

Specifications The specifications usually consist of general conditions, standard construction provisions, and special provisions.

General conditions refer to the basic legal and operating rules under which the contractor and agency will work. These sections cover the respective rights and obligations of the parties, authority of the engineer, progress and final payments, money retentions, completion time versus damages, safety, change orders, and suspension or termination of the contract. Matters applicable to each project (actual time allowances and liquidated damage amounts, for example) are placed in the bid documents or special provisions.

The general conditions must be preapproved by the agency's legal counsel, and in some instances portions may have to be modified (in the special provisions) or an entirely different set used to comply with certain laws or regulations. Some professional organizations have prepared "model" specifications that include general conditions, but these should be used with considerable care because they may be directed more toward the interests of a design consultant than those of public agency clients, and they probably do not adequately cover various requirements under which such agencies must operate.

Standard construction provisions set forth the requirements for items commonly used in construction such as asphalt, concrete, fencing, pipe, and so on. Because the general conditions or standard construction provisions seldom cover all the details or items needed for a given project, special provisions are used to state modifications, additions, or deletions.

Since the drawings may not always agree with the sections of the specifications, a precedence of documents is included in the general conditions; this often consists of (1) the special provisions, (2) the drawings, (3) the general conditions, and (4) the standard construction provisions. Typically, the specification of an item will contain all the information needed to ensure delivery of a product of the desired character and quality. Reference is often made to the published standards of the American Society for Testing and Materials. When numbers or descriptions from manufacturers' catalogs are being referred to, or some of the specifications have been prepared by others, make sure that the material is current, applicable to the subject project, not improperly restrictive, and readily available to bidders.

The purpose of drawings and specifications is to describe the work required fully and clearly, enhance bidding competition, and avoid undue expense to the agency for excess quality or unexpected maintenance or operation. A good rule to follow to minimize difficulties during construction is: "In case of a question in preparing plans and specifications, err on the side of *more* detail." In some areas, local governments work through chapters of the American Public Works Association or other groups to develop standard specifications and drawings tailored to their needs, which can create savings through common description of items and contractor appreciation of the greater uniformity in bidding.

Technical considerations in design

Design involves many decisions of a technical nature that require professional judgment. Reasonable care must be taken in making these decisions because the designer can be held professionally, legally, and personally responsible if the facility fails during construction or use. There is no substitute for detailed information and study when it comes to design decisions. A number of technical considerations must be taken into account:

1. Different, unusual, or mandated standards may apply.
2. Innovative new products or methods should not be ignored, and expertise and common sense must be applied in evaluating them to ensure confidence in both the ultimate cost and the soundness of the work.
3. Local handicapped interest groups should be consulted to enhance project usability and to avoid later controversy or revision.
4. Public facilities should be attractive because of their visibility. It is always appropriate to consider ways to enhance appearance (which often costs very little extra).
5. Mere compliance with environmental assessment procedures is not enough to ensure that a facility will be an environmental asset throughout its life. The designer must evaluate the project setting and its short- and long-range impacts and take reasonable steps to prevent problems.
6. Design alternatives should be compared with projected operation and maintenance of facilities. It is wise to seek the advice and assistance of line managers who will be responsible for the completed facility.
7. Cost tradeoffs should be made. Design of a system of fire stations is a prime example of *first* versus *long-term* costs because the amortized cost of land and building is much less than that of personnel and equipment over twenty or thirty years. Optimum locations are the key.
8. Increased public agency liability exposure requires careful study of ways to improve safety. It is far better to invest initially than to spend large amounts paying claims later.
9. Many projects are so large and complex that certain major questions cannot be adequately assessed with specialized advice. Retention of value engineering or construction management consultants to review and comment on methods, materials, and construction alternatives can pay big dividends at bid time.

Contract planning

Contract planning should be done thoroughly for each project. Careful preparation at this stage will facilitate the bidding process, award of contract, and construction. This process involves decisions on the kinds of pricing to be used, estimates, legal requirements, schedules, and special conditions for each project.

Contract pricing

There are several options for organizing project prices for bidding and eventual payment to the contractor.

With unit prices, the project is broken down into its distinctive elements by type of material or activity, and the amount of each item is estimated in an appropriate unit. Bidders quote a price per unit, and the full price is calculated by multiplying each unit by its related quantity and totaling the figures for all of the items. Prudent bidders will use their experience or their own computations to verify bid quantity estimates. Unit prices allow quantity adjustments to meet field conditions without pricing questions, but if a quantity has been miscalculated or a major segment of work can be completed early, a bidder can "unbalance" the unit prices, raising some and lowering others, within a total amount deemed low enough to secure the contract. Unbalancing provides a windfall for the contractor through unearned profit or early cash flow; either way, there is a potential disadvantage for the agency. Some items may be better paid under "extra work" (contractor's cost plus a set profit) to permit the construction manager to tailor the amount of activity to actual field needs; examples are job fencing, traffic control, and dust mitigation.

Lump sum pricing may be used for the entire work or for some items in an otherwise basically unit price contract. With lump sums, plans must be even more explicit than for unit price contracts, because bidders must estimate quantities of materials and assess work difficulty; a contingency is normally added to the bid to cover uncertainties. The main disadvantage of lump sum bidding is that sometimes the price has to be adjusted because of unexpected field conditions or the amount of work has to be changed. Supplemental unit prices can be requested for particular items so that changes can be made without causing a price dispute.

If additive or deductive alternate prices are used, project content can be increased or decreased to obtain the maximum work possible within the budget allocation (this is especially useful for lump sum projects). Bid documents must specify whether the award will be made on the base bid amount or the base adjusted for any selected alternates.

Contract payments can also be based on actual cost plus a fixed or sliding scale fee or percentage to cover profit and overhead, with a stated maximum. This arrangement is suitable for emergency work but is otherwise undesirable because it forces agencies to increase their monitoring and gives the contractor little incentive to control costs.

Bid documents must spell out any unusual circumstances related to payments that can affect bid prices and cash flow to the contractor. Some capital funding sources allow payment to the agency only when part or all of the work has been completed. If the finance officer cannot arrange interim financing so that the contractor can receive progress payments, bid prices will likely be higher to compensate for the contractor's carrying costs. Whether grant reimbursements are based on a percentage of an approved estimate, a percentage of the final cost, or a fixed amount, the degree of eligibility of some project elements may not be certain until an audit is made after the work has been completed. Because disallowed costs become the agency's sole responsibility, advice must be sought regarding acceptable levels of financial risk before bids are solicited.

The frequency of progress payments (usually monthly, although one may be skipped if little or no work has been done) and the time frame from the close of the estimate period to payment should be clearly stated. Public works agencies with a reputation for expediting payments often enjoy better-than-average bid price experience.

Estimates

As design proceeds, financing must be kept in mind because every project has a specific budget allowance. If, on one hand, the original capital program estimate is found to be simply inadequate, the design should not be carried too far without more money being approved. If, on the other hand, the budget is overly generous, the design must not become slipshod nor should features be added simply to use up all the funds.

Construction costs are usually predictable within an acceptable range, but when the overall budget is limited, unexpected right-of-way expenses can force an agency to scale back the scope of the project. It is critical that the best available data be used to prepare estimates. Because buildings and other lump sum projects are more difficult to estimate, some agencies retain professional estimators, particularly if debt financing must be secured. Intermediate estimates are important for keeping the design within the established budget as it progresses, and the final (or "engineer's") estimate is even more critical because it is used to evaluate the bids received for the project.

Legal and procedural requirements

In matters such as competition, payment of minimum wages, listing of subcontractors or suppliers, and amounts of work that can be undertaken with local forces, local bidding is usually governed by state law. Federal regulations sometimes supersede state and local requirements. Bid documents must clearly identify special items such as prequalification, affirmative action, or participation by designated groups. Legal counsel should advise on the bidding and award process to avoid last-minute problems.

Construction factors and time allowances   Construction planning should take account of factors which are critical to successful use of project plans and specifications and to meeting project schedules. During design, advice must be sought from agency construction management personnel and, if appropriate, from knowledgeable contractors. There must be a safe and practical way to accomplish the work involved; if a project is intended for construction by agency forces, their capabilities must be considered. Construction methods may be mandated or left up to the contractor, but where an innovative or unusual design has been selected, a usable method should be stated. Procedures for handling traffic also need to be spelled out for most work in public streets to ensure reasonable access to the site and other affected properties and to avoid public safety or convenience problems. Any conditions affecting hours of work, dust and noise control, or special worker protection must be detailed because they influence bid prices. If the contractor is permitted to offer alternate methods, materials, schedules, or sequences, the result can be shorter work times, less disruption, and even cost credits.

It is essential to set realistic time allowances that take into account the needs of the owner, the contractor, and the public. Too short a time will drive up bid prices or discourage potential bidders, whereas too long a time can inconvenience the public and cause unnecessary delays in using the facility. Contract time can be stated as a fixed date, calendar days, or working days. The latter two are the most common, but "working" must be defined. A monetary bonus can be provided for finishing ahead of the stated time if there is a clear public benefit; damages are normally assessed when the contractor fails to meet the deadline. If actual damages are difficult to determine, "liquidated" damages are used, expressed as a penalty of so many dollars per day of inexcusable overrun. When damages are assessed, controversy often arises because not all factors leading to delay (weather and strikes, for example) are within the control of the contractor. Even though reasons for excusable delay may be specified in the general conditions, there can be uncertainties and therefore dispute.

Fast track projects   Sometimes a "fast track" approach is used if a project is so urgent that construction must be started before the overall plans and specifications have been completed. In such cases the designer has the added burden of making sure that all the documents are coordinated because multiple contracts will almost always be required. Total construction cost can be expected to go up on a fast track project, and special problems may develop in debt financing if bonds must be sold before all bids are in and the total price is established. Fast track specifications usually make the agency responsible for some of the tasks normally done by a general contractor (such as site fencing, safety, access, scheduling, and contractor coordination).

Contract bidding and awards

The major steps in the bidding and award of a construction contract are soliciting bids, submitting bids, reviewing and evaluating bids, and awarding the contract. Because each step is concerned with plans and specifications, these must be made available to all interested firms to foster competition and to permit realistic costing. A refundable deposit can be requested to discourage any who are not seriously interested and to minimize losses on the cost of reproducing documents.

Soliciting bids

The agency makes its formal request for proposals in the form of a "notice to bidders." The notice includes the project title and location, date, time, and place for opening bids, how long bids will remain open for agency consideration, supplemental items to be submitted with the bid or immediately following the opening, the office to contact for information and for the plans and specifications. The notice will also specify that the agency reserves the right to accept or reject any bid if such action best serves the public interest. The notice is accompanied by forms for bidding and related lists and certificates.

Bidding periods must be long enough to meet with legal requirements and to enable bidders to cost the work and obtain quotations from specialty contractors and suppliers. If the time is too short, there will be fewer bidders (and therefore less competition), and higher bids if contingencies are added because of lack of confidence in price estimates. When large or complex projects are involved, the bidding plans of others must be taken into account since many contractors are limited in bonding capacity or are unwilling or unable to prepare too many large bids at one time. (Bid preparation is expensive, and contractors can only afford the effort if they see a reasonable chance of success.) Availability of the contract should be published widely through legal notices in newspapers with a broad circulation and mailed to contractors in the area. In addition, trade journals and technical publications can be used. The advertisements and legal notices include essentially the same information as the notice to bidders. Whatever method is used to request proposals, it must reach enough contractors to ensure active competition.

Bid forms and requirements   The bid form has spaces in which to enter the prices for each unit or a lump sum in the base bid and alternates. Bidders should be required to fill out all the spaces unless specific exceptions are made for partial bidding. Amounts should be entered in both words and figures to confirm the bidder's intentions (in case of conflict, the words should prevail). The notice can call for bids on the entire work or it can ask for separate bids in specialty areas such as plumbing or electrical work (which are then set out in distinct schedules); this arrangement allows the agency to choose the combination that best fits its needs. Spaces are provided for address, telephone, and license information and signature of an authorized agent or officer of the contractor.

Separate forms are furnished for listing subcontractors and suppliers (along with the work or material each is responsible for) and other data to be submitted with the bid. Such lists guard against "bid shopping" by the low bidder after the opening in an effort to increase profits. The contractor is normally required to do all work not listed under a sub-bid.

A bidder's bond is always required as a guarantee of good faith that the bidder will execute the contract if awarded; ten percent of the bid amount is usual. It may be a certified or cashier's check or a surety bond.

Participation by disadvantaged business enterprises (DBEs) Most federally assisted projects require participation by DBEs, as do many state and local projects. DBEs are firms owned and controlled by minorities or women. When applicable, the bid submittal must list DBE participants, the work each will do, and the related percentage of the total bid price. DBE lists can also be required only from the lowest bidder(s) within a day or two after the opening. In either case, problems can arise. If the lists come with the bids, efforts to contact potential DBEs can interfere with last-minute efforts to trim price. If the submittal arrives later, a low bidder who feels his or her bid was too low can escape without penalty simply by failing to document adequate participation or attempts to secure it.

Bidder prequalification If an agency is concerned about receiving proposals from irresponsible or unqualified contractors or if it wants special assurance regarding financial or technical capability, bidders can be prequalified. This takes extra time and effort (for solicitation and evaluation of qualifications statements), and it may lead to favoritism or may restrict competition if there are not enough finalists. Prequalification may also be subject to legal advertising requirements.

Prebid conference Prebid conferences are valuable for all but the smaller or less complicated projects as a means of explaining the work involved, the agency procedures and requirements, and any unusual circumstances or contract provisions. Attendance can be made optional or mandatory (the latter *must* be stated in the notice to bidders), but when it is optional, clarifications and answers to questions must be made available to all plan holders before the bid date.

Addenda It is preferable to make changes and clarify interpretations before bids are opened rather than attempt to adjust prices after the award. Addenda should be sent to all plan holders notifying them of significant interpretations, additions, deletions, modifications, and extension of the bid date. Addenda have the same force as other contract documents and for that reason cannot be issued so close to the bid deadline that they cannot be distributed to all concerned. Bidders must be required to submit a countersigned copy of all addenda with their proposals as verification that the changes were taken into account.

Bid openings

Bid openings should be held at a location convenient for bidders as well as other interested parties, such as the media. Sealed bids are accepted up to the hour set for opening, and any bids turned in after that time are returned unopened. No change is allowed in a bid once it is exposed, but upon the written request of a submitter, that proposal can be returned sealed prior to the deadline. Bid envelopes must be identified on the outside with the project and bidder's names. At the established hour, a designated official will open the envelopes one at a time in some appropriate order, announcing the bidder's name, bid total, any alternate prices, presence of the required bond, and any obvious exceptions taken. Once all bids have been opened and declared, attendees may request that unit prices and the names of subcontractors and suppliers from the apparent low bid be read. The bids are then taken under submission for review. All bid securities are retained until an award is made or the bids are rejected. Bonds and bids can lapse, however, if action is not taken within the time stated in the notice to bidders (bidders may agree to an extension if one is needed).

Review and recommendation Each bid must be reviewed for completeness and accuracy of figures and totals and compared with the final estimate. Decisions must be made regarding award or rejection of additive or deductive alternates, if any, and the lowest bid must be identified. If the low bid exceeds the final estimate, it can be accepted or all bids can be rejected, in which case the agency may wish to request new bids based on the same or modified plans. Minor irregularities may be overlooked, but major irregularities or exceptions normally disqualify the offending bids. Licensing, bid security, experience, capability, and reliability of the contractor are reviewed and verified.

Whereas award is usually made to the lowest responsible bidder, under disadvantaged business enterprise regulations this is changed to lowest "responsive" bidder because a successful bidder must offer a good price *and* demonstrate attainment of the required percentage of participation goals or document good faith efforts to do so. A lowest *responsible* bidder who fails to comply or show sufficient efforts may be bypassed in favor of a lowest *responsive* bidder.

Once all reviews are complete, a recommendation to the awarding authority can be formulated. Selection (for whatever reason) of other than the lowest bidder is potentially controversial and may require explanations to the awarding body, the media, and the public. Prior approval to award must be secured for certain federal or state funding.

Construction contract　After the award is announced, the successful bidder is sent a written notice and advised to make all further required submittals and be prepared to execute the contract. The contract sets forth details of the relations between the parties and includes, by reference, other documents that are part of the agreement, such as the plans and specifications and the verified bid with its attachments. Two contract bonds are usually required: one guaranteeing faithful contract performance (normally 100 percent of the contract amount) and the other ensuring payment of workers, suppliers, and subcontractors (in an amount specified in the bid notice or general conditions). An insurance certificate must be furnished showing specified amounts of coverage for liability, worker compensation, and property damage or loss (with the agency as a named insured). Once all contract documents have been approved by the attorney and executed on behalf of both owner and contractor, construction can begin.

Construction management

The purpose of construction management is to facilitate and control the execution of the contract so that the intended work will be completed within a reasonable time and within the planned expenditure. Inspection is the central element of construction management (see the next section) and, together with all the other elements, it requires care, integrity, patience, tact, expertise, and a willingness to approach the job as a team with the contractor. The best interests of both parties are served if no contract violations occur. Good management is just as important when agency forces do the work as they, too, must comply with the plans and specifications.

Except for small or uncomplicated projects, a preconstruction meeting is recommended to establish a good working basis. The contractor, subcontractors, major suppliers, affected utilities, and project and outside agency staffs should attend. Meeting minutes should be recorded, and they should include names, affiliations, addresses, and phone numbers for all attendees. The sequence of activities and schedule for the project should be discussed and all contract procedures outlined. Any problems or needs that have been identified should be brought up and dealt with immediately if possible.

Construction is then formally initiated with the issuing of a "notice to proceed" that states the time allowed to complete the contract (which normally starts on the date of the notice), the computed date of completion, and any intermediate dates noted in the specifications.

Coordination and monitoring

Construction managers have more complex responsibilities if there is more than one general contractor on the site, if another agency in the area also is doing work, or if the contractor must work around the agency's regular operations. Unless the agency has the necessary staff expertise, multiple contracts may be best handled by securing the services of a professional construction manager to assist with the "housekeeping," coordination, and other work usually done by a single general contractor. Some aspects of construction contracts almost always require regular monitoring; for example, payrolls are often reviewed so that compliance with minimum wage, affirmative action, and disadvantaged business enterprise provisions can be checked. Job safety is another ongoing concern that cannot be left entirely up to the contractor because of owner liability exposure; on large and very complex jobs, a separate safety inspector may be needed. Constant attention must also be given to proper traffic handling and noise, dust, and dirt control.

Communications Good communication between contractor and agency personnel expedites the project, and scheduled job meetings (with minutes kept) are one of the most effective ways to maintain it. Each side's authority must be clearly defined, and most questions, interpretations, and decisions should be made or confirmed in writing. It can be extremely difficult to resolve issues later if they are not recorded promptly. Although subcontractors and suppliers are seldom referred to in the contract, they will have to be contacted frequently, and when such contacts occur, a representative of the contractor should be present or the contractor should be fully briefed. All *instructions* must be given to the contractor.

Contract time Failure to meet contract completion dates is a common cause of disputes. Completion on schedule has definite advantages, including on-time income flow if the project is a revenue-producing facility, savings on short-term borrowing, ability to meet bond and other debt payments on schedule, and ability to open as promised. Delayed completions often bring public criticism that can be bitter if special events have to be postponed or canceled.

The contractor should report immediately anything that might cause delay, and the agency should respond by making every effort to resolve problems so as to maintain the schedule. The contractor is expected to place orders for equipment and materials early enough so that items will be available when needed. Prompt agency response to contractor submittals is essential. There should be an established agency policy on criteria and authority for granting time extensions.

Contractors cannot be held responsible for delays beyond their control, for example, because work done by separate parties (such as independent contractors, utilities, other agencies) was late or because of adverse weather or strikes. Most contracts call for damages for delays the contractor *could have* controlled. If the amount of damages is large or the delay is long, the contractor often may try to place blame on the agency, its staff, or others. Upon the advice of counsel, the agency may seek actual damages rather than the liquidated damages stated in the contract. As soon as an unacceptable delay becomes known, any damages assessed should be withheld from payments due.

Payments Payments to the contractor demand careful attention because a public trust is involved. Acceptable completed work is evaluated periodically on the basis of measurements, calculations, estimates, or job records, depending on the nature of the items. Compensation can be made for materials and equipment delivered to and stored securely on the site but not yet incorporated in the work. A percentage is deducted from each progress payment (to cover undiscovered defects or failure to pay bills), after which the balance, less previous payments, is paid to the contractor.

Changes to the contract

Unexpected site conditions or other unpredictable circumstances frequently necessitate modifying the contract during construction. This is done through a contract change order. The contract price may decrease, increase, or be unaffected, and the contract time may be modified.

A policy should be formally established to govern change orders for all projects and to authorize approvals by the public works director within stated limits (as an aid to keeping the work moving); in some cases, however, approval will have to be granted by a higher authority. Although change orders are best limited to those needed for proper completion of the construction work contemplated at the time of award, some agencies take a broader view. Change order integrity must be scrupulously maintained because change orders processed improperly or for improper purposes can arouse criticism and require legal investigation. If work costs are reduced, the order should contain an appropriate credit, but if they increase, they can be paid at bid, negotiated lump sum, or unit prices, or they can be based on the actual costs of personnel, equipment, and materials (extra work).

A change order form should be used, and no order should become effective until fully executed on behalf of both owner and contractor. Should the contractor refuse to sign an order for a needed change, contract provisions covering disputes will have to be utilized.

Special contract situations

Contracts can be the subject of claims, disputes, stop work orders, defaults, or terminations. If the contractor enters bankruptcy or otherwise abandons the work, the performance bond ensures that the work will be completed, usually through another contractor; in such cases the bonding company or deposit defrays any costs the owner incurs in restarting and finishing the work, including damages. If the owner terminates or suspends the contract, the contractor may be entitled to compensation for lost profits and unrecoverable costs.

A stop work order can be issued to suspend activity temporarily if weather, strikes, fund shortages, or other problems make it undesirable to keep work forces and agency staff at the site continuously. Depending on the circumstances, contract time may also be suspended, and damages may be due one of the parties. Disputes can arise over interpretations, instructions, the rejection of work or materials, delays, withheld payments, or other problems, and they often lead to claims for extra compensation. The "general conditions" to the contract usually specify procedures for the resolution of claims, such as negotiation or arbitration, because the cost and time inherent in litigation make it desirable to reach agreement as soon as possible. Legal counsel should always be consulted on contract conflicts.

Job records are important. They are a permanent file for future maintenance or remodeling reference; if conflicts should arise, the records must contain enough details to support the agency's position. Daily inspection diaries should record weather, activity under way, numbers and types of personnel engaged, safety or construction incidents, decisions and interpretations, meetings held, and job visitors. Both correspondence and measurement and payment records should be organized for easy retrieval. A final report is valuable to summarize project construction and to bring both good and bad job experiences to the attention of designers and inspectors.

Contract completion

Before completing the contract, it is useful to conduct a comprehensive "final" inspection with the contractor (and the facility user if appropriate). This inspection will produce a "punch list" of the remaining deficiencies, which, when corrected, will complete the contractor's obligations (although minor repairs or missing items that do not unreasonably delay or interfere with occupancy can be handled through a separate bonded agreement).

A notice of substantial completion should be prepared at the time the owner has beneficial use or occupancy, and any assessments for damages due to delay should then stop. In conjunction with final acceptance, the contractor must deliver any required warranties and equipment manuals and pay all outstanding project bills. A final payment then is prepared showing the total amount due the contractor, which may include a further brief retention of funds so that claims can be filed under mechanics lien laws.

Inspection

The purpose of inspection is to verify that work quality meets the intent and requirements of the plans and specifications and that the quantities of material used are reasonable (considering site conditions) in relation to the estimated amounts.

Construction inspectors are communicators, facilitators, and overseers with a great obligation to both owner and designer to ensure that the finished work meets all expectations. Inspectors must be firm but fair and use their authority properly. Although inspectors need some discretion to make adjustments and changes to meet field conditions, their sole *authority* rests in requiring compliance. All questions and interpretations that might affect design integrity must be referred to someone qualified to judge the matters involved (often, the designer). Inspectors must be thoroughly familiar with the plans and specifications and applicable laws and regulations, and be able to spot construction problems and deal effectively with the public, affected property owners, the contractor, and other people at the site.

Inspection controls

Inspection is concerned with controlling two main factors: quality and quantity. Materials are normally subjected to specified test procedures. Although many tests are performed onsite, others are done elsewhere on samples obtained at the site or prior to site delivery. In some cases testing may be done at a point of manufacture. The options for testing services include inspectors (if properly trained and equipped), public or private laboratories, and professionally qualified engineers. Engineers and laboratories normally give written certification of conformance. Persons or firms chosen for certification and commercial testing must be carefully evaluated. Most are reliable professionals, but a few are not and they should be bypassed because the agency must have complete confidence in test results.

If materials are tested before site delivery, the samples must be truly representative of the materials eventually used in the work. Materials placement must also comply with specifications, whether governed by the documents or standard practice. The contractor bears the sole responsibility if materials that have not yet had testing approval are covered by other materials.

Quality control includes correct positioning of every project element, large and small, at the intended location, elevation, and alignment. Quantity control must ensure that there is enough material to achieve expected strengths but not an excess that would balloon costs. One source of problems is materials densities differing from the assumptions used for estimating. The inspector should learn the contractor's planned placement sequence and precalculate the yield that should occur for a given area or bulk. By comparing the calculations and actual data on "as delivered" quantities, inspectors can quickly spot problems.

At the same time, no agency can afford to inspect every detail of every project, but sufficient staff must be present to make certain that no *significant* step or detail is unchecked. Random inspection is acceptable (but a recognizable pattern of inspection will encourage contractors to take shortcuts), as long as the level of examination provides confidence in the whole. Inspection time should be devoted to examining strength, durability, function, and quantity control (not necessarily in that order).

Specifications usually stipulate that failure to inspect does not reduce the contractor's exposure to making corrections. Nevertheless, the contractor must rely on staff clearance to some extent before proceeding to the next step. Assignment of a proper number of inspectors is a critical management responsibility.

Inspector training

Inspection experience is valuable but it cannot fully substitute for formal training. Personnel should have general instruction in traffic control, job safety, construction and testing methods, materials, and procedures and policies for project paperwork (including change orders, submittals, payments, and correspondence). Strong emphasis must be placed on public relations because many affected citizens consider the inspector to be their source of project information and a personal "problem solver." Specialized training courses such as those offered by the American Public Works Association are particularly valuable.

Surveys, maps, and records

The purpose of surveys, maps, and records is to provide controls and data for planning, design, maintenance, and other engineering tasks performed by public and private parties, and for general public information.

Surveys

Local public works engineering includes several types of surveying: control, boundary, physical data, and construction.

Control surveys, which are essential for consistent, coordinated work throughout the community, create and use systems of permanent monuments and bench marks to establish horizontal and vertical positions on which other surveys are based. Local government is usually responsible for community controls, which are tied to higher order networks established by the state and federal governments. Most agencies require that control monumentation be installed as part of land development projects.

Boundary surveys, which recover or set corners and lines for parcels of land or public rights-of-way, are highly specialized and are usually done by private surveying firms, although an agency may carry out boundary surveys if it has staff professionally qualified for such work.

Physical data surveying is done to plot topography and natural and man-made objects for purposes of records, planning, and design. Aerial mapping is often cost-effective for physical data needs.

Because of the ease of coordination, construction surveys to place project elements are best done by the public works agency, but the contractor can be required to do some or all of the project staking. All construction surveys require great care because errors are embarrassing and often quite expensive to correct.

There have been great advances in optical and electronic surveying instruments and in methodology, but adequate work can still be done with older, more traditional equipment. Costs and benefits should be weighed carefully before investing in expensive new gear.

Maps

Public works departments create and maintain several types of maps for the benefit of planners, designers, surveyors, maintenance and operating personnel, and the public. Maps of the community's streets and other public facilities will be widely used. Detailed, large-scale maps of street features, utility lines and appurtenances, right-of-way widths, and other basic information are essential both for records and as an operating and emergency aid to other local government departments. Such maps should show both horizontal and vertical data, as appropriate. Other useful maps depict land divisions, political boundaries, official street width lines, and special situations such as areas in which all utilities must be placed underground.

Computerized mapping (such as the CAMRAS technique) is becoming common. Although the initial cost of transferring information from hard copy records can be high, there are great advantages and long-range savings for map additions, corrections, and deletions, and the ability to vary the form of reproduction to meet special needs.

Records

Good records management is a critical public works responsibility, which if properly handled can assist in avoiding legal problems. Survey data, maps, facility plans, land plats, assessment records, utility connection information, and the status of fee payments are examples of important public records that must be kept organized, safe, and accessible.

The public works department will receive frequent requests for information about its surface and underground facilities, and it should be able to respond fully, promptly, and accurately. Many will also want to inspect records and will ask for copies, and there must be careful control to prevent unauthorized removal or changes. For example, original drawings should never be out of direct public works control except for release to approved reproduction companies for copying. Copies of filed drawings, never the originals, should be used for design or remodeling.

Special records should be kept on matters relating to emergencies and the environment, such as hillside slippage, groundwater levels and quality, earth faults, and flood-prone areas. All maps and drawings on permanent record should be on archival stock, but microfilming and separate storage of the films is advised as protection against possible loss of the originals. Before any obsolete records are destroyed, persons qualified to judge their historical significance should be consulted.

Engineering management and private activity

Although this chapter is primarily concerned with design and construction conducted by, or on behalf of, local public agencies, another significant public works responsibility is engineering management vis-à-vis land development, street work permits, and other activity by private parties. Private efforts—especially privately financed streets, sewers, water, and utilities—sometimes provide more public infrastructure additions and modifications than do government projects. They may directly serve shopping centers, large office buildings, and residential subdivisions. Engineering management considerations presented in this chapter are largely applicable to private activity which is regulated by government.

Public agency and developer perspectives

Development is a logical, profit-motivated outgrowth of the need for buildings and other facilities to support community life and commerce. Most public agencies welcome development because it provides new taxable wealth and jobs and accommodates population and economic growth. Despite this linkage, there are some unavoidable differences in the perspectives of developers and local public works engineers.

Cost control is vital to the development industry, which often views government requirements and procedures as excessive and public personnel as overly conservative and unreceptive to new materials and technology. Developers face stringent financial problems in creating a product at a saleable figure because of interest charges and commitments of financial resources well ahead of sales and occupancy. For a given market price, more developer money in public improvements or carrying charges can mean less of the on-site amenities that increase sales and profits. For these reasons, demands can be made on public works departments for changes or reductions in standards and discretionary requirements, for the use of new products, and for faster processing of maps and plans. There may even be real or perceived political pressure to modify judgments on general or project-specific matters.

The public works engineer's first duty is to the general public to maintain a reasonable, balanced, and sound professional position regardless of demands and pressures. Consent to use innovations should not be withheld without valid reason, however, and effective administrative steps should be taken to ensure prompt review of developer applications and submittals.

Working with developers

Public works engineering managers must work with developers courteously and cooperatively while at the same time ensuring that private construction of public facilities meets proper design and service criteria. They should not approve experimentation with untried ideas or products if failure could lead to significant future public costs, nor should comparison of first cost with long-range operation, maintenance, and rehabilitation costs be overlooked.

The department should establish efficient procedures for reviewing plans and plats and for relaying comments and corrections to the submitter. It is particularly important to cooperate on systems planning and to work through the sometimes conflicting needs and objectives of two or more developers. Suspense files should be used to track due dates and commitments and to provide warning signals on the prospective expiration of surety bonds. Most differences with developers can be resolved with tact, integrity, and a willingness to listen.

Permit administration

Permits should be required for all physical work in public rights-of-way to protect against damage and unsafe conditions, ensure proper placement and operations, provide managed access to underground facilities, and control construction and encroachments on the surface. The costs of permits and inspections are normally met, at least in part, by fees.

An effective permit system should be established and coordinated with a "one-call" utility location and marking system. Scarce underground space must not be wasted by poor placement of new installations; working with all of the street users to preplan standard locations is an excellent preventative measure. Appropriate permit conditions can be attached for traffic control and public convenience, including hours of operation. Backfill and surface restoration, both temporary and permanent, requires thorough inspection because off-grade areas can be hazardous, a source of complaint, and a generator of future maintenance costs.

Retention and use of consultants

The usual reason for using consultants is to obtain professional services and technical know-how not available on staff. Few local agencies can handle every type of engineering and architectural work and special studies they need with in-house personnel. With fluctuating program levels, it is uneconomical or impractical to retain excess staff during low periods or to recruit employees for peak work loads. Most public works agencies maintain staff for a basic design and construction program and use consultants for other work; other agencies limit their staff to checking plans and administering consultant contracts. Some small agencies cannot afford a full-time staff engineer at all and use a consultant on retainer, but this is a sensitive authority-responsibility situation where very careful negotiation is required.

The selection process

Successful consulting services depend on qualifications, professional responsibility, avoidance of conflicts of interest, and proper placement of authority. The selection process must focus on qualifications, not price or politics. Engineering and architectural services are equally as professional as those provided by lawyers and doctors. Once the scope of services has been agreed upon, a hard bargain can be driven on professional fees, but selection based *primarily* on competitive bidding or some other basis emphasizing cost is inconsistent with securing requisite quality. A consultant who negotiates solely on price will surely have to cut corners somewhere, to the client's detriment. Even if local preference is possible under law, qualifications should be paramount.

Consultants should rarely be given authority to act as the owner's agent; their most appropriate role is to provide services and advice. Any final decisions, especially decisions relating to policy and finance, should rest with qualified agency officials. If the agency lacks such personnel, a separate and independent consultant can be retained to review the main consultant's work.

Potential conflicts of interest should be anticipated. Thus if full services are needed for both design and construction management for a project, a separate consultant should be retained for each phase. A single consultant allowed to do both on a project could mask design errors and omissions when working with the contractor or acting on change orders without the owner's knowledge. Avoid situations where a consultant has a proprietary interest in a construction material or method to be used on a project. Most consultants accept and maintain full professional responsibility for their work, and an agency (or review consultant working for the agency) must always understand and respect that professional position. An important recommendation should never be overturned without careful consideration (and perhaps advice of counsel). Fortunately, consultants seldom create serious problems if they have been carefully selected and the contract is managed properly. Thus the use of consultants for public agency work is by and large mutually profitable and satisfying.

The essence of selection is to determine consultant reliability, integrity, and expertise. Because selection can be a very sensitive matter, the legislative body or the public works director should establish a formal written selection policy, which should give confidence in consultants and protect staff from political forces.

Figure 10–1 Criteria for evaluating consultants.

1. Educational background of personnel to be used on the work.
2. Experience record of consultant's firm.
3. Demonstrated success on previous work for this or other agencies.
4. Who will be in responsible charge of the work.
5. Adequacy of consultant's staff to perform on schedule.
6. Method of attack proposed for problem or study.
7. Ability of key persons to make effective public presentations.
8. Ability to work with agency staff and other people involved.
9. Any pertinent new ideas offered.
10. Adequacy of consultant's knowledge of local and site conditions.
11. Technical adequacy of personnel and subconsultants.
12. Showing that consultant continues to have an interest in the success of previous projects.
13. Whether the consultant is currently involved in another project that is significantly related.
14. Whether it is important in modifying existing facilities to use the original consultant (if available) or a new one.
15. Demonstrated record of keeping costs within budget and estimates.
16. All other things being equal:

    Local consultants are preferred over nonlocal ones.
    Nonlocal consultants who associate with a local firm for the work are preferred over those who do not.
    Preference shall be given to consultants who have not done recent work for the agency.

Note: Agency policy may also include consideration of affirmative action or disadvantaged business enterprise participation.

Such policies can be general, covering only such matters as emphasis on qualifications and authority to enter into contracts, or they may spell out detailed criteria and processes. Both engineers and architects can be selected under a single policy, but it should be a detailed one if consultants are used frequently. Figure 10–1 shows the selection criteria used successfully by a middle-sized city that relies on consultants for most of its design work.

Staff should be extensively involved in the selection process, and can be authorized either to bring a fully negotiated agreement to the legislative body for approval or to present a group of prequalified consultants to that body for interview and final selection (after which the staff will negotiate).

Screening and interviews Because the number of candidate consultants should be large enough to offer options on qualifications and fees, but not so large that processing and interview is unwieldly, a two-step process is often used.

The first step is to determine consultant interest in submitting a proposal by using data on file, mailed notices, telephone contacts, a formal request for proposals, or, in some states, advertising the availability of a design contract. Information submitted by interested firms is screened and, along with knowledge gained from past experience, is used to narrow the group down to an appropriate number for formal interview. The policy may call for interviewing a minimum number of firms, depending on projected construction costs or other criteria. When a capital improvement program includes a large number of projects, time can be saved by using a single set of interviews for multiple contracts, providing the candidate consultants are qualified to handle all the projects.

The second step matches a consultant with each project for purposes of contract negotiation. Selection (or prequalification) interview panels should include staff persons who will manage the consultant contracts, representatives from using departments, and others such as interested citizens who can help make the best decision. For important projects, a department head might participate personally. The panel (a maximum of six is adequate in most cases) should discuss in advance the objectives of the interview and how it is to be conducted as well as the rating procedures; one of the panel should act as chairperson to make introductions and keep the interview moving. Any available written project information should be distributed to the panel and consultants in advance.

A good interview can be completed in less than an hour. A typical format begins with introductions and preliminaries (five minutes), which are followed by the consultant's uninterrupted presentation of qualifications and other information such as the design approach (twenty to thirty minutes), questions by the panel (as desired), and a summary by the consultant (three minutes maximum). Consultants should be allowed to use audiovisual aids, and there should be at least a brief discussion about fees (such as alternative methods of compensation and order-of-magnitude figures). Best results are obtained by considering and evaluating only the project team *as proposed* by each consultant because efforts to substitute or add specific individuals or subconsultants can result in unworkable combinations. Following the last interview, the panel discusses and rates the candidate firms (and matches them with projects if more than one contract is involved). When negotiations with a selected consultant cannot be completed successfully, they should be terminated and new discussions undertaken with the next ranked firm, or a new selection process should be started.

Consultant contracts The key points in the contract cover the scope of work, schedule, fees, payments, and responsibilities and relations of the parties. The first (and most difficult) negotiating step is defining the scope of work in terms of content and tasks to be performed. The work can range from a single unit to a phased task that includes initial studies and investigations, schematic, preliminary design, final design, specifications, assistance during bidding, and services during construction. Fees and schedules should be keyed to the tasks, and each task or phase should be contracted for separately in the overall agreement so that the agency may stop after any task without penalty (an individual notice would be required to proceed).

Separate estimates should be prepared for agency approval in the schematic, preliminary, and drawing phases of a design contract and, if the low bid received for construction exceeds the final approved estimate by more than a stated percentage, the agency should have the right to require the consultant (without additional fee) to redesign or modify the plans and specifications in an acceptable manner so that a rebid will fall within the budget. Other important contract details include information or services to be provided by the agency, consultant attendance at meetings or public appearances, penalties on *either* the agency or consultant for unacceptable delay, names of the persons in charge and any subconsultants (who can be changed only with agency approval), insurance for liability and errors and omissions, payments, contract outputs such as submittals or reports, agency approval authority (either an official or the legislative body), and the terms of contract termination or modification. The agency must take possession of all original drawings, field books, and other data that are costly to duplicate because all too often such documents are destroyed when a consultant goes out of business. An additional fee may be paid to the consultant if building or other plans are used for further work that duplicates the original. The consultant must be required to carry a predetermined amount of "errors and omissions" insurance to protect the agency.

Consultant fees Fees can be a fixed sum, a percentage of construction cost, the consultant's cost plus a fixed fee or percentage, consultant's wage payments times a multiplier (to cover fixed costs and profit), or some other reasonable formula. Costs of items such as travel, long-distance calls, and production of extra copies of reports are usually paid separately. A fee based on a percentage of construction cost is illogical because a skilled design that holds down costs lowers the fee, whereas a poorer design that is more expensive raises the fee. Cost-plus and multiplier arrangements make it difficult for the client to predict and control costs. Any fee other than one based on a fixed sum requires inclusion of an agreed-upon maximum payment, and the work may not be finished at that point. Most agencies find fixed sum fees most satisfactory, but the scope of work must be carefully defined and a provision included to adjust payments for changed conditions or extra work. In any event, payments should not be made in advance of delivery of acceptable work.

Working with consultants

Staff and consultants must maintain mutual respect and use a "team approach" because their common objective is service to the public. The work must be under agency control at all times, and communications must flow easily and often enough so that the consultant is given prompt decisions and the agency knows what is going on. Both parties should stick to the agreement, and if it proves unworkable, they should negotiate amendments and have them approved. The consultant must work with and through designated contract administration staff who are trained in management and know how to give clear instructions. It can be disastrous for a consultant to reach side agreements or undertake unauthorized work unknown to the management staff.

It is often necessary for a consultant to contact materials or equipment suppliers or manufacturers as the work progresses; the agency must be assured that such contacts do not lead to noncompetitive bids. Whenever other persons or firms have to be called in to prepare drawings and specifications, such situations should be reported to and accepted by the agency *in advance*. Correspondence is preferred to oral exchanges, especially for summarizing meetings and phone conversations and documenting instructions given and decisions made.

Keeping on schedule requires prompt agency review, comment, and approval of submittals. The public works staff is responsible for getting all affected parties within and outside the agency involved in reviews and decision making. The consultant must be able to rely on sign-offs so as not to be subjected to later changes of mind without additional compensation and time for making revisions. Each submittal should be reviewed by competent personnel checking for accuracy and compliance with design standards, clarity, completeness, and other matters that affect successful use of plans or reports. A detail-by-detail check may not be needed, however, because the consultant is contractually accountable to the agency for errors and omissions. When all is in order, plans and reports should be accepted for the agency and using departments for purposes of bidding and/ or payment. Now and then a consultant will offer meals or other gratuities, but the best rule regarding gifts and gratuities is not to accept any.

Common sense and consideration of professional responsibility dictate that the design consultant should act as an advisor (but not an agent) during bidding and construction. The consultant can help with prebid meetings, preparation of addenda, clarification, use of contacts to increase the number of bidders, and evaluation of bids. During construction, the designer should review and make recommendations on contractor submittals, disputes, change orders, and other matters that affect successful use of the plans and specifications. Occasionally, problems will arise because inadequacies or errors in the contract documents necessitate changes and extra payment to the contractor. The design consultant should not be penalized for costs the agency would have paid anyway had the plans been correct, but the consultant may be financially responsible if the agency is exposed to undue expense (during or after construction) or if the facility cannot be used as intended. Questions of consultant financial responsibility are so sensitive that the public works director must be scrupulously objective in analyzing any project problems suspected of having been caused by consultant errors or omissions.

Summary

Managers are employed to guide and direct work so that it is done properly and on time. Local public works engineering managers can discharge their responsibilities only through and with other people: professional and technical staff, consultants, contractors, the legislative body, the agency administrator, people from other departments, utility and outside agency staff, and the public. A strong and consistent impression of personal integrity, competence, and professionalism can greatly enhance the reputation and effectiveness of the manager and the unit for which he or she is responsible.

11 Equipment management

Equipment management encompasses a wide variety of functions, usually associated with fleet operations, that include maintenance, replacement, cost recovery, utilization, and operations control. The objectives of equipment management are not only to minimize costs but also to provide effective and dependable equipment that is properly designed to furnish the necessary service. It is this overall view of fleet operations relative to service delivery and cost that makes this a major management function in public works.

Organizational structure

The structure of the equipment management organization should fit the operational needs of the public agency. These needs will vary considerably, depending upon the size and overall management structure of the organization, but there does not seem to be a top limit on the size of the organization that can effectively utilize equipment management concepts. Even smaller agencies with a competent head of public works can effectively utilize basic equipment management principles on a scaled-down basis to fit their specific needs.

During the 1980s there has been a strong movement toward centralized management of the equipment fleet. This management structure works well in the council-manager form of government, where the city manager delegates the fleet ownership to one department (usually the public works department), which establishes a management system to control costs. Centralized fleet management is also effective in a mayor-council form of government. The key to the success of any program, however, is a strong public works director with management commitment.

This centralized approach allows the manager to set citywide priorities in decisions concerning equipment replacement as well as equipment maintenance. The manager can adjust equipment priorities as organizational equipment needs change in response to community service needs. The strong centralized approach provides the manager with enough flexibility to meet the changing needs of a dynamic organization. In addition to reducing costs, an effective equipment management program will extend the life of equipment and will support multiple-use operations that provide the agency with a higher degree of flexibility.

Cities and counties may use a centralized maintenance garage but allow individual departments to retain equipment replacement decisions. In a more traditional environment, some departments (usually police and fire) will direct and operate independent maintenance shops themselves. In these shops priorities are set to meet departmental goals and needs, and although these needs may be satisfied, costs are usually higher than in a centralized operation and flexibility is lost.

The size of the organization also has a direct effect on the degree of flexibility that can be permitted in setting up an equipment management program. It is obvious that each department cannot handle its own maintenance if there are not enough mechanics to go around. Moreover, maintenance shops require specialized employees, such as welders, and specialized equipment, such as lathes, presses, test equipment, and special tools.

Total equipment management

The form of a piece of equipment makes little difference from the point of view of management, which sees most equipment as a "black box" that takes in money at one end and puts out work at the other. The basic job of the fleet manager is to develop a program that will provide the maximum amount of work output for the minimum amount of money input.

This simplistic analysis can be refined further to cover not only the cost of providing the work, but also of taking into consideration the quality of work output and the availability and reliability of equipment. This approach is built on cost, quantity, and quality and can be called "total equipment management." Total equipment management thus involves equipment maintenance, equipment performance (specifications), equipment availability (downtime), and equipment utilization by those providing service to the taxpayers.

Even though a total equipment management program may represent the most cost-effective way to manage a fleet, few agencies have actually implemented such a program, although many have adopted basic equipment management principles and have made strides in the direction of controlling fleet costs. For a variety of reasons, however, many others still concentrate on maintenance alone and do little to evaluate and control fleet costs. Factors that influence the type of program favored are tradition, organizational structure, size, politics, managerial expertise, and organizational climate.

The total equipment management approach cannot be successfully implemented unless a close working partnership is established between the operational departments of the local government and the equipment management organization. This can be done through equipment coordinators in each equipment-using department whose job is to relay equipment needs and operational considerations of their departments so that equipment availability will match crew availability and citywide or countywide operational needs.

In some organizations the problems in day-to-day communications may create a "gap" between the equipment coordinator and the department head. To ensure that department heads are not isolated from their equipment and that they have a high level of "equipment awareness" at all times, the interfacing between departments must be reviewed continuously.

Studies of operational equipment needs relative to manpower utilization for maximum productivity will determine the proper amount of equipment needed. A detailed analysis of equipment downtime, turnaround time, and effectiveness will determine proper spare parts ratios and maintenance priorities for the shop. With a detailed review of the using department's operations, the equipment manager will be able to meet that department's needs in the most cost-effective manner because the "total" equipment needs, from the perspective of both the equipment user and the equipment manager, will be satisfied. Furthermore, this coordinated approach provides the most cost-effective use of manpower and equipment in providing services to the taxpayer.

Rental system

Agencies utilizing the centralized equipment management approach will find that a rental system simplifies procedures and provides improved cost control.

Traditionally, the using department was responsible for the upkeep of equipment, and furnished the fuel, repairs, and capital for its eventual replacement. In many agencies, a central garage provides these services to the using departments on a direct charge basis. In both cases, budgeting involves projecting last year's experience forward on a line-item basis. This approach does not identify the cost of operating each category of equipment on the basis of performance. The using organization needs to know how its fleet is performing with respect to operational costs as well as reliability. At the same time, the equipment management organization needs to measure the effectiveness of its fleet maintenance and management programs. The rental system provides the information needed to manage equipment effectively on the basis of actual performance.

In recent years the development of centralized equipment ownership and management has refined the rental system concept so that the centralized equipment organization "owns" the fleet and rents each unit to each using department on a cost per mile, cost per hour, or flat monthly charge. The rental system has enough flexibility to recover equipment operating, maintenance, and replacement costs, or any portion thereof, depending on the accounting system in place. The rental rates include all costs assigned to the fleet, and thus the equipment management organization's budget is totally recovered from the rental rate structure.

The rental rates can include replacement charges in addition to operating and maintenance charges. If the funds are kept separate, however, the system will have a greater degree of flexibility, and in case of a revenue shortfall, adjustments can be made to maintain an overall effective program.

The rental system simplifies the budget process considerably. Before budget preparation begins, the equipment management organization issues a rental rate schedule for all units in the fleet. The equipment-using departments determine what equipment will be needed to meet the organization's work plans for the coming year. The rental rate multiplied by the projected utilization for each unit will provide a projected annual cost for each unit in the department's fleet. This information, when combined with labor and other costs, will provide operating departments with the means to cost out all their programs.

An accurate rental system cannot be developed and maintained, however, unless a management information system is used to analyze all costs. For medium and large agencies, such analysis has to be done with rather sophisticated computer systems, but smaller agencies can use manual record-keeping systems, possibly assisted by a microcomputer.

Equipment replacement

A given piece of equipment has a number of "lives." It has a *service life*, which refers to the amount of time the vehicle is capable of operating and rendering service. This life may be nearly infinite if the unit receives adequate maintenance and if worn-out components are dutifully replaced.

A unit also has a *technological life*, which represents the relative productivity decline of the unit when compared with newer models on the market.

This discussion is concerned with another type of equipment life, the *economic life*. The economic life of a unit is of critical importance to equipment managers, for it relates to the total stream of costs associated with the unit through time. Therefore, it has a significant impact on both capital and operating budgets. The economic life of a unit refers to the length of time that the average total vehicle cost is at a minimum.

In the early years of ownership, costs are dominated by the declining resale value (depreciation) of the vehicle; in later years the decline in resale value slows, whereas operating and maintenance costs continue to rise. Figure 11–1 illustrates the relations between these costs. In this example, a minimum average annual cost is reached after about five years, followed by a steady increase in average annual costs. It is important to recognize the distinction between the total per period costs and the average period costs of a vehicle. The economically optimum replacement point is reached when *average* period costs are at a minimum, not when total period costs are at a minimum.

Data for completing a replacement analysis may come from a variety of sources such as the agency's shop records and fuel tickets, staff estimates, and blue book

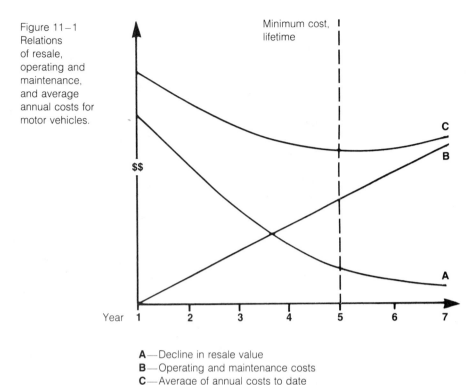

Figure 11–1
Relations
of resale,
operating and
maintenance,
and average
annual costs for
motor vehicles.

A—Decline in resale value
B—Operating and maintenance costs
C—Average of annual costs to date

analysis. Agencies with an equipment management information system may have all the historical data necessary for a proper analysis.

The development of replacement analysis curves can be as detailed and complex as desired, depending upon the amount of detailed information available. In many cases, however, a simplified approach utilizing only key data can be used to make priority replacement decisions.

Another approach to vehicle costing is the nomogram. A nomogram is a graphical representation of a complicated algebraic equation (see Figure 11–2). It is essentially an alignment chart consisting of a number of calibrated scales arranged in such a way that when a straight edge is laid across them, the set of values where the edge intersects the scale represents the solution to an equation.

Nomograms are inexpensive, straightforward, and easy to use. Staff can be easily trained to use nomograms, and no special mathematical or statistical background is required. The nomogram process is as simple as drawing three straight lines through points on scales representing the capital cost of the present unit, total maintenance cost to date, the age of the unit, the maximum cost of projected repairs for next year, and the capital cost of a replacement unit. The projected cost of repairs for the coming year will determine whether replacement is necessary.

Another approach for agencies with rental systems is to plot the rental rates for categories of equipment over a period of time. Substantial increases in rental rates will show which categories of equipment are becoming costly to maintain and operate. All categories can then be entered onto a priority list based on a ranking according to the percentage of increase in rates. The results of this analysis will place various units in priority categories. Those categories with the highest ranking will provide the highest return on investment of the replacement dollar. This approach, although simple, may provide a method that will best fit the realities of the competitive budget process.

In summary, the replacement process can be as complicated or as simple as the situation warrants. It is the responsibility of equipment managers to select

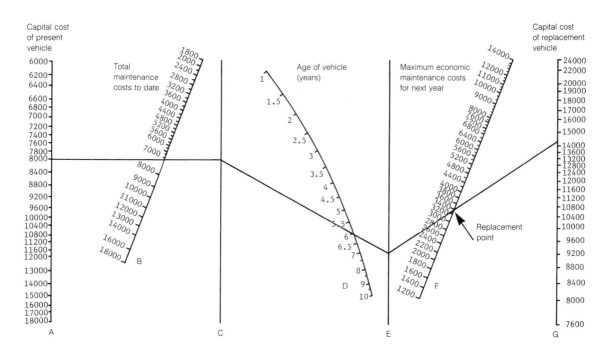

Figure 11–2   Nomogram for vehicle replacement. Initial cost: $8,000. Total maintenance cost to date: $7,200. Age: 6 years. Replacement cost: $14,000. Replace the vehicle when the maintenance cost for the next year is projected at $3,300 or more.

the process that will best serve their organizations by providing the greatest return on the replacement dollar.

Management information systems

A modern fleet of equipment cannot be managed without the assistance of an equipment management information system (EMIS). The size of the fleet being managed will determine the type and complexity of the system needed.

For larger fleets, the choice would be either a centralized mainframe system or a dedicated stand-alone minicomputer. In either case, a substantial amount of memory or storage would be required. For medium to small fleets, a microcomputer system will provide all that is necessary to manage the fleet. A number of software programs and microcomputer hardware systems have been developed for fleet management and are available in the marketplace.

The equipment management information system will help the equipment manager make proper and cost-effective decisions concerning equipment procurement, utilization, maintenance, and replacement that have a significant effect on local government expenditures. Typical systems include the following:

Equipment list by activity	Billing
Detailed equipment history	Revenue projections
Work code analysis	General ledger interface
Shop labor utilization	Preventive maintenance schedules
Manpower staffing analysis	Fuel-usage control

Accident experience   Parts-inventory control

Equipment depreciation and   Exception reporting.
replacement

Managers can use the equipment management information system to monitor operations and to analyze operational data. As with any tool, its effectiveness will be limited by the quality of its design, the extent to which it is designed for the task at hand, and the ability of the user.

The new technology can gather, sort, and present large volumes of data to the equipment manager, but there is a danger in this, because the sheer volume of data can be a deterrent to its use. A stack of computer printouts several feet thick will scare off any fleet manager. Thus, management information must be summarized or brought forward as exception reports. Managers need not know what went right or the details of how the "bottom line" was reached. They want to know what went wrong so it can be corrected. Summary information that can be used for planning and current management decisions also is needed. The most effective way to deal with the excess paper problem is to view the data on a computer terminal screen and print out only the information that is needed in the proper report format.

A well-designed and properly utilized equipment management information system will provide the equipment manager with a wealth of information about, and control over, the equipment fleet, which is the largest capital investment in most organizations.

Utilization balancing

The typical motor fleet for a city or county government is quite diverse, a mixture of types that range from motor scooters to bulldozers, with everything in between. Even with similar equipment (for example, four-door passenger cars), the kind and intensity of use can vary widely.

"Utilization balancing" is another management tool to reduce fleet costs by balancing usage of all units with a specific class or type and within a specific year. This is done by exchanging like units having dissimilar utilization at various points in time to achieve a balanced utilization at the completion of the unit's economic life. This program will avoid the "hand-me-down" activity involving older units with low utilization. Here is an example: Several new vehicles are purchased at the same time. Two are assigned to supervisors who have office responsibilities, and the others are assigned to active field use. In a five-year period, the field units will have covered 60,000 to 80,000 miles, whereas the supervisors' units will have covered 20,000 miles. The field units are replaced and the supervisors' units become "hand-me-downs." Because these units are kept for many more years, parts have to be stocked, and failures occur as a result of age alone.

With utilization balancing, the units would have been assigned to different locations at regular intervals and all would have been replaced at the same time. In this way the agency can get its money's worth out of each piece of equipment. Unfortunately, not all employees approve of this process. Staff must be cooperative and well-disciplined to make this approach completely successful. Because the attitudes of individuals driving vehicles vary widely, it is not realistic to expect that this concept will work in all cases. Some supervisors will still want the newer vehicles. It is worth a try, however.

Vehicle equivalents

Another useful management tool in the equipment manager's tool bag is the concept of "vehicle equivalents." Originally developed by the military, it has

Table 11–1 Vehicle equivalent rating.

Vehicle	Avg. no. of mechanic-hours per year
Staff sedan (base unit of 1.0) =	23
Light-duty truck =	69
Heavy-duty truck =	161

69/23 = 3 vehicle equivalents for light-duty trucks

161/23 = 7 vehicle equivalents for heavy-duty trucks

been successfully used in managing local government fleets. Vehicle equivalents compare labor requirements for maintaining a variety of equipment units in a fleet. The concept is extremely useful in supporting budget requests for additional personnel and in projecting future facility needs.

The concept requires that a base unit of 1.0 vehicle equivalents first be established. For example, most agencies would use a standard four-door sedan as a base unit and give it a 1.0 unit designation. Past maintenance records are then examined to determine the average number of mechanic-hours required to maintain the base unit sedan. (If work standards are being used, they can be substituted for past labor records to determine what should be done rather than what has been done.) Average hours of labor required for other units in the fleet are also determined from an analysis of past labor records. The ratio of the labor requirements for each category of equipment to the base unit determines the vehicle equivalent rating for each unit in the fleet (see Table 11–1). In this manner, the vehicle equivalency and number of mechanics can be determined for the entire fleet.

In a typical organization, one mechanic-year = 2,080 hours. After deductions for vacation, sick leave, training, and nonproductive time, approximately 1,679 mechanic-hours are available each year.

$$\frac{1,679 \text{ annual productive hours}}{23 \text{ hours for base unit (staff sedan)}} = \frac{73 \text{ equivalents}}{\text{per mechanic.}}$$

We have now determined that each mechanic can maintain seventy-three vehicle equivalents of equipment each year. This can be a combination of units ranging from seventy-three staff sedans to ten heavy-duty trucks or any combination totaling seventy-three vehicle equivalents.

These figures can be used to support a budget request for the mechanics needed to maintain the new vehicles added to the fleet each year. For example, a group of new units ranging from scooters to bulldozers with a combined total vehicle equivalency of 365 would justify the following:

$$\frac{365 \text{ vehicle equivalents}}{73 \text{ vehicle equivalents}} = 5 \text{ mechanics needed.}$$
$$\text{per mechanic}$$

If more than one shop is used, we can determine how many mechanics are needed at each location simply by calculating the total vehicle equivalents of the equipment maintained at that shop and dividing it by 73.

We can further define this process by using heavy-equipment mechanics in addition to auto mechanics and develop different mechanic-to-vehicle-equivalent ratios. Thus a staff sedan with 20,000 miles might have a vehicle equivalency of 1.0, while a similar unit with 75,000 miles might have a vehicle equivalency of 1.7.

Facility growth projections can be made by using the bay/shift approach to vehicle equivalents. Projections of fleet growth are made by correlating past fleet growth with community population growth or some other available measure. The projected fleet growth is then converted to vehicle equivalents using the above process. From this, the number of mechanics is determined. Using the principle that each mechanic needs a work bay and a work shift, we can determine the number of bay/shift units needed to support the projected fleet growth. Fleet managers may now evaluate the options of adding a graveyard shift or building a new shop with additional bays. Thus they have another management tool at their disposal.

This should be treated as only one of many management tools, however. It is the supervisor's job to evaluate the performance of individual mechanics. This individual evaluation can be further incorporated into the system by placing mechanics into rating groups, such as A,B,C, and so on.

In summary, vehicle equivalents are used to monitor the utilization of labor, relative to the work load requirement, and to plan ahead for any changes in operations that might be required.

Preventive maintenance

The most important phase of the maintenance system is scheduled periodic preventive maintenance (PM). PM is accomplished through careful operation and timely servicing of equipment and by systematic inspection, detection, and correction of potential equipment failures before major defects develop. The purpose of PM is to keep equipment in satisfactory operating condition at all times. If major breakdowns can be prevented, using departments will be able to carry out their assigned duties in the quickest and most efficient manner possible.

PM consists of (1) daily maintenance and inspection services performed by assigned drivers, operators, and maintenance personnel, and (2) scheduled services performed by maintenance mechanics, drivers, and operators.

PM services properly applied will keep vehicles and equipment in the best possible operating condition and ready for use at all times. PM reduces the incidences of unscheduled servicing with accompanying downtime. As a result, repair time and capital investment are saved; the life of equipment is prolonged considerably; and parts do not wear out as quickly, so fewer parts need to be replaced. For these reasons, PM programs should be followed closely and all employees should recognize the important part they play in accomplishing their maintenance duties.

The driver has the foremost responsibility for keeping a vehicle in proper operating condition. Public service vehicles should be able to operate under the most rugged working conditions, both on and off the road, but even the best equipment maintained by skilled mechanics will be subject to breakdowns and excess wear when improperly or unsafely operated. Any vehicles that are improperly operated or poorly maintained will eventually fail in their mission. Yet many who neglect to keep equipment at the proper standards of operational readiness frequently blame defective vehicles, insufficient or unskilled mechanics, difficult terrain, and excessive use.

Practically all unscheduled maintenance arises from either an operator's trouble report or emergency road calls. Unscheduled maintenance service is the correction of deficiencies that occur between scheduled safety or other inspections and the scheduled preventive maintenance servicing prescribed by management. Unscheduled maintenance service generally involves correcting only the specific items reported to be deficient by an operator and confirmed to be so by qualified inspection personnel. Other reported deficiencies observed by the inspector at the time of an unscheduled service, particularly those affecting safety, must be corrected before the vehicle is released for service. However, the costs of trouble reports and road calls should be summarized separately from scheduled maintenance to allow for the effective measurement of the scheduled maintenance program, the skill of the diagnosticians, and the quality of shop maintenance work. Maintenance personnel should take a "negative attitude" when inspecting equipment. By looking for improperly adjusted fan belts, cracked hoses, body corrosion, and other indicators, they can apply the "preventive" approach to their maintenance activities.

Scheduled maintenance is the systematic inspection and servicing of motor equipment at intervals compatible with manufacturers' recommendations for lubrication and mechanical services. However, any such program should be flexible enough to meet current operating conditions.

Automotive equipment is scheduled for maintenance on the basis of mileage, time, fuel consumption, or calendar period, or a combination of these elements. Off-highway and motorized maintenance and construction equipment are scheduled on the basis of engine-hour or time. Since the odometer or hourmeter is often the key to the entire program, all personnel associated with equipment operation and maintenance should determine that these instruments are in satisfactory operating condition. In some smaller operations, it may not be advisable to base maintenance on mileage because of low utilization. In some large operations, the maintenance agency may schedule PM on the basis of time to increase the efficiency of shop operation. A minimum or even a specific time must then be established for servicing vehicles. Some operations will experience high idle time on some units.

Scheduled maintenance inspections normally are divided into three classes:

Class A includes all lubrication and mechanical services recommended by the manufacturer, plus inspection and checking of all components and parts related to the safe operation of the equipment.

Class B includes all the elements of Class A service plus a check and inspection of components having a high rate of wear or deterioration or a proven need for frequent adjustment.

Class C includes all the elements of the A and B inspections plus a thorough check and inspection of all remaining components and assemblies of the unit.

In addition, inspections on safety, exhaust emissions, and other items may be required at regular intervals. Depending on the complexity of these requirements, they may be added to the B or C inspection.

The usual pattern of inspection is A, B, A, B, A, C. The C inspection should be scheduled at least once every twelve months.

Corrective adjustments and repair actions taken as a result of serviceability inspections generally are limited to those items prescribed by the manufacturer, and only to the extent necessary to restore the equipment to an optimum degree of serviceability consistent with achieving the highest degree of cost effectiveness. Repairs should be authorized by maintenance supervisors only after thorough diagnosis and detection of the malfunction, wear, or deterioration.

When the manufacturer specifies optional adjustments such as "engine tune-up," such adjustments should not be made unless a specific malfunction is reported by the operator and is confirmed by the inspector's diagnosis. Under adverse local conditions, however, normal maintenance operations may include preventive adjustments such as "tune-ups" to prevent hard starting and resultant service calls. In such cases, the requirement should be determined by the fleet manager. When the manufacturer recommends an hourly, daily, or weekly routine servicing and/or adjustment, the work may be performed by a properly trained operator.

If PM is to be effective and efficient, the scheduling system must cover all vehicles maintained by the equipment maintenance shop. Management can contribute to the success of the program by:

1. Establishing a complete equipment inventory with systematically assigned equipment code numbers that are similar to the equipment code of the American Public Works Association
2. Purchasing special tools and equipment required for servicing
3. Providing updated training procedures
4. Determining and establishing service intervals
5. Establishing repair time standards for each type of equipment.

After new shop equipment has been installed and personnel trained, time standards should be established for servicing each category of equipment so that an assortment of vehicles can be scheduled daily in order to keep a balanced shop load.

Making certain that equipment is available for service according to a predetermined schedule is often difficult. To achieve some measure of success, all using organizations should collaborate with shop management in selecting a time and day for servicing vehicles and then should arrange the shop schedule accordingly. PM schedules should be distributed at least one week prior to appointment so that operating supervisors will have time to make work adjustments and to furnish standby vehicles when necessary. If PM service inspection can be performed on a night shift, both the user organization and the maintenance shop will benefit because downtime will be minimized.

Work measurement/maintenance management

The main purpose of a work measurement/maintenance management program is to preplan work, layout of tools and working environment, and time for standard maintenance jobs so that individual employees achieve greater production. Feedback on what is happening in the shops can be used to correct soft spots, perform critical self-analysis, measure progress, and undertake future planning.

At the heart of the maintenance management program is the *repair order*, which:

1. Clearly defines and authorizes the work to be performed
2. Provides planning and scheduling control
3. Serves as an input document to the management information system
4. Serves as a parts-issue control document in the purchase and supply system.

In order to manage maintenance activities, it is necessary to develop work standards. In a large and complex organization with trained analysts, industrial engineering techniques can be used to develop standards from the data on jobs performed. In most organizations, however, this is not the case and predetermined standards are used.

Predetermined standards are commonly called "flat rates" and are listed in flat-rate manuals. Examples are Mitchell, Chilton, Motor, and manufacturer flat rates. These flat rates will apply to a range of time from "Warranty" to "Customer Pay." The experience of the user will determine where a particular shop should be placed in the time range. In most government shops, the high end of the range is used because of the variety of equipment serviced and the lack of repeat work experienced by automobile dealerships.

For jobs that don't have standards, new standards are "slotted" between jobs that are estimated to require more or less time than the job at hand. The time standards should include time for job preparation and road testing in addition to the actual repair function.

The procedure in using time standards is as follows:

1. Incoming vehicles are diagnosed by a service writer who initiates the repair order.
2. The repair order is sent to the employee responsible for planning and controlling shop work (analyst, superintendent, or foreman). Work is preplanned with time standards. Preplanned time is put on the repair order, availability of parts is checked, and parts are ordered if not in stock.
3. The job is assigned to a mechanic who does the work and enters the actual time required on the repair order.
4. The foreman reviews the repair order and compares standard and actual times.
5. Information from the repair order is entered into the equipment management information system.
6. Reports are generated from data input for management actions.

Standards enable the maintenance manager to measure the work of mechanics, the effectiveness of supervision, and shop layout efficiency. This information can be used to justify changes in layout, work flow, and the purchase of labor-saving tools. In a word, standards are effective in improving work methods. Knowing how to do a common job effectively in less time will mean ongoing labor savings and reduced costs.

Specification preparation

From the managerial viewpoint, writing equipment specifications provides another means of lowering equipment operating expense and downtime and of raising effectiveness in service delivery.

The American Public Works Association, in its *Equipment Management Manual*, sets forth two commonly accepted methods of preparing equipment specifications: the vehicle performance specification and the vehicle hardware specification. A summary of the procedures follows.

If an organization has a large fleet and a generous budget to support it, staff may be wise to prepare the specifications themselves. Automotive engineers are commonly employed in this capacity these days. For smaller fleets, specifications can be prepared and contracts reviewed by someone in the private sector. Such services have only recently become available and consequently are not widely known. This discussion focuses on vehicle hardware specifications because performance specifications are more costly to verify in terms of compliance and are not likely to be used except for large fleets.

Figure 11–3 is an example of detailed hardware specifications.

Parts-inventory control

Fleet maintenance consists primarily of labor and parts, which are therefore the main concerns of overall equipment management. Work measurement pertaining to the management of labor has been covered in another section of this chapter. This section deals with auto parts, the "lifeblood" of a vehicle maintenance program, with respect to the availability and control of parts inventory and the responsibilities of the maintenance manager.

The common inventory problem in most agencies can be stated as follows:

The operating agency (public works, police, other) has little or no standby equipment and a minimum amount of downtime. The maintenance manager believes that to operate efficiently a shop must have an adequate parts inventory on hand or the parts should be available from local sources. The chief fiscal officer wants to keep inventory to a minimum in order to reduce the cash investment. This may be offset somewhat, however, by inflation, which will increase the value of the cash investment over a period of time.

Thus, the agency's task is to balance these conflicting views so as to obtain maximum service at minimum operating cost and inventory investment.

Whether an inventory is needed or not depends on several factors. First, certain parts should be on hand to meet emergency seasonal needs—for example, snowplows in winter and mowers in summer. Second, the sources of parts and the time needed for delivery have considerable bearing on the need for maintaining an inventory and on the size of the inventory. The larger the inventory, the less coordination is needed to keep the process running smoothly.

The third factor is cost. Characteristically, the costs that influence inventory policy are not those recorded by an accounting system. The cost of inventory may be divided into two categories: (1) inventory and storage costs, and (2) downtime or interruption of service costs.

In most cases, the space used to store parts could be used for other purposes; such space requires heating, lighting, and other services that can be expensive when reduced to cost per square foot. These costs plus the cost of handling parts must be considered when evaluating the appropriate stock level for a particular agency. Inventory obsolescence costs must also be considered. The cost of a part that is no longer needed and that cannot be returned for credit represents a loss.

The cost of capital invested in the inventory is the product of three factors: (1) the capital value of a unit of inventory, (2) the time a unit of inventory is kept, and (3) the computed interest rate that could be earned on the investment.

The cost of equipment downtime must also be analyzed when determining the cost-effectiveness of various sizes of inventories. Through analytical means, the equipment manager should develop a relation between parts inventory and equipment downtime. This is a complex procedure that requires a close working relation with the equipment-using agency as described above under "Total Equipment Management." The dependability of parts suppliers and the length of time it takes to receive a shipment are also important cost factors.

In developing parts inventory control, management should divide the inventory into three groups:

1. Parts used in quantities
2. Security parts, that is, parts used infrequently, mainly because there are few similar vehicles in the fleet
3. Insurance parts, that is, parts for obsolete equipment and parts for essential equipment with unacceptable parts delivery histories.

Effective inventory control depends on records to identify parts on hand and provide cost accounting data on the parts that flow through the system. In addition, a good system will discourage theft.

Physical segregation and security are needed for maximum control. Up to now most systems have used cards to indicate bin or stocking levels and record the flow of parts. With the recent developments in computer software and the integration of data base facilities, the techniques of controlling parts inventory costs have been improved. The size of the agency and the size and complexity of the fleet will determine what type of parts-control system will be most effective. Smaller agencies will find it effective to convert from the card system to micro-computers, while larger agencies should consider integrating parts inventory

Figure 11–3 Sample specification for 3/4 ton capacity utility truck.

Component	Specification body	Offered
General	This specification has been prepared to represent a utility vehicle to be used by municipal work crews. Compartments and their construction must be consistent with tool and parts storage and security of same.	
Chassis	V8 gasoline- or diesel-powered having a minimum engine displacement of 5.0 L	
	80 amp alternator, minimum	
	550 CCA battery, minimum	
	HD dry-type oil filter	
	HD radiator and clutch fan	
	Power steering	
	Power-assisted brakes	
	HD automatic transmission (3) speed with in-radiator cooling	
	130″ minimum wheelbase	
	8600 GVWR, minimum	
	Unmounted spare wheel	
	Front bumper (painted)	
	HD-reinforced rear step bumper with Holland 60 AOL Pintle hitch-bolt on only—no welding to chassis frame or crossmembers or drilling of frame flanges	
	Pollak 77 series receptacle-wired per ICC regulation flush-mounted in bumper face adjacent to hitch location	
Cab	(3) man bench seat configuration with seat belts—all positions	

control with an equipment management information system. These large systems can utilize stand-alone minicomputers or can be built into a "mainframe" system.

Downtime and turnaround time

Both downtime and turnaround time can be used effectively in measuring and managing equipment, but there is widespread confusion about the term "downtime." For many, the term means the time that a vehicle or unit is in the shop and is unavailable for service, but this interpretation leads to problems. Downtime is properly defined as the actual time that a vehicle or unit is out of service during a work shift when its services are required. This means that if equipment is normally used only during an eight-hour shift each day, there can only be a maximum of eight hours of downtime during each twenty-four hour perid. For example, a staff car would have a maximum of eight hours of downtime each day while a police car used on three shifts has a maximum potential of twenty-four hours of downtime during each twenty-four-hour day.

Figure 11–3
(continued).

Component	Specification body	Offered
Cab (continued)	Gauge-type instrumentation	
	Heater, defroster, and OEM installed air-conditioning	
	Tinted glass	
	L & R outside tilt mirrors 7 1/2″ × 10″ below eye level	
	Rearview mirror	
	Dual sun visors	
	Windshield wipers and washers	
Body	Reading model 967ABSW (c) or equal service body. Diamond plate (steel) floor, 12 ga. minimum	
	Adjustable compartment shelves with dividers	
	Tailgate	
	All required light wires in compartments to be protected in conduit	
	Body installation by bolting to chassis frame webs—no drilling of frame flanges, no welding or cutting of chassis frame or crossmembers	
Finish	OEM white all over including wheels	
Warranty	OEM chassis and cab warranty as provided standard	
Service compliance	Offered cab and chassis and service must be represented locally by factory-authorized sales and service outlet	
Guarantee	Successful bidder shall guarantee compliance to all specification items unless waived by city during bid acceptance procedure	

According to this definition, a vehicle that is assigned to an eight-hour shift could have preventive maintenance and repair work done on the off shifts and have little or no downtime. In other words, the unavailability of this vehicle due to repair has no impact on operational requirements, and thus no downtime is recorded.

Turnaround time, on the other hand, is the time that a vehicle or unit is under the control of the shop rather than the operational unit. It consists of the actual clock hours that have elapsed over a period of twenty-four hours from the time the vehicle or unit is turned into the shop until it is put on the ready line for return to service.

Vehicle maintenance facilities

As a city or county government grows, so does the motor fleet that is needed to provide police, fire, road maintenance, code inspection, and other local government services. Such growth entails not only more pieces of motor equipment but also a greater range and diversity of equipment. Such changes are bound to back up on the motor equipment garage and necessitate expansion or replacement. The local fleet manager may be aware of the need for a new maintenance facility long before anyone else. A number of conditions, including high costs and chronic delays, may be symptoms of the underlying cause—inadequate facilities. This is evident when:

1. Work is unfinished and there is little point in hiring additional mechanics because there is no work space.
2. There is no effective preventive maintenance because all available space and equipment are tied up with breakdown repairs.
3. Building maintenance costs for the hydraulic lifts, the vehicle washers, and other equipment are excessive.
4. Mechanics are using an undue amount of time jockeying vehicles in and out of bays.
5. The time and costs for routine repairs are significantly higher than published standards.
6. High mechanic turnover exists because of poor working conditions and out-of-date equipment.
7. Vehicle downtime is increasing.
8. More maintenance is done away from the shop, via emergency road vehicles, because of inadequate shop space and equipment.
9. Work that could be done economically in-house is farmed out.
10. Long lines exist at fueling facilities, and productive labor and vehicle time are wasted at fueling lines.
11. Engines are damaged owing to contaminated fuel from corroded tanks.
12. Inadequately sized fuel tanks are preventing the agency from taking advantage of volume-purchase discounts.

Issues that should be faced in considering a new maintenance facility are:

1. The fleet size and composition to be served by the facility
2. The frequency of maintenance and the amount of preventive maintenance versus breakdown maintenance
3. Whether maintenance and fueling are centralized or decentralized
4. How much maintenance is contracted out to private vehicle maintenance facilities
5. The organization of the equipment management function.

A new facility, if properly designed, will reduce maintenance costs through improved efficiency in moving vehicles through the facility. The investment is large and will fix a base of operations for years to come. Therefore this investment must be thoroughly planned to accommodate future operations as efficiently as possible. A study of vehicle maintenance operations either by qualified staff or by consultants will provide the architect with the necessary input for designing a useful facility that will last for many years.

Use of consultants

The concept of *managing* public agency fleets has been in wide use since the early 1970s, but many agencies have not exploited it and continue to operate only a vehicle maintenance program. This is due in part to a lack of adequately trained administrative staff.

By tradition, the enemy of the mechanic is paperwork. Those who "get their hands dirty" do not like any form of paperwork. If they did, they would be "pushing pencils" rather than "turning wrenches." In today's environment, however, records must be kept in order if an organization expects to manage its affairs properly, control costs, and deliver good service.

In most shop operations, the fleet has grown in both size and complexity. Costs have risen at an exceedingly high rate, and what used to be a small repair shop is now a multimillion-dollar operation. Anyone in the refuse collection business can attest to the high cost of refuse collection trucks and landfill equipment. Other equipment has become far more complex with the arrival of on-board computers and sophisticated hydraulic systems. Even small operations with just a few units are using costly equipment that must be properly managed.

Most garage superintendents and maintenance managers come up through the ranks, usually from mechanic to supervisor to superintendent to manager. This promotion from within, while providing maintenance experience, does not provide the basic managerial perspective that is critical in developing an effective equipment management program.

Quite often, the initial step of converting a maintenance-oriented operation to an effective equipment management program requires the services of a skilled and experienced consulting firm. A good consultant will point out needed changes and provide a workable plan for implementation. The outside opinion of those experienced in developing successful equipment management programs will go a long way in providing essential credibility.

The process for obtaining consulting services can be simple or complex, depending on the type of assistance needed. For smaller agencies, a simple request for proposals (RFP) can be prepared and sent to a list of firms experienced in the equipment management field. Some firms will provide assistance or make sample RFPs available for modification to fit local circumstances.

It may be more helpful to retain a consultant on a daily basis to provide an initial review and assist in outlining the scope of work prior to preparing an RFP. By contacting other agencies, you can obtain useful advice on how to proceed. A sample of cities that have successfully used equipment management consultants are St. Louis; St. Paul; Scarsdale, New York; Olathe, Kansas; Columbia, Missouri; Norfolk, Virginia; Indianapolis; and Naples, Florida.

Regardless of the size of the program, outside advice will help remove many stumbling blocks and save money in the long run.

Summary

This chapter began with an explanation of total equipment management. Subsequent sections covered the basic elements of a comprehensive equipment management program as it applies to local government.

Broadly speaking, the managerial functions of planning, directing, and controlling are utilized by the public agency to ensure that the equipment necessary to keep the public agency "running" is operating at maximum efficiency. The key word is "management," whether it refers to managing the operation or the maintenance of equipment. In regard to maintenance, a primary concern is the preventive maintenance program that will directly affect both cost and reliability.

By striving to encompass the total equipment management concept, a public agency will provide the taxpayers with the highest level of service at the least possible cost.

12 Buildings and grounds management

A little neglect may breed mischief;
for want of a nail the shoe was lost;
for want of a shoe the horse was lost;
for want of a horse the rider was lost;
for want of a rider the battle was lost;
for want of a battle the kingdom was lost;
and all for want of a horseshoe nail.

First four lines attributed to Jacula Predentum (1640);
last three lines added by Benjamin Franklin (1758).

The term *maintenance*, in its broadest sense, includes all work that sustains and restores, where necessary, buildings, the equipment housed within them, and the grounds around them so that they can function safely and economically and give an appearance that inspires public confidence.

Construction creates a building. When it is complete, deterioration begins. Maintenance checks the deterioration and keeps the building sound and functioning. Good management will develop a maintenance program that retains and enhances buildings and their grounds.[1]

But some, in a misguided effort to cut expenses, argue for an appealing program of "deferred maintenance." This actually means neglect, a disreputable appearance of the buildings and grounds, greater hazards for those working in the buildings, and a much higher reconstruction and replacement cost when buildings and equipment finally fail. Damage suits also can be expected.

Still others who callously want to neglect maintenance argue in loud, bellicose voices, "If it ain't broke, don't fix it." Leave the equipment and the building alone, they say, even if the heating and air-conditioning equipment is struggling to perform, or the bearings are pounding on the sides of the engine.

Another obstacle to proper maintenance is the unwarranted reliance on the "handyman"—allegedly a multitalented, undiscovered genius who can repair everything better than the professionals, from heating and air-conditioning equipment to electrical switchgear, from plumbing fixtures to computer-controlled electrical equipment. The difficulty is that the handy-man doesn't do it well enough to meet today's exacting maintenance needs.

Buildings and grounds management has changed drastically since the 1970s. Technology has generated remarkable improvements in equipment, materials, and tools, and in their applications. Three examples are computer monitoring and feedback for energy conservation, the use of plastics as an effective and economical replacement for other materials, and structural design for energy conservation and user security.

These changes provide more durability and reliability at lower cost, but they demand better qualified engineers, mechanics, technicians, and custodial personnel. These employees need a much broader range of skills to maintain, service, and repair the sophisticated equipment and machines that "operate" today's structures. With utility costs at permanently higher levels (in constant dollars), and with buildings and grounds security a constant concern, both management and first-line supervision entail much greater responsibility.

Centralized maintenance

The responsible maintenance manager, particularly one who has charge of several buildings, must avoid responding to maintenance needs in a fragmented manner. To do so will create problems of accountability and complications in budgetary and administrative processes. Even worse, it can lower maintenance performance as well.

Administrators will find that by assigning responsibility for the care and maintenance of public buildings to one department, they are gaining value at low cost and emulating the successful patterns of many cities and counties.

Controlled maintenance   The term "controlled maintenance" was introduced by K. L. Smuland of the Los Angeles Bureau of Public Buildings to cover the following purposes of an effective building management program:

Protect capital investment

Reduce incidence of equipment failure and trouble calls

Anticipate major repairs or replacements

Maintain continuous building operation with a minimum of inconvenience to the users

Eliminate excessive travel and overtime

Insure effective use of personnel and equipment

Provide accurate records of work accomplishment

Establish a work measurement system for budget preparation, review of accomplishments, and comparison of costs with published standards.

One of the prime objectives of controlled maintenance is to eliminate unscheduled or emergency maintenance. . . .

The second objective is to increase the productivity of the maintenance force.

Source: Excerpted, except for the first paragraph, from Institute for Buildings and Grounds, American Public Works Association, *Centralized Administration of Public Buildings*, Special Report no. 50 (Chicago: American Public Works Association, 1984), p. 12.

What the building services organization does

Although their exact organizational structure in each local government agency can vary, building services have certain objectives in common.

First, the building services organization must protect the public's investment in buildings and property used to respond to its needs.

Second, it must improve managerial effectiveness by consolidating functions to reduce duplication, planning future requirements, increasing productivity in maintenance activities, establishing effective reporting procedures, and implementing more effective control and use of resources.

Every manager responsible for buildings and grounds must provide the following basic services:

1. Supply master planning for physical growth or adjustment for new conditions

2. Program and administer construction and renovation
3. Operate and maintain facilities associated with mechanical systems
4. Establish housecleaning levels to assure a pleasant work environment
5. Oversee major and minor repairs
6. Provide security for all buildings and grounds
7. Establish an effective energy conservation program.

Performance of central management

The buildings and grounds manager can divide work activities into six groups.

Contractual construction   Construction by contract requires the buildings and grounds manager to negotiate, oversee, and coordinate outside architectural and engineering contracts. Management must maintain liaison between the architectural and engineering firms and the user agencies and coordinate and provide technical assistance and advice in the review of plans and specifications during construction. In small cities, these responsibilities may rest with the engineering department.

Management prepares and reviews cost estimates for new work, checks payment estimates during construction, and recommends final acceptance of the completed work.

Central administration and control   Management needs to receive and record work requests and issue needed work orders. Management must coordinate and schedule work, maintain a follow-up system for each project, assemble and analyze cost and performance data, develop performance standards, maintain budget control, and administer personnel and records activities.

Architectural planning and design   Management should assist other city and county departments when developing long- and short-range building requirements and space needs and when programming the larger projects to be in harmony with master plans. Management must directly develop plans and specifications for remodeling, renovation, and small construction projects; coordinate and review plans and specifications for new buildings prepared by outside architects; and recommend improvements in existing buildings and surrounding areas.

Custodial maintenance   Custodial maintenance means that management schedules and supervises day-to-day housekeeping services, including procedures and methods that assure physical safety and a clean, healthful environment.

Management must maintain data on costs and performance of custodial work, develop and conduct training programs, and supervise the work of contractors to ensure that they are fulfilling their contract responsibilities.

Operations and general maintenance   Scheduled operations and preventive maintenance on all structures and movable equipment are part of operations and general maintenance. Buildings today utilize new materials such as longer lasting paints that can provide longer life and that require less maintenance. At the same time, buildings now contain more electronic devices and controls that improve efficiency but require more exacting maintenance by skilled personnel. New hazards also exist that are not observable to the untrained eye.

Security   Security is a sensitive, serious, and constant problem. Management must help prevent thefts, damages, and assaults, and guard against disruption of vital services at any time, particularly during emergencies.

Buildings and grounds management must investigate and report all security violations to the director of public works or a similar responsible official, as well as evaluate procedures for adequate protection and weigh the cost against the risk if such services are not supplied.

In reviewing their position on security, managers should not neglect assistance available from the local police, state police, and the FBI.

Management methods

This section examines three of the major management methods used today both in maintenance and, in more general terms, in the field of public works management. These methods are management by objectives (MBO), life-cycle costing (LCC), and quality circles (QCs).

Management by objectives (MBO)

Management by objectives is a process that appeals to many administrators. The manager ascertains, from those in charge of the activities conducted in the building, the objectives of the organizations and then determines how the buildings and grounds department can function in concert with these objectives. Invariably, the plans of the operating departments conflict, and it is up to the buildings and grounds manager to reconcile legitimate differences. The manager also uses the objectives to define tasks and clarify responsibility and accountability. The benefits of MBO are that it assists operating department heads, improves productivity, leads to the discovery of innovative methods, and helps improve the performance of both management and employees.

The manager should formulate the objectives that the program is striving to attain. A well-formulated objective is specific, short-range in nature, and sets a date for completion.

The objective is worthwhile if it generates benefits, poses challenges to management, and can win support of the next higher level within the organization.

Management must consult not only with supervisors but also with those involved in performing the tasks. As a result of the consultation, the program review will disclose whether the plan is on schedule and what revisions or adjustments are required. All must be convinced that the program will work. Those who have used MBO have found that from three to five years may be required to implement it successfully.

Life-cycle costing (LCC)

With life-cycle costing, the manager identifies and quantifies all costs associated with acquiring, owning, using, and disposing of an item, system, or service over its useful life. When LCC is applied to buildings, the manager is able to evaluate the net dollar effect of purchasing, constructing, maintaining, operating, and replacing buildings. Building costs are hard to estimate when labor, materials, and energy costs rise dramatically. Escalating costs impel the manager to identify the best building designs and systems to provide long and useful lives.

To determine LCC, management first establishes the objectives of the analysis, which must embrace alternatives and bring out constraints that may limit available options.

The second step is to formulate the criteria for applying LCC to the total investment problem. These criteria will fix the time period over which the evaluation is to be made.

To determine the total LCC of an alternate building system, or building practices, management must investigate cost categories such as these:

1. Investment costs—costs of planning, design, engineering, construction, inspection, purchase, installation, finance, and salvage or trade-in returns

2. Nonfuel operation and maintenance costs—materials and labor for routine upkeep and operation other than energy
3. Repair and replacement costs if the building develops excessive maintenance costs or becomes obsolete
4. Energy costs
5. Initial cost-reduction features such as grants or subsidies
6. Depreciation
7. Financing.

Management can employ the total LCC to determine whether an investment is cost-effective. For example, LCC could show that when insulation is introduced to a building energy costs are reduced enough to outweigh the cost of the insulation. Managers who wish to choose between a conventional heating system and a solar energy system with a conventional heating backup can select a system with the lower total LCC if other factors remain equal. Operating data must also be examined carefully to determine whether equipment usage will be intense, with high load factors, or casual, as on a standby basis.

Management can also utilize LCC to award contracts on the basis of the lowest LCC value rather than the lowest initial contract bid. Unfortunately, too often goods and services are purchased on the basis of first cost rather than life-cycle costs.

Management must be prudent when gathering information to be used for a reference file. The method requires a large file of information on manufacturers' products. The manufacturers in turn constantly revise and improve these products, and thereby tend to make the information file obsolete.

Quality circles (QCs)

Quality circles refer to regular meetings at which employees and supervisors share ideas about work-unit priorities. Managers and employees discover viable solutions to most of their work-unit problems by listening to each other and working together.

Those who have used the system warn that discussions should be limited to eligible subjects. Extraneous topics, such as grievances about labor contracts, should be ruled out (in this case, other remedies are available to labor).

The presence of labor representatives can be an advantage in QC discussions. The QC recommendations may call for changes in the work organization that will affect employees who have not participated in the discussion, and labor representatives can ease these tensions and help implement the new ideas.

Robert Moses, who built many impressive projects for the New York area, had few labor problems. He settled all labor differences at the start of construction. When the project was completed and dedication plans were formulated, the president of the Building Trades Council was invited to be on the platform along with the mayor, the governor, and other dignitaries. Labor generally appreciates being recognized as a working part of a program.

Management in turn must help overcome the anxiety of some supervisors and employee leaders who fear that they will lose their influence with the workers if they participate in QC discussions. All must be persuaded that the communication is truly open, and it may be desirable to keep minutes of meetings.

Routine and preventive maintenance

It is often helpful, in work planning and budgeting, to separate building maintenance into routine, ongoing work and preventive maintenance. This section of the chapter takes this approach, first summarizing work orders, which authorize special jobs, and then reviewing routine and preventive maintenance.

Work orders

The work order is the documentary heart of good maintenance. It is a written record showing what, where, and when. It prevents confusion among differing levels of maintenance personnel, often a problem in smaller communities.

The two general types of work orders are the specific maintenance assignment and the "open" work order for tasks performed on a regular basis. Generally the latter order should not be written for more than one year.

A work order should give the employee all the information needed to complete the task, and also should give management the following information as a minimum: originator's name; authorization; work-order number; location of the work to be performed and the department requiring the work; identification of equipment, structure, or grounds being maintained; completion date; description of the work; estimate of labor, material, equipment, and overhead required; time actually spent on the job; parts and materials used; costs; and personnel actually performing the work.

These work orders provide management with a history of the performance of specific items and a comparative guide covering the cost of repetitive repairs. In addition, the record of materials, labor, and parts used offers a budgeting tool.

Management may be forced by circumstances to bypass the work order in an emergency. As soon as the emergency is over, however, the information should be compiled and the order filed.

Routine building maintenance

The purpose of building maintenance is not only to protect the physical integrity of the structure and equipment but also to help employees, visitors, and others use the properties efficiently and pleasantly. "Routine" building maintenance means regular maintenance, often day to day, with established procedures. The following procedures are generally a part of most good building maintenance practices:

1. Place furnishings, tools, and equipment where they will not hamper the movement of those using the building.
2. Keep traffic areas free of obstructions such as cabinets, desks, racks, bins, benches, boxes, and baskets.
3. Keep wastebaskets and ashtrays empty and clean. Regularly clean and dust radiators, desks, cabinets, louvers, exhibit cases, panels, and displays.
4. Keep all metal surfaces polished.
5. Keep all drinking fountains clean, clear of debris, and in good working order. Keep a trash receptacle nearby.
6. Keep storage areas clean and in order.

Rest rooms   Management must give special attention to cleanliness in rest rooms, shower rooms, and locker rooms because of threats to health. These instructions are minimal:

1. Keep soap, paper, and towel racks filled, mirrors clean, and shelves clean, polished, and free of debris.
2. Check regularly to make sure that the showers, toilets, and washbasins are properly vented, and that the plumbing does not leak.
3. Check the enamel on all fixtures for breaks, chips, and cracks.
4. When installing new fixtures, check drywall and floors for cracks, and check other areas that might need repair.

In general, all housekeeping maintenance should be subject to daily inspection, and management should encourage crews to look for potential trouble areas.

Floor maintenance   Most experienced managers of buildings and grounds agree that maintenance of floors and their coverings is expensive. What begins as a loose tile or moist spot in a corner of a room can develop into costly repair. With the introduction of new materials and methods of floor installation, maintenance procedures can change, but the following should be considered basic:

1. Instruct maintenance personnel to keep areas of flooring free of loose, damaged, or missing bases, binding strips, and thresholds; projecting nails, bolts, and screws; slippery surfaces; and loose or missing nosings and treads.
2. Insist that carpets and rugs be free of raveling, cuts, and tears; facing and discoloration; loose anchorage; and obvious insect damage. Establish regular schedules for vacuuming and shampooing.
3. Insist on regular inspection to ensure that wood floors are not sagging, splintering, warping, rotting, or scratched. Request prompt investigation and repair, if needed. Look for developing wet spots, stains, and discolorations. Check for signs of termite or other insect infestations. Establish a regular schedule for cleaning, waxing, and buffing.
4. If the building has resilient flooring, insist that it be checked for signs of cracking, shifting, and breaking.
5. Floor framing should also be inspected on an established schedule. The principal points to look for are evidence of decay, deterioration, sagging, and of course termite invasion as well as overall soundness. If joists require replacing, the work should be done in accordance with the current building code. In older buildings, the joists often have been installed at spacings that are excessive and potentially dangerous.

A little background on floor polish should be of interest in this section. Originally floors were "waxed" with beeswax. This worked well but left the floor too slippery so maintenance crews of that time devised a crude method of measuring slipperiness. They filled a cloth sack with 10 pounds of shot and pulled it across the floor by a fish scale. If the scale recorded a resistance of less than 3 pounds, the floor was considered dangerous. If it exceeded 3 pounds, it was satisfactory.

Now the chemists have developed synthetic polishes and can make them as slipproof as desired, and the bees have lost a market.

Interior walls, ceilings, and attics   Interior walls and ceilings generally require less attention than other areas. Nevertheless, managers must establish routines for inspection and maintenance. These are suggested:

1. Inspect routinely for leaks, cracks, decay, insect infestation, stains, scuff marks, and loose fastenings. If feasible, place furniture so that it is a minimum of 4 to 6 inches from the wall.
2. Plan to repaint at intervals of one to three years. Clean and dust regularly, as the need dictates. Repair abrasions, punctures, tears, or adhesive failures.
3. Check attic ventilation. Make certain that boxes or other stored articles do not obstruct the flow of air.
4. Establish a regular attic inspection schedule to look for defective roof sheathing, water penetration, warped floor covering, loose collar ties, and warped attic access doors. Check plumbing stacks, chimneys, and plaster.
5. Remove graffiti as soon as it appears. Graffiti repellant coatings and graffiti removal compounds are available commercially.

Door and window maintenance   Doors and windows are access points that aid in the safe movement of personnel. As a minimum, inspection schedules should cover these points:

1. Insist that any splits, cracks, or rot in the wood sash be repaired immediately.
2. Establish a schedule for oiling door hinges and checking hinge bolts. Instruct the maintenance crews to see that the bottom and door-facing closing strips are clean and tight. Insist on regular checks of doorknobs and locks for evidence of corrosion or spot breakage.
3. Set a schedule of cleaning screens and inspecting them for holes in the mesh or breaks in the casing.
4. Insist that broken glass in windows or doors be replaced immediately.
5. Schedule cleaning of venetian blinds. Check the pull cords to see that they have not tightened. Lubricate the mechanisms when needed. Schedule cleaning of draperies and check them for loose fastenings, broken strands, and frayed cords.

Stairway maintenance   Maintenance management must be cognizant of the risks of injuries to employees and the public if stairs are poorly maintained. As a minimum a maintenance schedule should see that:

1. Defects in stringers, risers, and treads are repaired immediately.
2. Handrails are routinely inspected for stability. Concentrate on the base of the rail pole, checking for stripped threads on the screws or for cracked concrete below the base cap.
3. Light fixtures and switches are inspected to see that they are working.

Exterior wall maintenance   The type of maintenance needed for the exteriors of buildings depends on the material used to build the wall. If the wall is constructed of masonry, management should emphasize inspection practices that detect cracks, spalling, eroded or sandy joints, stains, and evidence of water passing through the walls themselves. Crews must be trained to know when a pointing repair will suffice and when patching with appropriate material is needed.

If there are wood walls, management must establish a repainting program, usually at intervals of three to five years. However, if the paint shows evidence of blistering or peeling, maintenance crews must investigate to determine evidence of moisture entering the walls and take corrective action. They should also keep an eye out for loose and missing fasteners and either repair or replace them.

If the wall has a metal facing, maintenance may be restricted to washing to eliminate grime and stains. The crews should inspect for pitting, punctures, and loose fasteners. They should also be alert for evidence of rust or corrosion.

Gutters, downspouts, and roof drains   Gutters, downspouts, and roof drains are items that the public sees and understands. Although neglect may cause only minimal damage to the building, it will substantially lower the maintenance department's credibility in the eyes of the taxpayer. It thus falls on management to schedule the cleaning, maintenance, and replacement of these items.

When establishing these schedules, management should (1) check the alignment and fastening of the drains; (2) establish either quarterly or semiannual cleaning programs to remove leaves and other debris and ensure that the wire guards are in place; (3) inspect the connections of the spouts to the storm sewers if this method of disposal is permitted; and (4) schedule repainting every three to four years.

Preventive maintenance

Preventive maintenance is a more exacting form of general maintenance. Its aim is to ensure that the normally expected breakdown doesn't happen.

To ensure that it doesn't, management must train personnel to think in terms of preventive maintenance and develop a thorough understanding of the materials and equipment placed under their care. Recommendations in suppliers' manuals provide a good starting point. Interviews with maintenance crews serving buildings and grounds may help. Equipment with a history of recurring problems clearly indicates the need to intensify preventive maintenance.

Heating, ventilation, and air-conditioning   Most buildings today have heating, ventilation, and air-conditioning equipment, identified by the unpronounceable acronym, HVAC. Frequently, HVAC equipment is sufficiently complex to require the services and advice of the supplier, but some general rules apply:

1. Inspections should be made on a monthly basis. These should be in addition to inspection by housekeeping crews.
2. Air filters should be kept clear of dust, grease, and lint. Inspectors should clean or replace filters as needed.
3. Inspectors should keep mechanical elements free of dust, dirt, soot, grease, lubricant drippings, rust, corrosion, and chemicals. Loose, broken, or missing parts should be repaired or replaced.
4. Wiring and electrical elements must be inspected for loose connections, frayed or worn braid, and improperly sized fuses; these deficiencies must be corrected immediately.
5. Exposed piping must be checked for clogged, rusted, corroded, or leaking parts. Valves, traps, and strainers must be clear of scale and leaks.
6. Inspectors should keep all air ducts free of soot, dirt, and grease. Loose connections in joints and seams should be repaired.
7. Inspectors should become familiar with boiler standards such as those provided in the *Heating, Ventilating and Air Conditioning Guide* of the American Society of Heating, Refrigerating, and Air Conditioning Engineers, and should base their inspection of boilers on information that the guide contains.

Temperature controls   In older buildings, temperature controls generally are simple and perform few functions. Newer controls are required for more complex modern heating and cooling systems. In both cases, however, management should base inspection on standards such as these:

1. Do not tamper with the controls; protect them with glass or box enclosures. Investigate controls that can be adjusted only by key.
2. Keep control boxes clean so that the dials or gauges can be easily read.
3. Control the air temperature in the rooms by thermostats except when units use solid fuel. Check the thermostats regularly to see that they are in good working order.
4. Be absolutely sure that all heating elements are vented to the outside by means of an adequate chimney, vent pipe, or smoke pipe. Do not allow combustion gases to escape into the building.
5. Inspect all safety devices used by the heating units to ensure that they are operating properly.
6. If the inspectors are not confident of their maintenance procedures, retain someone who is knowledgeable to perform the maintenance, and write up the procedures as a safeguard against court action in case something goes wrong.

7. In summer instruct that temperatures be maintained at 78° F. Winter temperatures should be no more than 70° F, and 68° F is acceptable.

Electrical maintenance As a guide, these inspection procedures are basic:

1. Instruct electricians to inspect fuse panels regularly to see that they are not overfused. Inspectors should also look for frayed or bare wire, especially in attics and basements, and repair it immediately.
2. Routine maintenance for wiring deficiencies should include detection of improperly spliced wire and rotted or cracked insulation; improperly grounded electrical contacts, especially convenience outlets; inadequate lighting; use of extension cords for permanent wiring; and breaker boxes and fuse panels that are incorrectly labeled and not identified by circuit.

Management must prepare electrical inspection procedures for the maintenance and control of outside electrical systems involving such facilities as parking-lot lighting, safety illumination, and outside electrical outlets. Light poles should be examined for cracks and spalling, and anchor plates and bolts on the poles should be inspected for evidence of rust, corrosion, and loose bolts.

Electric service panels should be examined for improper labels, and all outside electrical services should be inspected twice a week.

Plumbing maintenance Inspectors should routinely look for leaks, breaks, corrosion, stoppages, odors, and gases; examine insulation for unsealed portions and evidence of moisture; test for valves and traps that do not operate; look for cracks in china and chips in porcelain fixtures; and report stains that have not been removed during routine housekeeping.

Roof maintenance Managers of buildings and grounds should maintain accurate inventories of *all* roofs, including maintenance and replacement needs for at least five years so that any unusual expenditures can be identified in advance.

Roofs carry warranties, but this does not eliminate the need for a few simple roof-maintenance practices that will avoid major repairs and disruptions of operations. These elementary maintenance practices should be followed:

1. On metal portions, look for broken seams, rust, and corrosion. Repair holes, open joints, and loose, broken, or missing fastenings immediately.
2. On roofs with wood, tile, or slate shingles, replace those that are warped, broken, split, or loosened.
3. On built-up roofs, look for and repair cracks, exposed coatings, blistering, curling, and buckling.
4. On flashings, look for rust, corrosion, open joints, and missing fastenings. Repair immediately.

Maintenance crews must be instructed that water will go through unbelievably small openings in a roof, and when it enters, it can cause major damage. The maintenance crew's goal is a watertight roof.

Elevator maintenance Because of the high risk, the maintenance of elevators remains a task for licensed mechanics; in most cities, elevators are inspected and certified by city inspectors.

Management still has certain responsibilities, however. Every elevator cab must carry a notice telling passengers what to do in case of an elevator malfunction. It also must carry warnings about passenger load limits. Notices of this nature should be at the elevator entrances as well as in the cabs.

Other maintenance tasks should be to clean and wax the cabs and doors, generally the duty of the housecleaning crews.

Some buildings have elevators called dumbwaiters that do not carry passengers but move material from floor to floor. Licensed, professional crews generally perform maintenance for them, ensuring that motors, pulleys, and stops perform properly.

Fire-control apparatus   Most buildings have sprinkler systems that local fire departments inspect regularly. Maintenance personnel should be sufficiently familiar with them to know when parts are defective, but manufacturers' representatives or the equivalent should perform the repairs.

Fire extinguishers are available in four different types.

Class A extinguishers can control fires of wood, paper, rubber, and many plastics. They utilize water, foam, or dry chemicals and are designed to cover a maximum of 3,000 square feet. Generally they are placed at intervals no greater than 75 feet.

Class B extinguishers are designed to extinguish fires fueled by liquids, gases, and greases. They may contain foam, compressed gas, dry chemicals, or vaporizing liquids. The extinguishers should be separated by no more than 50 feet.

Class C extinguishers are designed for electrical fires and contain a nonconducting flame suppressant. Using water on such a fire is extremely dangerous and might electrocute the operator.

Class D extinguishers should be used at special locations where combustible metals are found. These can include magnesium, titanium, zirconium, sodium, and potassium. Maintenance crews should inspect the extinguisher nameplate to determine its degree of effectiveness.

Fire alarms can be highly sophisticated or simple bells. The sophisticated types can have an annunciator in each main entrance of the building that tells where the fire is located, and also a connection with the local fire and police departments.

Maintenance crews should learn how sprinkler systems are activated, and how to shut them off if the fire is small so as to prevent the sprinkler system from causing unnecessary water damage. They also should be told what minor repairs they might make. Rigid, regular inspections must be management's policy on fire protection.

Smoke alarms are a valuable supplement to sprinklers. In many buildings, such as libraries or offices where files important to the community are kept, sprinklers can cause as much damage, and often more than the fire itself. In certain cases, smoke alarms are legitimate alternates to sprinklers.

Custodial maintenance

Custodial service workers, more frequently called by the disparaging term *janitors*, are often neglected by management. Personnel tend to be hired at the lowest possible wage, with the result that employee turnover is high. These workers receive virtually no training, and no effort is made to make them feel an important part of the buildings and grounds organization.

Management must be cognizant of these shortcomings and be prepared to rectify them. The first basic step is to design a rational custodial program. Four steps deserve consideration.

1.   Inventory the physical components of each building to determine the source and extent of the work load.
2.   Estimate the work-hour requirements.
3.   Establish the number of positions required to perform the tasks.
4.   Make personnel assignments on the basis of work areas and schedules.

Assignments

Once the worker requirements have been determined, employees can be organized into two basic groups according to their assignments: fixed stations and the gang system. In the first case, a custodian is assigned to a fixed work area; in the second, a crew of several custodians reports to a supervisor and moves from one work area to another.

The first type of assignment gives the custodian a sense of individual responsibility and a feeling of confidence. The second may be combined with the first from time to time, with the gang performing intermittent maintenance work and the fixed-station worker performing the daily tasks.

High turnover of custodial workers is a concern to management. Such workers are generally at the bottom rung of the organization's employment ladder and accordingly receive minimum wages. Moreover, they have little chance of moving up the career ladder.

In-house or contract custodial work

The buildings and grounds manager has the responsibility of recommending to the department of public works whether the best interests of the department are served by using day-labor custodial employees or a private contractor to perform custodial work. Basically the difference between the two is that the latter must earn a profit, whereas the former need not.

Many argue that the city can avoid direct union problems by using private contractors. This may be true until the unions organize the private crews, as they have done in such services as refuse collection.

When investigating private contractors, check their reputation among clients, their employee turnover, their financial statements, the duration of the contract offered and whether it includes a contract-renewal clause, and the experience record of the company.

Energy conservation

The issue of energy conservation has lost much of the intensity that it had amidst the panic caused by the oil boycott of 1973. Since the mid-1980s, however, the nation has been facing another energy situation that will not go away. The cost of building electrical generating stations to meet the increased demand for power has quietly but spectacularly risen. And if the demand rises further, the cost of electricity delivered from these new plants will rise also.

The experience of the Allegheny Power Company, a relatively small electrical utility, illustrates this price rise. Allegheny Power reports that in 1968 the construction cost per kilowatt of generating capacity was under $130. By 1980 the cost had risen to over $600. Furthermore, the utility reports that in 1970 it could buy coal for $5.70 per ton. Ten years later, the cost of coal had risen to $31.55 per ton. The costs incurred to meet environmental restrictions had nearly quadrupled over the late 1960s.[2]

As a result of these escalating costs, many utilities are promoting energy-saving programs, hoping to postpone the day when they will be forced to enlarge their plants and raise their rates.

For buildings and grounds managers, energy budgeting[3] for a building is one way of attacking this problem. The energy budget analysis requires setting energy consumption limits in Btus per square foot of building area. This type of analysis is based on (1) annual consumption, (2) peak hourly demand of the cooling cycle, and (3) peak hourly demand of the heating cycle. It embraces all forms of energy required in the building, such as power for elevators, food preparation, and operation of equipment.

Actual energy use should be monitored and compared to the energy budget. Significant deviations from the budget on the high side may indicate problems in the construction or operation of the facility.

In the design of new facilities, the obligation of the design engineer is to save as much energy as possible without increasing the cost of construction or reducing the comfort levels. This can be done by introducing energy load-trimming procedures, heat recovery equipment, or solar energy collectors. Cogeneration also is a cost-effective technique in many applications.

The potential effectiveness of energy cost-reduction measures can be determined by analyzing local energy rate structures. A high electric-demand (kw) charge, for example, would indicate the need for demand-control techniques, such as generation peak shaving, which respond to load dynamics; whereas a low demand charge or a flat electric rate based only on consumption (kwh) would indicate a need for measures that would reduce total connected loads and the running time of equipment.

Roofs account for most of the heat gain and loss in a building, thus justifying the use of additional insulation. This must be placed to avoid problems with dewpoint condensation and heat buildup in unvented spaces. Roofs also may be coated with a reflective paint or sprayed with water intermittently.

In their efforts to reduce energy requirements, buildings and grounds managers should consider whether it would be cost-effective to replace single-pane glass with insulating double or triple glazing, or to tint the single-pane glass. In the case of skylights, new insulated glass deserves investigating. The energy-saving value of skylights as a means of reducing the need for artificial lighting should not be overlooked.

Security management

The greatest building security risks occur when the building is closed. Consequently, the first line of defense is the maintenance and housekeeping personnel, who should be instructed to be alert for doors left open to offices or areas normally closed for security reasons; desk drawers left unlocked or conspicuously open; doors to safes or other normally locked equipment not fully closed; items or equipment conspicuously out of place; individuals not known to maintenance personnel who are found within the building or on the grounds after working hours and who offer vague reasons for being there; items, equipment, or obviously valuable papers found in trash receptacles; and unfamiliar vehicles found in parking lots.[4]

Sometimes maintenance people breach security by propping exterior doors open when they leave temporarily to discard refuse or for other reasons.

Management should appraise each building to determine what items a high-risk burglar would want to take. Any equipment or material that can be transported easily and disposed of quickly would be attractive and would include typewriters, word processors, calculators, office furniture, bulk food supplies, tools, equipment parts, cash, negotiable notes and bonds, computer tapes or printouts, confidential reports, and even automobiles.

Management should not discount the possible threat of violence to key personnel if information or material kept within the building is sufficiently attractive to those who want it. If these violence-prone individuals cannot obtain it by theft, they will not hesitate to threaten injury or murder to obtain what they want.

Basic security measures should embrace door locks with deadbolts, high fencing, window grills, ultrasonic alarms, radioactive sensors, heat sensors, smoke sensors, infrared alarms, electronic eyes, silent alarms, fire alarm pull stations, safes and vaults, and radio-controlled openers. Computers and computer programs can provide additional ways to assist those responsible for building security.

Managers should arrange for frequent spot checks on security requirements. These will disclose personnel needing refresher courses on existing security procedures.

Grounds maintenance

Many public buildings have substantial grounds with attractive trees and shrubbery. These amenities have more than decorative value. Trees and shrubbery cool and freshen the air. If they are carefully placed to shield the building from intense sunlight, they can reduce air-conditioning costs, sometimes by as much as 30 percent. These grounds should be policed to remove accumulations of debris, including branches, leaves, and miscellaneous trash.

In the spring, management should schedule remulching of trees, shrubs, and other planted areas and should instruct the maintenance personnel to turn over the mulch and add more if needed. The mulch depth should not be greater than 2 or 3 inches.

A little planning can reduce mowing costs. Maintenance crews can eliminate sharp corners around walls and buildings and other above-grade landscape features; paved mowing strips against walls and buildings will eliminate hand trimming. Keep grass surfaces flush with paved areas such as walks and parking lots. Space groups of trees or shrubberies far enough apart to accommodate mowing equipment.

Eliminate hand trimming around trees by using grass barriers such as flush metal edging. Use ground cover on steep slopes and other areas difficult to mow. Provide ramps for mowing equipment in areas with sharp differences in elevation. Plan for roads, walks, and entrances that are wide enough for passage of mowing equipment. Keep lawn areas clear of unnecessary obstructions where they interfere with mowing.

Transplanting trees and shrubberies is a continuous task. A 5 percent annual loss of trees is normal. Trees that are to be transplanted successfully in public grounds must have trunk diameters of 2 to 2½ inches, and the trunks should be wrapped to prevent vandalism. The root ball should be kept moist during transport and should be placed in a hole large enough to provide the roots with enriched soil consisting of a good loam mixed with peat moss or other organic material. The soil around the root ball should be soaked and tamped during backfilling to remove air pockets. The soil should be saucer-shaped when the backfilling is completed to catch rainwater. The transplanted trees should be pruned back by no more than one-third to compensate for root loss.

Buildings and grounds managers cannot expect city or county snow removal crews to plow their walks and driveways. The crews will have their hands full keeping the arterial roads clear and then plowing and clearing the feeder roads and side streets. Buildings and grounds personnel should therefore plan to acquire motor equipment that can be used for several tasks—mowers that have attachments for snow plowing or snow blowing; a jeep that can be fitted with a plow or a blower; a snowplow for a front-end loader that can quickly be clamped on.

Management must form a snow-fighting and ice-control crew under the direction of a supervisor, probably the person in charge of grounds maintenance. When the weather reports predict snow, the supervisor must alert the crew, calling them at home if necessary. If the snowfall is light, an application of salt or calcium chloride will probably melt it. Salt performs best in an ambient temperature range of 20° to 32° F. It loses its effectiveness when the temperature drops, and at 6° F it reacts scarcely at all. At the lower ranges, the crew should mix the salt with calcium chloride at a ratio of three parts salt to one of chloride. The latter goes to work at once while the salt will remain effective for a longer period.

Snow fences should be considered for buildings that lie in the open where winds can develop drifts that will thwart snow-clearing efforts. Unfortunately, few people use these fences effectively.

Drifting snow travels only a well-defined distance. Snow particles undergo evaporation, or sublimation, depending on the solar radiation, ambient temperatures, relative humidity, and the size of the snow particles. Scientifically developed formulas can determine this distance with some precision. However, certain rule-of-thumb guidelines will work in most cases.

1. Measuring from the roadway edge or the property line, place the fence at a distance twenty-five times the height of the fence from ground level.
2. Place the bottom of the fence from 6 to 18 inches above the ground. Blowing snow tends to concentrate close to the ground where the wind has little effect.
3. Maintain a fence porosity of 50 percent.
4. Place the fence perpendicular to the prevailing wind.

Normally the drift will extend twenty to twenty-five times the height of the fence, measured from the ground. Tall fences, about 12 feet, are obviously more effective than shorter fences that range from 4 to 6 feet.

Conclusion

Buildings and grounds managers oversee a multitude of activities and tasks. The neglect of any one of them will damage the usefulness of the structures and grounds entrusted to them. Such damage will in turn interfere with the performance of the service departments using the facilities, impede the delivery of services to the public, and create dissatisfaction with the governing body.

The quotation at the start of the chapter shows how the loss of a horseshoe nail caused the loss of a kingdom. Buildings and grounds managers are responsible for many horseshoe nails. Their performance has a direct bearing on the ability of the municipality to supply, through other departments, services needed by the community.

1   The information on building maintenance comes primarily from the American Public Works Association, Institute for Buildings and Grounds, *Centralized Administration of Public Buildings*, Special Report no. 50 (Chicago, 1984).

2   Allegheny Power System, Inc., *Annual Report* (New York, May 10, 1984).

3   Williams S. Foster, "Energy Budget, Municipal Buildings," *American City & County*, April 1978, p. 40.

4   William S. Foster, ed., *Handbook of Municipal Administration and Engineering* (New York: McGraw-Hill, 1978), p. 11–37.

13 Transportation

As far back as the Middle Ages and the Renaissance, the cities of Europe were faced with transportation problems not unlike those of today. Although their streets were adequate for pedestrians and the occasional man on horseback or mule, they could not handle the growing numbers of carts, wagons, and carriages, partly because of the irregular layout of streets. To cope with these problems, cities issued many decrees regarding parking, speeding, and even U-turns. In 1540, for example, Francois I forbade wagoners and drivers, whether of carts, drays, or other vehicles, to turn in the streets except at intersections and corners.

Another problem was the surface of streets. For centuries, street paving was unknown, although it had been used in the sacred ways of ancient Memphis, Babylon, and pre-Christian Rome. As a result, pedestrians in medieval cities were choked by clouds of dust in dry weather and were equally inconvenienced by mud during wet spells. Little by little, paving was introduced to important thoroughfares, but most European rulers were unwilling to build or pay for heavy paved roads and instead commanded landowners to maintain the roads that ran past their property. Most citizens, however, preferred to spend their money and time in other ways than keeping up their city. Attempts to make citizens pave the streets in front of their homes proved ineffectual. When hauled before the courts, the householders wailed that they had no money to pay the pavers and that, in any case, that stretch of road had never been paved so there was actually no need to do so. Moreover, the homeowners had to put up with dishonest pavers whose boldness grew from the mandates of the king. It was not unusual for pavers to dig up perfectly good paving to compel the householders to hire them to replace it! Even though such destruction of pavement had been made a capital crime, the racket flourished.

What do these historical minutiae have to with an up-to-date chapter on the management aspects of transportation? The answer is, "Everything."

Transportation makes it possible to have urban centers and to get around in them. This chapter deals with four of the most important elements of urban transportation—planning, street maintenance, traffic, and airports. These elements are in constant use and under the pressure of widely fluctuating demands and intense citizen expectations.

The first section looks at the transportation planning process from the public works point of view, street classification, transportation systems management, subdivisions and street patterns, parking, pedestrian systems, public transit, and other aspects of urban transportation.

The next section deals with street maintenance, particularly with respect to pavements, street surfacing, street cleaning, snow removal, and bridge maintenance. One of the themes of this section is that comprehensive maintenance brings long-run benefits both to the economy and to the citizens of cities and towns.

The third topic is traffic management, which is reviewed from the standpoint of traffic studies, traffic control devices, street lighting, and methods for organizing traffic flow and relieving traffic congestion.

The final section summarizes airport classifications and ownership patterns, management responsibilities, financing, and relations with the community and the federal government.

Transportation planning

Over the past two centuries, transportation in the United States has evolved from ocean and river transport to the automobile, truck, railroad, and airplane. Good harbors and access by water were the major determinants in the location of Philadelphia, New York, Chicago, San Francisco, St. Louis, New Orleans, and other large cities.[1]

During the last half of the nineteenth century, thousands of miles of railroad track were laid, reaching into remote corners of almost every state. Hundreds of towns and villages sprang up alongside the track to serve as loading and transfer points for agricultural products, raw materials, and finished goods. From the 1870s to the 1920s, intercity trolley cars (often known as "interurbans") and commuter railroads were strong forces in shaping metropolitan areas.

Since the 1920s, it has been the automobile that has changed cities, spreading urban and suburban development over enormous areas. The average family now has its suburban villa on a large lot with yards on all sides, thus increasing the size of the utility system the public works department has to provide and maintain.[2] The automobile has decentralized the central business district (CBD) of many cities, and, following Raymond Vernon's predictions of the 1950s, the "gray areas" around the CBD are expanding rapidly. The new shopping malls of the 1950s in the far suburbs of large cities have long since reached the outskirts of smaller cities. In the metropolises, business and industrial parks have developed in profusion. The interstate highway system has facilitated the spread of urbanization into what appeared to be fringes only thirty years ago.

Since the 1930s, trucks have supplanted railroads in many markets and raised new problems for traffic engineers in older cities with narrow streets. Highway engineers have had to contend with longer trucks carrying much heavier loads; predictably, maintenance costs have accelerated while highway revenues have lagged behind. The shift to cars and trucks has affected city development as old, small railroad yards are eliminated or consolidated into larger facilities.

As of the mid-1980s, the nation is securely bound together by low-cost passenger and freight air transport.

The transportation planning process

Such massive changes in a relatively short time should leave no doubt about the importance and need for a transportation plan that addresses the movement of people and goods. Yet many public works and city and county planning officials did not have sound transport plans until the federal government required and began to fund them in the 1950s. With the current decline in federal planning funds, the frequency, if not the quality, of the process is slipping.

The key to transportation planning was discovered several decades ago—that is, the frequency of trips varies with the type and intensity of land use.[3] Cities have been controlling land use, primarily through zoning, since the 1920s. Today cities and counties rely on extensive data, analysis, and regulations to control land use. Each public works official would intuitively know that a multifamily apartment house will need more off-street automobile parking and generate more trips than would a single-family residence. Thus the core of the concept is widely known. Land use, actual or planned, is used to generate the number of trips expected from residential, commercial, and industrial areas. As expected trips are quantified they are factored into the present and/or planned network of streets and transit systems. Complicated computerized mathematical models are utilized in this iterative process, for each decision is likely to affect other decisions and many decisions will have an adverse impact on areas and neighborhoods.

The planner constructs a model to predict what is likely to happen by some future date; the model is calibrated by checking its estimates for the present against the actual traffic counted in the origin and destination (O-D) survey. Computers are essential for large cities and more recently have been available in smaller ones. However, the same results can be obtained in simpler ways, especially for smaller towns or neighborhoods of larger cities. Some of the possibilities are discussed later in this chapter, but it is important to mention the linkage between theory and practice here. Although public works officials may be able to apply their plans to the street system, it may be more difficult to change the transit system, which may be operated privately or by another public agency, perhaps a regional authority. In this case, more detailed plans may be made by the transit operator and these may be in conflict with those of the public works department or the city or county planning agency.

Some differences are expected; transit operators consider the short-range impact of cash flow whereas the street agency obtains the appropriation and expects to construct the link soon after design. Transit operators will look at an incremental link or extension and will want to test it for months before agreeing to keep it on "their" system. The operator may even object to new modes (i.e., paratransit, express bus lines, or light-rail transit) because their cost-revenue potentials do not fit the cash flow.

Large metropolitan areas often have problems with boundaries, not only between municipalities and counties, but also within service areas bisected by state lines. The transportation system is a connector and all boundary issues must be resolved to provide the designed service. A well-prepared planning process acceptable to political decision makers will help resolve these problems.

Public works and the transportation planning process

Implicit throughout this chapter is the thought that broad resolution of a variety of problems should take place in the planning process and be refined in the design process. Many cities or counties deal with particular problems through ad hoc studies. In very large areas these studies may take place simultaneously at regional, city, and neighborhood levels. Oftentimes ad hoc studies are put to the operational test since they are truly transportation systems management (TSM) related.

Other issues can be resolved in the subdivision process as owners divide or assemble property for new uses. Wooneruf, a technique being developed in Europe, limits residential access to a single path that serves several purposes, including recreation, shade trees, and the like. Consequently, through traffic is much more subordinated to other factors than is usual in the United States.[4]

Ad hoc and less comprehensive plans are not sufficient, however. The federal and some state governments call for a comprehensive, continuing, and cooperative planning process (the 3 Cs) to qualify an area for certain federal grants. The genesis of this requirement was first articulated in the Federal-Aid Highway Act of 1962.

Origin and destination studies were developed in the 1930s and 1940s, using home interviews and brief questionnaires administered along roadways and on transit vehicles. The purpose of origin and destination studies was to determine the beginning and end points of a substantial number of the trips made in a city. By the 1960s, these simple studies had evolved into expensive planning exercises costing hundreds of thousands or even millions of dollars. The ad hoc groups in charge of these studies occasionally spent so much money collecting data that they had to skimp on the analysis phase because of a lack of funds. As staffs were demobilized and leases canceled, much of the accumulated knowledge disappeared.

Soon it was apparent that if such studies could be made continuous and comprehensive (that is, if they could cover land uses, transit, and pedestrians), the knowledge would be more useful to more organizations and would be more readily available.

This led to new demands for governmental structures that could accommodate a revised process and reduce bureaucratic infighting. The earlier studies were usually accomplished by the state transportation agency; local governments were strongly involved in a few. A very few left major aspects of control in the hands of local government. Several agencies contributed funds and staff, but in many instances the local public works official played a minor role, perhaps because the importance of the work was underestimated or there were not enough staff or funds to contribute. The transit agency was more often the stepchild of the process.

Costs were usually shared, leading to the cooperative term, but the state(s) and the federal government had the major share. The city planning agency often had a more modest role than seemed appropriate to many local governments, but cities thought they had to choose as their representative the head of the streets agency. The alternative appeared to be that the city's representative would be designated by the state.

Whether it is metropolitan in scope or smaller, the transportation planning process is complex and involves many agencies, not all under the control of a single executive.[5] Thus a team has to be assembled consisting of capable representatives of all pertinent agencies. Many good examples exist of successful groupings. The leader is the key appointment. It is his or her responsibility to see that the work of the group moves steadily forward so that the goals and objectives are attained.

Rarely does a public works agency control the entire transportation planning process, and this is the way it should be. Nearly everyone is interested in the outcome, and in large metropolitan areas, the stakes can be hundreds of millions of dollars. Because land use is related to transportation needs, large-scale transportation facilities create high land values, often almost immediately. Thus landowners, planning agencies, transit agencies, multistate authorities, public utilities (privately owned in most areas), mortgage holders on large plants or buildings, tenants, truckers, and politicians are concerned about the distribution of values brought about by changes in the transportation system.

Ideally, transportation planning goals, especially those at the regional level should be determined or at least proposed by the metropolitan planning organization (MPO). This agency has been given the mandate to do so by federal legislation, usually buttressed by state legislation. Moreover, it has been designated by the governor to carry out such assignments. In large metropolitan areas, the formulation and adoption of goals is a complex process, but well-articulated and reasonable goals are readily accepted.

Citywide goals are usually the product of the city-planning process. In some areas, Houston and Los Angeles, for example, the municipality constitutes the important economic area and its plan is likely to be a determining factor in establishing regional goals. Elsewhere, the city is a lesser part of the region—as in Denver, Pittsburgh, and Boston. In some cities, as in Pittsburgh, the county may be strong enough to establish its goals as paramount. Regardless of the size of the cities or regions, planning agencies must work effectively with the MPO so that the approved plan becomes an action document and not one that is placed on the shelf and occasionally opened by historians.

Once written goals have been accepted, the role of the public works agency or agencies becomes much more important. Generally, such a group has money appropriated for ongoing maintenance and reconstruction. During the preparation of construction plans, broad issues are identified and resolved—for they may have an impact on an existing bus route, major underground utility lines, or a private landowner's plan. New construction is even more likely to affect others and thereby the plan. This major role gives the public works agency an important voice in effectuating the plan. The short-term decision does have an impact; many think it is the determining factor in plan implementation.

The city planning agency may choose a variation to a public works proposal. Progress will be more rapid if the two departments work together through open discussion rather than at cross-purposes. The operating budget may not go before the planning commission, even for comment, so the public works department will have the funds for force account work, contractual work, materials, design engineering, and staff analysts. Clearly, these are powerful tools that can be and have been used to preempt the planning process. The capital budget, on the other hand, is more likely to be controlled by the planners. Ultimately, it is the city council that will determine the projects to be built and that may provide sufficient appropriations for engineering and property acquisition.

Planners also play an important role in long-range capital improvements programs. Long-range plans include proposed funding for projects that are envisioned five to ten years hence. As transportation projects may be among the largest a city carries out, the public works transportation team will put considerable effort into this area.

A word of caution is in order here. Many city and county officials may promote glamorous projects such as professional baseball or football stadiums because they have strong public and political appeal. But the reconstruction of an undersized sewer or repairs to a dilapidated building are just as important. The public works or transportation planner may have to fight for the unglamorous or soon see these needs greatly exceed the government's ability to finance them. If more cities in the United States had not ignored such needs for so long, there would be less concern about the deteriorating infrastructure.

Street classification

Street systems serve a variety of purposes. For a long time streets were constructed to different standards, and it was not until recently that the classification concept came into use.[6] Only a few cities are thought to be "planned cities" (e.g., Philadelphia and Washington, D.C.), and their original plans encompass only a small part of today's conglomeration. Most streets were laid out to serve the abutting properties, but soon it was observed that certain streets connected small villages or served many other people. The "through trips" became a large share of the total trips and overshadowed the service to local users. Early in this century, with the pressure to "get the farmers out of the mud," it became clear that these differences had to be recognized in a systematic way so that limited funds could be concentrated on those roads serving the most people. Then, as now, approximately 80 percent of the total trips were made on 20 percent of the mileage, both on urban streets and rural roads. As our understanding of traffic dynamics grew, it became obvious that "systems" were desirable or even essential to facilitate decisions on funding, set priorities on street links, and attempt to concentrate trips on the streets best able to handle them.

In this effort, two classifications emerged: functional and administrative. The functional is more the province of the traffic engineer and the city planner, who must consider how the street will be used. The administrative is concerned with who will construct and pay for the work—city, county, state, or federal government. After the concept was accepted and applied, design standards and other criteria were defined, in part to ensure that the funds granted by a government bought what was intended.

Local public works managers, especially the engineers, became enthusiastic supporters of the functional/administrative concept, and state and federal agencies encouraged its spread. As the interstate highway system was funded and urban extensions added thereto in the mid-1950s, the engineers' logical application of the concept began to hit insuperable road blocks. A multitude of social and economic factors peripheral to many engineers' interests began to block design and operating decisions. This was exacerbated by the requirements for public hearings, which gave a forum to opponents. The issues were often so strongly felt that even in the mid-1980s some major freeways, authorized two or three decades ago, have not yet been built. Many urban links have been abandoned. These opportunities were not overlooked by politicians who either tried to balance the needs of competing groups or to further their own careers by utilizing the new forums. The classification concept is still useful when applied judiciously as it aids the traffic engineer and planner in finding other solutions, but the term *judicious* must be stressed. At this time so much of the city's circulation system has been constructed that little flexibility may be available.

A good classification plan calls for a network of streets that integrates commercial and industrial development, schools, parks, residential areas, and intercity highways—that is, the traffic generators. The following classification is a reasonable one:

Traffic streets
   Freeways and expressways
   Major arterials
   Arterials

Service streets
   Major collectors
   Minor collectors
   Loop streets
   Cul-de-sacs

Connectors
   Major connectors
   Minor connectors
   Parking connectors.

Criteria for design and specifications for construction vary with the type of service to be rendered—width and number of lanes, types of curbs, thickness of paving. These factors are major determinants of the cost of building the street or highway. Obviously, a freeway with controlled access requires both a wide and costly right-of-way and a heavy paving, which is also costly. But its benefit-to-cost ratio will justify such expenditures because the freeway can handle so many trips more efficiently. A rural two-lane highway will cost much less, but, since it may carry only several hundred vehicles a day, the cost per trip is likely to be far higher.

Transportation systems management

Another concept in planning is transportation systems management (TSM).[7] It was developed in part because of the opposition to new freeways and/or funding constraints. TSM is acceptable to the efficiency-minded public works manager who has long attempted to get the most out of a limited budget and who should embrace the federal requirements nearly automatically. In part, the federal pressures for TSM came from both the transit and highway funding agencies who were looking for a means of reducing claims for new, expensive construction.

TSM was an outgrowth not only of the search for efficient operations, but also of the efforts of conservationists, who wanted to make do with less, and of

Mobility dominant goal	Conservation dominant goal
Larger cities	
"Add-a-lane" preferential facilities for high occupancy vehicles (HOV)	"Add-a-lane" preferential facilities for high occupancy vehicles (HOV)
Preferential parking for HOV	Preferential parking for HOV
Ride-sharing promotion	Ride-sharing promotion
Improvements in local bus fares, routes, and schedules	Improvements in local bus fares, routes, and schedules
Park–ride with express bus	Park–ride with express bus
Express bus operations	Express bus operations
Bicycle paths	Bicycle paths
Signal improvements	Ramp metering with HOV bypass
Pedestrian separations	Automobile restricted zones with HOV preference
One way streets	Exclusive HOV ramps
Reversible streets	Through traffic restrictions with HOV preference
Turn restrictions	"Take-a-lane" HOV preferential facilities
Ramp metering	Parking duration limit with HOV preference
Channelization and widening	Facility and area tolls and taxes with HOV preference
Curb parking restrictions	Parking duration pricing with HOV preference
Bus stop relocation	
Loading zones	
Speed limits	
Truck enhancements, controls	
Work rescheduling	
Motorists' aids, advisories	
Smaller, less congested cities	
Ride-sharing promotion	Ride-sharing promotion
Improvements in local bus fares, routes, and schedules	Improvements in local bus fares, routes, and schedules
Bicycle paths	Bicycle paths
Signal improvements	
Pedestrian separations	
One way streets	
Turn restrictions	
Right turn on red	
Channelization and widening	
Curb parking restrictions	
Bus stop relocation	
Loading zones	
Speed limits	

Figure 13–1   TSM actions by goals category.

neighborhood leaders, who thought the automobile had been given undue emphasis over neighborhood values. These pressures have forced highway planners to look for solutions in a new context because of the severe limitations on construction funds.

TSM calls for more alternatives, not fewer. It puts more emphasis on less costly short-term projects rather than capital-intensive long-term projects. TSM strategies include paving marking, improved signal systems, carefully considered traffic regulations, and the like (see Figure 13–1). Transit is even considered for some trips, usually via buses on existing streets rather than by building new streets or fixed-guideway transit lines. Obviously, TSM is more applicable to a mature city than to a rapidly developing city.

Many larger cities are changing as the transportation system changes. Some needs may be declining or moving away from the central business district (CBD), leaving facilities underutilized in one area and creating a need for new facilities in another. TSM can offer low-cost relief in one place to permit the expenditure of greater funds to solve a problem in another area. Unfortunately, this practice may lead to charges of the unequal distribution of funds, particularly if low-cost TSM solutions are repeatedly used in minority or low-income neighborhoods.

Subdivisions and street patterns

In some ways the problem in the mature city is different from that in the developing one.[8] Subdivisions in the older city are not restricted to undeveloped land, for estates may be too large for multifamily uses and may have to be demolished and thus the land is subdivided. The arterial street probably is already present in the older city whereas it will have to be constructed in the new.

In some of the older cities in the eastern United States, high-capacity rapid transit lines or commuter railroads may already exist to attract riders from a dense apartment project to be constructed in a former single-family area. Or a new transit system may cause developers to seek a land use change from low density to much higher density, especially near stations (Washington, D.C., and Toronto, Ontario, have many examples).

Thus the transportation planner addresses different problems in different types of cities. In growing cities, the expansion into undeveloped areas may be very rapid, forcing public works to build new arterial streets, sewers, parks, libraries, and other public facilities. Generally, the construction of minor collector streets is the sole responsibility of the developer. The cost to construct large capacity arterial streets may be shared between the developer and the public agency. In some instances the local agency pays the total cost.

Public transit

There are many other new public works for the manager to be concerned about— water, schools, firehouses, refuse disposal plants—each of which may be politically sensitive as well as difficult to finance. In the developing city, one issue that is often overlooked is the need for a street system that is capable of handling public transportation. Many subdivisions of the past five decades have been constructed on the premise that every family will own one or more automobiles. Yet, changing family situations, the cost and availability of petroleum, and city and state finances may force significant transportation model changes in the future. Although buses require slightly wider lanes and greater turning radii, the most important factor to consider may be the availability of connectors and the location of arterial streets. Unfortunately, many residents want convenient bus service providing the bus does not operate on their residential street.

As noted above, public transit has some special requirements, especially in a newer city or in the developing suburbs of the older city. The transit operator should have a member on the transportation planning team who can explain the proper role of public transit services. The traffic planner is likely to have this ability, partly because the street system has changed so little and partly because he has been trained to think of new and effective ways to move traffic.

The first consideration should be the need for special treatment of bus stops, a design rather than a planning function. However, the transit operator and traffic engineer must agree on whether it is better to place bus stops on the near side of the intersection rather than the far side (or vice versa) and if the bus should stop at every corner. A stop at every corner may be too frequent, particularly when the blocks are short; yet, the riders want the last leg of their trip home to be as short as possible. Wear and tear at the stop will require a heavier street section or more frequent maintenance.

A second point to consider is whether preference should be given to high-occupancy vehicles (trolley cars, buses, vans, or carpools known as HOV) in the timing of the traffic signal system or whether lanes can be dedicated for HOV during rush hours. Money and space are often too tight to make such decisions when an arterial is designed. Taking a lane that has been available for general use and dedicating it to a special purpose can cause an outcry, even though the group being aided should be and usually is the larger group. Nonetheless lanes in larger cities are reserved for buses at peak hours and might be considered for all day in some locations.[9]

More than a dozen cities have high-speed transit systems that require special planning considerations. Since new systems demand large capital investments, the budget (or budgets, for several municipalities are likely to be involved) may dictate where the line and stations are likely to be located. The traffic engineer and planner have special concerns about station designs. Where are the entrances and exits? Is space to be provided for transit rider drop-off from automobiles and buses? Will WALK signals be required? As usual, the objective is to balance the needs of diverse groups.

Western cities are facing such issues, and several of them are building light-rail transit lines (San Diego, San Jose–Santa Clara, and Sacramento, California, and Portland, Oregon). Others are planning for such lines (Denver and Dallas). The limited availability of petroleum may force more cities to follow that path, if the predictions of conservationists are proved to be correct.

If the transit operator is a regional agency with a broad mandate to build a system, the same questions will arise, and the public works transportation team will be involved in resolving them. If they are not involved, the new system may not function well at critical locations.

Parking

Parking for automobiles is a recent addition to the planner's menu, and in a few locations bus parking must also be considered (at areas with a large number of tourists) along with occasional bicycle parking (especially at or near colleges and in some major cities abroad).

In smaller cities, parking is a municipal problem only in the central business district, and in such places a few surface lots will suffice. In the largest cities, parking is needed in the CBD and in outlying commercial areas as well as in dense residential areas. Here, expensive, multilevel garages are likely to be necessary.

Because underground parking structures are so expensive, they are usually located in places with the highest land values. Balancing is again the problem. Suburban apartments, shopping centers, and office parks were initially built in locations where land values were lower and parking was provided as a cost of the location. As these centers became popular and competitive with parts of the older city, pressure developed for expensive parking at the municipality's expense and usually was acceded to.

Until World War II, on-street parking was looked upon as a right; at most the motorist expected to pay only a modest price for that convenience. On reflection, it should be realized that streets are the most valuable land in the city. The cost of constructing new lanes is inordinately high in most CBDs so the price for convenience should be high. What appears to be a true economic price seems to be too high to many, especially the lower income groups. This leads to underpricing and requires enforcement of regulations designed to share street space equitably.

Such enforcement includes meters and time-limited parking to force turnover. Infractions result in towing, which is costly but necessary at peak hours to free lanes for their prime function—moving vehicles. This is another TSM strategy, but it appears difficult for many cities to consistently enforce such regulations.

Many larger cities have turned to special authorities to operate their parking structure and lots, hoping to insulate the problem from the city government. A few cities, usually the larger ones, have given such independent agencies control of parking meters (installation, operation, and maintenance), regulations and signage, and the lower levels of the traffic court function—that is, collecting fines.

The automobile may impinge adversely on residential neighborhoods at transit stops and commuter rail stations. If the stations have been located properly, they will be near potential riders. After the line is put into operation, usage usually expands and becomes denser. As drivers from some distance come to take advantage of the transit service, inevitable conflicts occur. Some can be mitigated by building larger lots, but then land costs are often prohibitive—in this case adequate planning should have reduced if not eliminated the problem. Otherwise, it becomes a matter for regulation and policing, which is difficult at best.

Pedestrian systems and bikeways

Pedestrians appear to be given short shrift in many cities, even in newer suburbs where land is less expensive. It is dangerous for one to walk in many such areas, especially so for children. The transportation planner should not ignore the rights of pedestrians. Sidewalks should be required on one side of the street in the lowest density areas and on both sides in all others. Walk widths should be adequate for two people to pass easily. In commercial areas, the building setback should give much more space for a wider sidewalk since it has to serve not only many more pedestrians but often delivery, shipping, and bike storage needs as well.

In commercial areas WALK signals may be needed, and special regulations and signage may be required in places where the pedestrian is at risk because of an unusual street layout. Special treatments may be needed on park paths, especially where there may be a conflict with cyclists.

Curbs protect pedestrians, but now have to be cut at intersections to give access to the handicapped. Location should be chosen to minimize danger to either. Center islands, transit loading zones, and the like are protected with curbs but not against high-speed automobiles where other treatments (poles or other barriers) may be essential.[10]

The transportation planner should consider the possibility of transit malls and pedestrian malls for some unusual problems. A few decades ago, such malls would have been considered unusual except by a few who had seen them in western Europe, but today a variety can be found in the United States, many of which are worthy of duplication—such as those in Cincinnati and Minneapolis (which are above ground), Chicago (at grade), and Philadelphia (which has extensive underground concourses in the city center).

Bikeways are important throughout the world, particularly in developing countries and in Japan and Holland. In some university and tourist cities of the United States, the bicycle is a significant transportation mode. A great concern is how to keep the bicyclist safe from vehicular traffic and minimize interference with pedestrians. In some cities, cyclists clubs have made their case sufficiently strong to win the rights for separate lanes and occasionally for special roadways. Some observers think the trend promoted by organized cyclists has peaked, but the transportation planner should give them careful consideration. Limited availability of petroleum is one factor that may influence the amount of bicycle traffic; cycling as a means to maintain physical fitness is another.

Airports and harbors

A city or county is not likely to be able to plan and locate a new airport or a new harbor, yet major improvements or changes in such facilities will have an impact on other transportation facilities. These terminals generate traffic, which at times is acute. The airport serves many people (both travelers and employees) and thereby needs a large parking facility. The harbor is the site of a large amount of truck and railroad traffic that can have an impact on the street system if there are grade crossings at inconvenient locations on nearby arterial streets or highways.

The transportation plan must consider all sources of heavy traffic, including the above. Added lanes may be necessary near airports, even in smaller cities, to enable both air travelers and airline companies to utilize their time fully. Air fleets produce peak-hour street demands. Building a new terminal at a different location within an existing airport can have a significant impact on the street system—favorable or unfavorable.

Similarly, the transportation planner should consider the needs of the harbor and find out how to handle them. Fortunately, container ships are not likely to draw enough trucks to create a backup on the street system. This was not true when general cargo and bulk cargo arrived in the same ship at the small harbor. The concentration of heavy trucks near piers may be a problem for the engineer designing the paving, however, and may also have an impact on the plan. Since the plan has to encompass the movements of both goods and people, these problems should receive full consideration. Trucking terminals are also large generators of traffic with specialized requirements.

Even though a water transport system may appear mature, unusual shifts can occur and create problems. For instance, the concentration of cruise ships docking in Fort Lauderdale led to higher peak trips on its street system. Meanwhile New York found after building a new terminal for passenger ships that nearly all transatlantic passengers had moved to the airport. The sunk capital of the passenger terminal was of no assistance in moving passengers to J. F. Kennedy Airport.

Elderly and handicapped

The effort to make public and private facilities more accessible to the elderly and handicapped is still in progress. The planner must consider their special needs. The federal requirements for curb cuts have been mentioned. In addition, public works managers have tried to meet the need for ramps at public buildings. Ramps are also needed for transit platforms. If the city is the transit operator, it will have to deal with the difficulty of finding an operable lift system for buses. Because such lifts are not always reliable, the city may have to consider a special, small-bus, demand-operated system similar to the system used for transportation to welfare or social service facilities.

If the city has a rapid transit system, the desire for accessible transit raises even greater problems for the planner and operator alike. Elevator service at stations, platform-train gap fillers, and hold-downs for wheelchairs on vehicles to protect the handicapped from rapid acceleration of any electric-powered vehicle create costly and difficult issues for the operator.

The planner will soon realize that the mere fact a solution is difficult to find is no excuse in the eyes of the handicapped, who are fighting for what they feel is their due after long being ignored.

Sources of information

A wealth of information is available to transportation planners, especially to those situated near a state DOT library or one of the few colleges with specialized transportation programs and libraries. There are hundreds of specialized studies and reports to consult when a problem arises. An overview of a solution might be found in a traffic engineer's handbook.[11] If that does not contain enough detail, there is bound to be a specialized report somewhere else that will be useful.[12] The task is to find it; the telephone is one means of reaching acquaintances who may have solved a similar problem or who can suggest another source.

Summary

This section has presented an overview of the transportation planning process for the public works manager, not the technician. It has included the historical development of the process and its conversion to a legislated mandate. It indicates that the movement of people and goods make up the two essential elements of a transportation plan. The complexity of the process and the large number of individuals and agencies involved make it as difficult an analytical process as any in the public works field. The array of actions required to develop and implement the plan require top managerial skills in the public works manager and transportation planner. While models and related computer programs are available to the technician, the promulgation and acceptance of goals requires dedicated leadership. In addition, striving to attain approved goals with limited funds is a difficult challenge for a public works manager.

The kit of available tools is extensive, however, and includes classification of streets, O-D studies, subdivision planning and controls, traffic systems management, transit and parking models, bikeways and pedestrian way standards, airport and port planning, and trucking terminal siting and access.

Street maintenance

The value of good highways, streets, and roads is taken so much for granted that most people tend to forget the year-round work that is required to keep transportation systems open. When the potholes occur, however, or when a bridge collapses, public attention suddenly is focused on streets and roads. This section describes the major functions of street maintenance with respect to the responsibilities of the public works director and managers of street and bridge maintenance.

The section opens with a review of pavement maintenance that stresses pavement condition inventory and ways of putting maintenance tasks together in a systematic way. Street surfacing then is reviewed with particular attention to options for resurfacing. Next is a brief discussion of the cost-benefit factors in keeping streets and roads in good condition.

Street cleaning and snow removal are then covered with emphasis on service levels and budgetary decisions. This section concludes with a review of bridge maintenance that stresses levels of inspection.

Pavement maintenance

In the past three decades, pavement maintenance has been the forgotten child in local government public works. The glamor has been in building new and more elaborate roadways. That the road system has lasted as long as it has under this benign neglect is a tribute to the men and women who have worked unnoticed in this field over this period. Despite their efforts, however, the technical and system support has not been built up, most often because the public agency has put its priorities elsewhere.

The cardinal rule in pavement maintenance is knowing *when* to carry out *what* type of maintenance or rehabilitation and then carrying out the planned program *on time*. Failure to observe all three of these points will result in a more costly or lower quality street. It is the pavement maintenance manager's job to put together the package that will convince legislators to approve an effective program.

There are many pavement maintenance systems now developed or in stages of development. The principal one is called PAVER (not an acronym), developed by the U.S. Army Corps of Engineers for military pavements. The American Public Works Association (APWA), with the help of the corps, adapted PAVER to the municipal scene in a major research and demonstration project. Because of APWA's interest, pavement maintenance systems are now available to most local government agencies at a reasonable cost. The first step for the street agency should be to check into this system by contacting APWA.

Many smaller street agencies have maintained their systems by using the knowledge of the street superintendent or "seat-of-the-pants" judgment. That approach alone will not obtain the best pavement maintenance program. No system, no matter how sophisticated, will remove the need for the final judgment of experienced supervisors. The basis of maintenance will continue to be a regular patrol, as indicated in Figure 13–2. During the patrol, usually once a week, defects in the street system are noted and the accumulated reports form the basis for the following week's work program. These forms are also used in the weekly meeting of supervisors to plan work and keep track of overall street conditions.

Inventory   The basis for any pavement maintenance system is a complete inventory by road and street sections. Section lengths can vary from a city block in an urban area to several miles for low-volume rural roads. The inventory should include all relevant physical characteristics, including design cross sections where available. The inventory should be updated regularly with data on conditions such as roughness, deflection measurements, skid resistance, and traffic type and volume.

When the patrol report in Figure 13–2 indicates surface stress, a detailed pavement evaluation is made once yearly. Figure 13–3 outlines a pavement condition evaluation report that could serve as one part of the inventory.

With a good inventory of the system, including the condition evaluations, one can predict the service life remaining in each section of the street or roadway. Knowing the projected life, the next step is to decide what action to take on each section each year.

1. For the good sections, a prediction of what is required in the five- and ten-year period is required for fiscal planning purposes. As the road ages, it will require work above the routine level. The alternatives must be identified and chosen.
2. The next step is to estimate the cost and benefits of each alternative. For example, a road or street section may receive extended life from a slurry seal or a 2-inch (5-centimeter) asphalt overlay. The slurry seal is much lower in cost but does not increase structural carrying capacity and wears out much faster. Which is better? Each situation must be analyzed. There is no one answer.
3. Next, develop a priority list of street sections for the entire street network for the planning period, usually five years.

REGIONAL MUNICIPALITY OF OTTAWA-CARLETON
ROAD MAINTENANCE PATROL REPORT

DATE PATROLLED: _____
DAY PATROLLED: _____

AREA: **PATROL – ONE**
PATROLLED BY: _____

ROAD Nº and LOCATION	ROAD SURFACE									SHOULDERS				DRAINAGE					BRIDGES & STRUCTURES			SAFETY DEVICES				ROADSIDE				WINTER CONDITIONS										REMARKS
	PATCHING	SPRAY PATCHING	CRACK SEALING	GRADING	SWEEPING	WASHOUTS	BASE	DUST CONTROL	UTILITY CUTS	PATCHING	GRADING	DUST CONTROL	WASHOUTS	DITCHING	CATCH BASINS	CURB&GUTTER	CULVERTS	MANHOLES	CLEANING	PAINTING	OTHER	SIGNS	GUIDE POST	FLEX RAIL	LIGHTING	MOWING	TREE REMOVAL	BRUSH CUTTING	LITTER	RAILWAY CROSSING	MAIL BOXES	BARE	CENTRE BARE	SNOW COVERED	DRIFTING	ICE COVERED	ICE PATCHES	SNOW REMOVAL	SIGHT LINES	
ROAD 5 STITTSVILLE TO ROAD 7																																								
ROAD 5A ROAD 5 TO HWY. 7																																								
ROAD 7 ROAD 22 TO OTTAWA RIVER																																								
ROAD 9 ROAD 22 TO HWY. 17																																								
ROAD 109 ROAD 9 TO ROAD 21																																								
ROAD 21 ROAD 109 TO ROAD 129																																								
ROAD 129 ROAD 21 TO ROAD 9																																								

J.J028

Figure 13–2　Road maintenance patrol report.

REGIONAL MUNICIPALITY OF OTTAWA-CARLETON
ROAD MAINTENANCE BRANCH
PAVEMENT CONDITION EVALUATION

STREET: WELLINGTON   DATE: Oct. 21 19 77
LOCATION: CHAMPAGNE TO FLEET
AREA: 15530 sq. yds. SURFACE: type - HL-3 width - 36'-48' SHOULDER WIDTH:

	DISTRESS MANIFESTATIONS	SEVERITY RATINGS	FAILURE DENSITY
1	IRON FAILURE	1 2 3 4 5 6 7 8 (9) 10	4¾%
2	DISTORTION BY CONSTRUCTION	1 2 3 4 5 6 7 8 (9) 10	20 - 50%
3	DIFFERENTIAL SETTLEMENT	1 2 3 4 5 6 7 8 (9) 10	50 - 80%
4	CRACK HEAVING FROST ACTION	1 2 3 4 5 6 7 8 (9) 10	50 - 80%
5	ALLIGATOR CRACKING	1 2 3 4 5 6 7 8 (9) 10	10 - 20%
6	TRANSVERSE CRACKING	1 2 3 4 5 6 7 8 (9) 10	80 - 100%
7	EDGE CRACKING	1 2 3 4 (5) 6 7 8 9 10	10 - 20%
8	LONGITUDINAL CRACKING	1 2 3 4 5 6 7 8 (9) 10	80 - 100%
9	CHANNELIZATION	1 2 3 4 5 6 7 (8) 9 10	80 - 100%
10	RIPPLING	1 2 3 (4) 5 6 7 8 9 10	< 10%
11	SHOVING	1 2 3 (4) 5 6 7 8 9 10	< 10%
12	RAVELLING	1 2 3 4 5 6 7 (8) 9 10	20 - 50%
13	PITTING	1 2 3 4 5 6 7 8 (9) 10	80 - 100%
14	OXIDIZATION	1 2 3 4 5 6 7 8 (9) 10	80 - 100%
15	RIDE COMFORT	SMOOTH / COMFORTABLE / UNCOMFORTABLE / ROUGH & BUMPY / (DANGEROUS)	
16	POLITICAL INPUT	NONE / INQUIRIES / (DIRECTION)	
17	VIBRATION COMPLAINTS	NONE / FEW / FREQUENT	
18	CO-ORDINATION WITH OTHER CONSTRUCTION	NONE / FUTURE / IMMEDIATE	
19	TRAFFIC VOLUME INCREASE	LIGHT / (MODERATE) / HEAVY	
20	GENERAL APPEARANCE INCLUDING CURBS	ACCEPTABLE / POOR / (SEVERELY DETERIORATED)	

Severity scale (left margin): 9 & 10 = VERY SEVERE; 7 & 8 = SEVERE; 5 & 6 = MODERATE; 3 & 4 = SLIGHT; 1 & 2 = VERY SLIGHT; NONE; EXPLANATION OF RATINGS

COMMENTS:-
RECOMMEND FOR O'L /77   Note: COUNT OVER 80 = PRIME CANDIDATE FOR RESURFACING
(OVERLAYED IN 1978)

INSPECTED BY:

MA818

Figure 13-3 Pavement condition evaluation report.

Inventory components   The elements that make up the inventory help in planning street maintenance operations. The inventory elements that are essential for work planning include:

Distinctive sections

Geometry—cross section, width

Structure—materials, depths

History—construction, maintenance

Drainage

Surface distress

Deflection

Roughness

Traffic—current and projections.

It is also helpful to include other information in the inventory such as color-coded maps on system condition, multiyear plan maps, and complete profiling.

Color-coded maps are very effective in selling decision makers. These people typically have time constraints, so that displaying information in a clear, concise manner can assist a program. A multiyear plan map is also useful. It can clearly show that delay of this year's program will mean increasing the next and future years' programs.

Alternative strategies   A number of courses are open to the street maintenance agency. The choice depends on the analysis of the street in question. The street agency official should identify the advantages and disadvantages of all the alternatives. From routine maintenance, slurry seal, chip seal, overlay, reworking of in-place materials, and surface rejuvenation to reconstruction, each alternative has an original cost, a life expectancy, and a total cost.[13]

Rehabilitation   The inventory will point up deficiencies in the street system and these will help determine a course of action. If structural capacity is inadequate, an overlay or complete reconstruction may be needed. It should be noted that an overlay does not mean putting down 1 or 2 inches of asphalt to hide blemishes. It is a designed thickness to return to a specified structural capacity. Placing a 2-inch overlay when the design calls for 4 inches might not extend the road life at all or might extend it for a shorter period than two applications of 2 inches, a few years apart.

Excessive distress may be the result of age, structural weakness, poor drainage, failure to seal cracks, or other reasons. Where distress is evident, the reasons should be identified and action taken at the determined time. Delay will result in increased cost.

When excessive maintenance costs exist, it is in the street agency's interest to develop a plan to reduce costs to the lowest level required to operate the system effectively. When excessive user costs exist, the street agency must take action to reduce these costs.

For example, as a street becomes congested, user costs skyrocket. It is not unusual to see excess user costs of $700,000 per mile per year in urban areas. Should the street agency spend, say, $1,500,000 of property tax revenue to widen a congested road that is in good condition, so that the congestion is removed and users save $500,000 per year? It is an extremely attractive investment. However, the property taxpayer sees the $1.5 million cost and may not see the $0.5 million per year saving in vehicle costs. Vehicle costs are increased in cents per day whereas the tax bill is one lump sum.

Is the city council or county board interested in lowering the total overall cost or lowering the tax rate in your jurisdiction? By leaving the congestion, they save a $1.5 million construction bill.

Putting the system together   The inventory is the heart of effective and economical street maintenance. It provides the framework for regular patrol and inspection, a constant monitoring so that small expenditures now can forestall huge expenditures later. Figure 13–2 shows the kinds of information that are needed.

Pavement condition inventory helps in planning both routine maintenance and rehabilitation of roadways ranging from heavily traveled city arterials to rural roads under county jurisdiction. Figure 13–3 suggests a simple scoring mechanism for pavement evaluation that can lead to continuing improvement in design, construction, and maintenance.

Figure 13–4 shows quality standards (more generally known as performance standards) for bituminous surfaces that are suggestive of standards that can be developed for other maintenance operations and pavement types.

Street surfacing

Almost all urban roads are developed with asphalt or Portland cement concrete surfaces. For rural areas, when the average annual daily traffic volume (AADT) rises above ten vehicles, an applied surface is warranted. In the past, this has been a gravel surface; in rural counties gravel will continue to be the preferred surface.

When the AADT reaches 200 and is expected to rise, studies by the World Bank in developing countries suggest adding an asphalt surface. Somewhere after 200 and before 500, the economics favor the capital cost of the asphalt surface. Definite factors in this choice are the makeup of traffic. A high percentage of school bus, milk truck, and produce trucks would indicate an asphalt surface at the lower number, while few trucks in the total would indicate waiting for a higher AADT.

It is beyond the scope of this chapter to cover the many ramifications of street and road construction, maintenance, and reconstruction, but the major concerns are set forth in the following paragraphs dealing with surface treatment, options for surface treatment, reconstruction and maintenance, and slurry seal.

Surface treatment   When there is sufficient drainage and surface material, the process of surface treatment (also known as chip sealing) has served many agencies well. Surface treatment consists of a thin coating of asphalt with stone chip rolled in. This treatment will give a five-year life under moderate traffic conditions. It is best to start with a double-life surface treatment. Because a chip seal adds no appreciable structural strength, its primary purpose is to provide an all-weather surface, minimize surface water infiltration, and prevent dust.

If the public works department has not had experience with surface treatment, it is prudent to check with the county, state, or provincial street or highway department to explore when and where to use it. The first applications should be made in road or street sections that are in good condition with respect to surface condition, edges, and drainage. As experience is gained, surface treatment can be extended to roads and streets that are in less desirable condition to see if the treatment will hold.[14]

The chip-seal surface treatment typically costs 10 to 20 percent of a 2-inch (5-centimeter) hot asphalt treatment. Although its average life is only five years, the low cost makes it the best buy for low-volume roads with average to low truck traffic. Additionally, chip seals can be repeatedly applied without great concern of building up an excessive roadway crown. Surface treatments are not suitable, however, where the road drainage and strength of base distort the road surface.

QUALITY STANDARD
for

BITUMINOUS SURFACES

EFFECTIVE DATE: November 1984	
MUNICIPALITY: Ottawa-Carleton	
PAGE 1 OF 1	

OBJECTIVE

The Major Objectives for maintaining BITUMINOUS SURFACES Are:

° To provide a smooth, safe, riding surface free from defects.
° To eliminate hazards to vehicular traffic.
° To protect the investment in the road surface.

SUMMARY OF QUALITY STANDARD

The Level-Of-Service For BITUMINOUS SURFACES Shall Be In Accordance With The Following:

° Cracks wider than 6 mm shall be sealed.

° Depressions or bumps greater than 5.08 cm over a distance of 3.05 m or less shall be corrected.

° Bumps or depressions occurring at bridge approaches, catch basins, manholes, or similar rigid structures shall be corrected.

° Ruts, corrugations, or pushing greater than 2.54 cm in the wheel paths shall be corrected.

° Surface alligatoring or checking shall be repaired. Conditions causing extensive areas of these deficiencies shall be investigated and corrected.

° The cause for water ponding to a depth greater than 2.54 cm shall be eliminated or repaired.

° Broken pavement edges, potholes, breaks or ravelled areas larger than 7.62 cm in diameter shall be repaired.

° Crossfall of pavement from the centre line to the edge of the pavement shall be uniform over the section of road.

° Severe surface polishing causing excessively slippery conditions when wet shall be corrected.

° Bleeding surfaces constituting a hazard to the road user shall be corrected.

Figure 13-4 Quality standard, bituminous surfaces.

Options for surface treatment Some agencies surface-treat a candidate road section with some soft spot locations (weak base) for the entire length and return the following year to carry out permanent repairs only on the sections where failures occurred. For example, a 6-mile (10-kilometer) section is withheld from permanent surfacing owing to the need for base work. The high maintenance costs continue during the delay. The road agency surface-treats the section and 0.6 mile (1.0 kilometer), in total, of soft spots appear. The road agency then repairs these spots by removing bad base or improving drainage as soon as funds are available.

This method should be carefully chosen; it is not suitable unless the surface treatment works well on the best locations. The city council and the public should be informed of this method to ensure that the agency is not criticized for wasting funds. Rather, the agency is looking for methods that will produce the lowest overall cost.

This method of applying a uniform approach to a road design and returning after a few years to strengthen a few selective spots has been suggested for asphalt roads. The theory is that roads are designed for the soft spots and that throughout much of its length, the base is stronger than required. The chief problem with this approach would be failure to carry out the remedial work, which would reduce the economic advantage and the road agency's credibility.

Reconstruction and maintenance When a street reaches the economic point where full reconstruction is warranted, the pavement maintenance manager should decide if a flexible material (asphalt concrete) or a rigid material (Portland cement concrete) should be used.

From the day the new street is finished, the maintenance starts. The first few months will consist of patrol reports to pick up any construction deficiencies that may appear. These should be reported to those responsible for the construction.

Soon the first cracks will appear and a decision will have to be made on their causes and how best to treat them. In cold climates, crack sealing is a routine part of street maintenance. All streets exhibit cracking at some point in their life cycle. For urban streets the man-made cracks of utility cuts must be maintained.

Crack-filling used to consist of pouring asphalt of varying types on the crack and dusting this with sand. This type of treatment lasted for one or two years, at most. Proper crack-filling requires a sufficient depth of a compressible, expandable asphalt-based material that adheres thoroughly to the sides of the crack. All methods now utilize either a router or blower to clean debris out of the crack.

In the past, recommended practice was to fill the crack just below the road surface to prevent tracking. One of the latest approaches recommends applying a band, 2–3 inches wide, over the crack or injecting the material into the crack to obtain a thicker strip. Also, the crack is heated to evaporate moisture and obtain better initial adhesion.

The purpose of crack-filling is to prevent water from entering into the base and weakening the street. The moisture reduces the load-carrying ability and leads to premature failure of the pavement. In areas with freeze-thaw cycles, cracks allowing moisture into a road base cause ice lenses, which accelerate road deterioration.

Slurry seal Slurry seal is a method of sealing a street surface that has many hairline cracks and perhaps oxidation. An emulsion of asphalt and sand is "painted" on the surface by means of a distributor and drag. It is important to note where this method will work and where it will not. Therefore, it is advisable to check with agencies that have used this method to seek their advice and gain from their experience. It is important to note that this is not a substitute for an asphalt surface, but it can extend the life of the existing surface.

In Ottawa-Carleton, slurry seal has been placed over a chip-sealed road to extend its surface life. This has proven quite successful. The usual conditions apply—good drainage, uniform base, and relatively low traffic volume.

The value of good streets and roads

Since the late 1970s, there has been intense debate about the extent of the deterioration of the public works infrastructure in the United States and Canada. The problem first surfaced in the early 1970s when state highway officials in the United States pointed out that the interstate system had deteriorated to the point where extensive maintenance was needed to bring the highways back to standard. Although the federal government had paid for 90 percent of the original cost, the maintenance costs were entirely the responsibility of the states.

Many cities, counties, and other local governments face the same problem of mounting maintenance costs, but the problem is exacerbated by the refusal of many public officials to deal with it. It is always so much easier to defer the maintenance "for just one more year."

Public works managers can draw on a number of methods to explain and convince elected officials and others that the need is real and the costs a few years down the road too high to contemplate without a shudder. Here are three examples.

Figure 13–5 portrays the normal life cycle of a pavement as indicated primarily by its surface condition. The vertical scale of 0 to 5 is the condition index, the surface of the road as rated by professionals in the field. The index ranges from "very good," which represents a road or street in fine condition, to "very poor," which shows a broken potholed road or street. The mid-to-fair level, or 2.5, is the lowest acceptable level for high-volume roads, and the low-to-fair level, or 2.0, is acceptable for low-volume roads.

Note in Figure 13–5 that the curve begins to fall rapidly at the point where the road deteriorates to the fair category. Put another way, if your road is at the lowest acceptable level, you have probably undertaken rehabilitation too late to achieve the lowest cost.

Figure 13–5   Pavement life cycle as measured by the performance curve.

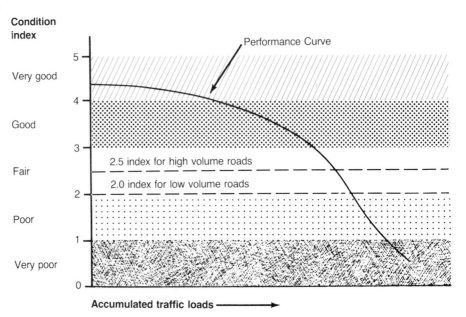

Figure 13–6 Pavement life cycle as measured by time and quality.

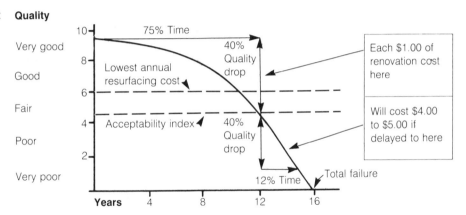

Surveys on road condition, cost of maintenance, and rehabilitation have shown what might appear to be obvious, that it costs more to rehabilitate if we delay until a street is in very poor condition. What is not obvious is that the cost escalates three, four, or five times higher the longer the delay. The surveys also show that this period of rapidly escalating cost is very short in terms of the life of the street.

Figure 13–6 emphasizes time in relation to road quality and deterioration. The same road condition index that appears in Figure 13–5 is used here, and the acceptability index level is at fair. At this point, 40 percent of the quality has been lost over a period of twelve years. The next 40 percent drop in quality takes place in only two years. At the acceptability level, each $1 of renovation will jump to $4 or $5 if the work is delayed just two more years. Further neglect will cause the road to fail.

The third way to look at street costs is to consider the costs to the automobile driver. Figure 13–7 shows that poorly maintained street and road surfaces exact

Figure 13–7 Costs of road deterioration as measured by automobile operating costs.

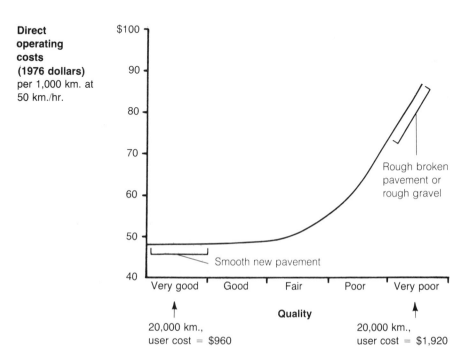

QUALITY STANDARD for

STREET CLEANING

| EFFECTIVE DATE: November 1984 |
| MUNICIPALITY: Ottawa-Carleton |
| PAGE 1 OF 1 |

OBJECTIVE

The Major Objectives for STREET CLEANING Are:
- To prevent injuries and annoyances arising from street dirt.
- To prevent damage to pedestrians, property and vehicles caused by loose objects being thrown up by traffic.
- To promote safety by removing debris which could create a fire hazard or cause skidding conditions.
- To reduce the obscuring of pavement markings and to prolong the life of these markings.
- To prevent the clogging of sewers.
- To enhance the appearance of the community.

SUMMARY OF QUALITY STANDARD

The Level-Of-Service For STREET CLEANING Shall Be In Accordance With The Following:

SPRING CLEANUP

- Spring cleanup shall be completed by May 1st.

CENTRAL BUSINESS AREA

- Shall be cleaned daily generally between May 1 and November 30.
- Street sweeping in central business area will begin at midnight.
- Street flushing in central business area will begin at 2 a.m.
- Market area flushing shall begin at 10 p.m.
- Sidewalk sweeping in central business area shall be carried out daily.
- Manual cleanup shall be carried out each day of the week, Monday to Friday, and all streets will be cleaned once every 10 days.

GENERAL

- Street sweeping and flushing shall be carried out at various levels-of-service, generally between May 1 and November 30, based on the traffic volume, pedestrian volume and on the amount of litter which has been observed on the roads over a period of years.
- Urban sections with curb and gutter shall normally be cleaned from one to three times a week.
- Rural sections with curb and gutter shall normally be cleaned once every ten days.
- Non-curb and gutter sections shall not normally be cleaned except at specific locations, where required.

Figure 13-8   Quality standard, street cleaning.

a high price from automobile owners. The same road condition scale is used, but the scale runs horizontally from "very good" to "very poor." The direct operating costs are shown on the vertical scale at dollars per 1,000 kilometers, driving at 50 kilometers per hour. The point is clear: good roads run at $960 for 20,000 kilometers whereas poor roads cost $1,920 for the same mileage. The costs increase sharply after the road or street goes from fair to poor.

Street cleaning

Cleanliness may be next to godliness, but to many elected and appointed officials in local government street cleaning is a program at the margin, an item that can be cut during the annual budget process.

The positive features of street cleaning, however, include safety, economy, and community appearance. Clean streets help citizens take pride in their communities and neighborhoods. Clean streets help promote civic consciousness. An unbroken, smooth street surface encourages citizens to take an active part in keeping a good appearance.

Dirt and litter, on the other hand, lead citizens to believe that a poor appearance does not matter. Littering and vandalism of street furniture often are the result.

Keeping streets clean involves practical economic considerations. Dust, dirt, and litter left on the street find their way into catch basins and can clog sewers or be washed into the receiving water, thus creating pollution. Dirt acts like sandpaper and obscures pavement markings, advancing the time when they must be redone. Dust storms created by wind around buildings cause eye and throat injury to citizens. These and other targets of street cleaning are outlined in Figure 13–8.

Service levels   With a tight budget, how can you maintain the desired level of service? By targeting your street patrol to the areas that need cleaning. For example, two residential streets in similar neighborhoods are the same except for one item. One has a preponderance of paved driveways, the other gravel driveways. They will require different levels of street cleaning because gravel will be tracked onto the street. As a more permanent solution, could the residents be encouraged to pave their driveways?

Some like the rustic look of gravel. In that case, how about a rule that the first 20 feet should be paved?

Other steps   There are other steps your community can take to reduce street cleaning.

1. Educational campaigns can help create a spirit of community pride that will result in a reduction in litter. Investigate the possibility of having one of the service groups in the community take on a clean community as one of their projects.
2. Provide a network of trash receptacles strategically placed. Many communities obtain these by allowing advertising companies to place advertisements on the receptacles. Some communities use these receptacles to advertise public messages from requests to keep the community clean to the latest cultural event.
3. Check the number and location of trash receptacles and how often they are emptied. Do not let the receptacles become litter zones; empty on a targeted basis.
4. Does your community require that corner stores, fast-food outlets, and other high users of immediately disposable packaging have litter receptacles? Enough receptacles that are emptied as required? Litter

from one or two such outlets can discourage a whole neighborhood. Target these areas for preventive action and regular patrol. Follow up with the owners and managers of these outlets to ensure they control all the litter generated on their property.

Flushing and hand sweeping Examine your flushing operations. In Ottawa-Carleton, a 50 percent reduction in street flushing, while maintaining the same sweeping patrol, resulted in an undetectable drop in service level.

Flushing is a marginal part of street cleaning. Traffic movement causes most debris to move to the gutters. Flushing washes the fine dust particles to the gutter, and the vacuum sweepers can now pick up almost all fine dust previously left by mechanical sweepers.

There will always be a spot for hand sweeping. In today's efforts to reduce personnel costs and the worker's aversion to being a "street-sweeper," it is difficult to keep personnel interested, but congested downtown sections require a hand-sweeping patrol to pick up litter behind the curb, around street furniture, and in the midst of crowds where equipment would be awkward or unable to do the job.

Regulations Are there other causes of high street litter, dirt, and gravel? How about construction sites? Do you have a street ordinance that says that tracking of dirt from construction sites is prohibited? Do you vigorously enforce it? A single construction site with trucks tracking and dropping excavated material can ruin miles of street cleaning.

Let it be known that you will enforce regulations strictly. Contact builders and contractors and outline how they can avoid costly shutdowns because their trucks are fouling the streets. The more people in the community who know you are serious, the cleaner the community will be.

Snow removal

Snow removal will vary in importance depending on location. In the Sun Belt winter is a time to be smug and brace for the influx of northern tourists. In the Snow Belt it can be a life-and-death struggle.

In some Snow Belt communities more funds are expended on snow removal than on all other street maintenance activities combined. Whether snow removal is the major item for your agency, or an occasional one, you know that snowstorms can stop business in your community. This makes snow removal a high profile activity that requires a high level of planning.

Levels of service The first step in a good snow removal program is to establish levels of service. These should be established by agency staff for submission to the governing body for approval. Figure 13–9 suggests levels of service that can be considered. These service levels are drawn from the Regional Municipality of Ottawa-Carleton, Canada, with breakdowns for urban roads (arterials and collectors), rural roads, bus bays, crosswalks and intersections, and other categories. The standards cover such factors as bare pavements, snow depth, priorities, allowable snow accumulations, salting, sanding, and other elements of service levels and quality.

The costs and tradeoffs for various options should be developed for review by the public works director, the finance and budget staffs, the city manager or other chief administrator, and the city council, county board, or other local governing body. To the extent possible, the costs, experience in prior years, and other data should be organized to show that snow removal is labor intensive, that storms are unpredictable except through the use of long-term averages, and that costs are high because equipment and personnel are often on a standby basis plus overtime.

Armed with this and similar information the council or board can decide what funds are needed. The council can also explain to their constituents why various levels of service were chosen. The elected officials are typically the best communicators.

Different levels of service will probably be required by class of roadway. Arterials will almost always be cleared curb to curb with bare pavement. On residential streets snow could be plowed as close to the curb as possible but without any application of salt or abrasives.

Once the levels of service have been approved, these levels should be publicized in the local newspapers.

The budget and expenditure decisions Since no two winters are the same, the budget must establish that snow removal continue at the level of service approved, even when the budget is overspent. One method of expenditure forecasting is to set the amount required for an average year, place funds in reserve in the years of light snowfall, and draw from the reserve fund in heavy years.

Whatever method is used, the policy should be clearly stated. The middle of a snowstorm is no time to have funding worries and to be looking for a decision from the city council.

The next step is the division of the street system into categories of level of service. Primary and secondary plow beats should be laid out to arrive at the minimum deadheading of nonproductive time. The amount of equipment needed to carry out this activity is then calculated for an average storm. This is compared to the equipment available in the fleet.

It is common to discover that there is not enough equipment to cover the average snowstorm. It is also common to find that you cannot, perhaps should not, augment your fleet for this activity. Shortfall of equipment should be made up by rentals or contracts from the private sector.

Many construction activities slow down or stop during snowstorms, and contractors are anxious to keep their equipment working. Street agency officials should be familiar with what equipment is available in their area and what is needed to have the private sector provide this equipment.

In the heavier snowfall areas, contractors may have a supply of equipment outfitted with plows and spreaders because of constant demand. In areas of lower and sporadic snowfall, the street agency may be required to supply plows and spreader boxes for mounting on contracted equipment.

Some high-cost items will force the street agency into hard decisions. High-volume snowblowers are essential in heavy snowfall, but this equipment is very expensive. Such equipment cannot be costed in the traditional way; a few communities in the heart of the Snow Belt are an exception. Look at the tradeoff, however. If the snowblower is not available to clear the street, all other emergency activities are slowed down or stopped.

Contracting out Another method of handling snowplowing is to contract it out, either partially or wholly. A street agency can contract out its entire winter-control operation (except quality control). This method is used by a few municipalities, Metropolitan Toronto, for one, and involves a complicated setup to ensure that the right equipment and personnel are available when needed.

A control center, staffed twenty-four hours a day during the winter, with crew and equipment on-site may be required. The street agency will be required to pay a fixed cost plus an hourly rate for each piece of equipment used. This method of setting up winter control requires a careful, detailed approach, and a visit to an agency already using this approach is a must.

```
┌──────────────────────────────────────────────────────────────┐
│                                    ┌─────────────────────────┐ │
│     QUALITY STANDARD               │EFFECTIVE                │ │
│           for                      │DATE:   November 1984    │ │
│                                    ├─────────────────────────┤ │
│                                    │MUNICIPALITY:            │ │
│      WINTER OPERATIONS             │    Ottawa-Carleton      │ │
│                                    ├─────────────────────────┤ │
│                                    │PAGE    1   OF    4      │ │
│                                    └─────────────────────────┘ │
```

OBJECTIVE

The Major Objectives For WINTER OPERATIONS Are:

o To reduce the hazards of icy road conditions to motorists and pedestrians.
o To reduce economic losses to the community and industry caused by workers not being able to get to their jobs.
o To facilitate the handling of emergencies by fire and police officials.
o To maintain safe, passable school bus and winter recreation routes.

SUMMARY OF QUALITY STANDARD

URBAN ROADS

In order to assign specific levels of service for WINTER OPERATIONS to roads based upon their importance in the total transportation system, Urban Roads have been classified according to the following table:

CLASS I ROADS (Arterials)	CLASS II ROADS (Collectors)
Carry large volumes of traffic. Serve as major traffic flows between principal areas of traffic generation.	Provide both traffic and land service.
Connect with major routes of other jurisdictions.	Collect traffic from Class III roads and distribute to Class I roads.
Generally have a winter average daily traffic greater than 6000 vehicles per day.	Generally have full access.
Serve as emergency routes to hospitals and for fire equipment.	Generally have a winter average daily traffic of between 1000 and 6000 vehicles per day.

The Level-of-Service For The Various Classes Of Roads For WINTER OPERATIONS Shall Be In Accordance With The Following:

CLASS I - BARE PAVEMENT

1. Surfaces shall be maintained AS BARE AS POSSIBLE through the CONTINUED USE of all assigned workers, equipment and materials suited to the conditions.

Figure 13–9   Quality standard for winter operations, Regional Municipality of Ottawa-Carleton, Canada. The first two pages of this four-page form are shown to suggest the factors and elements to be considered in drafting standards to meet local conditions.

QUALITY STANDARD
for

WINTER OPERATIONS

EFFECTIVE DATE: November 1984
MUNICIPALITY: Ottawa-Carleton
PAGE   2   OF   4

SUMMARY OF QUALITY STANDARD (CONTINUED)

2. The maximum allowable snow accumulation for commencing winter operations is 2.54 cm (1 inch).

3. Frequency of coverage (either plowing or spreading) shall not exceed 3 hours, except in extreme conditions.

4. Roads shall be given FIRST PRIORITY TREATMENT and shall be plowed full width to an acceptable level of service before attention is given to CLASS II roads.

5. Parking lanes and road shoulders where no sidewalks are provided shall be plowed when there is an appreciable accumulation of snow after one or more light snow falls.

6. Snow removal shall be carried out immediately following any total accumulation of 10.16 cm (4 inches) or greater, or when a windrow is formed which is 91.44 cm wide and 45.72 cm high above the road surface, encroaching 60.95 cm to 76.20 onto the travelled roadway, except where storage areas are available on roads with no sidewalks and/or no parking.

CLASS II - BARE PAVEMENT

1. Surfaces shall be maintained AS BARE AS POSSIBLE through the CONTINUED USE of all assigned workers, equipment and materials suited to the conditions.

2. The maximum allowable snow accumulation for commencing winter operations is 5.08 cm (2 inches).

3. Frequency of coverage (either plowing or spreading) shall not exceed 4 hours, except in extreme conditions.

4. Roads shall be given SECOND PRIORITY TREATMENT and shall be plowed full width to an acceptable level of service.

5. Parking lanes and road shoulders where no sidewalks are provided shall be plowed when there is an appreciable accumulation of snow after one or more light snow falls.

6. Snow removal shall be carried out immediately following any total accumulation of 10.16 cm (4 inches) or greater, or when a windrow is formed which is 91.44 cm wide and 45.72 cm above the road surface, encroaching 60.96 cm to 76.20 cm onto the travelled roadway, except where storage areas are available on roads with no sidewalks and/or no parking.

Figure 13-9 (continued).

Another method is to have street-agency crews handle one or more sections and contract for other sections. This can build up a healthy competition to provide good service.

Some of the contract options are (1) payment per lane (by mile or kilometer) of plowing and sanding, based on snowfall measured at an agreed site; (2) payment per lane with a fixed fee; (3) payment on an hourly basis for equipment used, with use based on snowfall; and (4) payment on an hourly basis for equipment used with a fixed fee.

Getting ready for winter The preceding paragraphs have described planning for service levels, budgeting and expenditure forecasting, and the option of contracting out for snow removal. These are management tasks that should be undertaken in the off-season when the weather is warmer and emergency and crisis conditions are absent.

Other steps should be taken every year in the early fall to make sure that procedures, personnel, equipment, and backups are checked out and ready to go. Here is a checklist that can be expanded and adapted to meet the specific needs of cities and counties from the extreme north to the variable weather conditions of the middle-zone states.

1. Recheck and confirm service levels (see Figure 13–9).
2. Draft and check your "battle plans"—routes for streets and roads; priorities for snow removal by streets and roads; personnel, including emergency phone numbers; city- or county-owned equipment and equipment on standby with contractors; on-line and hard-copy maps; and radio and telephone.
3. Train and retrain street crews and their supervisors.
4. Inspect all city- or county-owned equipment. Verify that maintenance and repair work has been completed and that equipment is ready to go.
5. Inspect and verify that contractors' equipment is serviced and ready to go.
6. Draft and check communication plans so that prompt, concise, and accurate reports on street and road conditions can be sent to radio and television stations, newspapers, and members of the city council or county board.

Bridge maintenance

That bridge maintenance has been neglected in North America is now accepted.[15] Now that time and neglect have slowly eroded the load-carrying ability of bridges, a few catastrophic collapses have convinced road authorities to introduce comprehensive bridge maintenance programs.

The public rightly expects the enormous investment in bridges to be used in the most economic way possible at an acceptable level of safety. To achieve this, an efficient modern management programme is required which has to rely on three basic precepts: bridge inspection, evaluation of load-carrying capacity and bridge maintenance.[16]

A bridge maintenance program requires the development of life-cycle engineering in order to optimize available resources. The basic steps in this program are design, evaluation, maintenance, inspection, and operation.

Bridges are complex structures that always require evaluation by a specialist. A street maintenance supervisor can take a chance on fixing a soft spot on the street and have it fail at the cost of esteem and extra cost to carry out remedial work. A seat-of-the-pants decision on a bridge repair, however, could have much more serious consequences.

Bridges are of such importance that most public works agencies will be governed by federal, state, and provincial requirements and guidelines in this regard.

Public works agencies and their consultants should be thoroughly familiar with the regulations and guidelines covering bridge standards.

Design The bridge maintenance agency may be integrated with the design or be a separate organization. In all cases there should be a continuous flow of information from designers, to maintenance personnel and back, completing a cycle that will facilitate modification of future designs and development of plans to retrofit existing bridges. Thus when the time for rehabilitation arrives, a complete picture of the bridge's life cycle will be available.

It is customary to think of the bridge as if it were a single unit, but it is made up of many material and structural components. Each material and structure type requires a separate analysis and in all probability a separate maintenance cycle. For this reason, it is important that bridge maintenance personnel understand the relations of design to maintenance.

In the absence of maintenance, bridges will wear out just as buildings and streets do. As the years go by, urbanization, traffic changes, fatigue brought on by constant loading, thermal reactions, chemical reactions, nearby building construction, and other changes in the immediate environment will affect strength and stability. Therefore, various components of the bridge will have different life cycles that must be identified for maintenance and rehabilitation schedules. Figure 13–10 shows the major kinds of maintenance that are required to keep bridges in good condition.

Inspection Inspection is based on trained observation. The inspector is trained to know the visible signs of distress in a bridge and when to probe beneath the surface. It is a critical link in the chain of events that keeps the bridge operating at full load-carrying capacity. It is critical to examine the bridge and its components to detect any deterioration, to find its true behavior, and to note any change since the last inspection.

The first step in planning bridge inspection is to divide the bridge into its components. (The design function will have provided this information.) Next, the elements within the components are listed and the properties of each material and the probable design life are listed.

As bridges in each area will be of different ages and components, it follows that inspection frequency will vary according to age "distress" and use. In Ottawa-Carleton, for example, five levels of inspection have been developed, A to E. The levels were set by structural engineers of the Regional Municipality of Ottawa-Carleton. Level E was set to coincide with the requirement of the American Association of State Highway and Transportation Officials for inspection of every bridge once every two years. Level A consists of an inspection each month and a half. These structures were obviously of great concern; many were just a short time from rehabilitation.

Where any doubt exists about the safety of the bridge, additional inspections are scheduled, and bridge structural engineers are empowered to temporarily close down any bridge at any time, if in their judgment it poses a safety hazard to the public.

Inspection content Although inspections should be consistent and periodic, the content of each inspection will vary. Initial inspections do much to determine how the bridge and its various components will act throughout the life cycle. Such inspections can be divided into three phases: overall review of the structural assembly, detailed review of components, and collation of design and inspection data. These will include:

QUALITY STANDARD
for

BRIDGE MAINTENANCE

EFFECTIVE
DATE: November 1984

MUNICIPALITY:
Ottawa-Carleton

PAGE 1 OF 1

OBJECTIVE

The Major Objectives for BRIDGE MAINTENANCE Are:

° To provide safety to the user through preventive maintenance.
° To protect the investment in structures.

SUMMARY OF QUALITY STANDARD

The Level-Of-Service For BRIDGE MAINTENANCE Shall Be In Accordance With The Following:

° Structure cleaning and painting shall be performed during summer months.

° Exposed metal surfaces on structures shall be painted once every four years, subject to field investigation.

° Damage to structures resulting from traffic accidents or deterioration shall be repaired and/or damaged section replaced.

° Timber abutments shall be repaired when evidence of failure is observed.

° Pilings which show deterioration caused by erosion, corrosion, or attack by organisms shall be replaced.

° Bridge drains shall be inspected twice per year in the fall and spring and cleaned if required.

° Bridge seats, rollers and other expansion elements shall be inspected once per year by the Regional Roads Design Branch and repairs made if required.

° Cleaning and flushing of expansion joints and bearings shall be carried out annually in the spring when winter sanding is complete.

Figure 13–10   Quality standard, bridge maintenance.

1. A dimensional survey qualifying vertical and horizontal alignment
2. Detailed survey of all primary, secondary, and auxiliary components
3. Diagnosis, categorization, and collation of all initial defects
4. Assurance of design tolerance limitations
5. Organization of construction documentation such as material test reports, proprietary products designations, and shop drawings.

The follow-up inspections for each bridge depend on age, condition, location, traffic, and other factors. Typically, the most frequent inspections will be needed to monitor components that have deteriorated rapidly because of accidents or extraordinary environmental conditions.

Some of the follow-up inspections may be designated "condition inspections." These inspections usually begin at the mid-life of a bridge when loss of resistance and reliability accelerate. Condition inspections help identify the bridge components that can be refurbished or replaced to extend the life of the bridge.

The combination of initial inspection of the total structure, follow-up inspections of component parts, and condition inspection at mid-life will ensure that problems are identified at a time that corrections can be made at the lowest cost and disruption to the public.

Rehabilitation   Your bridge inspections have led to the proper level of routine maintenance. Cleaning drains and joints, painting, bearing lubrication, wearing surface repair and sealing, and other services have all prolonged the life of the bridge. In addition, component parts with a short life have been replaced. Such items as wear surface, seals, and membranes have a ten- to fifteen-year life, and their replacement protects primary components.

It is inevitable, however, that at some point, major rehabilitation will be required. The fifty-year period seems to be indicated from surveys. Rehabilitation involves extending the bridge life for the lowest cost by locating the deterioration at a point where the fewest resources are needed to return the bridge to service.

In Ottawa-Carleton, it has been found that deficiencies in newer structures occur earlier and with more frequency than in older structures. This tells planners that more maintenance resources will have to be provided in the future to maintain bridge serviceability.

The rehabilitation design is often more complex than the original. It requires the examination of all components, a decision on their repair or replacement, and a totaling of all these parts to see if replacement would be the better alternative. The original design incorporated materials of known properties at that time. The rehabilitation designer must determine the properties of each component, because each will have been affected differently over fifty or more years.

Because this is a long process, rehabilitation design should be scheduled with sufficient time to ensure that delay does not produce accelerated deterioration that forces a structure to be replaced at much higher cost.

As problems arise during the life cycle of a bridge, it may be possible to make short-term corrections to the structure to overcome design deficiencies, accident damage, or environmental damage. These methods are stop-gap and should only be used to provide time to complete the rehabilitation design. In each case the effect of the modification should be carefully assessed. Here are some examples:

Structural members can be stiffened; foundations can be shored or strengthened.

A bridge agency could rationalize its truck-routing system and reduce load ratings on some bridges to extend the bridge life for small vehicles.

The number of lanes of traffic on the bridge could be reduced.

Traffic management

This section is devoted primarily to traffic studies, including street evaluation, land use as a traffic generator, accident studies, on-street and off-street parking, and other studies that help in the management of motor vehicle traffic. This is followed by a brief discussion of traffic control devices and street lighting.[17]

Street transportation is vital to the life of a community. Hence, it is important to have the best possible street system and to maintain optimum effectiveness of operation of that system. Such operation means safe, orderly, efficient, and convenient traffic conditions.

In most communities, new or widened arteries are now very expensive—and so are other street construction projects. There are more and more demands on local government funds, which are generally not increasing at a pace consistent with needs. Moreover, it is being demonstrated increasingly in various communities that major advances in meeting traffic needs can be secured by better traffic management. And many traffic operational improvements are relatively modest in cost. Consequently, there is a growing emphasis on doing a much better job of traffic management. Such a goal is achievable, and numerous substantial benefits can be attained thereby. The first essential is a firm commitment by the city or county executive to develop and carry on a progressive traffic operations or traffic management program.

There are many ways of improving traffic operations. Yet developing and maintaining effective operations is a large, complex undertaking. The only solid bases for high-quality traffic operations are pertinent facts, and many kinds are needed. Hence, studies are very important. There must be good organization and administration for effective operations. Basic is the need for continuous direction of the operations program by a professionally qualified and experienced person—presumably a traffic-transportation engineer. Large cities need a full-time traffic engineering staff. Small cities may assign traffic operations responsibilities to the city engineer or public works director.

There should be legislation creating a traffic engineering unit, no matter how small, and specifying its powers and duties. The traffic engineer must have authority consistent with responsibilities, reasonable staff and funds, and executive support. In a word, he or she must be given the opportunity to give fully of professional competence and experience.

It is essential that there be cooperation among agencies of community government and coordination of their activities related to traffic. An effective citizens traffic advisory committee is highly desirable, and it too should be created under appropriate legislation.

Traffic studies

Good, up-to-date traffic-transportation studies and records are essential in maintaining effective transportation system operations. Surprising numbers of kinds of studies and records are needed—far more than can be discussed here. Some of the most basic and important will therefore be outlined. Further information can be obtained from the cited reference materials. It should also be realized that some kinds of studies, to be most effective, should range beyond the boundaries of an individual city or county.

Most of this section on traffic management is an abridged version of Chapter 13 in *Urban Public Works Administration*, the predecessor edition to this book. The chapter needed only small changes and updating to make it fully useful for public works managers. This work was done by Christopher F. Fernandez, traffic engineer, City of Santa Clara, California.

Street plan evaluation   One basic study investigates the adequacy of the urban street system in serving community needs and objectives. This evaluation will be aided by assigning all streets to one of these three categories: arterial streets, collector streets, or local streets.

Arterial streets, including freeways and expressways, are those major facilities of limited mileage on which most non-neighborhood traffic flows. Is the community's arterial system adequate? Does it serve all sections of the city satisfactorily? Is continuity provided? Is capacity in all of its parts sufficient to keep through or long-distance movements from spilling over onto collector or even some local streets? Does the arterial system provide suitable ways for through-destined traffic to keep off major business streets? Does the arterial network hook up well with arteries at city limits? Strong emphasis should be given to the arterial system and to how to improve operations where there are deficiencies. The more that abutting properties can be served from other streets or alleys, the more effective those arterial streets will be.

Collector streets serve neighborhoods or subdivisions, providing for substantial traffic movements between arteries and local streets. They also serve abutting properties. Are they located and designed to serve those functions invitingly, with suitable neighborhood continuity?

Local streets should provide only for short-distance local traffic movements, mainly for service of abutting properties. To discourage through or long-distance traffic, roadways should be narrow; such design features as cul-de-sacs, T intersections, curvature, and no direct arterial access should be introduced. Even in already developed residential districts, it may sometimes be desirable to physically close the entrance to a residential street from an arterial street.

As part of the street plan evaluation, there should be an inventory and appraisal of terminal and transfer facilities. Included, where they exist, should be rail, bus, and truck terminals; airports and ship ports; and parking facilities.

Arterial streets are generally shown on a large-scale map of the community. It is helpful to show thereon the various terminal transfer facilities. Suitable symbols, notes, and other markings can be used to indicate evaluations or ratings of the various parts as to their operational effectiveness. If such a map exists, it will be helpful to update it and continue to keep it current. Whether or not collector streets are shown will depend on map scale, on availability of even larger scale sectional maps, and on how much importance is foreseen for use of collector street information. Where substantial land use changes are anticipated, collector streets should have an especially strong role.

Land use and development study   Land use is a basic factor in determining traffic needs and patterns, and a map showing existing land uses should be prepared. It should show residential, business, and industrial areas; schools; playgrounds; hospitals; parks; and sports and other recreational areas.

Changes in land use can substantially modify traffic flow in an area. Therefore any proposal for substantial change in land use should be thoroughly evaluated as to probable effects on traffic operations. Two kinds of effects should be examined: effects on the existing street system and terminals and effects within the proposed new development.

Consider, for example, a proposed large shopping center. Will entering and departing traffic produce confusion, congestion, delays, or accident hazards? How much new traffic will the shopping center attract or generate?

As to effects within the new development, is there a sound plan for movement of vehicles and pedestrians? Is adequate off-street parking provided?

Subdivision street plans   A good street plan for a new subdivision will keep through traffic out, keep speeds low, and make for both pedestrian and vehicle safety and for pleasant living. Proposals for subdivision plans should be examined to see if local streets are noncontinuous; local street roadways are narrow and involve curvature; cul-de-sacs are used; T intersections are used and distances between intersections are made substantial (300 feet or more); percentage of land devoted to streets is kept low; arterial streets are kept at the perimeter of the subdivision; the number of intersections is kept at a minimum; and pedestrian hazards are minimized. There should not be an excessive number of collector streets. Where subdivision streets meet arterial streets, conflicts should be minimized by designs permitting right turns only.

Origin-destination (O-D) studies If ten times as many people want to go from *A* to *B* as want to go from *S* to *T*, then clearly operational measures to facilitate trips between *A* and *B* should have high priority over *S–T* trips. Those responsible for traffic operations need to know trip facts. Providing such information is one major objective of origin-destination studies (see Figure 13–11). Such studies also provide the local government manager with other important information: how or by what mode are trips made (public transit, truck, automobile, taxi)? When are trips made (by time of day)? Why are trips made (to work, to shop, to attend school, etc.)?

O-D studies produce information of importance in planning and improving bus routes and schedules, appraising transportation deficiencies, and determining locations and importance of new or improved streets, bridges, and terminal facilities. O-D studies are valuable in planning, including land development.

The smaller the city, the simpler can an O-D study be. A large-city comprehensive origin-destination study is the most complex and time-consuming of all traffic studies. Hence it should be thoroughly weighed and planned under informed professional direction.[18]

Accident studies Traffic accidents are facts of life—and death. They are of course deplored, but some say that not much can be done about them. Why, then, should local governments, with their many other responsibilities, devote much effort to studying accidents and developing countermeasures?

Experience seems to indicate that, unfortunately, such viewpoints govern or at least significantly affect the thinking of many key officials and citizen leaders. Yet evidence abounds that well-designed and well-conducted accident studies and sound countermeasures can be most valuable. Part of the evidence is the dramatic reduction in motor vehicle deaths since the 1920s. The motor vehicle death rate was 18.20 per 100 million vehicle miles for the five-year period of 1923–27. By 1969 this rate had dropped to 5.21. By 1984 this rate was almost cut in half and had dropped to 2.68. As encouraging as these reductions are, the motor vehicle death rate shows startling differences between cities. For example, in sixty-seven cities of 100,000 to 200,000 population, the death rate per 10,000 registered motor vehicles in 1984 ranged from 0.1 to 5.0.[19]

Traffic crashes are very expensive—and many leave tragic consequences. Moreover, they often cause serious, irritating delays; and many involve expensive repairs or replacements of local government property and costly expenditures of time by police and other personnel. Hence traffic accidents deserve thorough study—this is an area in which almost all communities need to do better. Usually much can be accomplished.

The first need is for good accident reports and records. Fortunately the local police have for years prepared reasonably satisfactory reports of at least the more serious traffic crashes so that much countermeasure work can be done without delay. Nonetheless, the existing police traffic crash report form should be checked as to its adequacy, and any necessary updating or other changes should be made. Contacts with the state agency that receives accident reports from drivers and with the National Safety Council will be helpful.

Presumably the police department has worked out a cooperative arrangement with the appropriate state agency as to combining the traffic accident reports which each receives.

Under the Highway Safety Program Standards of the U.S. Department of Transportation, developed in compliance with the Highway Safety Act of 1966 (PL 89–564), each state in cooperation with its political subdivisions is to maintain a traffic records system, including accident records. This system, which may consist of compatible subsystems, is to include data for the entire state (Standard 10). Standard 9 provides that "each state, in cooperation with county and other local governments, shall have a program for identifying accident locations and for maintaining surveillance of those locations having high accident rates or losses."

Finding high-rated accident locations   Accident reports can be filed in a number of ways (chronologically, by drivers' names, or by some serial number system). Experience has shown that by all odds the most useful method is by accident location. Indeed a location file is essential to attaining full value from the records.[20] From the location file, one or more accident spot maps can be prepared. In addition to spotting all recorded crash locations on one map, with perhaps different designations for fatal, nonfatal injury, and property damage crashes, separate spot maps may be prepared for crashes involving darkness, pedestrians, schoolchildren, or elderly persons. Such maps help identify special problem areas and locations. Accident spot maps are usually based on a calendar year, but for smaller communities a longer period may be more useful.

The location file also provides the basis for developing a very useful high-rated accident locations list. Such a list can be based on the number of crashes at various locations. Or accidents can be rated according to severity, with, for example, twelve points for a fatality, three for a nonfatal injury accident, and one for an accident involving only property damage. The customary way to describe accident severity is by the most serious injury to any person in the accident. Other weighting factors, such as number of traffic units involved, are also used. Even listing by numbers of crashes gives some weight to severity since the lesser accidents are usually less fully reported or are not reported at all.

The period of time for which the high-rated accident locations list is prepared is important, especially for small municipalities where a period of several years may be needed to provide sufficient data for productive study. Usually conditions at an accident location do not change markedly over a period of several years.

Whatever the chosen basis for rating, it is urged that a considerable number of locations (usually intersections) be placed on a high-rated accident locations list in descending order of seriousness. Those locations topping the list should be the ones studied, the number depending on available resources. But other locations near the top-level group will often be useful in helping to answer demands for unwarranted expenditures for locations further down the list or not listed at all.

Studying high-rated accident locations   Effective procedures have been developed to study a high-rated accident location:

1. Prepare a collision diagram. This is a diagram showing by conventional symbols the directions and kinds of traffic unit movements involved in the accident, the kind of accident, its severity, time of day, date, pavement condition, and weather. Accident totals by type, severity, and day-or-night may helpfully be tabulated on the diagram.
2. Prepare a condition diagram. This is a to-scale drawing showing all traffic-important physical features at and near the high-rated accident location.

Figure 13–11
Origin-destination
projections (see caption
on facing page).

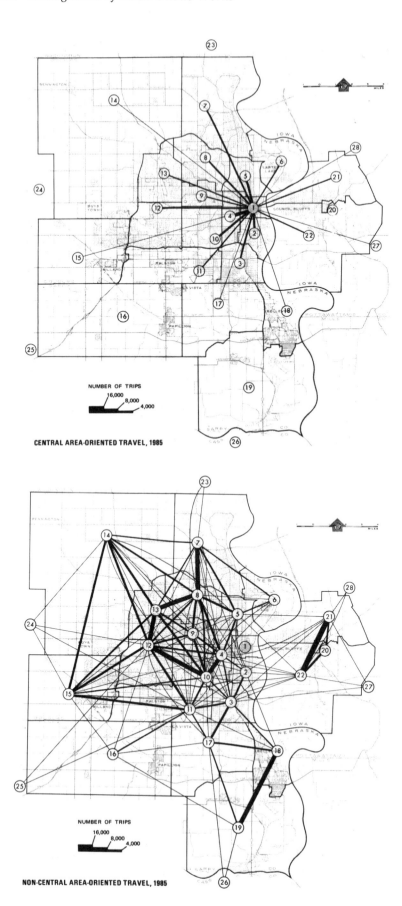

NUMBER OF TRIPS

16,000
8,000
4,000

CENTRAL AREA-ORIENTED TRAVEL, 1985

NUMBER OF TRIPS

16,000
8,000
4,000

NON-CENTRAL AREA-ORIENTED TRAVEL, 1985

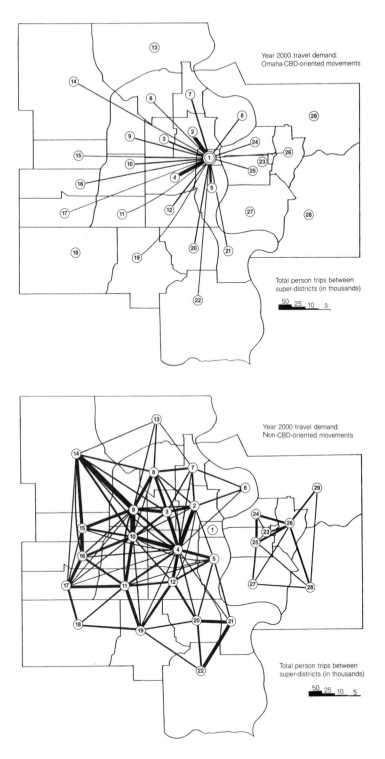

Figure 13–11 Origin-destination projections for auto travel, Omaha, Nebraska, metropolitan area, 1985 and 2000. The maps on the facing page were drawn in 1970 to show auto trip movement projections for 1985 with projections to and from the central area (top) and between points outside the central area (bottom). Both projections have been generally borne out on the basis of data gathered in 1985. The maps on this page (with Council Bluffs, Iowa, added to the metropolitan area) were drawn in 1985 to show auto trip movement projections for 2000 with projections to and from the central area (top) and between points outside the central area (bottom). These maps show a continuing decentralization of travel in the metropolitan area.

3. Summarize the available facts and circle or red-mark those that are especially significant.
4. Visit and study the location with the collision and condition diagrams and summary at hand. Drive and, if pertinent, walk the most involved pathways. If darkness is a factor, include a night study.

Preparing findings and proposed action   The outcome of indicated studies of high-rated accident locations will be the preparation of findings, conclusions, and proposed remedial action.

Making and using before-and-after studies   All pertinent materials relating to each high-rated accident location studied should be carefully filed (see Figure 13–12). One year after remedial action has been taken, parallel data should be compiled and a careful analysis made of data for the year before and the year after remedial action. For small municipalities the comparison periods might be longer. Much can be learned from such comparisons. And they are excellent in informing the public.

Summarizing accident records   What kinds of actions of drivers and pedestrians are most frequently involved in traffic crashes? What age groups are most prominent? What are the most hazardous times of night or day, days of the week, and months or seasons? In terms of numbers, which kind of vehicle is most frequently involved in a crash?

Answers to these and many other general questions are essential to a progressive program for reduction of traffic crashes. Moreover, answers applying to one's own community will carry more weight than if state or national figures are used. Also, although such facts usually do not change rapidly, it is desirable to use reasonably up-to-date information.

If information from traffic accident records has been computerized, desired summaries can be quickly obtained. Often answers will be desired for certain variables or groups only. For example, as has been noted it will often be desirable to study accidents involving pedestrians, the elderly, children, or hours of darkness only.

For what period of time should such summaries and accompanying spot maps be prepared? A calendar year is a suitable period for all but small cities. A statistician can guide a small city as to what time period will produce large enough numbers so that findings will be significant.

This discussion of accident studies is limited, but other sources will provide further useful information.[21]

Traffic volume counts   Knowledge of vehicular volumes is fundamental to most measures for improvement of traffic operations—and for some purposes, the same is true of pedestrian volumes. Is a stop sign or a traffic control signal warranted? Should re-routing of buses involve use of certain streets? From a traffic viewpoint, what should be done about curb parking on various downtown streets? What major traffic changes are suitable in the central business district? In answering these and many other practical operations questions, traffic volume data—often for both vehicles and pedestrians—are essential.

The most frequently used vehicular traffic counts are of average daily traffic, though for some purposes peak hour counts are more important. In preparing a vehicle volume map for an artery, area, city, or county, it would not be economically feasible to make twenty-four-hour counts at all selected count locations.

Fortunately, satisfactory economical methods have been found that utilize (1) a few continuous counting control locations (state highway department count-

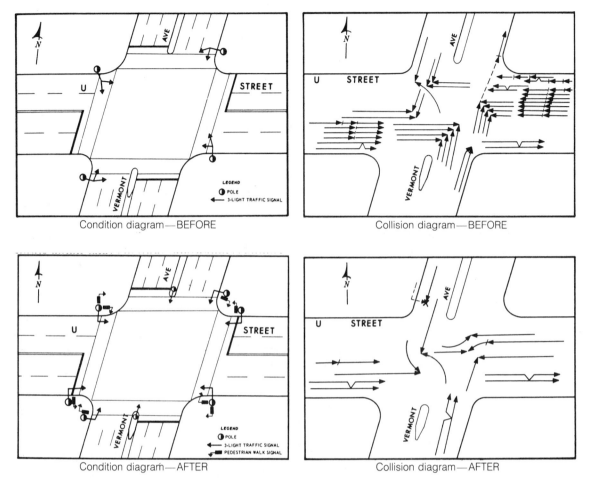

Figure 13–12 "Before" and "after" sets of condition and collision diagrams for a busy intersection in Washington, D.C. The top figures illustrate a situation hazardous to both motor vehicles and pedestrians due to poor visibility of primary and supplementary signals and inadequate yellow clearance interval time. The bottom diagrams show the vehicle and pedestrian control measures adopted to improve the situation and indicate the resulting improvement in traffic movement. In the year following installation of the new controls, accidents, injuries, and accident costs each decreased about 66 percent.

ing stations may serve), (2) a modest number of key stations at which counts cover a goodly number of hours, and (3) the remaining locations at which short-time counts are made. The short-time data are extrapolated to a twenty-four-hour basis using factors developed from the long-time counts. Various kinds of counts are made. Examples are given immediately below.

Cordon counts   A cordon count is one in which a particular area—such as the central business district—is completely encircled and counts are made on all roads crossing the cordon. This study shows the daily volume of traffic entering and leaving, by what mode (including walking), on what streets, and at what hours.

Screen counts   The number of crossings of a major barrier, such as a river or railroad, are recorded by mode (vehicular or pedestrian), by time of day, and by direction of travel. An example of screen counts is checking accuracy of origin-destination data.

   Various methods of making traffic counts are available, including manual tallying, use of a variety of vehicle detector devices, and photographic recording.

Making proper decisions and choices as to conducting traffic volume counts is important, both in dollar implications and in terms of the effectiveness of street system operations.

Speed and delay or travel time studies   Many complaints are received about how much more slowly traffic moves on one or more arteries than it used to. A parent-teacher group calls for better controls against excessive speeds on certain streets in the school area. How much benefit will be achieved as a result of a planned program of operational measures along a main arterial street?

These examples are among the many situations calling for some type of speed and delay or travel time study. Sometimes spot speed studies are suitable. Using such studies, the variances and averages of speeds are ascertained for a selected short stretch of street. Sometimes studies cover long distances, as along an arterial street; variances in speeds for different segments are recorded as well as delay points and reasons for delays. For some purposes the total travel time for a designated trip will suffice. Generally all such studies will include peak hour data. Various methods of study exist involving widely differing time requirements and costs.

Terminals studies   Terminal facilities for automobile parking, truck loading, interurban bus loading, and mode changing are very important components of a city transportation system. Often too little attention is devoted to the overall terminals situation. Parts of that picture are examined next.

Compact parking dimension standards   In the 1970s the traditional trend of longer and wider automobiles was reversed. As a result of the growing number of smaller standard-sized and compact cars, many municipalities have reduced their standard parking stall and aisle dimensions to reflect the smaller-sized cars. The percentage of allowed compact stalls in some municipalities is as high as 50 percent of the required off-street parking requirements.

Automobile parking   Practically every community has parking problems—and usually they are troublesome. They affect just about everybody—drivers, retail merchants, downtown property owners and other businessmen, truckers, transit interests, taxi drivers, and pedestrians—but often in widely differing ways. In many areas special efforts are now being made to convince commuters traveling to downtown locations to use transit vehicles. One idea is to reduce the amount of parking available to automobile drivers (except drivers of group ride cars) or to make parking in the central business district (CBD) considerably more expensive (except for group ride cars).

There are, of course, widely differing viewpoints about parking policies and conditions. Under such situations it is highly desirable to have parking facts on hand. Although parking problems may be considerable in various areas, the main problems are in the CBD. This discussion is limited to that area and to the fringe just outside the CBD in which long-time or all-day parkers leave their cars and walk to their CBD destination. Such fringes should be included in study areas.

Parking inventory   The initial step, if it has not recently been taken, is to prepare an inventory of existing parking facilities, both on-street and off-street, in useful forms including visualization on one or more large-scale maps. This inventory will be a compilation of facts pertaining to the location, type, design, and any restrictions on use of all parking spaces.

Parking use studies Studies of present usage of parking facilities in the study area should follow. These studies should cover all instances of parking—the hour and duration of parking, location, type of parking space (curb, lot, or garage), type of vehicle, legal or illegal space utilized, and instances of hazardous parking.

Parking demand study This study identifies the parking vehicle, indicates its type and the type of parking, when parked and unparked, trip origin and destination, distance walked in study area to destination, purpose of trip, and home address. The study permits ascertaining parking demand in terms of the trip purposes of individual drivers, how much parking time is associated with different trip purposes, what origins the study area serves for different purposes, how far parkers walk for different purposes, and what trip purposes are mainly served by said parking. The above are not the only parking studies that may be desirable. For example, a parking accumulation study may also be desirable.[22]

Freight terminals The effective handling of wares, merchandise, and other freight in a community is essential to that community's continuing viability. Most urban freight is handled by trucks, and a large proportion moves through terminals. City-destined freight is usually brought to numerous separate terminals by railroad trains, intercity trucks, ships, or airplanes. After being sorted, most freight is delivered by a variety of local service trucks. For outbound freight the process is reversed.

For most freight movements on (and deliveries from) city streets, inadequate account is taken of their effects on traffic operations. In some areas at certain times, these effects are seriously detrimental. Hence, it is desirable to study freight terminals and street operations relating thereto. Consolidations of terminals, for example, often could lead to a substantial increase in efficiency with decreases in vehicle miles of local truck travel, lowered costs, and street operational benefits.

Transit terminals and mode-change stations It is often quite an ordeal to pick up by car a relative or friend scheduled to arrive at an interurban bus terminal at a certain time. Often there is no place nearby to park and you are one of many trying to spot a person, get his or her attention, and then pick up the person and luggage. If the bus is late, the situation is worse. Sometimes interurban buses adversely affect traffic operations because of inadequacies of their terminals.

At some "park-and-ride" or "kiss-and-ride" stations on public transportation routes, street traffic is clogged at certain times because of inadequate capacity or bad design of such mode-change stations. Hence, studies of such facilities are needed, it is hoped before the designs and plans are completed if new facilities are to be created.

Studies relating to traffic control devices

What are traffic control devices? "Traffic control devices are all signs, signals, markings, and devices placed on or adjacent to a street or highway by authority of a public body or official having jurisdiction to regulate, warn or guide traffic."[23] All communities have traffic control devices, generally in considerable numbers. And the cities have had many of them for years. Why should studies be needed in this field? Effective traffic control devices indicate good local government. They significantly affect the convenient movement and safety of people. Moreover, citizens are exposed to these devices daily. Hence they deserve high importance ratings and warrant thorough study.

Effectiveness and liability   Are all traffic control devices effective? To be effective, the official *Manual on Uniform Traffic Control Devices for Streets and Highways* states, each device should do the following: fulfill a need; command attention; convey a clear, simple meaning; command the respect of road users; and give adequate time for proper response.[24] Five basic considerations are employed to ensure that the above five requirements are met: design, placement, operation, maintenance, and uniformity.

Lest the importance of the above not be realized, consider a relatively recent development—the growing problem of liability of a governmental agency or of governmental officials for some failure relating to a traffic control device in an accident. Some very high dollar judgments have been rendered. The immunity once relied upon by local jurisdictions has eroded. In numerous states the immunity doctrine does not apply to local governments.

Clearly there should be accurate inventories of all traffic control devices and records showing inspections, cleanings, adjustments, repairs, and replacements to prove that reasonable programs are carried out. Records should also be kept of all studies made as to the justification of devices at designated locations, of complaints and what outcomes resulted, of new installations and their warrants, and of removals and justifications for such actions.

Required uniformity   Do all devices conform with standards issued or endorsed by the Federal Highway Administration? Acting under provisions of the Highway Safety Act of 1966 (PL 89–564), the Secretary of Transportation promulgated eighteen highway safety program standards. Standard 13, "Traffic Engineering Services," specifies that:

Each State, in cooperation with its political subdivisions . . . shall have a program for applying traffic engineering measures and techniques, including the use of traffic control devices. . . . The program as a minimum shall consist of . . . periodic review of existing traffic control devices, including a systematic upgrading of substandard devices to conform with standards issued or endorsed by the Federal Highway Administrator, . . . a maintenance schedule adequate to insure proper operation and timely repair of control devices, including daytime and night-time inspections.[25]

Some target dates have been specified for compliance, and there are eventual penalty possibilities for not instituting a program for compliance. Perhaps the target dates need to provide more time, but the intent is clear.

High degrees of observance   Traffic control devices can perform their objectives of regulating, warning, or guiding traffic well when there is a high degree of voluntary observance. There are far too many applications of devices to depend on enforcing their messages at each location.

It is important periodically to conduct observance studies to ascertain what the situation is for various devices in various locations at various hours. Results of such studies can be used in many ways. One example is to justify removal of an unwarranted, ineffective device.

Saving money   Often there is strong neighborhood pressure for installation of unwarranted YIELD or STOP signs or a traffic control signal. The *Manual on Uniform Traffic Control Devices* provides criteria or warrants for such installations.[26] Studies may show clearly that such warrants are not met and thus may provide factual bases for denying such requests. These studies will often indicate other less costly ways of meeting the needs.

Upgrading traffic signals and signal systems involves various methods. Studies may show that the most costly option may not be the best choice.

Pavement marking is one of the best, lowest cost, and most appreciated ways of aiding drivers. But such markings wear off. Yet some remain effective much longer than others. Some longer lasting paints may cost more originally but may save money in the end. Use of glass beads in or on the paint not only greatly improves night visibility but increases the effective life of the markings, possibly long enough to save money. Thermoplastic markings have advantages and disadvantages. In some situations raised reflector markers are warranted. They improve night visibility, especially for wet pavement conditions. From the managerial perspective, the point to emphasize is that there should be careful studies of the various options as to pavement markings. Sound decisions could save significant amounts of money over the years.

Traffic controls during construction and maintenance   Special and often serious problems of traffic operations are produced when vehicular traffic must be routed around or through locations where street or other construction, maintenance, or utility work involves closing streets or lanes. Not too many years ago, drivers often experienced confusion, delays, discomfort, and irritation when trying to proceed on their trip in such situations. All too often such driver troubles existed in large measure because of bad pavement or other traffic conditions on a prescribed detour, including unsatisfactory signs, markings, and guide devices such as cones and barricades. Such deficiencies were usually most serious at night.

Fortunately, traffic controls during construction, maintenance, and utility work are now receiving much better consideration in most places—though further improvements are usually warranted, particularly when massive construction work on a subway is involved.

Should Part VI standards be adopted by the local government office responsible for street construction and for street system operations? Should these standards be incorporated (as by reference) in specifications for all street contract work—and enforced? Is it important to have all responsibilities clearly assigned and understood by those involved? When, under what authority, and by whom should temporary traffic control devices be removed or otherwise made ineffective?

Whose responsibility is it to see that weeds, brush, construction materials and equipment, and the like do not interfere with driver ability to see the traffic control device in ample time to respond properly? Who determines which signs shall be reflectorized and which adequately illuminated—and whose responsibility is it to see that this very important provision is carried out and kept in effect? What signs must be of the specified orange color? What purpose does the diagonal aspect of striping on barricades serve?

When a reduction in usable pavement width is required, how important is the rate of taper and what minimum standard should be adhered to? Should a longer taper ever be required? How are drivers to be guided into and through the taper?

Under what conditions should construction or maintenance work be done at night—and what special problems must then be dealt with? Is special lighting necessary or highly desirable, and if so for what situations and purposes? How important is flagman training and supervision? Whose responsibility is it? What police needs will there be? What about adequately informing the public in advance?

The above are some of the matters on which decisions need to be made in advance.

Street lighting

The decision as to where and how to improve a street-lighting system should not be made without knowledge of where the greatest needs lie and what the total annual costs will be. As the factors of nighttime visibility become better understood and as street-lighting equipment becomes more sophisticated and of higher intensity, it becomes more important than ever to use competent personnel for the careful planning and design that are essential. Experienced assistance usually is available from the local utility, the municipal engineering department, independent engineering firms, or manufacturers of street-lighting equipment.

Planning Planning should include a classification of all roadways, an analysis of traffic accident and crime statistics, and consideration of the needs of business and recreation centers. Future civic planning also should be considered if the plan is to have long-range effectiveness. The design of the lighting system must take into account the visibility task to be accomplished on each class of roadway, including light levels, glare, surrounding light conditions, uniformity of lighting, and color. The existing facilities may determine much of the design and future operating practice. Future operating and maintenance costs should be determined for alternative systems because these costs will probably be greater than those of the initial installation—although a properly designed new system could provide the required lighting at no added cost. Table 13–1 shows lumen and wattage ranges, average life, initial and operating costs, and other characteristics for eight types of street and highway lighting.

Designers must include the daytime appearance of the new system in their

Table 13–1 Typical area and roadway lighting lamp characteristics.[1]

Type of lighting	Lumens per watt			Wattage range	Rated average life (hrs.)[3]	% maint. output at end of life	Color rendition	Optical control	Cost	
	Includ. ballast losses[2]	Lamp only	Lumens						Initial (lamp)	Operational (power)
Incandescent[4]	N/A	11-18	655-15300	58-860	1500-12000	82-86	Exc.	Excellent	Low	High
Tungsten-halogen	N/A	20-22	6000-33000	300-1500	2000	93	Exc.	Exc. vertical Poor horiz.	Moder.	High
Fluorescent	58-69	70-73	4200-15500	60-212	10000-12000	68	Good	Poor	Moder.	Moder.
Mercury-clear	37-54	44-58	7700-57500	175-1000	24000+	62-82	Fair	Good	Moder.	Moder.
Mercury-w/phosp.	41-59	49-63	8500-63000	175-1000	24000+	50-73	Good	Fair	Moder.	Moder.
Metal halide	65-110	80-125	14000-125000	175-1500	7500-15000	58-74	Good	Good	High	Low
High pressure sodium	60-130	83-140	5800-140000	70-1000	20000-24000	73	Fair	Good	High	Low
Low pressure sodium	78-150	131-183	4650-33000	35-180	18000	100[5]	Poor	Poor	High	Low

Source: U.S., Department of Transportation, Federal Highway Administration, *Roadway Lighting Handbook* (Washington, D.C.: Government Printing Office, 1978), p. 44.

1 All figures show operating ranges typical for lamp sizes normally used in area and roadway applications.

2 Ranges shown cover low wattage lamps with regulated type ballasts (worst condition) through high wattage lamps with reactor type ballasts (best condition).

3 Rated average life is based on survival of at least 50% of a large group of lamps operated under specified test conditions at 10 or more burning hours per start.

4 Larger sized incandescent lamps (up to 2000 watts) for floodlighting applications are available. Depending on operating conditions, the luminous efficacy and life change considerably for these lamps from the typical values shown. Lamp schedules should be consulted for details.

5 Low pressure sodium lamps maintain initial lumen rating throughout life, but lamp wattage increases. Considering this change in wattage, the luminous efficacy of these lamps (including ballast losses) at 18000 hours is 67–117 lumens per watt.

considerations. Community groups often exert pressures to obtain a unique styling in street-lighting components that are inefficient light sources. If safety—the prime purpose of the lighting—is not to be compromised, the costs will rise considerably with the use of special ornamental lighting components.

Financing   Municipal or county officials responsible for financing public street lighting must determine whether a proposed modernization system will provide benefits greater than the cost, and which parts of the system will provide the greatest cost-benefit ratio. It will probably be necessary to assign high priorities to relighting certain classes of roadways and to postpone relighting others. The financing must account for not only the initial installation costs but also the ongoing maintenance and energy costs. The funds for installation usually are provided by bond issues or special assessments on property. The funds for maintenance and operation are usually charged against the general taxes or against street and highway revenues.

Many utilities have established rates for street lighting that include either the total annual costs or the costs of operation and maintenance only if the municipality owns the fixtures.

Local subscription in a business or residential area is a method often used to raise funds for installation and construction costs, but this method of raising funds is not reliable for future maintenance costs.

The required lighting on new freeways and major arterials and in civic centers can be financed as part of roadway projects; such costs may be as low as 1 percent of the total project cost.

Conclusion

This section has reviewed the traffic studies and other measures that help organize traffic flow on city and county streets and roads for automobiles, trucks, vans, buses, and other motor vehicles. The overriding objectives are to prevent injuries and deaths, reduce damage to motor vehicles and other property, and enhance the economic strength and social qualities of community life.

Traffic congestion everywhere seems to be chronic. The remedial measures are expensive, and many members of the public resist effective measures and promote wasteful and ineffective measures. The record, however, is extraordinarily good. The National Safety Council reports that from 1913–17 to 1975, motor vehicle deaths per 10,000 registered vehicles in the United States fell from 24 to 3. Between 1923–27 and 1984, the death rate per 100 million vehicle-miles fell from 18.2 to 2.7. This record shows what can be done.

Airports

An airport is the centerpiece in any community's efforts to attract and maintain new industry and tourism. The airport's success is not determined by its size, but rather by acceptable management procedures and techniques that must be interwoven with those of many diverse interests within the airline industry and the community the airport serves. Notwithstanding the size and scope of an airport, the chief ingredient in achieving successful recognition is management's emphasis on guiding a safe operation for air transport users and those who provide the services. An unsafe airport is not saleable so it is little wonder that the successful airport manager appears to concentrate so much time and effort on every facet of safety in the facility's day-to-day operations.

Airport managers combine public works, public relations, and customer affairs in their daily assignments. As public works directors, they are responsible for the construction and maintenance of runways, taxiways, aircraft parking and loading ramps, access roadway systems, and terminal and hangar facilities, not to mention parking lot and security facilities. In public and customer relations, all airport managers must be able to deal forthrightly with every sector of the community.

The airport is a unique physical, social, and economic phenomenon. The airport manager must facilitate scheduled airline service in a deregulated environment with fluctuating fares and daily peaks and valleys in arrivals and departures that generate airport rush hours. Particularly significant is the reduction in governmental regulation of airline service. This is not to suggest that government has no role or interest in airport management. The Federal Aviation Administration (FAA), for example, works almost daily with airline managements in monitoring the development of airports and awarding federal grants for construction and land acquisition. State governments have a similar role. Also, airport managers must cope with various federal, state, and municipal laws and ordinances regarding the quality of life that surrounds an airport, particularly the impact of noise and pollution.

The airport management job includes the operation of the airport itself and the many facilities that serve the primary function of the airport—safe and timely arrivals and departures. This must be done within the federal regulations governing myriad aspects of security and safety.

With the phenomenal growth of both airline travel and general aviation, including commuter and regional services, business aircraft, and general aviation, airport facilities at cities both large and small have developed at a fantastic rate.

Classification of airports

An airport may be defined as any space adopted and used primarily for aircraft takeoffs and landings, and equipped with facilities necessary for the hangar storage, parking, and servicing of aircraft; the handling of passengers; and the receipt and transfer of cargo.

There were 12,653 airports on record in 1983 with the Federal Aviation Administration, a part of the U.S. Department of Transportation. Of this number, 4,812 or 38 percent are publicly owned. Air carriers serve approximately 677 certificated airports under Part 130 of the Federal Aviation Regulations. Of this number, 409 receive scheduled commercial service and an additional 268 receive unscheduled service.

The tremendous growth of air travel is also reflected in the following statistics: 2,918 heliports, 392 seaplane bases, and 66 airports designated for use by aircraft capable of short takeoffs and landings. For those involved in pleasure flying there are 12 ultralight flight parks, 32 gliderports, and 7 balloon parks.

Air traffic hubs   The Civil Aeronautics Board (CAB) has classified the geographical areas in which airports are located into large, medium, small, and nonhubs (See Figure 13–13). These classifications are the CAB's principal method of operations control in economic and operations research procedures. Within this medium are consolidated the social and economic factors that influence a community's ability to generate air carrier or general aviation traffic. Air traffic hubs are not airports, but the cities and metropolitan statistical areas (MSAs) requiring aviation services.

Individual communities fall into these four hub classifications as determined by each community's percentage of the total enplaned, revenue passengers in all services and operations of the U.S. certificated route air carriers within the fifty states, the District of Columbia, and the other U.S. areas designated by the FAA. Classification is based on the percentage of total enplaned passengers for the nation. The dominance of the hub areas is shown in the 1983 figures, which reveal that 96.2 percent of the 303,720,634 passenger enplanements took place at the 121 large, medium, and small hubs and only 3.6 percent at the

Figure 13–13
The national
system of airports.

Classification	Annotation
Air traffic hubs. Developed by the Civil Aeronautics Board to reflect socioeconomic factors that generate air traffic. Based on number of enplaned passengers.	
Large hub	1.0 percent or more of total enplaned passengers for the nation
Medium hub	0.25 to 0.99 percent
Small hub	0.05 to 0.24 percent
Nonhub	Less than 0.05 percent
Airport and Airway Improvement Act of 1982. Established by the Federal Aviation Administration for eligibility to be included in the Airport Improvement Program.	
Commercial service airport	Public airport enplaning 2,500 or more passengers annually
Primary airport	Public service airport enplaning 0.01 percent of total number of passengers enplaned annually at all commercial service airports
Reliever airport	An airport designated by the FAA as having the function of relieving the congestion at a commercial service airport

nonhubs. Considering enplanements at hub areas only, the 26 large hubs accounted for 72.6 percent; the 36 medium hubs, 17.6 percent; and the 59 small hubs, 6.9 percent.

Under the Airport and Airway Improvement Act of 1982, the FAA has established the airport classifications shown in Figure 13–13, which relate primarily to eligibility for inclusion in the Airport Improvement Program (AIP): commercial service airport, primary airport, and reliever airport. To be eligible for funding under the Airport Improvement Program, each airport must be included in the National Plan of Integrated Airport Systems (NPIAS).

General aviation airports   The largest number of airports, public and private, serve only general aviation activity. All civil aviation other than that of certificated air carriers, including recreational, instructional, commercial, and business flying, is considered general aviation. Thousands of communities throughout the country are served by general aviation, which accounts for 98 percent of all civil aircraft registered in the United States. The dimension of general aviation can best be illustrated with reference to operations (landings and takeoffs). General aviation is credited with over 80 percent of the total operations at the nation's 392 airports that have FAA control towers. General aviation operations have more than tripled in the last two decades, rising to more than 53 million operations in 1983. During the same period, air carrier operations went from 7 million to over 9 million.

Because general aviation aircraft are smaller and handle smaller groups of passengers than those of the scheduled airlines, they are able to use smaller airports and do not require the facilities necessary at air carrier airports. They do, however, use the various hub airports and feed passengers and cargo to both trunk and regional airlines.

Airport ownership

Types of airport administration   The ownership and management of airports in the United States is handled in many ways.

Port authority   This type of organization operates a number of public services, including airports, bridges, tunnels, docks, and tollways. Members of its governing body usually are appointed and it has the power to obtain long-term financing through the issuance of revenue bonds. A port authority operates much like a business in the finance, planning, development, and day-to-day management of the airport. Its entrepreneurial nature derives largely from its relative freedom from political influence and its strong financing base free from municipal budgetary control.

Airport authority   Another entrepreneurial type of airport administration is the airport authority, which is very similar to the port authority except that it deals exclusively with the operation of airports. The authority is responsible for providing aviation facilities for a large district; frequently this includes the operation of several airports. Although many airport authorities are self-sustaining through user charges, most have the power of taxation and may levy a certain millage on the tax rolls, subject to a maximum established in the authority's charter. The power and the authority to sell general obligation and revenue bonds give the airport authority financial flexibility that often produces enough income for both capital improvements and operating expenses.

The staff of an airport under the aegis of an airport authority, like that of a port authority, derives broad policy direction from, and reports to, an appointed board. The airport staff thus has wide latitude in operational decision making and is relatively free from political and outside budgetary control.

Division of city government   Most U.S. commercial airports operate as a division of the city government, under either a city manager or a department of aviation. In the latter case, a commissioner of aviation may sit on the city council. The mayor often appoints an aviation advisory committee as well, but responsibility for all major airport policy decisions rests with the mayor and the alderman. In some states the laws allow the mayor to appoint a board of aviation commissioners who have the authority to enter into contracts and establish policy. Financing an airport operation of this kind is usually restricted by the same limitation encountered by other divisions of city government. Airport bond issues, for example, must compete with streets, water service, and other capital expenditures within the city's bonded debt limit. Aside from certain federal aid available to all public-use airports, city airport funding, both operations and capital improvements, often is controlled by annual appropriations in the city budget.

Division of county government   The administration of an airport under county government is similar to a city airport operation. Many county airports, however, are operated in a more entrepreneurial manner under a county airport commissioner. The airport commissioners are either elected or appointed, and they act more or less autonomously in managing the airport. On major issues or policy decisions, they must go back to the highest county officials for approval. Generally, however, the operation is independent of county political control and functions to a substantial degree in the same manner as the airport authorities.

Combination of city and county governments   There are an increasing number of combined sponsorships of airports. A county government and a city government, or several county governments, or several city governments share the ownership and operation of an airport or a system of airports. Many regional airports have joint sponsorships.

Division of state government Some state-operated airport systems and airports tend to parallel the city-county type of operation in that their staff has day-to-day operational responsibilities under established policy directions. State airport administration goes through the same budget processes as do other departments of state government. The airport or airport system thus is operated under capital programming approvals and restrictions that are strictly controlled by state law. Airports are ordinarily a division of state government in only the smaller states, in which statewide administration is more feasible geographically.

Division of federal government In Washington, D.C., the FAA, through the Bureau of National Capital Airports, operates Washington National and Dulles International Airports. These are the only federally operated airports in the United States. Budget approval comes through the normal federal appropriations process, which seeks to operate the airports on a balanced budget. Thus, revenues are available to offset operating expenses; but problems arise in obtaining approval of capital expenditures, which must undergo tedious Senate and House committee budget review processes. Capital expense requests often are reduced or delayed prior to approval.

Privately owned airports Privately owned and operated airports make up the largest percentage of airports in the country. With few exceptions, they are small and cater almost exclusively to general aviation interests. If the level of traffic dictates, a privately owned airport may have a control tower built, staffed, and operated by the FAA.

The federal government did not have the flexibility to assist in developing private aviation facilities until passage of the Airport and Airway Improvement Act of 1982. Private airports thus are usually financed through private funds, either as a corporate entity, an individual partnership, or a joint venture investment.

In the broadest sense, private airports are generally entrepreneurial in nature and free from governmental operating control. Their location, of course, must conform to local zoning codes, and a state-issued operating license or certificate is usually a prerequisite to commencing business.

Airspace conflicts stemming from the proximity of a private airport to a public airport fall under FAA jurisdiction. Although the FAA cannot prohibit a private airport from locating near a public airport, the Federal Aviation Act of 1958 requires that reasonable prior notice be given the administrator for the establishment or construction of a private airport or alteration of the runway layout. This is required so that everyone will be aware of the effects of such construction on the use of airspace by aircraft. Any airspace conflicts are then resolved by the FAA.

Private airports are less permanent than public airports because of the flexibility of private ownership. That is to say, if the airport becomes engulfed by urban growth and an opportunity for capital gains arises, the land may be sold for other uses. In addition, a private airport is not protected by laws that bar obstructions from its approach zone, nor does it have the power of eminent domain.

Management responsibilities

The management of an airport, especially one that is publicly owned and has scheduled airline service, is complex. The complexity increases with size. The person who is responsible to the ownership is known as the airport manager, airport director, director of aviation, or in some states, the commissioner of aviation. In many instances, this person is a professional who has been accredited by the American Association of Airport Executives (AAAE) as an accredited airport executive (AAE). Although this accreditation is not required, many employers have found that those who are accredited are particularly adept at handling the problems of managing an airport. To begin the process of accreditation, an applicant must have a four-year college degree and must have been employed at an airport for one year. To complete the accreditation, the applicant must have three years of employment at an airport in a management position, pass written tests in three subjects, write a thesis, and pass an oral examination. As of 1985 there were 220 accredited airport executives in the United States.

Only a limited number of colleges offer degrees in airport administration, but many offer degrees in business administration or transportation, and courses in various aspects of airports and air transportation are available in these fields of study. AAAE sponsors national and regional meetings and seminars on a number of related subjects dealing with airport management. The National Airports Conference held each year in Norman, Oklahoma, is jointly sponsored by AAAE, the Federal Aviation Administration, and the University of Oklahoma.

The AAAE is basically an organization of airport professionals. Based in Washington, D.C., the association maintains an extensive reference library available for the use of members. In addition, the association has committees to deal with technical matters, airport safety and security, public relations, commuter airports, and general aviation airports.

Another organization, the Airport Operators Council International (AOCI), located in Washington, D.C., has a membership of governmental organizations whose airports account for 90 percent of the domestic passengers enplaned and generate 75 percent of the free world passengers. AOCI represents 218 airport legislative bodies operating more than 800 airports in five continents. This organization is considered the voice of airports. It conducts meetings in which the important matters of airports are discussed and provides information on airport economics, public relations, security, problems of small airports, environment, and governmental affairs.

Administration   Airport managers are responsible for establishing and maintaining the public service capability through qualified administrative, public relations, management, and marketing skills. They must also recommend and supervise the development of periodicals, press releases, and other promotional matter to assure that the airport will have a public image of the highest quality.

Supervision of a continuing evaluation of the adequacy of air service being provided to the community is an important function of airport management. Other functions include the development and implementation of minimal acceptable standards for public services to assure that air passengers and airport visitors are served in the best manner, particularly in and about the terminal building.

The manager also should establish policy and manage appropriate work systems and files throughout the offices of the airport to achieve conformity of activities, efficiency of operation, and simplicity but completeness in all departmental administrative activities.

Fiscal management   It is essential to develop and supervise a staff qualified to handle airport property management, budgeting and accounting, and personnel administration activities. The airport manager must administer all property management activities of the airport. These will include:

1. Maintaining property management records related to each item of airport property

2. Developing lease and contract terms
3. Establishing rates and charges related to the use of all airport properties
4. Promoting the development and use of airport properties
5. Negotiating lease and contract terms with the prospective users of the airport properties and services.

The airport manager must also administer the budgeting, accounting, and personnel activities for the airport, including:

1. Supervising the preparation of the annual maintenance and operations budgets of the airport and its administrative function
2. Supervising the budgetary accounting system
3. Establishing subsidiary accounting records to produce special financial data necessary for revenue development and cost control and to provide criteria for establishing airport rates and charges
4. Developing fiscal plans and forecasts to establish the financing capability of the airport
5. Maintaining the airport's personnel records
6. Developing and recommending the staffing requirements of the airport and preparing job descriptions for each established staff position.

The operation of an airport and the leadership role of the airport manager, airport director, or director of aviation are unique in the area of public works administration. Managing an airport is much like managing a city in that most of the services and facilities necessary to the smooth functioning of a city are present at the airport. In addition to possessing this management expertise and the ability to administer aviation operations, the airport manager also must be able to function efficiently in the area of business management. The business management or financial management division of airport administration does not parallel that of public administration. Rather, it involves the risk-taking, lease-negotiating, and revenue-raising functions of business administration.

The responsibilities of an airport manager depend on the size and activity of the airport and the support of other departments and agencies.

Operations and maintenance The manager is responsible for all airport operations and maintenance. These functions are directly related to the safety of all those who use the airport, primarily with respect to the flying activities.

Included in these responsibilities are a minimum of once-a-day inspection of runways, ramps, and taxiways; dissemination of information about field conditions to all aviation users; custodial services; electrical systems; buildings and grounds; heating, ventilation, and air conditioning; security and police services; and crash, fire, and rescue services. In the winter season, snow and ice control requires close supervision, and the dissemination of information about field conditions is essential.

The manager is also responsible for traffic and accident reports and the enforcement of airport regulations.

Financing

Airports often are considered to be similar to a public utility and generally enjoy a monopolistic position; users may not have an alternative facility in the immediate area. Rates and charges, however, are not regulated by the state or federal governments.

An April 1974 FAA survey of ninety-two air carrier airports and eighty-four general aviation airports found that many large hub airports and some medium hub airports generate sufficient revenues to be both self-supporting and self-liquidating. Other airports, nonhub and general aviation usually, generate income sufficient to pay only for costs of maintenance and operation (self-supporting), and the capital costs are borne by the local taxpayers in recognition of the value of the airport to the community. Because of limited activity, the income at most small airports is insufficient to totally support the facility. At these locations, the community underwrites the airport costs for its value to the local economy and convenience to local residents.

Sources of income   Fees and charges that generate income are derived from users and commercial enterprises. Depending on the size and activity of the airport, revenues may come from both landing area and terminal area sources.

Landing area sources of income include landing fees, as established or determined by agreement between the airlines and airport management, aviation fuel fees, and tenant fees, such as hangar rentals, ramp tie-down charges, and fixed-base operator fees.

Terminal area sources of income are primarily fees paid by passengers and visitors for automobile parking near the terminal, by airport tenants for the lease of commercial space in the terminal building, and by business for the privilege of renting cars and transporting passengers to and from the terminal in buses, taxis, limousines, and courtesy cars. Airport tenants include airlines, food and drink concessions, flight insurance, motels, coin machines, space advertising, and specialty and general merchandise shops.

The airport may also have other sources of income, such as rental of office space, airport buildings, ground rent for buildings, sale of utilities to tenants, and the rental of surplus airport land for farming, recreation, or light manufacturing.

The airport and the community

An airport served by scheduled air carriers is recognized by local, regional, and state interests as an important community asset. It not only serves as a connecting link with other cities but also generates commercial and industrial development, enlarges the job market, and improves the tax base.

The great concern expressed by communities in which airline service has been withdrawn or reduced is another example of recognition of the airport as an economic asset. An airport served by only general aviation is also an asset in that it serves as a connecting link in the air transportation system. However, it does not provide the same degree of economic stimulation as an airport with air carrier service.

The growth of aviation has outpaced the development of new airports and the improvement of facilities at existing airports throughout the country. FAA forecasts indicate that aviation activity (takeoffs and landings) at airports with FAA air traffic control towers will almost double between 1985 and 1996.

A new or enlarged airport breeds activity and development of adjacent areas. Many cities are now faced with problems of congestion and land use that could have been forestalled by enlightened planning. New industrial, commercial, and residential developments have hemmed in existing airports so that expansion has become economically infeasible and nearby residents are annoyed by aircraft noise.

The solution of existing problems and the prevention of a repetition of similar problems relating to airports require that long-range airport needs be considered during the planning process, not only at the local level but also at regional, state, and federal levels.

Master plan   At the local level, a comprehensive or master plan for the city or region should allow for future aviation needs, including provision for access facilities, for airport expansion, and for compatible land uses adjacent to the airport. In the past, master plans often have omitted this important city subsystem, bringing on the present problems of congestion and land use.

Development and implementation of airport improvement programs should be consistent with goals determined through areawide planning programs. In that way, aviation will be placed in its proper perspective relative to a balanced, multimodel transportation plan and will be located and improved so as to minimize ecological impairment and intrusion of unacceptable levels of noise and air pollution. To be effective, the airport planning process must be totally coordinated with the other planning efforts on the local, regional, and state levels and must involve the units of government responsible for implementing the plan in a systematic fashion.

System plan In certain metropolitan areas of over 500,000 population or over 250,000 annual enplaned passengers, metropolitan airport system plans are recommended. The metropolitan airport system plan is a representation of the aviation facilities required to meet the immediate and future air transportation needs of the metropolitan area. It recommends the general location for and characteristics of new airports and the nature of and expansion for existing ones. It shows the timing and estimated costs of development and relates airport system planning to the policy and coordinative planning for the area, and particularly to ground transportation and land use planning and the urban environment. It provides the basis for definitive and detailed individual airport planning.

Vicinity plan In general, land in the vicinity of an airport is used compatibly when it is occupied by enterprises and activities that derive benefits from their nearness to air transportation services and facilities and are of such character that they do not inhibit the efficiency of airport operations. A land use plan can be said to, be consistent with a community's long-term interest if it channels the growth and development of the community along lines that exploit the topographical and other natural advantages of an area to the best advantage.

The airport and the federal government

The relationship of the federal government to civilian airport management, with particular regard to the safety of air navigation, is embodied in the Federal Aviation Act of 1958 and amendments thereto. Under its terms, the FAA administrator is to consider the following as being in the public interest:

1. The regulation of air commerce in such manner as best to promote its development and safety and fulfill the requirements of national defense
2. The promotion, encouragement, and development of civil aeronautics
3. The control of the use of the navigable airspace of the United States and the regulation of both civil and military operations in such airspace in the interest of safety and efficiency of both
4. The consolidation of research and development with respect to air navigation facilities, as well as the installation and operation thereof
5. The development and operation of a common system of air traffic control and navigation for both military and civil aircraft.

As it affects civilian airport management, the act authorizes the airport administrator to:

1. Assign by rule, regulation, or order the use of navigable airspace under such terms, conditions, and limitations as he or she may deem necessary

to ensure the safety of aircraft and the efficient utilization of such airspace
2. Acquire, establish, and improve air navigation facilities wherever necessary; operate and maintain such air navigation facilities; and provide necessary facilities and personnel for the regulation and protection of air traffic
3. Prescribe air traffic rules and regulations governing the flight of aircraft.

On a day-to-day basis, the FAA exercises its regulatory powers at civilian airports in (1) the operation and staffing of the air traffic control tower; (2) the control of all landings, takeoffs, and taxiing of aircraft at the airport; (3) the regulation of flight patterns around the airport; and (4) the operation, maintenance, and control of all air navigation facilities on, and in the vicinity of, the airport.

Other federal relations to civilian airport management include the development of a national system of airports, federal environmental legislation, federal grant programs for airport planning and construction, airport certification, airport security, and military use of civilian airports.

National system of airports   The national system of airports comprises those airports within the United States and its territories considered necessary by the federal government to meet civil requirements. These airports are identified in the NPIAS developed by the FAA and scheduled to be updated every two years. The plan identifies the composition of a national system of airports and the airport development required to meet the present and future needs of civil aeronautics. To be eligible for federal aid, an airport must be included in NPIAS. The plan also can serve as a guide to Congress for appropriations and to the FAA for allocations of funds under the Airport Improvement Program.

Airport security   In response to aircraft bombings and hijackings, the president on 9 March 1972 issued a proclamation establishing certain aviation security standards for operators of airports regularly serving scheduled air carriers and for commercial operators engaging in interstate common carriage operating large aircraft other than helicopters.

The presidential order, later issued as FAA Regulation, Part 107, assigned primary responsibility for airport security to the airport operators. In general, they required that airport operators establish adequate security for all air operations areas except those that are occupied or controlled exclusively by a certificate holder required to have its own security program under other regulations.

Military use of civilian airports   Except for a customary waiver of landing fees, military aircraft have neither special privileges nor rights at civilian airports. A military unit, typically a National Guard or Reserve unit, is frequently based at a civilian airport. In such an instance, the military has the same status as any other tenant at the airport. Its rights, duties, benefits, and obligations are governed by the terms and conditions of the lease agreement with the airport management. The lease is usually long term with the right of renewal, thereby enabling the federal government to make a long-range military commitment at a particular geographical location for defense, training, or other purposes.

Military flights at civilian airports are subject to the same rules and regulations as civilian flights. At large airports, both civilian and military aircraft are subject to the direction and control of the air traffic control tower.

Summary

This section has emphasized the managerial aspects of airport operations and maintenance. Treated first were the subjects of airport classification and ownership, public and private. Discussion of overall management responsibilities and financing followed. The discussion concluded with a review of the links between the airport, the community, and various government agencies.

Administration of an airport requires both technical familiarity with airport operations and a thorough knowledge of specific state and local regulations and of community needs and priorities.

1 A discussion on transportation as a factor in city location, especially for those with an interest in history, can be found in Lewis Mumford, *The City in History: Its Origins, Its Transformations, Its Prospects*, 1st ed. (New York: Harcourt, Brace and World, 1961), pp. 59–70, 92–94. A briefer treatment is given in Vukan Vuchic, *Urban Public Transportation: Systems and Technology* (Englewood Cliffs, N.J.: Prentice-Hall, 1981), pp. 2–4.

2 Lewis Mumford, *The Highway and the City* (New York: The New American Library, 1963).

3 Robert B. Mitchell and Chester Rapkin, *Urban Traffic—A Function of Land Use* (New York: Columbia University Press, 1954).

4 The role of subdivision control in the planning process is explained best by William Lamont, Jr., "Subdivision Regulation and Land Conversion," in *The Practice of Local Government Planning*, Frank S. So et al., eds. (Washington, D.C.: International City Management Association, 1979), Chap. 14, pp. 389–415. Lamont sees the need for coordination of public transport and pedestrian and bicycle paths, p. 393.

5 The best primer for the process is National Committee on Urban Transportation, *Public Administration Service: Better Transportation for Your City* (Chicago, 1958).

6 This is paraphrased from the much more extensive treatment in "Urban Transportation," by Alan M. Voorhees, Walter G. Hansen, and A. Keith Gilbert, Chapter 8 in *The Practice of Local Government Planning*, pp. 214–45. A briefer treatment is in National Committee on Urban Transportation, *Public Administration Service*, pp. 42–46.

7 Frank S. So et al., eds., *The Practice of Local Government Planning*, pp. 222–24; Richard L. Oram, *Transportation Systems Management: Bibliography of Technical Reports*, sponsored by Urban Mass Transportation Administration and Federal Highway Administration (Washington, D.C.: UMTA, Office of Policy and Program Development, 1976).

8 See note 4.

9 American Association of State Highway and Transportation Officials, *Guide for the Design of High Occupancy Vehicle and Public Transfer Facilities* (Washington, D.C., 1983).

10 American Association of State Highway and Transportation Officials, *Guide for Selecting, Locating, and Designing Traffic Barriers* (Washington, D.C., 1977); U.S. Department of Transportation (Urban Mass Transportation Administration), *Auto Restricted Zones—Background and Feasibility*, vol. 1, UMTA-VA-06-0042-78-1 (Washington, D.C.: Government Printing Office, 1977).

11 John E. Baerwald, ed., Matthew Huber and Louis E. Keefer, assoc. eds., *Transportation and Traffic Engineering Handbook*, Report of the Institute of Traffic Engineers (Englewood Cliffs, N.J.: Prentice-Hall, 1976), esp. chaps. 6, 12, and 13.

12 The wide variety of specialized studies is typified by Michael N. Aronson and W. S. Homburger, *The Location and Design of Safe and Convenient Park and Ride Lots* (Berkeley, Calif.: University of California Institution of Transportation Engineering, 1983); George E. Kanaan, *Parking and Access at General Hospitals* (Westport, Conn.: Eno Foundation for Transportation, Inc., 1973); Metropolitan Association of Urban Designers and Environmental Planners, *Planning, Design and Implementation of Bicycle and Pedestrian Facilities* (New York, 1978).

13 For an overview of pavement management systems, see Christine Johnson, *Pavement (Maintenance) Management Systems* (Chicago: American Public Works Association, n.d.). Includes step-by-step instructions, charts, diagrams, and examples.

14 For an excellent introduction to pavement types, methods of street maintenance, street construction and reconstruction, and soil types, see William S. Foster, ed., *Handbook of Municipal Administration and Engineering* (New York: McGraw-Hill, 1978), chaps. 1–5.

15 This section on bridge maintenance was prepared with the assistance of D. C. Marett.

16 Organization for Economic Cooperation and Development, *Bridge Evaluation* (Paris, 1979).

17 For a practical and concise review of traffic control and street lighting, see William S. Foster, "Traffic Control and Street Lighting," in William S. Foster, ed., *Handbook of Municipal Administration and Engineering* (New York: McGraw-Hill, 1978), chap. 14. The definitions, photos, and diagrams are especially helpful.

18 For further information, see Wolfgang S. Homburger, ed., Louis E. Keefer and William R. McGrath, assoc. eds., *Transportation and Traffic Engineering Handbook*, 2d ed. (Englewood Cliffs, N.J.: Prentice-Hall, 1982), pp. 539, 544–46; Paul C. Box and Joseph C. Oppenlander, *Manual of Traffic Engineering Studies*, 4th ed. (Arlington, VA: Institute of Transportation Engineers, 1976), chap. 9.

19 National Safety Council, *Accident Facts, 1985 Edition* (Chicago, 1985), pp. 59, 65–66.

20 Instructions for developing and maintaining a traffic accident location file may be obtained from the National Safety Council, 444 North Michigan Avenue, Chicago, Illinois 60611.

21 Edward J. Cantilli, "Transportation Safety," in Homburger, *Transportation and Traffic Engineering Handbook*, chap. 18, pp. 555–68, 581–84; Box

and Oppenlander, *Manual of Traffic Engineering Studies*, chap. 4; U.S. Department of Transportation, National Highway Traffic Safety Administration and Federal Highway Administration, *Highway Safety Program Standards* (Washington, D.C.: Government Printing Office, 1974), Standard 9, p. 10; Standard 10, pp. 11–12; Standard 18, pp. 27–29.

22 See James M. Hunnicut, "Parking, Loading, and Terminal Facilities," in Homburger, *Transportation and Traffic Engineering Handbook*, chap. 21; Box and Oppenlander, *Manual of Traffic Engineering Studies*, chap. 10.

23 U.S. Department of Transportation, Federal Highway Administration, *Manual on Uniform Traffic Control Devices for Streets and Highways* (Washington, D.C.: Government Printing Office, 1978, with periodic revisions), p. 1.

24 Ibid., p. 3.

25 U.S. Department of Transportation, *Highway Safety Program Standards*, Standard 13, pp. 16–17.

26 U.S. Department of Transportation, *Manual on Uniform Traffic Control Devices*, pp. 32–33, 34–35.

14

Water resources

This chapter deals with three vital community services: potable water supply; wastewater collection, treatment, and disposal; and urban drainage and flood control. It is possible to live without governmental provision of these services, and in many parts of the world people do live, on a primitive level, without water and waste disposal. But the developed areas of the world depend for their very survival on water supply, wastewater disposal, and, to an increasing extent, control of drainage and floods.

The first section of this chapter, "Potable water," reviews planning for water service, operations, and budgeting and financing. The second section, "Wastewater systems," deals with collection systems, treatment and disposal methods, and operation of treatment works. The final section, "Drainage," examines governmental and management responsibilities for urban drainage and flood control, stormwater detention and retention, planning and implementation, maintenance of facilities, and data needs and analysis.

Potable water

This section reviews the steps that local government managers can take to plan, operate, and finance a potable water system. The water system supplies a vital service to the people, and it is the water purveyor who is basically responsible for providing safe water that will not impair health in any way. The objective of the water system, therefore, is to deliver safe, potable water to customers.

People generally give little thought to the water system supplying their needs. It is an unspoken tribute to the many people connected with the thousands of water systems throughout the country who, day after day, deliver potable water in quantities and at pressures desired by the customers with so few disruptions.

In most cities and counties the need for water will continue to increase. Many of the existing water sources will not be capable of supplying the extra need. New, expensive sources will have to be developed or production from existing ones increased at high cost. The federal Safe Drinking Water Act of 1974 as amended has resulted in the establishment of strict water quality standards. Many water sources will require additional expensive treatment in order to achieve the new standards.

Just about all water systems are energy intensive. It is often necessary to pump the water, sometimes more than once, from source through treatment and storage to the distribution system. The chemicals used for treatment and disinfection require energy to produce. It is highly probable that power costs and therefore water supply costs will continue to increase in the future.

Communities and their water departments are faced with the compelling need to resolve the conflict between higher costs due to the factors noted above with

The section on potable water is an abridged version of Chapter 16 in *Urban Public Works Administration*, the predecessor edition to this book. The chapter needed only small changes and updating to make it fully useful for current public works managers. This work was done by Lloyd C. Fowler, General Manager and Chief Engineer of the Goleta Water District, California.

the reluctance of the general public to accept higher rates, charges, and fees. Only good management of all phases—planning, treatment, distribution, financing, and so on—can be relied on to keep costs to a minimum.

It is management's responsibility to take a personal interest in the entire water system and to make certain it is well managed so that the maximum economies are realized. Planning at all levels is essential. Long-term planning, ten years or more ahead, is required to develop a cash flow that proves reliable to both the agency involved and the customers. Under the financial conditions facing cities and counties, good long-term planning is more important than ever.

This section is divided into three main parts. The first concerns planning for the water system. The second and third parts discuss, respectively, the operational program and budgeting and finance.

Planning for the water system

Objectives and goals   The first item of business for the management of a water system is to determine goals. These are best presented as carefully considered, *written* general objectives. Since the efforts of every person employed by the water system will be directed by the objectives and goals, they should be brief, clear, and concise so that everyone can understand them. It takes the cooperation of all employees to deliver the water to the customer. The goals should be tied into specific time periods and money expenditures wherever possible. A few examples of objectives and goals are shown below.

Objectives   Deliver potable water of approved quality at the established pressures, and in the quantities and at the rates of flow that the customers desire and are willing to pay for; operate the water department so the total cost of the delivered water is less than the median cost experienced by other cities of approximately the same size with similar source and distribution conditions.

Goals   Identify the customers. Provide municipal water service during the period 1986 to 2005 to domestic, industrial, and commercial customers within the incorporated limits of the city and in the unincorporated area of the county for one lot depth along both sides of "X" Highway between the city limits and "Z" River.

System   Operate the water system 24 hours per day, 365 days per year in an effective and professional manner.

Source   Design and implement by stage construction an intake structure and pumping station capable of producing 10 million gallons per day (MGD) in 1986 and 14 MGD in 1996.

Treatment   Design and operate the water treatment plant (1) to produce a treated water that meets all health and quality standards of state health departments and the Federal Safe Drinking Water Act and (2) to meet the average and peak demands for water by the distribution system.

Distribution system   Deliver water in the quantity and at the rate desired by the customer while maintaining pressure between 40 and 60 pounds per square inch (psi), except that the pressure can drop to 20 psi when supplying water to fight a major fire.

Firefighting capabilities   Consider requirements for firefighting facilities during design of water distribution system. Coordinate design with local fire departments and fire underwriters to assure implementation of national standards for fire protection.

A master plan for the water system The objectives and goals for the water system have to be implemented. Even small water systems are complicated and expensive operations. It is not possible for management to develop the water system so that it will be efficient and will carry out the objectives and goals—and also meet the other requirements of the customers—without a long-term master plan. It would be much simpler for management if it could develop the objectives and goals, prepare the master plan, and establish a workable organization before it was called on to operate the system and deliver water to the customers.

Water, a squandered resource The Northeast, according to experts, is sitting on almost enough water to float away, but the resource of water in the ground is being thoughtlessly squandered. "Scattered below the nation's surface are an estimated 8 million storage tanks containing literally billions of gallons of petroleum products, hazardous wastes and industrial process chemicals," said Michael R. Deland, regional administrator of the Environmental Protection Agency. "It is estimated that 25 percent of these tanks will leak their toxic contents into the ground water in the next five years."

A single gallon of gasoline, Mr. Deland said, can contaminate a million gallons of ground water to a level detectable by taste and smell. . . . There are also problems from so-called nonpoint sources, . . . such as pesticides and fertilizers, and acid rain. In addition, the geologic conditions created by glaciers thousands of years ago have made the region's groundwater vulnerable to chemicals leaching from dumps. Some towns used abandoned gravel pits as landfills directly over aquifers, or underground pools, said Ivan C. James 2d, chief of the New England District of the United States Geological Survey's Water Resources Division. "From their consideration, it was an excellent place for a landfill," he said, adding, "the mistakes are very dear in terms of what it takes to correct them."

According to Mr. Deland, "By comparison, the surface water challenge of the early 1970s now seems simpler. We knew the pollutants by name, measured them in tons. Today, if we know the names of the toxic threats we often can't pronounce them. We measure them in parts per million, parts per trillion, or parts per quadrillion."

Source: Matthew L. Wald, "In Eastern States, the Water Supply Is Topic A," *New York Times*, September 1, 1985. Copyright © 1985 by The New York Times Company. Reprinted by permission.

Except on rare occasions, the key management personnel are hired after the water system has been in operation for some time, so the preparation of a new master plan or modification of an existing one has to take place simultaneously with operations. Conscientious planning is even more critical under these circumstances than when starting from scratch. Flexibility has to be built into the planning process if the plan is to be implemented at a reasonable cost.

Future events cannot be predicted exactly, if at all. Economic and social changes are occurring regularly in our society. Management has to modify its methods of operations on an almost continuous basis to keep up with the times. The master plan has to cover a period of at least ten years if the objectives and goals are to be achieved and logical changes can evolve. Short-term planning cannot tolerate major problems or new trends requiring substantial changes.

The master plan can be prepared by the water department if there are a sufficient number of experienced employees available. An alternative method is to have the plan prepared by a consultant with experience in the water field. Engineers have, over the years, acquired a great deal of knowledge and experience in the design and construction of water works.

The master plan has to provide the basic information required to develop all facets of the water system. The more important topics that should be included are discussed below.

Water resources are limited The United States has about 600 billion gallons of water available daily. In a *Forbes* article (August 20, 1979), K. C. Wiegner reported that in 1960, the demand for water reached 270 billion gallons. In 1970, this had risen to 370 billion gallons, and for 1985, the author quoted estimates that would place the demand at 422 billion, or uncomfortably close to the top available supply.

As of the mid-1980s, shortages became apparent throughout the nation. New York City is prepared for water restrictions. California reports water shortages in several areas of the state. Denver is planning for the reuse of wastewater, treating it for potable use.

This lack of water has had a crippling effect on commerce and industry, especially in the West. Coal is abundant in Wyoming and eastern Montana, and the most effective way to distribute it is by pipeline in a slurry form, according to the *Forbes* account. But the water is not available.

Domestic usage represents only about 9 percent of total demand, while agriculture requires 43 percent and industry 47 percent. The nation has experienced serious conflicts over water rights in the past, and urban governments must be prepared to defend their rights to this need.

Source: William S. Foster.

Estimating future water needs Management must have a relatively accurate estimate of the customers' future needs for water in order to implement the correct source, treatment, and distribution facilities. Both the total volume of water and the rate of purchase have to be known. Many factors affect the total volume of water that is delivered to the customers. Expensive water encourages conservation and intelligent use of water. Cheap water, particularly if paid for at a flat rate per customer unit, supports high use and wasteful practices such as leaks that are not fixed, hoses left running, and water allowed to run off the property. A water system is a utility, and in common with other utilities it experiences very large fluctuations in demand for its product. The daily average need for water used inside living units and for most commercial and light industrial establishments is relatively constant throughout the year. However, there is a great variation in water use during different periods of the day and night because most people eat, work, wash, and sleep at about the same time. Certain industries, such as canneries, have tremendous peak seasonal needs for water and then require practically no water between seasons. Fire flows are sporadic, yet can reach very high rates during a major fire—a factor that can be a problem if such flows coincide with the peak water uses of the other customers. Heavy industry can use large volumes of water but factories often have private water sources that meet most of their needs. Single-family residences on large lots with extensive landscaping are responsible for exceptionally high water use on hot summer afternoons and evenings.

The engineer calculating water needs has to take all existing conditions into consideration as well as such potential future effects as rezoning; annexations; different types and sizes of future commercial and industrial establishments; and building of more single-family houses or apartments, and so on. The estimate of the need for water has to be relatively accurate since substantial sums of money could be wasted if the system is built too large or too small. Actual domestic water use can vary between 40 and 120 gallons per person per day. Average per capita per day consumption of water for all uses (domestic, commercial, and industrial) generally is within the range of 170 to 300 gallons per capita per day but can be as high as 500 or 600, or even more. The variations in the rates of water use by the customer can also be very large, with maximum hour use rate being two and a half to four times the yearly average. It is necessary to have a dependable population forecast when estimating future water needs.

Policies and procedures needed to meet health and water quality standards
Management cannot tolerate—and is not allowed legally to tolerate—compromises with public health. At all times the water system has to deliver safe water to customers. A "safe" water is free from pathogenic (disease-causing) organisms, toxic material, and any other substances that could be harmful to customers. Historically, state and/or local health departments have established the quality standards for potable water. These standards must be consistent with the federal Safe Drinking Water Act of 1974 as amended. Compliance with the standards that have been and continue to be developed under this law is mandatory. The state can accept more responsibility or delegate it to local agencies. Extensive monitoring of the water as well as public notification of deficiencies by the water system is required.

Water, even after full treatment (including filtration), is disinfected to ensure destruction of pathogenic organisms. Most systems rely on some form of chlorine for disinfection. Ozone is used where trihalomethane formation is a problem. In other cases chlorine dioxide is used or ammonia is added with the chlorine. A free chlorine residue in the water throughout the distribution system is desirable since it helps maintain the quality of the water and can guard against minor amounts of accidental pollution.

Bacteriological, physical, and chemical tests have to be performed on water samples collected regularly from the source, during treatment, and from the distribution system. The results of the tests have to prove conformity with regulatory agencies' standards. At least once, and preferably two or more times, per year a sanitary survey should be made of all the water system facilities to check for potential cross connections. Any potential source of pollution or contamination has to be eliminated. All treated water (potable water) storages should be covered and their vents screened. Wells should not be subject to flooding or be near septic tanks or sanitary sewers. Facilities to bypass a surface water source when spills of toxic materials occur should be in operating condition.

There have been a number of documented occasions when the distribution systems of certain water works were contaminated by pathogenic organisms or toxic materials originating on a customer's property. High pressure pumps can force contaminated water back through service lines into the distribution system, or low pressure in the distribution system (due to main breaks, fire flows, peak demands, etc.) may permit contaminated water from cross connections to flow back into the distribution system. High-rise buildings are particularly vulnerable to this type of problem. All water systems should have an active cross-connection control program to protect the quality of the water. Approved backflow prevention devices should be installed on all service lines where potentially hazardous conditions exist on the customer's premises.

Water sources It is management's responsibility to make certain that the water supply is capable of producing the quantity of water that the customers are

Contamination of water supplies

Many synthetic organic compounds and other hazardous chemicals are increasingly being detected in drinking water sources, particularly in groundwaters that have been long considered pristine. A 1982 study by the U.S. Environmental Protection Agency estimated that 15 to 20 percent of the groundwater supply systems in the United States contain synthetic organics. These pollutants enter into the groundwater as a result of improper storage and handling of chemicals, improper disposal of these materials, and leaks from underground tanks and pipelines.

All water supply managers must be aware of the threat to surface and groundwater quality from hazardous chemicals. This threat is especially prevalent in urban areas where these materials are heavily used by industry and commerce. Even rural and residential areas are affected by agricultural and household uses of these chemicals. Synthetic organic chemicals are produced at a rate of over 20 billion pounds per year; because these materials are used in a multitude of ways and produced in great amounts, they are readily introduced into the environment and into water supplies.

All water supplies should be monitored to check for potential contamination. However, just checking is not enough. Water managers should work to assure that potential polluting chemicals are properly handled, that transport and storage are safe, and that potential spills and leaks can be safely contained. This requires monitoring and checking by qualified health authorities in cooperation with the water purveyors.

It is in the best interest of the water purveyor and the consumer that water supplies be uncontaminated. Water managers should consider management and treatment strategies to ensure that this goal is reached. Some of these strategies are as follows: (1) eliminate potential sources of contamination from the watersheds; (2) if they cannot be eliminated, contain the potential contaminants so they cannot enter the water supply; (3) find new water supplies that are away from potential sources of contamination; and (4) if problems arise, blend water supplies so that any pollution is reduced by dilution.

Obviously if a water supply is found to be contaminated and a new supply cannot be immediately found, then the water supply has to be treated to remove the offending agent. The treatment strategy will depend on the chemical involved, the acceptance of regulatory agencies, cost, reliability, ease of implementation, and public opinion. The water manager should not hesitate to call on specialty consultants to ensure that public water supplies are protected.

Source: Lloyd C. Fowler, P.E., General Manager and Chief Engineer, Goleta Water District, California.

---

willing to pay for. The origin of all water available for municipal uses is rain or snow. Most of the water used by cities is obtained from surface sources. The source has to produce sufficient volumes of water to meet water needs on a continuous basis. Engineers can calculate the perennial yield of a surface source. Every area periodically experiences periods of lower than average rainfall and at times the condition can be severe enough to be classified as a drought. It takes good planning and design to provide the storage required in ponds, lakes, or reservoirs for most surface sources to meet customer needs during an extended drought.

The quality of the water is not uniform at all depths in most rivers and reservoirs. The intake structure should be designed to take water from the level of best quality. This level can fluctuate depending on season and water level;

therefore the intake structure should be capable of taking water from several different depths. Historically, certain surface waters have been subject to gross contamination or pollution from effluents of industrial plants and sanitary sewers. Enforcement of the requirements of the Federal Water Pollution Control Act of 1972 as amended have resulted in a higher quality of surface water. Nevertheless, surface waters generally require full treatment to produce potable water. Acquisition of rights to water from a river or lake is often a complicated procedure and is best handled by attorneys specializing in water rights.

There is much more groundwater available than surface water on the North American continent. About 80 percent of the community water systems rely on groundwater for part or all of their supply, but only about one-third of the population in the United States is served by such systems. Groundwater might be used to a greater extent in the future as the availability of new surface sources is exhausted. The source of groundwater is that portion of snowmelt and rainwater that percolates into the ground. The yield of an aquifer, a formation that holds water, which can be removed from it by wells, can be increased by artificial recharge; surface waters can be spread over soils with high infiltration capacities that are continuous to the aquifer; or treated water can be injected through wells into the aquifer. Pumping more water from the ground than can be replaced by natural or artificial recharge is overdraft and can result in subsidence of the ground surface, water quality degradation, and higher pumping costs. Groundwater used should be within the perennial yield of the basin or the undesirable results from overdraft noted before may occur.

Groundwater can be obtained from wells, springs, or infiltration galleries. The quality of most groundwaters is good. However, dissolved minerals and hardness can be a problem. In some areas groundwater basins are subject to pollution.

Methods of water treatment   Management has to provide a treatment plant capable of producing a safe, healthful, potable water in the volumes and at the rates desired by customers.

Flexibility of operation is essential since there can be wide variations in the quality of the raw water and in the rate of use of the treated water. Sufficient storage for treated water can level out the high peak flows normally experienced in urban water supply.

The quality of the raw water determines the type of treatment required. Some well waters and surface waters of exceptional quality require no treatment other than chlorination. Raw waters subject to pollution have to receive extensive treatment in order to make them safe and remove color, odor, taste, and so on.

Much research is being directed toward solving the potential health problems connected with using wastewater treatment plant effluent as a source of potable water. It is possible that water treatment plants in the future will be capable of producing, from effluent, a potable water that is acceptable to public health authorities.

Water distribution system design concepts   The water distribution system must be capable of delivering the desired quantities of water at the flow rates and pressures acceptable to the customers while maintaining acceptable water quality. The distribution mains and appurtenances should be designed to deliver these required volumes of water to the service areas during their entire design life; this could be twenty-five to forty years or more depending on the type of pipe used. The distribution system in most locations is required to maintain a minimum residual pressure of 20 pounds per square inch (psi) during peak fire demand and to not exceed 120 psi at any time. Customer complaints can be expected if the pressure falls below 20 psi. The optimum range is between 40 and 60 psi. It is desirable to maintain a minimum pressure at least 20 psi during fires. Too high a pressure can cause excessive leakage and failure of older hot water heaters. The maximum main pressure should not exceed 100 psi.

Management has to make a decision on the number and location of gate valves in the system. Valves are expensive but the more valves used the better the distribution system can be controlled. When sufficient valves are available, only a minimum number of customers need be without service during the repair of a main break or other emergency. Without sufficient valves, three, four, or more blocks in residential and commercial areas may have to be shut down and a great many customers will be out of water.

The pipes that carry the water throughout the distribution system can be made of many different materials. It takes an engineering study to determine the best pipe for a particular system. A few of the more frequently used materials are iron, concrete, plastic, and steel. The type and location of fire hydrants should be determined by the fire department. Many conditions and factors have to be considered when calculating the sizes of the pipes in the system. A few of the more important questions to be answered are:

1. Can the treatment plant or storage facility be located at a high enough elevation to serve the system by gravity?
2. Are pump stations required to pressurize all or part of the system?
3. Is it economically feasible to provide additional storage capacity in order to reduce the size of the pumping facilities and the water mains?

Water stored at critical points in the distribution system can reduce peak loads on pumps, water transmission pipes, and treatment facilities. It can also provide extra volumes of water to fight fires and feed portions of the distribution system during repairs to mains, pumps, or transmission pipes. The size of distribution system storage facilities may vary from a few thousand gallons to more than 10 million gallons. Storage units are usually constructed of reinforced concrete or of steel. These units can be installed underground, at ground level, or elevated as necessary to provide the required pressure. Low-level structures may require pumps to maintain the desired pressures.

Coping with adverse climatic and geological conditions   Each area of the country has its own climatic and geological conditions that have to be considered when designing and operating a water system. In the colder parts of the country pipes have to have an earth cover of 5 to 7 feet, or even more, so that the water will not freeze and break the pipe. Also in cold areas fire hydrants must be of the dry barrel type; the water drains out of the portion of the fire hydrant above ground through a drip hole when the hydrant is not being used, thereby eliminating water that may freeze in the hydrant. There are special water meters available that are not badly damaged if the water inside freezes. In extremely cold areas water pipes near the surface have to be insulated. Operating crews must be equipped to thaw customer service lines.

In areas subject to hurricanes or tornadoes, treatment plants, pumping stations, and other buildings have to meet special building code requirements so that they will survive the high velocity winds. In areas of high seismic activity the buildings have to meet earthquake building code requirements. No one can guarantee that structures designed and constructed pursuant to the special codes will not be damaged during these events, but the structures should experience little damage from light to moderate winds or earthquakes. Pipelines installed near or across active geologic faults have to be specially designed with flexible joints and correct bedding. Soils that are very corrosive to metals are found in many areas. When water mains have to be installed through such soils, pipes made of noncorrosive materials such as plastic can be used; metal pipes can be protected by special wrappings or coatings applied to the outside of the pipes. In addition metal pipelines can be protected by impressed current or sacrificial anodes.

Customer service lines can be made of many materials, including copper and plastic. The size of the line should be calculated in order to ensure the desired flows without excessive pressure loss. Corporation stops are required at the mains to permit installation of the line and to shut off abandoned or broken lines. A curb stop at the property line is necessary to shut the water off to the customer in case of an emergency, the replacement of a meter, or repairs to water lines.

Facilities and operational methods to ensure dependability   Management has to provide a water system that is dependable. Dependability starts with adequate design standards and the use of good materials and equipment installed in a skillful manner. Water mains have to be large enough to carry the designed flows within allowable pressure losses. The right kind of pipes have to be used in order to resist the action of corrosive soils. The thickness of the pipe has to be great enough to stand up against water hammer and external loads imposed on the pipes.

At least two separate electric power sources should be provided for treatment plants and major pumping stations. Many water systems provide sufficient extra pumps to meet peak demands if the largest pump is not operating at any one time. Treatment plants and larger pump stations should have emergency electric generators. The capacity of the generators should be sufficient to provide the power for the minimum number of pieces of electric equipment and lights required to keep the plant in operation if the regular power source fails. In some areas power companies have parallel transmission lines that may be utilized.

There should be sufficient storage tank capacity to permit normal delivery of water during all but the most severe emergencies. None of the equipment can be considered dependable unless it receives preventive maintenance on a regular basis. There should be sufficient gate valves in the system so that emergencies and construction will not require extensive areas to be shut down and many customers to be out of water while repairs or new connections are made.

Safety standards   It is a basic responsibility of management to provide a safe working environment for all employees. The potential for accidents in a water system is high. The water system has to be operated so that the safety standards of the regulatory agencies are met. The federal Occupational Safety and Health Act (OSHA) now serves as the basis for most state and local safety standards. All employees have to receive training in safe working practices. Safety is a subject that has to be rediscussed with employees on a regular basis or it is soon forgotten and not practiced. Informal weekly sessions with the employees are a good means of reviewing safety precautions. All serious accidents should be reviewed by a committee consisting of three or more members picked from the supervisors and other employees. If possible, the cause of the accident should be determined and action taken to prevent similar accidents from occurring in the future.

Safety equipment—proper clothing, shoes, eye protection, approved railings, safety harnesses for fixed ladders, machinery guards, safety signs, etc.—must also be provided. Management has to make the required effort to ensure that employees develop a good attitude toward safety. "Good housekeeping" in all areas tends to improve morale and reduce the number of accidents.

Policy on water meters   The customer should pay for all water delivered to his or her property. An accurate measurement of the water delivered is required in order to prepare a water bill that is fair to both the customer and the jurisdiction. The water meter is a practical device for accurately measuring quantities of water; all customer service lines should be metered.

The water department should be certain that the particular meter chosen will accurately measure the water delivered to the customer. All meters require periodic maintenance and repairs, which the water department can either provide in its own meter shop or contract out to companies specializing in meter repairs. Every meter should have its own file and all inspections and repairs should be recorded. A specific time period between testing for each size and type of meter should be established, with the larger meters being tested more frequently since they have more potential for loss of revenue because of the large volumes measured.

Records system and preventive maintenance   Water systems cannot function efficiently if the only records of locations and sizes of mains, valves, and services are stored in the minds of a few employees. Management has to devise and carry out a procedure that will generate a complete record system of maps and files that can be used by any trained person.

No water system can operate effectively without accurate maps. Maps on the scale of 50 feet to the inch on a good grade reproducible material such as Mylar are the basis of many map programs. The maps should show lot lines; house numbers; location, size, and type of mains; valves; fire hydrants; blowoffs; location and size of customer service lines; pressure control valves; pumping stations, etc. Maps on the scale of 200 feet to the inch are useful for planning studies. Larger scale maps showing the mains and their sizes are suited for wall displays and for explaining the facilities available to prospective developers. Special maps showing fire hydrant locations are useful for maintenance scheduling and for the fire department.

Without a preventive maintenance program for all equipment and facilities, the general condition of the system would soon degenerate to a point where it would no longer be dependable and would be very expensive to restore. Management has to control potentially critical conditions to the best of its ability. A thorough preventive maintenance program allows the supervisors to determine when a piece of equipment should be taken out of service for maintenance. Maintenance can be scheduled for a time when the piece of equipment is least needed. The alternative to preventive maintenance is "operation by emergency," since unmaintained equipment often breaks down during periods of peak demand, when the need for the equipment is at a maximum. The costs of repairs and the resulting problems are more expensive than the provision of good preventive maintenance.

A separate preventive maintenance schedule should be prepared and implemented for each type of equipment and facility. Extensive records are required to accomplish this task. Every fire hydrant should be inspected twice a year. The hydrant should be flowed to check its condition and to make certain that the separate gate valve on the water line is open and the hydrant can be operated without excessive force. Each fire hydrant has to have its own record card, and all work done on the hydrant has to be recorded.

Every gate valve should be checked and operated every one to three years depending on size and importance. The number of turns to open and close the valve should be counted to make certain that the valve is fully open. All valves should close in the same direction to avoid mistakes that result in improperly closed valves in the system. Leaking valves or ones that stick or are difficult to close and open should be repaired. A separate maintenance card should be kept for each valve. Good housekeeping is an important part of preventive maintenance. Any deterioration in the long-term level of housekeeping might be a clue to management that the general condition of the entire system is slipping. Billing and fiscal records have to meet all accepted auditing standards.

Replacement of equipment and facilities   No vehicle, piece of equipment, or water supply facility will last indefinitely. The life of an individual item can vary from three to five years for a pickup truck to fifteen to twenty-five years for pumps, motors, and similar equipment. Some buildings, pipelines, and other structures can have a useful life of forty years or more. Preparing a table listing each vehicle, major piece of equipment, building, and the like; the economic life of each item; and the year that it should be replaced is a convenient way of ensuring that management is made aware of the aging of the system. Cost estimates of the equipment and facilities to be replaced can be prepared for each year and the money required for replacement can be included in the long-term budget prepared by the department.

It is one of management's responsibilities to see that the system does not become obsolete. Managers of water systems should receive a system in good condition; they should maintain it in good condition; and later they should hand over the system in good condition to their successors. Practically no agency can afford to replace a large obsolete water system. It is financially feasible to spend smaller amounts of money each year for replacements and avoid the ruinous costs of replacing a major portion of the system at a later time.

Least-cost alternatives for various classes of work   The water system has to meet the requirements of all regulatory agencies, the customers, and the fire department. It is possible to design several different systems that would be capable of meeting all such requirements. One of the solutions would nevertheless provide the desired level of service over the given time period for the lowest annual cost. Management has to find that solution. Each proposed solution has to consider all costs. These include capital costs of the equipment and facilities, operation and maintenance costs, replacement costs, and debt service costs. In order to be able to compare alternatives with equal capabilities, the costs for each should be calculated for the same time period, usually annually. The number of alternatives available to a water system can be substantial. The choice of water sources might be wells in several locations, surface water, or purchase of water wholesale from another agency. There might be two or more methods to treat each different water source. The distribution system could use larger pipe sizes with lower friction losses, smaller pumping stations, and less power usage, or vice versa. Some of the alternatives can be eliminated without much study because of high costs or dependability problems. Ingenuity on the part of the design engineer can pay off in this phase of planning a water system.

Priority list of equipment, facilities, and procedures required for implementation of the master plan   The fruit of the master plan process is a priority list of the new capital projects, major pieces of equipment, and new facilities required first to develop the water system, and second to prepare the long-term budget, cash flow calculations, and method of financing the water system. For each item on the priority list there should be a written statement of need, a written description of the project or piece of equipment, a map showing location in which it will be used, a decision as to the year that the item will be required, and a cost estimate for purchase and installation as well as for the yearly operation and maintenance cost, all based on the value of the dollar at the time the master plan was developed. When the budget is prepared, the year of proposed construction will be determined and the cost estimate modified to reflect the value of the dollars at that time.

Environmental assessment   A determination has to be made whether an appropriate environmental impact report (EIR) or a negative declaration as to environmental impact has to be prepared for the master plan. There are many factors that go into this decision. If the master plan is for a water system that will experience substantial growth in the future and will need many construction projects, an EIR probably will be required. On the other hand, if the physical facilities are substantially completed and the water system is in conformity with the approved general plan for the community, then a negative declaration might suffice. The city attorney should be consulted in each specific case.

It is generally preferable to prepare an EIR or negative declaration for the entire master plan rather than preparing separate EIRs or negative declarations for each construction project prior to the time that the project is constructed. By consideration of the entire master plan at one time, the number of EIRs to be prepared is reduced to one and the public has a better idea of what is going to take place over the next few years. In addition the public is able to make its ideas known on the entire plan at the public hearings.

The section of the EIR that discusses possible growth-inducing effects is practically always controversial, and it is desirable to have public discussion on the subject before the major items of the master plan are ready for design. Management has to decide who will prepare the EIR or negative declaration. Relatively few water departments have sufficient experienced personnel available to prepare an EIR for a complex master plan. There are consultants available who specialize in the preparation of EIRs and who can assist at the public hearings.

Written emergency plans   Water systems can be adversely affected by hurricanes, floods, droughts, earthquakes, tsunamis, tornadoes, extensive electric power failures, contamination (or pollution), conflagrations, major main breaks, loss of water source, labor strikes, and so on. Management has to determine which emergencies are likely to affect its water system.

A *separate* contingency plan should be prepared for each potential type of emergency before the emergency occurs. Every type of emergency has special features and must be considered separately. After a major emergency occurs, it is too late to prepare a plan or even to schedule effectively the steps to be taken. Emergency plans should include reciprocal agreements with adjacent water purveyors so that emergency water connections can be installed with the neighboring water system to ensure that some water will be available during emergencies afflicting just one agency. Informational statements for each type of emergency should be prewritten for radio, television, and the newspapers. Public address systems in police patrol cars are a good means of disseminating information quickly throughout an area. If there are sufficient numbers of non-English-speaking people in the service area, bilingual informational statements should be prepared. Procedures should be worked out with the news media so that information can be distributed quickly in cases of emergency. This would be particularly important if the water in the distribution system were to become contaminated.

Labor strikes and walkouts are a special problem. Management has to make certain that a good plan evolves so that the water system will continue to deliver potable water to the customers during a strike. The plan should include an organizational chart and a method of spreading shift work. Only a minimum amount of preventive maintenance can be accomplished during a strike. The water system will be in competition with other departments for managerial staff during a general strike.

Emergency funds may be available from federal and state agencies under certain conditions. Before federal or state funds become available, the community generally has to be designated as a disaster area. If at all possible, heavy expenditures of money should wait until the jurisdiction is eligible for the special funds. Good records of all expenses have to be kept. During the emergency it is desirable to assign administrative aides and clerical help to keep the records in the required form.

The emergency plan for the water system must be coordinated with local and regional emergency plans. The water system cannot stand alone in an emergency.

Standard specifications and details A current set of standard specifications and details should be maintained by the management of a water system. This is required to ensure uniformity of construction, materials, and equipment whether the work is accomplished by contract or by water department employees. Since new materials and equipment are constantly being developed, the specifications and details should be reviewed periodically and updated. For legal reasons and to obtain the best prices, the specifications have to be written in such a way that competition is not excessively restricted or eliminated. An attorney should review the specifications, particularly the legal sections.

A large number of model specifications and standards are prepared by organizations and public agencies that can be wholly or partially incorporated into the system's specifications and details by reference. These include (but are by no means limited to) those prepared by the American Water Works Association (AWWA), whose standards are very comprehensive and cover the entire water field; the American Public Works Association (APWA); and the American Society for Testing and Materials (ASTM).

The operational program

Management has to implement the objectives and goals of the water system first by providing the equipment, facilities, and process listed in the master plan, and second by choosing and employing a group of people who will cooperate with one another and channel their efforts to ensure that the system's objectives and goals are achieved. The second of these steps is very important; it takes well-trained, *motivated* employees to make the system operate effectively. No two water systems are organized in exactly the same way. The organization has to be molded around the knowledge, experience, attitudes, and aptitudes of the key personnel in order to be successful. Organizational changes are inevitable when key personnel are replaced. Sufficient authority should be delegated to employees at all levels to assure that the work can be accomplished in a minimum of time. Good management practices are applicable to both large and small departments but organization of functions can vary substantially. Whether small or large, water departments should be willing to cooperate and work with other departments, particularly the fire department, in solving problems that cross departmental lines of authority.

Management should spend the time and effort to prepare a written, detailed estimate of the man-hours in the different classifications required to operate each of the various services and functions of the water system. Sufficient personnel to cover all services and work have to be employed, but every excess employee is a financial drain on a system, particularly a small one. Conversely, understaffing can result in increased costs owing to the neglect of proper maintenance. Working only on emergency or crisis projects can be very expensive. Careful staffing is required to keep total costs at a minimum.

It is frequently possible for a telemetering system to control water transmission and distribution systems with sufficient accuracy and dependability that no operators have to be on duty at night, on weekends, or even during a three-day holiday. There should be an experienced operator on standby at home with a fully equipped truck. The telemetering system should be connected to an alarm system at police headquarters or an answering service so that the standby operator can be notified as soon as a problem occurs.

Management has to provide on-the-job and formal training for employees. Certain states require certification of water treatment plant operators and distribution system operators. The training programs should be coordinated to ensure that the employees have an opportunity to become certified and then advance to higher ratings. It is the responsibility of management to train employees even though some of the employees might transfer to another water system in the future.

Good public relations are worth the effort and cost. There should be trained individuals in the office to receive service requests and answer complaints. Good public relations require that complaints be investigated and corrective action taken promptly. Most criticisms and complaints are the result of special problems or emergencies such as low water pressure due to a main break, turbidity, or air in the water.

Management should make certain that preventive maintenance programs are carried out. If there are many emergencies of the type that could be avoided by planning or preventive maintenance, something is wrong with the method of management. Construction should be coordinated with the street department and other utilities so that the minimum number of street cuts are made. No utility cuts should be made soon after a street is resurfaced. The mains have to be flushed periodically through the fire hydrants in order to remove accumulations of sand, silt, and other material that settles out during periods of low flow. If not removed, the settled material is picked up again during peak flows and delivered to customers.

Management has to make every attempt to produce, treat, and deliver no more water than is paid for by the customer. Water is expensive. There is no such thing as "free water." Even the water required for such city facilities as parks, city hall, etc., should be metered and the cost of the water charged to the respective programs. This will balance the income to the water department and provide a more accurate cost picture for the other departments.

Water meters are the "cash registers" of the water system. They have to be accurate. Practically all inaccurate meters register low and therefore the jurisdiction is not paid for all the water delivered through inaccurate meters. The losses can be limited by a good meter shop operation with well-trained repair personnel. Pipes and appurtenances tend to leak in time, and leak surveys by department personnel or consultants specializing in this type of work should be carried out if there appears to be a significant loss of water. Contractors who fill their tank trucks from fire hydrants should be required to obtain a permit from the jurisdiction and pay for the water used as measured by a portable meter with a backflow prevention device provided. Management should take all the steps necessary to keep the percentage of "unaccounted for" water to less than 10 percent and preferably nearer 5 percent. There will always be some lost water. The water system should also have a complete operations and maintenance manual.

Budgeting and financing

It takes money, and generally large amounts of money, for a water system to deliver potable water to the customers. The facilities and equipment listed in the master plan have to be acquired; the employees have to be paid and materials and supplies bought. The best way for the water system to meet its financial obligations is to prepare a sound budget. The time period covered in the budget should be long enough, preferably eight to ten fiscal years, to permit the development of a logical financing plan. Budgeting on a short-term basis can be very misleading. Management has to have a good estimate of future cash flows for the water system.

The first step in the budget process each year is for management to review the objectives, goals, and master plan to determine if modifications are necessary. If changes are made, all affected persons should be notified. At this point a public meeting to obtain feedback from the customers could be beneficial. The department then prepares a draft of a budget that can be financed and will meet all the approved needs of the system; it should have a high probability of being accepted by the manager and the council or board of directors. The special items that the customers want and are willing to pay for, such as water softening, should be included. All calculations, policy decisions, and estimates used in the preparation of the budget should be recorded so that the information will be available to explain the budget at a later date or to be used in the preparation of a future one. The budget should be based on the master plan and the personnel requirements compiled for the operational program. The costs of supplies and materials for each activity have to be estimated. Good estimates are possible if past fiscal year expenditures for items are modified to reflect future needs and cost differentials due to inflation. Water systems often spend substantial sums of money for such items as chemicals, electric power, pipes, and meters. The expenditures should not exceed the revenue. The budget has to include all direct and indirect costs.

The draft budget is reviewed by the manager and other officials and the required changes are made. The manager and other officials and water department director now review the manager's budget with the council or directors, preferably in a study session. The final step is the public hearing on the budget, with modifications being made as required, and approval by the council or directors. Every three to six months management should review the expenditures and compare them with the approved budget to determine the extent of any discrepancies. Changes in the rate of expenditures may be in order, or the budget may be modified to reflect more accurately the expenditures to the end of the year.

The water system is a utility. The revenue produced by the system should be sufficient to pay all capital expenditures, operation and maintenance costs, debt service, and administrative costs as well as to build up a reserve for special "pay-as-you-go" capital projects and to meet emergencies. The principal source of income is from the sale of water. The customers should pay for the amount of water they use. Flat monthly rates for water used by residential units result in greater use of water than is required or desired. This system is not equitable since one family can use two or three times as much water as another and yet pay the same monthly charge. A good policy is to require that all customer service lines be metered. Establishing the correct rate for water is not always an easy process. If the agency does not have experienced personnel to determine the rate, there are consulting firms specializing in this work. The finance department in many smaller and medium-sized agencies handles the financing, billings, and collections for the water system, whereas the water department itself handles these matters in the larger agencies.

A number of agencies realize a savings by billing every other month or quarterly rather than monthly and by having one combined bill for all utilities instead of having a separate water bill. Many municipal water systems charge higher rates for water service outside the city limits. The reasons most often given are the higher costs of delivering water because of main extensions and the possibility of an incentive to annex to the city. Some cities and agencies will not serve customers outside the city or agency limits. Customers requiring very large volumes of water often pay a demand charge to offset the costs of the larger facilities needed. Water systems also collect other charges and fees from the customers, including connection charges, frontage fees, fees for installation of the service lines, and the like.

It is common practice to require developers of subdivisions to install the water mains and appurtenances through or along the tract and deed the facilities to the agency. Some water systems credit the developer with a portion of the costs if the water mains are larger than required for the subdivision alone or if a main is installed along the edge of the tract and will serve the other side of the street. There are many different policies on water meters. In most utilities the utility owns the meter and the rate is adjusted to collect the original cost; most water systems maintain the meters.

In order to construct major enlargements and modifications, water systems generally have to borrow money by selling bonds. Two common types of bonds are available to cities and public agencies: the municipal general obligation (GO) bond and the revenue bond. GO bonds may usurp a portion of the bonding capacity of the area, depend on property taxes for redemption (not a popular solution if the tax rate has to be increased), and in most areas require a two-thirds majority vote of the people. Revenue bonds are secured exclusively by the revenue from the sale of water and fit the policy of having the customer pay for all costs of the water used. The interest rates paid on the bonds will depend on the agency's financial rating and the general economic conditions at the time of the sale of the bonds.

Conclusion

The potable water system is a *system*, and the most effective and well-managed contemporary water supply systems are those whose managers have been able to take a system-wide view and act accordingly. Such management takes a considerable degree of skill, not least because few managers are afforded the opportunity to be in on the development of a new water system from the planning stage to operation; they thus have to work within the technological, administrative, and political environment that they inherit. This discussion has applied a systematic approach to potable water systems operation. It has reviewed the planning process and placed appropriate emphasis on that function and has also analyzed features of the operational program and of budgeting and other financial operations. The managerial approaches described will be modified in application to the circumstances of a particular community, but their overall impact will be to improve delivery of a municipal service in a vital area of urban life in our changing society.

Wastewater systems

Effective sanitary wastewater systems are indispensable for community health. Vital to a community's total service delivery system, they maintain the quality of a community's natural waters and natural environment. Essentially, proper management of water-borne waste includes operating, maintaining, expanding, and replacing components of the wastewater system to assure uninterrupted wastewater collection and transportation, adequate waste processing treatment, and proper disposal or reuse of reclaimed waters and of waste treatment by-products. Each component of a wastewater system must function properly, efficiently, and continuously—following sound environmental policy and methodology—if wastewater service is to be provided efficiently and safely and if the health of the community is to be protected.

Since the late 1960s, national, state, and local leaders have expressed concern about the deteriorating condition of the nation's natural waters. This concern has led to nationwide efforts for tougher and more effective water quality management programs. The early federal and state programs exerted authority over the communities involved, and at the same time placed on them final obligation and responsibility for getting the job done. To this end, the federal and state programs provided financial incentives, such as grants-in-aid for the planning, design, and construction of publicly owned wastewater system improvements.

These incentives were designed to encourage the communities themselves to assume both a greater commitment to and financial obligation for building the necessary collection, treatment, and disposal projects.

With the infusion over the past two decades of substantial public and private funds, the burden of responsibility for the protection of the nation's water has shifted from national and state governments to local governments—cities, counties, and special districts. Communities that fail to assume the additional responsibilities and costs may face intensive monitoring and enforcement efforts and punitive enforcement tools: legal action, state or federal administrative orders, and monetary penalities.

Future prospects for sanitary wastewater systems are clear; current trends will continue; and cities, counties, and their wastewater agencies will assume still greater responsibility for complying with national water quality policy. While each community will respond to this challenge in its own way, greater local resourcefulness and better wastewater system management by local public officials will be a key ingredient in successfully addressing these obligations.

Wastewater system objectives

In general, domestic sewage is highly organic; as such, it is unstable, putrescible, and capable of carrying disease-bearing microorganisms. Because of its high organic energy value, domestic sewage will rapidly deplete available oxygen, decompose, and produce noisome odors and noxious gases. Industrial spent waters may range from completely innocuous flows to extremely hazardous process discharges that require specialized treatment and disposal techniques. Dangerous materials, especially hazardous industrial waste discharges, may present either immediate or future public health risks. The existence of water-borne pathogenic (disease-producing) microorganisms and certain vectors of infectious diseases makes careful handling of wastewater essential. Especially in view of the available pollution control and waste treatment technologies, exposure of a community's population (including its nearby food chains and downstream residents) to mismanaged water-borne wastes is an unnecessary and avoidable health risk.

Essentially, wastewater service delivery systems are designed to fulfill two central objectives. The first objective is to protect the quality of the natural waters and waterways, that is, the quality needed to allow their continued use. Natural water quality standards are usually established by a state water quality agency and then approved by the U.S. Environmental Protection Agency (EPA). Under state and federal laws, the quality of natural waters is subject to a high degree of regulation. For example, each wastewater system that discharges into a receiving water must apply for a permit to discharge, under the National Pollution Discharge Elimination System administered by EPA. Each discharge permit specifies both the general requirements and the particular permit conditions that the wastewater system must fulfill, including the effluent standards for the reclaimed water discharge. Furthermore, each discharger must (1) collect samples and perform laboratory analyses in order to properly describe the quality of discharges, (2) frequently report this information to state and federal water quality management agencies, and (3) undergo periodic inspections by state and federal enforcement officials to assure compliance with regulatory requirements. Wastewater systems that fail to comply with adopted requirements may be subject to administrative orders, monetary penalties, legal action, or all three. The pressure for permit compliance is substantial.

The second objective is to assure cost-effective service delivery that protects the health and welfare of the community's families, businesses, and institutions—all of whom rely on the wastewater system. At first blush, the major objectives of customer service delivery and water quality assurance seem to be wholly compatible, and generally they are. But this is not always the case, for a waste-water system manager can be caught between motivating factors that are at cross purposes. For example, the goal of maintaining high water quality in the receiving waters may receive enthusiastic community support—until the costs of improving the wastewater system mandate substantial increases in local taxes or in waste-water user charges. Under these circumstances, the public works manager must inform local public officials and work with them to help develop consensus for effective action. The community must set short- and long-term priorities for developing wastewater system components that will reduce and finally eliminate these potential conflicts.

Common terms and definitions

Natural water   Water of natural water bodies—oceans, lakes, ponds, rivers, streams, etc.

Waterway   Body of running water; a watercourse

Service area   Geographical extent of a service delivery system, the ultimate size of which is most often described by watersheds circumscribing a drainage area

Wastewater   Drainage of all kinds from an area, including storm drainage and sanitary wastewater

Sanitary wastewater   Used or spent water from residences, businesses, industries, institutions, and other system users within the community: from households, commonly called domestic sewage; from commercial, manufacturing, or industrial establishments, called industrial waste

Receiving water   Natural water bodies—oceans, lakes, ponds, rivers, streams, etc.—and their man-made extensions—watercourses, canals, ditches, channels, etc.—into which wastewaters are discharged

Reclaimed water   Wastewater of any kind that has been treated to a level of water quality to allow its reuse

Building sewer   Underground pipeline that drains a structure's plumbing system

Lateral, branch, and trunk sewer   Underground gravity pipeline; part of a public/community sewer system.

Wastewater physical facilities

The major wastewater system components—summarized below—are similar from system to system and are subject to regulation and control.

On-site building plumbing   The on-site drainage system collects domestic spent water flows from individual water closets, sinks, and other water-using appliances. In a commercial or industrial structure, the system would include not only collection of domestic type wastewaters but also drain spent water from product storage and other manufacturing processes. On-site plumbing is privately owned by a property owner, but its installation or subsequent modification usually is governed by local plumbing codes.

Local, state, and federal regulations govern the management of industrial waste discharges. For example, industrial wastes may be subject to specific types of waste treatment prior to being discharged into a public wastewater system. If the wastes are classified as hazardous, they may require separate, special methods of treatment and disposal that are not normally provided by publicly owned wastewater systems.

On-site plumbing relies on gravity collection of spent or used wastewaters through drains installed to flow downhill. An on-site drainage system is not intended to operate under water pressure or to accommodate continuous flows.

Three protective measures generally are installed in on-site plumbing: (1) vent stacks permit the system to "breathe" and to equalize pressures; (2) water traps protect a system user from noxious gases, odors, fumes, and vermin in the sanitary collection system; and (3) special traps collect sand, grease, and oil, and they protect the sanitary collection system from undesirable discharges. On-site plumbing should be installed to handle wastewater only, not to commingle stormwater runoff with wastewater, unless specifically permitted.

Building sewer   A building sewer is a collector pipeline that conveys wastewater via downhill flow from the on-site plumbing to the public sewer. Building sewers are installed underground, below the frost line. Most of a building sewer is installed on private property and is privately maintained to the property line, unless local utility policy specifies otherwise. The ownership of the physical connection to the public sewer and that part of the building sewer in the public way usually belongs to the city, county, or special district providing the service. The construction of a building sewer may be subject to local utility sewer connection permit fees and inspection.

The building sewer portion of the wastewater system is usually one of the most poorly maintained parts of the system. Many collection system problems can be traced to improperly constructed building sewer connections. This has prompted some wastewater agencies to assume the responsibilities for installation of connections, or at least careful inspection prior to acceptance. Many local government agencies use smoke testing to detect illegal connections.

A properly installed and well-maintained building sewer and sewer connection will assure conveyance of only sanitary wastewaters. It will not allow the introduction of groundwater or extraneous surface water runoff caused by roof or yard drain connections, separated joints, or poor maintenance.

Public sewer mains   Sanitary sewer systems are designed to convey wastewater by gravity. They may be classified as separate sanitary systems or combined sewer systems. A separate sanitary wastewater system collects only sanitary wastewater. A combined sewer system collects not only sanitary wastewater, but also intermittent stormwater runoff. Combined sewer systems must be much larger than separate wastewater collection systems since stormwater runoff design flows are substantially larger than normal sanitary wastewater design flows.

The effectiveness of a separate sanitary wastewater collection system can be measured by how well it serves without stoppage or obstruction and by its watertightness, whereas the effectiveness and function of a combined sewer system is dictated by its capacity to drain storm runoff. Separate sanitary collection systems with very high flows during and after rainfalls may be showing the effects of extensive deferred maintenance or upstream inflow due to interconnection with storm runoff sources. Large inflow responses use up available hydraulic capacity, thus causing surcharged sewer mains and manholes. Since sanitary system flows must be treated, a community may end up paying for treating more wastewater flow than necessary.

The true challenge of sanitary wastewater collection is to assure that the collection system has the hydraulic capacity and the physical integrity to convey all sanitary wastewater flows to the wastewater treatment plant without bypassing these flows into receiving waters and without causing waste backups that store sanitary sewage on private property.

An overloaded sanitary sewer will require a relief or alternative sewer to provide additional hydraulic capacity and to eliminate unpermitted discharges. A leaky sanitary sewer or one that accepts too much groundwater infiltration or too much storm runoff may require extensive repair or renewal. If badly deteriorated, it may require complete replacement using normal open-cut pipeline construction techniques. Sewer renewal may be accomplished by installing a sliplining or, in some instances, by in situ pipe liner fabrication methods.

A variety of materials are used in the construction of sanitary sewers, but they must be strong enough to be installed underground, below the frost line. Sewer materials must also be inert and resistant to the chemical and biological processes that occur as sanitary wastewater decomposes in transit. Materials such as concrete, clay, cast iron, ductile iron, polyvinyl chloride, polyethylene, and a variety of new synthetic materials may be found in contemporary sewer construction. Pipe manufacturers have developed pipe joints that are virtually infiltration proof.

Modern equipment and methods are now available to help in the planned maintenance and cleaning of sewer systems. Some of these include hydraulic cleaning machines, powered rodding and bucket machines, mobile vacuum units, and better, smaller backhoes for excavation. Manholes provide access to an underground sewer system. They are usually constructed at junctions; changes in direction, diameter, or slope; and at specified distances from one another in straight sewer mains. An increasing number of public works departments are using a soil fumigant to inhibit the growth of roots in sewers. The fumigant, a root inhibitor and a foaming agent, is introduced into the sewer pipe where it comes in intimate contact with the roots.

Approximately 70 to 80 percent of the potable water supplied by the community's water distribution system is returned to the sanitary wastewater collection system. Sanitary wastewater collection systems may be sized to accommodate average wastewater flows of about one hundred gallons per capita per day. Short-term variations can result in wastewater flows three or four times as large as the average daily flow. Sewer systems are usually utility owned and regulated through some form of connection and use permitting system.

Pumping stations and pressure mains   Collection system pumping facilities are used under two circumstances. First, a pumping station and a pressure main may be used to convey sanitary wastewaters to locations that cannot be reached in a normal downhill gravity collection system. Second, a pumping station may be built when projected underground sewers would be too far below the ground surface to allow for economic construction or future extension. In this situation, a pumping station is used to lift sewage to a sewer at a higher elevation.

Pumping stations are expensive to build and operate. Their use occurs most often in flat terrain where it is difficult to maintain minimum sewer grades. The decision to use a pumping station is largely economic, but a properly designed and constructed pumping station can also be valuable for sanitary wastewater flow management. System cost savings may be achieved through the timing of pumping operations and use of in-system storage that provides for even loading of waste treatment facilities. In either case, the detention time of quiescent sewage should take into account the loss of oxygen, generation of gases, and septicity.

Wastewater treatment plant facilities   Wastewater treatment attacks the unstable and decomposable constituents in sanitary sewage in a controlled environment. Treatment is usually designed to speed up the natural processes of water cleansing, remove the noisome attributes of sewage, and, properly operated, destroy disease-bearing microorganisms prior to the discharge of reclaimed water into a receiving water.

Wastewater treatment facilities are usually local government operations although individual waste treatment facilities may be used to treat specific types of industrial waste. Modern wastewater treatment includes physical, chemical, biological, and radiological treatment methods such as screening, odor control, sedimentation, chemical precipitation, biological trickling filtration, biological waste activated sludge, filtration, and disinfection. Modern wastewater treatment facilities include a broad variety of stationary equipment, tankage, and machinery.

Although wastewater treatment appears to be industrial in nature, waste treatment plant operational requirements are often more stringent than industry's. Operating treatment facilities is complicated, too, by the need for continuous, twenty-four-hour operation. Scheduled or emergency closedowns are difficult to handle unless extra capacity and some component redundancy within the wastewater treatment plant are available.

Wastewater treatment facilities are designed to meet the specific discharge requirements established by state and federal regulatory agencies. Discharge requirements are determined by the assimilation capabilities of the receiving waters, that is, the amount of wastewater constituents for reclaimed waters that a receiving water can accept under the severest conditions—without harming its water quality. Although receiving water includes natural water bodies (e.g., oceans, lakes, rivers, streams, ponds, etc.) and their man-made extensions (e.g., watercourses, canals, ditches, channels, etc.) in which wastewaters are discharged, the development of effluent discharge standards is always predicated on receiving water quality. For example, when a stream fulfills a public purpose—availability for swimming, boating, or drinking water supply—the stream's ambient dissolved oxygen levels must be maintained under the severest conditions of low flow and high temperature; the presence of enteric microorganisms must be nil.

In order to ensure continued use and quality of a receiving waterway, the following conditions must be analyzed to determine effluent discharge standards: the physical characteristics of the stream, stream hydrology, reaeration capacity, velocity, chemical makeup, and oxygen demands. In some instances, the effluent quality required for reclaimed water discharges into a large, broad, full-flowing stream of substantial volume, velocity, and high ambient water quality may be less stringent than the quality level required for discharges into a small, limited waterway of low volume and velocity. The latter stream is more sensitive because of its limited ability to accept pollutant discharges. Discharge, however, must be of a quality equal to or higher than the minimum standards established under federal law.

Handling waste treatment by-products

Waste treatment operations produce not only reclaimed water but by-products as well, which must be processed and disposed of in an environmentally sound manner. Minor amounts of floating materials result from wastewater treatment, but the most significant by-product is waste treatment plant sludge. Treatment plant sludge is highly organic and putrescible and, as a by-product of waste activated sludge treatment, may be largely composed of microorganisms or "biomass."

Sludge processing usually involves controlled decomposition of the putrescible fraction of the sludge, processing to reduce volume by removing water, and final stabilization and disinfection of the sludge materials to assure that the threat of disease-bearing microorganisms is eliminated. Final disposal of treated sludges may be by direct burial in a sanitary landfill, by areal application to the land, by further processing for use as a soil conditioner, or by further processing for use in energy production.

Sludge management is encumbered by the many pollutant constituents that may compose waste treatment sludges. For example, uncontrolled industrial discharges may produce high concentrations of heavy metals within sludge by-products. Some heavy metals may have toxic effects upon some vegetative growth, and others may have extended negative health effects—if they are absorbed into a food chain and concentrated within food plants or livestock. Accordingly, the final decisions for the disposal of these materials must take into account whether hazardous constituents exist in the sludges at concentrations high enough to be dangerous. Finally, due care must be accorded the proper treatment and disposal of the sludge by-products of waste treatment to assure that the sludge materials are properly handled so as to minimize risk.

Wastewater system planning

Wastewater system planning must address (1) the preservation of the existing system and its financial requirements, (2) the expansion of the wastewater collection system, and (3) the specific waste treatment requirements that are needed to fulfill existing and projected quality needs for the area's natural waters. Wastewater service delivery depends on local topography; hydrology; geology; the receiving water body, its water quality requirements, and the proximity of the receiving water body to the plant; the existing wastewater service area, its limits, size, population, land use, and projected growth; and the most cost-effective combination of system elements to produce continuous, high quality wastewater service throughout the service area.

Service area topography reflects the shape of the land, and it may dictate the ultimate size of a wastewater system. Topography also may dictate system energy needs and the rate of system deterioration due to chemical corrosion. Geology may influence the cost of facility construction. A system's closeness to its receiving waters, as well as the nature of receiving waters and their quality needs, will dictate the extent and expense of waste treatment. An area's climate may affect the size of system facilities: an area of high annual rainfall may require larger pipelines and plant facilities because of the direct effects of unavoidable inflow.

Planners should anticipate growth of the service area as well as probable changes in land use. The size and the character of the community being served has a decided effect upon the makeup of a wastewater system. A manufacturing city, for example, may produce more difficult-to-treat waste flows due to industrial wastes than would a bedroom community in which wastewaters are predominantly domestic in character.

Effective wastewater planning should cover system finances, including construction, operating, and maintenance costs; technical alternatives to produce the most cost-effective plans; and cost impacts on future tax rates and user service charges. Wastewater system planning is a periodically renewable obligation. Data should be updated regularly, and system plans should be subject to public review and comment followed by approval and adoption by the city council or county board.

Wastewater plan implementation

Wastewater plans are implemented by the wastewater capital improvements program or the wastewater renewal and replacement program, often in response to plans adopted by the wastewater agency. However, *community* decision makers play a major role in shaping the final form of the wastewater program and daily operation of the service delivery system.

Wastewater agency characteristics   A wastewater agency may be either a generalized or a specialized service delivery agency. A generalized agency may bear responsibility for all or most aspects of the wastewater system, while a more specialized agency may bear responsibility for only one or just a few aspects of the service delivery system.

The more general agencies are retailers of wastewater services, while the more specialized agencies are more often wholesalers of wastewater services. Specialized agencies are usually wastewater treatment specialists that provide for treatment operations and maintenance. Generalized agencies bear a broader planning obligation, while more specialized agencies restrict their scope of planning. The existence of both types of agencies within a single service delivery area may require substantial coordination between agencies.

Organization for sanitary wastewater systems The city is probably the most common agency operating the wastewater function as a part of its public works department. . . . The city not only serves those within its territorial limits but will often contract with special districts to serve the area surrounding its boundaries.

Special districts, most often called "sanitary districts," . . . often serve several cities and the contiguous area between them. Some are single-purpose districts while others serve a variety of needs. Some only collect wastewater and contract with a city for treatment and disposal; others operate treatment and disposal facilities while cities and other special districts perform the collection function.

Joint exercise of powers enables agencies in some states to combine activities. This basically consists of two or more agencies, which are empowered by law to perform services and levy taxes to pay for these services, joining together in a common activity such as wastewater treatment.

Counties often perform the wastewater collection, treatment, and disposal functions for all their residents. Again, separate functions may be divided between cities and the county.

Source: Ronald N. Doty, "Wastewater Collection, Treatment, Disposal, and Reuse," in William E. Korbitz, ed., *Urban Public Works Administration* (Washington, D.C.: International City Management Association, 1976), p. 385.

Wastewater activities—direction and control The direction and control of wastewater activities represent essentially the challenges of motivating employees and coordinating their efforts to attain quality performance. Standards setting and performance measurement are time consuming but necessary activities for wastewater service delivery systems and many of these standards and measures are controlled by laws and administrative regulations.

1. Performance measures in a wastewater service delivery system lend themselves to straightforward countable items, i.e., citizen complaints, response times, number of gallons of quality reclaimed water produced, and so on.
2. Wastewater service delivery systems are highly regulated by state and federal water quality management agencies. The consequences of agency failure in this system of regulation provide a lot of motivation for "actuating" employees.
3. Performance standards are well defined for a wastewater agency's treatment plant discharge since they are set forth in the plant discharge permit.
4. The performance of the wastewater system plant facilities are routinely monitored, sampled, laboratory tested, reported, and evaluated.
5. Failure to adjust plant performance to meet discharge standards may result in administrative orders, fines, or penalties.

Wastewater system financing and service extensions The revenues for a wastewater system must cover capital improvements to enlarge the system, capital improvements to renew and replace system facilities, and day-to-day operation and maintenance of the system. Four major revenue sources are available for this work: (1) property taxes and other local tax revenues; (2) user service charges; (3) agency contracts to provide wastewater services to other local governments in the area, with reimbursement based on usage; and (4) cost-sharing arrangements with two or more agencies sharing several aspects of wastewater service as public partners. It is of course possible to use a combination of these methods. For example, an agency might levy a user charge that does not cover all costs and the balance would be paid from the city or county general fund. In addition, the agency might sell some of its services outside its jurisdictional boundaries to a contiguous city, county, or special district.

Policy decisions are made by the wastewater agency, the chief administrator of the city or county government, and the city or county governing body. Like most questions involving revenues and expenditures, paying for wastewater service can be controversial. Some argue that wastewater service is a community obligation, not just an amenity but a vital part of public health. Others argue that wastewater service is a public utility with all the attendant costing, pricing, and servicing responsibilities. Only users should pay, they argue, and for the full cost of service.

Several kinds of user charges are available, but the one that is the most workable is based on water usage. It is simple to measure (based on the water meter readings), fair to apply, and generally acceptable. By far the most important advantage of this financing method is that it provides a stable and predictable revenue source.

Some capital improvements, especially wastewater service extensions, can be paid for as part of the negotiations with developers. Subdivision regulations for residential and commercial development commonly require installation of sewers that will at least serve the immediate area of development. Sometimes additional requirements can be imposed on developers as part of the negotiations for large office/commercial developments, shopping centers, and apartment buildings.

A community's attitude to extension of wastewater service reflects its land use policies. Should existing users be required to subsidize, wholly or in part, new users of the system? A community seeking revenue producing growth and development may offer subsidized service extension as an incentive to attract commercial and industrial development. Other communities may require all developers to pay their equitable share of wastewater collection and treatment facilities. Regardless of the extent of subsidy, most developer obligations take the form of completed facility construction, development impact fees, plat application charges, or particular charges related to the wastewater system, such as sewer connection charges and capital recovery charges.

A community's service extension policy directly affects its ability to implement short- and long-range planning. Capital improvements costs that a community will pay for may expand the wastewater system more rapidly. The greater the subsidy, however, the higher the cost to existing users.[1]

Wastewater reserve capacity   Capital improvements may be planned that accommodate future growth by constructing facilities with reserve capacity. The commitment of additional funds to provide reserve capacity depends on projections for population growth, greater employment, and industrial, commercial, and residential development. Using additional funds to provide reserve capacity in transmission sewers, pumping stations, or other facilities that cannot be readily expanded may be a prudent financial decision.

Modularization provides an alternative approach for wastewater treatment planning. It is predicated on a precise understanding of waste treatment plant discharge requirements. The translation of discharge requirements into waste treatment unit process characteristics can produce the "least-size" wastewater treatment plant expansion that can be constructed to comply with discharge quality requirements. This is largely a function of existing waste treatment plant geometry and the most cost-effective combinations of waste treatment plant unit process sizes needed to meet a given discharge requirement. The idea behind modularization is to construct smaller scale waste treatment plant expansions on the basis of one or more modules that will accommodate immediate demands, and perhaps some additional short-term growth; it does not include a large reserve capacity.

On this basis, the wastewater system can provide additional waste treatment capacity to accommodate existing and predictable short-term demands. In order to use this approach, however, the service delivery agency must be ready to respond to demands for additional service and to begin construction on short notice. This approach, in conjunction with a long-term plan for the system, allows a wastewater agency to better distribute its capital expenditures and to cover more of its immediate priorities with limited financing.

Organization and management

Effective operation of a sanitary wastewater service delivery system includes management responsibilities for planning; engineering; plant and systems operations and maintenance; finance and accounting; revenue planning and forecasting; wastewater evaluation and quality control; and various supporting services. These responsibilities are described in earlier chapters of this book dealing with organization, information, finance, and other management responsibilities common to all public works activities.

The same major management considerations, service objectives, and tools applicable to other areas of governmental (i.e., public) service apply to the wastewater service agency as well, but there are some differences inherent in the very nature of wastewater service delivery systems.

Sanitary wastewater service delivery systems are continuous operations that must function day-in and day-out, twenty-four hours a day. Wastewater service delivery systems are highly constrained by the degree of regulation and control that is exercised by federal and state agencies. Finally, the success of a community's wastewater service delivery system depends on the importance assigned to effective wastewater programs within the community and the community's view of its responsibilities to water quality and the environment. Community attitudes and their influence on local public policy are telling considerations in the management of sanitary wastewater systems.

Drainage

Drainage has become a major consideration in the management of local public works. Drainage is significantly affected by urbanization because the same amount of rainfall produces much more stormwater under developed conditions than it does when an area is undeveloped. If this increase is not anticipated, rain storms of relatively small magnitude can flood streets, interrupt traffic, and damage streets and property. Storms of larger magnitude can overflow once-small gullies and creeks, cause property damage, and threaten lives.

If development is controlled and adequate facilities are provided, problems can be largely avoided. If problems already exist, then remedial actions have to be evaluated and implemented to mitigate them.

Urban drainage and flood control system

The urban drainage and flood control system can be divided into the "minor" system and the "major" system.[2] The minor system is designed to carry runoff from frequent storms and provide relief from the nuisance and inconvenience caused by minor flooding. The typical minor system consists of curbs and gutters, street inlets, underground pipes, and roadside ditches. On-site detention storage and small detention facilities can be used to reduce storm runoff from developments that can have an impact on the minor system.

Minor drainage systems are tributary to major systems serving larger areas. Major flood routes are normally along creeks and rivers that are prone to intermittent flooding. Minor systems are designed to accommodate flows that occur fairly frequently, such as the two- and five-year events. Major systems are evaluated for rarer events such as the 100-year storm.[3] Elements of the urban drainage system are shown in Figure 14–1.

Urban drainage system components are listed in Figure 14–2. The minor drainage system is divided into a surface runoff component and a transport component. The major drainage system is also referred to as the receiving water component.

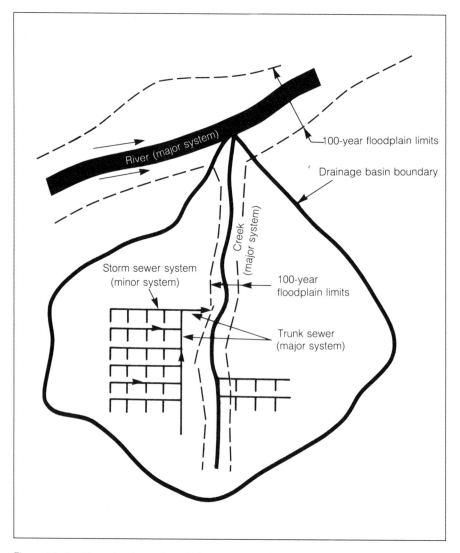

Figure 14–1   Elements of an urban drainage system. Small detention and retention facilities are often used in the minor system to reduce downstream flows and in some cases to provide initial treatment to improve stormwater quality.

Figure 14–2 Principal components of major and minor urban drainage systems.

The minor system
A. Surface runoff component
   1. Natural conditions—overland flow
   2. Developed conditions
      a. Lots
      b. Dwellings and other structures
      c. Streets
      d. Alleys
      e. Parking lots
      f. On-site detention
      g. Parks and open spaces
B. Transport component
   1. Natural conditions
      a. Swales
      b. Gullies
   2. Developed conditions
      a. Streets
      b. Ditches
      c. Stormsewer systems

The major system (receiving water component)
A. Rivers, streams, creeks
B. Wetlands
C. Lakes, ponds
D. Marshes
E. Ocean
F. Estuary

Drainage is an important consideration in urban road and street design, construction, and maintenance. Stormwater must be diverted from well-traveled roadways in order to prevent traffic hazards and to minimize damage to the streets. Standing or flowing water makes normal travel unsafe. Consideration must be given to the type of roadway and the frequency and depth of flooding that can be tolerated. For example, on a major arterial it may be necessary to keep the road open under all conditions to allow passage of emergency vehicles. In such a case it may be arbitrarily decided to design for a 100-year event regardless of the cost.

On the other hand, a storm sewer system in a residential area might be designed to handle a two-year storm. Major storm events would exceed the capacity of the storm sewer system and flood the streets. On lightly traveled residential streets, this would not cause traffic hazards and would be tolerable as long as no damage occurred. Design criteria for streets and highways are not the same everywhere but vary from local government to local government and for various street classifications.

The damaging effect of high water also is an important consideration in the design and maintenance of streets and highways. Potential and actual damage from storms that exceed the capacity of drainage facilities can be estimated, and if potential or actual damage to the roadway exceeds the cost of construction of larger facilities, then it would be more cost effective to install a larger drainage facility than to repair damages. Drainage facilities should be considered on a cost-effective basis, if other conditions are equal.

Responsibility for urban drainage and flood control

The responsibility for management of the urban storm drainage and flood control system is not clear-cut. Other urban systems such as water supply, transportation, and sewerage are provided because a house or office building cannot be sold without them. For these services a management system is created. Stormwater facilities are needed and should be provided, but houses can be sold without them, and in many cases stormwater facilities are not provided until need is demonstrated by flooding and subsequent inconvenience or hardship. Thus, construction of systems for urban stormwater often lags behind other urban systems. Maintenance of stormwater facilities is often neglected because of inadequate management.

Local governments should insist that developers provide adequate drainage facilities for both major and minor systems. The need for such facilities cannot be emphasized enough. If a developer is allowed to provide less than adequate facilities, local government will inevitably be faced by angry citizens demanding to have the flooding problem solved.

Liability Case law has in some situations held local governments liable for damages to properties that are caused by increased runoff from upstream developments approved by the local government. Typically, local government will approve or accept drainage facilities in a development and once developers sell lots to builders or homes to homeowners they are not perpetually involved in the project. After the area is fully developed, flows that are greater than usual pass through the municipal drainage system. If the drainage system is not safely connected to an outfall point, then the increased flow may discharge onto a downstream property and cause more harm than might otherwise be expected. Local governments may be called upon to make restitution and may even end up being sued and having to foot the bill both for the damages and for correcting the problems.

Legal responsibility varies from state to state, and the city or county attorney should be asked to find out whether the local government would be held responsible for such damages if it approved and accepted developer-designed and developer-constructed drainage systems. If a local government is potentially liable for downstream damages, it should ensure that the facilities installed do not cause downstream damages. Case law by its nature depends on the particular facts, but common sense suggests that the potential for liability would be greatest when drainage flows that were formerly sheet flows are increased, concentrated, and discharged onto an adjacent landowner in such a manner as to cause harm.

Local government liability can arise in several ways:

1. The local government may itself alter the existing drainage conditions.
2. The local government may undertake to regulate drainage and do so improperly.
3. It may approve a drainage system.
4. It may accept a dedication of a street and storm drainage system that causes damage.
5. It may fail to properly maintain drainage facilities.
6. Through zoning and subdivision approval, it may merely have permitted the development of property in a particular way that infringes on adjacent or downstream property owners.[4]

If a local government is not liable for a drainage problem for one of the reasons set forth above, it generally does not have to construct facilities to remedy a flooding problem, but if it undertakes to do so, then it must do so properly or liability may be incurred.[5]

Management responsibility The primary responsibility for urban stormwater management lies with local government. Any stormwater activity involves various management system components, but effective urban drainage and flood control management depends on effective local government.

Many metropolitan areas contain several local governmental entities, and it may be desirable to have an agency that can address the multijurisdictional aspects of urban drainage and flood control. Multijurisdictional problems are difficult to solve if local governments are unable to work together to solve interrelated problems. Multijurisdictional drainage planning, therefore, must be addressed on a multijurisdictional basis and should involve all entities related to the problem. In some cases, implementation may be accomplished by individual local governments as long as conformance to a master plan is maintained.

A regional planning agency or council of governments can coordinate the implementation of drainage projects and provide a mechanism for defining solutions. Regional agencies also can assist smaller local governments that cannot afford to hire experts in the field of drainage and flood control.

Metropolitan areas with complex multijurisdictional drainage and flood control problems should consider establishing regional agencies if none exist. Examples of such agencies include the Albuquerque Metropolitan Arroyo Flood Control Authority of Albuquerque, New Mexico, and the Urban Drainage and Flood Control District of the metropolitan area in Denver, Colorado.

Drainage system management Urban drainage and flood control is no respecter of city and county boundaries. The problem—and the solution—is bounded by floodplains, stream valleys, and other natural configurations that channel and disperse water. Consequently, many public and private agencies, corporations, and other groups are involved in drainage system management. Figure 14–3 shows the major parties to the process. Land use planning, flood prevention,

Figure 14–3 Management system components for urban drainage and flood control.

Private sector
A. Developers
   1. Large tracts
   2. Small tracts or individual lots
B. Property owners
C. Manufacturers, contractors
D. Consulting engineers
E. Irrigation and drainage companies
F. Special districts (for a development)

Public sector
A. Local government
   1. Incorporated communities
      a. Cities
      b. Towns
      c. Villages
   2. Unincorporated areas of counties
   3. Special districts (regional)
   4. Improvement districts
B. State agencies (varies from state to state)
C. Federal agencies
   1. U.S. Army Corps of Engineers
   2. Federal Insurance Administration and Federal Emergency Management Agency
   3. Federal Housing Administration
   4. Department of Housing and Urban Development
   5. U.S. Geological Survey
   6. Environmental Protection Agency
   7. Federal Highway Administration
   8. Soil Conservation Service
   9. Bureau of Outdoor Recreation
   10. Bureau of Reclamation
   11. U.S. Fish and Wildlife Service
   12. National Marine Fisheries Service

housing construction, insurance, environmental protection, fish, game, parks, and many other interests are represented in the figure.

These interests come together (not always in a friendly way) in two broad kinds of drainage systems: minor drainage systems and major drainage systems.

Minor drainage system interface   The minor drainage system usually is part of the development of large tracts of land in rapidly growing areas. The developer often initiates the process by requesting a zoning change to accommodate the proposed development. Since the proposal is likely to include intensive land use, the natural drainage in place through stream valleys and other natural features will be quickly overloaded. The developer therefore is expected to show feasibility before rezoning or other actions will be taken by the city or county government.[6]

Once the development is approved, however, it is the developer's responsibility to have specific drainage plans prepared by competent and experienced engineers. These plans are then submitted by the developer to the local government for review. The developer must also satisfy Federal Housing Administration (FHA) drainage requirements if FHA financing is involved. State, regional, and other local agencies may also be involved in the approval process, depending on local requirements. Before buildings are occupied, local government must ensure that the development has been constructed in conformance with approved plans.

Many kinds of local governments are involved in this process, including counties, townships, large cities, and small towns. Regardless of the type or size of the jurisdiction, the critical factor is the ability of the local government to control and ensure the preparation of sound plans and the construction of adequate drainage facilities. This may be difficult for local governments with small staffs, but it still must be done even if it is necessary to obtain outside consulting help.

In developed urban areas with flooding problems that involve the minor drainage system, property owners usually initiate action through local government. It is then up to the local government to determine whether to respond and if so how to fund the improvements.

Major drainage system interface   In relatively undeveloped floodplains along major drainageways, effective floodplain land use accomplished via floodplain ordinances and regulations can prevent serious problems from occurring. In practically all cases floodplain regulation is partly or entirely the responsibility of local governments. Individual property owners and developers of large tracts (the regulated) interface with local government (the regulators). Local government in turn works with the Federal Emergency Management Agency (FEMA) or a state government agency with regard to flood insurance requirements, and it works with state land use agencies to determine state requirements. Effective floodplain regulation depends on the experience and motivation of local government.

Many urban floodplains along major drainageways are developed to the extent that remedial measures are necessary to reduce property damage. Major flooding problems usually are conveyed to local government by the floodplain occupants. Local government may seek the assistance of state and federal agencies, such as the U.S. Army Corps of Engineers, but they must generally rely on their own resources to solve the problem.

Drainage and flood control planning

Planning for urban drainage and flood control must be considered in terms of overall community goals and objectives. The urban drainage and flood control system is closely related to many other urban systems and cannot be considered and planned in isolation. General community and regional policies and goals should be formulated; planning principles for guiding the planning process should be clearly stated; and drainage criteria should be developed to provide a basis for consistent and uniform planning, design, implementation, and operation.

Planning approaches vary for different situations. Planning for undeveloped areas must be approached differently from planning for developed areas. Planning for the minor drainage system differs from planning for the major system. Planning for multijurisdictional problems is different from planning for problems contained entirely within a single political jurisdiction. Even so, all planning should take place within a framework of established community and regional policies, goals, principles, and criteria.

Stormwater detention and retention

Stormwater detention and retention basins in developing areas retard storm runoff, and in this way counter the increased rate and volume of runoff from impervious surfaces. Detention or retention of runoff involves the collection of stormwater in holding areas prior to releasing it into the drainage system. Detention refers to the temporary holding of stormwater, and retention to the holding of stored water for much longer periods of time. Most detention and retention basins constructed by developers are in the 1-to-10 acre-foot capacity range (see Figure 14–4). Larger detention facilities generally built by public-sector agencies can be "regional" facilities (see Figure 14–5).

Detention and retention basins are generally designed to control short, high-intensity storms from urban watersheds. Basins can be classified as wet or dry. Examples of dry basins are shown in Figures 14–4 and 14–5; a wet basin is shown in Figure 14–6. Dry basins hold back water only for short periods after storm events. A wet basin would have a permanent pool of water below the level needed to store flood waters. Detention and retention basins may have other beneficial features such as recreation, groundwater recharge, irrigation, industrial uses, water supply, erosion control, and pollution control when the total urban system is considered. Detention basins can be integrated into developments, as was the basin in downtown Denver, Colorado (see Figure 14–7).

Detention and retention basins are most effective when they can be built at

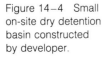

Figure 14–4 Small on-site dry detention basin constructed by developer.

Figure 14–5   Regional
dry detention basin.

the time of development. Local ordinances can set forth criteria for the design
of retention and detention facilities and require developers to provide such
facilities when current and potential drainage problems are encountered.

Detention and retention systems cannot be considered a substitute for a drainage system. They have their greatest impact immediately downstream of the
basin, but their effectiveness in reducing flood peaks diminishes rapidly further
downstream. If downstream facilities are to be designed on the assumption that
detention or retention basins will be built, then a guarantee must be provided
that all such facilities will remain in place and will be effectively maintained. If
this cannot be done, downstream facilities should be designed as if the basins
did not exist.

To be most effective, detention and retention basins should be designed in
conjunction with the drainage system that they affect. This can be accomplished

Figure 14–6   Wet
detention basin
constructed in
conjunction with
park uses.

Figure 14–7 Detention basin as integral part of development in downtown, Denver, Colorado.

for larger developments because the system of downstream conduits can be reduced in size to carry the amounts of water to be released from the detention facilities. When small detention and retention basins are randomly placed, however, their beneficial effects are much more difficult to identify.

Small detention basins have little impact on the peak flows of larger streams and rivers because increases in total runoff volume are not affected by small detention basins, and total flows swell as the many small detention basins add their flows to the major stream. Unless retention is provided over a prolonged period, all that can be expected is a delay in the timing of flood peaks of the larger streams, with little change in the peak flow rate.

Maintenance must be seriously considered by the local jurisdiction before requiring detention or retention. After detention or retention facilities are installed and the development is complete, the facilities must be maintained in perpetuity. Otherwise they will become more of a liability or hazard than an asset. Funds must be provided for maintenance, which in this case includes routine inspection, mowing, mosquito control, clearing and repairing of outlet works, removing sediment and debris after storm events, erosion control on the embankment, maintaining grass covers, and keeping motorcycles off embankments.

Preventive measures for major drainageways

One approach to floodplain management is to try to prevent problem situations from occurring. Preventive measures are generally most effective in undeveloped floodplains, but they also can be used in the management of partly developed floodplains. They include floodplain regulations, the National Flood Insurance Program, and other measures (floodplain acquisition, development review, and bridge and culvert design).

Floodplain regulation   The most important and basic preventive tool is floodplain regulation. The purpose of floodplain regulation is to manage, not prevent, development within a defined floodplain (usually the 100-year floodplain) so as to preclude or mitigate future flood damages. Legal justification for floodplain regulation is the health, safety, and welfare of the public. Regulation should not be used to keep floodplains in an open, undeveloped state.

The authority to regulate floodplains is generally delegated by the state government to local governments. Some states have minimum requirements; some do not. In a few states local governments must regulate floodplains or the state will do it for them. Statutory requirements vary among states and should be checked by local government legal counsel.[7]

The first step in implementing a floodplain regulation program is to define the 100-year floodplain. Accurate delineations are particularly important in urban and urbanizing areas. In rural areas where development pressures are less severe, accuracy requirements are not as stringent, and the cost of floodplain delineation is correspondingly less.

A floodplain is regulated through an ordinance adopted by the local government. Such an ordinance can take the form of rezoning or an overlay approach. The latter leaves the underlying zoning unchanged, but overlays a floodplain area that affects the uses permitted in the underlying zone. The overlay approach is recommended because it does not carry as many adverse connotations as a rezoning. Changing a residential zone to a floodplain zone can be politically traumatic.

Before a floodplain map is adopted, public hearings should be held to provide those affected with an opportunity to challenge the technical data if they think it is wrong. Another important reason for publicizing a floodplain delineation is to warn the floodplain occupants of the potential hazard. In fact, local governments may open themselves to legal suits if they do not advise citizens living in a flood hazard area of the situation. Floodplain maps should be widely published, and each property owner should be advised of the hazard in the area.

Floodplain ordinances can take a one-district or a two-district approach. A one-district regulation treats the entire floodplain being regulated in the same way. A two-district regulation recognizes a floodway and a flood fringe. The floodway is that portion of a floodplain required to pass the regulation flood, usually the 100-year flood, with reasonable depths and velocities. Under the two-district regulation, no building is allowed in the floodway that would cause the water surface to rise, but fewer restrictions are applied to the flood fringe.

The two-district approach is recommended because it distinguishes between a high-hazard area and a low-hazard area, and reserves an area to pass the 100-year flood. A disadvantage of the two-district approach is that the floodway has to be defined, and this somewhat complicates the floodplain delineation process.

National Flood Insurance Program   The National Flood Insurance Program (NFIP) was established pursuant to the National Flood Insurance Act of 1968, as substantially modified by the Flood Disaster Protection Act of 1973.

The NFIP makes flood insurance available at reasonable rates to individuals within communities that meet eligibility requirements by adopting floodplain management regulations. The NFIP is subsidized and seeks to encourage floodplain management that reduces the risks of flooding. Communities entering the program first become eligible for flood insurance in the emergency program, in which all insurance is subsidized but only limited coverage is available. Once a community is in the emergency program, the Federal Emergency Management Agency (FEMA) identifies areas within the community that are subject to flooding and provides the information necessary to establish actuarial insurance rates. The floodplains delineated in the study serve as a minimum base for regulating the 100-year floodplain.

Once the flood hazard areas are defined, the community enters the regular program under which buildings constructed before a specified date remain eligible for subsidized rates. Buildings constructed after the specified date are charged actuarial rates, which can be substantial depending on the elevation of the structure relative to the elevation of the 100-year flood.

Whatever a community's actions with regard to the program, FEMA will prepare flood hazard boundary maps for the community, but will not provide federal financial assistance for buildings within flood hazard areas unless the community has entered the program and insurance has been purchased. For example, Small Business Administration, Veterans Administration, and Federal Housing Administration assistance and other federal grants, loans, or guarantees are prohibited unless the community participates in the program.

For all practical purposes, the regulation of floodplains has become a matter of necessity for local governments rather than a matter of choice, as it once was. Local governments should become familiar with the NFIP, take steps to enter the program, and ensure their continued eligibility. Agencies should not join the program, however, unless they intend to meet NFIP requirements. If an agency fails to meet requirements, the NFIP might bring a suit against the local agency to recover NFIP flood-related losses.

Other preventive measures   Other preventive measures are floodplain acquisition, development reviews, and bridge and culvert design.

Acquisition of undeveloped floodplains is generally difficult to justify solely on the basis of flood control. The value of floodplains in urban areas is related more to recreation, environmental, and open space requirements. Floodplain acquisition, however, is the surest method of keeping floodplains free from development and associated damage. Those responsible for floodplain management should aggressively encourage open space groups to acquire floodplains. Effective floodplain regulation can make this task easier. Where open space acquisition funds are available, some of these funds should go toward floodplain acquisition.

Most developers are willing to "play by the rules" if the rules are defined ahead of time and are applied fairly to all developments. Developers should be encouraged to stay away from floodplains and to dedicate floodplains as open space or recreation areas. If it is necessary to build in a floodplain, developers should be required to abide by the existing floodplain ordinance. In general, development activities should in no way adversely affect adjacent, upstream, or downstream property owners and should not subject the proposed development to damage during the 100-year flood. The local government should require that plans be prepared by qualified registered professional engineers and should thoroughly review the developer's plans prior to approval. The local government should also require a post-project inspection by a registered professional engineer to ensure compliance with approved plans.

Local government traffic departments and state highway departments should be advised of flow requirements at road and highway crossings. Bridges and culverts should be designed to pass the regulation floods, usually the 100-year floods, either through, or through and over, the crossing without significant upstream ponding unless the roadway is designed as a detention embankment and right-of-way upstream of the roadway is acquired. Opportunities for detention at roadway crossings do exist, but they must be planned and guaranteed to remain in place. Local governments should take the initiative in advising those responsible for the design of bridges and culverts of flood flow requirements.

Implementation of remedial projects

Remedial activities relate to both major and minor drainage systems and can be either structural or nonstructural in nature.

The drainage and flood control plan should specify areas in need of immediate attention, improvements that can be constructed independently of others, estimated construction costs, and probable benefits from the recommended improvements. Implementation strategies then can be formulated on the basis of available funds. The pressure to implement improvements usually comes from affected property owners, and the urgency to implement is usually related to the amount of pressure being applied.

One factor that controls the timing of implementation is the cost of improvements. If improvement costs are high, outside assistance may be needed, such as that provided by the U.S. Army Corps of Engineers. Federal funding for flood control as well as for other programs is difficult to obtain; local funding therefore should be developed if at all possible. Some improvements, such as new culverts and minor channel modifications, can be made by local government forces.

The challenge to the public works manager is to know and understand the problems and to take advantage of the political pressures to obtain required funding for implementation. The basic principle for the public works official to remember is this: Nothing will be accomplished unless effective efforts are initiated at the local level.

Some remedial measures are nonstructural in nature and do not take large funding commitments. When structural solutions are not appropriate, a flood warning system and evacuation plan may be more acceptable. Again, the initiative lies with local government. A flood warning system may consist of rainfall gauges and high-water indicators on local streams that can send signals directly to police headquarters. Rising waters can trigger warning signals that can in turn set in motion a previously prepared plan that could ultimately lead to the evacuation of floodplain occupants. The National Weather Service (NWS) can provide weather information on an up-to-date basis and can give advice regarding the installation of flash flood alarm systems.

Evacuation plans should be developed, and all affected local officials should be kept up to date. The importance of a well-conceived evacuation plan was demonstrated in 1972 during flooding in Rapid City, South Dakota, where more than 250 lives were lost. Some lives might have been saved had a well-rehearsed plan familiar to all been available.

Another nonstructural measure is flood insurance. Flood insurance does not mitigate flooding but does provide assistance for the victims of flooding.

Financing urban drainage and flood control projects

Many well-conceived drainage and flood control plans are never implemented because of the lack of funds. Flood control, generally associated with major drainageways, is one of the few areas of public expenditure in which it is usually necessary to show that tangible benefits exceed expenditures. Flood control or drainage improvements are sometimes difficult to fund because relatively few people are directly affected. Flooding, however, is aggravated by increased runoff caused by impervious surfaces in the upper portions of the drainage basin, and upper-basin landowners should be required to share in the flood control costs.

The beneficiaries vary with the project, and potential sources of funding vary accordingly. For example, it may be difficult to justify using general tax funds to finance a project of limited local benefit. General fund expenditures may be justified, however, if project benefits are distributed more widely.

The concept of who benefits and who pays can provide a basis for addressing funding problems. If the relation between project costs and the beneficiaries can be established, then equitable funding approaches can be developed. If the benefits can be defined and bounded (geographically), then funding sources can be pursued with clear cost/benefit justifications.

Potential benefits of urban drainage and/or flood control projects include:

1. Increasing the market value of property

Figure 14–8   Sources of funds for urban drainage and flood control projects.

Development phase	Sources of funds by projects
	Minor drainage system projects
Existing development	General tax fund Special assessments Service charges or fees Federal or state grants Municipal bonds
New development	Developer responsibility Basin fees Bonds
	Major drainage system projects
Existing development	General tax fund Special assessments Service charges or fees Federal or state grants Municipal bonds
New development	Developer responsibility Basin fees Dedications Floodplain zoning Bonds

2. Allocating the cost of providing for increased runoff caused by impervious surfaces on uphill lands to owners of uphill land
3. Adapting property to superior or more profitable uses
4. Alleviating health and sanitation hazards
5. Reducing maintenance costs
6. Facilitating access to and travel over streets, roads, and highways
7. Providing recreational and open space improvements for particular property owners.

The costs and benefits for urban drainage and flood control are difficult to measure and controversial to apply. It is difficult to convince upstream and uphill landowners that they too must participate in the financing of runoff control. It can be done, however, and must be done in many areas if flood damage is to be controlled. State and local governments in the West have had years of experience in water resource allocation and the correlative problems of drainage and flood control. Local governments in other parts of the country can learn from their experience.

Potential funding sources for both minor drainage system projects and major drainage system projects are shown in Figure 14–8. In addition, several publications provide valuable reference information on costs, benefits, and other aspects of funding. A Colorado State University publication addresses the definition and quantification, where possible, of urban drainage and flood control projects and is a good reference for the analysis of benefits and costs.[8] Financing urban drainage and flood control projects is covered in the American Public Works Association's *Urban Stormwater Management.*[9] A Water Resources Council publication discusses ordinances for selected financing techniques,[10] and a standard reference on local government finance is available.[11]

Maintenance of facilities

The importance of maintenance cannot be emphasized enough. Regardless of the type of facility, funding must be provided. Without maintenance, facilities will deteriorate and eventually will not function properly and in some cases may even pose a hazard. If damage results because a local government did not adequately maintain a facility, the local government could be held liable for that damage.

Detention facilities   Local detention facilities are in most cases constructed by developers. Local government may agree to assume maintenance responsibilities, or it may require the developer or a homeowner's group to assume the responsibility. In either case, the local government should ensure that someone will be responsible for maintaining the completed facility.

Maintenance activities may include cleaning the facility after major storms, mowing grass or cutting weeds, replacing and repairing recreation equipment, controlling mosquitos, checking outlet work facilities, and posting and maintaining various signs. Facility ownership may be accompanied by other problems, such as keeping motorcycles or other motorized vehicles off embankments and other areas. Owners may also be liable for injuries to persons while they are on or near the facility.

Flood control facilities   A local sponsoring agency is required to make a maintenance commitment in the form of a signed agreement before the Army Corps of Engineers will construct flood control facilities. Such facilities may include dams, flood channels, or levees. Dams require maintenance similar to localized detention facilities but on a larger scale. Flood control channels must be kept free of growth and debris. In an urban environment channels should be kept neat, clean, and free of trash, and regular mowing and cleaning may be necessary. Levees must also be mowed, and they should be checked routinely for possible erosion.

There is usually a tradeoff between facilities that have high capital cost but low maintenance cost and facilities that have relatively low capital cost with higher maintenance cost. The desired facility will depend on the local situation, but maintenance should not be over looked during the evaluation of alternative solutions to a flood problem.

Storm drainage facilities   Underground conduits probably require less maintenance than most drainage facilities if they are properly designed. Inlets and catch basins must be cleaned, however, and storm sewer outlets sometimes cause erosion problems that must be remedied.

Stormwater quality considerations

The effect of urban stormwater discharges on the quality of creeks, gulches, rivers, and lakes (receiving waters) is gaining more and more attention. "Simply stated the problem is, . . . when a city takes a bath, what do you do with the dirty water?"[12] Three types of discharges are involved:

1.   Overflows from sewers that carry both sanitary sewage and stormwater (combined sources)
2.   Storm runoff from separate storm sewer systems
3.   Overflows or bypasses from sanitary sewers that have been infiltrated by stormwater.[13]

Discussion in this section is limited to the quality effects of storm runoff from separate storm sewer systems. Combined sewer and infiltration problems are discussed in the section of this chapter dealing with wastewater.

The potential water quality problem created by stormwater was recognized by Congress in the Water Quality Act of 1965 (P.L. 89–234). Section 62 of that act authorized the federal government to make grants for the purpose of "assisting in the development of any project which will demonstrate a new or improved method of controlling the discharge into any water of untreated or inadequately treated sewage or other waste from sewerage which carry stormwater or both stormwater and sewage or other waste." This was essentially an intuitive conclusion because the impact of stormwater on receiving waters was not well documented or well understood at that time, as became clear when Congress deleted federal funding for the treatment of separate stormwater discharges in the Clean Water Act of 1977 (P.L. 92–217). Congress stated that not enough was known about urban runoff loads, impacts, and controls to warrant major investments in structural control systems.

Additional data were needed, and in 1978 the Environmental Protection Agency (EPA) initiated the Nationwide Urban Runoff Program (NURP). The NURP was implemented to build on previous work in order to provide practical

. . . information that would help provide local decision makers, states, EPA, and other interested parties with a rational basis for determining whether or not urban runoff is causing water quality problems, and in the event that it is, for postulating realistic control options and developing water quality management plans, consistent with local needs, that would lead to implementation of least cost solutions. It is also hoped that this information base will be used to help make the best possible policy decision on Federal, State, and local involvement in urban stormwater runoff and its control.[14]

The NURP effort was completed in December 1983 and the project was fully reported by EPA.[15] The NURP concluded that excessive urban runoff causes quality problems.[16] This conclusion must be tempered, however, by consideration of whether these problems deny beneficial uses or cause water quality standard violations. The presence of a pollutant in urban stormwater does not necessarily mean that remedial action is necessary. The NURP report stated that "the effects of urban runoff on receiving water quality are highly site specific. They depend on the type, size, and hydrology of the water body; the urban runoff quantity and quality characteristics; the designated beneficial use; and the concentration levels of the specific pollutants that affect that use."[17]

Potential effects of pollution   Urban streams, gulches, rivers, lakes, and estuaries are community resources. They provide water supplies for domestic or industrial use, recreation sites for water contact activities and open space enjoyment, and habitats for many forms of life, such as fish, water plants, and water fowl. Pollution should be measured by its effect on these various uses.

Water supplies should meet minimum water quality criteria as set forth in U.S. Public Health Service standards. Because stormwater may adversely affect water supplies, greater treatment of the drinking water supply is required and higher costs usually result. Water supplies can be protected from potential stormwater pollution through land use controls in the tributary watershed.

Water-related body contact sports such as swimming and diving require certain minimum water standards. Stormwater may contribute enough pollutional load to a receiving water to bring the quality below minimum standards and make it necessary to close the area to body contact sports.

Bodies of water are an important part of the ecosystem. Stormwater discharges may raise concentrations of certain substances to the detriment of water-dependent life. For example, the toxicity of discharges may induce high mortality rates and thereby reduce biological populations.

Stormwater pollution emanates from two principal sources: (1) pollutants deposited on the surface and washed into receiving waters and (2) erosion-induced sediments. Street litter, oil, fertilizers, pesticides, chemicals, airborne debris, and other deleterious material are deposited on the surfaces of an urban environment. Storm runoff may wash these contaminants into tributary receiving waters. Soils stripped of their protective vegetative cover are particularly susceptible to erosion. Construction practices that expose soil for long periods of time are the primary cause of erosion and the resulting sedimentation. Sediment washed into receiving waters may contain deleterious materials, may cause silting, and may substantially increase turbidity.

From NURP studies of the potential effects of water pollution in twenty-eight cities in the United States, as well as previous research efforts, it appears that the effects of urban stormwater are site specific. Local governments will therefore have to acquire additional data and conduct further analyses to determine the source, nature, and effects of stormwater pollution for their situations. In particular, data are needed on rainfall, runoff quantity and quality, and basin parameters. Programs should be designed to obtain such data and should be adequately funded, supported, and encouraged.

Potential courses of action   What can be done to mitigate the effects of stormwater pollution? The first step is to decide where to attack the problem. This may be at the source (streets, gutters, parking lots, etc.), within the collection system, at the terminus of a watershed, at strategic locations within a watershed, or combinations of these. The second step is to decide how much control or treatment to apply. The third step is to assess the impact of pollution on receiving waters—to determine if beneficial uses of the receiving waters are being hindered, to compare the costs of reducing the impacts of stormwater pollution with the benefits obtained, and to establish priority rankings with regard to other community needs.

The intermittence and variability of stormwater runoff make it impossible to determine average design conditions for stormwater treatment facilities. Moreover, stormwater runoff is difficult to characterize precisely because of the variability in types of watersheds and storm events. Therefore, a treatment process that functions correctly only under controlled conditions will be too restrictive for stormwater treatment.

In addition, the magnitude, debris content, force of storm flows, and cost will limit the desirability and practicability of central treatment facilities. The same factors will probably render sophisticated and complex equipment ineffectual or impossible to maintain. Furthermore, the large number of stormwater discharge points will preclude or limit the practicability of individual treatment facilities for each discharge point. In other words, treatment facilities for stormwater runoff do not appear possible or practical.

The NURP looked at a few techniques for controlling the quality of urban runoff in the twenty-eight cities it studied. These were primarily practices that appear practical and feasible from a local perspective. The techniques examined during the NURP included detention, street sweeping, recharge devices, and use of grass swales and wetlands. The NURP report[18] contains an evaluation of the effectiveness of these various techniques.

Basic data needs and data analysis

Urban storm drainage practices suffer from a lack of basic data, which are needed to develop reliable design tools, define and understand problems, and evaluate solutions. City or county managers need not have a thorough understanding of data collection and analysis programs, but they should be fully aware of the need.

Substantial amounts of money are spent each year on storm drainage and flood control facilities in urban areas. The procedures used to design these facilities, however, are in many cases very crude. If facilities are underdesigned as a result of such procedures, the stated level of protection will not be provided. If facilities are overdesigned, money is wasted. It is the responsibility of local government to provide the best possible design within the constraints of available funds and existing technology.

The United States Geological Survey (USGS) runs a cooperative program whereby it will establish and maintain rainfall and runoff data collection programs if local or state governments will share one-half of the cost. These programs are managed by USGS district offices. Information regarding such assistance can be obtained from the office of the USGS district chief in each state. Local government managers should be aware that these are usually long-term programs lasting ten years or longer.

Many urban areas lack an inventory of the physical system. Before meaningful planning can be completed, facts regarding the existing physical drainage system must be established. The exact nature of the information needed will vary from locale to locale.

Detailed information should be obtained about flooding problems. Pictures of flooding events and documentation of damages are particularly helpful when funding is being sought from city councils, boards of commissioners, or the public. Such damages should be related to depth and velocity of water. Damages consist of both private and public damages to roads, streets, bridges, culverts, buildings, water and sewer facilities, and homes. Damage data should be collected immediately after a storm event while memories are fresh and documents and records are readily available.

1   For further information on financing sanitary waste-water systems through user charges, see Paul Downing, "User Charges and Special Districts," Chapter 9 in J. Richard Aronson and Eli Schwartz, eds., *Management Policies in Local Government Finance* (Washington, D.C.: International City Management Association, rev. ed., forthcoming).

2   D. Earl Jones, Jr., "Urban Hydrology—A Redirection," *Civil Engineering* 37 (August 1967): 58–62.

3   The 100-year event has a 1 percent chance of occurring each year, the 5-year event has a 20 percent chance, and the 2-year event has a 50 percent chance.

4   Matthew D. Glasser, "Development and Drainage Issues," (Broomfield, Colo.: City Attorney's Office, November 1984): 3–4.

5   Legal aspects of drainage are addressed in these references: John R. Sheaffer et al., *Urban Storm Drainage Management* (New York: Marcel Dekker, Inc., 1982), pp. 7–33; Wright-McLaughlin Engineers, *Urban Storm Drainage Criteria Manual, Urban Drainage and Flood Control District, Denver, Colorado* (1969), vol. 1, chap. 2; and American Public Works Association, *Urban Stormwater Management*, Special Report no. 49 (Chicago, 1981), pp. 248–59.

6   The zoning ordinance no longer is the sole authorization for large-scale land development. Such development is increasingly negotiated by the developer and the local government. For further information on this point, see Chapter 5 on zoning.

7   For a basic reference, see Jon A. Kusler et al.,

Regulation of Flood Hazard Areas to Reduce Flood Losses, vol. 1 (1971), vol. 2 (1972), vol. 3 (1982) (Washington, D.C.: Water Resources Council).

8   Neil S. Grigg, Leslie H. Bothum, Leonard Rice, W. J. Shoemaker, and L. Scott Tucker, *Urban Drainage and Flood Control Projects: Economic, Legal and Financial Aspects* (Fort Collins, Colo.: Colorado State University Environmental Resources Center, July 1975).

9   American Public Works Association, *Urban Stormwater Management*, pp. 260–63.

10   Kusler et al., *Regulation of Flood Hazard Areas*.

11   The best overall reference on local government finance is J. Richard Aronson and Eli Schwartz, eds., *Management Policies in Local Government Finance*, rev. ed., forthcoming. See especially chaps. 9, 10, and 11, and the bibliography.

12   Richard Field and John Lager, "Urban Runoff Pollution Control—State-of-the-Art," *Journal of the Environmental Engineering Division*, Proceedings of the American Society of Civil Engineers 101 (February 1975): 107.

13   Ibid.

14   United States, Environmental Protection Agency, Water Planning Division, *Results of the Nationwide Urban Runoff Program*, Executive Summary (Washington, D.C., December 1983), p. 1.

15   Ibid., vol. 1, Final Report; vol. 2, Appendices; and vol. 3, Data Appendix.

16   Ibid., vol. 1, Final Report, p. 3–3.

17   Ibid., Executive Summary, p. 7.

18   Ibid., pp. 13–16.

15 Solid waste management

The disposal of solid waste has become one of the most critical problems facing local governments in the 1980s. Their decisions regarding disposal methods will have a significant impact on other elements of the solid waste service chain. This chapter presents a brief review of the events that have led to the present disposal crisis.

Evolving concepts and responsibilities

Traditionally, solid waste disposal was a local government responsibility regulated by local or state public health agencies. In 1965, the federal government enacted Public Law 89-272, the Solid Waste Disposal Act, which provided funds for planning and research in solid waste management and established a bureau in the federal government to administer the act. When the Environmental Protection Agency was established, the Solid Waste Bureau was incorporated into EPA. Since 1965, the federal government has amended the Solid Waste Disposal Act with laws passed in 1970, 1971, and 1972. Eventually the passage of Public Law 94-850, the Resource Conservation and Recovery Act of 1975 (RCRA), added significantly to the federal government's involvement in and control of solid waste management and added the control of hazardous waste to the scope of EPA's responsibility. In 1984, RCRA was reauthorized and EPA's responsibilities were redefined with the passage of Public Law 98-616.

Other federal laws that impinge on solid waste management pertain to the protection of the air, water, and oceans; to energy; and to the conservation of resources. With the passage of air pollution laws in the 1960s, many of the incinerators serving municipalities, institutions, and residences had to be shut down. Restrictions against dumping at sea added significantly to the need for land disposal space. At the same time, the quantities of waste to be disposed of by solid waste service agencies increased because sludges and residues were designated as a solid waste.

Under RCRA the federal government has set minimum standards for waste disposal facilities, which, through state-promulgated rules and regulations, restrict the location and size of solid waste processing and disposal facilities. Because of these restrictions, coupled with an unprecedented and sometimes irrational public concern about the potential degradation of the environment and danger to public health from the presence of trace quantities of known hazardous materials in solid waste, there is a serious shortage of both acceptable space for the disposal of waste and process facility locations. Consequently, planning for the management of solid waste by municipalities, counties, or regional organizations invariably starts with the selection of viable sites for the process and/or disposal facilities that are acceptable to the residents of a community.

RCRA identified hazardous waste as a growing environmental and health problem and established federal standards for the handling, transport, processing, and disposal of these wastes. The effect of these standards on the management of the more traditional municipal wastes is now widely recognized and therefore will be included among the topics in this chapter.

What are hazardous wastes? What are the traditional municipal wastes? What is the definition of solid waste? Definitions have been formulated by EPA and each state. In addition, EPA has prepared a list of hazardous wastes that is updated periodically and reported in the *Federal Register*. Universal definitions of various categories of waste can be found in the *Thesaurus on Resource Recovery Terminology*, which defines solid waste as follows:

A general term for discarded materials destined for disposal, but not discharged to a sewer or to the atmosphere. Solid waste(s) can be composed of a single material or a heterogeneous mix of various materials including semi-solids.[1]

The accompanying sidebar defines the components of solid waste.

Solid waste service elements

It is convenient to describe the solid waste service by identifying the several separate but related elements of which it is composed, namely: storage, collection, transfer, process, and disposal.

RCRA has mandated (and economics at times supports) the addition of resource recovery as an element of the solid waste service. It should be noted that the economic justification for resource recovery includes both the value of the recovered resource and environmental benefits of increasing the usable life of disposal areas.

The goal of the public works manager is to develop and implement a plan that will provide a level of service that will protect public health and the environment, that will meet the convenience levels residents are willing to pay for, and that can be carried out by the personnel, equipment, and facilities available to the administrator. The factors that must be evaluated for each service element and for total service include:

1. Cost, notably capital, operating and maintenance, and financing alternatives
2. Environmental and health factors
3. Resource conservation and recovery potential and reliability
4. Institutional factors, particularly political and public feasibility, legislative constraints, and administrative reliability.

The balance of this introductory section briefly reviews the public/private service question (drawing on experience in Philadelphia) and resource recovery. The chapter then covers the six major elements of solid waste service—storage and collection, transfer, process, disposal, hazardous waste, and financing. Throughout the discussion of service elements, the relations between public and private sectors will be identified.

Public/private service—one city's experience

The first record of solid waste service in this country is found in Ben Franklin's *Poor Richard's Almanack*, in which Franklin describes the hiring by a group of merchants of a "poor and industrious man" to clean the streets of Philadelphia and dispose of the collected waste, a private-sector undertaking.

A recent special committee report on the solid waste management service in Philadelphia provides a useful history of the changing popularity of public versus private service. Recognizing that unsanitary streets contributed to periodic disease epidemics, the city council in 1821 ordered that "the street be scraped at least once a week, and when required, twice or oftener."[2] Subsequently,

In 1826, Philadelphia began cleaning its own streets, but city officials returned to street

Definitions of solid waste

Ash Residue from burning of combustible materials.

Bulky waste (oversize waste) Large discarded materials; appliances, furniture, junked automobile parts, diseased trees, large branches, stumps, etc.

Commercial waste From businesses, office buildings, apartment houses, stores, markets, theaters, etc.

Combustible waste The organic content of solid waste, including paper, cardboard, cartons, wood, boxes, excelsior, plastic, textiles, bedding, leather, rubber, paints, yard trimmings, leaves, and household waste, all of which will burn.

Domestic refuse (household solid waste) Putrescible and nonputrescible waste originating from a residential unit, and consisting of paper, cans, bottles, food wastes and may include yard and garden waste.

Food waste (garbage) Animal and vegetable discards from handling, storage, sale, preparation, cooking and serving of foods. . . .

Hazardous waste Any waste material, or combination thereof, which pose a substantial present or potential hazard to human health or living organisms because such wastes are non-degradable or persistent in nature or because they can be biologically magnified, or because they can be lethal, or because they may otherwise cause or tend to cause detrimental cumulative effects. Includes, but is not limited to, explosives, pathological wastes, radioactive materials and chemicals which may be harmful to the public during normal storage, collection or disposal cycle.

Industrial waste Discarded waste materials from industrial processes and/or manufacturing operations.

Infectious waste (pathological waste) Waste materials from a medical facility, hospital or laboratory which may contain pathogens or other disease infected wastes.

Litter Solid wastes that are scattered about in a careless manner.

Municipal solid waste (MSW) Domestic refuse and some commercial waste.

---

cleaning by contractor in 1840. Despite these changes, the elimination of contagious diseases was not achieved. Between 1849 and 1853, cholera, smallpox, yellow fever, typhus, dysentery, scarlet fever, and tuberculosis—all believed to be caused by unsanitary conditions—killed over 5,000 people. The Sanitary Committee of the Board of Health, after cleaning up after the cholera epidemic of 1849 which killed 1,012 people, left little doubt over its opinion on the cause of the epidemic.

Following consolidation in 1854, street responsibilities were placed in a new Department of Highways, Bridges, Sewers, and Cleansing of the City and the city again performed its own street cleaning until 1874, when the legislature made contract work obligatory. The Bullitt Bill of 1887 transferred responsibility for supervision of street cleaning and waste disposal to the Department of Public Works, where responsibility shifted from bureau to bureau.

During this period, contracts for street cleaning and waste disposal were traditionally combined, setting a precedent under which these functions have been performed by the same division of city government ever since.[3]

The report indicates that the contracts for the collection of trash and garbage and the cleaning of streets were usually awarded as political favors without regard for ability to perform the function capably and economically. Thus, sanitary conditions during this period "left much to be desired." Things changed, however, with the adoption of a reform charter in 1919: "In the new charter, the city won the right to collect its own trash and clean its own streets. With this new power, the city began its own collection program, with full operations underway by 1922."[4]

Noncombustible waste Inorganic content of solid waste, including glass, metal, tin cans, foils, dirt, gravel, brick, ceramics, crockery and ashes.

Residential waste Discarded materials originating from residences. Also called domestic or household refuse.

Refuse Term sometimes used in place of "solid waste." Used to define general community waste which includes kitchen/food wastes and rubbish.

Rubbish Term for non-putrescible materials collected from residences, commercial establishments and institutions, consisting of cans, paper, glass, magazines, packaging materials, brick, wood.

Rubble Rough stones of irregular shape and size, broken from larger masses either naturally or artificially, as by weathering action or by demolition of buildings, pavements, roads, etc.

Sludge A semi-liquid sediment resulting from the accumulation of settlable organic/inorganic solids deposited from wastewaters or other fluids in tanks or basins.

Street refuse Material collected by manual and mechanical sweeping of streets and sidewalks, litter from public litter receptacles and dirt removed from catch basins. *Also see* Litter.

Toxic waste Waste that causes unnatural genetic activity, has the potential for bioaccumulation in tissue, or could cause acute and chronic toxicity to various organisms, including humans.

White goods Discarded kitchen and other large, enameled appliances, as washing machines, and refrigerators. *See* Bulky Waste.

Yard waste Plant clippings, prunings, grass clippings and leaves, and other discarded material from yards and gardens.

Source: American Society for Testing and Materials, *Thesaurus on Resource Recovery Terminology*, pp. 53, 85–87. Definition of toxic waste from U.S. Environmental Protection Agency, *Hazardous Waste Guidelines*.

A new Charter Commission (1949) prepared a new Philadelphia Home Rule Charter, which was adopted in 1951 and which addressed the question of public- and private-sector sanitation services as follows:

The [Street] Department shall itself, or when specifically authorized by Council, by contract, clean and sand City streets, remove and dispose of ashes, garbage, and refuse, remove and dispose of ice and snow from City streets, design, construct, repair, maintain and operate incinerators or other plants or equipment for the disposition of ashes, garbage and refuse, and administer and enforce statutes, ordinances and regulations for maintaining the cleanliness of city streets.[5]

Since the adoption of the charter in 1951, Philadelphia has utilized both public and contract service for all aspects of its solid waste service. The Philadelphia experience is typical of that in many municipalities throughout this country.

Resource recovery

Resource recovery is "a general term used to describe the extraction of materials or energy from wastes."[6] Resource recovery may be accomplished by recycling or energy recovery. Recycling involves "separating a given waste material . . . from the waste stream and processing it so that it may be used again as a raw material for products which may or may not be similar to the original."[7] Energy recovery may be defined as "resource recovery where a part, or all, of the waste stream is processed to utilize its heat content to produce hot air, hot water, steam, electricity, synthetic fuel or other useful energy form."[8]

Recycling can be accomplished (1) by the method called source separation, "sorting at point of generation of specific discarded materials such as newspapers, glass, metal cans, vegetative matter, etc., into specific containers for separate collection";[9] or (2) by delivery of the recyclable by the generator to collection centers. Either method of recycling can significantly influence all elements of solid waste service.

For counties and municipalities that may wish to add recycling to their operations, how should they proceed? First, check out the markets that exist for recyclables. The most common recyclables from municipal waste are newspapers, aluminum, glass, ferrous metals, and some plastics. Contact the scrap industry and those who handle secondary materials directly or the state agency responsible for recycling and obtain information on the demand for recyclables. Then organize a citizens group to help set up test programs for source separation, community institution, or neighborhood recycling centers. Publicize the test effort. On the basis of the success of the test, work with the citizens group to expand the operation.

Storage and collection

Storage and collection processes reflect on health and environmental considerations, population density, on-site storage capability, resource recovery practices, local customs, the physical structure of communities, climate, and the distances from collection centers to transfer, process, and disposal facilities. A brief discussion of each of these factors follows.

Factors in planning

Solid waste containing putrescible matter may be stored in closed containers for up to one week in order to control fly propagation and related health problems.[10] Weekly collection of solid wastes will meet this time limitation. Residents in humid areas of the South, however, generally prefer more frequent collections.

Densely populated urban areas, particularly in older cities that have experienced the conversion of large single-family dwellings to multifamily houses, often contain living areas that do not provide space for the proper storage of solid waste. Such a condition should be recognized in determining the frequency of refuse collections.

Resource recovery, particularly the source separation procedure in which residents separate and store newspapers, bottles, cans, and glass, significantly affects the storage controls and collection procedures for solid waste.

Local custom, the refuse storage and collection practices that residents are familiar with, is an important factor in the management of the solid waste service. When new types of containers, collection vehicles, and collection systems are introduced, people often have to change well-established habits.

The physical structure of a community—including the width of roadbeds, the availability of common driveways and alleys for collection vehicles, and the availability of convenient spaces for placing large communal containers—affects storage and collection practices. Even the space in shopping malls, bus stations, and recreation centers, where recycling containers could be located, influences storage and collection practices.

Climate, particularly precipitation and humidity, affect the generation of garden wastes and the length of time required between collections. Areas of the country that produce large quantities of garden waste may require special seasonal storage and collection procedures.

The distance from a collection route to a transfer station, process plant, or disposal site could influence the type of collection equipment and crew sizes that would most efficiently serve a community.

Finally, as noted at the beginning of this chapter, the willingness of people to pay for quality service must be recognized. Regulations governing refuse collection in Philadelphia are shown in Figure 15–1.

The U.S. Environmental Protection Agency (EPA) has developed recommended regulations in accordance with RCRA that provide for the storage of waste in a manner that will "not constitute a fire, health or safety hazard or provide food or harborage for vectors"; establish a seventy-five-pound limit, when filled, on the weight of a container to be manually emptied; and stipulate that "single-use plastic and paper bags should meet the National Sanitation Foundation Standard No. 31 for polyethylene refuse bags and Standard No. 32 for paper refuse bags respectively."[11]

The EPA recommended regulations specify that collection equipment and operating procedures must protect the health and safety of personnel assigned to the collection task. Standards of the Occupational Safety and Health Administration for personal protective equipment must be met; scavenging should be prohibited; and equipment used for the collection of solid waste and source-separated recyclables should be enclosed or provided with suitable covers to prevent spillage. In addition, collection equipment must meet American National Standard Institute (ANSI Z245.1) Safety Standards for Refuse Collection Equipment.[12]

Collection frequency requirements are also addressed as follows:

Solid wastes (or materials which have been separated for the purpose of recycling) shall be collected with frequency sufficient to inhibit the propagation or attraction of vectors and the creation of nuisances. Solid wastes which contain food wastes shall be collected at a minimum of once during each week. Bulky wastes shall be collected at a minimum of once every 3 months.[13]

Equipment and storage

The equipment available for the storage and collection of solid wastes varies from rigid containers small enough to be picked up manually, to disposable bags made of plastic and paper, to large, rigid containers that are hoisted and unloaded into a collection vehicle with mechanical equipment.

Of the various collection vehicles the major types are:

Rear loading, closed compactor vehicles that have either manual or mechanical loading and range in capacity from 10 to 40 cubic yards

Side loading, closed compactor vehicles, either manually or mechanically loaded, that range in capacity from under 10 yards to 40 cubic yards

Large refuse collection trucks that load mechanically from the front end, generally in the range of 25 to 40 cubic yards

Large refuse-hauling trucks with equipment that hoists containers onto flat beds and dumps the contents of the containers.

Many of the mechanical unloading and hoisting vehicles can be operated by one person, the driver. Other collection vehicles are designed to be operated by crews of one to four persons per vehicle.

Often waste is stored in locations other than the collection location. Containers can be stored next to the residence, in an alley or driveway accessible by the collection vehicle, or at the curb. For large, mechanically hoisted containers, the storage location is generally the collection point. When the collection point and storage area differ, the first step in the collection process is to move the container to the pickup point. Generally this is the resident's responsibility,

Figure 15–1 Regulations governing municipal refuse collection in Philadelphia.

REGULATIONS GOVERNING
MUNICIPAL REFUSE COLLECTION

Pursuant to Section 10-717 (1) of the Philadelphia Code, the Department of Streets adopts the following regulations:

1. SEPARATION OF REFUSE. Refuse shall be separated into the following four categories prior to being set out for collection:

    a. *Garbage*
    b. *Household bulk items*
    c. *All other refuse*

2. TYPES AND SIZES OF RECEPTACLES. The following shall be acceptable as "authorized private receptacles" for the types of refuse indicated, provided that they are used in such a manner as to prevent their contents from being scattered or being carried by the elements upon any public place or upon private premises.

    a. *Rubbish* can be set out in a metal or other non-corrodible receptacle having a tight-fitting lid or cover or may be securely bundled in a substantial leak-proof bag. Each receptacle shall have a capacity of not more than thirty-two gallons. No receptacle having ragged or sharp edges or any other defect liable to hamper or injure the person collecting the contents thereof shall be used. No one receptacle shall exceed 75 lbs. in weight. Household material which is too bulky for a container such as large appliances may be set out with the regular rubbish. These bulk items will be collected separately by special crews.

    b. *Garbage* shall be set out in a metal or other non-corrodible, leak-proof container with a tight-fitting lid. Receptacles for garbage shall have a capacity of not more than ten gallons and shall not exceed 50 lbs. in weight when filled. Garbage receptacles shall be kept clean, neat, and in a sanitary condition.

    c. *Newspapers, Magazines or Collapsible Cardboard Boxes or Containers* can be set out in securely-tied bundles. No one bundle shall exceed 25 lbs. in weight.

    d. *Yard Dirt* (i.e. tree trimmings, hedge clippings and similar materials) shall be cut to a length not to exceed 4 ft. and securely tied in bundles not more than 2 ft. thick before being set out for collection. Leaves, grass clippings and similar garden refuse shall be set out for collection in a receptacle similar to that required for rubbish. No one receptacle shall exceed 75 lbs. in weight.

    e. *Highly flammable or explosive materials* shall not be placed in containers for regular collection, but shall be disposed of as prescribed by the Fire Department.

3. MAXIMUM QUANTITIES TO BE COLLECTED

    a. *Rubbish.* On each collection day the Department of Streets will collect a maximum of the six 32-gallon receptacles or ten $30'' \times 37''$ plastic bags or any equivalent amount from each residential or business building. Buildings occupied by manufacturers and wholesalers and apartments shall not be included, except that rubbish will be collected from apart-

(continued on next page)

Figure 15–1 (continued).

ments where the whole building or complex (if more than one building) contains no more than six (6) units. The total weight of rubbish collected from any one unit shall not exceed 450 lbs. not including bulk items. Retail stores, service stations, hotels and office buildings shall be limited to one collection day per week.

b. *Yard Dirt.*   On each collection day, the Department of Streets will collect a maximum of five 20-gallon receptacles of yard dirt, with a weight not in excess of a total of 375 lbs. from each unit as specified in paragraph 3a above.

c. *Garbage.*   On each collection day, the Department of Streets will collect ten gallons or approximately 50 lbs. of garbage from each dwelling, retail store, service station, hotel, rooming house, apartment and office or other type building except those occupied by manufacturers and wholesalers.

d. No collections will be made from

(1) Manufacturers, i.e., anyone who sells articles or products made or produced by him.

(2) Wholesalers, i.e., anyone who sells articles to a purchaser who retails or resells them.

(3) Establishments which are part manufacturing and part wholesale.

(4) Large apartment houses, i.e., more than six (6) units in one building.

(5) Apartment complexes, i.e., more than six (6) units in adjoining or contiguous buildings under the same management.

4. COLLECTION DAYS AND "SET-OUT" TIME

a. *Refuse* (other than garbage)

(1) Will be collected in accordance with a definite schedule which will be announced from time to time by the Department of Streets.

(2) When collections are made during the day, all authorized private receptacles must be placed on the sidewalk adjacent to the curb before 7:00 a.m. on the day of collection but not before 7:00 p.m. on the previous day.

(3) When collections are made at night, authorized private receptacles must be placed on the sidewalk adjacent to the curb between 4:00 p.m. and 6:00 p.m. prior to collection.

(4) In those areas where the Department permits such collections, authorized private receptacles may be placed in the rear of buildings or private driveways.

b. *Garbage*

(1) Will be collected twice a week in accordance with a definite schedule which will be announced from time to time by the Department of Streets.

(2) Authorized private receptacles for garbage will be set out for collection according to the prevailing custom by neighborhoods, as follows:

(a) on the sidewalk adjacent to the curb wherever this is feasible.

(b) in alleys, driveways or in yards adjacent to alleys where receptacles are easily accessible.

although in some communities the collection employees move the containers either to or to and from the pickup point as part of the collection service.

A variety of options are available to the manager who is planning a new system of storage and collection or modifying an existing one. In addition to determining which of the many alternatives for equipment, procedures, and crew sizes are best suited, managers are concerned with collection route layouts and the location and operational restrictions of transfer, process, and/or disposal facilities.

Public and private service

Service can be provided by local government, private contract, or a combination of the two. The private contract service can be performed by franchise, with one or more contractors providing the service, or by contract, under which the service is provided by a private firm under contract with the local government.

Another alternative is commonly referred to as private collection. This kind of service is intended for the customer who is not served by the local government. When a city or county decides that it will not serve a part of the community, such as the business sector, private refuse collectors, generally licensed by a local regulatory agency, will negotiate directly with the customer to provide the collection service. The quality and frequency of such service may be determined by some regulatory agency standards—such as Health Department regulations—but, except for such standards, would not be controlled by the local government.

Private collection is a common practice for commercial and industrial waste produced in medium and large cities because the quantities generated are often large enough to warrant more frequent collections than are available from municipalities and because waste disposal is recognized to be a part of the service that should not be provided by local tax funds.

Routing

The task of deciding on the best solid waste management system for a community rests on many factors related to the storage and collection of waste plus the routing of collection vehicles, transportation, and the type and location of process and/or disposal facilities. The route design of collection systems should recognize traffic patterns, parking requirements, street widths, availability of through driveways and alleys, and of course, crew sizes. Routing can be designed using mathematical evaluations, observation and experience, or a combination.

Routes can be serviced by collection vehicles using the "task system" in which a single vehicle is assigned to a route for each work shift; the crew's work is completed when the service is completed.

Alternatively, crews can be assigned routes for a designated time period. Under this system the crews follow defined routes that may take anywhere from two to ten days to service completely, depending on the weather, season of the year, and other factors. The crews go home after an eight-hour shift and then resume collections the next day from the location where they ended their work the day before. This method is generally used in conjunction with collection service from a building or storage space adjacent to a building.

A third collection system, called the group task system, uses several crews to collect along a single route. When the collection is completed, all crews on the route have completed their assignment. This procedure is generally restricted to densely populated areas.

Putting the system together

No single system can be identified as the most efficient for all communities. In fact, the most efficient overall solid waste system for large communities will probably consist of combinations of storage methods, collection vehicles, and collection frequencies, and even mixes of public and private collection responsibilities. The best system for your community can be determined by listing and matching all the combinations of storage, collection, transport, and disposal, including the use of private contractors, and determining the cost of each combination or alternative. When all alternatives have been analyzed systematically, the most efficient ones that are also consistent with the desires and customs of the community can usually be determined.

Alternatives can be evaluated using a simple systems analysis in which the elements of each are identified, and the costs of the elements are added together to determine the overall cost of each system. Alternatively, the decision maker can use computer programs to evaluate and compare many complex combinations of elements. In evaluating alternative systems, it is essential to factor reliability into each system evaluated. Such factoring often requires professional assistance, but can be accommodated by using a pass-fail method of accepting and rejecting elements of the system or assigning a reliability facctor to each element.

Solid waste service is one of the most dangerous work areas in the country. A 1982 report for the U.S. Department of Health and Human Services[14] describes the danger as follows: "Collectors incur injuries at a rate 7 times higher than the average for all industries. Collectors may also risk serious short and long-term illnesses."

Work in process and disposal facilities is equally hazardous, and in planning for and managing solid waste service operations it is important to recognize and provide for this condition. The Health and Human Services report provides useful information on the subject of the hazards associated with the service and equipment as well as the procedures that are available to reduce the danger.

Transfer

Once collected, the solid waste must be delivered to a process plant or disposal facility. If the process or disposal facility is located a reasonable distance from the collection route, the collection vehicle can economically carry its load directly to the facility. Otherwise it may be more efficient to deliver the waste to a transfer station where it will be loaded onto large, over-the-road trailers or other large-bulk conveyance bodies for delivery to process or disposal facilities.

What is considered a reasonable distance from collection route to facility cannot be defined in miles. Rather, it is defined in terms of time and manpower. The workweek in the solid waste service is usually forty hours, generally spread over five eight-hour days, although four-day workweeks of ten hours per day are not unusual. If during a normal workday the time taken to fill a collection vehicle represents 70 percent or more of the working shift, and the collection vehicle can be driven to and returned from the process or disposal facility within the remaining time left in the working day, there would probably be no need to provide a transfer operation. Conversely, if 50 percent or less of the workday is devoted to collections, a transfer operation would probably be economical. Actually, the only way to determine whether a transfer operation is required is to compare the cost of hauling directly from the collection route with the cost of transferring.

Transfer stations are available or can be designed in a number of ways. Basically, a transfer station is a two-level operation. Collection vehicles dump their loads from an upper level, and the transfer trailers are loaded at a lower level. The transfer can take place at the same level if storage pits and conveyors or cranes are used. However, the most common methods are direct dumping into an open trailer or the receiving hopper of a compactor trailer; dumping into compactor hoppers that are used to store and feed the refuse into trailers equipped with ejectors or dumping or discharge devices; dumping into troughs with conveyor feed bottoms; or dumping into push pits.

Where direct dumping into an open trailer is the practice, a backhoe equipped with a tamping device is often used. Floor space is generally provided for the storage of refuse, and front-end loaders are used to move the refuse from the floor to the trailer-feeding mechanism.

Two types of trailers are used for waste transfer, the open-top trailer and closed compactor unit. Open-top trailers are filled by direct dumping from the collection vehicle or by material-handling equipment at the transfer station. For maximum transfer efficiency, open trailers are designed to carry approximately 100 cubic yards of uncompacted refuse. Supporters of this method claim it has greater payloads than the closed compacter type of trailer because ejection mechanisms are not required and the absence of compaction pressure reduces the structural requirements of the body. However, the addition of mechanical top-closing panels to produce a closed vehicle for transport and the use of moving floors (conveyors) or ejection panels for unloading purposes add to the weight of the trailer, which tends to offset the claimed weight advantage of the open-top trailer. These trailers have been fabricated of aluminum in order to save weight and reduce corrosion.

Two types of compactor trailers are available. One is a combined unit in which the compactor is built into the trailer. The compactor compacts refuse as it is dumped into the trailer and also ejects the refuse at the disposal site or process plant. The second type is a separate stationary compactor equipped to accommodate trailers that are anchored to the compactor during the refuse-loading process. These trailers must have an auxiliary means of unloading, such as an ejection conveyor or dumping mechanism.

Solid waste can also be transferred by rail and barge. The hauling of refuse by rail, a practice followed in other parts of the world, has been studied and tested in North America, but is not popular at present. Research into this method of transport, often conducted in cooperation with railroad companies, has considered baled refuse, containerized refuse, and open dumping gondolas. Much of this research has been based on the use of transfer stations specially designed to receive refuse from collection vehicles and to transfer it, with or without further processing, to either standard railroad cars, such as gondolas or flatbed cars, or to special cars that can accommodate a container.

Solid waste, both refuse and sludge, is transported by barge in a number of locations in the United States. Refuse barging from transfer station to a landfill area is practiced in New York City, and a number of cities use barges for hauling sludge for sea disposal. Although sea disposal may be banned in the future, barging is still a solid waste management tool that could be of value to seaside municipalities.

Transfer stations can accommodate recycling activities in several ways. With respect to waste delivered by residents of a community, for example, it would be convenient to provide bins for the storage of separated recyclables. The transfer station could also include a bulky waste removal service in its operations. Properly segregated, discarded refrigerators and other white goods can often be sold, and this type of separation could easily be incorporated into a transfer station. Where source separation and separate collection of recyclables are practiced, the transfer station could be used for the consolidation of recyclables and as the pickup point by purchasers of the recyclables or as the loading station for the trucks used to haul the recyclables to the purchasers' facilities.

Processing

Solid waste is processed for a number of reasons, including volume reduction, sanitation, conversion to useful products, and alteration for ease of disposal.

Many disposal processes have been developed, and, as solid waste disposal problems become more acute, new processes will continue to be introduced. The increased demand for solid waste processing, the result of disposal space shortages and of the growing desire to conserve energy and resources, has encouraged "inventors" to develop new ways to use waste. The public works administrator is often the first to learn of a new process that will allegedly solve solid waste disposal problems economically and without damage to health and the environment.

Undoubtedly, new inventions are introduced that live up to the expectations of their developers, and the public works manager should be aware of such developments. However, reliability is one of the most important considerations in selecting a waste-processing system because the heterogeneity of the solid waste affects the materials-handling capability of any solid waste process. The reliability of a solid waste process is often subject to expert interpretation. Therefore, public works managers interested in selecting a solid waste process should obtain the assistance of experienced professionals in evaluating the reliability of processes under consideration.

Two processes that have been used for many years are composting and incineration. Composting—the biochemical degradation of organic materials under controlled conditions to a sanitary, humus-like, nuisance-free material—has been used since time immemorial. Farmers and horticulturalists have been composting leaves, animal manure, decayed fish, and other organic wastes for hundreds if not thousands of years. However, few areas in this country have used composting to convert municipal solid waste to a useful product. In recent years sewage sludge composting has gained in popularity because of the ban on ocean dumping, landfill shortages, and the growth of a limited market for organic soil conditioners. But until such time as a significant demand for the end product is developed, composting must be recognized as a process with limited application in solid waste management.

Incineration has been used in this country for the disposal of solid waste for approximately one hundred years. Incineration is a controlled combustion process designed to reduce the weight and volume of solid waste by the destruction of organic materials. The resulting products are gases, chiefly carbon dioxide, and water vapor, which are discharged into the atmosphere, and a relatively noncombustible residue.

A typical incinerator has a storage pit or tipping area, cranes with buckets or grapples to transfer wastes to a charging hopper, a furnace or combustion chamber, grates of various design to agitate and move the burning materials, and a controlled air supply to regulate combustion and furnace temperatures. Combustion and temperatures may be regulated by the natural draft of a chimney or by forced-draft or induced draft fans. In addition, air pollution control devices must be employed to remove noncombustible particulate matter entrained in the exiting gas stream. A means of residue removal is also necessary.

The development of sophisticated gas-testing equipment coupled with an awareness of the potential danger from the emission of harmful gases has resulted in the establishment of gas quality emission standards in a number of government agencies.[15]

Incineration is available with and without heat recovery (resource recovery) in several major designs (see Figure 15–2). Since the 1970s, mass-burn, modular furnaces in sizes ranging from less than 1 ton/hour to 100 tons/day have become popular. In a short period of time, a number of manufacturers have had enough experience to test the reliability of their designs.

The more traditional mass-burn, custom-designed incinerators have been used successfully to reduce waste volumes and to generate steam since they were introduced in the nineteenth century. They feature continuous feed grates, strokers, and rotary kilns, with and without water wall-boilers and waste heat boilers.

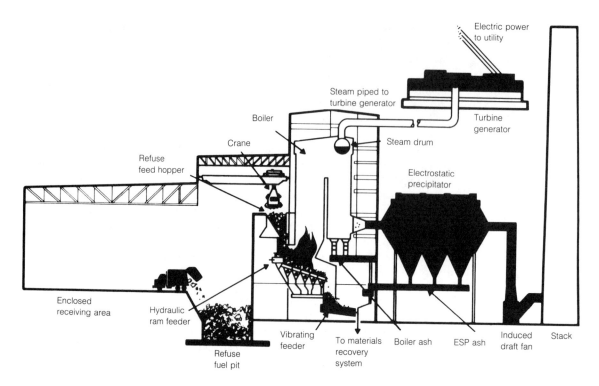

Figure 15–2   Mass burn, waste-to-energy plant, cross-sectional schematic, Baltimore facility.

A third incineration process, the fluidized bed furnace, has been successfully for the incineration of industrial wastes and sludges and has been tested for the incineration of municipal solid waste. The incinerator consists of a bed of sand in a refractory-lined housing. The introduction of heated air through a distribution piping system located at the bottom of the sand bed fluidizes the bed, and when waste is introduced in the bed, it is subjected to the heated sand environment and thus begins to burn. The solids remain in the bed and gradually drop to the bottom, where they can be removed, and the hot gases emerge from the top of the bed for eventual cleaning, utilization, and dispersion into the atmosphere.

Although efforts have been made to generate electricity directly from the hot gases produced in the incineration process, the only successful experience has been to utilize the steam produced from waste-to-energy installations. Cogeneration, the production and use of both steam and electricity, has been effective, however. As for the most efficient use of solid waste as a fuel, steam generation alone will provide the best efficiencies, 55 to 70 percent of heat value; straight electricity generation will normally be quite low, 20 to 35 percent of heat value; and cogeneration may vary between the straight steam and straight electricity efficiencies.

The residue from incineration contains ferrous metals that can easily be removed magnetically for recycling if the markets exist. Efforts have been made to separate and utilize the ash from the residue, but traces of heavy metals have been found in the residue, and many states prohibit the use of this material for any purpose.

In an effort to improve the handling characteristics of solid waste for separation and recycling, waste is shredded using hammer mills, drum pulverizers, crushers, and wet pulverizers. Further improvement for storage purposes is accomplished by pelletizing or briquetting, primarily, the combustible fraction of the waste. The combustible fraction of the waste produced through these processes is the refuse-derived fuel (RDF), which is used to generate steam either as an exclusive fuel in a dedicated boiler or in combination with other fuels, particularly coal in coal-fired boilers.

The shredding process does simplify the process of separating the waste mechanically for future recycling purposes. However, the quality of the separated recyclables has often failed to meet the standards of the secondary materials industry owing to contamination from other wastes. In considering the desirability of utilizing this process for the production of recyclables, it is important to determine the quality of recyclables generated and the market for the product produced.

Pyrolysis is a thermal process in which heat is used without the introduction of oxygen to produce low-sulfur gaseous, liquid, and solid products. Such products might be used as fuels, or possibly as chemical raw materials. Pyrolysis has been tried as a waste-processing procedure. Although useful in some industrial applications, such as the production of charcoal and gas from coal, it has not been successful in the processing of mixed solid waste. It has, however, been used successfully to convert used tires to fuels.

Baling for the purpose of conserving landfill space, reducing transfer costs, and reducing environmental degradation has been in use for some time but has never become popular. Baled waste can be transported economically by truck, train, or barge, and can be disposed of in a specially designed landfill called a balefill. It has all the advantages and flexibility of conventional landfills coupled with a density characteristic that reduces leachate and gas generation, highly desirable environmental features.

Disposal

After source separation, resource recovery, and waste processing have been completed, there is always some waste left that must be disposed of. Solid waste is properly disposed of by sanitary landfilling, which is defined by each state utilizing procedures developed by EPA.[16] Sanitary landfilling is a procedure in which waste is deposited on land, is confined and compacted, and is covered each day with suitable material, generally earth, to resist vector penetration and odors. Equipment is available to excavate, transport, deposit, and spread the earth, and to compact the waste prior to covering. A properly designed and operated sanitary landfill will be located on a site that will not adversely affect ground and surface waters, will be readily accessible to good access roads, and will be acceptable to the public.

The physical properties of a sanitary landfill site to be used for municipal waste are generally defined by state regulatory agencies. The primary factors are proximity to surface waters, floodplains, and marshlands; distance from groundwater and drinking water wells; and the type and quality of the rock formations under the proposed site. The disposal of hazardous waste must meet minimum federal regulations as promulgated under RCRA. Restrictions for hazardous waste are more stringent than those for municipal waste.

Many states require that all new landfills be constructed on impervious liners fabricated of clay with specified permeability or manmade materials such as asphaltic or plastic sheeting. These landfills must be provided with leachate collection systems and gas venting. Surface runoff must be controlled, and leachate treatment or disposal capability must be provided.

The gas generated by the natural decomposition of organic waste in the landfill had been considered both a nuisance and a potential hazard to vegetation and structures. At many landfills, the gas has been collected, treated, and used as a fuel. The gas-generating capability of a landfill can be estimated on the basis of gas samples from test wells and a record of the operations of the landfill. Landfills that have received 1 million or more tons of waste would probably generate enough salable gas to warrant the installation of a gas collection and treatment system.

The major problem associated with sanitary landfills is location. The public has become so conscious of the health and environmental problems associated with the improper disposal of hazardous wastes that there is an immediate adverse reaction to the siting of landfills any place near dwelling areas, recreation facilities, and surface waters. The public reaction to siting landfills and waste-processing facilities generally is, "Not in my backyard" (NIMBY). The "back-yards" seem to extend farther away from dwelling areas with each passing year. Public works managers should involve the community in the site selection process early in the planning period to reduce the NIMBY syndrome.

In 1981, the Japanese National Diet passed the Law of Regional Offshore Environmental Improvement Centers,[17] which permits waste to be disposed of in bodies of water behind shore protection walls. In view of the fact that many shorelines have been altered by filling with solid waste in this country, this may represent a siting opportunity for the future.

Hazardous waste

Subtitle C of the Resource Conservation and Recovery Act of 1976 (RCRA) directs the U.S. Environmental Protection Agency to promulgate regulations establishing a federal hazardous waste management system. In 1980 EPA published regulations that classified hazardous wastes into two main categories: "acutely hazardous" and "other."

Acutely hazardous wastes are those that may "cause or significantly contribute to an increase in serious irreversible or incapacitating reversible illness," regardless of how they are managed. Other hazardous wastes are considered hazardous only because they "pose a substantial present or potential hazard to human health or the environment when improperly managed."

The RCRA reauthorization bill was passed by Congress and signed into law in 1984. RCRA regulations and identification of hazardous wastes are published in the *Federal Register*. The regulations identify wastes that are excluded from the hazardous list, such as household waste, septage (septic tank contents), agricultural wastes, animal wastes (including manures), mining overburden, ash from the burning of fossil fuels, and drilling fluids associated with crude oil, natural gas, and geothermal energy.

The 1984 law changed the designation of the quantity of hazardous waste to be monitored in transport and disposal from 1,000 kilograms/month (2,200 pounds/month) to 100 kilograms/month (220 pounds/month). This change should help to reduce the quantity of hazardous waste in municipal facilities, but it also increases manyfold the responsibility of regulatory agencies to control the transport and disposal of hazardous waste and thereby prevent more illegal dumping. When quantities are relatively low—that is, less than 100 kilograms/month—lead acid batteries discarded by automotive repair shops usually comprise the greatest portion of hazardous waste.

Hazardous wastes can be disposed of by landfilling, lagooning, incineration, chemical processing, and recycling. All of these processes are controlled by state and federal agencies in accordance with RCRA. Furthermore, the 1984 law conveys to the regulated community and the EPA the congressional intent that land disposal be used as a last resort.

Financing

The traditional means of financing solid waste service is to pay for employee salaries and wages and equipment from the annual operating budget and to use general obligation bonds for land acquisition, site preparation, and facility construction. The equipment used for collection, transfer, and landfill can be privately leased rather than purchased from operating funds or can be purchased from capital funds.

From the mid-1970s on, however, the traditional financing methods have been augmented by other methods to offset the problems of inflation, which has escalated the capital cost of process and disposal facilities, restrictive environmental regulations, and the high cost of borrowing because of fluctuating interest rates. Some cities and counties have established public authorities to exploit the low-interest borrowing available through municipal bonds while drawing on the vehicle maintenance and replacement experience in private industry. Other agencies have explored contract collection, user fees, comparative pricing, and other approaches.

The collection service, as has been noted, can be provided by franchised contract collectors who charge the customer directly for the collection service performed. It is also common for municipalities to employ user fees for collection and disposal services.

The relations between private and public service and the potential to reduce costs by switching from one type of service to another are recognized. Some municipalities such as Kansas City, Missouri, and Pittsburgh, Pennsylvania, operate private and public collection services simultaneously in an effort to maintain a healthy competitive relationship.

The Phoenix public works department has used another technique to produce competition between the municipal and private sectors.[18] The Phoenix approach to landfill contracting incorporates a number of management techniques that have value individually and, when combined, produce what appears to be a most cost-effective process. The technique consists of a bid procedure that permits the city's own operations department to submit a bid, an operations aspect that rewards high-density compaction or landfill life extension, and a "penalty equation" that enables the city to charge the contractor for failure to meet obligations.

Private funds are available for the construction and operation of facilities, including waste-processing facilities, through a procedure called "privatization," which involves private-sector financing, ownership, and operation, and public-sector regulation of major infrastructure facilities including resource recovery plants. The private sector's investment is protected by contracts in which the municipality agrees to a "put or pay" tipping fee[19] for the waste disposal service provided. It is also common to provide a return to the municipality for income realized from the sale of energy.

Conclusion

This chapter has reviewed evolving concepts of solid waste service and has covered the principal steps of storage, collection, transfer, process, and disposal. Looking ahead, the public works director, the manager of the solid waste service, the planning director, the budget officer, the finance director, and others involved in long-range financial planning should be anticipating three elements that are likely to profoundly affect the service during the 1980s and 1990s: long-range planning, hazardous wastes, and NIMBY.

The first step, if it has not already been done, is to develop a ten-year solid waste plan to cover purchase and amortization of motor equipment, wage and salary costs, projected streets and highways, and other cost and service elements. The plan should be flexible so that it can easily be altered as conditions change and should be reviewed and updated at least once a year.

Second, hazardous wastes should be monitored constantly. This involves keeping track of not only the technical and legal aspects but also the economic and social aspects of change. For example, most local governments seek new factories and other industrial employers, but the primary and secondary effects may include hazardous wastes with litigious and costly effects. State and federal oversight is likely. Costs versus benefits need to be measured.

Finally, the not-in-my-backyard (NIMBY) syndrome has to be anticipated. The NIMBY acronym is not intended to be sarcastic. People are much more concerned about and involved in their homes, immediate neighborhoods, and adjacent surroundings than they were a generation ago. The public works director and the solid waste manager know that somewhere, sometime, a landfill site may have to be designated; citizen involvement, public hearings, and other steps can make the process much more workable. In the last two decades, the state highway departments have learned a great deal about public involvement in public decision making; much can be learned from their experience.

1 Herbert I. Hollander, ed., *Thesaurus on Resource Recovery Terminology*, American Society for Testing and Materials, Special Publication 832 (Philadelphia: American Society for Testing and Materials, 1983), p. 85.

2 Sam Bass Warner, Jr., *The Private City: Philadelphia in Three Periods of Its Growth* (Philadelphia: University of Philadelphia Press, 1968), p. 75.

3 Bureau of Municipal Research, *Municipal Street Cleaning in Philadelphia* (Philadelphia, 1924), p. 10.

4 Ibid., p. 32.

5 Philadelphia Home Rule Charter, Par. 5-500 (2) (C).

6 Hollander, ed., *Thesaurus*, p. 74.

7 Ibid., p. 71.

8 Ibid., p. 33.

9 Ibid., p. 88.

10 Institute for Solid Wastes, *Refuse Collection Practice*, 3d ed. (Chicago: American Public Works Association, 1966), p. 49.

11 *Code of Federal Regulations*, Title 40, Protection of Environment, Chapter 1, EPA, Part 243, "Guidelines for the Storage and Collection of Residential, Commercial and Institutional Solid Waste" (Washington, D.C.: Government Printing Office, July 1984).

12 Ibid.

13 Ibid., p. 275.

14 United States, Department of Health and Human Services, Public Health Service, C.D.C., NIOSH, *Residential Waste Collection: Hazard Recognition and Prevention* (Washington, D.C.: Government Printing Office, 1982), p. 1.

15 For authoritative information on the subject of gas emissions from incineration, see Edward T. Wei, *Resource Recovery Facilities, Air Pollution and Public Health Safety* (Berkeley, Calif.: University of California, School of Public Health, 1984).

16 Code of Federal Regulations, Title 40, Chapter 1, EPA, Part 241, "Guidelines for the Land Disposal of Solid Wastes" (Washington, D.C.: Government Printing Office, July 1984).

17 Katsumi Yamamura, "Current Status of Waste Management in Japan," in *Proceedings, International Solid Wastes and Public Cleansing Association Congress* (Philadelphia: Institute of Solid Waste, American Public Works Association, September 1984), p. 1.

18 "Entrepreneurs Can Do Everything Government Can Do, Only Better. Or Can They?" *INC.*, December 1984, pp. 169–74.

19 "Put or pay" is a contractual term for the requirement that the city or county guarantee a certain quantity of solid waste. If the local government fails to deliver the guaranteed quantity, it still must pay for the guaranteed amount.

16 Air quality control

Air pollution—these words have an immediate negative connotation. However, probably very few people can define what they mean by air pollution. Some believe that cigarette smoke is air pollution, and others associate it with acid rain or smoke from an industrial plant. For the purposes of this discussion, air pollution can be considered "any constituent in the atmosphere that is harmful to man or the environment." Of course, this would include natural sources of air pollution such as volcanoes or forest fires, but these are not normally under the control of the public works official. This chapter focuses on man-made sources of air pollutants, specifically those that affect outdoor air. Air pollution in the workplace is not discussed, even though this can be a very serious problem, nor is the issue of municipal or state legislation to prohibit smoking in public places, which is also important but is not normally handled by the public works department.

The types of air pollution a public works official has to deal with are found mostly in urban areas and usually in areas of heavy industrial concentration and heavy automobile traffic. In the United States, these types of air pollution come under the authority of the federal Clean Air Act, which defines the roles of various levels of government in identifying and controlling air pollution. The act places considerable responsibility for identifying and removing air pollutants on state and local officials. This chapter therefore reviews the process for determining which constituents are hazardous to health and the role of cost-benefit analysis in identifying pollutants and establishing the appropriate standard. A number of pollutants are described that already have standards established. The sources of the designated pollutants and the major regulatory processes for control are also discussed.

Although most regulations deal with stationary sources such as smokestacks, the mandated planning processes focus on nonstationary sources such as the automobile. It is in these planning processes that the public works official is most likely to become involved. The two types of plans are designed to address areas with existing pollution problems or areas that are at present clean but may be facing new sources. Both planning efforts are described.

It should be noted at the outset that air quality control is a specialized activity. Most states have established entire departments and commissions for the sole purpose of protecting air quality. The local public works official must work with these state and federal personnel who may not recognize the multiple concerns at the local level. It is hoped that this chapter can assist the local person in working with such air quality officials.

Standard setting

Before the federal Clean Air Act was passed in 1972, the adoption of air quality standards was the responsibility of the states. Now the standards set in Washington must be used in every state, unless more stringent values are adopted by a state. Because the results of a standard can have a major impact on a local community, the public works official must have a general understanding of the process involved in establishing the standard. In fact, the local official can directly affect the standard-setting process at a number of points, either at public hearings or in technical committees.

Section 109 of the Clean Air Act gives the administrator of the U.S. Environmental Protection Agency (EPA) broad powers to set national air quality standards for pollutants that are widely dispersed and emitted by large numbers of sources. Referred to as the National Ambient Air Quality Standards (NAAQS), these values are meant to protect both public health and public welfare. Because the act does not specify the meaning of "public health," it falls on the EPA administrator to define the aspects of health that are to be considered in setting a national standard. To carry out that responsibility, EPA has prepared a "criteria document" for each pollutant designated to date.

The criteria document contains a detailed analysis of the current scientific data relating to the health effects of the pollutant. To assist EPA in evaluating this information, Congress has created a Scientific Advisory Committee, a seven-member group that includes one member of the National Academy of Sciences, one physician, and one state air quality administrator. Once the document has been reviewed by the committee, it is made available to the general public for comment. If a local community is concerned about its air quality or about the potential effects of a national standard on the community, it is essential that someone in that community obtain the criteria document and provide comments to EPA.

To date, NAAQS have been established for carbon monoxide, ozone, sulfur dioxide, total suspended particulates, hydrocarbons, nitrogen dioxide, and lead. The first six were required by the act in 1972; lead was regulated as the result of a lawsuit brought by the Natural Resources Defense Council in 1975.[1] Each of these standards must be reviewed every five years, at which time a new criteria document is prepared. This provides another opportunity for the local community to review and comment on national standards.

Each of these pollutants is unique and requires different methods for measuring and setting the standard. For example, carbon monoxide has both a one-hour standard and an eight-hour standard. These might be labeled short-term and long-term exposure levels, although eight hours may not be a very long time. Total suspended particulates have an annual average standard and a one-hour standard. Ozone has a one-hour standard but no long-term value, whereas nitrogen dioxide has a long-term standard but no short-term value has been set. Figure 16–1 provides the standards in effect at the time of this printing. State health departments monitor these priority pollutants regularly and can provide local officials with information on their communities.

Why have these seven been designated pollutants? A brief review of their health effects will explain the national concern. In extreme cases, any of these pollutants can cause death.[2] Carbon monoxide from automobile exhausts has frequently been the cause of death or serious injury.

Although the NAAQS have been set well below the levels that caused these incidents, each of the seven pollutants is capable of causing physical harm. Carbon monoxide reacts with the blood to prevent oxygen from reaching vital organs. It can, therefore, impair heart functions, especially in those already suffering from heart disease. It can reduce mental alertness and may alter the body's defenses, leaving the body more susceptible to infection. It is particularly dangerous to those already vulnerable—children, the elderly, those suffering from heart and lung disease, pregnant women, and fetuses.

Nitrogen dioxide also irritates the lungs and other mucous membranes. In so doing it reduces the body's resistance to respiratory infections. Ozone, which is formed when nitrogen dioxide and hydrocarbons react with sunlight, also affects the respiratory tract and irritates the eyes. It can cause structural and chemical changes in the lungs and some alterations of blood components.

Figure 16-1 National
ambient air quality
standards.

Pollutant	Averaging time	Standard
Carbon monoxide	1-hour[1]	35 ppm[2]
	8-hour[1]	9 ppm
Ozone	1-hour[1]	0.12 ppm
Nitrogen dioxide	Annual	0.05 ppm
Sulfur dioxide	Annual	0.03 ppm
	24-hour[1]	0.14 ppm
	3-hour[1]	0.50 ppm
Total suspended particulates	Annual	75 μg/cu m[3]
	24-hour	260 μg/cu m
Hydrocarbons	3-hour	160 μg/cu m
Lead	Quarter	1.5 μg/cu m

1   Not to be exceeded more than once per year.
2   ppm—parts per million.
3   μg/cu m—micrograms per cubic meter. (These particulate standards are currently under revision.)

Total suspended particulates are small solid or liquid particles that can enter the respiratory tract. Larger particles can cause constriction of the airways and production of increased or thickened mucus. Smaller particles may enter the lungs and damage the oxygen transfer capability. Recent research has suggested that some types of particulates may cause lung cancer. Lead is a particulate that can enter the bloodstream through the lungs. It is especially hazardous to children, who may develop brain damage after exposure.

In the criteria documents, EPA reviews the scientific information and determines an appropriate standard. The act requires that the standard provide an adequate margin of safety to protect public health, but considerable controversy surrounds the determination of this "adequate" margin of safety. EPA is attempting to utilize modern risk assessment techniques in setting standards. Risk assessment involves establishing the probabilities of various outcomes on the basis of the available scientific evidence. Although not yet a universally accepted procedure, risk assessment may remove some of the more subjective elements of standard setting.

Cost-benefit analysis is also involved in the standard-setting process. Although the act does not allow EPA to consider the economic impacts on pollutant sources when setting a standard, EPA has been including an assessment of the economic impact of the proposed standard in its regulatory analysis. In some communities this may be a major impact. For example, because of the present lead standards some smelting operations have not found it economical to improve their facilities and instead have closed their smelters. For a small mining community this could mean economic disaster. Under the current act, however, the health effects alone determine the standard and economic considerations are not to be taken into account.

Another important point to note regarding standard-setting procedures is that prior to the federal act, a number of states were already establishing air quality standards. Under the Clean Air Act, these state standards are recognized only if they are more stringent than the federally established value. California is probably the most active state in setting independent standards. One example is its high-altitude carbon monoxide standard. Carbon monoxide is more hazardous at high altitudes since there is less oxygen in the ambient air. California has set a one-hour standard of 6.0 parts per million for high-altitude areas, which is one-third more stringent than the national standard. Local officials should be aware of state-established standards and should also recognize that state legislation may be available to deal with unique local pollution problems.

Sources of emissions

The air pollutants described in the previous section can be traced to a number of sources. These sources can be classified into three large groups: stationary, mobile, and area sources. This section provides a general overview of these classes and their particular effects on air quality.

Stationary sources are defined in the Clean Air Act (Sec. 111[a][3]) as "any building, structure, facility, or installation which emits or may emit any air pollutant." This is a very broad definition, but in practice stationary sources are taken to be major industrial and commercial facilities that emit specific pollutants, either as part of fuel combustion or as part of a manufacturing process. Examples of the first case include electric generating stations that burn fuel oil, coal, or natural gas; solid waste incinerators; and space heating of large industrial buildings. Process emissions may include hydrocarbons from dry cleaning establishments, lead and other particulates from metal smelters, and dust from mining activities. Industrial sources are major contributors of sulfur dioxide, nitrogen dioxide, hydrocarbons, and particulates. They contribute a limited amount of carbon monoxide to the atmosphere.

The amount of pollutant emitted by a particular stationary source can vary depending on the age of the facility, the type of process or boiler used, or the application of various control techniques. A good example of these variables can be found in steel-making furnaces. Older open-hearth furnaces are a significant source of sulfur oxides and particulates. Newer open-hearth furnaces can reduce these emissions through better fuel utilization and emission control devices such as baghouses. (A baghouse is a building containing a large fabric "bag." Air from the furnace is filtered through the bag to remove particulates and gases.) In addition, modern electric furnaces have changed the manufacturing process so that much less pollution is generated.

Mobile sources of air pollution tend to be the major source in areas where manufacturing activity is limited or where stationary sources have implemented significant control measures. The gasoline-powered automobile, the most obvious mobile source, emits carbon monoxide and hydrocarbons. But there are a number of other mobile sources. Diesel-powered automobiles, trucks, and buses do not add much carbon monoxide to the atmosphere but do contribute nitrogen dioxides and particulates. Rail activities usually rely on diesel fuel and can be a major source in a limited area. Airport operations contribute heavily to air pollution, although their impact is usually limited to the vicinity of the airport. Restrictions on newer aircraft, which are being required to reduce the emissions from their engines, should help reduce airport pollution.

Restrictions are also being imposed on direct emissions from other mobile sources. The controls on automobile manufacturers are discussed in more detail later, but it should be noted that both gasoline and diesel engines are becoming cleaner as a result of such changes. The continued improvement in emission levels will, in many cases, prevent future violations of the standards.

The last group of emission sources are called area sources since they are distributed widely across an area. As individual units, they may produce little effect, but, when concentrated, they can cause air quality violations. Space heating of residential areas is one of the most common area sources. The burning of natural gas in home heating contributes carbon monoxide and hydrocarbons. If coal or fuel oil is the home heating fuel, the emissions will also include sulfur oxides and particulates. And, as wood becomes a more frequent choice for home heating, wood smoke will add increasing amounts of particulates to the atmosphere. In fact, in some areas such as mountain communities wood smoke is the reason that air quality standards (usually particulates) are violated.

Other area sources of particulates include street salting and sanding, individual burning of solid waste, other incineration facilities, and dust from construction activities. Evaporative losses from petrochemical service operations (gas stations, fuel oil delivery, etc.) can be a hydrocarbon source. As a result, a number of areas have placed controls both on the delivery of gasoline to gas stations and on the pumps that are used to fill the automobile gas tanks. In areas with extreme carbon monoxide or ozone problems, some consideration has even been given to regulating area sources such as lawn mowers.

Air quality data needs

If a community or region has an air quality problem or anticipates a problem in the future, local officials will need certain information to deal with the situation. Three types of information are most important to good air quality planning: background air quality information; an emissions inventory that helps define the sources of pollution already present in the community; and meteorological information that defines how those emissions interact in the atmosphere. This section explains the importance of this information and summarizes the methods used to gather it.

Air quality information

Without adequate data on the existing air quality in a community, it is impossible to evaluate the need for controls or to predict future air quality.

Because the entire decision-making process relative to air quality is directly affected by this determination, it is important that the planner use air quality data that is the most accurate, complete, and representative information available. In most cases, state air pollution control agencies have operational air quality monitoring systems and have been collecting air quality data for the past few years. Where this is not the case, or where such data are judged not to be consistent with the requirements of the planning decisions, it may be necessary to seek the services of an air pollution specialist with air quality monitoring capabilities.[3]

For a small region, data collected by the state may not be adequate since the state may not have sampled a sufficient number of locations or may not have collected data frequently enough. In such circumstances, the community may need to establish its own monitoring system. EPA provides guidelines for establishing such systems for each of the major pollutants in their regulations (40 CFR 53). Regional EPA offices, as well as the state air pollution control agency, can assist local governments in setting up a monitoring network.

Emission inventory

The second important data collection effort is an emission inventory, which identifies the major and minor sources of emissions within the community. The stationary source inventory is probably the easiest to complete, although for a large region there may be hundreds of stationary sources. Again, EPA has provided guidelines for such inventories (40 CFR 51). These guidelines list major stationary sources by industry type. The following list, for example, has been compiled for food and agricultural industries:

Alfalfa dehydrating

Ammonium nitrate

Coffee roasting

Cotton ginning

Feed and grain

The pollution standards index   In many metropolitan areas, the air quality agency provides the media with a "pollution standards index," or PSI, that may appear in the newspaper or on the television news. This index is intended to give the general public an indicator of the air quality for that day. An example of the PSI graphic for the Denver metropolitan area is shown below:

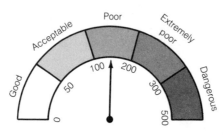

The PSI is divided into five air quality categories—good, acceptable, poor, extremely poor, and dangerous. An index number is calculated based on the values of the various pollutants monitored in the community. The value reported to the public is usually that of the worst pollutant that day. In Denver,

values have been calculated for carbon monoxide, ozone, particulates, and sulfur dioxide. However, the index may be based on different pollutants in other years or other communities.

One hundred on the index represents the primary ambient air quality standard set by the U.S. Environmental Protection Agency. Therefore, a PSI greater than 100 indicated that the standard has been violated. Air pollution alerts, which inform the public that persons most susceptible to the particular pollutant should avoid outside air, are called when the index reaches 200, or extremely poor. Values of over 300 will trigger the implementation of an emergency plan. This plan grants the governor the power to shut down industries and close other offices on a staggered schedule.

Source: Based on *PSI . . . What It Is, How It Works, What It Means for You* (Denver: Air Pollution Control Division, Colorado Department of Health, January 1982).

Fermentation processes

Fertilizers

Fish/meat processing

Meat smoke houses

Starch manufacturing

Sugarcane processing (40 CFR 51, Appendix C).

For each industrial facility, the inventory should determine the location of various emission points such as smokestacks, vents, or engine exhausts; the types of manufacturing processes used; the heating fuels and other chemicals used; the operating schedule; and the existing air pollution controls in place. Since most major sources are already regulated by the state agency, this information should have been collected by that agency. If that is the case, the agency will also have determined the tons per year or per day of each pollutant emitted by that source. If the state has not made such an estimate, the local agency can estimate the emissions from standard rate tables for the industry or processes involved.

To inventory the emissions from mobile sources, a community must have information on the composition of the vehicle fleet, that is, the types of vehicles and their ages. These data can be obtained from the state department of motor vehicle registrations. Emission rates for various types and ages of vehicles are available from EPA or the state air pollution control agency. The local transportation planning agency or state highway department can provide the other needed information: the average vehicle miles of travel per day in the community. Since automobile emission rates are generally given in grams per mile or a similar unit, the rate times the daily travel will yield a daily emission total.

Emissions from area sources are probably the most difficult to estimate since it is impossible to measure all of the individual units. However, the inventory can separate the various area sources and provide a general estimate of the number and emission rate of each type. For example, an estimate of the number of housing units in the community can provide the basis for estimating the emissions from home heating. Sources such as the U.S. Census can provide a starting point for determining the number of homes using various kinds of home heating fuels. Local data-gathering efforts can then be tailored to the specific types of housing and fuels found in that community. The rate of emissions from a single home for a given fuel is available in many air pollution reports. A similar process can be used for other area sources such as gas stations, dry cleaning establishments, and degreasing operations.

Meteorological information

Finally, meteorological information is needed since the actual air quality depends not only on the volume of pollutants released into the air but also on weather conditions. For example, a single automobile idling in a closed garage can produce sufficient carbon monoxide concentrations to cause death. However, millions of automobiles can be driving throughout a region, and the mixing of the carbon monoxide in the air can keep concentrations well below the dangerous level. If the air is stable and there is little mixing, however, the same number of automobiles, driving the same number of miles, can produce unhealthy levels of carbon monoxide. Therefore, it is important for the person concerned with air pollution to have some knowledge of local weather conditions.

Four meteorological variables are necessary to describe the mixture of pollutants in the atmosphere: wind direction, wind speed, atmospheric stability, and mixing height.

Wind direction determines the general direction of pollutant transport. Wind speed determines the amount of initial dilution of the pollutants and also the height to which the plume rises. Atmospheric stability is a measure of turbulence, which in turn determines the rate at which the effluent is dispersed as it is transported by the wind. Mixing height is the vertical depth of the atmosphere through which pollutants can be dispersed.[4]

Ozone, because it is a product of hydrocarbons and nitrogen oxides reacting with sunlight, is also affected by the amount of solar radiation.

The effect of wind direction and speed on air pollutants is straightforward, but the concept of atmospheric stability needs further explanation. If the pollution problem under consideration is the impact of a particular stationary source, say a power plant, atmospheric stability may refer to the amount of turbulence in the vicinity of the plant. If the area downwind of the plant is flat, with very few buildings or trees to break up the wind patterns, the pollution from the plant will form a "plume" with relatively little dispersion (see Figure 16–2). If the area contains hills and valleys, or is greatly built up with high-rise structures, the wind patterns should create a dispersed "plume." This would be described as a very unstable atmospheric pattern.

At the regional level, atmospheric stability is usually related to the concept of the "inversion layer." Under normal conditions, atmospheric temperature decreases with altitude. At times, however, a layer of warmer air may develop over a layer of cooler air and trap the cooler air at the surface. This phenomenon, which is known as inversion, arises from two types of conditions.

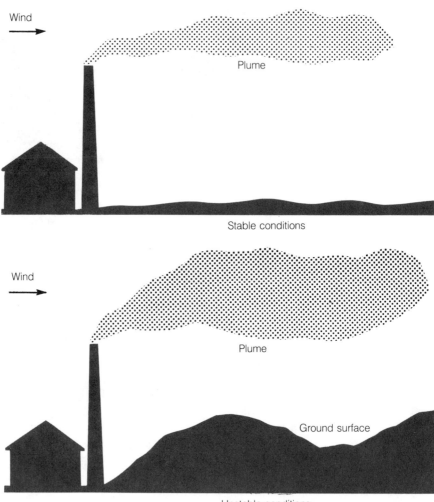

Figure 16–2   The plume
from a pollution
source is affected
by atmospheric
stability.

"The strong inversions typical of West Coast summers are caused by downward vertical motion called subsidence which compresses and heats the air."[5] The other condition occurs in winter as air at the surface becomes cooled when in contact with the earth's cold surface. The inversion remains in place until solar heating can cause the temperature of the surface air to rise to a level sufficient to "break" the inversion. If daytime temperatures do not reach adequate levels, the inversion can remain in place for a number of days. During that time, the mixing height remains very low and pollutants are trapped at the surface.

In order to understand the local air pollution situation, the local official needs to have a good understanding of the local weather pattern. The local weather department will probably have detailed information on wind speed and direction.

Data on atmospheric stability may not be as readily available since temperature at different altitudes must be measured by weather balloons or other difficult methods. It is known, however, that inversion layers are associated with certain topographic features. Urban areas in deep valleys tend to have frequent inversions because the coldest air sinks into the lowest part of the valley (see Figure 16–3).

The hills around Los Angeles or around San Francisco Bay, the mountains around Denver, and the Appalachian valleys all play a role in the air pollution episodes common in these areas. If local officials are aware of the relationship

Figure 16–3 Wind patterns in valley areas.

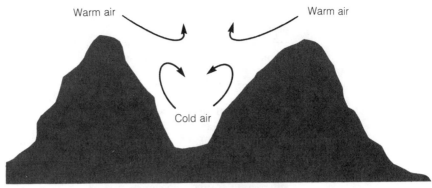

Atmospheric inversion

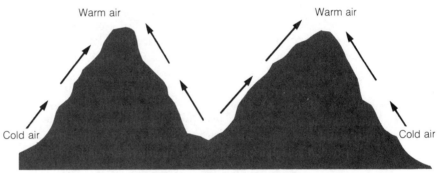

Normal daytime airflow out of valleys

between topography and inversion they will be able to tell whether this factor is a dominant cause of poor air quality in an area.

The details presented in this section concerning existing air quality, emission inventories, and meteorological conditions represent the basic information needed to deal with air pollution problems. These problems are dealt with in the context of a federal regulatory program that addresses pollution directly at the source and through control of the distribution of those sources both in a region and between regions.

Regulatory programs

As mentioned earlier, the Clean Air Act establishes the air quality program for the United States. The national standards are adopted in Washington and are implemented throughout the country through a two-part regulatory program.

The first part regulates the amount of pollutant that can be released by the various sources. The second part oversees the development of plans that ensure that clean air areas remain within the standards and that areas not achieving the standards implement a program to reach them. This section describes the roles of the various levels of government in regulating the sources themselves.

The National Commission on Air Quality summarized the regulatory process as follows:

Congress establishes national policy.

The Environmental Protection Agency conducts research, sets ambient and certain emissions standards, develops guidelines and adopts regulations for achieving and maintaining ambient standards, disburses funds, approves and oversees the carrying out of state implementation plans, and enforces the Act's requirements.

States develop, adopt, and enforce control strategies for achieving and maintaining ambient standards and incorporate those measures into their state implementation plans.

Local governments may develop and enforce control strategies for stationary and mobile sources within their jurisdictions.[6]

For stationary sources, EPA fulfills its regulatory responsibilities by establishing "new source performance standards" for each major industrial group. Two levels of standards have been set that the states can require in the appropriate circumstances. The first level consists of reasonably available control measures that EPA considers technologically feasible and not unreasonably expensive for the affected industry to implement. These controls are detailed descriptions of measures that can be designed into a new plant or added onto an existing source. The measures are industry specific; for example, EPA has described reasonably available control measures for twenty-five categories of hydrocarbon-emitting industrial facilities.

EPA has also set forth control regulations that mark the limit of currently known technology. These controls are known as lowest achievable emission rates and are usually required only in areas that cannot meet the NAAQS. These controls do not take into account the economic impact on the facility, since without this level of control the facility would not even be allowed to operate.

Mobile sources are also regulated by EPA, which sets allowable emissions from various classes of vehicles. The act restricts the motor vehicle pollutants for which EPA can set limits to carbon monoxide, hydrocarbons, oxides of nitrogen, and particulates. Standards are to be set for both light- and heavy-duty diesel and gasoline engines. According to the Clean Air Act, the levels set are to

. . . reflect the greatest degree of emission reduction achievable through the application of technology which the Administrator determines will be available for the model year to which such standards apply, giving appropriate consideration to the cost of applying such technology within the period of time available to manufacturers and to noise, energy, and safety factors associated with the application of such technology (Sec. 202[a][3][A][i]).

The establishment of mobile source standards in the program known as the Federal Motor Vehicle Emissions Control Program has been one of the most controversial elements of the air quality program. Automakers have been concerned about the cost of control equipment and about their ability to develop the technologies needed to meet the limits. At the same time, environmental quality groups have worried that EPA will not set the limits low enough to protect public health. Issues such as high-altitude controls and fleet-versus-model averages have been debated since the Clean Air Act was passed. Standards for some engine types are still in the process of being adopted by EPA, which means it will be a number of years before models meeting the standard are on the road.

The state role in this regulatory process consists of both additional standard setting and enforcement activity. The only state that is allowed to regulate mobile source emissions is California, which had such standards prior to adoption of the federal act. California continues to have different automobile standards than the remainder of the United States, although other states can adopt the California standard if they believe it would better serve their needs.

The regulation of stationary sources is the major function of the state air pollution control agencies. State statutes allow the agency either to match the federal emission limits or to set even stricter limits. The agency can then develop control technologies (working with industry scientists), negotiate individual permits, and conduct surveillance of the pollution sources. Enforcement involves taking legal or administrative actions against sources that exceed allowable emissions limits, do not use adequate control measures, fail to implement controls, or use controls improperly. State agencies can carry out all of these activities, although the level of involvement varies from state to state.

Local agencies can be involved in the same types of air pollution control activities, depending on the delegation of authority from the state. In California, for example, the state has delegated almost all enforcement powers to regional air quality control boards. Such boards can deal with the special sources and problems of their regions. However, in most states, the powers of local agencies are much more limited. Local health departments may carry out inspection and enforcement actions, but the control regulations and permits are set by the state. A special local situation, such as outdoor trash burning, may be regulated through the city or county. Transportation control measures, discussed in more detail below, are one area in which the control is primarily at the city or county level.

Planning for improved air quality is a special function defined by the act as a state activity with a specific requirement for local participation. This provision (Section 121) was added to the act in 1977 because local government was not being consulted or involved in the air quality process prior to that date. Each state is now required to develop a mechanism for local participation in the development of the state implementation plan. In most cases, this involvement takes place through a council of governments or other regional agency. The following sections describe the two major elements of the state implementation plan—(1) dealing with nonattainment areas and (2) the prevention of significant deterioration—and the roles of state and local governments in these elements.

Nonattainment area plans

The Clean Air Act divides the nation into two types of areas: those that meet the national standards and those that do not, called nonattainment areas. In the nonattainment areas, states are required to develop plans that will result in attainment by certain deadlines. These nonattainment area plans are likely to have a significant impact on local governments and on public works departments.

Nonattainment areas are defined through ambient air monitoring programs. If an area is already failing to meet any one of the NAAQS, it is or will be classified as a nonattainment area. The limits of the nonattainment area are intended to encompass not only the area actually exceeding the standard but also the area that contains the sources causing the violations. For example, carbon monoxide violations tend to occur in areas of intense traffic congestion, especially central cities, but the nonattainment area for carbon monoxide is usually defined as the entire metropolitan commuting area, since this is the area that generates the traffic in the central city.

The nonattainment area is defined for each pollutant so that a community may be listed as attaining some standards but may be in nonattainment for others. The state implementation plan will define the nonattainment areas for each pollutant. Nationally, ozone problems account for the largest number of nonattainment counties. More than 500 counties, including the entire northeastern United States and most of the West Coast, were unable to attain the ozone standard.[7] At the other end of the scale, nitrogen dioxide nonattainment areas were limited to seven counties (Chicago, Denver, and five counties in southern California). The plan for each area must therefore be directed to the specific pollutants of concern to that area.

The basic information described earlier in this chapter must be gathered for the nonattainment area. The emission inventory, the ambient data, and the meteorological information will all be used to determine the maximum amount of pollutants the area's air system can handle without exceeding the standards. A model is usually used in the analysis to predict the air quality of the area

Control of smoke from residential wood burning   One source of air pollution—residential wood burning—has been almost exclusively under the control of local jurisdictions. There are no federal standards for wood stoves or fireplaces and, until recently, no state regulations. Therefore, communities where wood smoke is a major cause of air pollution must deal with it directly.

Since the energy crisis of the early 1970s, the use of wood and sometimes coal as home heating fuels has increased dramatically. Between 1977 and 1980, it has been estimated that the percentage of households in Colorado using firewood increased from 36 to 49 percent. The increase in total cords of firewood burned was even greater, from 568,200 cords to 913,500 cords. Similar increases have occurred in other areas, especially where fuel is readily available, and many of these communities have noticed significant declines in air quality.

The most obvious declines have been reported from communities in mountain valleys where both large numbers of stoves and fireplaces are used and meteorological conditions are likely to concentrate the smoke in the valley. Such conditions can occur in small towns such as Aspen, Colorado; medium-sized towns such as Missoula, Montana; or large cities such as Denver. Because the sources of air pollution are so complex in large cities, it has been the smaller communities that have dealt most directly with wood burning.

There are essentially three ways to reduce wood smoke problems: (1) improve the emissions from wood-burning units; (2) improve the knowledge of the wood stove owner, and (3) control the number or use of wood-burning units. The control of emissions has been both a state and a local issue. As of 1985, two states (Colorado and Oregon) and a number of cities and counties had adopted performance standards for wood stoves and fireplace inserts. These usually required the use of catalytic converters or secondary combustion zones. A secondary combustion zone has sufficiently high temperatures to cause combustion of the unburned particles and gases.

Even the best-built stove will emit large amounts of smoke if improperly used and maintained. The second approach to reducing wood-burning emissions is operator education. Such education programs stress the use of proper fuels; the importance of using dry, seasoned wood; proper loading of the stove; and control of air inlets. Many areas have used cable television and informational brochures to reach owner-operators. In Colorado, the wood stove dealers have helped develop and distribute such a brochure.

In many cases the control of performance standards and the education of owners are insufficient to protect health

under different conditions. Air quality models can be very complex representations of the area's physical and meteorological features or a very simple mathematical formula.

The simplest model currently accepted by EPA is called the "rollback" model. Data from the emissions inventory are used to develop a historical relation between the amount of emissions and the resulting levels in the air. For example, 150 tons of carbon monoxide emitted into the air from all sources may result in a level of 15 parts per million in the atmosphere. At another time, 120 tons may have produced 12 parts per million. The rollback model would then predict that the level in the air would drop 1 part per million for every 10-ton reduction in emissions. Although the rollback model is accepted by EPA for planning, it ignores many of the mechanisms at work in the atmosphere. Its use should be standards. Some approaches to the control of wood burning are described below:

In some areas of Sweden, no wood-burning appliances are allowed in any building located within 25 meters of a house, because of concern with smoke downwash.

Since 1976, Telluride, Colorado, has limited fireplaces and wood stoves in new buildings to one per building.

Vail, Colorado, limits the number of fire-places that may be installed by residential unit.

In Crested Butte, Colorado, only one wood-burning device is allowed per building and that is allowed only if the building is extremely well insulated (i.e., the city regulates the type of building in which wood burning is allowed).

In Jackson County, Oregon, all homes with wood heaters must be weatherized and must undergo energy audits. Stove use is prohibited on days when health standards are violated, unless there is no back-up heat source.

In Missoula, Montana, when certain pollution levels are reached, wood burning is prohibited and failure to comply results in warnings and fines.

In Reno, Nevada, when inversions combine with high pollution levels, the 75 percent of the residents who burn wood will be asked not to do so.

One of the most elaborate control programs has been instituted by the Beaver Creek Ski Area in Colorado. A Forest Service permit to operate the ski area limits the number of fireplaces allowed in the Beaver Creek Valley. In addition, an extensive monitoring system has been installed to anticipate high pollution periods. Every fireplace or stove is equipped with a warning light and a heat sensor. In the event of high pollution, the warning light will alert the resident to douse the fire. The heat sensor will allow the ski area to monitor compliance and, if the fire is not doused within a reasonable time, the fire department can enter the residence to put it out.

Such elaborate controls are probably necessary only in a few valleys with poor natural air circulation. However, if wood becomes more common as a home heating fuel, other communities may be faced with developing some kind of controls for wood stoves and fireplaces.

Source: Derived, in part, from *A Recommended Program for Colorado Leading to a Regulatory Position on Air Pollution Control from Residential Wood and Coal Combustion: Report to the Colorado Air Quality Control Commission* (Denver: Advisory Committee on Residential Wood and Coal Combustion, 27 January 1983).

---

limited to generalizations about a region, and its calibration should be based on data from days of similar weather conditions.

Once a model has been selected and calibrated, the nonattainment area must identify control measures that will reduce emissions to the level of the national standard and that can maintain them there. It is at this point that the involvement of local officials is most important. Although the collection of background data and the calibration of a model can be carried out by air quality technicians, the preparation of a control strategy must involve the region's public and private policymakers. Because the control strategy is likely to contain elements that will affect the general citizens and specific interest groups, their representatives should participate in the selection process.

In most nonattainment areas, the process has been coordinated by the local

Figure 16–4   Potential air pollution control measures.

Transportation systems management actions
1. Improved public transit
2. Exclusive bus and carpool lanes and areawide carpool programs
3. Private car restrictions
4. Long range transit improvements
5. On-street parking controls
6. Park and ride fringe parking lots
7. Pedestrian malls
8. Employer programs to encourage carpooling and vanpooling, mass transit, bicycling, and walking
9. Bicycle lanes and storage facilities
10. Staggered work hours (flexitime)
11. Road pricing to discourage single-occupancy auto trips
12. Controls on extended vehicle idling
13. Traffic flow improvements

Direct automotive emissions controls
14. Inspection/maintenance programs (AIR)
15. Control of vapor emissions from fuel transfer and storage and operations using solvents (vapor recovery)
16. Alternative fuels or engines, and other fleet vehicle controls
17. Retrofit of emission control devices on other than light duty vehicles
18. Extreme cold start emission reduction programs

council of governments or regional planning commission. These entities have representation from the public sector and have formed special committees or task forces to involve other interests in the preparation of the air quality plan. Such a group will develop a list of potential control measures for possible inclusion in the plan. The Clean Air Act contains a listing (Sec. 108) of types of measures that should be considered, many of which are related to transportation. Figure 16–4 shows eighteen such measures that are meant to reduce emissions either by reducing the amount of travel or by reducing automotive engine emissions directly.

One strategy that is mandatory in areas with severe carbon monoxide and ozone problems is a motor vehicle emission inspection and maintenance program. Such a program requires the state to inspect all or certain classes of motor vehicles on a regular basis, such as annually, to determine if the vehicle's emission control devices are functioning properly. If they are not, some type of adjustment is made to improve their performance. A well-run inspection and maintenance program is considered to be the second best control strategy for carbon monoxide and hydrocarbons, exceeded only by the Federal Motor Vehicle Emissions Control Program.

The local community must select a package of control measures that is capable of reducing emissions to the level specified in the model for attainment. Within the nonattainment area, the stationary sources are required to adopt controls that will bring emission rates to the lowest achievable levels. The transportation control package must ensure the implementation of "all reasonably available control measures as expeditiously as practicable," as stated in the act.

Some controversy surrounds the local determination of which strategies are reasonably available. For example, in Denver, the local committee determined that "no-drive days" were not reasonably available. These are days on which a certain group of drivers (e.g., those with a certain license plate number) are asked not to drive. However, the state air pollution control agency overruled the regional group and placed this strategy in the state plan. Although unusual, this example shows how difficult it may be to select the control package.

Once selected, the control package must be implemented by the appropriate agencies, which may include the state legislature, state transportation departments, local governments, transit agencies, and private businesses. EPA oversees this implementation and can impose certain sanctions if the plan is not followed. For example, it can cut off federal highway, wastewater, and air quality funds and shut down new construction of any facility requiring an air pollution permit.

Nonattainment area plans probably represent the most current control technology available to address the nationally designated pollutants. They are revised periodically as more becomes known about the pollutant and its control. They are meant to achieve the standards by specified deadlines set in the act. Someone interested in the control of a particular pollutant would do well to review the nonattainment plans for areas similar to the affected community.

Prevention of significant deterioration

Areas that are not at present violating the national standards are dealt with in a program known as the Prevention of Significant Deterioration (PSD). This effort is intended to guarantee that these areas will never violate the standards. Although the PSD program is also part of the state implementation plan, it contains elements very different from those of the nonattainment area plans.

The PSD program takes all attainment areas and creates a three-tiered classification. Most of the country is initially placed in class II, with the exception of large national parks and wilderness areas above a certain size that were in existence when the act was passed and were placed in class I, the most protected. Additional areas may be classified as class I through a complicated review process. In a similar way, states may reclassify areas as class III, which is the least protected, although no state has done so to date.

After areas are classified, increments are established that determine the amount of additional pollutants that may be emitted. In class I areas, the increments are very small, especially for particulates and sulfur dioxide that restrict the visibility at these national parks. Increments become larger for class II and III areas but are still small enough to protect national standards.

The PSD program can affect local public works officials in two ways. First, some public improvement facilities may require PSD permits. For example, solid waste incinerators emitting 100 tons or more per year of particulates would need a permit. Before public works officials could select the incinerator as the best approach to dealing with a solid waste problem, they would have to work with air pollution staff to determine if enough increment is available for the incinerator's emissions. Second, a community may be trying to attract new industry that would need a PSD permit. The public works official can assist such industries in dealing with the air pollution staff, but must be familiar with the program to some extent to be effective in either of these situations.

Just as in the nonattainment plan, the PSD program needs a good base of information to determine the effect of a new source on the local air quality. Once the effect is known, it may be mitigated by applying controls to other sources, if needed. At that point the PSD program could use techniques similar to a nonattainment plan so that the total effect of the new source would be below the allowable increment.

It should be noted that in most cases, the PSD program will not produce transportation control measures. Most increments can be met through the use of best available control technologies on the stationary sources. In some cases, transportation measures may be useful in providing additional offsets but not the major efforts required in nonattainment areas.

Conclusion

The control of air quality is a major national undertaking involving complex scientific information and complicated intergovernmental cooperation. Although this chapter has tried to discuss air quality control in a general context, the issue is so closely related to decisions made by the federal government that no presentation can remain valid for long. Local officials who recognize an air quality problem should use that information as a starting point but should also contact their state or regional air pollution agency for the latest information.

Air quality is only one aspect of the environmental protection program. As we learn more about the relationship of human activity to the environment, we find that controlling air pollution may introduce land or water pollution. For example, the disposal of waste from smokestack scrubbers is a solid waste problem. Air quality officials tend to be single-service oriented, but the local public works person must deal with multiple environmental effects. This task can be frustrating, but because it is so complex the local official often can come up with the most creative solution.

Today, in the air quality field, we know much more about both the health effects of air pollutants and their control. Local public works officials can do much to increase awareness of air quality and to improve the control of pollution sources. As more is learned about the health effects of the various air pollutants, air quality standards are likely to change, and as the control of pollutants from all sources continues to improve, transportation control measures may become more effective at reducing travel and vehicle emissions. In all of these cases, the community with air quality concerns will be ahead if its officials are aware of and implement the appropriate measures.

1 U.S., National Commission on Air Quality, *To Breathe Clean Air* (Washington, D.C., March 1981), p. 3.1–4.
2 Lester B. Lave and Eugene P. Seskin, *Air Pollution and Human Health* (Baltimore: Resources for the Future, Johns Hopkins University Press, 1977), p. 188. The authors summarize a number of major air pollution incidents that have resulted in fatalities.
3 A. H. Epstein, C. A. Leary, and S. T. McCandless, *A Guide for Considering Air Quality in Urban Planning* (Research Triangle Park, N.C.: U.S. Environmental Protection Agency, March 1974), p. 33.
4 David Strimaitis, Robert Bibbo, and Robert McCann, *Air Quality Modeling: What It Is and How It Is Used* (Research Triangle Park, N.C.: U.S. Environmental Protection Agency, September 1980), p. 9.
5 Milton Feldstein, "Air Pollution: Sources, Effects, and Control," Chapter 20 in *Urban Public Works Administration*, ed. William E. Korbitz (Washington, D.C.: International City Management Association, 1976), p. 464.
6 U.S., National Commission on Air Quality, *To Breathe Clean Air*, p. 3.2–4f.
7 Ibid., p. 3.4–6.

Code administration

The construction, maintenance, and alteration of houses, apartment buildings, office buildings, retail stores, and other structures are done within a framework of city and county ordinances, regulations, forms, procedures, examinations, inspections, and, where necessary, enforcement. The word "codes" is generally used to cover the major parts of this framework involving building structure and integrity, mechanical equipment, electrical systems, plumbing systems, and fire protection.

When code administration is well done, architects, contractors, and others in the private sector can anticipate predictability in reviews, approvals, and other steps. Code administration therefore can be viewed as a team effort on the part of the local government, property owners, builders, and others in improving the quality of community life.

Code enforcement is backed by the police power of state and local government; where necessary, enforcement is applied to secure the health, safety, and welfare of the public. But good codes, well administered, are a positive force in helping ensure orderly land development, prevent structural disasters, control incipient blight, and provide building standards.

The implementation of such aims, however, is fraught with considerable difficulty. Three areas of managerial and administrative challenge may be noted briefly at the outset. In its legal aspect, to take a first example, local government code enforcement raises issues that go to the heart of our constitutional system, notably the delicate relationship between what is held to be the public good (represented in this case by the police power of government) and the rights of the individual (often represented by the owner of property). All managers would therefore agree that it is necessary, because regulatory codes embody the law, to have as complete an understanding as possible of the legal aspects of programs and to rely on the expert advice of legal counsel whenever appropriate. Cities or counties obtain their legal right to code enforcement from the police power of the state, delegated by various enabling acts to governmental agencies and subject to the interpretations of the courts. The regulatory function of governments is designed to control the use of property in the broad public interest. This function has expanded rapidly in recent years. The growing dependence on governmental regulatory agencies has arisen in part from the failure of the private sector of the economy to regulate itself.

A second point is that code enforcement management has been affected by general administrative discussions concerning the decentralization or centralization of public works activities, a theme touched on in several chapters of this book. The consensus of professionals now seems to be that a code enforcement program under the administration of a single agency, rather than a number of agencies, can often more efficiently coordinate code enforcement activities. Much

Most of this chapter has been taken from Chapter 21 in the 1976 edition of *Urban Public Works Administration*. A few additions and changes have been made to bring it up to date on the basis of reviews by Building Officials and Code Administrators International, International Conference of Building Officials, Southern Building Code Congress, and the city of Savannah, Georgia.

will depend, however, on the nature of the community involved, especially its size.

A third point is that the detailed language of codes often impedes rather than clarifies routine code enforcement. After a survey of examples of poor code writing, one authority on the subject rightly draws the following conclusion:

A primary responsibility of those engaged in the production of codes is to carefully select language that will minimize the chances of misunderstanding, with its resulting progeny—misinterpretation and misapplication.[1]

Given this general context, the present chapter presents a discussion of the managerial factors involved in code enforcement, using practical examples wherever possible. It does not attempt to present detailed legal discussions or enter into the detailed aspects of code administration, both topics beyond the scope of a single chapter.[2] The chapter is divided into sections progressing from general to specific aspects of code enforcement. It begins with an overview of code enforcement in the modern community; discusses the unique organizational and managerial problems involved in code enforcement; analyzes basic aspects of codes and standards; describes the examination function and then the inspection function; and concludes with treatment of violations and with some guidelines for effective code enforcement.

Code enforcement in the modern community

The governmental context

In size and in organization the code enforcement group is usually a relatively small component of local government. As a result, except in the larger cities, the prevailing practice has been to make the group a division within another department, rather than a separate department. Not unexpectedly, the group has tended to become a part of the public works department. It is also true, however, that a large number of agencies may have some degree of responsibility in the regulatory code area. A central coordinating agency may greatly facilitate code enforcement. If the agency operations are subsumed under the broader administrative responsibilities of a public works department, of course, there is a possibility that code enforcement will be given a low priority in the department. As a result, there may be little or no growth in organization or salaries. The arguments for and against a separate code enforcement department are set out by Robert E. O'Bannon, who summarizes a survey conducted by Gerald B. Wilson.

Arguments in favor [of including code enforcement in the public works department]:
1. "Improves coordination."
2. "Allows combination of some inspection functions. Cuts down time for processing permits."
3. "Reduces city manager's span of control."
4. "Should be a part of public works if not headed by a licensed engineer."
5. "Reduces operating expenses."
6. "Improves efficiency."

Arguments against [i.e., in favor of a separate code enforcement agency]:
1. "Functions are too dissimilar: one is a design and service organization, the other is concerned with enforcement; one is a proprietary, the other regulatory; one deals with public property, the other with private property."
2. "Sufficiently unique and important to rate direct contact with the city manager."
3. "Building regulation becomes lost and less effectual when a subsidiary of public works."
4. "If combined with anything, should be planning [department] in the interest of coordination and maximum efficiency."

5. "Distinct from public works in design, concept, financing, etc."
6. "Relationship between public works and building too minor to justify combination."
7. "Building official is an orphan in public works."
8. "Permit fees may be used to defray unrelated costs of municipal government."
9. "Reduces efficiency of operations."[3]

It is interesting to note that of the various managerial and other groups surveyed, the overall opinion was about three to one in favor of excluding code enforcement functions from the public works department.[4]

Code enforcement as law enforcement

Whatever the administrative environment within which code enforcement activities are carried out, it is important to emphasize that, ultimately, code enforcement is law enforcement. However, even though a violation of the code is subject to criminal action, the *object* of code enforcement is code compliance rather than punishment. From a managerial perspective, court action should be taken only as a last resort, when no other remedial action can be taken. In practice, this means that continued and willful violations of the code have occurred after due and written warnings to cease and desist have been given to the individual or individuals concerned.

Because the objective of code enforcement is to ensure conformity to minimum technical standards legally established to protect the health, safety, and welfare of the public, it is usually unnecessary and undesirable to impose punishment after a violation has been abated.

Unfortunately few code enforcement officials, and practically no members of the general public, realize that ultimately a court can determine whether a violation occurred or exists. Code enforcement officials can only allege that this was or is the case. Courts have held that the property owner or other person accused of a violation must take his or her case to an appeals board before he or she can bring it before the courts. The code official can, of course, qualify as an expert witness in matters involving code enforcement. When an appeals board upholds the code official's position, a board representative might assist in court action. The local government manager involved in such matters will sometimes find that professional assistance from the jurisdiction's attorneys will be necessary, particularly where substantive legal issues are involved.

The changing social and political environment

Inept administration is one of the ills in contemporary code enforcement in the United States. Good code administration requires the application of principles of rational management; a clear appreciation of the political realities of the community is also involved.

In many cases, for example, administrators of code enforcement agencies have continued to cater to their traditional clientele (builders, contractors, and property managers) without fully responding to such newer citizen groups as environmentalists, block clubs, and tenant unions. Such administrators may soon find, however, that their traditional "clients" may have taken their votes and their businesses to what are perceived as the greener pastures of the suburbs.

In most of our older cities, both large and small, the most recent emphasis has been on maintenance, conservation, rehabilitation, and renewal of older neighborhoods. Yet many code enforcement agencies have failed to "shift gears" to accommodate the changed emphasis. In cases where an administrator or a party has been long entrenched in power, such unresponsiveness or inflexiblity may characterize the entire governmental hierarchy, from the administrator and council downwards.

The primacy of the public good

A related and even more subtle problem in regulation arises from the fact that code enforcement agencies deal with clientele groups having interests that often are at odds with what are held to be the best interests of the public. Ironically, some of the regulations enforced by the agencies may actually advance rather than hinder the interests of these client groups. For example, the licensing of contractors and tradesmen, such as plumbers and electricians, ostensibly protects the public by imposing minimum standards of experience and workmanship. In practice, however, it is alleged that such licensing is used in many cases by tradesmen and unions controlling the licensing boards to limit entry into the trades (not least where minorities and women are concerned), and thus maintain an artificial shortage of skilled tradesmen. When such regulations prohibit property owners from doing their own work even when they are capable of doing it properly, and when the code enforcement agency is responsible for seeing that it is done properly, the true purpose of the regulations is open to serious question. The entire license qualification regulations also are, of course, subject to court review. The local government agency concerned must therefore exercise care in enforcement. Homeowners, provided that oral communication with the code official has established that they are qualified, must be permitted to do work on their own abode.

A code enforcement agency cannot protect tradesmen, developers, contractors, and other such groups and at the same time serve the public. In general, code enforcement probably is the area of local government most open to improper and/or criminal actions on the part of officials. It is incumbent on code officials and other responsible managers to prevent vested interests from controlling or manipulating codes and code-related work. As previously noted, government agencies have been taken to court in recent years and the result has been changes in codes and regulations where discrimination has been involved. The code officials can be weakened by such moves.

In spite of all these changes, however, the primacy of the public good remains an effective overall principle for code officials and all managers involved in this area to bear in mind.

The complexities of modern code enforcement

The need for systematic code enforcement by honest and competent inspectors has never been greater than it is today. Not only are more complex construction methods and systems being used and more sophisticated types of equipment being installed, but also the entire set of architect-engineer-contractor-owner relations is in flux. Responsibility for the actual performance of any of the functions necessary to complete a construction project depends on the contractual agreements between those involved. As far as a code enforcement agency is concerned, however, the person to whom a permit is issued is held responsible for the work authorized by the permit.

Nevertheless, because real property is always involved in construction, the owner of record of the real property (land and improvements, including buildings and other structures) bears ultimate responsibility. He or she may perhaps be regarded as an "innocent bystander" in a practical sense, only to be involved after the architect, engineer, or contractor fails to meet his or her obligations. Managers again will recognize the need to draw upon expert legal advice in such cases.

Further complexities have emerged in recent years because of economic and social changes within the private sector; a new breed of owner-developer has emerged. Such owner-developers may employ their own architects, who may not have the same authority as architects in private practice if owner-approved deviations from the original plans occur during construction. These new owner-developers also may act as their own contractors and may tell subcontractors just what they want and how much they are prepared to pay. Subcontractors in turn may employ craftsmen who, although technically paid by the hour, are paid, in effect, on a piece-rate basis (this procedure is sometimes called "lumping"). The net result of these trends has been an erosion of independent authority and systematic inspection and enforcement, not least because of the pressure on many of the parties concerned to finish the job in a hurry.

Whatever the problems occasioned by this "get-in-and-out-quickly" development philosophy (somewhat modified by economic difficulties and growth controls in the later 1970s), certain basic managerial principles of code enforcement retain their validity. Effective control can be exercised only when there are adequate regulations that are knowledgeably enforced. The necessary regulations are:

1. Subdivision regulations: a comprehensive, unambiguous document that specifies in detail the minimum requirements for sanitary sewers, storm drains, paving, sidewalks, water mains, streetlighting, rights-of-way, easements, and the like
2. A realistic zoning ordinance designed to accomplish the long-range goals established by a community master plan
3. A complete set of model regulatory technical codes, including building, plumbing, electrical, mechanical, fire prevention, and housing codes.

The governmental context, legal parameters, a rapidly changing social and political environment, the special needs of the concept of the public good, and the sheer complexity of code enforcement operations—all help shape the day-to-day administrative and decision-making environment of local government personnel involved in this challenging field. Bearing this background in mind, it is now possible to move on to a discussion of the specific, if not unique, organizational and managerial problems involved.

Unique organizational and managerial problems

The following discussion describes some of the basic organizational and managerial factors that must be taken into account if the code enforcement function is to be carried out in a realistic and effective manner. It thus sets the scene for the remainder of the chapter, which discusses detailed aspects of the code enforcement function in themselves.

Organization for administration

One of the biggest headaches experienced by persons dealing with local government code enforcement agencies, and perhaps the biggest single obstacle to code enforcement, is the fact that no one agency can handle all code enforcement. Most communities lack even a central information agency that could direct someone to all of the agencies involved in some aspect of code enforcement. For example, the owner of a new building may be issued a certificate of occupancy by the building department, and then be ordered by the fire marshall to install costly and unsightly sprinkler systems, exit signs, and the like, or by the health department to install amended sanitary equipment.

Such situations represent faulty organization that is not responding to the realities of the situation. Fortunately, however, good leadership and the increasing professionalism in the code enforcement field can help break down the inter-

and intradepartmental barriers to effective operation. The general organizational principles involved are well set out as follows:

Good codes and competent personnel must be placed in a proper organizational arrangement to achieve an administration that will result in good and efficient inspections. The main organizational problems experienced by both large and small communities are usually inter-departmental in nature and pertain to the building, health and fire functions. In addition, attention should be given to administrative problems of an intra-departmental nature since these can be a frequent cause of criticism from the public affected by the inspectional services.[5]

Savannah: a case study

How can such problems be overcome in practice? Obviously, much will depend on the size of the community concerned and the traditional practices prevailing—and the degree to which tradition is guarded by entrenched departmental heads jealous of departmental prerogatives. One particular method of reorganization in the case of the city of Savannah is detailed below.

How was the Code Enforcement Section of the city of Savannah originally organized? The personnel of this unit were attached originally—perhaps for the simple administrative reason that a place had to be found for them—to the Engineering Section of the Department of Public Works. Observers held that the personnel involved thus tended to lack leadership or a sense of direction. Organizationally, things tended to amble on through the years until some crisis occurred and either decisions or codes were changed, perhaps as a result of political pressure or bad judgment on the part of one of the inspectors involved. The group did not grow, and there was little if any upgrading of codes, administrative practices, or personnel salaries.

In the mid-1960s, the city manager concluded that the Code Enforcement Agency should become an organizational entity of itself, headed by a professional engineer with construction experience who could meet architects, engineers, contractors, homebuilders, and related groups on an equal professional basis.

It was clear at the time that the codes were not up to date, the forms involved were inadequate, and administrative control of the enforcement operation was virtually nonexistent. A frank appraisal revealed that there was mistrust and lack of communication, both inter- and intradepartmentally, and also with the client groups outside of the city government that the codes and the personnel were serving. This situation presented an administrative and managerial challenge. Like many crises in local government, it was necessary for the new professional administration to become thoroughly familiar—by study, and by attending code conferences and workshops—with the latest technical information necessary to run an efficient operation.

Under the reorganization that followed, forms were redesigned, the codes were brought up to date, the barriers between the various specialist groups of inspectors were broken down, and inappropriate restrictions on the use of materials were lifted. The functions of examining boards were also investigated. It became clear that the need for such boards was diminishing in areas where the state of Georgia had responsibilities for determining qualifications, as in the case of warm air heating, plumbing, and electrical contractors and journeymen. The only examination given in Savannah after the reorganization was in such areas as air conditioning, boiler work, refrigeration, and the other mechanical trades. Further, the examinations now included only those questions applicable to the actual work in the fields mentioned, rather than outdated topics.

The fact that the Code Enforcement Department now was headed by a professional engineer did indeed help to break down the barriers that had hitherto existed between the organization and various client groups. (With the retirement of the professional engineer, a professional architect was hired as director of inspections.) Good communication and mutual respect were enhanced by such procedures as meeting with architects and other interested parties before plans were finalized. Potential code problems were minimized in this fashion. Savannah has a large historic district. Restoration work in this area involves not only homes but also multistory apartment houses and the conversion of warehouses for shops and restaurants. Code problems, where they arose, were solved in a pragmatic manner through the medium of good communication.

Today, good use is made of the professional code boards by encouraging appeals when an individual thinks that there has been a misinterpretation of the codes or, as the codes themselves put it, where a strict interpretation would manifest an injustice. Such procedures are carried out on an impersonal basis and any differences have been resolved as far as possible in a logical manner.

The organization of the department is such that each code has its own plan reviewer in addition to the certified/licensed inspector for that discipline. The plan reviewer examines the plans for code compliance and works with the designer when there are questions. The inspector verifies that the project has been built to the approved plans and specifications and issues the occupancy permit. The function of the director is to administer the Code Enforcement Department itself. A primary responsibility, of course, is to ensure that no injustice is done, either to the code enforcement officers or their decisions, or to the citizens of the community. An appeal is only begun after the fullest discussion with all concerned persons, including the aggrieved party, the code official, and the director. If the discussion does not resolve the differences, then an appellant is encouraged to proceed further—as indeed is his or her right.

The reorganized Department of Inspections enforces the electrical, building, plumbing, mechanical, and fire prevention codes and the zoning ordinance. The housing code also is budgeted out of the department, and activities are coordinated with the policies of the city because the department is under city contract with the Health Department to perform the housing code inspections. The department also coordinates relations with other city agencies whose activities are involved, as in the cases of the city engineer, the traffic engineer, or the sanitation director. There is also contact with the local representatives of the state health department and the state department of agriculture, whose approval is sometimes required prior to permit issuance. Finally, it may be noted that the department has a sworn deputy state fire marshal who is concerned with work on new construction that is of interest to the state fire marshal's office.

In order that applicants may have speedy service, all applications are coordinated through the department. Only on rare occasions does the applicant have to contact such other departments as those of the city engineer or traffic engineer. Efforts also are made to issue provisional permission for work on site preparation, interior demolition, and foundation work while final legal requirements in other areas are being met—of course with the clear understanding that a final decision must be made about the whole project. Finally, if a code violation does occur, no legal action is ever taken if the violation can be corrected. It may also be noted that—through close work with the utility companies—electrical and gas services are not provided to a project unless first approved by the chief electrical and mechanical inspectors. As the water system is owned by the city, water service is not connected until the plumbing work is in compliance with the code. Zoning and building code violations in fact are cause for nonprovision of utility services.

Although some aspects of the Savannah experience are specific to that community, it is suggested that some of the procedures described may be of use to managers in other communities as they consider ways of improving the organizational efficiency of their code enforcement departments.

The code enforcement official

To adopt regulatory laws is a relatively simple matter. Their true value, however, depends on the judgment, efficiency, impartiality, and continuity with which they are administered. Unfortunately, a large segment of the public still retains a naive belief that the legal system is automatically self-enforcing. The effectiveness of a code enforcement agency depends essentially on its plan review and inspection processes.

Plan review is a complex technical process that is usually performed by a trained engineer or architect who is competent in structural analysis and fire protection. Plan review involves checking drawings, specifications, and other materials to assure conformance to code requirements—not only the building code but also electrical, mechanical, and plumbing systems, zoning requirements, and special features, such as elevators, that are found in multistory office buildings and other large structures.

Inspection is the process of checking to see that the plans that have been approved by the plan examiner are adhered to. Inspection involves checking work in progress for conformance to code provisions, plans, specifications, and other requirements; certifying conformance for structural, electrical, and other components; issuing warning notices and conducting reinspections; and inspecting existing buildings.

The best of regulations are of little value unless they are enforced. The official generally charged with the enforcement of the zoning ordinance and the various regulatory codes is commonly known as a code enforcement official. An older term—"building official"—is too limited to convey the range of duties that may well involve plumbing and electrical matters as well as standard construction procedures. Building officials, plumbing officials, and so on, may work under the direction of an agency head, particularly in the larger communities where the agency director may be heavily involved in overall management and administration.

In some smaller cities and counties it has long been the custom for building inspections to be handled by a one-person department. This person would do it all—structural, electrical, plumbing, and so on. There were risks in this approach because no one can be an expert across the board, but the hazards are much greater in the 1980s because of the rapid advances in building technology and the complexity and detail that today's construction entails. The small local government that can afford only one inspector will be better off to contract for their work with a neighboring city, the county or state government, or a private firm.

Whatever the background of the official, he—and in spite of affirmative action, it usually is a "he"—must learn the profession on-the-job in the particular community concerned. Every community has its unique physical heritage, and its own code practices. The tasks of the code enforcement official are many and varied. The official may be involved in the licensing and examining of plumbers, electricians, air-conditioning and refrigeration contractors, television repairmen, sign erectors, and steeplejacks. Officials also may test, evaluate, and approve or disapprove new materials, systems, and devices. They review applications, examine plans, and issue building permits of various kinds. They issue land use permits, inspect places of public assembly from nightclubs to jails, and are often heavily concerned with substandard slum dwellings in older urban cores, as well as with new construction.

Such officials have as much direct personal contact with as great a cross section of community citizens as any other local government personnel. The public relations aspect of their activities in the community is crucial. In addition to an effective sense of public relations, such officials must possess personal integrity and administrative ability if their tasks are to be carried out effectively.

Although every code enforcement official will learn much during the course of his or her work, the qualifications brought to that work are important. Unqualified employees, or employees serving vested interests rather than the general public, are clearly a barrier to effective operation at any level. The code enforcement official who is a professional engineer or an architect may well be able to deal with client groups as a professional equal. In those larger departments where supervision of the work of the code enforcement personnel is important, familiarity with the technical nature of the work performed may be of significant assistance in managerial work. Supervision of such personnel is usually a difficult task. Esprit-de-corps, dedication, and spot checking of the many tasks being carried out all help to make the work of the head official proceed smoothly. Such officials should not be overburdened with paper work and reports. Simple forms usually suffice, and full written reports can be kept to a minimum and only used for unusual cases. Breaking down the barriers to communications between the various specialist code officials is another major task of the head of the code enforcement agency.

Staffing the agency

Personnel selection for the agency is difficult, especially in the case of the building code. Low salaries are one reason for this problem. The lack of experienced applicants is another. Such people often have to be recruited from other cities or counties. One reason for this situation is the dearth of courses in code enforcement—even in architectural, engineering, and vocational technical schools. Another is the time needed to master the intricacies of a complicated professional activity. The rapid advances in construction methods, equipment, and materials make the inspection job a continual learning experience. All the major branches of building—structural, mechanical, electrical, and plumbing—have changed radically in their sophisticated use of heavy equipment, modular components, factory-assembled items, and precise schedules for delivery of materials and flow of work. It often takes up to five years to become a first-rate building inspector. Mechanical and electrical inspectors usually have sufficient background experience to reduce that five-year period to a year or less, assuming supplemental on-the-job training in administrative procedures.

Because of these factors, heads of code enforcement agencies face difficulties in building up their staffs. Perhaps such factors will continue until there is greater demand for formal training and state certification of inspectors, supplemented by workshops and institutes. Code enforcement is becoming increasingly complex, and it is unfortunate that government leaders have not placed sufficient emphasis on this area of local government service.

Whatever the difficulties encountered by the head of the agency, the agency must be staffed and administered. O'Bannon cites the importance of careful planning for administration. He suggests, for example, the organization of a building department into four major components: administration; engineering; office management (permit section); and inspection. Each division named would normally have a supervisor and each could be assigned key functions. For example, the administrative section could be made responsible for preparing the annual budget; establishing standards of production for the department; assigning areas of responsibility to supervisory personnel; assuming responsibility for the hiring and dismissal of personnel; and developing and/or reviewing all systems or procedures.[6]

Desirable qualities of an inspector   The general personal qualities required of a code enforcement inspector are self-respect; a tolerant, pleasant personality with an understanding of human nature (it will be needed); a neat personal appearance; integrity and honesty in a field where such characteristics have not always held sway; and motivation—a genuine belief in the mission of the agency. More specialized characteristics also are necessary. These include good observational ability and familiarity with the field; an ability to digest and interpret the technical language of codes and ordinances; the ability to read and understand blueprints and technical drawings; the ability to write concise and effective narrative reports as needed, and to fill in forms accurately; and, not least, the ability to issue clear instructions—verbal or written—if further action is necessary following the field visit.

Certification for building officials and inspectors In the late 1970s building officials and inspectors, through their code associations, took decisive steps toward full-scale professional certification with the development of two groups of training programs and examinations. Although the programs are voluntary, it is expected that they will profoundly influence recruitment, training, advancement, and qualitative standards for thousands of building officials and inspectors.

One program, sponsored by the Council of American Building Officials (CABO), provides an examination series in law, technology, and management for code administrators and other building officials with significant management responsibilities. Known as the Building Official Certification Program, it is recognized by the three model code organizations: Building Officials and Code Administrators International (BOCA), International Conference of Building Officials (ICBO), and Southern Building Code Congress International (SBCC).

The second program is the National Certification Program for Construction Code Inspectors (NCPCCI). The sponsors include BOCA, SBCC, the National Conference of States on Building Codes and Standards, and several other organizations. Thirteen tests are offered in general building inspection, building plan review, and related topics. The examinations provide the basis for certification in any of nine areas: One- and Two-Family Combination Inspection, One- and Two-Family Electrical Inspection, Building Inspection, Electrical Inspection, Plumbing Inspection, Building Plan Examination, Electrical Plan Examination, Plumbing Plan Examination, and Elevator Inspection.

Training In an age of ever-changing technology, training is an essential part of any agency personnel program. Regulatory code enforcement agencies are no exception. New employees have to be briefed and trained in the agency mission, with a delicate balance maintained between classroom instruction and in-the-field experience. Group training and self-education must also be taken into account, although the format and scope of training programs will vary according to the size of the jurisdiction. Preparation of a training manual may also prove a useful step. The emphasis on continuing education in recent years has helped to enhance training programs of all kinds, including the professionalization of code enforcement activities.[7]

Evaluation The problem of evaluating the productivity and performance of field inspectors is, as is the case in many other service professions, complicated by the many variables involved. For example, there is no one simple answer to the question: What constitutes a thorough inspection? No arbitrary rule can prescribe a certain number of inspections per person per day. The kind of inspection, the travel distance, the amount of office time, and the complexity of reports forms—all have a bearing on productivity. The inspector in the field in fact has a considerable degree of freedom, and must therefore exercise an equivalent amount of self-discipline if the agency mission is to be carried out.

Although a supervisor of inspectors without personal field experience has problems in trying to evaluate the productivity of the inspectors supervised, certain criteria do exist for judging productivity. Basically, it is necessary to remember that an inspection is the observation of conditions and recording of facts necessary to determine the conformity or nonconformity of a specifically designated property, building, structure, or piece of equipment to the provisions of an applicable ordinance or ordinances. Bearing this definition in mind, it can be noted that an inspection is not, therefore, a follow-up on a violation notice written as the result of an inspection; nor is it a stop made by an inspector without gaining entry to the premises. In fact, when an inspector makes a stop, the official concerned either makes an inspection or makes a reinspection (follow-up), or is unable to do one of the above for some reason beyond his or her control. The kind of inspection made—progress or maintenance; call or discretionary; periodic, complaint, or survey (as discussed later in this chapter)—is also a factor, as is the time taken to make an inspection. This may vary from a fifteen-minute inspection of a small air-conditioning unit to an inspection of a building that could take an hour, a day, or a week. Given such basic variables, at least some estimate and evaluation of the productivity of the agency inspectorate can be made.

Codes and standards

As the ultimate objective of a code enforcement agency is to secure total compliance with all ordinances under its jurisdiction, it must devise means to prevent and abate violations. An effective prevention mechanism based on well-designed codes and standards will reduce substantially the need for abatement activities. The purpose of the following section is to describe something of the basis for code enforcement; to discuss building codes, model code organizations, standards, and the distinction between fire and building regulations; and to characterize the basics of code enforcements. This discussion sets the scene for the sections immediately following, which deal with the examination and inspection functions and with violation procedures.

A comprehensive set of codes and ordinances will prohibit all construction, uses, or occupancies except those which are specifically permitted under well-defined conditions. These ordinances must be exclusive rather than inclusive. Anything not specifically permitted is prohibited.

Building codes

O'Bannon provides a useful answer to the question: What is a building code?

The "building code" has come to mean collectively all the local laws regulating the construction of a building, including all of its auxiliary components such as electrical wiring, plumbing, and mechanical. Although electrical, plumbing, and mechanical installations are governed by other codes, many persons do not draw a distinction and refer simply to all codes as the building code. The building code governs not only the construction of a building but also its use and occupancy. The essential purpose of a code is to provide for the classification of a building's use, its type of construction, and to impose certain requirements as to its design and safety features, sufficient to reduce threats to life and property to an acceptable minimum.[8]

Because of the importance of local building codes, and because of the constant need to update such codes in the light of changing technology, code review is a managerial function as significant as any other agency organizational or administrative function. If the codes are out of date, unreasonable, or difficult to enforce, then the inspectional service program may fail, however well organized the rest of the agency may be. Revision should be a top priority for the administrative officer concerned; conferences with department heads will soon reveal areas of weakness. The local government administrator also has obligations to the general public and other interested parties. The public needs to be informed, through normal public relations procedures and educational programs, of the overall benefit of efficient, modern codes. Local interests affected by codes—contractors, trade associations, labor, material and equipment suppliers, landowners, tenants, and others—must be satisfied as far as possible that their justified interests will not be adversely affected by the code revision. Uniformity of code application and a proper appeals procedure also need stressing. All these factors move parallel to the required legislative procedures leading to the adoption of a new code.

Model code organizations

There was a time when codes were locally generated—a procedure that more often than not led to difficulties. Codes might vary from jurisdiction to jurisdiction, and in any case were generally "specification" codes because they stated requirements in terms of specific materials and methods. Nationally recognized model building codes, known as "performance" codes (because they prescribe only what must be accomplished, not the methods to be followed), later came into being. They serve a useful purpose in establishing the functional performance of fire protection, structural safety, and health safety required, without specifying the kinds of materials or methods to be used.

For many years, continuous revision of model building codes has been carried on by the three national organizations: Building Officials and Code Administrators International (BOCA), International Conference of Building Officials (ICBO), and Southern Building Code Congress International (SBCC). Brief summaries of the activities and services of these organizations are shown annually in ICMA's *The Municipal Year Book* in the section on directories under the heading "Professional, Special Assistance, and Educational Organizations Serving Local and State Governments."

These organizations have issued three major model building codes: Basic National Building Code, first published in 1950 by BOCA; Uniform Building Code, first published in 1927 by ICBO; and National Standard Building Code, first published in 1945 by SBCC. Each of these organizations also publishes mechanical, plumbing, and housing codes and related plan documents.

The model codes have been developed to take care of the code requirements of all local governments. Meetings of the organizations concerned serve as a sounding board for new concepts of code administration and enforcement and code changes appropriate to changing modern design and technological advances in construction. Code organizations also sponsor seminars, workshops, and institutes that provide invaluable help for the code enforcement official, whether the official be a veteran or a novice.

The codes, used in combination with proper administrative procedures and controls, including adequate salaries, and qualifications for enforcement personnel, are a key element in meeting the objectives of the code enforcement agency.

Standards

Standards are intricately linked to code matters. As O'Bannon points out:

The word "standard" has at least 17 different meanings . . . [but] . . . the main definition . . . when related to code requirements, is: "something established for the use as a rule or basis of comparison in measuring or judging capacity, quality, content, extent, value, quantity, durability, capability, etc."[9]

There are over sixty agencies promulgating standards for every conceivable type of material, from concrete to wood and from steel to welding. Standards fall into three broad categories: testing standards; engineering practice standards; and, most significant, materials standards. Development of standards in a technologically innovative society is an immensely complicated task, carried out under the aegis of such major agencies as the American Society for Testing and Materials; the National Fire Protection Association; the National Bureau of Standards (of the United States Department of Commerce); and the American National Standards Institute.

From the managerial viewpoint, the main interest—as in the case of building codes—is not so much in the technical details of standards but in the successful integration of this technical material into the overall administrative function of the agency.

The distinction between fire and building regulations

The terms *building regulations* and *fire prevention regulations* are often used interchangeably, whereas each has a separate, well-defined meaning. As has been noted, building regulations relate to the erection, construction, enlargement, alteration, repair, improvement, conversion, or demolition of buildings or structures.

Fire prevention regulations cover building occupancy, maintenance, and use with respect to heating and air-conditioning; doors and exits; housekeeping standards for flammable liquids, rubbish, and the like; occupancy limits for theaters, arenas, restaurants, and other public buildings; and other aspects of building operations. The major objectives are to minimize fire and other hazards that threaten life and property. For simplicity, these regulations may be thought of as pertaining to the housekeeping and maintenance of buildings with respect to fire hazards and exit provisions.

Clearly, a close working relationship is necessary between officials concerned with building codes and the fire department official who supervises fire prevention regulation enforcement. For example, the design of modern buildings is limited by building regulations that include, it is hoped, the best notions of how to prevent the spread of fire and facilitate the safe escape of occupants. After a building has been completed and the building department has finally indicated compliance with pertinent building department regulations, the building will come under periodic inspection by the fire prevention official for the rest of its life. Officials in both agencies must understand each other's needs, in terms of code enforcement. It may be noted that the fire department official's inspections must be made at the time the building is in maximum use so that it may be determined if exit requirements, occupancy criteria, and other fire regulations are in fact being adhered to.

Enforcing the codes

Code enforcement activities can be divided into two categories. The *examination* function occurs before the fact. Its purpose is to predetermine the possibility of compliance. The *inspection* function occurs after the fact. Its purpose is to determine whether compliance has been achieved, and, if not, to take action for compliance. The examination function includes review of proposal documents— plans and applications—to determine conformity to regulations. The inspection function is necessary to secure both initial and continuing compliance. Both examination and inspection functions operate within the organizational and administrative framework outlined earlier in this chapter and have, of course, direct and practical links with the codes described above. These functions are examined in detail in the next two sections of this chapter.

The examination function

The following discussion approaches the examination function from several angles. It starts off by analyzing three kinds of permits: building permits, conditional permits, and mechanical permits. It then discusses plan examination, touching on such matters as zoning, housing, structural engineering, and other considerations. The permit issuance process is then illustrated by a case study, and the discussion concludes with a look at licenses.

Permits

Permits are a vital administrative tool. Nothing can be constructed, altered, or installed and no uses or occupancies established or changed unless a permit is secured. The basis on which a code enforcement agency issues a permit and what rights accrue to the permittee are of prime importance. In effect, a permit is a covenant between the agency and the applicant whereby permission is given to perform a specific act on assurance that it will be done according to applicable standards and that the applicant has the legal authority to secure the permit. Permits cannot be issued to unauthorized persons or for work that does not conform to all applicable codes and ordinances. A comprehensive form that combines the applications for a building permit and a plan examination is reproduced in Figure 17–1.

Permits must be secured for everything from the installation of a gaslight in a front yard to the complete construction of large building complexes. In the case of the larger projects, every local government agency that has code enforcement responsibilities and every agency that will be affected by its construction must examine the plans.

Building permits   Proper control of the issuance of building permits is essential to enforcement of the building code, housing code, and zoning ordinance. In addition to the technical aspects of proposed construction, it is the applicant's responsibility to establish that:

1.   The applicant for a permit is indeed the owner of the real property involved or his or her authorized agent
2.   Satisfactory evidence of ownership has been presented to the permit-issuing agency
3.   The property legally described in the document presented as evidence of ownership corresponds in every detail with that described in the permit application and on the site plan.

Conditional permits   Many building and use permits can only be issued on approval of the zoning board of appeals, the planning commission, the city council, or related bodies. Subject to legal provisions, these special approvals—which must not be arbitrary—usually impose conditions considered necessary by the authoritative body to meet the intent of the ordinance. It is essential, in ensuring initial and continuing compliance, that these conditions be an integral part of the permit and be listed in permanent records. Permits should not be issued unless a copy of the special approval is attached to the permit application. When the permit is issued, a copy of the special approval should be attached to the inspector's field copy of the permit. It is important to emphasize that permits should not be completed nor certificates of occupancy issued until all special conditions have been fulfilled.

Mechanical permits   Proper control of the issuance of mechanical permits substantially reduces illegal changes in the uses and occupancies of buildings. Mechanical permits, especially plumbing and electrical permits, should not be issued unless the city or county can determine that proposed work will not contribute to such a change. Properly designed application forms, reference to open building permits and departmental records, and an inspection of the property or installation in question will all help to effect such control.

It should be noted that individual subcontractors on a project—electricians, plumbers, heating and refrigeration specialists, and the like—must take out their own permits to perform work approved by plan examiners. These procedures are in addition to the issuance of a building permit to a general contractor and the start of general construction work.

Plan examination

Efficient plan examination, coupled with accurate permanent records, is the key to effective code enforcement. The purpose of plan examination is to permit the predetermination on the part of a code enforcement agency that, upon completion, any proposed construction, alteration, installation, or use will meet the requirements of all applicable codes and ordinances.

Permits cannot legally be issued by a code enforcement agency for work that is in violation of a code or ordinance under its jurisdiction or the jurisdiction of some other agency. If the purpose of plan examination is to be accomplished, full use should be made of properly designed permit application forms. Furthermore, plans and applications submitted as supporting data with the application must provide sufficient detail.

Plan examiners need special knowledge of a wide field—zoning, housing, exits, structural design, fire protection, fire prevention, elevators, escalators, heating equipment, refrigeration equipment, air pollution, electrical installation, sanitation, and traffic patterns. Complex project plans may be routed to other agencies, from the departments of the fire marshal and the safety engineer to those of the air pollution control specialist, the sanitarian, and the traffic engineer. From the managerial viewpoint, the code enforcement agency can and should render a service by coordinating work flows and approval decisions involving other agencies. This applies where large agencies or very small departments are involved. Good records management and modern techniques will also help.[10]

Zoning   The zoning specialist checks the legal description on the application against the site plan and the site plan against the zoning map to determine in what zoning district the property is located. After determining that the legal description is correct and the proposed general use is permitted in the zoning district, the official begins a systematic analysis of the proposed construction. Requirements that must be considered include:

1. The permissibility of each individual business proposed to occupy the subunits of the complex
2. Location of the buildings in relation to the property lines
3. Size and location of signs
4. Size and location of service areas, loading docks, and the like
5. Off-street parking facilities (no small task in shopping centers when zoning ordinances typically have different requirements for each occupancy)   [Text continues on page 369]

APPLICATION FOR
PLAN EXAMINATION AND
BUILDING PERMIT

NO.

STREET

IMPORTANT – *Applicant to complete all items in sections: I, II, III, IV, and IX.*

I. LOCATION OF BUILDING

AT (LOCATION) _____ ZONING DISTRICT _____
  (NO.)   (STREET)

BETWEEN _____ AND _____
          (CROSS STREET)   (CROSS STREET)

SUBDIVISION _____ LOT _____ BLOCK _____ LOT SIZE _____

II. TYPE AND COST OF BUILDING – *All applicants complete Parts A – D*

A. TYPE OF IMPROVEMENT

- 1 ☐ New building
- 2 ☐ Addition *(If residential, enter number of new housing units added, if any, in Part D, 13)*
- 3 ☐ Alteration *(See 2 above)*
- 4 ☐ Repair, replacement
- 5 ☐ Wrecking *(If multifamily residential, enter number of units in building in Part D, 13)*
- 6 ☐ Moving (relocation)
- 7 ☐ Foundation only

B. OWNERSHIP

- 8 ☐ Private (individual, corporation, nonprofit institution, etc.)
- 9 ☐ Public (Federal, State, or local government)

D. PROPOSED USE – *For "Wrecking" most recent use*

Residential

- 12 ☐ One family
- 13 ☐ Two or more family – *Enter number of units* – – – – → _____
- 14 ☐ Transient hotel, motel, or dormitory – *Enter number of units* – – – – – – – → _____
- 15 ☐ Garage
- 16 ☐ Carport
- 17 ☐ Other – *Specify* _____

_____

_____

Nonresidential

- 18 ☐ Amusement, recreational
- 19 ☐ Church, other religious
- 20 ☐ Industrial
- 21 ☐ Parking garage
- 22 ☐ Service station, repair garage
- 23 ☐ Hospital, institutional
- 24 ☐ Office, bank, professional
- 25 ☐ Public utility
- 26 ☐ School, library, other educational
- 27 ☐ Stores, mercantile
- 28 ☐ Tanks, towers
- 29 ☐ Other – *Specify* _____

C. COST

(Omit cents)

10. Cost of improvement.............. $ _____

   To be installed but not included in the above cost
   a. Electrical....................... _____
   b. Plumbing .... _____
   c. Heating, air conditioning......... _____
   d. Other (elevator, etc.)............. _____

11. TOTAL COST OF IMPROVEMENT $ _____

Nonresidential – Describe in detail proposed use of buildings, e.g., food processing plant, machine shop, laundry building at hospital, elementary school, secondary school, college, parochial school, parking garage for department store, rental office building, office building at industrial plant. If use of existing building is being changed, enter proposed use.

_____

_____

_____

_____

III. SELECTED CHARACTERISTICS OF BUILDING – *For new buildings and additions, complete Parts E – L; for wrecking, complete only Part J, for all others skip to IV.*

E. PRINCIPAL TYPE OF FRAME

- 30 ☐ Masonry (wall bearing)
- 31 ☐ Wood frame
- 32 ☐ Structural steel
- 33 ☐ Reinforced concrete
- 34 ☐ Other – *Specify* _____

F. PRINCIPAL TYPE OF HEATING FUEL

- 35 ☐ Gas
- 36 ☐ Oil
- 37 ☐ Electricity
- 38 ☐ Coal
- 39 ☐ Other – *Specify* _____

G. TYPE OF SEWAGE DISPOSAL

- 40 ☐ Public or private company
- 41 ☐ Private (septic tank, etc.)

H. TYPE OF WATER SUPPLY

- 42 ☐ Public or private company
- 43 ☐ Private (well, cistern)

I. TYPE OF MECHANICAL

Will there be central air conditioning?

- 44 ☐ Yes   45 ☐ No

Will there be an elevator?

- 46 ☐ Yes   47 ☐ No

J. DIMENSIONS

48. Number of stories................ _____
49. Total square feet of floor area, all floors, based on exterior dimensions .... _____
50. Total land area, sq. ft. .... _____

K. NUMBER OF OFF-STREET PARKING SPACES

51. Enclosed .... _____
52. Outdoors........................ _____

L. RESIDENTIAL BUILDINGS ONLY

53. Number of bedrooms .... _____
54. Number of bathrooms { Full.......... _____   Partial........ _____ }

Figure 17–1 Application for plan examination and building permit. In addition to requesting information on building structure and use, this form provides for illustration of the site plan, a record of plan review, and notations by the zoning plan examiner regarding compliance with local zoning ordinances. It also includes a checklist for additional mechanical permits and other agency approvals.

IV. IDENTIFICATION – *To be completed by all applicants*

	Name	Mailing address – *Number, street, city, and State*	ZIP code	Tel. No.
1. Owner or Lessee				
2. Contractor			Builder's License No.	
3. Architect or Engineer				

I hereby certify that the proposed work is authorized by the owner of record and that I have been authorized by the owner to make this application as his authorized agent and we agree to conform to all applicable laws of this jurisdiction.

Signature of applicant	Address	Application date

DO NOT WRITE BELOW THIS LINE

V. PLAN REVIEW RECORD – *For office use*

Plans Review Required	Check	Plan Review Fee	Date Plans Started	By	Date Plans Approved	By	Notes
BUILDING		$					
PLUMBING		$					
MECHANICAL		$					
ELECTRICAL		$					
OTHER _____		$					

VI. ADDITIONAL PERMITS REQUIRED OR OTHER JURISDICTION APPROVALS

Permit or Approval	Check	Date Obtained	Number	By	Permit or Approval	Check	Date Obtained	Number	By
BOILER					PLUMBING				
CURB OR SIDEWALK CUT					ROOFING				
ELEVATOR					SEWER				
ELECTRICAL					SIGN OR BILLBOARD				
FURNACE					STREET GRADES				
GRADING					USE OF PUBLIC AREAS				
OIL BURNER					WRECKING				
OTHER _____					OTHER _____				

VII. VALIDATION

Building
Permit number _____

Building
Permit issued _____ 19 _____

Building
Permit Fee $ _____

Certificate of Occupancy $ _____

Drain Tile $ _____

Plan Review Fee $ _____

FOR DEPARTMENT USE ONLY

Use Group   _____

Fire Grading   _____

Live Loading   _____

Occupancy Load   _____

Approved by:

_____

_____
                              TITLE

Figure 17–1   (continued).

VIII. ZONING PLAN EXAMINERS NOTES	
DISTRICT	
USE	
FRONT YARD	
SIDE YARD	SIDE YARD
REAR YARD	
NOTES	

IX. SITE OR PLOT PLAN – *For Applicant Use*

N

BOCA FORM APEBP – 669   C1969 BUILDING OFFICIALS & CODE ADMINISTRATORS INTERNATIONAL, INC.

Figure 17–1   (continued).

6. Special requirements imposed by the planning commission or similar bodies.

Managers will recognize the pitfalls in such a complex administrative process. Thoroughness on the part of the examiner—particularly the ability to comprehend a mass of detail, synthesize information, and proceed with meticulous logic—will therefore help achieve the zoning ordinance intent.

Housing The housing plan examiner is concerned with the following:

1. Occupancies
2. Room sizes and arrangements
3. Light and ventilation (including open spaces such as yards and courts)
4. Sanitary facilities
5. Supplied facilities (heat, hot water, screens, etc.).

Again, the characteristics noted as desirable for zoning plan examiners are applicable.

Structural engineering Plans are checked by the structural plan examiner to determine whether:

1. The structural design of the building is satisfactory.
2. The use of fire-resistant materials as protection for such members and as components in wall and floor–ceiling assemblies meets code requirements
3. The special protections required by the building code because of the inherent hazards of certain uses or occupancies have been provided for.

Clearly, a registered professional engineer is best qualified for at least the first of such determinations, and many state and local legal requirements demand just such a qualification. Certification by an engineer or architect is intended to augment, not replace, independent plan review by the building inspection agency. The local government cannot abdicate its responsibility for plan review. "Recent court cases have emphasized the fact that local communities have an obligation for determining, independently, whether a project has been properly designed and are not home free from the liability that attends the process when they are casual in handling such a responsibility."[11] Some of the other determinations mentioned, within the legal framework of the jurisdiction concerned, may be made by nonengineering personnel with good reading comprehension and training in blueprint reading. Finally, it must be emphasized that code enforcement agencies are required only to advise the architect or engineer on code requirements, not to help in actual design work. Once the architect or engineer becomes aware that this is the case (it is hoped before and not after having had plans returned and permits disapproved for noncompliance), he or she may make a rapid investment in, and study of, one or more of the appropriate code books.

Similar examination functions must, of course, be carried out in the case of plumbing, electrical installations, and safety engineering, as well as in relations with other concerned agencies such as those of the sanitarian or traffic engineer. The managerial principles involved remain fairly constant, however, although the specialist knowledge will differ in each case.

The permit issuance process: a case study

The operations of complex administrative procedures are sometimes illuminated by an illustrative case study. The following brief description indicates how the building permit issuance process works in Savannah, Georgia.

An applicant is required to complete the building permit application form and submit it with two copies of plans and specifications, properly certified (when this is required by law) by a registered architect or engineer licensed by the state of Georgia.

The plans must be sufficient to show code compliance. They must include a site development plan showing drainage, water and sewer lines, parking configuration, and the location of structures. The plans are checked for all code compliance matters.

Prior to submission for a building permit, the proposed project must be reviewed for zoning ordinance compliance and, when necessary, to receive approval from the zoning board of appeals, the planning commission, and other agencies where required. These could include the county health department, the state department of agriculture, the department of the sanitation director for refuse storage and collection method matters, and other agencies, including those of the traffic engineer and the city engineer (for water, sewer, and drainage adequacy). When it is required, the building official, who is a sworn deputy state fire marshal, gives state permits.

The code enforcement department coordinates all approvals and minimizes possible travel by the applicant to other agencies in other locations. After approval by the authorities noted and by code officials, the permit is issued. One approved copy of the plans is returned to the applicant and is to remain at the job site. No electrical or mechanical inspections may be performed without a building permit. The forms shown in Figure 17–2 illustrate the procedure involved in obtaining permission for and inspection of electrical work. As noted above, the request for authorization to proceed with the work cannot be completed before the issuance of a building permit.

The applicant is permitted to make minor modifications on the plans, but the plans must be returned for correction if major changes are contemplated. Mill certificates, laboratory certification, and the like are submitted at the earliest practical time, but prior to issuance of a certificate of occupancy. A certificate of occupancy is issued only upon completion of work to the satisfaction of code officials. A sample certificate of approval for occupancy is seen in Figure 17–3.

Licenses

Licenses are issued for tradesmen, operators of certain equipment, and the proprietors of certain businesses. The aim is to help prevent violations. A license is a legal device used to prevent unqualified persons from engaging in occupations or businesses whereby the public health, safety, or welfare might be endangered. To secure a license an applicant must submit satisfactory evidence of his or her competence in the field and of good moral character. Written and oral examinations are used often. Refusal, suspension, or revocation may be used in connection with the right to a license, and can be powerful deterrents to code violations.

The inspection function

Inspection is an administrative tool used to enforce public policy. The ingredients of an effective code enforcement program are the same regardless of the code that is being enforced, the size of the code enforcement agency, or the kind of inspection that reveals a violation. Inspection practices, however, vary substantially, depending on the size of the agency and the size and complexity of the building, equipment, or installation involved.

It is important to understand that the concern in code enforcement is not with the details of what is right about a situation. A simple "OK" followed by the date and the inspector's initials should suffice to indicate that everything is acceptable. Only when something is wrong is a written statement required. When something is wrong, a concise narrative statement of fact is needed; a checklist alone is inadequate.

Some code enforcement agencies, especially those that are experimenting with data processing equipment, burden their inspectors with bedsheet-size, paper-ballot-type report forms that appear to have as many boxes for the inspector to check as the data processing equipment can accommodate. This might be good for the data processing equipment industry but its contribution to code enforcement can be negative if the inspector must devote a disproportionate amount of his or her time to putting check marks in little boxes.

The inspector needs a set of approved plans to make worthwhile inspections, which fall into two broad categories: progress inspection, concerned with new construction, and maintenance inspection, concerned with existing buildings and other structures.

Progress inspections

Inspection at specified stages of construction is yet another tool for preventing violations. Work requiring inspection must be approved by permit before it is covered. When corrections are required, the permit holder, or his or her agent, must be notified in writing, on standard forms. If work proceeds without authorization before the required corrections are made, a "stop work order" must be posted on the job site. If work still continues, a warrant may be secured and the offender arrested.

The inspector in the field must use the plans approved by the plan examiner as the basis for inspection, and many managers would welcome inspectors with in-depth knowledge equivalent to that of the plan examiner.

There are two kinds of progress inspections: (1) called and (2) discretionary. The called inspections occur when the general contractor (or a subcontractor) has completed work up to a certain point and cannot proceed until the work has been inspected and approved. The point of progress at which such inspections are deemed necessary is predetermined by codes and ordinances, or by code enforcement agency rules. Discretionary or surprise inspections are what their name suggests. They may be made when called inspections are required, but are in such cases directed to areas of activity other than the one called. The called inspection method is used principally in the construction of one- and two-family dwellings and garden-type apartments.

The discretionary method is more common in the construction of high-rise and other major buildings. These buildings and structures require more specialized, detailed, and technical inspections than the building inspection agency can provide. To meet this situation, the Uniform Building Code requires the use of "special inspectors" for the critical phases of construction such as high-strength bolting, field welding, and placing concrete.

Maintenance inspections

The maintenance inspection of existing buildings, structures, or equipment comprises three types: (1) periodic; (2) complaint; and (3) survey.

Periodic inspections are those that are made routinely at time intervals established either by ordinance or policy. Complaint inspections are made as the result of a citizen's complaint to the code enforcement agency that an unlawful condition exists. Survey inspections are those made of all buildings within a designated area. This is the type used in concentrated code enforcement programs. The difference between maintenance and construction (or "progress") inspections was well stated in *Municipal Public Works Administration:*

Maintenance inspections of buildings are different from construction inspections in two important respects. First, they are less technical to perform and this should facilitate consolidations. Second, they are not of an emergency nature and are susceptible to

[Text continues on page 374]

REQUEST FOR
ELECTRICAL INSPECTION

DEPARTMENT OF INSPECTIONS
CITY OF SAVANNAH
P. O. BOX 1027, 31402

Date _____

I hereby make application for permission to install or change electrical wiring in or on the premises described below and I agree to comply with all rules and regulations governing electrical installations in the City of Savannah.

Bldg. Permit No. _____ State License No. _____ Class _____

Street _____ No. _____

( ) Builder
( ) Owner _____ Building Occupied As _____ ( ) Tenant _____

( ) New Construction

( ) Smoke Detector	( ) Exit Lights	
( ) Electric Welder	( ) Electric Oven	
( ) Electric Rectifiers	( ) Electric Range Top	
( ) Water Heaters	( ) Electric Range	
( ) Bath Heaters	( ) Electric X-Ray	
( ) Sign Circuits	( ) Loud Speaking Systems	
( ) Bell Transformers	( ) Intercommunication System	
( ) Built in Package Heating	( ) Motors - Attach separate itemized	
( ) _____ Ton Air Conditioner (Central)	list.	
( ) Air Conditioning Window Units		

( ) Old Construction

( ) Electric Washing Machine	( ) Each New Service
( ) Electric Dryers	( ) Change in Service
( ) Electric Dish Washers	From: _____
( ) Exhaust Fans	To: _____
( ) Electric Disposals	( ) K.W. Load
( ) Ceiling Outlets	
( ) Bracket Outlets	
( ) Receptacles	
( ) Flush Switches	
( ) Sockets on Fixtures	

TEMPORARY SERVICE   Time Allowed ( ) days   ( ) Emergency Lighting
What purpose   ( ) Building Saw   ( ) Floor Sanding   ( ) Gospel Service   ( ) Circus   ( ) Others _____

( ) Rough in wiring   ( ) Fixtures   Will be ready for inspection _____

Application filed by _____

Mailing Address _____

Phone No. _____

Fees $ _____

I hereby certify that I have personally supervised this installation and found it to pass all City Electrical Ordinances of Savannah, Georgia, and the National Electric Code.

Certified Electrician _____

Approved _____
Electrical Inspector

DEPARTMENT OF INSPECTIONS

CITY OF SAVANNAH

P. O. BOX 1027
SAVANNAH, GEORGIA 31402

Date _____

The electrical installation at _____
is found on inspection to be defective and must be made to conform to City Ordinance. Ten days are allowed in which to correct the following defects:

_____

_____

_____

_____

Re-inspection Fee $ _____

On or after _____, I will re-inspect the premises for the purpose of ascertaining if these defects have been corrected.

Respectfully

_____
Electrical Inspector

Figure 17–2 These forms used by the city of Savannah, Georgia, illustrate the steps involved in undertaking electrical work. The application for permission to begin work (top) requires that a building permit be obtained before application is made and requests information about the nature and purpose of the work. When the Department of Inspections is notified by the contractor that the work is completed, a department inspector checks the job for compliance with local standards. The inspection report (bottom) is used where defects are found that must be corrected before approval can be given. The certificate of final inspection and approval (opposite page, top) is signed by both the contractor responsible for the work and the electrical inspector. The inspection and approval stickers (opposite page, bottom) are posted at the site at appropriate stages.

Certificate of Inspection

CITY OF SAVANNAH ELECTRICAL DEPARTMENT

Savannah, Georgia,_____ , 19____

This certifies that the electrical installation described below has been inspected by me and found to conform to the ordinances of the City of Savannah governing same.

For whom work was done_____

Location of work_____

Description of work_____

_____

_____

_____

Electrical Contractor_____

Electrical Inspector_____

Rough Wiring

Electrical Inspection Report

DO NOT COVER

REASON _____

_____

_____

DATE_____

Another inspection will be made when signed defect notice is received stating that defects have been corrected.

Electrical Inspector
CITY OF SAVANNAH

(OVER)

THE ROUGH WIRING
IN THIS _____
HAS BEEN INSPECTED AND APPROVED. THE BUILDING CONTRACTOR IS HEREBY PERMITTED TO CONCEAL

DATE_____

ADDRESS_____
INSPECTOR_____

CITY OF SAVANNAH
Electrical Inspection Department

THE COMPLETION WIRING IN THIS _____
HAS BEEN INSPECTED AND APPROVED.

DATE_____

ADDRESS_____
INSPECTOR_____

CITY OF SAVANNAH
Electrical Inspection Department

Figure 17–2 (continued).

CERTIFICATE OF OCCUPANCY

DEPARTMENT
OF
INSPECTIONS

SAVANNAH,
GEORGIA

Location of Building_____

Major Occupancy of Building_____Type of Construction_____

Height of Building_____Ground Floor Area_____

    I certify that the building located at the above address has been inspected and complies with the require-
ments of the Savannah Building Code.

In addition to the major occupancy, the building is approved for_____

_____

_____

The maximum number of persons permitted to occupy each floor is_____

_____

Date_____.

Building Official.

Figure 17–3   Certificate of occupancy, city of Savannah, Georgia.

better scheduling and programming. The great volume of these maintenance inspections, which are made monthly, quarterly, or annually, depending on the nature of the problem, relate to fire and health hazards and are made to ascertain and eliminate such hazards. Inspections related to the housing code and for urban renewal purposes are also of this general maintenance type. It would be desirable if all maintenance inspections could be centralized in a single division or department along with construction inspections.[12]

Periodic inspection of existing structures is a useful method of encouraging preventive maintenance, particularly where absentee landlords of slum properties are involved. It is also a great deterrent to "bootleg" construction. Further, an ongoing building inspection program is a valuable asset to any code enforcement agency because it provides a constant supply of work and helps in the retention of trained personnel. A program of this type is best utilized by new, growing communities as a stabilizer when new construction is slow and by older communities as the prime function of the building or code enforcement department. In sum, a properly administered existing building inspection program (1) prevents deterioration of buildings; (2) prevents illegal construction; (3) prevents zoning violations; (4) conserves existing housing stock; (5) eliminates slack work periods; (6) provides a record of building occupancies; and (7) provides a constant source of revenue for the department concerned.

Housing and zoning inspections

To be effective, an inspector assigned to zoning ordinance or housing code enforcement must be a skilled investigator. Some skill is required to walk through a building and observe if violations exist. It takes considerably more skill, however, to write a report that describes in detail exactly what the violations are and where they are, and even more skill to compose a legal notice of violation that will inform the person responsible for the violations exactly what he or she must do to correct them. Once a violation notice is written, it takes determination and perseverance to secure compliance, right up to the preparation of a properly prepared, watertight court case.

Building conservation and maintenance Traditionally, and almost universally, the manpower allocation of building departments is dependent on and governed by the revenue received from the issuance of permits. The intent is to make the building department as nearly self-supporting as possible. This is a commendable but impractical concept. The problem lies in the cyclical nature of building construction, which has highs and lows that produce erratic levels in the issuance of permits and income. When the level of construction recedes or is depressed the problem is severely aggravated because of the inevitable reduction in working staff.

Unfortunately, the special and expensive training efforts expended on staff can be lost if they must seek employment elsewhere. This results in a new training effort (when construction is again accelerated) with its attendant costs. What then is to be done with building department personnel, when there is little or no new construction to oversee? The answer lies in building conservation programs. There are few cities that have escaped the ravages of

building deterioration and the resulting slums both in residential and commercial buildings. The social and law enforcement problems associated with such deterioration are well known, but they need not occur to the extent that they do.

Building conservation or maintenance programs can materially assist in retarding blight in buildings and the attendant problems this brings. Unfortunately, few cities have instituted such activities for one reason or another, but quite likely because they are unpopular with almost everyone and, more importantly, politically unpalatable. However, the positive aspects of such a program should be the guiding principle, not the unpopularity.

Source: Richard Kuchnicki, "Perspectives on the Problems and Promises in Code Administration," in *Code Administration and Enforcement: Trends and Perspectives*, Management Information Service Special Report no. 10 (Washington, D.C.: International City Management Association, August 1982), p. 91.

Inspecting government projects

One final point may be made about the inspection function. Many managers would agree that there is often a real or apparent misunderstanding about inspections of projects of other municipal agencies, especially public works projects. To put the matter bluntly, however, if the public works projects are covered by the codes, then code compliance is required. For example, the city water and wastewater pump stations must comply with building and electrical codes, obtain electrical and utility releases, and be given building permits and certificates of occupancy if this is what the law demands. This holds true for state and federal projects that require water supply, fire protection, and other city or county services. In such cases, the city or other government, through its codes, has jurisdiction and requires code compliance. Such projects, if they do not want the city's inspectional services, may well be on their own if it comes to obtaining electrical service releases and certificates of occupancy.

Dealing with violations

The question of how to deal with violations is crucial. As stated in *Municipal Public Works Administration*:

Good public relations requires administration of regulations with understanding, tact, and restraint, as well as fairness and firmness. The responsible official must not shrink from or be dilatory in citing code and ordinance violators and bringing offenders to justice. The major objective is to see that the regulations are observed and not that citizens are punished for failure to observe the regulations. The official should strive toward securing compliance. . . . When this fails, it may be necessary to issue violation notices or prosecute those who persistently refuse to comply with the requirements.[13]

The following brief discussion therefore considers two basic topics: the role of supportive legal services in violation procedures, and the function of an appeals board.

Supportive legal services

It is important for the code enforcement officer to have good communication with the legal department and to use counsel whenever necessary. Counsel should be available and sympathetic to the needs of the code enforcement department, its chief executive, and its staff. The legal counsel may be assigned to the agency on a full- or a part-time basis. Legal actions of many types may, of course, be involved in code enforcement and experienced legal advice and services are essential. Code enforcement agencies in large cities may have their own legal staffs to assist them with court complaints and also in the provision of codes and ordinances. In smaller jurisdictions, one member of the legal staff must be assigned responsibility for the code enforcement agency.

One matter of no small interest in this area is the question of right of entry, a matter of some discussion in our courts in recent years. This is not the place to enter into a detailed discussion of the legal questions involved, for which the reader is referred to the standard law reports and legal sources. Most managers would probably agree that whatever the right of entry given by a particular ordinance, if actual right of entry is forbidden, the code official in question should exercise prudence and withdraw to seek legal advice. Forced entry may lead, of course, to very serious legal consequences. Also, there is a practical question of the distinction between refusal of right of entry and a particular time of entry not being convenient to the occupant. Legal advice should always be sought in these matters if there appears any substantial doubt as to the course that the code enforcement official should take.

The function of an appeals board

As O'Bannon points out:

With hundreds of different persons administering the codes, different interpretations are inevitable. As a consequence, an interpretation rendered by a building official, under certain circumstances, may be challenged. . . . These are situations in which a member of the public is entitled to a hearing before a qualified Board to determine the validity of the action of the building official. . . . The Appeals Board can play a very important role in helping to keep the building department on an even keel.[14]

Some general points can be made about the appeals board. For example, there is a clear advantage if the board is comprised of persons who are thoroughly familiar with the technical procedures involved in the subject matter under discussion. This might seem an obvious factor, but the ever-changing pace of modern technology makes it an important one. Formal appointment of the board of course will be a matter of the appropriate legislature, but it is certainly in the interests of a code enforcement agency to do everything possible to facilitate contacts with the professional bodies concerned so that the best qualified candidates may be appointed. The actual duties of such boards may be set out in the requisite code, particularly when the question of what matters may be appealed comes up. As far as the liability of board members for legal action is concerned, professional advice should be sought in the light of prevailing legal opinion.

Guidelines for effective code enforcement

Code enforcement is a complex field. There is no single right way of doing the job. Much will depend on the character of a particular community, and the discretion of the executive concerned is a vital factor. Nevertheless, some guidelines may be offered. The following list is not intended to be exhaustive, or indeed the only perspective on the subject. But it is offered in the hope that it may guide managers who have contemplated developing similar lists for their own communities and, it is felt, end this chapter on a realistic and practical note.

1. Establish a central "active" file for all open permits, violation notices, and complaints.
2. Establish a systematic uniform procedure for processing of code violations.
3. Establish fees for the inspection of all existing buildings except one-family dwellings and minor accessory buildings.
4. Make periodic inspections of all existing buildings.
5. Require inspectors to write a brief narrative report, clear enough for a person of average education to understand, as a basis for any violation notice they write. Require that each item on a violation notice be followed by the number of the specific section of the code that has been violated.
6. Require that every legal notice of violation be approved by the inspector's supervisor before is is typed and mailed.
7. Relieve field inspectors of all discretionary authority and place this responsibility on the bureau director.
8. Use multicopy correction notices to secure compliance with simple construction violations. Keep one copy in the office until compliance is secured.
9. Require a thorough examination of plans prior to the issuance of permits.
10. Check department records before issuing permits.
11. Put all violation notices in writing.
12. Redesign permit application forms to include all necessary information.
13. Require submission of plans that are sufficiently detailed to ensure code compliance.
14. Establish a procedure for processing plans through all agencies having a legitimate interest, coordinating same.
15. Require the plan examiner to check all legal descriptions on ownership documents against permit applications and plans prior to accepting plans

for detailed examination, and certify the nature and identification number of the document.

16. Require plan examiners to use correction sheets and discontinue the practice of marking changes on plans.
17. Require plan examiners to cite code section numbers when plan changes are indicated.
18. Provide permit applicants whose applications have been denied with a written denial, specifying all of the deficiencies by code section number.
19. Provide such applicants with an application for appeal to the appropriate appellate body if they desire to appeal.
20. Require reference to a building permit number of departmental occupancy records before issuing mechanical permits. If no records are available, an inspection should be made prior to issuing a permit.
21. Require that copies of all special approvals granted by the city council, the zoning board of appeals, or other regulatory boards be attached to the permit application and to the inspector's field copy of the permit.
22. Do not issue certificates of occupancy until all required special conditions have been fulfilled.
23. Relieve inspectors of all filing duties.
24. Require inspectors to leave route sheets in the office indicating in sequence where they are going and why.
25. Require inspectors to turn in all records every day.
26. Require that all correction notices be in writing and that one copy of the notice be left in the office at all times until compliance has been obtained.
27. Number complaint forms in sequence, make them out in duplicate, and keep one copy in the office until the complaint is resolved.
28. Accept referral forms from other departments as complaints; attach them to complaint forms and keep them together until disposition.
29. Notify referring department of disposition.
30. Establish a "date file" for open violations and reinspect on compliance dates.
31. When work is done without a permit, issue a violation notice to both the property owner and the contractor. If the contractor is unknown, issue the notice to the owner only. Upon failure to obtain proper permit, issue stop work order.
32. Reinspect properties in violation on the established compliance date.
33. Require inspectors to contact the responsible party when there has been no compliance or only partial compliance.
34. Require each inspector to recommend a course of action to his supervisor based on contact with the responsible party.
35. Require the supervisors to review and approve or modify the recommendations of the inspectors.
36. Repeat the reinspection process as long as satisfactory progress and good faith are demonstrated by the violator.
37. If compliance cannot be secured, require the bureau directors to hold a hearing to permit the violator an opportunity to show cause why a complaint should not be entered in municipal court.
38. If cause is not demonstrated, require the chief inspector of the division involved to prepare the court complaint.
39. Require the bureau director to approve the complaint and submit it to the city attorney.
40. Require the city attorney to conduct a pre-trial hearing to determine whether to file the complaint, grant additional time for compliance, or return the complaint to the department for clarification.

41. If the complaint is filed, require that the chief inspector and the city attorney appear in court.
42. Use only the chief inspectors as court officers.
43. Establish a certain day of each week as court day for code violations.
44. Give code violation cases priority on that day so that inspectors will not have to lose any more time than necessary.
45. Require the department administrator to propose ordinance amendments to update code requirements continually.
46. Require the city attorney to review and approve the form of ordinance amendments submitted by the building department.
47. Alert the police department to watch for construction work proceeding with no permit posted and to require that a ticket be issued or that the condition be referred to the building department.
48. Require utility companies to secure a written release from the department of buildings before turning on utilities.
49. Require building inspectors to check the location of buildings on the first inspection for conformity to the site plan.
50. Require the posting of a cash bond before issuance of a demolition permit to ensure proper site restoration.

1   Robert E. O'Bannon, *Building Department Administration* (Whittier, Calif.: International Conference of Building Officials, 1973), p. 97. All references to this source, copyright 1973, were reproduced with permission of the publisher.

2   For further discussion of legal cases bearing on code enforcement, see Chapter 12, "Legal Aspects," pp. 422–505 in O'Bannon, *Building Department Administration; Legal Aspects of Code Administration*, published jointly in 1984 by BOCA, ICBO, and SBCC; and Richard L. Sanderson, *Codes and Code Administration: An Introduction to Building Regulations in the United States* (Chicago: Building Officials Conference of America, Inc., 1969).

3   O'Bannon, *Building Department Administration*, pp. 22–23.

4   Ibid., p. 22. See also pp. 23–36 for a full discussion of the factors involved.

5   International City Managers' Association, *Municipal Public Works Administration*, 5th ed. (Chicago: International City Managers' Association, 1957), p. 394.

6   O'Bannon, *Building Department Administration*, p. 196. See also pp. 196–99 for more detailed organizational suggestions.

7   See the detailed discussion in O'Bannon, *Building Department Administration*, pp. 251–59.

8   Ibid., p. 88.

9   Ibid., p. 128.

10   See the discussion in Chapter 3 of this volume.

11   Letter dated January 4, 1985, from James E. Bihr, Executive Director, International Conference of Building Officials.

12   International City Managers' Association, *Municipal Public Works Administration*, p. 408.

13   Ibid., p. 400.

14   O'Bannon, *Building Department Administration*, p. 563.

Selected bibliography

1 What Is Public Works?

Armstrong, Ellis L., ed., Michael C. Robinson, and Suellen M. Hoy, assoc. eds. *History of Public Works in the United States, 1776–1976*. Chicago: American Public Works Association, 1976. Prepared by professional historians and organized thematically in twenty chapters on streets, highways, waterways, railroads, airports, water supply, sewers, public buildings, parks, military installations, irrigation, and other subjects.

Hodges, Henry. *Technology in the Ancient World*. New York: Alfred A. Knopf, 1970.

Kranzberg, Melvin, and Carroll W. Pursell, Jr., eds. *Technology in Western Civilization*. Vols. 1 & 2. New York: Oxford University Press, 1967. (See especially Chapter 2, "The Beginnings of Technology," by R. J. Forbes.)

Payne, Robert. *Ancient Rome*. Rev. ed. (Orig. titled *The Horizon Book of Ancient Rome*.) New York: McGraw-Hill, 1971.

Singer, Charles, E. J. Holmyard, A. R. Hall, and Trevor I. Williams, eds. *A History of Technology*. 7 vols. New York: Oxford University Press, 1954–78.

Von Hagen, Victor W. *The Roads That Led to Rome*. London: Weidenfeld & Nicolson, 1967.

2 Public Works Organization

American Public Works Association. *Public Works Management: Trends and Developments*. Special Report 47. Chicago, 1981.

Connellan, Thomas K. "Management by Objectives in Local Government: A System of Organizational Leadership." *Management Information Service Report* 7, no. 2A. Washington, D.C.: International City Management Association, February 1975.

Foster, William S., ed. *Handbook of Municipal Administration and Engineering*. New York: McGraw-Hill, 1978. Emphasizes maintenance methods for streets, bridges, motor equipment, sewer and water lines, parks, buildings, street lighting, and traffic controls. Generously illustrated with photos and diagrams.

Jun, Jong S., ed. "A Symposium: Management by Objectives in the Public Sector." *Public Administration Review* 36 (January/February, 1976).

Poister, Theodore H., and Robert P. McGowan. "The Use of Management Tools in Municipal Government: A National Survey." *Public Administration Review* 44 (May/June, 1984).

Roll, Joyce, and David Roll. "The Potential for Application of Quality Circles in the American Public Sector." *Public Productivity Review* 7 (June 1983).

Sheeran, F. Burke. *Management Essentials for Public Works Administrators*. Part III. *The Organization Function*. Chicago: American Public Works Association, 1975.

3 Information Systems

Arthur Andersen and Co. *A Guide to Selecting and Using Microcomputers in Government*. Washington, D.C.: Government Finance Officers Association, 1984.

Churchman, C. West. *The Systems Approach*. Rev. and updated. New York: Dell Publishing Company, 1983.

Griesemer, James R. *Microcomputers in Local Government*. Washington, D.C.: International City Management Association, 1983.

Kraemer, Kenneth L., William H. Dutton, and Alana Northrup. *The Management of Information Systems*. New York: Columbia University Press, 1981.

Murdick, Robert G., Joel E. Ross, and James R. Claggett. *Information Systems for Modern Management*. 3d ed. Englewood Cliffs, N.J.: Prentice-Hall, 1984.

Schmitt, Rolf R., and Harlan J. Smolin, eds. *Practical Application of Computers in Government: Papers from the Annual Conference of the Urban and Regional Information Systems Association, August 22–25, 1982*. Washington, D.C.: International Science and Technology Institute for the Urban and Regional Information Systems Association, 1982.

4 Public Works Finance

Aronson, J. Richard, and Eli Schwartz, eds. *Management Policies in Local Government Finance*. Washington, D.C.: International City Management Association, 1981.

Hatry, Harry P., and George E. Peterson, eds. *Guides to Managing Urban Capital Series*. 6 vols. Vol. 1, *Guides to Managing Urban Capital: A Summary*, Harry P. Hatry and George E. Peterson; Vol. 2, *Guide to Assessing Capital Stock Condition*, Stephen R. Godwin and George E. Peterson; Vol. 3, *Guide to Benchmarks of Urban Capital Condition*, George E. Peterson, Mary John Miller, Stephen R. Godwin, and Carol Shapiro; Vol. 4, *Guide to Selecting Maintenance Strategies for Capital Facilities*, Harry P. Hatry and Bruce G. Steinthal; Vol. 5, *Guide to Setting Priorities for Capital Investment*, Harry P. Hatry, Annie P. Millar, and James H. Evans; Vol. 6, *Guide to Financing the Capital Budget and Maintenance Plan*, George E. Peterson, Rita Bamberger, Nancy Humphrey, and Kenneth M. Steil. Washington, D.C.: The Urban Institute Press, 1984. An authoritative reference for managing the streets, bridges, and water and sewer lines that make up most of the local government capital plant. Based on extensive survey work and first-hand observations by staff from the Urban Institute and Public Technology, Inc., and loaded with practical steps and examples.

Lynch, Thomas D. *Public Budgeting in America*. 2d ed. Englewood Cliffs, N.J.: Prentice-Hall, 1985.

Mikesell, John L. *Fiscal Administration: Analysis and Applications for the Public Sector*. Homewood, Ill.: Dorsey Press, 1982.

Municipal Finance Officers Association. *Governmental Accounting, Auditing, and Financial Reporting*. Chicago, 1980.

Mushkin, Selma J., ed. *Public Prices for Public Products*. Washington, D.C.: Urban Institute, 1972.

Petersen, John E., and Wesley C. Hough. *Creative Capital Financing for State and Local Governments*. Chicago: Government Finance Officers Association, 1983.

Wildavsky, Aaron B. *The Politics of the Budgetary Process*. 4th ed. Boston: Little, Brown, 1983.

5 Public Works Planning

Catanese, Anthony James, and W. Paul Farmer, eds. *Personality, Politics and Planning: How City Planners Work*. Beverly Hills: Sage Publications, 1978.

DeGrove, John M. *Land, Growth, and Politics*. Chicago: Planners Press, 1984.

Freilich, Robert H., and Peter S. Levi. *Model Subdivision Regulations: Text and Commentary*. Chicago: Planners Press, 1975.

Godschalk, David R., and David J. Brower. *Constitutional Issues of Growth Management*. Chicago: Planners Press, 1979.

Jacobs, Allan B. *Making City Planning Work*. Chicago: American Planning Association, 1978.

Slater, David C. *Management of Local Planning*. Washington, D.C.: International City Management Association, 1984.

So, Frank S., Irving Hand, and Bruce D. McDowell, eds. *The Practice of State and Regional Planning*. Chicago: American Planning Association, 1986.

So, Frank S., Israel Stollman, Frank Beal, and David S. Arnold, eds. *The Practice of Local Government Planning*. Washington, D.C.: International City Management Association, 1979.

6 Managing People

Bent, Alan E., and T. Zane Reeves. *Collective Bargaining in the Public Sector: Labor-Management Relations and Public Policy*. Menlo Park, Calif.: Benjamin/Cummings, 1978.

Dresang, Dennis L. *Public Personnel Management and Public Policy*. Boston: Little, Brown, 1984.

Greiner, John M., Harry P. Hatry, Margo P. Koss, Annie P. Millar, and Jane P. Woodward. *Productivity and Motivation: A Review of State and Local Government Initiatives*. Washington, D.C.: Urban Institute, 1981.

Hays, Steven W., and T. Zane Reeves. *Personnel Management in the Public Sector*. Newton, Mass.: Allyn and Bacon, 1984.

Klingner, Donald E., and John Nalbandian. *Public Personnel Management: Contexts and Strategies*. 2d ed. Englewood Cliffs, N.J.: Prentice-Hall, 1985.

Lieberman, Myron. *Public-Sector Bargaining: A Policy of Reappraisal*. Lexington, Mass.: Lexington Books, 1980.

Matzer, John, Jr., ed. *Creative Personnel Practices: New Ideas for Local Government.* Washington, D.C.: International City Management Association, 1984.

Morrisey, George L. *Performance Appraisals in the Public Sector: Key to Effective Supervision.* Reading, Mass.: Addison-Wesley, 1983.

7 Communication Management

American Public Works Association, Task Force on Communication. *Public Works Communication Manual.* Chicago, 1984.

Arnold, David S., Christine S. Becker, and Elizabeth K. Kellar, eds. *Effective Communication: Getting the Message Across.* Washington, D.C.: International City Management Association, 1983.

Banovetz, James M., ed. *Small Cities and Counties: A Guide to Managing Services.* Washington, D.C.: International City Management Association, 1984.

International City Management Association. *Effective Supervisory Practices: Better Results Through Teamwork.* 2d ed. Washington, D.C., 1984.

8 Legal Aspects of Public Works

Affiliated Capital Corporation v. *City of Houston,* 735 F.2d 1555 (5th Cir. 1984), and *Scott* v. *City of Sioux City, Iowa,* 736 F.2d 1207 (8th Cir. 1984). Cases providing clear analyses of the difficulties of applying the federal antitrust laws to the actions of local governments; with the citations above, these opinions are readily available from the local government attorney or from the local law library.

Banovetz, James M., ed. *Small Cities and Counties: A Guide to Managing Services.* Washington, D.C.: International City Management Association, 1984. A handbook on local government management, including a particularly enlightened chapter on the legal structure of local governments and the legal aspects of daily government operations.

McQuillin Municipal Corporations. 22 vols. Chicago: Callaghan and Co., 1967. One of the prime sources available to city and county attorneys.

Sands, C., and Michael Libonati. *Local Government Law: 1981.* 4 vols. Wilmette, Ill.: Callaghan and Co., 1981. An in-depth discussion and analysis of local government law; less detailed than *McQuillin* but a thoughtful critique of the legal problems facing local government managers.

9 Purchasing

National Association of State Purchasing Officials. *State and Local Government Purchasing.* Prepared by NASPO and Peat, Marwick, Mitchell & Co. Lexington, Ky.: Council of State Governments, 1975. A report of the study that was the basis for the American Bar Association's project for A Model Procurement Code for State and Local Governments.

――――. *State and Local Government Purchasing.* 2d ed. Lexington, Ky.: Council of State Governments, 1983. An update of the original report and a valuable resource for all public officials concerned about the role of law and correct practice in the acquisition of goods and services.

National Institute of Governmental Purchasing, Inc. *General Public Purchasing.* Falls Church, Va., 1977. Provides information on the "basics" of public purchasing; designed primarily for classroom use.

――――. *Public Procurement Management.* Part 1. Falls Church, Va., 1985. Provides information on operations and project management, evaluation of public purchasing systems, communications, and other relevant concerns for public purchasing managers; designed primarily for classroom use.

――――. *Public Purchasing and Materials Management.* Falls Church, Va., 1983. Provides information on planning for purchases, contracting for services, transporting purchased materials, quality assurance, and inventory management; designed primarily for classroom use.

Page, Harry Robert. *Public Purchasing and Materials Management.* Lexington, Mass.: Lexington Books, 1980. An overview of the purchasing and materials management systems employed at the several levels of government.

10 Engineering and Contract Management

Ahuja, Hira N. *Project Management: Techniques in Planning and Controlling Construction Projects.* New York: John Wiley & Sons, 1984.

American Public Works Association. Institute for Municipal Engineering. *Guidelines for Retaining Consultants to Provide Architectural and Engineering Services.* Chicago, 1973.

――――. *How to Create Standard Specifications.* Chicago, 1982.

————. Research Foundation. *CAMRAS II: Computer Assisted Mapping and Record Activity System*. Chicago, 1984.

American Society of Civil Engineers. Task Committee on the Revision of Manual No. 45. *Consulting Engineering: A Guide for the Engagement of Engineering Services*. New York, 1981.

Engineer's Joint Contract Documents Committee. *Standard Form of Agreement Between Owner and Engineer for Professional Services*. Washington, D.C.: National Society of Professional Engineers, 1984.

Hohns, H. Murray. *Preventing and Solving Construction Contract Disputes*. New York: Van Nostrand Reinhold, 1979.

McNulty, Alfred P. *Management of Small Construction Projects*. New York: McGraw-Hill, 1982.

11 Equipment Management

American Public Works Association. *Equipment Management Manual*. Chicago, 1977.

Bert, Kendall. "Replacement Analysis." In *Equipment Management Manual*, Section 1. Chicago: American Public Works Association, 1977.

Bremner, Ross, and Richard Sullivan. "Parts Inventory Control." In *Equipment Management Manual*, Section 4. Chicago: American Public Works Association, 1977.

Hartmann, John P., A. Dale Wade, and Walter Moore. *Vehicle Maintenance Facilities: A Planning Guide*. Special Report 51. Chicago: American Public Works Association, 1984.

Jensen, Ronald W., and James Armentrout. *Greenbook*. Phoenix, Ariz.: Public Works Department, Equipment Management Division, 1979.

Kahan, Cynthia V. "Vehicle Replacement: Three Techniques for Better Decision Making." *Management Information Service Report* 13. Washington, D.C.: International City Management Association, June 1981.

Perrone, Thomas, Kendall Bert, and Richard H. Sullivan. "Preventive Maintenance," in *Equipment Management Manual*, Section 3. Chicago: American Public Works Association, 1977.

12 Buildings and Grounds Management

American Public Works Association. Institute for Buildings and Grounds. *Centralized Administration of Public Buildings*. Special

Report #50. Chicago, 1984. Administration and management, building maintenance, custodial service, energy conservation, building design, and building security. Includes suggested forms and other illustrations.

Cristofano, S. M. "Urban Maintenance, Buildings." Chapter 7 in William S. Foster, ed., *Handbook of Municipal Administration and Engineering*. New York: McGraw-Hill, 1978. Emphasizes systems analysis in planning public buildings.

Professional Grounds Management Society. *Grounds Maintenance Management Guidelines*. 1st ed. Pikesville, Md., 1984.

U.S. Department of Agriculture, and U.S. Forest Service regional and local offices will provide information on pruning techniques and other tree-care programs free of charge.

13 Transportation

Airport Operators Council International. *Public Relations Handbook*.

American Public Works Association. *Guidelines for Developing a Bridge Maintenance Program*. Chicago, 1974.

————. Special Report 42. *Managing Snow Removal and Ice Control Programs*. Chicago, 1974.

————. Institute for Transportation. *Paying for Transportation at the Local Level: 17 Strategies*. Chicago, 1984.

————. *Street and Highway Maintenance Manual*. Part 1, "Managing Street Maintenance," L. G. Byrd; Part 2, "Street Maintenance Operations," George M. Briggs. Chicago, 1986.

————. *Street Cleaning Practice*. 3d ed. Chicago, 1978.

Box, Paul C., and Joseph C. Oppenlander. *Manual of Traffic Engineering Studies*. 4th ed. Arlington, Va.: Institute of Transportation Engineers, 1976.

Civil Aeronautics Board/Federal Aviation Administration. *Airport Activity Statistics of Certified Route Air Carriers*.

Harral, C. G., et al. *The Highway Maintenance Problem*. Washington, D.C.: World Bank, May 1980.

Highway Users Federation for Safety and Mobility. *Getting Around Town: Strategies for Urban Mobility*. Washington, D.C., 1986. Strategies used by cities to face urban transportation problems; intended for local government officials, mayors, city council members, county commissioners, regional planning council members, and others.

Homburger, Wolfgang S., ed., Louis E. Keefer, and William R. McGrath, assoc. eds. *Transportation and Traffic Engineering Handbook.* 2d ed. Englewood Cliffs, N.J.: Prentice-Hall, 1982.

Johnson, Christine. *Pavement (Maintenance) Management Systems.* Chicago: American Public Works Association, n.d.

———, ed. *The Hole Story: Facts and Fallacies about Potholes.* Chicago: American Public Works Association, n.d.

Kane, Robert M., and Allen D. Vose. 5th ed. *Air Transportation.* Dubuque, Iowa: Kendall/Hunt, 1976.

Levinson, Herbert S., and Robert A. Weant, eds. *Urban Transportation: Perspectives and Prospects.* Westport, Conn.: Eno Foundation for Transportation, 1982. Readings that include a balance between advocates of street/automobile and public transit systems.

Locklin, D. Philip. *Economics of Transportation.* 6th ed. Homewood, Ill.: R. D. Irwin, 1966.

Marett, D. C. "Bridge Management." American Society of Civil Engineers. Las Vegas, Nev., April 1982.

National Safety Council. *Accident Facts.* Chicago, annual.

Oglesby, Clarkson H., and R. Gary Hicks. *Highway Engineering.* 4th ed. New York: John Wiley & Sons, 1982.

Owen, Wilfred. *Cities in the Motor Age.* New York: Viking Press, 1959.

———. *The Metropolitan Transportation Problem,* rev. ed. Washington, D.C.: Brookings Institution, 1966.

Pushkarev, Boris S., Jeffrey M. Zupan, and Robert S. Cumella. *Urban Rail in America: An Exploration of Criteria for Fixed-Guideway Transit.* Bloomington: Indiana University Press, 1982.

Replogle, Michael A. *Bicycles and Public Transportation.* Washington, D.C.: The Bicycle Federation, 1983. Explores the interrelationship of bicycles and public transit and includes analyses from the United States and abroad.

Road Information Program. Publishes a variety of studies and news releases, as well as an annual, *State Highway Funding Methods.* Washington, D.C.

Sheflin, M. J. E. "Cost Justification of Pre-

ventive Street Maintenance." *National Road and Street Maintenance Conference.* Oklahoma State University, April 1980.

Smerk, George M. *Urban Mass Transportation: A Dozen Years of Federal Policy.* Bloomington: Indiana University Press, 1974. An examination of development and change in transportation policy; for another view, see Wilfred Owen, *Transportation for Cities: The Role of Federal Policy.* Washington, D.C.: Brookings Institution, 1976.

Smith, Wilbur, and associates. *Future Highways and Urban Growth.* New Haven, Conn.: Automobile Manufacturers Association, 1961. Excellent data for transportation planners.

Transportation Research Board. "Consequences of Deferred Maintenance." *NCHRP Synthesis of Highway Practices #58.* Washington, D.C., 1979.

———. "Distribution of Wheel Loads on Highway Bridges." *NCHRP Synthesis 111.* Washington, D.C. 1984.

———. "Running Costs of Motor Vehicles as Affected by Road Design and Traffic." *NCHRP Report 111.* Washington, D.C., 1971.

U.S. Department of Transportation. *Proceedings of the Fourth National Conference on Rural Transportation.* DOT-1-79-19. Washington, D.C.: GPO, 1979.

———. *Roadway Lighting Handbook.* Washington, D.C.: GPO, 1978.

———. *Transportation for the Elderly and Handicapped, Programs and Problems, 2.* 1981-0-727-309/1592. Washington, D.C.: GPO, 1980.

U.S. Department of Transportation, Federal Highway Administration. *Manual on Uniform Traffic Control Devices for Streets and Highways.* Washington, D.C.: GPO, 1978, with periodic revisions.

U.S. Department of Transportation, National Highway Traffic Safety Administration, and Federal Highway Administration. *Highway Safety Program Standards.* Washington, D.C.: GPO, 1974.

Utah Department of Transportation. *Good Roads Cost Less.* UDOT-MR-77-8. October 1977.

Vuchic, Vukan. *Urban Public Transportation: Systems and Technology.* Englewood Cliffs, N.J.: Prentice-Hall, 1981. Gives a current view of the components of a public transit system and how they may be used to meet current needs.

Weant, Robert A. *Parking Garage Planning and Operation*. Westport, Conn.: Eno Foundation for Transportation, Inc., 1978.

---

14 Water Resources

American Public Works Association. *Changing Directions in Water Management: An Infrastructure Financing Policy Statement*. Chicago, 1983.

———. *Planning and Evaluating Water Conservation Measures*. Special Report 48. Chicago, 1981.

———. *Urban Stormwater Management*. Special Report 49. Chicago, 1981. Comprehensive coverage of most aspects of stormwater management with an emphasis on detention systems. Includes planning; problems and solutions; urban hydrology; design, operation, and maintenance of collection systems; stormwater detention planning, design, construction, and maintenance; stormwater quality benefits of detention; costs; stormwater law, ordinances, and legal issues; and financing.

American Society of Civil Engineers. *Ground Water Management*. Manual 40. New York, 1972.

American Water Works Association. *Basic Management Principles for Small Water Systems*. Denver, 1982.

———. *Challenges in Water Utility Management*. Denver, 1980.

———. *Cross-Connections and Backflow Prevention Handbook*. Denver, 1974.

———. *Emergency Planning for Water Utility Management*. Denver, 1984.

———. *Financial Planning and the Use of Financial Information for General Management Personnel*. Denver, 1982.

———. *Getting the Most from Your Well Supply*. Denver, 1972.

———. *Managing Water Rates and Finances*. Denver, 1979.

———. *Safety Practice for Water Utilities*. Denver, 1983.

———. *Standard Methods for the Examination of Water and Wastewater*. Denver, 1984.

———. *Water Conservation Management*. Denver, 1980.

———. *Water Disinfection with Ozone, Chloramines, or Chlorine Dioxide*. Denver, 1980.

———. *Water Quality and Treatment*. Denver, 1971.

———. *Water Utility Accounting*. Denver, 1980.

California Department of Water Resources. *Water Well Standards*, Bulletin 74–81.

Foster, William S., ed. *Handbook of Municipal Administration and Engineering*. New York: McGraw-Hill, 1978. See especially Chapter 9, "Sewer Maintenance."

Kusler, Jon A., Douglas A. Yanggen, and other participants. *Regulation of Flood Hazard Areas to Reduce Flood Losses*. Washington, D.C.: Water Resources Council, Vol. 1, 1971; Vol. 2, 1972; Vol. 3, 1982. Volume 1: regulation of private and public land uses, draft statutes and ordinances for regulation of land uses in riverine and coastal flood hazard areas; volume 2: techniques of regulating subdivision of lands in flood hazard areas; volume 3: strategies for improving regulations and for combining regulations with other management tools to serve multipurpose state and local goals.

National Water Well Association. *Manual of Water Well Maintenance and Rehabilitation Technology*. Worthington, Oh., n.d.

Sheaffer, John R., Kenneth R. Wright, William C. Taggert, and Ruth M. Wright. *Urban Storm Drainage Management*. New York: Marcel Dekker, 1982. Addresses major drainage and floodplain management issues, including legal aspects, planning, hydrology, floodplain delineation and regulation, storage concepts, and water quality.

U.S. Environmental Protection Agency. Water Planning Division. *Results of the Nationwide Urban Runoff Program*. "Executive Summary"; Vol. 1, "Final Report"; Vol. 2, "Appendices"; Vol. 3, "Data Appendix." Washington, D.C., December 1983. Results of a five-year effort by the EPA to study methods of improving receiving water quality as affected by stormwater pollution. Includes discussion of pollutant types, loads, and effects on receiving water quality; the need for stormwater control; and alternatives for the control of stormwater pollution.

———. *Sewer Infiltration and Inflow Control*. Environmental Protection Technology Series, EPA–600/2–77–017c. Washington, D.C., July 1977.

Whipple, William, Neil S. Grigg, Thomas Grizzard, Clifford Randall, Robert P. Shubinski, and L. Scott Tucker. *Stormwater Management in Urbanizing Areas*. Englewood Cliffs, N.J.: Prentice-Hall, 1983. A book for municipal and county engineers, planners, and administrators as well as consulting engineers, state and federal engineers, and those who deal with land use control, urban drainage, water quality, and control of flooding at the local level. Covers governmental programs, hydrology, runoff pollution, stormwater models, erosion, detention facilities, floodplain management, and management aspects.

Wright-McLaughlin Engineers. *Urban Storm Drainage Criteria Manual*. 2 vols. Denver: Urban Drainage and Flood Control District, 1969. Used by cities and counties in the Denver metro area and the Urban Drainage and Flood Control District (UDFCD) as a basic reference for development of drainage and flood control facilities; also used by developers and their consulting engineers in preparation of plans and designs. Periodic updates prepared by UDFCD.

15 Solid Waste Management

American Public Works Association. Institute for Solid Wastes. *Hazardous Waste and the Public Works Official*. Chicago, forthcoming.

————. *Solid Waste Collection Practice*. 4th ed. Chicago, 1981.

Foster, William, S., ed. *Handbook of Municipal Administration and Engineering*. New York: McGraw-Hill, 1978.

U.S. Environmental Protection Agency. Office of Solid Waste Management Programs. *Decision-Makers Guide in Solid Waste Management*. 2d ed. Washington, D.C.: GPO, 1976.

Wilson, David C. *Waste Management: Planning, Evaluation, and Technologies*. New York: Oxford University Press, 1981.

16 Air Quality Control

Bevilacqua, Oreste M., and Edward C. Sullivan. *Proceedings of the Specialty Conference on Transportation and the 1977 Clean Air Act Amendments*. New York: American Society of Civil Engineers, November 1979.

Epstein, A. H., C. A. Leary, and S. T. McCandless. *A Guide for Considering Air Quality in Urban Planning*. Research Triangle Park, N.C.: U.S. Environmental Protection Agency, March 1974.

Feldstein, Milton. "Air Pollution: Sources, Effects, and Control." Chapter 20 in William E. Korbitz, ed., *Urban Public Works Administration*. Washington, D.C.: International City Management Association, 1976.

Lave, Lester B., and Eugene P. Seskin. *Air Pollution and Human Health*. Baltimore: Resources for the Future, Johns Hopkins University Press, 1977.

Strimaitis, David, Robert Bibbo, and Robert McCann. *Air Quality Modeling: What It Is and How It Is Used*. Research Triangle Park, N.C.: U.S. Environmental Protection Agency, September 1980.

United States Conference of Mayors. *Urban Air: A Guide to the Clean Air Act for Local Elected Officials*. February 1980.

U.S. Environmental Protection Agency, Office of Transportation and Land Use Policy, and Urban Mass Transportation Administration. *Transportation Air Quality Analysis—Sketch Planning Methods*. 2 vols. Washington, D.C., December 1979.

U.S. National Commission on Air Quality. *To Breathe Clean Air*. Washington, D.C.: March 1981.

17 Code Administration

Three national organizations have issued model building codes that are revised and updated on a continuous basis. These organizations also publish newsletters, technical bulletins, magazines, and training materials. The organizations are Building Officials and Code Administrators International, 4051 West Flossmoor Road, Country Club Hills, Illinois 60477; International Conference of Building Officials, 5360 South Workman Mill Road, Whittier, California 90601; and Southern Building Code Congress International, 900 Montclair Road, Birmingham, Alabama 35213.

International City Management Association. "Code Administration and Enforcement: Trends and Perspectives." *Management Information Service Special Report* 10. Washington, D.C., August 1982. Symposium papers on public and private perspectives; certification, ethics, and professionalism; code administration, liability, and inspection; enforcement strategies; and model codes.

————. *Code Administration and Enforcement*. Microcomputer training package. Washington, D.C., 1985. Computer simulations at three levels of difficulty for budgeting, code enforcement, and political and ethical decisions. Package includes training manual, gaming manual, and computer software.

Murphy, Michael J. "Reforming Local Development Regulations: Approaches in Five Cities." *Municipal Management Innovation Series* 35. Washington, D.C.: International City Management Association, 1982.

Sanderson, Richard L., ed. *Readings in Code Administration*. Vol. 1, *History/Philosophy/Law*, 1974; Vol. 2, *Fire Protection Technology*, 1975; Vol. 3, *Building Materials/Systems/Standards*, 1975. Chicago: Building Officials and Code Administrators International.

List of contributors

Sam M. Cristofano (Editor) is Director, Department of Public Works, Santa Clara, California. He holds a bachelor's degree from the University of Colorado and a master's degree from Santa Clara University. In 1984 he received the Distinguished Engineering Alumnus Award from the University of Colorado. Since 1982 he has served on the Board of Directors of APWA.

William S. Foster (Editor and Chapter 12) is the retired editor of *American City* magazine. He holds a civil engineering degree from Iowa State University, which awarded him a Professional Citation for achievements in engineering in 1984. An honorary member of ICMA and of the APWA Institute of Municipal Engineering, he is a Fellow in the American Society of Civil Engineers and a life member of APWA and the American Water Works Association. He also was a long-term trustee of the APWA Research Foundation.

John A. Bailey (Chapter 13, "Transportation planning"), a management consultant, is President of Transportation Systems Associates, Inc., Philadelphia. He specializes in transportation policy, long-range planning for public works, and feasibility studies of transportation and public works projects. He is a registered engineer in Pennsylvania and holds a B.S. degree from Texas A&M University and M.G.A. and Ph.D. degrees from the University of Pennsylvania. He has served as a principal in two engineering firms, director of the Transportation Center of Northwestern University, transportation coordinator for Philadelphia, and as a public works and transportation manager. He is a board member of the National Association of Railroad Passengers, Inc., and serves on the boards of several civic and educational agencies (where he specializes in financial matters). A former city manager, Bailey is also a member of ICMA and APWA.

Carey C. Burnett (Chapter 1) is a civil/sanitary/industrial engineer, working with the U.S. Army in Fort Jackson, South Carolina, as a Projects Management Consultant. He has served in both the public and private sectors, including positions as public works director/city engineer in several local governments; city manager in Albany, Georgia, and Columbia, South Carolina; vice-president in charge of municipal engineering for Wilbur Smith and Associates, Inc. (Columbia, S.C.); and project manager for the engineering firm Wiedeman and Singleton, Inc. (Atlanta, Ga.). He is a registered professional engineer with a bachelor of science degree from the University of Georgia. A life member of ICMA and APWA, he has served as ICMA regional vice president; President, Georgia and South Carolina City Managers' associations; and chairman, original Southern Building Code Congress. He has received *American City & County* magazine's Certificate of Merit for Leadership.

Myron D. Calkins (Chapter 2) has been Director of Public Works for Kansas City, Missouri, since 1964. Prior to that he was employed as City Engineer in Tacoma, Washington, for nearly ten years. He holds a degree in civil engineering from Washington State University and he is a registered Professional Engineer in Missouri and Washington. He has received numerous awards and honorary degrees and has served in many leadership positions, including National President of APWA, Chairman of the APWA Education Foundation Board of Trustees, President of the APWA Historical Society Board of Trustees, Fellow of the American Society of Civil Engineers, member of the Advisory Board for Graduate Studies in Public Works Management at the University of Missouri–Kansas City, and diplomate of the American Academy of Environmental Engineers. He was named as one of the Top Ten Public Works Leaders of the Year in 1973.

Stephen Chapple (Chapter 8) is an attorney with the firm of Cohen, Gettings, Alper & Dunham in Arlington, Virginia. He holds an A.B. degree from the University of Illinois and a J.D. degree from the University of Minnesota. He is a member of the bars of Illinois, Minnesota, Virginia, the District of Columbia, and the United States Supreme Court. Among others he represents the United States Conference of Mayors.

Robert H. Goodin (Chapter 7) is Director of Public Works for Rockville, Maryland, and was formerly Director of Public Works for Glencoe, Illinois. A registered professional engineer in Illinois and Maryland, he holds a Certificate of Qualification from the National Council of Engineering Examiners, an engineering degree from the University of Minnesota, and a masters degree in public administration from Roosevelt University, Chicago. He is Past President of the Virginia-District of Columbia-Maryland chapter of APWA, Past President (1977–78) and now Honorary Member of the APWA Institute for Administrative Management, and, starting in 1982, a member of the Board of Trustees of the Public Works Historical Society. He served as Managing Editor of *Current Municipal Problems* and was selected as one of the Top Ten Public Works Leaders of the Year in 1973.

Stephen B. Gordon (Chapter 9) is Manager, Research Services, for BidNet, a service offered by BidNet, Inc., and the Dun & Bradstreet Corporation. He holds bachelor's and master's degrees from Mississippi State University and a doctorate from the University of Maryland. For ten years he was director of professional development and procurement research for the National Institute of Governmental Purchasing, Inc. He has spoken and published extensively on public purchasing and contracting.

Ronald W. Jensen (Chapter 11) is Director of Public Works for Phoenix, Arizona. He holds a bachelor's degree in civil engineering from California State University at Fresno and has done graduate work at Arizona State University. He attended the Program for Senior Executives in State and Local Government at Harvard University. A nationally recognized expert in equipment management, he has served as a management consultant to numerous local governments.

Tina Ann Lamoreaux (Chapter 8) is an associate with the Santa Ana, California, law firm of Macdonald, Fabozzi & Prenovost. She holds a B.A. degree from San Diego State University and a J.D. degree from Cal-

ifornia Western School of Law. She is a member of the bar both of the District of Columbia and the Commonwealth of Virginia.

Martin J. Manning (Chapter 14, "Wastewater systems") is public works director in Clark County, Nevada. As deputy public works director in Houston, he was responsible for the city's water and wastewater utility systems. He holds a bachelor's degree in civil engineering from the University of Illinois and a master's degree in public works from the University of Pittsburgh, earned as an APWA fellow. Active in a number of associations, he is a twenty-year veteran of professional public works management.

Burton W. Marsh (Chapter 13, "Traffic management") has been a consulting engineer in traffic and safety since his retirement in 1970. He has served as Executive Director of the Institute of Traffic Engineers (Washington, D.C.), Executive Director of the American Automobile Association Foundation for Traffic Safety, Director of the AAA Traffic Engineering and Safety Department, and City Traffic Engineer of Philadelphia. He was the first full-time City Traffic Engineer (Pittsburgh, Pennsylvania) in the United States. He has received numerous awards and has been involved in many professional traffic engineering and safety activities. He was Chairman of the National Research Council's Highway Research Board and in 1954 received the board's Roy W. Crum Award for Distinguished Service. He holds a bachelor of science degree in civil engineering and an honorary doctorate from Worcester Polytechnic Institute.

James L. Martin (Chapter 10) is Director of Public Works and City Engineer in Fresno, California. In his 35 years of municipal practice he has been responsible for engineering design and construction and the maintenance and operation of public facilities (including several utilities). He graduated in civil engineering from George Washington University and is a registered professional engineer. He is a member of the American Society of Civil Engineers, the American Academy of Environmental Engineers, and APWA, of which he was President in 1983–84.

John Matzer, Jr. (Chapter 6) is City Administrator, San Bernardino, California. He was previously Distinguished Visiting Professor, California State University–Long Beach, where he now teaches graduate courses in personnel management. He has served as Deputy Assistant Director, U.S. Office of Personnel Management; City Manager, Beverly Hills, California; Village Manager, Skokie, Illinois; and City Administrator, Trenton, New Jersey. He received B.A. and M.A. degrees from Rutgers University, New Brunswick, New Jersey.

Abraham Michaels (Chapter 15), a professional engineer, is a solid waste consultant to local and state governments, federal agencies, international organizations, private industry, and public service organizations. He has served several local governments, most recently as the Streets Commissioner for Philadelphia, Pennsylvania. He is editor of the Solid Waste Forum in *Public Works* magazine and has served as adjunct professor at Drexel University, president of the Institute for Solid Waste, and diplomate of the American Academy of Environmental Engineers.

Ronald Miller (Chapter 4) is Chief Budget Officer for Indianapolis, Indiana. Prior to that he was Principal Planner for Economic and Fiscal Affairs for Indianapolis, and Town Manager for Newport, Maine. He also serves on the adjunct faculty of Indiana University's School of Public and Environmental Affairs, and was Director of the school's Financial Management Consulting Program. He holds a bachelor's degree in public management and a master's degree in public administration from the University of Maine.

Larry G. Mugler (Chapter 16) is Director of Development Services for the Denver Regional Council of Governments. He is responsible for the development and environmental planning programs and the economic and demographic information systems. He holds a bachelor's degree in civil engineering from Northwestern University and a master's degree in regional planning from the University of Wisconsin–Madison. He is active in the Urban Planning and Development Division of the American Society of Civil Engineers.

Wilfred M. ("Wiley") Post, Jr. (Chapter 13, "Airports") was manager of the Allentown-Bethlehem-Easton Airport for 47 years until his retirement in 1984. He attended the Massachusetts Institute of Technology, received a bachelor of science in aviation administration from Parks College of St. Louis University, and held a commercial pilot's license for many years. He was named a Distinguished Pennsylvanian and received both the Distinguished Service Award from the Federal

Aviation Administration and the President's Award from the American Association of Airport Executives.

William A. Ramsey (Chapter 3), Director of Public Works for Olathe, Kansas, holds a bachelor's degree in education from Emporia State University and a master's degree in public administration from the University of Kansas. He has previously served as City Manager of Centralia, Illinois, City Manager of Herington, Kansas, and Administrative Assistant to the City Manager of Emporia, Kansas. He has also taught management courses at Avila College and the University of Missouri at Kansas City and has lectured at Kansas University.

Mires Rosenthal (Chapter 17) was Director of Inspections and Zoning Administrator for Savannah, Georgia, until his retirement. His previous positions with the city of Savannah include Director of Central Services and Deputy Director of Streets and Sanitation. He holds a bachelor of science in civil engineering from Louisiana State University, and he is a registered professional engineer. He is a member of many professional associations, including APWA, the Southern Building Code Congress, the National Academy of Code Administrators, and the Georgia Society of Professional Engineers.

Michael J. E. Sheflin (Chapter 13, "Street maintenance") is Transportation Commissioner for the Regional Municipality of Ottawa-Carleton (Ontario, Canada). He has received engineering degrees from St. Francis Xavier University and the Technical University of Nova Scotia. He has given numerous presentations on street maintenance to federal, state, provincial, and local agencies, and he has served in the national and international offices of a number of public works organizations.

Frank S. So (Chapter 5) is Deputy Executive Director of the American Planning Association. He has worked previously in local and area-wide planning agencies. He holds a bachelor's degree in sociology from Youngstown State University and a master's degree in city planning from Ohio State University.

Donald M. Somers (Chapter 14, "Potable water") was Director of Public Works for Sunnyvale, California, from 1956 until his retirement in 1981. He is a life member of APWA and a member of the American Water Works Association. His educational background includes a bachelor's degree and a master's degree in civil engineering from Rensselaer Polytechnic Institute.

L. Scott Tucker (Chapter 14, "Drainage") has been Executive Director of the Urban Drainage and Flood Control District of Metropolitan Denver since 1972. He was formerly a Research Associate at Colorado State University in Fort Collins, and Deputy Project Director for the Urban Water Resources Research Program of the American Society of Civil Engineers. He has served as both Chairman and Secretary of the Urban Water Resources Research Council of the American Society of Civil Engineers. He is past president of the Colorado chapter of APWA, past president of the Colorado chapter of the American Society of Civil Engineers, and member and immediate past president of the Executive Council of the Institute for Water Resources of APWA. His educational background includes a bachelor of science in civil engineering from the University of Nebraska and a master of science in civil engineering from the University of Arizona.

Illustration credits

Chapter 1 Figure 1–1: Map drawn by Tom Stalker-Miller, appears in *The Roads That Led to Rome*, Victor W. von Hagen (London: Weidenfeld & Nicolson, 1967), permission granted by the Estate of Victor von Hagen; Figure 1–2: Spanish National Tourist Office; Figure 1–3: The Bettmann Archive; Figure 1–4: New England Water Works Association; Figure 1–5: Carey C. Burnett; Figure 1–6: Adapted from Donald Fisk, Herbert Kiesling, and Thomas Muller, *Private Provision of Public Services: An Overview* (Washington, D.C.: The Urban Institute, 1978).

Chapter 2 Figure 2–2: American Public Works Association, *Public Works Communication Manual* (Chicago, 1984).

Chapter 3 Figures 3–1, 3–2, 3–5, 3–6, 3–7, 3–8, 3–9, 3–10, 3–12, 3–13, 3–14, 3–15: City of Olathe, Kansas.

Chapter 4 Figure 4–1: "Type of Program or Service Continuum," from Dennis R. Howard, and John L. Crompton, *Financing, Managing and Marketing Recreation & Park Resources* (Dubuque, Iowa: Wm. C. Brown Publishers, [c] 1980), Fig. 20.1, p. 407. All rights reserved. Reprinted by permission; Figure 4–2: "An Analysis of Budget Formats," in Edward A. Lehan, *Simplified Governmental Budgeting* (Chicago: Municipal Finance Officers Association, 1981), p. 79.

Chapter 5 Figure 5–2: Peat, Marwick, Mitchell & Co., *Rebuilding New Orleans: Financing Public Facilities*, May 1982, p. 8.

Chapter 9 Figure 9–2: National Institute of Governmental Purchasing, *Public Procurement Management* (Falls Church, Va., 1985), pp. 2–6; Figure 9–3: "Environmental Report," *Nation's Cities Weekly*, March 15, 1982; Figure 9–4: National Institute of Governmental Purchasing, *Public Purchasing and Materials Management* (Falls Church, Va., 1983), p. 148; Figure 9–5: National Institute of Governmental Purchasing, *General Public Purchasing* (Falls Church, Va., 1977), p. 98.

Chapter 10 Figure 10–1: City of Fresno, California.

Chapter 11 Figure 11–2: Jack R. Graves.

Chapter 13 Figure 13–1: Alan M. Voorhees, Walter G. Hansen, and A. Keith Gilbert, "Urban Transportation," in Frank S. So et al., eds., *The Practice of Local Government Planning* (Washington, D.C.: International City Management Association, 1979), p. 224; Figures 13–2, 13–3, 13–4: Regional Municipality of Ottawa-Carleton, Canada; Figure 13–6: American Public Works Association, Institute for Transportation, *Paying for Transportation at the Local Level: 17 Strategies* (Chicago, n.d.), p. 3; Figures 13–8, 13–9, 13–10: Regional Municipality of Ottawa-Carleton, Canada; Figure 13–11: Metropolitan Area Planning Agency, Omaha, Nebraska; Figure 13–12: District of Columbia Department of Highways and Traffic, *Highway and Traffic Safety Improvement Program for the District of Columbia* (Washington, D.C., n.d.), p. 20; Figure 13–13: Federal Aviation Administration, National Plan of Integrated Airport Systems (NPIAS).

Chapter 14 Figures 14–4, 14–5, 14–6, 14–7: Photos courtesy of Urban Drainage and Flood Control District, Denver, Colorado.

Chapter 15 Figure 15–1: City of Philadelphia, Department of Streets, Division of Sanitation, n.d.; Figure 15–2: Klaus S. Feindler, "Baltimore Resource Recovery," *ISWA Proceedings* (Philadelphia, 1984).

Chapter 16 Figure 16–3: A. H. Epstein, C. A. Leary, and S. T. McCandless, *A Guide for Considering Air Quality in Urban Planning* (Research Triangle Park, N.C.: U.S. Environmental Protection Agency, March 1974), p. 29; Figure 16–4: U.S. Environmental Protection Agency and U.S. Department of Transportation, *Transportation–Air Quality Planning Guidelines* (June 1978).

Chapter 17 Figure 17–1: Building Officials & Code Administrators International, Inc., *Building Code Reform Kit* (Country Club Hills, Ill., n.d.); Figures 17–2, 17–3: Department of Inspections, City of Savannah, Georgia.

Index